DOLAN HUBBARD

FORM and

THOUGHT

Edited by

in PROSE ~ *Second Edition*

WILFRED H. STONE
Stanford University

ROBERT HOOPES
Michigan State University, Oakland

47415

THE RONALD PRESS COMPANY ~ NEW YORK

Library of Congress Catalog Card Number: 60–7612

PRINTED IN THE UNITED STATES OF AMERICA

Preface

When this book was originally conceived, it was our conviction that college students do not at any level have to be talked down to. Nothing has caused us to modify this view, and the reader may be assured that it is still reflected in the quality of the selections in this new edition. We have again tried to choose for the book readings which are not patronizing, which are, if anything, a teasing distance beyond the student's intellectual reach. But a collection of challenging essays alone is not enough to provide an adequate teaching aid for use in college composition classes. Our aim has also been to make a book that will assist the student to read critically, to think straight, to write well.

Although the book has not changed in *purpose* from the first edition, its contents have changed considerably. More than 30 new essays and stories have been added and some old ones dropped. The rhetorical introductions in Part II have been thoroughly revised, and nearly all of the *Problems for Thought and Writing* have been rewritten. In selecting new essays and stories, we have been guided primarily by a constant desire to find material which illustrates as effectively as possible our own rubrics and is, at the same time, particularly appropriate to the vital concerns of today's college students. We hope that our labors have produced a better book, and that it will please and serve well both those who have used it before and those who are coming to it for the first time.

The book is divided into two parts. Part I is mainly concerned with ideas and thought. The readings in this part of the book seek to lead the student from a world he knows and lives in to one of increasing complexity and distance. Along the way he encounters problems in style, reasoning, and logic, which will, we hope, assist him in coping more effectively—as a writer and as a thinker—with some of the disturbing social, religious, scientific, and moral issues dealt with. Part II is conceived as the second half of a composition course, and utilizes in a more specialized way the knowledge gained from the first half of the book. Here the readings are chosen to illustrate specific rhe-

iii

torical modes of controlling and organizing thought: definition and description, comparison and contrast, classification and division, process and narration, argument and persuasion, and evaluation. Each of the above sections is introduced by a chapter describing and analyzing that particular rhetorical mode and the intellectual problems it entails. So the book is an informal rhetoric as well as a volume of directed readings.

The questions—*Problems for Thought and Writing*—after each selection in both parts of the book have been carefully prepared to provoke thought and to assist in making cross-references to the ideas and organization of other essays in the book. The first section in each set of *Problems* centers on what seem to us the crucial questions and implications raised by the selection; the second section contains questions designed to develop the student's sensitivity to style and rhetorical techniques. The book is, therefore, conceived as a *course*—a set of readings and questions designed to stimulate both the mind of the writer and his developing craft.

It is, of course, impossible to acknowledge fully our indebtedness to all of the teachers who have used the book and offered helpful suggestions for its improvement. But once again we wish to thank those who helped us with the first edition: Miss Elizabeth Atwater, Mrs. Betty Behrmann, Mr. and Mrs. Norman Guinasso, Mrs. Ruth Headley, Mr. David Levin, Mr. James McNelis, Mr. John Loftist, Mr. James Schermerhorn, and Mr. Richard Scowcroft. And for invaluable criticism and advice in making this revision we extend our special thanks to Mr. Thomas R. Arp, Mr. Ross C. Brackney, Mr. Richard Kraus, and Mr. Edward Tayler, four teachers of writing who serve the cause of excellence in all they do. We are also grateful for the valuable aid rendered by Mrs. Irene Denne, Miss Dimitra Govenis, Miss Sandra Langeland, and Miss Marie Medina. In the first edition thanks were given for the assistance of Miss Cary Lee Laird. That name has since been changed to Mrs. Wilfred Stone, and thanks are once again given.

WILFRED H. STONE
ROBERT HOOPES

January, 1960

Contents

PART I

IDEAS AND ISSUES FOR THOUGHT

4. Humor and Satire   120

5. The Individual and Society   157

A. Freedom and Control

B. Man and the Mass

6. People and Population   225

A. Culture and Lebensraum

PART II

THE ORGANIZATION OF THOUGHT

6. Evaluation   629

FORM
and
THOUGHT in PROSE

PART I
IDEAS AND ISSUES FOR THOUGHT

PART I

Ideas and Issues for Thought

INTRODUCTION

Most of the essays that follow are concerned with crucial issues of human experience and are, as well, models of style and organization from which you can profit in your own writing. Some of the essays deal specifically with issues that confront the writer and therefore emphasize the intellectual and artistic discipline; others treat larger issues that confront us all as individuals and members of society.

Although we have permitted ourselves an occasional exception for pedagogical purposes, on the whole our aim has been to present essays which effectively illustrate good writing and good thinking in combination. We believe that any writer in his early maturity must be motivated by two things: (1) having something to say, and (2) really wanting to say it. He must care enough to learn all he can about his subject; he must care enough to want to communicate what he feels and thinks as clearly and cogently as he can. If he does so, he should have little difficulty mastering the technical problems of writing.

These essays—and the "Problems for Thought and Writing" which follow them—are designed to provide such motivation and to show how master craftsmen, who have something to say and want to say it, manage to shape a writing vehicle to their desire.

In Part II of this book the vehicle itself—the shaping forces of definition, classification, argument, and other modes of organization—gets our main attention. Part I is more general. We have delayed engaging with those specialized problems because we believe that the beginning writer must open his eyes before he begins to squint. Writing is a discipline, but it is also an act of love. The student who comes joyless to his theme will write sad themes. So while Part I is a preparation for Part II, it has its own reason for existence: it is designed to give the young writer (1) something to write about, and (2) the stimulation to write it.

3

College and Conscience

THE PRINCETON BICKER: VALUES IN FORMATION*

John McNees

> *My own ideals for the University are those of a genuine democ-
> racy and serious scholarship. The two, indeed, seem to me to go
> together. Any organization which introduces elements of social
> exclusiveness constitutes the worst possible soil for serious intel-
> lectual endeavor . . . Any organization that has the idea of ex-
> clusiveness at its foundation is antagonistic to the best training for
> citizenship in a democratic country . . . My conviction has been
> confirmed by everything that I have heard and inquired into, that
> the Clubs, as now organized, must go, or Princeton will cease to
> be an important element in University leadership in this country.*
> —THOMAS WOODROW WILSON

"Now I know you guys up at Harvard put an emphasis on individualism and that's fine," he said refusing to acknowledge my depreca-
tory gesture and attempt to interrupt. "But down here we like a
less impersonal way of living so you can be with who you want for
your friends and choose the guys you eat with."

It is the first night of "Bicker" at Princeton, and through the
windows glaring orange out of a hundred majestic black bastions,
the committees are seen as they come calling, catching sophomores
just accidentally attired from top to toe in immaculate tweeds, and
Exeter yearbooks displayed with casual prominence.

"Hello, we're from Cottage."

"Come right on in," and there is a cordial babble of welcome as
they all heartily seat themselves, and suddenly find a terrifying silence
left standing.

"Uh, that looks like an old Currier and Ives you've got up there."
(The walls, they always start with what you've got hanging on the

* From *The Harvard Crimson*, as reprinted in *Sequoia*, Stanford University
literary magazine.

walls, or with what you're majoring in or what you did last summer
or where you're from—but avoid that one, there's danger there.)

So it goes for ten or fifteen minutes. Total strangers confronting
total strangers, making nervous small talk with artificial poise, watching through narrow eyes for the wrong color of socks, a grammatical
slip or affectation, a pun or wisecrack in questionable taste. Then—

"Well, we really must be running along. A lot of men to see tonight, you know."

"Well, we've certainly enjoyed chatting with you."

Smiling and nodding and handshaking them out the door, roommates turn to each other with dread or accusations, while outside
in the hall the committees rate personalities on a grading system from
one to seven (except for Ivy, the top, which needs only a plus or
minus)—one even reports the decision, incredibly enough, on a
walkie-talkie:

"This is Pete calling in for Cottage. Negative on wonks in Patton
96. Dirty story, grubby room. That's right: negative."

It's a two-dollar, one-hour train ride from Princeton, New Jersey,
to either Philadelphia or New York City. The nearest thing to a girl's
college for miles around is the public high school, and there are only
three theaters in the entire town. When seeking relief from the
academic life, therefore, the average Princeton man invariably turns
to his club. There he not only takes all his meals, but forms friendships, watches television, plays squash or bridge or ping-pong, drinks,
parties, holds bull sessions, and even studies. Unless he's on a varsity
team, the club's intramural program is his only athletic outlet, and,
when he becomes an alumnus, it becomes the focus for fond memories, homecoming weekends, and pleas for financial support. More
than any other part of the campus, it is the center of his life at
Princeton.

"Bicker" is the annual process by which sophomores are chosen
for election to the unproctored, privately owned and operated eating
clubs. The college newspaper calls it "the most important single
value-forming experience of the average undergraduate's career at
Princeton."

The object of Bicker, according to a booklet published by the clubs
themselves ("Now That You Are Eligible") is to discover "personable-
ness in the individual" and "congeniality in the total section." It is a
method for assuring each club that any student to whom it offers a
bid is the "club type."

Immediately after finals—this year on Thursday, January 30—the Bicker committees of the clubs start to make their calls. These calls continue for ten days. Classes resume not long after Bicker has started, but they are largely ignored, sophomores finding it "hard to read anything more advanced than *Peyton Place.*"

The committees call between the hours of four and six in the afternoon at first, then between seven-thirty in the evening and midnight. On the basis of a few minutes of stereotyped small talk the committees rate the eligibles, and the clubs immediately begin cutting their lists, "from the top" as well as "from the bottom." Each night fewer clubs come calling at a given room. If, on the last night of the Bicker period, a sophomore is still receiving a committee, he has probably procured a "first-list bid." If not, and he has good friends whom a certain club is anxious to have, he may receive a "second-list bid" that will get him in if his friends accept their first-list bids, or if not enough first-list men accept that club's bids to fill its "section." Some sophomores receive bids from a number of clubs; others receive none at all.

Individual sophomores are associated together in complexes of friends known as "preferentials," all of whose members desire to remain together with varying degrees of zeal. The exigencies of Bicker rapidly force most of these preferentials into advanced states of disintegration, subjecting old friendships to severe strains and sometimes even shattering them. A sophomore's preferential group may also be used by the clubs to appraise and manipulate him throughout the Bicker procedure.

Saturday afternoon at Holder Court, club representatives and hundreds of sophomores shivering in the icy wind stand with hands thrust in pockets or holding frigid beer cans, grouping and regrouping, talking in fast desperate undertones, trying to bargain friends into the same group, unload undesirables elsewhere, bid a sad goodbye to classmates joining other clubs:

"Well best of luck, Chuck" (wet-eyed and swallowing hard). "I'm sure sorry you and George won't be going with me into Cannon."

"Ted's in trouble. He hasn't a bid yet. If you'd only turn down Tiger, Eldon, the two of us could get him into Charter."

"Hell, I hope Braddock does go to Key; I always thought he was a bastard anyhow."

There is a definite hierarchy among the clubs at Princeton which is universally acknowledged, though the existence of the implied caste structure is widely denied. The highest echelon consists of

"the big five." Ivy Club ("The Vine") is at the absolute summit;
then follow, in no particular order, Tiger Inn, Colonial ("The Pil-
lars"), Cap and Gown ("The Cap"), and Cottage ("The Cheese").
Graduates of the most famous Eastern prep schools, the scions of
stock hallowed by generations of fame and money, and other individuals who can sell themselves well in fifteen minutes or so, are
nearly assured admission to one of these. To make Ivy is social
apotheosis.

Then follow the host of "middle clubs," subject to gradation among
themselves, no doubt, though here any explicit ranking would be
less objective and not generally conceded: Campus, Cannon, Charter,
Cloister, Court, Dial, Elm, Key and Seal, Quadrangle, Terrace, and
Tower. Dial took this year's only Negro.

Certain stereotypes are associated with some of the clubs which,
like all stereotypes, do not hold in many individual instances. They
are, however, fairly reliable. Thus, the campus "doers" or activity
men are apt to be found in Cap and Gown or Quadrangle, and
athletes tend to turn up, according to their inmost natures, either in
Tiger Inn, the lair of "the gentlemen jocks," or in Cannon, home of
"the sweaty ones." The captain of this year's football team, however,
is in Ivy, which always has its pick of the entire class.

Sharing the bottom of the social scale with Prospect Club—though
ranking, if possible, even further down—is Woodrow Wilson Lodge,
or as it is commonly called, "the facility." Wilson Lodge was founded
last year by the University and supposedly provides "an alternative
to the club system" for those who want neither to renounce all social
activity for three years of college life nor to pass through the indignity·
of Bicker and accept membership in one of the seventeen eating
clubs. But anyone in the University, with the possible exception of
the administration, will freely admit that the three-room "facility" in
no sense provides a satisfactory alternative.

Last year, in an attempt to raise Wilson's prestige, Sophomore
Vice President Robert Hillier dramatically announced that he would
accept no bids from any club, but would join the Lodge and bring
"sixty or seventy of the good men in the class" along with him.
"Everyone's afraid that the facility will become a dumping ground,"
he stated. "Someone has to make the move to destroy the stigma that
will result." Today, Hillier has become a junior member of Quadrangle Club, there are only twenty-one people in the facility, and it,
along with Prospect, is a dumping ground.

The youngest, the cheapest, and the shabbiest of the clubs is Prospect. It is also the most democratically governed. Founded ten years ago, Prospect is unique in demanding neither undergraduate nor alumni dues, and its term rate is eighty dollars less than Tower's and a hundred and thirty dollars less than Ivy's, which otherwise represent the two extremes. More important, Prospect is unlike the other organizations on Prospect Street in that its policies are not determined privately by a small clique of officers and a powerful graduate board. Alone among the clubs, Prospect can hold the sort of Bicker its members actually want.

This year, Prospect announced that any sophomore who wished to join might do so by simply dropping in and signing the books, until either its capacity had been reached or the official deadline arrived. Isolated idealism of this sort, however, was naïve in a situation so inherently unprincipled. The thousand and one vices of the system have long been concealed by the democratic boast that "everyone who wants to, makes a club." Jim Ridgeway, chairman of *The Daily Princetonian*, published an editorial warning Prospect that its policy would prove disastrous, that one club would be used as a scapegoat and dumping ground by the irresponsible other sixteen, who could then continue the old boast without themselves doing anything to achieve it. As a result, the Interclub Committee summoned Ridgeway and his managing editor to their meeting place in the library of Ivy Club, hotly denounced them both for "incompetence," failure to "cooperate," a "negative" and "critical" attitude, and formally broke off all relations with the *Princetonian*.

Without once making specific criticisms of what had been written or charging factual inaccuracies, the ICC banned the press from all further Bicker events and information. Every one of Bicker's key decisions was made in personal anonymity and behind closed doors. The demands of the newspaper for an account of what was going on were flatly rejected, and the all-powerful ICC operated throughout without being responsible to anyone, least of all to the Princeton administration or student body.

Bicker reaches its colorful climax during Open House. At seven-thirty Saturday evening the entire class, bathed, brushed, shined, combed, and shivering, hurries through the dark night and biting wind across the campus to Prospect Street, where the grounds of sixteen plush clubhouses—and the not-so-plush Prospect Cooperative Club—stretch before them. The luckiest ones have received several bids, and join one of the big five.

A sophomore strolls with anxious expectation across the broad lawn up to the great white columns of Colonial's porch. The door swings open and he and his group (throughout Bicker, he moves in a group of three or four—they are judged, accepted and perhaps rejected collectively) are swept into the dazzling warm uproar inside. There is the soft depth of a rug beneath his feet and a bright, glittering, well-groomed haze all around him. Then he goes up the grand stairway, lined with clapping and cheering upperclassmen, until he reaches the top, where beaming and blushing he signs his name and receives the dark blue, red, yellow, and green striped club tie from the president. A final huzzah, then they all turn with relish to the serious business of the evening: consuming as much alcohol as possible. Everyone is shaking hands and slapping each other on the back. He is in.

The rest, the majority, must accept bids to lesser clubs, and a lesser number must go through the agonizing process of rushing from house to house hoping to be accepted from the second list after all their more desirable classmates have signed the books. When at last these too are in, they drink still more freely and shout more loudly—trying to forget, though they are in, how it was they got there.

Finally there are the Others—those who are "in trouble," as the euphemism goes, who must somehow be fitted in somewhere by somebody so the clubs can again point with pride to the precious statistic of 100 per cent—"100 per cent of those wishing to join a club did so." One hundred per cent is the single all-forgiving number by which the system can be justified. It must be able to claim the fact of 100 per cent, no matter how often or how strangely 100 per cent must be redefined.

A council of the club presidents, the ICC, directs all hundred per-centers to report to the back porch of Ivy at 9:30 sharp, not entering by the front door or being admitted to the parlor, but stumbling through the dark around the carousing house, and coming in through the servants' entry.

At first they joke about their predicament. "I'd feel pretty bad if I didn't see so many of my friends here." Kind, soft-spoken Ivy men take them aside and counsel them. Join Prospect, they gently urge (each adjusting his identical green and yellow striped tie). Join the poverty-stricken cooperative where you'll take turns waiting on your own tables and mopping the floor and be looked down upon for three years by the members of the real clubs. Join the wonk club, the club for left-overs, and—ever so gently—hurry up about it, so we can show 100 per cent and go back to the party. Resistance is firm, but in many cases gives way. Something in one resists being classified as a wonk, but something deeper cries out against exile.

What constitutes the Princeton definition of "wonk" at Bickertime? The traits of this varied species can be most clearly understood when combined into an extreme, idealized archetype, whose full obnoxious character each individual manifests but partially and then only for a brief time. To apprehend the Platonic essence of the utter antithesis of the approved club type, imagine an inarticulate, introverted, morbidly shy sophomore from a small provincial town. He wears outlandish ties, dirty sweaters, and baggy pants. Not only lacking a crewcut, he is in bad need of a barber nearly all the time and obviously shaves but rarely. Until he arrived at the University he was educated in mediocre public schools. The whole of life to him lies in doodling with mathematics, and his idea of relaxation is playing the violin. He is too undersized for athletics, has a horror, in fact, of both sports and drunken manly roughhousing, and his table manners, to put it kindly, are unpolished. The girls he dates are "dogs." His conversation, when he talks at all, is incessantly intellectual and hardly what the *New Yorker* calls "sophisticated." He is wholly unaware of his own inadequacies and ineptitudes; moreover, he wears thick glasses, has a large nose, and is flagrantly Jewish. None of the hundred percenters on Ivy's back porch were in so repugnant a state as this; even the sorriest of them participated in only a few of the characteristics of such an ideal form, and then in an attenuated degree. But one can clearly see why a social club would only be sensible in excluding such an individual, whatever the wisdom might be of admitting him to the university, and most of the officers on Prospect Street would agree that this precisely describes the sort of man who must be kept out at all costs. It is also a fairly accurate portrait of Albert Einstein.

On the back porch of Ivy, the brand, the taint of wonk, are clearly seen: the error of wearing white bucks for so solemn an evening, the misdemeanor of a soft stammering voice, the felony of one too loud and sure, the atrocity of a blue suit. Here sit a couple of silent boys with slanted eyes and yellow skin, from here the man who was academically first in the class leaves in discouragement to join Prospect, and here, recurring nearly two times out of every three, Israel's face is seen; the class has sixteen Merit Scholars, ten were "in trouble" on Thursday night, and five of them still are.

When they're sure you're not an unctuous agitator for Prospect Club, they are willing to talk to you freely, gathering round to tell you calmly about the fist fight at the meeting when Court Club decided to cut its Jewish quota in half because an unintentional influx one year was causing its prestige to flag; about what a club representative had just told one of them quite frankly: "We'd like to take you but our quota on you people is filled up."

The other heads abruptly part and there is suddenly only one single scowling face. The president of the sophomore class.

"Are you from the Harvard *Crimson?*"

"Yes."

"The ICC has voted the press completely barred here tonight. I'll have to ask you to leave."

"I'm not from the *Princetonian*, you know. I have nothing to do with the University."

"I know that. But you'll have to leave."

"Why?"

"I'm not at liberty to tell you."

"Why not?"

"Get out."

Someone standing nearby begins to shout.

"If it weren't for you damn newspaper guys, we wouldn't have this mess. These people wouldn't even be here tonight."

He has on a green and yellow striped tie. Ivy man. He's right. They'd be in Prospect.

"Shortly after that incident," the *Princetonian* reported, "the central headquarters committee decided that too many people were on the porch without a legitimate reason. They closed the doors and kept a careful tab on who went in and out. This immediately gave rise to the idea that the porch was a 'cage.' Even the men not in clubs began referring to themselves as 'cagers.'"

Around midnight, the clubs run out of liquor and every door on Prospect Street spews forth a jubilant stream of staggering sophomores, juniors and seniors. Leaning on each other, singing, shouting, a few pausing at the gutter to retch quietly for a moment, then loudly rejoining the buoyant inebriated throng, they totter off toward the campus or a cafe where they can calm down with a cup of coffee. The fraternal transport is now at its beatific height. Arm in arm they reel, indifferent to traffic or the piercing cold; one lifts his hands to the frigid heavens and races down the street backwards, his scarf and topcoat wildly flapping in the wind, crying out in ecstasy, "Lord,

Lord, Lord, Lord, Lord!" The unbroken tension of weeks—of a year and a half for some—has ended. Bicker is over at last, for them.

But on Ivy's back porch, for forty-two remaining sophomores, the suspense has reached its most pitiless climax. Since almost everyone who was inside has gone home now and the porch has long been growing chilly, the hundred percenters are permitted to move into the Ivy dining room. They can see the silver candelabras now and the rows of empty bottles. Prospect had electric lights and beer tonight. Somehow the number dwindles to thirty-five as the discouraging hours pass, then six give way and trudge toward Prospect, and another six are placed as a few clubs each make the sacrifice and consent to admit one lone hundred percenter. Above, in the library, the ICC meets in constant absolutely closed session. Below them, twenty-three hundred percenters remain, half of them Jewish. The list is gone over name by name: where are those to be placed?

An outsider observing Bicker finds it difficult to take the whole thing seriously. The enormous anxieties generated in every member of the sophomore class, the superficiality of its standards and ceremonies, the blatant injustices of the values and principles the system indicates—all would seem ludicrous in any civilized community, but they are doubly comic when set in one of the nation's greatest universities and practiced by what is supposed to be a substantial segment of this generation's intellectual elite.

At the heart of the system, unquestioned by even the hundred percenters themselves, lies the principle of selectivity. As a member of Key and Seal expressed it, "In a democracy, we are supposedly free to become as exclusive or as gregarious as we like, and if in a club situation we choose to be exclusive, this is our privilege." From that bit of casuistry—more often expressed as an innocent belief that "you've got a right to choose your friends and the guys you're going to eat with"—the code of values can be relentlessly deduced which summarily condemns certain personality traits, ethnic groups, and even scholarship, intellectualism and originality themselves *per se*.

A truly liberal education should not only reject bigotry and prejudice but also avoid the opposite extreme—the position that there are no significant differences between men in terms of personality, social charm, race, or religious conviction. Its task is rather to show that these factors have nothing to do with one's ethical worth or human dignity—to help the student remold his system of values so that none of these traits are the controlling factor in evaluating another human being—to deepen and expand his vision to the point where he rejoices in human diversity and creative individuality and actively seeks it out. Social insulation, a striving for comfortable homogeneous groups, the frank institutionalization of arbitrary and unreflective prejudices —these do not contribute to that aim. Even if racial discrimination were eliminated from Bicker, the general principle of an ill-founded discrimination would remain as an axiom of Princeton's entire social structure.

Perhaps the most unfortunate victims of Princeton's vicious rushing process are not those scores of students who are dumped in undesirable organizations or left altogether out in the cold. Perhaps the real victims of Bicker are the hundreds of students who happily make the most respectable and desirable clubs on the street. It is they who have consented to build their prestige, success, and social contentment on the hypocrisy, inhumanity, servility, and sheer unreason upon which Princeton's club system and Bicker procedure are obviously based. In letting her students, after months of reading Plato and Kant, Milton and Thoreau, pass complacently through the two weeks of Bicker, Princeton may well be defeating her own highest efforts at cultivating an operative system of values, and may be inducing in her sons the unrefined sort of ethical blindness which adjusts to the reality of what is, by tactfully refraining from seriously applying standards of what is right.

President Wilson tried to reorganize the clubs with a philosophy of education which viewed the student social structure as a primary concern and an area of legitimate jurisdiction for a great university. He sought to rebuild that structure on a principle which was the inverse of selectivity: the principle of geographical, academic, economic, and intellectual distribution within the House, with diversity of race and religion being considered relevant only insofar as they are eagerly sought after, and never forming a basis for exclusion. The same element which finally defeated him in 1908 would be sure to oppose vigorously any similar move by President Goheen to alter the clubs today.

The alumni of Wilson's time organized meetings of protest. One of the leading graduates of Princeton wrote to the *Alumni Weekly* denouncing the idea that students should be compelled to mix with their inferiors—"no one can make a gentleman associate with a mucker." In the pages of the *New York Sun*, an indignant letter signed "Ivy" appeared, demanding to know "Is it possible that the doctrines of the confiscation of property and the superior wisdom of those in high places which have recently been so characteristic of our political life are to be received with favour in one of the most historic and conservative of our institutions of learning?"

Then, as now, the overwhelming majority of the faculty favored the substitution of "the college plan" for the club system, and the great masses of Western alumni also supported Wilson's efforts.

But the Eastern alumni, working through the Board of Trustees and making free use of financial pressure, defeated Princeton's greatest president and the founder of her celebrated preceptorial system, in what he regarded as "nothing less than the most critical work of my whole administration, the work upon which its whole vitality and success depends."

Flurries of protest have arisen on the Princeton campus. In 1918 and again in 1949, the demands of the students themselves forced the clubs to consider the necessity of 100 per cent club membership and finally compelled them to adopt it over strong alumni opposition. The principle has long since degenerated, however, and this year it was openly exposed as a patent farce.

At 2:10 in the morning, the meeting in the library at last breaks up and the decision descends. The sophomores in Ivy's dining room are hushed as they hear the verdict:

". . . the ICC will take no responsibility for those who have re-fused to take bids to Prospect. They consider any reasons for refusing as invalid . . ."

So the sophistry predicted by the *Princetonian* is made complete. Prospect held an open Bicker. Therefore, in effect, every sophomore wanting to join a club could have gone to Prospect. Therefore 100 per cent.

". . . The ICC can determine no valid reason for distinguishing be-tween Prospect Cooperative Club and the other sixteen upperclass eating clubs, and holds that a bid to Prospect is as good as a bid to any other club. Nor can the ICC determine any valid reason for refusing an opportunity to join Prospect Club . . ."

They word the statement as firmly as possible, for they already know that no one, least of all themselves, believes a single word of it. But the lie sustains the system for another year.

A petition passes among the hundred percenters. It objects that racial and religious discrimination has been exercised in excluding them from the clubs, and pleads for a reply, a public review, a denial or an explanation. The ICC flatly refuses to recognize it.

After a Bicker that took five extra nights of haggling to get a bid for everyone in 1955, the *Daily Princetonian* and other university

organizations demanded the provision of an alternative to the club
system. The result was the creation of the now discredited Wilson
Lodge. It is in the rapid physical improvement of the Lodge plant,
however, and the dim hope that it may eventually evolve into Wilson's
conception of a House, that the *Princetonian* and most of the other
critics of the clubs still look for salvation. Just such a project was
placed before Woodrow Wilson as a suggested compromise with his
demand that the clubs be abolished altogether and the "Quad Plan,"
as he called it, be made universal. Wilson rejected it. He thought
such a "sample quad" would be doomed from the start since only
men not in the clubs would join it. The proposal merely dodged the
main issue—the principle of selectivity—and prolonged the evils of
exclusion for both club and non-club men. It did nothing toward
the solution of the problem that tormented Wilson at Princeton: "the
blighting of the intellectual interests of many of her best minds and
finest spirits."

A few hours pass and despite going late to bed and the throb of
stubborn hangovers, hundreds of undergraduates drag themselves to
chapel Sunday morning, signing little white cards at the door in order
to receive credit for having been there.

"The University is vitally concerned with all aspects of Bicker,"
says William D'O. Lippincott, Dean of Students, "but it has been,
and still is, the policy to leave the conduct of club elections completely up to the undergraduates. We do not plan to use pressure
to have these men integrated."

The light filters majestically down through the great blue stained-
glass windows. (Twenty-three sophomores still without a club, fifteen of these Jewish, five Merit Scholars.)

"The unfortunate allegations of religious discrimination . . . obscure the plain facts that there are today members of the three major
faiths in this country in each of the seventeen eating clubs and that
every one of the sophomores who has not joined a club in 1958 was
offered club membership."—Robert F. Goheen, President, Princeton
University—"It is fair to say that the seriousness of these allegations
has been exaggerated by several individuals who sought to impose
their wishes on the clubs . . ."

"The ICC recognizes the right of every club to be selective. Selectivity implies the right of a club to impose a religious quota, if it so
desires."—Text of a statement released by the Interclub Committee,
Princeton University, February 10, 1958—"The ICC does not approve
of religious and racial discrimination, but has no power to control

the Bicker policy of individual clubs. Ultimate responsibility for religious and racial discrimination rests with the individual members of the individual clubs."

(According to all present indications Bicker will be back next year.)

The voice of the organ echoes down the mighty, Gothic nave as the congregation rises to sing the Doxology—

"Praise God from whom all blessings flow . . ."

Problems for Thought and Writing

I

1. Of this article the author remarked: "It was my intention in writing this to raise the broader social issues which plague nearly every campus rather than merely to 'dump on Princeton' where they happen to be so nearly focused." Are issues similar to those raised here evident on your campus?

2. Do you think it possible or advisable to bring ideals of a "genuine democracy" (as Woodrow Wilson conceived it) to student organizations on a campus? Do you agree with Wilson in thinking that "social exclusiveness constitutes the worst possible soil for serious intellectual endeavor"?

3. Make a list of the values employed by most of the Princeton clubs. How many of these values do you accept as part of your personal code?

4. If you were a Princeton student and received an invitation from Ivy, but were at the same time seriously disturbed by the revelations in this article, what would be your course of action?

5. What is your reaction to the statement of President Goheen (pages 16–17)? How has the reading of the article affected your reaction?

6. Why should the solid clubmen be so concerned over the 100-per-cent figure?

II

7. The accusations of the ICC against the *Princetonian* included "incompetence," failure to "cooperate," a "negative" and "critical" attitude. What name would George Orwell (page 48) give to such terms? What name would James H. Robinson (page 461) give to the motives behind them?

8. On page 11 the author writes, "But one can clearly see why a social club would only be sensible in excluding such an individual. . . ." What term do we have for the particular *tone* of this statement? (See "Problems for Thought and Writing" after Powell, page 146.)

9. Define *euphemism*. What examples of it exist in this article?

10. Define or identify: casuistry, mucker, "wonk," attenuated, stereotype, anonymity, preceptorial.

11. This article was written by a Harvard sophomore. The editors have chosen it as an example of good undergraduate writing: an example of the level of expository excellence they hope this volume will help you to achieve. What, in your opinion, are the virtues of the article? Is the writing in your campus literary magazine—if your campus has one—this good?

~

THE APOSTATE*   *George Milburn*

Harry, you been jacking me up about how I been neglecting
Rotary here lately, so I'm just going to break down and tell you
something. Now I don't want you to take this personal, Harry, because it's not meant personal at all. No siree! Not *a*-tall! But, just
between you and I, Harry, I'm not going to be coming out to Rotary
lunches any more. I mean I'm quitting Rotary! . . .

Now whoa there! Whoa! Whoa just a minute and let me get in
a word edgeways. Just let me finish my little say.

Don't you never take it into your head that I haven't been wrestling
with this thing plenty. I mean I've argued it all out with myself.
Now I'm going to tell you the whyfor and the whereof and the how-
come about this, Harry, but kindly don't let what I say go no further.
Please keep it strictly on the Q.T. Because I guess the rest of the
boys would suspicion that I was turning highbrow on them. But
you've always been a buddy to me, Harry, you mangy old son of a
hoss thief, you, so what I'm telling you is the straight dope.

Harry, like you no doubt remember, up till a few months ago
Rotary was about "the most fondest thing I is of," as the nigger says.
There wasn't nothing that stood higher for me than Rotary.

Well, here, about a year ago last fall I took a trip down to the
university to visit my son and go to a football game. You know
Hubert Junior, my boy. Sure. Well, this is his second year down
at the university. Yes, that boy is getting a college education. I
mean, I'm all for youth having a college education.

Of course I think there is such a thing as too much education working a detriment. Take, for instance, some of these longhairs running
around knocking the country right now. But what I mean is, a good,
sound, substantial college education. I don't mean a string of letters
a yard long for a man to write after his John Henry. I just mean that
I want my boy to have his sheepskin, they call it, before he starts out
in the world. Like the fellow says, I want him to get his A.B. degree,
and then he can go out and get his J.O.B.

* From *No More Trumpets* by George Milburn. Copyright 1933 by Harcourt,
Brace and Company, Inc. Reprinted by permission of Paul R. Reynolds & Son.

Now, Harry, I always felt like a father has got certain responsibilities to his son. That's just good Rotary. That's all that is. You know that that's just good Rotary yourself, Harry. Well, I always wanted Hubert to think about me just like I was a pal to him, or say an older brother, maybe. Hubert always knew that all he had to do was come to me, and I would act like a big buddy to him, irregardless.

Well, like I was telling you, Harry, I started Hubert in to the university two years ago, and after he had been there about two months, I thought I would run down and see how he was getting along and go to a football game. So I and Mrs. T. drove over one Friday. We didn't know the town very well, so we stopped at a filling station, and I give Hubert a ring, and he come right on down to where we was to show us the way. Just as soon as he come up, I could see right then that he had something on his mind bothering him.

He called me aside and took me into the filling-station restroom, and says: "For the love of God, Dad, take that Rotary button out of your coat lapel," he says to me.

Harry, that come as a big surprise to me, and I don't mind telling you that it just about took the wind out of my sails. But I wasn't going to let on to him, so I rared back on my dignity, and says, "Why, what do you mean, take that Rotary button out of my lapel, young man?" I says to him.

"Dad," Hubert says to me, serious, "any frat house has always got a few cynics in it. If you was to wear that Rotary button in your lapel out to the frat house, just as soon as you got out of sight, some of those boys at the house would razz the life out of me," he says.

"Hubert," I says, "there's not a thing that this lapel badge represents that any decent, moral person could afford to make fun of. If that's the kind of Reds you got out at your fraternity, the kind that would razz a what you might call sacred thing—yes sir, a sacred thing—like Rotary, well I and your mamma can just go somewheres else and put up. I don't guess the hotels have quit running," I says to him.

By now I was on my high horse right, see?

"Now, Dad," Hubert says, "it's not that. I mean, person'ly I'm awful proud of you. It's just that I haven't been pledged to this fraternity long, see, and when some of those older members found out you was a Rotarian they would deal me a lot of misery, and I couldn't say nothing. Person'ly I think Rotary is all right," he says to me.

"Well, you better, son," I says, "or I'm going to begin to think that you're sick in the head."

The way he explained it, though, Harry, that made it a horse of a different tail, as the saying goes, so I give in and took off my Rotary button right there. Stuck it in my pocket, see? So we went on out and visited at Hubert's fraternity house, and do you know that those boys just got around there and treated we folks like we was princes of the blood. I mean you would of thought that I was an old ex-graduate of that university. And we saw the big pigskin tussle the next day, fourteen to aught, favor us, and we had such a scrumptious time all around I forgot all about what Hubert had said.

Ever'thing would of been all right, except for what happened later. I guess some of those older boys at the frat house begin using their form of psychology on Hubert. I mean they finely got his mind set against Rotary, because when he come home for the summer vacation that was about the size of things.

I mean all last summer, I thought Hubert never would let up. He just kept it up, making sarcastic remarks about Rotary, see? Even when we was on our vacation trip. You know we drove out to California and back last summer, Harry. Come back with the same air in the tires we started out with. Well, I thought it would be kind of nice to drop in and eat with the Hollywood Rotary—you know, just to be able to say I had. Well, do you know that that boy Hubert made so much fun of the idea I just had to give it up? That was the way it was the whole trip. He got his mother around on his side, too. Just to be frank with you, I never got so sick and tired of anything in all my born days.

Well, Harry, I had my dander up there for a while, and all the bickering in the world couldn't of shook me from my stand. But finely Hubert went back to college in September, and I thought I would have a little peace. Then I just got to thinking about it, and it all come over me. "Look here, Mister Man," I says to myself, "your faith and loyalty to Rotary may be a fine thing, and all that, but it's just costing you the fellowship of your own son." Now a man can't practice Rotary in the higher sense, and yet at the same time be letting his own son's fellowship get loose from him. So there it was. Blood's thicker than water, Harry. You'll have to admit that.

Right along in there, Harry, was the first time I begin to attending meetings irregular. I'll tell you—you might not think so—but it was a pretty tough struggle for me. I remember one Monday noon, Rotary-meeting day, I happened to walk past the Hotel Beckman just

at lunchtime. The windows of the Venetian Room was open, and
I could hear you boys singing a Rotary song. You know that one
we sing set to the tune of "Last Night on the Back Porch." It goes:

> I love the Lions in the morning,
> The Exchange Club at night,
> I love the Y's men in the evening,
> And Kiwanis are all right . . .

Well, I couldn't carry a tune if I had it in a sack, but anyway that's
the way it goes. So I just stopped in my tracks and stood there
listening to that song coming out of the Hotel Beckman dining room.
And when the boys come to the last verse,

> I love the Optimists in the springtime,
> The Ad Club in the fall,
> But each day—and in every way—
> I love Rotary best of all. . . .

I tell you, Harry, that just got me. I had a lump in my throat big
enough to choke a cow. The tears begin coming up in my eyes, and
it might sound ridiculous to hear me tell it now, but I could of broke
down and bawled right there on the street. I got a grip on myself
and walked on off, but right then I says to myself, "The hell with
Hubert and his highbrow college-fraternity ideas; I'm going back to
Rotary next week."

Well, I did go back the next week, and what happened decided me
on taking the step I decided on. Here's what decided me. You
know I never got very well acquainted with Gay Harrison, the new
secretary. I mean, of course, I know him all right, but he hasn't been
in Rotary only but about a year. Well, on that particular day, I just
happened to let my tongue slip and called him Mister Harrison,
instead of by his nickname. Well, of course, the boys slapped a dollar
fine on me right then and there. I haven't got no kick to make about
that, but the point is, I had a letter from Hubert in my pocket right
then, telling me that he had run short of money. So I just couldn't
help but be struck by the idea "I wish I was giving Hubert this
dollar." So that's what decided me on devoting my time and finances
to another kind of fellowship, Harry.

I get down to the university to see Hubert more frequent now.
I make it a point to. And the boys come to me, and I been helping
them a little on their frat building fund. There's a fine spirit of
fellowship in an organization like that. Some boys from the best

families of the State are members, too. You might think from what
I said that they'd be uppish, but they're not. No siree. Not a bit of
it. I been down there enough for them to know me, now, and they
all pound me on the back and call me H.T., just like I was one of
them. And I do them, too. And I notice that when they sit down
to a meal, they have some songs they sing just as lively and jolly as
any we had at Rotary. Of course, like Hubert said, a few of them
might have some wild-haired ideas about Rotary, but they're young
yet. And as far as I can see there's not a knocker nor a sourbelly
among them. Absolutely democratic.

It puts me in mind of a little incidence that happened last month
when the frat threw a big Dad's Day banquet for us down there.
All the fathers of the boys from all over the State was there. Well,
to promote the spirit of fellowship between dad and son, the fraternity
boys all agreed to call their dads by their first name, just treating
their dads like big buddies. So at the table Hubert happened to
forget for a minute, and says to me "Dad" something. Well sir, the
president of the frat flashed right out, "All right, Hubie, we heard you
call H.T. 'Dad.' So that'll just cost you a dollar for the ice-cream
fund." Ever'body had a good laugh at Hubert getting caught like
that, but do you know, that boy of mine just forked right over without
making a kick. That shows the stuff, don't it, Harry? Nothing
wrong with a boy like that.

And the whole bunch is like that, ever' one of them. I'll tell you,
Harry, the boys at that frat of Hubert's are the builders in the coming
generation. Any man of vision can see that.

Well, that's that. Now what was you going to say?

Problems for Thought and Writing

1. What is the basic irony of the story? How is it achieved? (See pages 146
   and 154.)

2. What is being satirized here? The father? The Rotary Club? Fraternities?
   The son? A set of values? Say precisely what the target of the story is.
   How does the language of the speaker serve to satirize these things? (See
   Powell, page 142.)

3. Read both "The Princeton Bicker" (page 5) and this story in conjunction
   with Erich Fromm's "The Illusion of Individuality" (page 198). In different
   ways, all three treat the question of personal *vs.* social values. How far are
   the people in "The Princeton Bicker" and "The Apostate" victims of the
   situation Fromm describes (page 207): "The loss of the self has increased the
   necessity to conform, for it results in a profound doubt of one's own identity"?
   Consult also Whyte (page 217) and Chiaromonte (page 225).

4. Does this story indicate in any way that the fraternity practices racial exclusiveness?

5. The story was first published in 1932. Does it strike you as dated?

6. Who is the "mock reader" of this story? See Gibson, page 70.

7. Are the father and son in the story snobs? What is snobbery? Is snobbery compatible with democratic values? (See Oscar Mandel, "Nobility and the United States," page 171.)

8. Since something seems to be satirized in this story, and since satire is always based on a standard of value, how do we find out what that standard is? On what standard of taste does the story rest?

~

GATE RECEIPTS AND GLORY *

Robert M. Hutchins

The football season is about to release the nation's colleges to the pursuit of education, more or less. Soon the last nickel will be rung up at the gate, the last halfback will receive his check, and the last alumnus will try to pay off those bets he can recall. Most of the students have cheered themselves into insensibility long ago.

This has been going on for almost fifty years. It is called "overemphasis on athletics," and everybody deplores it. It has been the subject of scores of reports, all of them shocking. It has been held to be crass professionalism, all the more shameful because it masquerades as higher education. But nobody has done anything about it. Why? I think it is because nobody wants to. Nobody wants, or dares, to defy the public, dishearten the students, or deprive alma mater of the loyalty of the alumni. Most emphatically of all, nobody wants to give up the gate receipts. The trouble with football is the money that is in it, and every code of amateurism ever written has failed for this reason.

Money is the cause of athleticism in the American colleges. Athleticism is not athletics. Athletics is physical education, a proper function of the college if carried on for the welfare of the students. Athleticism is not physical education but sports promotion, and it is

* From *The Saturday Evening Post*, December 3, 1938. Reprinted by permission of James Brown Associates, Inc.

carried on for the monetary profit of the colleges through the entertainment of the public. This article deals with athleticism, its cause, its symptoms and its cure.

Of all the crimes committed by athleticism under the guise of athletics, the most heinous is the confusion of the country about the primary purpose of higher education. The primary purpose of higher education is the development of the mind. This does not mean that colleges and universities should neglect the health of their students or should fail to provide them with every opportunity for physical development. The question is a question of emphasis. Colleges and universities are the only institutions which are dedicated to the training of the mind. In these institutions, the development of the body is important, but secondary.

The apologists of athleticism have created a collection of myths to convince the public that biceps is a substitute for brains. Athletics, we are told, produces well-rounded men, filled with the spirit of fair play. Athletics is good for the health of the players; it is also good for the morals of the spectators. Leadership on the playing fields means leadership in life. The Duke of Wellington said so. Athletes are red-blooded Americans, and athletic colleges are bulwarks against Communism. Gate receipts are used to build laboratories and to pay for those sports that can't pay for themselves. Football is purely a supplement to study. And without a winning team a college cannot hope to attract the students or the gifts which its work requires.

These myths have about them a certain air of plausibility. They are widely accepted. But they are myths. As the Carnegie Foundation has said, "The fact that all these supposed advantages are tinged at one point or another with the color of money casts over every relaxation of standards a mercenary shadow." The myths are designed, consciously or unconsciously, to conceal the color of money and to surround a financial enterprise with the rosy glow of Health, Manhood, Public Spirit and Education.

Since the primary task of colleges and universities is the development of the mind, young people who are more interested in their bodies than in their minds should not go to college. Institutions devoted to the development of the body are numerous and inexpensive. They do not pretend to be institutions of learning, and there is no faculty of learned men to consume their assets or interfere with their objectives.

Athleticism attracts boys and girls to college who do not want and cannot use a college education. They come to college for "fun."

They would be just as happy in the grandstand at the Yankee Stadium, and at less expense to their parents. They drop out of college after a while, but they are a sizable fraction of many freshman classes, and, while they last, they make it harder for the college to educate the rest. Even the earnest boys and girls who come to college for an education find it difficult, around the middle of November, to concentrate on the physiology of the frog or the mechanics of the price structure.

Worse yet, athleticism gives the student a mistaken notion of the qualities that make for leadership in later life. The ambition of the average student who grew up reading Stover at Yale is to imitate as closely as possible the attitude and manners of the current football hero. Since this country, like all others, needs brains more than brawn at the moment, proposing football heroes as models for the rising generation can hardly have a beneficial effect on the national future.

The exponents of athleticism tell us that athletics is good for a boy. They are right. But athleticism focuses its attention on doing good for the boys who least need it. Less than half of the undergraduate males—800 out of 1900 at the University of Chicago, for instance—are eligible for intercollegiate competition. But where athleticism reigns, as happily it does not at Chicago, 75 per cent of the attention of the physical-education staff must be lavished on that fraction of the student body who make varsity squads. The Carnegie Foundation found that 37 per cent of all undergraduates engage in no athletic activity, not even in intramural games. Since graduate and professional students are also eliminated from competition, we have more than half the college and university population of the country neglected because we devote ourselves, on the pretext that athletics is good for a boy, to overdeveloping a handful of stars.

And athletics, as it is conducted in many colleges today, is not even good for the handful. Since the fate of the coach sometimes depends on victory, players have sometimes been filled with college spirit through caffein tablets and strychnine. At least one case reached the public in which a coach removed a plaster cast from a star's ankle and sent him in "to win." The Carnegie Foundation found that 17.6 per cent of all football players in twenty-two colleges suffered serious injuries. The same report asserts that college athletes have about the same life expectancy as the average college man and not so good an expectancy as men of high scholarship rank.

Most athletes will admit that the combination of weariness and nervousness after a hard practice is not conducive to study. We can thus understand why athleticism does not contribute to the production of well-rounded men destined for leadership after graduation. In many American colleges it is possible for a boy to win twelve letters without learning how to write one. I need only suggest that you conjure up the name of the greatest college football star of fifteen years ago and ask yourself, "Where is he now?" Many of his contemporaries who made no ninety-yard runs enjoy at least as good health as our hero and considerably more esteem. The cheers that rock the stadium have a rapid depreciation rate.

The alleged connection between athletic experience and moral principles is highly dubious. At worst, the college athlete is led to believe that whatever he does, including slugging, is done for the sake of alma mater. He does not learn that it is sometimes better, both on and off the playing field, to lose than to win. At best, the college athlete acquires habits of fair play, but there is no evidence that he needs to join the football squad to acquire them; he can get them from the studies he pursues and from living in a college community which, since it is a community of comparatively idealistic people, is less tolerant of meanness than most. The football players who threw the campus "radicals" in the lake at the University of Wisconsin knew little of fair play, and incidents in which free speech in the colleges is suppressed have frequently shown the athletic group lined up on the side of suppression.

Even if it were true that athletics developed courage, prudence, tolerance and justice, the commercialism that characterizes amateur sport today would be sufficient to harden the purest young man. He is made to feel that his primary function in college is to win football games. The coach demands it, because the coach wants to hold his job. The college demands it, because the college wants the gate receipts. And the alumni demand it, because the test of a college is the success of its teams and they want to be alumni of a good college.

The university with which I am connected has a different kind of college and a different kind of alumni. I can make this statement because I am in no way responsible for its happy condition. When John D. Rockefeller founded the University of Chicago forty-five years ago, he told William Rainey Harper to run it as he pleased. It pleased Mr. Harper to appoint men of character and distinction. One of the men he appointed was Amos Alonzo Stagg. To the amazement of the country, Mr. Harper made Mr. Stagg a professor on life appointment. It was the first time such a thing had happened.

Secure in his position, whether he produced winning teams or not, Mr. Stagg for forty years kept Chicago an amateur university. Some of his teams were champions. Chicago still has the second best won-and-lost record in the Big Ten, although we are using it up pretty fast. But through all those years Chicago students learned that athletics is only one aspect, and a secondary one, of college education. The result is that today Chicago's alumni are loyal to their university and generous with their moral and financial support.

The prestige that winning teams confer upon a university, and the profits that are alleged to accompany prestige, are the most serious obstacles to reform. Alumni whose sole interest in their alma mater is its athletic standing lose their interest when its teams run on bad years. The result, which horrifies college presidents, is that the alumni do not encourage their children or their neighbors' children to attend the old college. The American public believes that there is a correlation between muscle and manliness. Poor teams at any college are supposed to mean that the character of its student body is in decay.

The myth that donors, like alumni and the public, are impressed by football victories collapses on examination of the report recently issued by the John Price Jones Corporation, showing gifts and bequests to colleges and universities between 1920 and 1937. Among the universities, Harvard, Yale and Chicago led the list, each having received more than $50,000,000. The records of these universities on the gridiron were highly irregular, to say the least; that of one of them was positively bad. Among the colleges, Williams, Wesleyan and Bowdoin led the list, each having received more than $5,000,000. Men of wealth were undeterred by the inconsequential athletic status of these colleges; it does not appear that philanthropists were attracted to their rivals by the glorious victories they scored over them.

If athleticism is bad for students, players, alumni and the public, it is even worse for the colleges and universities themselves. They want to be educational institutions, but they can't. The story of the famous halfback whose only regret, when he bade his coach farewell, was that he hadn't learned to read and write is probably exaggerated. But we must admit that pressure from trustees, graduates, "friends," presidents and even professors has tended to relax academic standards. These gentry often overlook the fact that a college should not be interested in a fullback who is a half-wit. Recruiting, subsidizing and the double educational standard cannot exist without the knowledge and the tacit approval, at least, of the colleges and universities themselves. Certain institutions encourage susceptible professors to be nice to athletes now admitted by paying them for serving as "faculty representatives" on the college athletic board.

We have the word of the famous Carnegie Report that the maxim "every athlete is a needy athlete" is applied up and down the land. Hard times have reduced the price of football players in conformity with the stock-market index. But when we get back to prosperity we may hope to see the resurrection of that phenomenon of the Golden Era, a corporation which tried to corner the market by signing up high-school athletes and auctioning them off to the highest bidder. The promoter of this interesting venture came to a bad end, and I regretted his fate, for he was a man of imagination and a friend of the football tramp, who has always been a victim of cutthroat competition.

Enthusiastic alumni find it hard to understand why a fine young man who can play football should be deprived of a college education just because he is poor. No young man should be deprived of an education just because he is poor. We need more scholarships, but athletic ability should have nothing to do with their award. Frequently the fine young man the alumnus has in mind can do nothing but play football. The alumnus should try hiring the young man and turning him loose in his factory. From the damage that would result he could gain some insight into the damage done his alma mater through admitting students without intellectual interests or capacity.

If the colleges and universities are to commend themselves to the public chiefly through their athletic accomplishments, it seems to me that they ought to be reorganized with that aim in view. Instead of looking for college presidents among educators, we should find them among those gentlemen who have a solid record of sports promotion behind them. Consider what Tex Rickard could have done for Harvard. I am rapidly approaching the retirement age, and I can think of no worthier successor, from the standpoint of athleticism, than Mr. Mike Jacobs, the sage of the prize ring. Mr. Jacobs has demonstrated his genius at selecting young men and developing them in such a way as to gather both gold and glory for the profession of which he is the principal ornament.

Another suggestion for elevating Chicago to the level of some of its sister institutions was advanced last year by Mr. William McNeill, editor of the student paper. Mr. McNeill proposed that instead of buying football players, the colleges should buy race horses. Alumni could show their devotion to alma mater by giving their stables to alma mater. For the time being, Yale would be way out in front, for both Mr. Jock Whitney and Mr. Cornelius Vanderbilt Whitney graduated there. But by a judicious distribution of honorary degrees horse fanciers who never went to college might be induced to come to the assistance of institutions which had not attracted students who had become prosperous enough to indulge in the sport of kings. Chicago could, for instance, confer the doctorate of letters upon that prominent turfman, Alderman Bathhouse John Coughlin, and persuade The Bath to change the color of his silks from green to maroon. The alumni could place their money on Chicago across the board. The students could cheer. Most important of all, the horses would not have to pass examinations.

The center of football strength has been moving, since the turn of the century, from the East to the Middle West, from the Middle West to the Pacific Coast, and from the Pacific Coast to the South and Southwest. According to a recent analysis by Professor Eells, of Stanford, the leading educational institutions of the country are, in order of their eminence, Harvard, Chicago, Columbia, Yale, California, Johns Hopkins, Princeton, Michigan and Wisconsin. None of these universities, except California, is close to the top of Professor Dickinson's annual athletic ranking, and California's success has something to do with the fact that it has a male undergraduate enrollment of 7500 compared with Harvard's 3700 and Chicago's 1900. We used to say that Harvard enjoyed its greatest years as an educational institution when Ted Coy was playing at Yale. If football continues to move to the poorer colleges, the good ones may be saved. Meanwhile it is only fair to say that some inferior colleges are going broke attempting to get rich—and famous—at football.

Athleticism, like crime, does not pay. Last summer St. Mary's College, home of the Galloping Gaels, was sold at auction and bought in by a bondholders' committee. This was the country's most sensational football college. Since 1924 it has won eighty-six and tied seven of its 114 games. Its academic efforts were inexpensive and its gate receipts immense. The bondholders were surprised to learn that it was running $72,000 a year behind in its budget. They were even more surprised to find that football expenses were almost equal to football income.

To make big money in athletics you have to spend big money. Winning coaches come high. The head coaches in our larger colleges and universities receive, on the average, $611 a year more than the highest-ranking professors in the same institutions. One famous coach of a small college was found, not long ago, receiving $25,000 in a year, between his salary and his percentage of the receipts. This situation is not without its advantages to the members of my hard-pressed profession. The president of one celebrated university was paid $8000 a year. A coach qualified to direct the football destinies of the institution could not be found for less than $15,000. Since the trustees had to have the coach, and since they couldn't pay the president less than the coach, they raised the president's salary to $15,000 too.

Subsidizing is expensive. Equipment, travel, advertising and publicity are expensive. These things have been known to run to $10,000 or $15,000, even in the smaller colleges, for football alone. Some of the more glorious teams carry a Pullman full of newspapermen across the country with them, paying the reporters' expenses.

The myth that football receipts support research, education, or even other sports has just been exploded by President Wilkins, of Oberlin. His analysis of football costs in twenty-two typical colleges shows that only two have a surplus of football income over football expense. The twenty others spend on football all they get from football and $1743 apiece a year additional. This is the income on $45,000 of their endowment.

President Wilkins' investigation of the colleges raises an interesting question. If most of the colleges lose money at football, is it not likely that most of the universities, with their proportionately heavy expense, are also playing a losing game? I know of only one university that ever claimed to have built a laboratory out of excess gate receipts, but many of our larger institutions claim that football finances their so-called minor sports. Perhaps it does in a few universities and in the years of their great teams. But I should like to see a study made of the universities along the lines of President Wilkins' investigation of the colleges; and I might suggest to those who make the study that they scrutinize the accounting methods of some of our educators to see if they are charging up coaches and even trainers as "professors," the purchase of players to "contingent expense," and the debt on the stadium to "real estate."

In 1925 the American Association of University Professors expressed the hope that colleges would in time publish the cost of stadiums. This hope has not been fulfilled, and for the most part the cost of stadiums remains one of the dark secrets of the athletic underworld. I understand that there are only two stadiums in the Big Ten which were not built with borrowed money, and that two have not yet been paid for. One cost $1,700,000.

Last fall I met a university president the day before his team was to play its opening game. All he could say was, "We've got to win tomorrow. We've got to pay off that $35,000 on the stadium this year." The necessity of packing these arenas has led colleges to schedule as many big games as possible. In order to establish the team's value as a spectacle as soon as possible, a big game must be played to open the season. The old scheme of playing easy games until the team is in shape has had to be abandoned. Consequently, practice must begin earlier to get the team in shape earlier. Harvard and Princeton have just extended preseason practice and have given a bad example to the country.

The reason that college stadiums can't be paid off is plain. They are built for one sport, football. A great team year after year might, in fifteen or twenty years, pay off the bond issue. But there are no great teams year after year. Athletic eminence is cyclical. College A has a great team and decides to build a great stadium, so that the entire population can watch it. But the alumni of College B, which is the traditional rival of College A, are irritated because their alma mater is being beaten by those thugs across the river.

So the alumni go out and buy a great team for College B. Colleges C and D also have alumni who also like to win.

In a few years College A is being beaten regularly and the stadium, except for those local citizens who can't afford to get away to watch B, C, and D, is empty. Then College B builds a great new stadium to cash in on its great new record, and goes through the same routine.

There are several factors already operating to reduce athleticism, whether or not we decide to do anything about it. The rise of the junior colleges, which educate freshmen and sophomores only, is reducing the supply of athletic material for the four-year colleges and universities.

Professional football, which is attracting larger and larger crowds, may ultimately do for college football what professional baseball has done for college baseball. And the United States Supreme Court, in a case involving the taxation of gate receipts, has clarified the national mind to some extent by indicating that intercollegiate football is business.

But neither the Supreme Court, nor professional football, nor the junior colleges can be depended upon to reform us. We must reform ourselves. How?

The committees which have studied the subject—and their name is legion—have suggested stricter eligibility rules, reduction of training periods, elimination of recruiting and subsidizing, easier schedules, limitation of each student's participation to one sport, and abandonment of the double scholastic standard for athletes. President-Emeritus Lowell, of Harvard, once proposed the Oxford and Cambridge system of limiting each sport to one game a season, and that one with the college's natural rival. Mr. Lowell's scheme might have the merit of enabling students and the public to work off their seasonal frenzy in one big saturnalia.

These reforms will never achieve reform. They may serve to offset athleticism at those few institutions which are already trying to be colleges instead of football teams. But it is too much to hope that they will affect the colleges and universities at large.

Since money is the cause of athleticism, the cure is to take the money out of athletics. This can be done only in defiance of the students, the alumni, the public, and, in many cases, the colleges themselves. The majority of the colleges and universities will not do it, because in the aggregate they dare not. Johns Hopkins, in Maryland, and Reed College, in Oregon, have dared, but nobody cares, athletically speaking, what Johns Hopkins or Reed does.

The task of taking the money out of athletics must be undertaken by those institutions which are leaders, institutions which can afford the loss of prestige and popularity involved. I suggest that a group of colleges and of universities composed, say, of Amherst, Williams, Dartmouth, Harvard, Yale, Chicago, Michigan, Stanford and California agree to take the following steps, to take them in unison and to take them at once:

1. Reduce admission to ten cents. This will cover the handling costs. For years prominent educators, all the way from Harper, of Chicago, to Butler, of Columbia, have insisted that college athletics should be supported from endowment like any other educational activity. Colleges should support athletics out of their budgets, or get out of athletics, or get out of education.

2. Give the director of athletics and the major coaches some kind of academic tenure, so that their jobs depend on their ability as instructors and their character as men and not on the gates they draw.

While these two steps are being taken, it might be well, for the sake of once more putting students instead of athletes on the college playing fields, to try to stimulate the urge to play for fun and health, instead of the urge to win at any cost. There are two ways to do this, and many colleges and universities are trying both with consider-able satisfaction to their students:

1. Broaden the base of athletic participation, so that all students, graduate and undergraduate, big fellows and little fellows, can play. The development of intramural athletics, which costs less than the maintenance of present programs, is a step in this direction. The English system of selecting a varsity from the intramural teams toward the end of the season and then playing a limited number of intercollegiate games suggests itself at this point.

2. Emphasize games which students will play in later life, when they need recreation and physical fitness as much as in college. Such sports are tennis, handball, skating, swimming, softball, bowling, rackets, golf and touch football. Few college graduates are able to use football, baseball or basketball, except as topics of conversation.

In a word: More athletics, less athleticism.

I think that after the steps I have suggested have been taken by the colleges and universities I have named, the rest of the country's educational institutions will not long be able to ignore their example.

Nor will the public, once the break has been made, attempt for long to prevent reform. The public, in the last analysis, pays for the colleges and the universities. It wants something for its money. It has been taught to accept football. It can, I am confident, be taught to accept education.

The public will not like ten-cent football, because ten-cent football will not be great football. The task of the colleges and the uni-versities, then, is to show the country a substitute for athleticism.

That substitute is light and learning. The colleges and universities, which taught the country football, can teach the country that the effort to discover truth, to transmit the wisdom of the race, and to preserve civilization is exciting and perhaps important too.

Problems for Thought and Writing

I

1. What is the primary purpose of higher education, according to Hutchins? Do you agree with him?

2. Would you characterize this essay as a statement of subjective opinion or as an example of a proposition followed by evidence and proof? Defend your choice. (See Argument and Persuasion, page 539.)

3. Examine as honestly as you can your own motives for having come to college (not to be confused with your present reasons for staying there).

4. On page 27 Hutchins writes, "The American public believes that there is a correlation between muscle and manliness." Is this a safe or accurate generalization? Does Shaw, in "The Eighty-Yard Run," suggest that the American public accepts or rejects such a correlation?

5. Hutchins' article was written in 1938. Does it now seem out-of-date or does it seem prophetic—or does it fall somewhere in between?

II

6. Is Hutchins guilty anywhere in the essay of slanting his meaning or of employing emotionally freighted language? (See Thouless, "Emotional Meanings," page 98.)

7. Find specific places where Hutchins exaggerates his facts. Do the tone and context of the passages usually make clear that the author knows that he is exaggerating, that he wants you to *know* that *he knows*? Is there such a thing as legitimate exaggeration, not dishonest or deceptive, in the interest of persuasion?

~

THE EIGHTY-YARD RUN *   *Irwin Shaw*

The pass was high and wide and he jumped for it, feeling it slap flatly against his hands, as he shook his hips to throw off the halfback who was diving at him. The center floated by, his hands desperately brushing Darling's knee as Darling picked his feet up high and delicately ran over a blocker and an opposing linesman in a jumble on the ground near the scrimmage line. He had ten yards in the clear and picked up speed, breathing easily, feeling his thigh pads rising and falling against his legs, listening to the sound of cleats behind him, pulling away from them, watching the other backs heading him off toward the sideline, the whole picture, the men closing in on him, the blockers fighting for position, the ground he had to cross, all suddenly clear in his head, for the first time in his life not a meaningless confusion of men, sounds, speed. He smiled a little to himself as he ran, holding the ball lightly in front of him with his two hands, his knees pumping high, his hips twisting in the almost-girlish run of a back in a broken field. The first halfback came at him and he fed him his leg, then swung at the last moment, took the shock of the man's shoulder without breaking stride, ran right

* Copyright 1941 by Irwin Shaw. Reprinted from *Mixed Company*, by Irwin Shaw, with permission of Random House, Inc.

through him, his cleats biting securely into the turf. There was only
the safety man now, coming warily at him, his arms crooked, hands
spread. Darling tucked the ball in, spurted at him, driving hard,
hurling himself along, his legs pounding, knees high, all two hundred
pounds bunched into controlled attack. He was sure he was going
to get past the safety man. Without thought, his arms and legs
working beautifully together, he headed right for the safety man,
stiff-armed him, feeling blood spurt instantaneously from the man's
nose onto his hand, seeing his face go awry, head turned, mouth
pulled to one side. He pivoted away, keeping the arm locked, dropping the safety man as he ran easily toward the goal line, with the
drumming of cleats diminishing behind him.

How long ago? It was autumn then and the ground was getting
hard because the nights were cold and leaves from the maples
around the stadium blew across the practice fields in gusts of wind
and the girls were beginning to put polo coats over their sweaters
when they came to watch practice in the afternoons . . . Fifteen
years. Darling walked slowly over the same ground in the spring
twilight, in his neat shoes, a man of thirty-five dressed in a double-
breasted suit, ten pounds heavier in the fifteen years, but not fat,
with the years between 1925 and 1940 showing in his face.

The coach was smiling quietly to himself and the assistant coaches
were looking at each other with pleasure the way they always did
when one of the second stringers suddenly did something fine, bringing credit to them, making their $2,000 a year a tiny bit more secure.

Darling trotted back, smiling, breathing deeply but easily, feeling
wonderful, not tired, though this was the tail end of practice and
he'd run eighty yards. The sweat poured off his face and soaked his
jersey and he liked the feeling, the warm moistness lubricating his
skin like oil. Off in a corner of the field some players were punting
and the smack of leather against the ball came pleasantly through
the afternoon air. The freshmen were running signals on the next
field and the quarterback's sharp voice, the pound of the eleven pairs
of cleats, the "Dig, now, *dig!*" of the coaches, the laughter of the
players all somehow made him feel happy as he trotted back to
midfield, listening to the applause and shouts of the students along
the sidelines, knowing that after that run the coach would have to
start him Saturday against Illinois.

Fifteen years, Darling thought, remembering the shower after the
workout, the hot water steaming off his skin and the deep soapsuds
and all the young voices singing with the water streaming down and

towels going and managers running in and out and the sharp sweet smell of oil of wintergreen and everybody clapping him on the back as he dressed and Packard, the captain, who took being captain very seriously, coming over to him and shaking his hand saying, "Darling, you're going to go places in the next two years."

The assistant manager fussed over him, wiping a cut on his leg with alcohol and iodine, the little sting making him realize suddenly how fresh and whole and solid his body felt. The manager slapped a piece of adhesive tape over the cut and Darling noticed the sharp clean white of the tape against the ruddiness of the skin, fresh from the shower.

He dressed slowly, the softness of his shirt and the soft warmth of his wool socks and his flannel trousers a reward against his skin after the harsh pressure of the shoulder harness and thigh and hip pads. He drank three glasses of cold water, the liquid reaching down coldly inside of him, soothing the harsh dry places in his throat and belly left by the sweat and running and shouting of practice.

Fifteen years.

The sun had gone down and the sky was green behind the stadium and he laughed quietly to himself as he looked at the stadium, rearing above the tree, and knew that on Saturday when the 70,000 voices roared as the team came running out onto the field, part of that enormous salute would be for him. He walked slowly, listening to the gravel crunch satisfactorily under his toes in the still twilight, feeling his clothes swing lightly against his skin, breathing the thin evening air, feeling the wind move softly in his damp hair, wonderfully cool behind his ears and at the nape of his neck.

Louise was waiting for him at the road, in her car. The top was down and he noticed all over again, as he always did when he saw her, how pretty she was, the rough blonde hair and the large, inquiring eyes and the bright mouth, smiling now.

She threw the door open. "Were you good today?" she asked.

"Pretty good," he said. He climbed in, sank luxuriously into the soft leather, stretched his legs far out. He smiled, thinking of the eighty yards. "Pretty damn good."

She looked at him seriously for a moment, then scrambled around, like a little girl, kneeling on the seat next to him, grabbed him, her hands along his ears, and kissed him as he sprawled, head back, on the seat cushion. She let go of him, but kept her head close to his, over his. Darling reached up slowly and rubbed the back of his hand against her cheek, lit softly by a street lamp a hundred feet away. They looked at each other, smiling.

Louise drove down to the lake and they sat there silently, watching the moon rise behind the hills on the other side. Finally he reached over, pulled her gently to him, kissed her. Her lips grew soft, her body sank into his, tears formed in her eyes. He knew, for the first time, that he could do whatever he wanted with her.

"Tonight," he said. "I'll call for you at seven-thirty. Can you get out?"

She looked at him. She was smiling, but the tears were still full in her eyes. "All right," she said. "I'll get out. How about you? Won't the coach raise hell?"

Darling grinned. "I got the coach in the palm of my hand," he said. "Can you wait till seven-thirty?"

She grinned back at him. "No," she said.

They kissed and she started the car and they went back to town for dinner. He sang on the way home.

Christian Darling, thirty-five years old, sat on the frail spring grass, greener now than it ever would be again on the practice field, looked thoughtfully up at the stadium, a deserted ruin in the twilight. He had started on the first team that Saturday and every Saturday after that for the next two years, but it had never been as satisfactory as it should have been. He never had broken away, the longest run he'd ever made was thirty-five yards, and that in a game that was already won, and then that kid had come up from the third team, Diederich, a blank-faced German kid from Wisconsin, who ran like a bull, ripping lines to pieces Saturday after Saturday, plowing through, never getting hurt, never changing his expression, scoring more points, gaining more ground that all the rest of the team put together, making everybody's All-American, carrying the ball three times out of four, keeping everybody else out of the headlines. Darling was a good blocker and he spent his Saturday afternoons working on the big Swedes and Polacks who played tackle and end for Michigan, Illinois, Purdue, hurling into huge pile-ups, bobbing his head wildly to elude the great raw hands swinging like meat-cleavers at him as he went charging in to open up holes for Diederich coming through like a locomotive behind him. Still, it wasn't so bad. Everybody liked him and he did his job and he was pointed out on the campus and boys always felt important when they introduced their girls to him at their proms, and Louise loved him and watched

him faithfully in the games, even in the mud, when your own
mother wouldn't know you, and drove him around in her car keeping
the top down because she was proud of him and wanted to show
everybody that she was Christian Darling's girl. She bought him
crazy presents because her father was rich, watches, pipes, humidors,
an icebox for beer for his room, curtains, wallets, a fifty-dollar
dictionary.

"You'll spend every cent your old man owns," Darling protested
once when she showed up at his room with seven different packages
in her arms and tossed them onto the couch.

"Kiss me," Louise said, "and shut up."

"Do you want to break your poor old man?"

"I don't mind. I want to buy you presents."

"Why?"

"It makes me feel good. Kiss me. I don't know why. Did you
know that you're an important figure?"

"Yes," Darling said gravely.

"When I was waiting for you at the library yesterday two girls
saw you coming and one of them said to the other, 'That's Christian
Darling. He's an important figure.'"

"You're a liar."

"I'm in love with an important figure."

"Still, why the hell did you have to give me a forty-pound dictionary?"

"I wanted to make sure," Louise said, "that you had a token of
my esteem. I want to smother you in tokens of my esteem."

Fifteen years ago.

They'd married when they got out of college. There'd been other
women for him, but all casual and secret, more for curiosity's sake,
and vanity, women who'd thrown themselves. at him and flattered
him, a pretty mother at a summer camp for boys, an old girl from
his home town who'd suddenly blossomed into a coquette, a friend
of Louise's who had dogged him grimly for six months and had taken
advantage of the two weeks when Louise went home when her
mother died. Perhaps Louise had known, but she'd kept quiet,
loving him completely, filling his rooms with presents, religiously
watching him battling with the big Swedes and Polacks on the line
of scrimmage on Saturday afternoons, making plans for marrying
him and living with him in New York and going with him there to
the nightclubs, the theatres, the good restaurants, being proud of

him in advance, tall, white-teethed, smiling, large, yet moving lightly, with an athlete's grace, dressed in evening clothes, approvingly eyed by magnificently dressed and famous women in theatre lobbies, with Louise adoringly at his side.

Her father, who manufactured inks, set up a New York office for Darling to manage and presented him with three hundred accounts and they lived on Beekman Place with a view of the river with fifteen thousand dollars a year between them, because everybody was buying everything in those days, including ink. They saw all the shows and went to all the speakeasies and spent their fifteen thousand dollars a year and in the afternoons Louise went to the art galleries and the matinees of the more serious plays that Darling didn't like to sit through and Darling slept with a girl who danced in the chorus of *Rosalie* and with the wife of a man who owned three copper mines. Darling played squash three times a week and remained as solid as a stone barn and Louise never took her eyes off him when they were in the same room together, watching him with a secret, miser's smile, with a trick of coming over to him in the middle of a crowded room and saying gravely, in a low voice, "You're the handsomest man I've ever seen in my whole life. Want a drink?"

Nineteen twenty-nine came to Darling and to his wife and father-in-law, the maker of inks, just as it came to everyone else. The father-in-law waited until 1933 and then blew his brains out and when Darling went to Chicago to see what the books of the firm looked like he found out all that was left were debts and three or four gallons of unbought ink.

"Please, Christian," Louise said, sitting in their neat Beekman Place apartment, with a view of the river and prints of paintings by Dufy and Braque and Picasso on the wall, "please, why do you want to start drinking at two o'clock in the afternoon?"

"I have nothing else to do," Darling said, putting down his glass, emptied of its fourth drink. "Please pass the whiskey."

Louise filled his glass. "Come take a walk with me," she said. "We'll walk along the river."

"I don't want to walk along the river," Darling said, squinting intensely at the prints of paintings by Dufy, Braque and Picasso.

"We'll walk along Fifth Avenue."

"I don't want to walk along Fifth Avenue."

"Maybe," Louise said gently, "you'd like to come with me to some art galleries. There's an exhibition by a man named Klee—"

"I don't want to go to any art galleries. I want to sit here and drink Scotch whiskey," Darling said. "Who the hell hung those goddam pictures on the wall?"

"I did," Louise said.

"I hate them."

"I'll take them down," Louise said.

"Leave them there. It gives me something to do in the afternoon. I can hate them." Darling took a swallow. "Is that the way people paint these days?"

"Yes, Christian. Please don't drink any more."

"Do you like painting like that?"

"Yes, dear."

"Really?"

"Really."

Darling looked carefully at the prints once more. "Little Louise Tucker. The middle-western beauty. I like pictures with horses in them. Why should you like pictures like that?"

"I just happen to have gone to a lot of galleries in the last few years . . ."

"Is that what you do in the afternoon?"

"That's what I do in the afternoon," Louise said.

"I drink in the afternoon."

Louise kissed him lightly on the top of his head as he sat there squinting at the pictures on the wall, the glass of whiskey held firmly in his hand. She put on her coat and went out without saying another word. When she came back in the evening, she had a job on a woman's fashion magazine.

They moved downtown and Louise went out to work every morning and Darling sat home and drank and Louise paid the bills as they came up. She made believe she was going to quit work as soon as Darling found a job, even though she was taking over more responsibility day by day at the magazine, interviewing authors, picking painters for the illustrations and covers, getting actresses to pose for pictures, going out for drinks with the right people, making a thousand new friends whom she loyally introduced to Darling.

"I don't like your hat," Darling said once, when she came in in the evening and kissed him, her breath rich with Martinis.

"What's the matter with my hat, Baby?" she asked, running her fingers through his hair. "Everybody says it's very smart."

"It's too damned smart," he said. "It's not for you. It's for a rich, sophisticated woman of thirty-five with admirers."

Louise laughed. "I'm practicing to be a rich, sophisticated woman of thirty-five with admirers," she said. He stared soberly at her. "Now, don't look so grim, Baby. It's still the same simple little wife under the hat." She took the hat off, threw it into a corner, sat on his lap. "See? Homebody Number One."

"Your breath could run a train," Darling said, not wanting to be mean, but talking out of boredom, and sudden shock at seeing his wife curiously a stranger in a new hat, with a new expression in her eyes under the little brim, secret, confident, knowing.

Louise tucked her head under his chin so he couldn't smell her breath. "I had to take an author out for cocktails," she said. "He's a boy from the Ozark mountains and he drinks like a fish. He's a Communist."

"What the hell is a Communist from the Ozarks doing writing for a woman's fashion magazine?"

Louise chuckled. "The magazine business is getting all mixed up these days. The publishers want to have a foot in every camp. And anyway, you can't find an author under seventy these days who isn't a Communist."

"I don't think I like you to associate with all those people, Louise," Darling said. "Drinking with them."

"He's a very nice, gentle boy," Louise said. "He reads Ernest Dobson."

"Who's Ernest Dobson?"

Louise patted his arm, stood up, fixed her hair. "He's an English poet."

Darling felt that somehow he had disappointed her. "Am I supposed to know who Ernest Dobson is?"

"No, dear. I'd better go in and take a bath."

After she had gone, Darling went over to the corner where the hat was lying and picked it up. It was nothing, a scrap of straw, a red flower, a veil, meaningless on his big hand, but on his wife's head a signal of something . . . big city, smart and knowing women drinking and dining with men other than their husbands, conversation about things a normal man wouldn't know much about, Frenchmen who painted as though they used their elbows instead of brushes, composers who wrote whole symphonies without a single melody in them, writers who knew all about politics and women who knew all about writers, the movement of the proletariat, Marx, somehow mixed up with five-dollar dinners and the best looking women in America and fairies who made them laugh and half-sentences immediately

understood and secretly hilarious and wives who called their husbands "Baby." He put the hat down, a scrap of straw and a red
flower, and a little veil. He drank some whiskey straight and went
into the bathroom where his wife was lying deep in her bath, singing
to herself and smiling from time to time like a little girl, paddling the
water gently with her hands, sending up a slight spicy fragrance from
the bath-salts she used.

He stood over her, looking down at her. She smiled up at him,
her eyes half closed, her body pink and shimmering in the warm,
scented water. All over again, with all the old suddenness, he was
hit deep inside him with the knowledge of how beautiful she was,
how much he needed her.

"I came in here," he said, "to tell you I wish you wouldn't call me
'Baby.'"

She looked up at him from the bath, her eyes quickly full of
sorrow, half-understanding what he meant. He knelt and put his
arms around her, his sleeves plunged heedlessly in the water, his
shirt and jacket soaking wet as he clutched her wordlessly, holding
her crazily tight, crushing her breath from her, kissing her desperately,
searchingly, regretfully.

He got jobs after that, selling real estate and automobiles, but
somehow, although he had a desk with his name on a wooden wedge
on it, and he went to the office religiously at nine each morning,
he never managed to sell anything and he never made any money.

Louise was made assistant editor and the house was always full
of strange men and women who talked fast and got angry on abstract
subjects like mural paintings, novelists, labor unions. Negro short-
story writers drank Louise's liquor, and a lot of Jews, and big
solemn men with scarred faces and knotted hands talked slowly but
clearly about picket lines and battles with guns and leadpipe at
mine shaft-heads and in front of factory gates. And Louise moved
among them all, confidently, knowing what they were talking about,
with opinions that they listened to and argued about just as though
she were a man. She knew everybody, condescended to no one,
devoured books that Darling had never heard of, walked along the
streets of the city, excited, at home, soaking in all the million tides
of New York without fear, with constant wonder.

Her friends liked Darling and sometimes he found a man who
wanted to get off in the corner and talk about the new boy who
played fullback for Princeton, and the decline of the double wing-

back, or even the state of the stock market, but for the most part he sat on the edge of things, solid and quiet in the high storm of words. "The dialectics of the situation . . . the theatre has been given over to expert jugglers . . . Picasso? What man has a right to paint old bones and collect ten thousand dollars for them? . . . I stand firmly behind Trotsky . . . Poe was the last American critic. When he died they put lilies on the grave of American criticism. I don't say this because they panned my last book, but . . ."

Once in a while he caught Louise looking soberly and consideringly at him through the cigarette smoke and the noise and he avoided her eyes and found an excuse to get up and go into the kitchen for more ice or to open another bottle.

"Come on," Cathal Flaherty was saying, standing at the door with a girl, "you've got to come down and see this It's down on Fourteenth Street, in the old Civic Repertory, and you can only see it on Sunday nights and I guarantee you'll come out of the theatre singing." Flaherty was a big young Irishman with a broken nose who was the lawyer for a longshoreman's union, and he had been hanging around the house for six months on and off, roaring and shutting everybody else up when he got in an argument. "It's a new play, *Waiting for Lefty*, it's about taxi-drivers."

"Odets," the girl with Flaherty said. "It's by a guy named Odets."

"I never heard of him," Darling said.

"He's a new one," the girl said.

"It's like watching a bombardment," Flaherty said. "I saw it last Sunday night. You've got to see it."

"Come on, Baby," Louise said to Darling, excitement in her eyes already. "We've been sitting in the Sunday *Times* all day, this'll be a great change."

"I see enough taxi-drivers every day," Darling said, not because he meant that, but because he didn't like to be around Flaherty, who said things that made Louise laugh a lot and whose judgment she accepted on almost every subject. "Let's go to the movies."

"You've never seen anything like this before," Flaherty said. "He wrote this play with a baseball bat."

"Come on," Louise coaxed, "I bet it's wonderful."

"He has long hair," the girl with Flaherty said. "Odets. I met him at a party. He's an actor. He didn't say a goddam thing all night."

"I don't feel like going down to Fourteenth Street," Darling said, wishing Flaherty and his girl would get out. "It's gloomy."

"Oh, hell!" Louise said loudly. She looked coolly at Darling, as though she'd just been introduced to him and was making up her mind about him, and not very favorably. He saw her looking at him, knowing there was something new and dangerous in her face and he wanted to say something, but Flaherty was there and his damned girl, and anyway, he didn't know what to say.

"I'm going," Louise said, getting her coat. "I don't think Fourteenth Street is gloomy."

"I'm telling you," Flaherty was saying, helping her on with her coat, "it's the Battle of Gettysburg, in Brooklynese."

"Nobody could get a word out of him," Flaherty's girl was saying as they went through the door. "He just sat there all night."

The door closed. Louise hadn't said good-night to him. Darling walked around the room four times, then sprawled out on the sofa, on top of the Sunday *Times*. He lay there for five minutes looking at the ceiling, thinking of Flaherty walking down the street talking in that booming voice, between the girls, holding their arms.

Louise had looked wonderful. She'd washed her hair in the afternoon and it had been very soft and light and clung close to her head as she stood there angrily putting her coat on. Louise was getting prettier every year, partly because she knew by now how pretty she was, and made the most of it.

"Nuts," Darling said, standing up. "Oh, nuts."

He put on his coat and went down to the nearest bar and had five drinks off by himself in a corner before his money ran out.

The years since then had been foggy and downhill. Louise had been nice to him, and in a way, loving and kind, and they'd fought only once, when he said he was going to vote for Landon. ("Oh, Christ," she'd said, "doesn't *anything* happen inside your head? Don't you read the papers? The penniless Republican!") She'd been sorry later and apologized for hurting him, but apologized as she might to a child. He'd tried hard, had gone grimly to the art galleries, the concert halls, the book-shops, trying to gain on the trail of his wife, but it was no use. He was bored, and none of what he saw or heard or dutifully read made much sense to him and finally he gave it up. He had thought, many nights as he ate dinner alone, knowing Louise would come home late and drop silently into bed without explanation, of getting a divorce, but he knew the loneliness, the hopelessness, of not seeing her again would be too much to take. So he was good, completely devoted, ready at all times to go anyplace with her, do anything she wanted. He even got a small job, in a broker's office and paid his own way, bought his own liquor.

Then he'd been offered the job of going from college to college as a tailor's representative. "We want a man," Mr. Rosenberg had said, "who as soon as you look at him, you say 'There's a university man.'" Rosenberg had looked approvingly at Darling's broad shoulders and well-kept waist, at his carefully brushed hair and his honest, wrinkleless face. "Frankly, Mr. Darling, I am willing to make you a proposition. I have inquired about you, you are favorably known on your old campus. I understand you were in the backfield with Alfred Diederich."

Darling nodded. "What happened to him?"

"He is walking around in a cast for seven years now. An iron brace. He played professional football and they broke his neck for him."

Darling smiled. That, at least, had turned out well.

"Our suits are an easy product to sell, Mr. Darling," Mr. Rosenberg said. "We have a handsome, custom-made garment. What has Brooks Brothers got that we haven't got? A name. No more."

"I can make fifty, sixty dollars a week," Darling said to Louise that night. "And expenses. I can save some money and then come back to New York and really get started here."

"Yes, Baby," Louise said.

"As it is," Darling said carefully, "I can make it back here once a month, and holidays and the summer. We can see each other often."

"Yes, Baby." He looked at her face, lovelier now at thirty-five than it had ever been before, but fogged over now as it had been for five years with a kind of patient, kindly, remote boredom.

"What do you say?" he asked. "Should I take it?" Deep within him, he hoped fiercely, longingly, for her to say, "No, Baby, you stay right here," but she said, as he knew she'd say, "I think you'd better take it."

He nodded. He had to get up and stand with his back to her, looking out the window, because there were things plain on his face that she had never seen in the fifteen years she'd known him. "Fifty dollars is a lot of money," he said. "I never thought I'd ever see fifty dollars again." He laughed. Louise laughed, too.

Christian Darling sat on the frail green grass of the practice field. The shadow of the stadium had reached out and covered him. In the distance the lights of the university shone a little mistily in the light haze of evening. Fifteen years. Flaherty even now was calling for his wife, buying her a drink, filling whatever bar they were in with that voice of his and that easy laugh. Darling half-closed his eyes, almost saw the boy fifteen years ago reach for the pass, slip the halfback, go skittering lightly down the field, his knees high and fast and graceful, smiling to himself because he knew he was going to get past the safety man. That was the high point, Darling thought, fifteen years ago, on an autumn afternoon, twenty years old and far from death, with the air coming easily into his lungs, and a deep feeling inside him that he could do anything, knock over anybody, outrun whatever had to be outrun. And the shower after and the three glasses of water and the cool night air on his damp head and Louise sitting hatless in the open car with a smile and the first kiss she ever really meant. The high point, an eighty-yard run in the practice and a girl's kiss and everything after that a decline. Darling laughed. He had practiced the wrong thing, perhaps. He hadn't practiced for 1929 and New York City and a girl who would turn into a woman. Somewhere, he thought, there must have been a point where she moved up to me, was even with me for a moment, when I could have held her hand, if I'd known, held tight, gone with her. Well, he'd never known. Here he was on a playing field that was fifteen years away and his wife was in another city having dinner with another and better man, speaking with him a different, new language, a language nobody had ever taught him.

Darling stood up, smiled a little, because if he didn't smile he knew the tears would come. He looked around him. This was the spot. O'Connor's pass had come sliding out just to here . . . the high point. Darling put up his hands, felt all over again the flat slap of the ball. He shook his hips to throw off the halfback, cut back inside the center, picked his knees high as he ran gracefully over two men jumbled on the ground at the line of scrimmage, ran easily, gaining speed, for ten yards, holding the ball lightly in his two hands, swung away from the halfback diving at him, ran, swinging his hips in the almost-girlish manner of a back in a broken field, tore into the safety man, his shoes drumming heavily on the turf, stiff-armed, elbow locked, pivoted, raced lightly and exultantly for the goal line.

It was only after he had sped over the goal line and slowed to a trot that he saw the boy and girl sitting together on the turf, looking at him wonderingly.

He stopped short, dropping his arms. "I . . ." he said, gasping a little though his condition was fine and the run hadn't winded him, ". . . Once I played here."

The boy and the girl said nothing. Darling laughed embarrassedly, looked hard at them sitting there, close to each other, shrugged, turned and went toward his hotel, the sweat breaking out on his face and running down into his collar.

Problems for Thought and Writing

1. What is the significance of Louise's remark, "I'm in love with an important figure"? Is she joking or serious? Is there any ambiguity in her words?

2. Was the date, 1929, of any significance in the personal trials of these characters? Does it symbolize other aspects of their lives or personalities?

3. Is the implication of this story that all football players are predestined to this kind of personal tragedy? Is football the real subject of this story or is Christian Darling?

4. Explain this statement: "He had practiced the wrong thing, perhaps. He hadn't practiced for 1929 and New York City and a girl who would turn into a woman" (page 46). Could Christian's education have given him the practice he needed to meet these problems of life? How? Is Shaw here making a valid criticism of the kind of education now prevailing in the United States? Is his story merely an instrument whereby such a critique can be made? Do Hutchins' criticisms (page 23) correspond with those implied here?

5. How can you explain the paradox that Louise, the rich girl, was a radical in political sympathies while Christian, who had no material advantages, was a Republican?

6. Would you say Christian or Louise was the greater failure? What does Christian's failure mean?

7. Does Christian's character have anything in common with that of the son or father in "The Apostate" (page 18)?

~

2 Writing and Reading

POLITICS AND THE ENGLISH LANGUAGE*

George Orwell

Most people who bother with the matter at all would admit that the English language is in a bad way, but it is generally assumed that we cannot by conscious action do anything about it. Our civilization is decadent, and our language—so the argument runs—must inevitably share in the general collapse. It follows that any struggle against the abuse of language is a sentimental archaism, like preferring candles to electric light or hansom cabs to aeroplanes. Underneath this lies the half-conscious belief that language is a natural growth and not an instrument which we shape for our own purposes.

Now, it is clear that the decline of a language must ultimately have political and economic causes: it is not due simply to the bad influence of this or that individual writer. But an effect can become a cause, reinforcing the original cause and producing the same effect in an intensified form, and so on indefinitely. A man may take to drink because he feels himself to be a failure, and then fail all the more completely because he drinks. It is rather the same thing that is happening to the English language. It becomes ugly and inaccurate because our thoughts are foolish, but the slovenliness of our language makes it easier for us to have foolish thoughts. The point is that the process is reversible. Modern English, especially written English, is full of bad habits which spread by imitation and which can be avoided if one is willing to take the necessary trouble. If one gets rid of these habits one can think more clearly, and to think clearly is a necessary first step towards political regeneration: so that the fight against bad English is not frivolous and is not the exclusive concern of professional writers. I will come back to this presently, and I hope that by that time the meaning of what I have said here will have become clearer. Meanwhile, here are five specimens of the English language as it is now habitually written.

These five passages have not been picked out because they are especially bad—I could have quoted far worse if I had chosen—but because they illustrate various of the mental vices from which we now suffer. They are a little below the average, but are fairly representative samples. I number them so that I can refer back to them when necessary:

(1) I am not, indeed, sure whether it is not true to say that the Milton who once seemed not unlike a seventeenth-century Shelley had not become, out of an experience ever more bitter in each year, more alien (*sic*) to the founder of that Jesuit sect which nothing could induce him to tolerate.

Professor Harold Laski (Essay in *Freedom of Expression*)

(2) Above all, we cannot play ducks and drakes with a native battery of idioms which prescribes such egregious collocations of vocables as the Basic *put up with* for *tolerate* or *put at a loss* for *bewilder*.

Professor Lancelot Hogben (*Interglossa*)

(3) On the one side we have the free personality; by definition it is not neurotic, for it has neither conflict nor dream. Its desires, such as they are, are transparent, for they are just what institutional approval keeps in the forefront of consciousness; another institutional pattern would alter their number and intensity; there is little in them that is natural, irreducible, or culturally dangerous. But *on the other side*, the social bond itself is nothing but the mutual reflection of these self-secure integrities. Recall the definition of love. Is not this the very picture of a small academic? Where is there a place in this hall of mirrors for either personality or fraternity?

Essay on psychology in *Politics* (New York)

(4) All the "best people" from the gentlemen's clubs, and all the frantic fascist captains, united in common hatred of Socialism and bestial horror of the rising tide of the mass revolutionary movement, have turned to acts of provocation, to foul incendiarism, to medieval legends of poisoned wells, to legalize their own destruction of proletarian organizations, and rouse the agitated petty-bourgeoisie to chauvinistic fervor on behalf of the fight against the revolutionary way out of the crisis.

Communist pamphlet

(5) If a new spirit *is* to be infused into this old country, there is one thorny and contentious reform which must be tackled, and that is the humanization and galvanization of the B.B.C. Timidity here will bespeak

canker and atrophy of the soul. The heart of Britain may be sound and of
strong beat, for instance, but the British lion's roar at present is like that
of Bottom in Shakespeare's *Midsummer Night's Dream*—as gentle as any
sucking dove. A virile new Britain cannot continue indefinitely to be tra-
duced in the eyes, or rather ears, of the world by the effete languors of
Langham Place, brazenly masquerading as "standard English." When the
Voice of Britain is heard at nine o'clock, better far and infinitely less ludicrous to hear aitches honestly dropped than the present priggish, inflated,
inhibited, school-ma'amish arch braying of blameless bashful mewing
maidens.

Letter in Tribune

Each of these passages has faults of its own, but quite apart
from avoidable ugliness, two qualities are common to all of them.
The first is staleness of imagery; the other is lack of precision.
The writer either has a meaning and cannot express it, or he in-
advertently says something else, or he is almost indifferent as to
whether his words mean anything or not. This mixture of vagueness and sheer incompetence is the most marked characteristic of
modern English prose, and especially of any kind of political writing. As soon as certain topics are raised, the concrete melts into
the abstract and no one seems able to think of turns of speech
that are not hackneyed: prose consists less and less of *words* chosen
for the sake of their meaning, and more and more of *phrases* tacked
together like the sections of a prefabricated hen-house. I list below,
with notes and examples, various of the tricks by means of which
the work of prose-construction is habitually dodged:

Dying metaphors. A newly-invented metaphor assists thought
by evoking a visual image, while on the other hand a metaphor
which is technically "dead" (e.g., *iron resolution*) has in effect
reverted to being an ordinary word and can generally be used without loss of vividness. But in between these two classes there is a
huge dump of worn-out metaphors which have lost all evocative
power and are merely used because they save people the trouble
of inventing phrases for themselves. Examples are: *Ring the changes
on, take up the cudgels for, toe the line, ride roughshod over, stand
shoulder to shoulder with, play into the hands of, an axe to grind,
grist to the mill, fishing in troubled waters, on the order of the day,
Achilles' heel, swan song, hotbed.* Many of these are used without
knowledge of their meaning (what is a "rift," for instance?), and
incompatible metaphors are frequently mixed, a sure sign that the
writer is not interested in what he is saying. Some metaphors now

current have been twisted out of their original meaning without those who use them even being aware of the fact. For example, *toe the line* is sometimes written *tow the line*. Another example is *the hammer and the anvil*, now always used with the implication that the anvil gets the worst of it. In real life it is always the anvil that breaks the hammer, never the other way about: a writer who stopped to think what he was saying would be aware of this, and would avoid perverting the original phrase.

Operators, or verbal false limbs. These save the trouble of picking out appropriate verbs and nouns, and at the same time pad each sentence with extra syllables which give it an appearance of symmetry. Characteristic phrases are: *render inoperative, militate against, prove unacceptable, make contact with, be subjected to, give rise to, give grounds for, have the effect of, play a leading part (role) in, make itself felt, take effect, exhibit a tendency to, serve the purpose of, etc., etc.* The keynote is the elimination of simple verbs. Instead of being a single word, such as *break, stop, spoil, mend, kill,* a verb becomes a phrase, made up of a noun or adjective tacked on to some general-purpose verb such as *prove, serve, form, play, render.* In addition, the passive voice is wherever possible used in preference to the active, and noun constructions are used instead of gerunds (*by examination of* instead of *by examining*). The range of verbs is further cut down by means of the *-ize* and *de-*formations, and banal statements are given an appearance of profundity by means of the *not un-*formation. Simple conjunctions and prepositions are replaced by such phrases as *with respect to, having regard to, the fact that, by dint of, in view of, in the interests of, on the hypothesis that;* and the ends of sentences are saved from anti-climax by such resounding commonplaces as *greatly to be desired, cannot be left out of account, a development to be expected in the near future, deserving of serious consideration, brought to a satisfactory conclusion,* and so on and so forth.

Pretentious diction. Words like *phenomenon, element, individual* (as noun), *objective, categorical, effective, virtual, basis, primary, promote, constitute, exhibit, exploit, utilize, eliminate, liquidate,* are used to dress up simple statements and give an air of scientific impartiality to biased judgments. Adjectives like *epoch-making, epic, historic, unforgettable, triumphant, age-old, inevitable, inexorable, veritable,* are used to dignify the sordid processes of international politics, while writing that aims at glorifying war usually takes on an archaic color, its characteristic words being: *realm, throne, chariot,*

mailed fist, trident, sword, shield, buckler, banner, jackboot, clarion.
Foreign words and expressions such as *cul de sac, ancien régime,*
deus ex machina, mutatis mutandis, status quo, gleichschaltung, welt-
anschauung, are used to give an air of culture and elegance. Except
for the useful abbreviations *i.e., e.g.,* and *etc.,* there is no real need
for any of the hundreds of foreign phrases now current in English.
Bad writers, and especially scientific, political and sociological writers,
are nearly always haunted by the notion that Latin or Greek words
are grander than Saxon ones, and unnecessary words like *expedite,*
ameliorate, predict, extraneous, deracinated, clandestine, subaque-
ous and hundreds of others constantly gain ground from their
Anglo-Saxon opposite numbers.[1] The jargon peculiar to Marxist
writing (*hyena, hangman, cannibal, petty bourgeois, these gentry,*
lackey, flunkey, mad dog, White Guard, etc.) consists largely of
words and phrases translated from Russian, German or French;
but the normal way of coining a new word is to use a Latin or
Greek root with the appropriate affix and, where necessary, the
-ize formation. It is often easier to make up words of this kind
(*de-regionalize, impermissible, extramarital, non-fragmentary* and
so forth) than to think up the English words that will cover one's
meaning. The result, in general, is an increase in slovenliness and
vagueness.

Meaningless words. In certain kinds of writing, particularly in
art criticism and literary criticism, it is normal to come across
long passages which are almost completely lacking in meaning.[2]
Words like *romantic, plastic, values, human, dead, sentimental,*
natural, vitality, as used in art criticism, are strictly meaningless,
in the sense that they not only do not point to any discoverable
object, but are hardly even expected to do so by the reader. When
one critic writes, "The outstanding feature of Mr. X's work is its
living quality," while another writes, "The immediately striking thing

[1] An interesting illustration of this is the way in which the English flower names
which were in use till very recently are being ousted by Greek ones, *snap-dragon*
becoming *antirrhinum, forget-me-not* becoming *myosotis,* etc. It is hard to see any
practical reason for this change of fashion: it is probably due to an instinctive
turning-away from the more homely word and a vague feeling that the Greek
word is scientific.

[2] Example: "Comfort's catholicity of perception and image, strangely Whit-
manesque in range, almost the exact opposite in aesthetic compulsion, continues
to evoke that trembling atmospheric accumulative hinting at a cruel, an in-
exorably serene timelessness . . . Wrey Gardiner scores by aiming at simple
bullseyes with precision. Only they are not so simple, and through this contented
sadness runs more than the surface bittersweet of resignation." (*Poetry Quarterly.*)

about Mr. X's work is its peculiar deadness," the reader accepts this as a simple difference of opinion. If words like *black* and *white* were involved, instead of the jargon words *dead* and *living*, he would see at once that language was being used in an improper way. Many political words are similarly abused. The word *Fascism* has now no meaning except in so far as it signifies "something not desirable." The words *democracy, socialism, freedom, patriotic, realistic, justice,* have each of them several different meanings which cannot be reconciled with one another. In the case of a word like *democracy*, not only is there no agreed definition, but the attempt to make one is resisted from all sides. It is almost universally felt that when we call a country democratic we are praising it: consequently the defenders of every kind of régime claim that it is a democracy, and fear that they might have to stop using the word if it were tied down to any one meaning. Words of this kind are often used in a consciously dishonest way. That is, the person who uses them has his own private definition, but allows his hearers to think he means something quite different. Statements like *Marshal Pétain was a true patriot, The Soviet Press is the freest in the world, The Catholic Church is opposed to persecution,* are almost always made with intent to deceive. Other words used in variable meanings, in most cases more or less dishonestly, are: *class, totalitarian, science, progressive, reactionary, bourgeois, equality.*

Now that I have made this catalogue of swindles and perversions, let me give another example of the kind of writing that they lead to. This time it must of its nature be an imaginary one. I am going to translate a passage of good English into modern English of the worst sort. Here is a well-known verse from *Ecclesiastes:*

I returned, and saw under the sun, that the race is not to the swift, nor the battle to the strong, neither yet bread to the wise, nor yet riches to men of understanding, nor yet favor to men of skill; but time and chance happeneth to them all.

Here it is in modern English:

Objective consideration of contemporary phenomena compels the conclusion that success or failure in competitive activities exhibits no tendency to be commensurate with innate capacity, but that a considerable element of the unpredictable must invariably be taken into account.

This is a parody, but not a very gross one. Exhibit (3), above, for instance, contains several patches of the same kind of English.

It will be seen that I have not made a full translation. The beginning and ending of the sentence follow the original meaning fairly closely, but in the middle the concrete illustrations—race, battle, bread—dissolve into the vague phrase "success or failure in competitive activities." This had to be so, because no modern writer of the kind I am discussing—no one capable of using phrases like "objective consideration of contemporary phenomena"—would ever tabulate his thoughts in that precise and detailed way. The whole tendency of modern prose is away from concreteness. Now analyze these two sentences a little more closely. The first contains 49 words but only 60 syllables, and all its words are those of everyday life. The second contains 38 words of 90 syllables: 18 of its words are from Latin roots, and one from Greek. The first sentence contains six vivid images, and only one phrase ("time and chance") that could be called vague. The second contains not a single fresh, arresting phrase, and in spite of its 90 syllables it gives only a shortened version of the meaning contained in the first. Yet without a doubt it is the second kind of sentence that is gaining ground in modern English. I do not want to exaggerate. This kind of writing is not yet universal, and outcrops of simplicity will occur here and there in the worst-written page. Still, if you or I were told to write a few lines on the uncertainty of human fortunes, we should probably come much nearer to my imaginary sentence than to the one from *Ecclesiastes.*

As I have tried to show, modern writing at its worst does not consist in picking out words for the sake of their meaning and inventing images in order to make the meaning clearer. It consists in gumming together long strips of words which have already been set in order by someone else, and making the results presentable by sheer humbug. The attraction of this way of writing is that it is easy. It is easier—even quicker, once you have the habit —to say *In my opinion it is a not unjustifiable assumption that* than to say *I think.* If you use ready-made phrases, you not only don't have to hunt about for words; you also don't have to bother with the rhythms of your sentences, since these phrases are generally so arranged as to be more or less euphonious. When you are composing in a hurry—when you are dictating to a stenographer, for instance, or making a public speech—it is natural to fall into a pretentious, Latinized style. Tags like *a consideration which we should do well to bear in mind* or *a conclusion to which all of us would readily assent* will save many a sentence from coming down with a bump. By using stale metaphors, similes and idioms, you save much mental effort at the cost of leaving your meaning vague, not only for your reader but for yourself. This is the significance of mixed metaphors. The sole aim of a metaphor is to call up a visual image. When these images clash—as in *The Fascist octopus has sung its swan song, the jackboot is thrown into the melting pot*—it can be taken as certain that the writer is not seeing a mental image of the objects he is naming; in other words he is not really thinking. Look again at the examples I gave at the beginning of this essay. Professor Laski (1) uses five negatives in 53 words. One of these is superfluous, making nonsense of the whole passage, and in addition there is the slip *alien* for *akin*, making further nonsense, and several avoidable pieces of clumsiness which increase the general vagueness. Professor Hogben (2) plays ducks and drakes with a battery which is able to write prescriptions, and, while disapproving of the everyday phrase *put up with*, is unwilling to look *egregious* up in the dictionary and see what it means. (3), if one takes an uncharitable attitude towards it, is simply meaningless: probably one could work out its intended meaning by reading the whole of the article in which it occurs. In (4), the writer knows more or less what he wants to say, but an accumulation of stale phrases chokes him like tea leaves blocking a sink. In (5), words and meaning have almost parted company. People who write in this manner usually have a general emotional meaning—they dislike one thing and want to express solidarity with another—but they are not interested in the detail of what they are saying. A scrupulous writer, in every sentence that he writes, will ask himself at least four questions, thus: What am I trying to say? What words will express it? What image or idiom will make it clearer? Is this image fresh enough to have an effect? And he will probably ask himself two more: Could I put it more shortly? Have I said anything that is avoidably ugly? But you are not obliged to go to all this trouble. You can shirk it by simply throwing your mind open and letting the ready-made phrases come crowding in. They will construct your sentences for you—even think your thoughts for you, to a certain extent—and at need they will perform the important service of partially concealing your meaning even from yourself. It is at this point that the special connection between politics and the debasement of language becomes clear.

In our time it is broadly true that political writing is bad writing. Where it is not true, it will generally be found that the writer is some kind of rebel, expressing his private opinions and not a "party line." Orthodoxy, of whatever color, seems to demand a lifeless, imitative style. The political dialects to be found in pamphlets, leading articles, manifestoes, White Papers and the speeches of under-secretaries do, of course, vary from party to party, but they are all alike in that one almost never finds in them a fresh, vivid, home-made turn of speech. When one watches some tired hack on the platform mechanically repeating the familiar phrases—*bestial atrocities, iron heel, bloodstained tyranny, free peoples of the world, stand shoulder to shoulder*—one often has a curious feeling that one is not watching a live human being but some kind of dummy: a feeling which suddenly becomes stronger at moments when the light catches the speaker's spectacles and turns them into blank discs which seem to have no eyes behind them. And this is not altogether fanciful. A speaker who uses that kind of phraseology has gone some distance towards turning himself into a machine. The appropriate noises are coming out of his larynx, but his brain is not involved as it would be if he were choosing his words for himself. If the speech he is making is one that he is accustomed to make over and over again, he may be almost unconscious of what he is saying, as one is when one utters the responses in church. And this reduced state of consciousness, if not indispensable, is at any rate favorable to political conformity.

In our time, political speech and writing are largely the defense of the indefensible. Things like the continuance of British rule in India, the Russian purges and deportations, the dropping of the atom bombs on Japan, can indeed be defended, but only by arguments which are too brutal for most people to face, and which do not square with the professed aims of political parties. Thus political language has to consist largely of euphemism, question-begging and sheer cloudy vagueness. Defenseless villages are bombarded from the air, the inhabitants driven out into the countryside, the cattle machine-gunned, the huts set on fire with incendiary bullets: this is called *pacification*. Millions of peasants are robbed of their farms and sent trudging along the roads with no more than they can carry: this is called *transfer of population* or *rectification of frontiers*. People are imprisoned for years without trial, or shot in the back of the neck or sent to die of scurvy in Arctic lumber camps: this is called *elimination of unreliable elements*. Such phraseology is needed if one wants to name things without calling up mental pictures of them. Consider for instance some comfortable English professor defending Russian totalitarianism. He cannot say outright, "I believe in killing off your opponents when you can get good results by doing so." Probably, therefore, he will say something like this:

While freely conceding that the Soviet régime exhibits certain features which the humanitarian may be inclined to deplore, we must, I think, agree that a certain curtailment of the right to political opposition is an unavoidable concomitant of transitional periods, and that the rigors which the Russian people have been called upon to undergo have been amply justified in the sphere of concrete achievement.

The inflated style is itself a kind of euphemism. A mass of Latin words falls upon the facts like soft snow, blurring the outlines and covering up all the details. The great enemy of clear language is insincerity. When there is a gap between one's real and one's declared aims, one turns, as it were instinctively, to long words and exhausted idioms, like a cuttlefish squirting out ink. In our age there is no such thing as "keeping out of politics." All issues are political issues, and politics itself is a mass of lies, evasions, folly, hatred and schizophrenia. When the general atmosphere is bad, language must suffer. I should expect to find—this is a guess which I have not sufficient knowledge to verify—that the German, Russian and Italian languages have all deteriorated in the last ten or fifteen years as a result of dictatorship.

But if thought corrupts language, language can also corrupt thought. A bad usage can spread by tradition and imitation, even among people who should and do know better. The debased language that I have been discussing is in some ways very convenient. Phrases like *a not unjustifiable assumption, leaves much to be desired, would serve no good purpose, a consideration which we should do well to bear in mind,* are a continuous temptation, a packet of aspirins always at one's elbow. Look back through this essay, and for certain you will find that I have again and again committed the very faults I am protesting against. By this morning's post I have received a pamphlet dealing with conditions in Germany. The author tells me that he "felt impelled" to write it. I open it at random, and here is almost the first sentence that I see: "[The Allies] have an opportunity not only of achieving a radical transformation of Germany's social and political structure in such a way as to avoid a nationalistic reaction in Germany itself, but at the same time of laying the foundations of a cooperative and unified Europe." You see, he "feels impelled" to write—feels, presumably, that he has something new to say—and yet his words, like cavalry horses answering the bugle, group themselves automatically into the familiar dreary pattern. This invasion of one's mind by ready-made phrases (*lay the foundations, achieve a radical transformation*) can only be prevented if one is constantly on guard against them, and every such phrase anesthetizes a portion of one's brain.

I said earlier that the decadence of our language is probably curable. Those who deny this would argue, if they produced an argument at all, that language merely reflects existing social conditions, and that we cannot influence its development by any direct tinkering with words and constructions. So far as the general tone or spirit of a language goes, this may be true, but it is not true in detail. Silly words and expressions have often disappeared, not through any evolutionary process but owing to the conscious action of a minority. Two recent examples were *explore every avenue* and *leave no stone unturned,* which were killed by the jeers of a few journalists. There is a long list of fly-blown metaphors which could similarly be got rid of if enough people would interest themselves in the job; and it should also be possible to laugh the *not un-*formation out of existence,[3] to reduce the amount of Latin and Greek in the average sentence, to drive out foreign phrases and strayed scientific words, and, in general, to make pretentiousness unfashionable. But all these are minor points. The defense of the English language implies more than this, and perhaps it is best to start by saying what it does *not* imply.

To begin with, it has nothing to do with archaism, with the salvaging of obsolete words and turns of speech, or with the setting-up of a "standard English" which must never be departed from. On the contrary, it is especially concerned with the scrapping of every word or idiom which has outworn its usefulness. It has nothing to do with correct grammar and syntax, which are of no importance so long as one makes one's meaning clear, or with the avoidance of Americanisms, or with having what is called a "good prose style." On the other hand it is not concerned with fake simplicity and the attempt to make written English colloquial. Nor does it even imply in every case preferring the Saxon word to the Latin one, though it does imply using the fewest and shortest words that will cover one's meaning. What is above all needed is to let the meaning choose the

---

[3] One can cure oneself of the *not un-* formation by memorizing this sentence: *A not unblack dog was chasing a not unsmall rabbit across a not ungreen field.*

word, and not the other way about. In prose, the worst thing one can do with words is to surrender them. When you think of a concrete object, you think wordlessly, and then, if you want to describe the thing you have been visualizing, you probably hunt about till you find the exact words that seem to fit it. When you think of something abstract you are more inclined to use words from the start, and unless you make a conscious effort to prevent it, the existing dialect will come rushing in and do the job for you, at the expense of blurring or even changing your meaning. Probably it is better to put off using words as long as possible and get one's meaning as clear as one can through pictures or sensations. Afterwards one can choose—not simply *accept*—the phrases that will best cover the meaning, and then switch round and decide what impressions one's words are likely to make on another person. This last effort of the mind cuts out all stale or mixed images, all prefabricated phrases, needless repetitions, and humbug and vagueness generally. But one can often be in doubt about the effect of a word or a phrase, and one needs rules that one can rely on when instinct fails. I think the following rules will cover most cases:

(i) Never use a metaphor, simile or other figure of speech which you are used to seeing in print.

(ii) Never use a long word where a short one will do.

(iii) If it is possible to cut a word out, always cut it out.

(iv) Never use the passive where you can use the active.

(v) Never use a foreign phrase, a scientific word or a jargon word if you can think of an everyday English equivalent.

(vi) Break any of these rules sooner than say anything barbarous.

These rules sound elementary, and so they are, but they demand a deep change of attitude in anyone who has grown used to writing in the style now fashionable. One could keep all of them and still write bad English, but one could not write the kind of stuff that I quoted in these five specimens at the beginning of this article.

I have not here been considering the literary use of language, but merely language as an instrument for expressing and not for concealing or preventing thought. Stuart Chase and others have come near to claiming that all abstract words are meaningless, and have used this as a pretext for advocating a kind of political quietism. Since you don't know what Fascism is, how can you struggle against Fascism? One need not swallow such absurdities as this, but one ought to recognize that the present political chaos is connected with the decay of language, and that one can probably bring about some improvement by starting at the verbal end. If you simplify your English, you are freed from the worst follies of orthodoxy. You cannot speak any of the necessary dialects, and when you make a stupid remark its stupidity will be obvious, even to yourself. Political language—and with variations this is true of all political parties, from Conservatives to Anarchists—is designed to make lies sound truthful and murder respectable, and to give an appearance of solidity to pure wind. One cannot change this all in a moment, but one can at least change one's own habits, and from time to time one can even, if one jeers loudly enough, send some worn-out and useless phrase—some *jackboot, Achilles' heel, hotbed, melting pot, acid test, veritable inferno* or other lump of verbal refuse—into the dustbin where it belongs.

Problems for Thought and Writing

I

On page 50 Orwell states that modern prose is a "mixture of vagueness and sheer incompetence." Actually the faults he itemizes are not exclusively modern, but the corruption of language in our time—abetted by radio, television, and the newspapers—is perhaps as serious as it has ever been. The faults he points out can be found everywhere—not just in politics. In all places where inhumanity is called by another name, where ignorance is disguised by pomposity, where dishonest or venal motives are smothered in verbal palliatives—in all these places we find stock language and the cliché expert. We find him also in polite society, but there he is less dangerous, for there we are conscious of his mannered deceptions and accept them. He is most dangerous where we perhaps least expect him—in the pulpit, in politics, as author of college textbooks. The ability to recognize stock language is often the ability to recognize a swindle. If we learn to demand concreteness and accuracy in the language we read and write and to reject "vagueness and sheer incompetence," we shall have advanced not only our education but the health of our society.

1. Evaluate the prose of one of your college textbooks, one that seems to you heavy with jargon and stock language. Try to determine the *motives* of the author in using this language. Was he just incompetent or was he trying to fake something?

2. Do you agree with Orwell's statement that "the word *Fascism* has now no meaning except in so far as it signifies 'something not desirable'"? Can you think of any other word that is frequently used in the same loose way? Examine the Chicago *Tribune* article by William Fulton (page 618) for examples.

3. Does Orwell overstate his case in the parody of *Ecclesiastes?* Do you think he wants everyone to write "poetic prose"?

4. "Orthodoxy," says Orwell, "of whatever color, seems to demand a lifeless, imitative style." Reflect on that statement. Is the "style" of the communion service "lifeless"? Have all religious sermons in history been lifeless and

colorless? Is Lincoln's Gettysburg Address, based on what may be called the orthodoxy of freedom, without life? Is Orwell's statement irresponsible?

5. Is Orwell justified in saying that the statement, " 'The Catholic Church is opposed to persecution,' [is] almost always made with intent to deceive"? Why or why not?

6. In what paragraph does Orwell make clear the specific nature of the relation expressed in his title between politics and language? What is that relation? Do you agree?

7. On the whole, would you say that this essay is *objective?* Or is the author guilty of smuggling in political prejudices under "literary" disguise? On the other hand, is it ever fair to accuse an author who includes the word "politics" in his title of "smuggling" political views?

II

8. Compare Orwell's remarks about emotional meanings (page 55) with Thouless, "Emotional Meanings" (page 98).

9. Students often mistakenly assume that imagery in writing is the exclusive concern of poets and artists and that business-like prose ought to be bare and matter-of-fact. Actually, imagery occurs in writing whenever an appeal is made to the five senses. Metaphors and similes are no more than convenient ways of expressing these sensory appeals. For example, H. L. Mencken in describing "style" remarks (page 67): "It hardens as his [the writer's] arteries harden. It is gaudy when he is young and gathers decorum when he grows old." All men tend to think and converse in images—and unfortunately these images are often clichés: it's hot as blazes, I'm limp as a dishrag, he's old as Methuselah, a bird in the hand is worth two in the bush, quick as lightning, slow as molasses. Perfecting one's writing, however, is not just a matter of (1) avoiding such clichés or (2) thinking up "fresh, arresting" images (as Orwell calls for). It is a matter of contemplating your experience honestly and recording it in the simplest and most natural image that comes to mind. If what comes to mind is a cliché or dying metaphor, then you are not really recording *your* experience but some one else's— long dead and gone.

Go through Orwell's own prose and underline every specific image that he uses. Do the same with Carson, "The Gray Beginnings" (page 526), and Bell, "In the Dark" (page 536). For a devastating attack on imagery when it becomes a disease of prose, read Thomas Reed Powell's, "Constitutional Metaphors" (page 142).

10. Study a group of magazine or newspaper advertisements for the kind of meaningless words Orwell lists. Listen to a radio or television announcer and copy down (if you can write fast enough) every piece of pretentious diction he drops in the course of a commercial.

11. Are there any "operators" or "verbal false limbs" in the following sentence from Orwell's essay: "In the case of a word like democracy, not only is there no agreed definition, but the attempt to make one is resisted from all sides"?

12. Which is the most important of the six rules listed at the end of the essay? Why?

~

THE CLICHÉ EXPERT
TESTIFIES ON POLITICS*   *Frank Sullivan*

Q. Mr. Arbuthnot, I hear you've become a campaign orator.

A. Fellow American, you have heard correctly. I've been on the stump all fall.

Q. In that case you ought to be up on your campaign-oratory clichés.

A. Well, sir, it is not my wont to brag, but I believe I may say with all due modesty that I can point with pride and view with alarm as sententiously and bombastically as any senator who ever thrust one arm in his frock coat and with the other called upon high heaven to witness the perfidy of the Other Party.

Q. Describe your candidate, Mr. Arbuthnot.

A. My candidate is a man four-square, a true representative of the people, a leader worthy of the trust which has been placed in him, and a standard-bearer who will carry the banner of our ga-reat and ga-lorious party to victory.

Q. Is he a man of prophetic vision?

A. He is indeed. He is also a man of sterling character and a champion of the rights of the people.

Q. What kind of champion?

A. A stalwart champion.

Q. What is he close to?

A. The soil.

Q. Is his name Jones?

A. It is not. I have nothing against Mr. Jones personally, but I can't see where he's fitted to be President.

Q. Why not?

A. He may be a first-rate businessman, but what does he know about government?

Q. Then your candidate's name is Brown.

A. Not at all. I'm a lifelong Democrat and I've always voted the straight Democratic ticket, but this year I'm taking a walk.

* From Frank Sullivan, *A Rock in Every Snowball* (Boston: Little, Brown & Co., Inc., 1946).

Q. Why?

A. Because old party lines are disappearing. What this country needs is a *businessman* in the White House.

Q. Then your man is Jones, after all.

A. Jones is all right personally, but I don't like the crowd he's tied up with.

Q. What crowd?

A. Oh, the public utilities, the Old Guard, and so on. Besides, what does he know about foreign affairs?

Q. Mr. Arbuthnot, I can't figure out *where* you stand. Let's get back to your campaign-oratory clichés. What kind of questions have you been discussing?

A. Burning questions. Great, underlying problems.

Q. What have you arrayed yourself against?

A. The forces of reaction. There must be no compromise with the forces of reaction.

Q. And now, Mr. Arbuthnot, may I ask you to characterize these times?

A. These are troubled times, sir. We are met here today in an hour of grave national crisis.

Q. What do you, as a campaign orator, propose to do in this grave hour?

A. I shall demand, and denounce, and dedicate. I shall take stock. I shall challenge, pledge, stress, fulfill, indict, exercise, accuse, call upon, affirm, and reaffirm.

Q. Reaffirm what?

A. My undying faith in the principles laid down by the Founding Fathers. And I shall exercise eternal vigilance that our priceless heritage may be safeguarded.

Q. Admirable, Mr. Arbuthnot. And that reminds me: What is it you campaign orators rise above?

A. Narrow partisanship. We must place the welfare of our country above all other considerations, including our desire to win.

Q. Mr. Arbuthnot, how do you campaign orators dedicate yourselves?

A. We dedicate ourselves anew to the task that lies before us.

Q. How does your party approach this task?

A. With a solemn realization of the awful responsibility that rests upon us in this hour of unprecedented national stress.

Q. When our country is—

A. Sore beset by economic ills.

Q. How else do you approach the task?

A. With supreme confidence that our ga-reat party will prove worthy of its ga-lorious tradition.

Q. And if your party failed to approach the task in that spirit, Mr. Arbuthnot, would you say that—

A. It would indeed be recreant to its sacred trust.

Q. Ah. But you feel that it won't be recreant?

A. No, my fellow American, a tha-a-o-u-sand times no! The ga-reat party of Washington, and Jefferson, and Lincoln, and Wilson, and Roosevelt, and Cleveland, and Grant, Garfield, Hayes, and Arthur will not fail our country in this, her hour of need.

Q. Hurrah for Jones!

A. The candidate of Big Business?

Q. Then hurray for Brown!

A. He wants to be a dictator.

Q. Then three rousing cheers for Green!

A. If elected, he couldn't even control his own party.

Q. Then hurray for Smith!

A. Elect him and you'll *never* get rid of him.

Q. I'm afraid there's no pleasing you today, Mr. Arbuthnot. Would you mind telling me who's to blame for our country's hour of need?

A. The Other Party.

Q. What has the Other Party proved?

A. Its utter incapacity to govern. Its record is an unbroken record of failure, of forgotten campaign pledges, of callous disregard for the welfare of the country.

Q. What is the Other Party undermining?

A. The American way of life. It is spending vast sums of the taxpayers' money.

Q. For what?

A. To build up a huge political machine. It has aroused class hatred. Fellow American, in this solemn hour, when the sacred institutions of democracy are challenged on every side and the world is rent by strife, I charge the Other Party with having betrayed the pee-pul of these Yewnited States.

Q. What must the pee-pul do?

A. They must rise in their wrath and elect my candidate.

Q. Mr. Arbuthnot, perhaps you'll tell us just what kind of leader the hour calls for?

A. A leader who will lead this country out of the wilderness, elimi-nate waste and extravagance in government, do away with red tape and bureaucratic inefficiency, solve the problem of unemployment, improve living conditions, develop purchasing power, raise the standard of living, provide better housing, and insure national defense by building a navy and air force second to none.

Q. What about the farmer?

A. The farmer must have relief.

Q. What kind of relief?

A. Farm relief. Labor must have the right to organize. Economy must be the watchword. Mounting deficits must cease; so must these raids on the public treasury. I view with alarm the huge and unwarranted increase in our national debt. Generations yet unborn! Those who would undermine our sacred institutions! Bore from within! Freedom of speech! Monroe doctrine! I call upon every patriotic American—

Q. Regardless of race or creed?

A. Be quiet . . . regardless of race or creed, from the snowcapped peaks of the Rockies—

Q. To the pine-clad shores of Maine?

A. Shut up! . . . to the pine-clad shores of Maine to have faith in the American way of life. Subversive doctrines! Undesirable aliens! Lincoln!

Q. What kind of Lincoln?

A. The Immortal Lincoln! The Immortal Washington! The Immortal Jefferson! The time for evasions has passed. We must face the facts, put our shoulders to the wheel, put our house in order, meet the challenge of the dictators, carry aloft the torch of liberty, fulfill our high destiny, face the future with confidence, and march forward to victory at the polls in November.

Problems for Thought and Writing

1. Frank Sullivan has written many pieces with Mr. Arbuthnot, the Cliché Expert, as leading character. Try your hand at this or a similar kind of exercise using the clichés relating to a certain profession or activity. Write the Gettysburg Address as a sociologist might write it; satirize the big man on campus who can't talk in anything but football lingo or the "Beatnik" who can't escape the language of jazz; describe a lawyer proposing marriage in legal jargon. See Donald Ogden Stewart, "How Love Came to General Grant" (page 125) for another example of the uses of clichés.

   Actually, there is nothing intrinsically laughable about stock language or the users of it. The man addicted to the prefabricated phrase or word, the conventional or euphemistic statement, the canned, overworked expression, is slave to self-imposed limitations. In chronic cases he may be incapable of fresh, original, or even honest thought. When asked what he "thinks" about something, he tries to remember some stock phrase that will help him to an answer. His answer, therefore, is what someone else thought in the dark past, not what he thinks. When asked what he "feels" about something, he will seek the same resource. He will try to react in the "approved" manner with a conventional phrase form—and he may never know he is deceiving himself as well as others. Honest feeling and honest thought are conditions of freedom; the man on the payroll of ready-mixed words and phrases is never free.

Yet we laugh. Perhaps we do so because we want to bring the dead back to life. We want the politician to be an intelligent and vital leader instead of a mechanical parrot. And we want the words he uses to be packed with meaning instead of cotton wool. Reasons for laughter are always complex, but we can be sure of this: the cliché (and its circle of relatives) is an enemy of all that is alive and fresh and honest in life. It is the enemy not only of clear and effective writing, but of clear and effective thinking as well.

Other pieces in this volume relevant to the discussion are: George Milburn, "The Apostate" (page 18), H. L. Mencken, "On Style" (page 166), Richard D. Altick, "Sentimentality" (page 109), Lee Strout White "Farewell My Lovely" (page 498), and most of Section 4, "Humor and Satire."

2. "The Cliché Expert" is a special kind of literary experiment, half pedagogical, half pure fun. Normally we don't find clichés in such concentrated solutions. But examine the text of a speech or sermon—as reported in a newspaper or such magazines as *Vital Speeches*—and underline all the words or phrases you would call clichés. Substitute fresh expressions, and see how the character of the speech is changed.

3. Define: hackneyed, jargon, gobbledygook, stereotype, cliché.

~

ON STYLE*   *H. L. Mencken*

With only one or two exceptions, all the books on prose style in English are by writers quite unable to write. The subject, indeed, seems to exercise a special and dreadful fascination over schoolma'ams, bucolic college professors, and other such pseudo-literates. In a thousand texts they set forth their depressing ideas about it, and millions of suffering high school pupils have to study what they say. Their central aim, of course, is to reduce the whole thing to a series of simple rules—the overmastering passion of their melancholy order, at all times and everywhere. They aspire to teach it as bridge whist, the flag-drill and double-entry bookkeeping are taught. They fail as

* Reprinted from *A Mencken Chrestomathy*, by H. L. Mencken. Copyright 1926, 1949, by Alfred A. Knopf, Inc.

ignominiously as that Athenian of legend who essayed to train a regiment of grasshoppers in the goose-step.

For the essence of a sound style is that it cannot be reduced to rules—that it is a living and breathing thing, with something of the demoniacal in it—that it fits its proprietor tightly and yet ever so loosely, as his skin fits him. It is, in fact, quite as securely an integral part of him as that skin is. It hardens as his arteries harden. It is gaudy when he is young and gathers decorum when he grows old. On the day after he makes a mash on a new girl it glows and glitters. If he has fed well, it is mellow. If he has gastritis it is bitter. In brief, a style is always the outward and visible symbol of a man, and it cannot be anything else. To attempt to teach it is as silly as to set up courses in making love.

The schoolma'am theory to the contrary is based upon a faulty inference from a sound observation. The sound observation is that the great majority of American high-school pupils, when they attempt to put their thoughts upon paper, produce only a mass of confused and puerile nonsense. The faulty inference is to the effect that what ails them is a defective technical equipment—that they can be trained to write clearly as a dog may be trained to walk on its hind legs. This is all wrong. What ails them is not a defective technical equipment but a defective natural equipment. They write badly simply because they cannot think clearly. They cannot think clearly because they lack the brains. Trying to teach them is as hopeless as trying to teach a dog with only one hind leg. Any human being who can speak English understandably has all the materials necessary to write English clearly, and even beautifully. There is nothing mysterious about the written language; it is precisely the same, in essence, as the spoken language. If a man can think in English at all, he can find words enough to express his ideas. The fact is proved abundantly by the excellent writing that often comes from so-called ignorant men. Such writing commonly arouses little enthusiasm among pedagogues. Its transparency excites their professional disdain, and they are offended by its use of homely words and phrases. They prefer something more ornate and complex—something, as they would probably put it, demanding more thought. But the thought they yearn for is the kind, alas, that they secrete themselves—the muddled, highfalutin, vapid thought that one finds in their own textbooks.

I do not denounce them because they write so badly; I merely record the fact in a sad, scientific spirit. Even in such twilight regions of the intellect the style remains the man. What is in the head

infallibly oozes out of the nub of the pen. If it is sparkling Burgundy
the writing is full of life and charm. If it is mush the writing is mush
too. The late Dr. Harding, twenty-ninth President of the Federal
Union, was a highly self-conscious stylist. He practised prose composition assiduously, and was regarded by the pedagogues of Marion,
Ohio, and vicinity as a very talented fellow. But when he sent a
message to Congress it was so muddled in style that even the late
Henry Cabot Lodge, a professional literary man, could not understand
it. Why? Simply because Dr. Harding's thoughts, on the high and
grave subjects he discussed, were so muddled that he couldn't understand them himself. But on matters within his range of customary
meditation he was clear and even charming, as all of us are. I once
heard him deliver a brief address upon the ideals of the Elks. It was
a topic close to his heart, and he had thought about it at length and
con amore. The result was an excellent speech—clear, logical, force-
ful, and with a touch of wild, romantic beauty. His sentences hung
together. He employed simple words, and put them together with
skill. But when, at a public meeting in Washington, he essayed to
deliver an oration on the subject of Dante Alighieri, he quickly became
so obscure and absurd that even the Diplomatic Corps began to
snicker.

A pedagogue, confronted by Harding in class, would have set him
to the business of what is called improving his vocabulary—that is, to
the business of making his writing even worse than it was. In point of
fact, he had all the vocabulary that he needed, and a great deal more.
Any idea that he could formulate clearly he could convey clearly.
Any idea that genuinely moved him he could invest with charm. But
style cannot go beyond the ideas which lie at the heart of it. If they
are clear, it too will be clear. If they are held passionately, it will be
eloquent. Trying to teach it to persons who cannot think, especially
when the business is attempted by persons who also cannot think, is a
great waste of time, and an immoral imposition upon the taxpayers of
the nation. It would be far more logical to devote all the energy to
teaching, not writing, but logic—and probably just as useless. For I
doubt that the art of thinking can be taught at all—at any rate, by
school-teachers. It is not acquired, but congenital. Some persons are
born with it. Their ideas flow in straight channels; they are capable
of lucid reasoning; when they say anything it is instantly understand-
able; when they write anything it is clear and persuasive. They
constitute, I should say, about one-eighth of one per cent of the human
race. The rest of God's children are just as incapable of logical

thought as they are incapable of jumping over the moon. Trying to teach them is as vain an enterprise as trying to teach a streptococcus the principle of Americanism. The only thing to do with them is to make Ph.D.'s of them, and set them to writing handbooks on style.

Problems for Thought and Writing

I

1. Mencken does not think much of books on English prose. "With only one or two exceptions, all the books on prose style are by writers quite unable to write." Do you agree?

2. Do you find Mencken's essay itself an example of the ability to think and the capacity for lucid reasoning that he claims is shared by only about one eighth of one per cent of the human race? If not, what do you find *illogical* about it?

3. Mencken says that only those who can think can write, and that the ability to think is itself congenital. Are his remarks about Harding, or their implications, consistent with this position?

4. Has Mencken really discredited the "schoolma'am theory" (that good writing can be taught)? He seems to imply that good writing is a product of good character. Does he anywhere suggest that good character can't be taught?

5. Do you think Mencken expects the reader to take his anti-intellectualism seriously? Is the tone of the whole essay, in fact, serious or the opposite?

6. Apart from references to specific topics and names, is there anything about the essay that makes it seem dated? If so, what?

II

7. Which among the following words or phrases would serve most accurately as a rubric under which Mencken's mode of treating his subject might be discussed: intolerable exaggeration, self-conceit, dogmatic irony, misanthropy, exhibitionism? Suggest others.

8. Do you find Mencken's use of similes and metaphors effective or ineffective?

9. Compare the techniques employed by Mencken and those by William Fulton (page 618). Which author would come off better on a truth scale?

10. Who, as examples, do you suppose Mencken had in mind in referring to the abundant writing produced by "so-called ignorant men"?

~

AUTHORS, SPEAKERS, READERS, AND MOCK READERS*

Walker Gibson

It is now common in the classroom as well as in criticism to distinguish carefully between the *author* of a literary work of art and the fictitious *speaker* within the work of art. Most teachers agree that the attitudes expressed by the "lover" in the love sonnet are not to be crudely confused with whatever attitudes the sonneteer himself may or may not have manifested in real life. Historical techniques are available for a description of the sonneteer, but the literary teacher's final concern must be with the speaker, that voice or disguise through which someone (whom we may as well call "the poet") communicates with us. It is this speaker who is "real" in the sense most useful to the study of literature, for the speaker is made of language alone, and his entire self lies on the page before us in evidence.

Closely associated with this distinction between author and speaker, there is another and less familiar distinction to be made, respecting the *reader*. For if the "real author" is to be regarded as to a great degree distracting and mysterious, lost in history, it seems equally true that the "real reader," lost in today's history, is no less mysterious and sometimes as irrelevant. The fact is that every time we open the pages of another piece of writing, we are embarked on a new adventure in which we become a new person—a person as controlled and definable and as remote from the chaotic self of daily life as the lover in the sonnet. Subject to the degree of our literary sensibility, we are re-created by the language. We assume, for the sake of the experience, that set of attitudes and qualities which the language asks us to assume, and, if we cannot assume them, we throw the book away.

I am arguing, then, that there are two readers distinguishable in every literary experience. First, there is the "real" individual upon whose crossed knee rests the open volume, and whose personality is as complex and ultimately inexpressible as any dead poet's. Second, there is the fictitious reader—I shall call him the "mock reader"—whose

* From *College English*, February, 1950. Reprinted by permission of author and publisher.

mask and costume the individual takes on in order to experience the language. The mock reader is an artifact, controlled, simplified, abstracted out of the chaos of day-to-day sensation.

The mock reader can probably be identified most obviously in sub-literary genres crudely committed to persuasion, such as advertising and propaganda. We resist the blandishments of the copywriter just in so far as we refuse to become the mock reader his language invites us to become. Recognition of a violent disparity between ourself as mock reader and ourself as real person acting in a real world is the process by which we keep our money in our pockets. "Does your toupee collect moths?" asks the toupee manufacturer, and we answer, "Certainly not! My hair's my own. You're not talking to *me*, old boy; I'm wise to you." Of course we are not always so wise.

Consider the mock reader in a case only slightly less obvious, the following opening paragraph from a book review of Malcolm Cowley's recent collection, *The Portable Hawthorne:*

Our thin self-lacerating and discontinuous culture automatically produces such uneasy collaborations as this one between Mr. Cowley, the hard-working scribe and oddly impressionable cultural sounding board, and the publishing industry with its concept of the "Portable." The Hawthorne who emerges has had such a bad fall between stools, or clichés, that he appears almost as giddy and shattered as we. . . .

The assumptions buried rather shallowly in this passage can very easily be brought to light. A nimble and sympathetic conversation is passing back and forth here—as always—between the speaker and the mock reader, a conversation that goes in part something like this:

You and I, in brave rebellion against the barbarousness of a business culture, can see this book for what of course it is—an "uneasy collaboration" and a defamation of that fine Hawthorne whom you and I know and love. *We* would not be content, would we, to be mere "scribes"; how stupid other people are to think that industry alone is sufficient. You and I are quickly able to translate "oddly impressionable" into what of course more literally describes the situation, though we were too polite to say so—namely, that Cowley is a weak sister. Nothing "odd" about it—you and I know what's going on all right.

It is interesting to observe how frankly the speaker throws his arm around the mock reader at the end of the passage I have quoted, as the two comrades experience their common giddiness at the appalling quality of this book. Remember that the *real* reader has in all likeli-

hood not even seen the book yet, and, if he takes his own mock-reader-
personality seriously enough, he probably never will.

An opening paragraph from another book review requires us to take
on another character:

I never got around to the early books of the Pasquier series, Georges
Duhamel's multigeneration history of a French family, but after reading
"Suzanne and Joseph" (Holt), the two-volume novel that closes the series,
I can't see any very pressing reason for flying in the face of prevailing opinion about M. Duhamel. He is, as has been claimed by such admirers of
his as Kate O'Brien and Sean O'Faolain, quite a good writer. He deals in
honored narrative methods and old truths, and he turns out the kind of
novel that can be recognized from afar as A Story. . . .

Again, some obvious portion of the between-the-lines dialogue between speaker and mock reader might be paraphrased as follows:

You and I are persons of leisure and taste, but unostentatious about it;
we make no pretense of having Big Ideas, and we "can't see any very pressing reason for flying in the face of prevailing opinion" (you'll excuse my
casual, homely phrase) merely because it *is* prevailing. We favor comfort,
after all, and we won't lament over the things we never got around to. On
the other hand we recognize competence and talent when we see it; we'll
certainly listen to whatever Kate O'Brien and Sean O'Faolain have to say;
and though we are enlightened enough to realize that A Story (you'll appreciate my capitals) won't in itself do in this complex age, nevertheless
the honored methods and old truths are after all the Honored Methods and
Old Truths. . . .

Here again it is worth pointing out that many successful readers of this
passage—perhaps most of them—never even heard of Kate O'Brien or
Sean O'Faolain. It is possible to imagine a reader saying, "I never
heard of Kate O'Brien; this review isn't addressed to the likes of me;
I'll read something else." But a more plausible response, I believe,
would be this: "It's true I never heard of Kate O'Brien, but in my
status as mock reader I'm going to pretend that I have; after all, it's
obvious how highly I would think of her if I had heard of her."

It will surprise no one to learn that the first passage was taken from
a recent issue of the *Partisan Review*, and that the second is from the
New Yorker. Perhaps it is fair to say that the mock readers addressed
by these speakers represent ideal audiences of the two periodicals. In
any case it seems plain that the job of an editor is largely the definition
of his magazine's mock reader and that an editorial "policy" is a
decision or prediction as to the role or roles in which one's customers

would like to imagine themselves. Likewise, a man fingering the piles at a magazine stand is concerned with the corollary question, Who do I want to pretend I am today?

(The mock reader of this article numbers among his many impressive accomplishments the feat of having participated at various times as mock reader of both the *New Yorker* and the *Partisan*.)

It is evident that imaginative literature too makes similar demands on its readers. There is great variation from book to book in the ease and particularity with which one can describe the mock reader, but he is always present, and sometimes is so clearly and rigorously defined as to suggest serious limitations on the audience. The mock reader of the opening paragraphs of *The Great Gatsby*, for instance, is a person determined within fairly rigid limits of time and space.

In my younger and more vulnerable years my father gave me some advice that I've been turning over in my mind ever since.

"Whenever you feel like criticising any one," he told me, "just remember that all the people in this world haven't had the advantages that you've had."

He didn't say any more, but we've always been unusually communicative in a reserved way, and I understood that he meant a good deal more than that. In consequence, I'm inclined to reserve all judgments, a habit that has opened up many curious natures to me and also made me the victim of not a few veteran bores. The abnormal mind is quick to detect and attach itself to this quality when it appears in a normal person, and so it came about that in a college I was unjustly accused of being a politician, because I was privy to the secret griefs of wild, unknown men. Most of the confidences were unsought—frequently I have feigned sleep, preoccupation, or a hostile levity when I realized by some unmistakable sign that an intimate revelation was quivering on the horizon. . . .

Here the mock reader must not only take in stride a series of "jokes" formed by some odd juxtapositions—vulnerable years, not a few veteran bores, etc.—but must also be quick to share the attitudes and assumed experiences of the speaker. For instance, the speaker by overt statement and the mock reader by inference have both attended a particular kind of college in a particular way; notice how "in college" appears grammatically as a dependent phrase within a dependent clause, supporting the casual, offhand tone.

Of course we remember, you and I, how it was in college, where as normal persons we certainly had no wish to be confused with campus politicians, yet were even warier of the wild unknown men, those poets, those radicals and misfits. You and I understand with what deliberate and delicate absurdity I make fun of both the wild unknown men and the formal-literary language to which you and I have been exposed in the course of our expensive educations: "an intimate revelation was quivering on the horizon."

It is probable that *Gatsby* today enjoys a greater reputation among real-life wild unknown men than it does among the equivalents of Nick Carraway's class. Somehow many people are able to suspend their antagonisms against Nick's brand of normalcy in order to participate in the tone. Yet it is neither necessary nor desirable to suspend all one's judgments against Nick and his society, for in so far as Nick himself is self-critical, of course we can and must join him. And, finally, Nick is not the speaker at all, I think, but a kind of mock speaker, as our mock reader is a more complex and discerning person than Nick himself. There is another speaker somewhere—almost as if this novel were written in the third person—and it is from this other speaker that the mock reader ultimately takes on some important attitudes. They speak right over Nick Carraway's head.

You and I recognize the weaknesses in Nick, do we not: his snobbery and his facile assumptions. But we like him pretty well, after all—and it's a question whether his shallowness is really his fault. . . .

The concept of the mock reader need not be "taught" in so many words to be useful to the teacher of literature. The question the teacher might well ask himself is no more than this: Is there among my students a growing awareness that the literary experience is not just a relation between themselves and an author, or even between themselves and a fictitious speaker, but a relation between such a speaker and a projection, a fictitious modification of themselves? The realization on the part of a student that he is many people as he reads many books and responds to their language worlds is the beginning of literary sophistication in the best sense. One crucial objective of the teacher, I take it, is simply the enlargement of his "mock" possibilities. But this is not to imply that one reading experience is as good as another or that there are not value discriminations that are appropriate among various mock readers. In fact, the term may be particularly useful in recognizing just such discriminations and in providing one way of pointing out what we mean by a bad book. A bad book, then, is a book in whose mock reader we discover a person we refuse to become, a mask we refuse to put on, a role we will not play. If this seems to say little more than "A bad book is a bad book," consider an example:

Alan Foster wanted to go to Zagazig. He wasn't exactly sure why, except that he liked the name, and after having spent four months in Cairo Alan was ready to go places and do things. Twenty-two years old, tall, blond, with powerful shoulders and trim waist, Alan found no difficulty in making friends. He had had a good time in Egypt. Now he wanted to leave Cairo and try out Zagazig.

What is so irritating about this? Many things, but if we isolate the third sentence and describe its mock reader, we can begin to express why this is bad writing. For the mock reader of the third sentence is a person for whom there is a proper and natural relation between powerful shoulders and making friends. No student in a respectable English course, I assume, should be willing to accept such a relation except perhaps as part of an irony. Only by irony could this passage be saved. ("You and I recognize that he makes friends all right, but what friends! This parody of a matinee idol is of course an ass.") No such irony is perceptible, however; the mock reader is expected to make one simple assumption only, and if the real reader has any sophistication at all, the passage collapses. It collapses precisely because the real reader finds in the mock reader a fellow of intolerable simplicity.

It is a question of rejecting the toupee ad, of recognizing that one's hair is one's own. However, the possibility must immediately suggest itself that a skilful control of tone could persuade us in an instant to don a fictitious toupee and to feel in all possible vividness the tug of a textile scalp against our own suddenly naked head. It is, finally, a matter of the details of language, and no mock reader can be divorced for long from the specific words that made him.

And the question remains: By what standard does one judge mock readers, how does one arrive at the decision that this one or that one is intolerable? Often it is as easy as in the case above—a case of oversimple assumptions. But obviously the problem is larger than that, and the tremendous importance, as it seems to me, of distinguishing for students between the mock world of the literary experience and the real world of everyday experience must not obscure the fact that in the end our appeals for decisions of value are toward sanctions of society in a very real world indeed. For the student, the problem of what mock reader—or part of a mock reader—it is proper for him to accept, and what to reject, involves the whole overwhelming problem of learning to read and learning to act. No terminology can remove his hesitations over attempting the enormously difficult job of becoming the mock reader of *Paradise Lost*, or *Antigone*, or Wallace Stevens.

The student's hesitation is no more than a part of a larger question that possibly no teacher can presume to answer for him: What do I want to be?

Problems for Thought and Writing

I

1. To whom is Gibson referring on p. 73 when he says, "(The mock reader of this article numbers among his many impressive accomplishments the feat of having participated at various times as mock reader of both the *New Yorker* and the *Partisan.*)"?

2. Reading literature is, by definition, vicarious experience. It permits the reader, so to speak, to live more than one life. Does Gibson's point seem to add up to this, or to this and something more?

3. Gibson makes his distinctions in an effort to *describe* what happens in the literary experience. What are the implications here, if any, for our assessment of the *value* of the literary experience?

4. Would it be possible to demonstrate the banality of the passage about Alan Foster without the mock-reader concept? Why or why not?

II

5. Try to rewrite Gibson's last paragraph, as he has rewritten others, in the form of a colloquy between the speaker (Gibson) and the mock reader (yourself as you read the paragraph).

6. Describe the mock reader of "The Winning of Barbara Worth," p. 134.

~

3 Reason and Emotion

LOGICAL FALLACIES*   *Robert Gorham Davis*

<small>UNDEFINED TERMS</small>

The first requirement for logical discourse is knowing what the words you use actually mean. Words are not like paper money or counters in a game. Except for technical terms in some of the sciences, they do not have a fixed face value. Their meanings are fluid and changing, influenced by many considerations of context and reference, circumstance and association. This is just as true of common words such as *fast* as it is of literary terms such as *romantic*. Moreover, if there is to be communication, words must have approximately the same meaning for the reader that they have for the writer. A speech in an unknown language means nothing to the hearer. When an adult speaks to a small child or an expert to a layman, communication may be seriously limited by lack of a mature vocabulary or ignorance of technical terms. Many arguments are meaningless because the speakers are using important words in quite different senses.

Because we learn most words—or guess at them—from the contexts in which we first encounter them, our sense of them is often incomplete or wrong. Readers sometimes visualize the Assyrian who comes down like the wolf on the fold as an enormous man dressed in cohorts (some kind of fancy armor, possibly) gleaming in purple and gold. "A rift in the lute" suggests vaguely a cracked mandolin. Failure to ascertain the literal meaning of figurative language is a frequent reason for mixed metaphors. We are surprised to find that the "devil" in "the devil to pay" and "the devil and the deep blue sea" is not Old Nick, but part of a ship. Unless terms mean the same thing to both writer and reader, proper understanding is impossible.

---

* From *Handbook for English A,* Harvard University. Reprinted by permission of Robert Gorham Davis, Theodore Morrison, and the President and Fellows of Harvard University.

ABSTRACTIONS

The most serious logical difficulties occur with abstract terms. An abstraction is a word which stands for a quality found in a number of different objects or events from which it has been "abstracted" or taken away. We may, for instance, talk of the "whiteness" of paper or cotton or snow without considering qualities of cold or inflammability or usefulness which these materials happen also to possess. Usually, however, our minds carry over other qualities by association. See, for instance, the chapter called "The Whiteness of the Whale" in *Moby Dick*.

In much theoretic discussion the process of abstraction is carried so far that although vague associations and connotations persist, the original objects or events from which the qualities have been abstracted are lost sight of completely. Instead of thinking of words like *sincerity* and *Americanism* as symbols standing for qualities that have to be abstracted with great care from examples and test cases, we come to think of them as real things in themselves. We assume that Americanism is Americanism just as a bicycle is a bicycle, and that everyone knows what it means. We forget that before the question, "Is Arthur Godfrey sincere?" can mean anything, we have to agree on the criteria of sincerity.

When we try to define such words and find examples, we discover that almost no one agrees on their meaning. The word *church* may refer to anything from a building on the corner of Spring Street to the whole tradition of institutionalized Christianity. *Germany* may mean a geographical section of Europe, a people, a governing group, a cultural tradition, or a military power. Abstractions such as *freedom, courage, race, beauty, truth, justice, nature, honor, humanism, democracy,* should never be used in a theme unless their meaning is defined or indicated clearly by the context. Freedom for whom? To do what? Under what circumstances? Abstract terms have merely emotional value unless they are strictly defined by asking questions of this kind. The study of a word such as *nature* in a good unabridged dictionary will show that even the dictionary, indispensable though it is, cannot determine for us the sense in which a word is being used in any given instance. Once the student understands the importance of definition, he will no longer be betrayed into fruitless arguments over such questions as whether free verse is "poetry" or whether you can change "human nature."

NAME-CALLING

It is a common unfairness in controversy to place what the writer dislikes or opposes in a generally odious category. The humanist dismisses what he dislikes by calling it *romantic;* the liberal, by calling it *fascist;* the conservative, by calling it *communistic.* These terms tell the reader nothing. What is *piety* to some will be *bigotry* to others. *Non-Catholics* would rather be called *Protestants* than *heretics.* What is *right-thinking* except a designation for those who agree with the writer? Social security measures become *creeping socialism;* industrial organizations, *forces of reaction;* investigation into Communism *witch hunts;* prison reform, *coddling;* progressive education, *fads and frills.* Such terms are intended to block thought by an appeal to prejudice and associative habits. Three steps are necessary before such epithets have real meaning. First, they must be defined; second, it must be shown that the object to which they are applied actually possesses these qualities; third, it must be shown that the possession of such qualities in this particular situation is necessarily undesirable. Unless a person is alert and critical both in choosing and in interpreting words, he may be alienated from ideas with which he would be in sympathy if he had not been frightened by a mere name.

GENERALIZATION

Similar to the abuse of abstract terms and epithets is the habit of presenting personal opinions in the guise of universal laws. The student often seems to feel that the broader the terms in which he states an opinion, the more effective he will be. Ordinarily the reverse is true. An enthusiasm for Thomas Wolfe should lead to a specific critical analysis of Wolfe's novels that will enable the writer to explain his enthusiasm to others; it should not be turned into the argument that Wolfe is "the greatest American novelist," particularly if the writer's knowledge of American novelists is somewhat limited. The same questions of *who* and *when* and *why* and under what *circumstances* which are used to check abstract terms should be applied to generalizations. Consider how contradictory proverbial wisdom is when detached from particular circumstances. "Look before you leap," but "he who hesitates is lost."

Superlatives and the words *right* and *wrong, true* and *untrue, never* and *always* must be used with caution in matters of opinion. When a student says flatly that X is true, he often is really saying that he or his family or the author of a book he has just been reading, persons of certain tastes and background and experience, *think* that X is true. If his statement is based not on logic and examination of evidence, but merely reproduces other people's opinions, it can have little value or relevance unless these people are identified and their reasons for thinking so explained. Because many freshmen are taking survey courses in which they read a single work by an author or see an historical event through the eyes of a single historian whose bias they may not be able to measure, they must guard against this error.

SAMPLING

Assertions of a general nature are frequently open to question because they are based on insufficient evidence. Some persons are quite ready, after meeting one Armenian or reading one medieval romance, to generalize about Armenians and medieval romances. One ought, of course, to examine objectively as many examples as possible before making a generalization, but the number is far less important than the representativeness of the examples chosen. The Literary Digest Presidential Poll, sent to hundreds of thousands of people selected from telephone directories, was far less accurate than the Gallup Poll which questioned far fewer voters, but selected them carefully and proportionately from all different social groups. The "typical" college student, as portrayed by moving pictures and cartoons, is very different from the "average" college student as determined statistically. We cannot let uncontrolled experience do our sampling for us; instances and examples which impress themselves upon our minds do so usually because they are exceptional. In propaganda and arguments extreme cases are customarily treated as if they were characteristic.

If one is permitted arbitrarily to select some examples and ignore others, it is possible to find convincing evidence for almost any theory, no matter how fantastic. The fact that the mind tends naturally to remember those instances which confirm its opinions imposes a duty upon the writer, unless he wishes to encourage prejudice and superstition, to look carefully for exceptions to all generalizations which he is tempted to make. We forget the premonitions which are not followed by disaster and the times when our hunches failed to select the winner in a race. Patent medicine advertisements print the letters of those

who survived their cure, and not of those who died during it. All
Americans did not gamble on the stock exchange in the twenties or
become Marxists in the thirties, and all Vermonters are not thin-
lipped and shrewd. Of course the search for negative examples can
be carried too far. Outside of mathematics or the laboratory, few
generalizations can be made airtight, and most are not intended to be.
But quibbling is so easy that resort to it is very common, and the
knowledge that people can and will quibble over generalizations is
another reason for making assertions as limited and explicitly conditional as possible.

FALSE ANALOGY

Illustration, comparison, analogy are most valuable in making an
essay clear and interesting. It must not be supposed, however, that
they prove anything or have much argumentative weight. The rule
that what is true of one thing in one set of circumstances is not necessarily true of another thing in another set of circumstances seems
almost too obvious to need stating. Yet constantly nations and
businesses are discussed as if they were human beings with human
habits and feelings; human bodies are discussed as if they were machines; the universe, as if it were a clock. It is assumed that what
held true for seventeenth century New England or the thirteen Atlantic colonies also holds true for an industrial nation of 160,000,000 people. Carlyle dismissed the arguments for representative democracy by
saying that if a captain had to take a vote among his crew every time
he wanted to do something, he would never get around Cape Horn.
This analogy calmly ignores the distinction between the lawmaking
and the executive branches of constitutional democracies. Moreover,
voters may be considered much more like the stockholders of a merchant line than its hired sailors. Such arguments introduce assumptions in a metaphorical guise in which they are not readily detected or
easily criticized. In place of analysis they attempt to identify their
position with some familiar symbol which will evoke a predictable,
emotional response in the reader. The revival during the 1932 presidential campaign of Lincoln's remark, "Don't swap horses in the
middle of the stream," was not merely a picturesque way of saying
keep Hoover in the White House. It made a number of assumptions
about the nature of depressions and the function of government. This
propagandist technique can be seen most clearly in political cartoons.

DEGREE

Often differences in degree are more important than differences in kind. By legal and social standards there is more difference between an habitual drunkard and a man who drinks temperately, than between a temperate drinker and a total abstainer. In fact differences of degree produce what are regarded as differences of kind. At known temperatures ice turns to water and water boils. At an indeterminate point affection becomes love and a man who needs a shave becomes a man with a beard. The fact that no men or systems are perfect makes rejoinders and counter-accusations very easy if differences in degree are ignored. Newspapers in totalitarian states, answering American accusations of brutality and suppression, refer to lynchings and gangsterism here. Before a disinterested judge could evaluate these mutual accusations, he would have to settle the question of the degree to which violent suppression and lynching are respectively prevalent in the countries under consideration. On the other hand, differences in degree may be merely apparent. Lincoln Steffens pointed out that newspapers can create a "crime wave" any time they wish, simply by emphasizing all the minor assaults and thefts commonly ignored or given an inch or two on a back page. The great reported increases in insanity may be due to the fact that in a more urban and institutionalized society cases of insanity more frequently come to the attention of authorities and hence are recorded in statistics.

CAUSATION

The most common way of deciding that one thing causes another thing is the simple principle: *post hoc, ergo propter hoc,* "After this, therefore because of this." Rome fell after the introduction of Christianity; therefore Christianity was responsible for the fall of Rome. Such reasoning illustrates another kind of faulty generalization. But even if one could find ten cases in which a nation "fell" after the introduction of Christianity, it still would not be at all certain that Christianity caused the fall. Day, it has frequently been pointed out, follows night in every observable instance, and yet night cannot be called the cause of day. Usually a combination of causes produces a result. Sitting in a draught may cause a cold, but only given a certain physical condition in the person sitting there. In such instances one may distinguish between necessary and sufficient conditions. Air is a necessary condition for the maintenance of plant life, but air alone is not sufficient to produce plant life. And often different causes at different times may produce the same result. This relation is known as plurality of causes. If, after sitting in a stuffy theatre on Monday, and then again after eating in a stuffy restaurant on Thursday, a man suffered from headaches, he might say, generalizing, that bad air gave him headaches. But actually the headache on Monday may have been caused by eye-strain and on Thursday by indigestion. To isolate the causative factor it is necessary that all other conditions be precisely the same. Such isolation is possible, except in very simple instances, only in the laboratory or with scientific methods. If a picture falls from the wall every time a truck passes, we can quite certainly say that the truck's passing is the proximate or immediate cause. But with anything as complex and conditional as a nation's economy or human character, the determination of cause is not easy or certain. A psychiatrist often sees a patient for an hour daily for a year or more before he feels that he understands his neurosis.

Ordinarily when we speak of cause we mean the proximate or immediate cause. The plants were killed by frost; we had indigestion from eating lobster salad. But any single cause is one in an unbroken series. When a man is murdered, is his death caused by the loss of blood from the wound, or by the firing of the pistol, or by the malice aforethought of the murderer? Was the World War "caused" by the assassination at Sarajevo? Were the Navigation Acts or the ideas of John Locke more important in "causing" the American Revolution? A complete statement of cause would comprise the sum total of the conditions which preceded an event, conditions stretching back indefinitely into the past. Historical events are so interrelated that the isolation of a causative sequence is dependent chiefly on the particular preoccupations of the historian. An economic determinist can "explain" history entirely in terms of economic developments; an idealist, entirely in terms of the development of ideas.

SYLLOGISTIC REASONING

The formal syllogism of the type,

> All men are mortal
> John is a man
> Therefore John is mortal,

is not so highly regarded today as in some earlier periods. It merely fixes an individual as a member of a class, and then assumes that the individual has the given characteristics of the class. Once we have decided who John is, and what "man" and "mortal" mean, and have canvassed all men, including John, to make sure that they are mortal, the conclusion naturally follows. It can be seen that the chief difficulties arise in trying to establish acceptable premises. Faults in the premises are known as "material" fallacies, and are usually more serious than the "formal" fallacies, which are logical defects in drawing a conclusion from the premises. But although directly syllogistic reasoning is not much practiced, buried syllogism can be found in all argument, and it is often a useful clarification to outline your own or another writer's essay in syllogistic form. The two most frequent defects in the syllogism itself are the undistributed and the ambiguous middle. The middle term is the one that appears in each of the premises and not in the conclusion. In the syllogism,

> All good citizens vote
> John votes
> Therefore John is a good citizen,

the middle term is not "good citizens," but "votes." Even though it were true that all good citizens vote, nothing prevents bad citizens from voting also, and John may be one of the bad citizens. To distribute the middle term "votes" one might say (but only if that is what one meant),

> All voters are good citizens
> John is a voter
> Therefore John is a good citizen.

The ambiguous middle term is even more common. It represents a problem in definition, while the undistributed middle is a problem in generalization. All acts which benefit others are virtuous, losing money at poker benefits others, therefore losing at poker is a virtuous act. Here the middle term "act which benefits others" is obviously used very loosely and ambiguously.

NON-SEQUITUR

This phrase, meaning "it does not follow," is used to characterize the kind of humor found in pictures in which the Marx Brothers used to perform. It is an amusing illogicality because it usually expresses, beneath its apparent incongruity, an imaginative, associative, or personal truth. "My ancestors came over on the Mayflower; therefore I am naturally opposed to labor unions." It is not logically necessary that those whose ancestors came over on the Mayflower should be opposed to unions; but it may happen to be true as a personal fact in a given case. It is usually a strong personal conviction which keeps people from realizing that their arguments are non-sequiturs, that they do not follow the given premises with logical necessity. Contemporary psychologists have effectively shown us that there is often such a wide difference between the true and the purported reasons for an attitude that, in rationalizing our behavior, we are often quite unconscious of the motives that actually influence us. A fanatical antivivisectionist, for instance, may have temperamental impulses toward cruelty which he is suppressing and compensating for by a reasoned opposition to any kind of permitted suffering. We may expect, then, to come upon many conclusions which are psychologically interesting in themselves, but have nothing to do with the given premises.

Ignoratio Elenchi

This means, in idiomatic English, "arguing off the point," or ignoring the question at issue. A man trying to show that monarchy is the best form of government for the British Empire may devote most of his attention to the charm of Elizabeth II and the affection her people felt for her. In ordinary conversational argument it is almost impossible for disputants to keep to the point. Constantly turning up are tempting side-issues through which one can discomfit an opponent or force him to irrelevant admissions that seem to weaken his case.

Begging the Question; Arguing in a Circle

The first of these terms means to assume in the premises what you are pretending to prove in the course of your argument. The function of logic is to demonstrate that because one thing or group of things is true, another must be true as a consequence. But in begging the question you simply say in varying language that what is assumed to be true is assumed to be true. An argument which asserts that we shall enjoy immortality because we have souls which are immaterial and indestructible establishes nothing, because the idea of immortality is already contained in the assumption about the soul. It is the premise which needs to be demonstrated, not the conclusion. Arguing in a circle is another form of this fallacy. It proves the premise by the conclusion and the conclusion by the premise. The conscience forbids an act because it is wrong; the act is wrong because the conscience forbids it.

ARGUMENTS AD HOMINEM AND AD POPULUM

It is very difficult for men to be persuaded by reason when their interest or prestige is at stake. If one wishes to preach the significance of physiognomy, it is well to choose a hearer with a high forehead and a determined jaw. The arguments in favor of repealing the protective tariff on corn or wheat in England were more readily entertained by manufacturers than by landowners. The cotton manufacturers in New England who were doing a profitable trade with the South were the last to be moved by descriptions of the evils of slavery. Because interest and desire are so deeply seated in human nature, arguments are frequently mingled with attempts to appeal to emotion, arouse fear, play upon pride, attack the characters of proponents of an opposite view, show that their practice is inconsistent with their principles; all matters which have, strictly speaking, nothing to do with the truth or falsity, the general desirability or undesirability, of some particular measure. If men are desperate enough they will listen to arguments proper only to an insane asylum but which seem to promise them relief.

After reading these suggestions, which are largely negative, the student may feel that any original assertion he can make will probably contain one or several logical faults. This assumption is not true. Even if it were, we know from reading newspapers and magazines that worldly fame is not dimmed by the constant and, one suspects, conscious practice of illogicality. But generalizations are not made only by charlatans and sophists. Intelligent and scrupulous writers also have a great many fresh and provocative observations and conclusions to express and are expressing them influentially. What is intelligence but the ability to see the connection between things, to discern causes, to relate the particular to the general, to define and discriminate and compare? Any man who thinks and feels and observes closely will not want for something to express.

And in his expression a proponent will find that a due regard for logic does not limit but rather increases the force of his argument. When statements are not trite, they are usually controversial. Men arrive at truth dialectically; error is weeded out in the course of discussion, argument, attack, and counterattack. Not only can a writer who understands logic show the weaknesses of arguments he disagrees with, but also, by anticipating the kind of attack likely to be made on his own ideas, he can so arrange them, properly modified with qualifications and exceptions, that the anticipated attack is made much less effective. Thus, fortunately, we do not have to depend on the spirit of fairness and love of truth to lead men to logic; it has the strong support of argumentative necessity and of the universal desire to make ideas prevail.

Problems for Thought and Writing

1. How many of the fallacies listed here can you detect in Antony's speech from *Julius Caesar* (page 622)?

2. Read the introductory essay on "Definition and Description" in Part II and relate to it what Davis says about "Undefined Terms" and "Syllogistic Reasoning."

3. All of the logical fallacies Davis describes are examples of unwarranted conclusions resulting from faulty reasoning. The list could be expanded and other terms used. But this is a useful check-list and the terms are traditional ones. In the following statements, identify the logical fallacies by reference to Davis' list.

   a) "Don't tell me that I overbid my hand! You aren't so perfect yourself, you know!"
   b) *Hamlet* is one of the greatest plays ever written, because Shakespeare wrote it.
   c) Bill ought to make a good husband. He doesn't drink or smoke.
   d) "For I doubt that the art of thinking can be taught at all—at any rate, by school-teachers." (H. L. Mencken, page 68)
   e) Titian's "Pope Paul III" is one of the greatest paintings in the world. Critics have often said so.
   f) Wilson must have been a good President; he read the same books Abraham Lincoln read.
   g) If you want to know my basic reason for not joining the Methodist Church, it's that I refuse to be associated with the bandits who run it.
   h) The whole movie colony is corrupt! Look at the divorces!
   i) I must be a criminal sort of person because I hate policemen.
   j) Telegrams always bring bad luck. I got one last week saying that my admission to college had been refused.
   k) War is inevitable because we can't change human nature.
   l) We are peace lovers and we'll defend it with our lives if necessary.
   m)   When my love swears that she is made of truth
                    I do believe her, though I know she lies. . . .
   n) After we gave women the vote we had ten years of immorality, political corruption, gangsterism, irreligion, and family disintegration. That ought to have taught us a lesson!

~

LOVE IS A FALLACY*   *Max Shulman*

Charles Lamb, as merry and enterprising a fellow as you will
meet in a month of Sundays, unfettered the informal essay with
his memorable *Old China* and *Dream Children*. There follows an
informal essay that ventures even beyond Lamb's frontier. Indeed, "informal" may not be quite the right word to describe this
essay; "limp" or "flaccid" or possibly "spongy" are perhaps more
appropriate.

Vague though its category, it is without doubt an essay. It develops an argument; it cites instances; it reaches a conclusion.
Could Carlyle do more? Could Ruskin?

Read, then, the following essay which undertakes to demonstrate that logic, far from being a dry, pedantic discipline, is a
living, breathing thing, full of beauty, passion, and trauma.

—AUTHOR'S NOTE

Cool was I and logical. Keen, calculating, perspicacious, acute and
astute—I was all of these. My brain was as powerful as a dynamo,
as precise as a chemist's scales, as penetrating as a scalpel. And—
think of it!—I was only eighteen.

It is not often that one so young has such a giant intellect. Take,
for example, Petey Burch, my roommate at the University of Minnesota. Same age, same background, but dumb as an ox. A nice enough
fellow, you understand, but nothing upstairs. Emotional type. Unstable. Impressionable. Worst of all, a faddist. Fads, I submit,
are the very negation of reason. To be swept up in every new
craze that comes along, to surrender yourself to idiocy just because
everybody else is doing it—this, to me, is the acme of mindlessness.
Not, however, to Petey.

One afternoon I found Petey lying on his bed with an expression
of such distress on his face that I immediately diagnosed appendicitis.
"Don't move," I said. "Don't take a laxative. I'll get a doctor."

"Raccoon," he mumbled thickly.

"Raccoon?" I said, pausing in my flight.

"I want a raccoon coat," he wailed.

* From *The Many Lives of Dobie Gillis,* by Max Shulman. Copyright 1951 by
Max Shulman. Reprinted by permission of Doubleday & Company, Inc.

I perceived that his trouble was not physical, but mental. "Why do you want a raccoon coat?"

"I should have known it," he cried, pounding his temples. "I should have known they'd come back when the Charleston came back. Like a fool I spent all my money for textbooks, and now I can't get a raccoon coat."

"Can you mean," I said incredulously, "that people are actually wearing raccoon coats again?"

"All the Big Men on Campus are wearing them. Where've you been?"

"In the library," I said, naming a place not frequented by Big Men on Campus.

He leaped from the bed and paced the room. "I've got to have a raccoon coat," he said passionately. "I've got to!"

"Petey, why? Look at it rationally. Raccoon coats are unsanitary. They shed. They smell bad. They weigh too much. They're unsightly. They—"

"You don't understand," he interrupted impatiently. "It's the thing to do. Don't you want to be in the swim?"

"No," I said truthfully.

"Well, I do," he declared. "I'd give anything for a raccoon coat. Anything!"

My brain, that precision instrument, slipped into high gear. "Anything?" I asked, looking at him narrowly.

"Anything," he affirmed in ringing tones.

I stroked my chin thoughtfully. It so happened that I knew where to get my hands on a raccoon coat. My father had had one in his undergraduate days; it lay now in a trunk in the attic back home. It also happened that Petey had something I wanted. He didn't *have* it exactly, but at least he had first rights on it. I refer to his girl, Polly Espy.

I had long coveted Polly Espy. Let me emphasize that my desire for this young woman was not emotional in nature. She was, to be sure, a girl who excited the emotions, but I was not one to let my heart rule my head. I wanted Polly for a shrewdly calculated, entirely cerebral reason.

I was a freshman in law school. In a few years I would be out in practice. I was well aware of the importance of the right kind of wife in furthering a lawyer's career. The successful lawyers I had observed were, almost without exception, married to beautiful, gracious, intelligent women. With one omission, Polly fitted these specifications perfectly.

Beautiful she was. She was not yet of pin-up proportions, but I felt sure that time would supply the lack. She already had the makings.

Gracious she was. By gracious I mean full of graces. She had an erectness of carriage, an ease of bearing, a poise that clearly indicated the best of breeding. At table her manners were exquisite. I had seen her at the Kozy Kampus Korner eating the specialty of the house —a sandwich that contained scraps of pot roast, gravy, chopped nuts, and a dipper of sauerkraut—without even getting her fingers moist.

Intelligent she was not. In fact, she veered in the opposite direction. But I believed that under my guidance she would smarten up. At any rate, it was worth a try. It is, after all, easier to make a beautiful dumb girl smart than to make an ugly smart girl beautiful.

"Petey," I said, "are you in love with Polly Espy?"

"I think she's a keen kid," he replied, "but I don't know if you'd call it love. Why?"

"Do you," I asked, "have any kind of formal arrangement with her? I mean are you going steady or anything like that?"

"No. We see each other quite a bit, but we both have other dates. Why?"

"Is there," I asked, "any other man for whom she has a particular fondness?"

"Not that I know of. Why?"

I nodded with satisfaction. "In other words, if you were out of the picture, the field would be open. Is that right?"

"I guess so. What are you getting at?"

"Nothing, nothing," I said innocently, and took my suitcase out of the closet.

"Where are you going?" asked Petey.

"Home for the weekend." I threw a few things into the bag.

"Listen," he said, clutching my arm eagerly, "while you're home, you couldn't get some money from your old man, could you, and lend it to me so I can buy a raccoon coat?"

"I may do better than that," I said with a mysterious wink and closed my bag and left.

"Look," I said to Petey when I got back Monday morning. I threw open the suitcase and revealed the huge, hairy, gamy object that my father had worn in his Stutz Bearcat in 1925.

"Holy Toledo!" said Petey reverently. He plunged his hands into the raccoon coat and then his face. "Holy Toledo!" he repeated fifteen or twenty times.

"Would you like it?" I asked.

"Oh yes!" he cried, clutching the greasy pelt to him. Then a canny look came into his eyes. "What do you want for it?"

"Your girl," I said, mincing no words.

"Polly?" he said in a horrified whisper. "You want Polly?"

"That's right."

He flung the coat from him. "Never," he said stoutly.

I shrugged. "Okay. If you don't want to be in the swim, I guess it's your business."

I sat down in a chair and pretended to read a book, but out of the corner of my eye I kept watching Petey. He was a torn man. First he looked at the coat with the expression of a waif at a bakery window. Then he turned away and set his jaw resolutely. Then he looked back at the coat, with even more longing in his face. Then he turned away, but with not so much resolution this time. Back and forth his head swiveled, desire waxing, resolution waning. Finally he didn't turn away at all; he just stood and stared with mad lust at the coat.

"It isn't as though I was in love with Polly," he said thickly. "Or going steady or anything like that."

"That's right," I murmured.

"What's Polly to me, or me to Polly?"

"Not a thing," said I.

"It's just been a casual kick—just a few laughs, that's all."

"Try on the coat," said I.

He complied. The coat bunched high over his ears and dropped all the way down to his shoe tops. He looked like a mound of dead raccoons. "Fits fine," he said happily.

I rose from my chair. "Is it a deal?" I asked, extending my hand.

He swallowed. "It's a deal," he said and shook my hand.

I had my first date with Polly the following evening. This was in the nature of a survey; I wanted to find out just how much work I had to do to get her mind up to the standard I required. I took her first to dinner. "Gee, that was a delish dinner," she said as we left the restaurant. Then I took her to a movie. "Gee, that was a marvy movie," she said as we left the theater. And then I took her home. "Gee, I had a sensaysh time," she said as she bade me good night.

I went back to my room with a heavy heart. I had gravely underestimated the size of my task. This girl's lack of information was terrifying. Nor would it be enough merely to supply her with information. First she had to be taught to *think*. This loomed as a project of no small dimensions, and at first I was tempted to give her back to Petey. But then I got to thinking about her abundant physical charms and about the way she entered a room and the way she handled a knife and fork, and I decided to make an effort.

I went about it, as in all things, systematically. I gave her a course in logic. It happened that I, as a law student, was taking a course in logic myself, so I had all the facts at my finger tips. "Polly," I said to her when I picked her up on our next date, "tonight we are going over to the Knoll and talk."

"Oo, terrif," she replied. One thing I will say for this girl: you would go far to find another so agreeable.

We went to the Knoll, the campus trysting place, and we sat down under an old oak, and she looked at me expectantly. "What are we going to talk about?" she asked.

"Logic."

She thought this over for a minute and decided she liked it. "Magnif," she said.

"Logic," I said, clearing my throat, "is the science of thinking. Before we can think correctly, we must first learn to recognize the common fallacies of logic. These we will take up tonight."

"Wow-dow!" she cried, clapping her hands delightedly.

I winced, but went bravely on. "First let us examine the fallacy called Dicto Simpliciter."

"By all means," she urged, batting her lashes eagerly.

"Dicto Simpliciter means an argument based on an unqualified generalization. For example: Exercise is good. Therefore everybody should exercise."

"I agree," said Polly earnestly. "I mean exercise is wonderful. I mean it builds the body and everything."

"Polly," I said gently, "the argument is a fallacy. *Exercise is good* is an unqualified generalization. For instance, if you have heart disease, exercise is bad, not good. Many people are ordered by their doctors *not* to exercise. You must *qualify* the generalization. You must say exercise is *usually* good, or exercise is good *for most people.* Otherwise you have committed a Dicto Simpliciter. Do you see?"

"No," she confessed. "But this is marvy. Do more! Do more!"

"It will be better if you stop tugging at my sleeve," I told her, and when she desisted, I continued. "Next we take up a fallacy called Hasty Generalization. Listen carefully: You can't speak French. I

can't speak French. Petey Burch can't speak French. I must therefore conclude that nobody at the University of Minnesota can speak
French."

"Really?" said Polly, amazed. "*Nobody?*"

I hid my exasperation. "Polly, it's a fallacy. The generalization is
reached too hastily. There are too few instances to support such a
conclusion."

"Know any more fallacies?" she asked breathlessly. "This is more
fun than dancing even."

I fought off a wave of despair. I was getting nowhere with this girl,
absolutely nowhere. Still, I am nothing if not persistent. I continued. "Next comes Post Hoc. Listen to this: Let's not take Bill on
our picnic. Every time we take him out with us, it rains."

"I know somebody just like that," she exclaimed. "A girl back
home—Eula Becker, her name is. It never fails. Every single time
we take her on a picnic—"

"Polly," I said sharply, "it's a fallacy. Eula Becker doesn't *cause*
the rain. She has no connection with the rain. You are guilty of Post
Hoc if you blame Eula Becker."

"I'll never do it again," she promised contritely. "Are you mad at
me?"

I sighed deeply. "No, Polly, I'm not mad."

"Then tell me some more fallacies."

"All right. Let's try Contradictory Premises."

"Yes, let's," she chirped, blinking her eyes happily.

I frowned, but plunged ahead. "Here's an example of Contradictory Premises: If God can do anything, can He make a stone so heavy
that He won't be able to lift it?"

"Of course," she replied promptly.

"But if He can do anything, He can lift the stone," I pointed out.

"Yeah," she said thoughtfully. "Well, then I guess He can't make
the stone."

"But He can do anything," I reminded her.

She scratched her pretty, empty head. "I'm all confused," she admitted.

"Of course you are. Because when the premises of an argument
contradict each other, there can be no argument. If there is an irresistible force, there can be no immovable object. If there is an
immovable object, there can be no irresistible force. Get it?"

"Tell me some more of this keen stuff," she said eagerly.

I consulted my watch. "I think we'd better call it a night. I'll take you home now, and you go over all the things you've learned. We'll have another session tomorrow night."

I deposited her at the girls' dormitory, where she assured me that she had had a perfectly terrif evening, and I went glumly home to my room. Petey lay snoring in his bed, the raccoon coat huddled like a great hairy beast at his feet. For a moment I considered waking him and telling him that he could have his girl back. It seemed clear that my project was doomed to failure. The girl simply had a logic-proof head.

But then I reconsidered. I had wasted one evening; I might as well waste another. Who knew? Maybe somewhere in the extinct crater of her mind, a few embers still smoldered. Maybe somehow I could fan them into flame. Admittedly it was not a prospect fraught with hope, but I decided to give it one more try.

Seated under the oak the next evening I said, "Our first fallacy tonight is called Ad Misericordiam."

She quivered with delight.

"Listen closely," I said. "A man applies for a job. When the boss asks him what his qualifications are, he replies that he has a wife and six children at home, the wife is a helpless cripple, the children have nothing to eat, no clothes to wear, no shoes on their feet, there are no beds in the house, no coal in the cellar, and winter is coming."

A tear rolled down each of Polly's pink cheeks. "Oh, this is awful, awful," she sobbed.

"Yes, it's awful," I agreed, "but it's no argument. The man never answered the boss's question about his qualifications. Instead he appealed to the boss's sympathy. He committed the fallacy of Ad Misericordiam. Do you understand?"

"Have you got a handkerchief?" she blubbered.

I handed her a handkerchief and tried to keep from screaming while she wiped her eyes. "Next," I said in a carefully controlled tone, "we will discuss False Analogy. Here is an example: Students should be allowed to look at their textbooks during examinations. After all, surgeons have X rays to guide them during an operation, lawyers have briefs to guide them during a trial, carpenters have blueprints to guide them when they are building a house. Why, then, shouldn't students be allowed to look at their textbooks during an examination?"

"There now," she said enthusiastically, "is the most marvy idea I've heard in years."

"Polly," I said testily, "the argument is all wrong. Doctors, lawyers, and carpenters aren't taking a test to see how much they have learned, but students are. The situations are altogether different, and you can't make an analogy between them."

"I still think it's a good idea," said Polly.

"Nuts," I muttered. Doggedly I pressed on. "Next we'll try Hypothesis Contrary to Fact."

"Sounds yummy," was Polly's reaction.

"Listen: If Madame Curie had not happened to leave a photographic plate in a drawer with a chunk of pitchblende, the world today would not know about radium."

"True, true," said Polly, nodding her head. "Did you see the movie? Oh, it just knocked me out. That Walter Pidgeon is so dreamy. I mean he fractures me."

"If you can forget Mr. Pidgeon for a moment," I said coldly, "I would like to point out that the statement is a fallacy. Maybe Madame Curie would have discovered radium at some later date. Maybe somebody else would have discovered it. Maybe any number of things would have happened. You can't start with a hypothesis that is not true and then draw any supportable conclusions from it."

"They ought to put Walter Pidgeon in more pictures," said Polly. "I hardly ever see him any more."

One more chance, I decided. But just one more. There is a limit to what flesh and blood can bear. "The next fallacy is called Poisoning the Well."

"How cute!" she gurgled.

"Two men are having a debate. The first one gets up and says, 'My opponent is a notorious liar. You can't believe a word that he is going to say.' . . . Now, Polly, think. Think hard. What's wrong?"

I watched her closely as she knit her creamy brow in concentration. Suddenly a glimmer of intelligence—the first I had seen—came into her eyes. "It's not fair," she said with indignation. "It's not a bit fair. What chance has the second man got if the first man calls him a liar before he even begins talking?"

"Right!" I cried exultantly. "One hundred per cent right. It's not fair. The first man has *poisoned the well* before anybody could drink from it. He has hamstrung his opponent before he could even start. . . . Polly, I'm proud of you."

"Pshaw," she murmured, blushing with pleasure.

"You see, my dear, these things aren't so hard. All you have to do is concentrate. Think—examine—evaluate. Come now, let's review everything we have learned."

"Fire away," she said with an airy wave of her hand.

Heartened by the knowledge that Polly was not altogether a cretin, I began a long, patient review of all I had told her. Over and over and over again I cited instances, pointed out flaws, kept hammering away without letup. It was like digging a tunnel. At first everything was work, sweat, and darkness. I had no idea when I would reach the light, or even *if* I would. But I persisted. I pounded and clawed and scraped, and finally I was rewarded. I saw a chink of light. And then the chink got bigger and the sun came pouring in and all was bright.

Five grueling nights this took, but it was worth it. I had made a logician out of Polly; I had taught her to think. My job was done. She was worthy of me at last. She was a fit wife for me, a proper hostess for my many mansions, a suitable mother for my well-heeled children.

It must not be thought that I was without love for this girl. Quite the contrary. Just as Pygmalion loved the perfect woman he had fashioned, so I loved mine. I determined to acquaint her with my feelings at our very next meeting. The time had come to change our relationship from academic to romantic.

"Polly," I said when next we sat beneath our oak, "tonight we will not discuss fallacies."

"Aw, gee," she said, disappointed.

"My dear," I said, favoring her with a smile, "we have now spent five evenings together. We have gotten along splendidly. It is clear that we are well matched."

"Hasty Generalization," said Polly brightly.

"I beg your pardon," said I.

"Hasty Generalization," she repeated. "How can you say that we are well matched on the basis of only five dates?"

I chuckled with amusement. The dear child had learned her lessons well. "My dear," I said, patting her hand in a tolerant manner, "five dates is plenty. After all, you don't have to eat a whole cake to know that it's good."

"False Analogy," said Polly promptly. "I'm not a cake. I'm a girl."

I chuckled with somewhat less amusement. The dear child had learned her lessons perhaps too well. I decided to change tactics. Obviously the best approach was a simple, strong, direct declaration of love. I paused for a moment while my massive brain chose the proper words. Then I began:

"Polly, I love you. You are the whole world to me, and the moon and the stars and the constellations of outer space. Please, my darling, say that you will go steady with me, for if you will not, life will be meaningless. I will languish. I will refuse my meals. I will wander the face of the earth, a shambling, hollow-eyed hulk."

There, I thought, folding my arms, that ought to do it.

"Ad Misericordiam," said Polly.

I ground my teeth. I was not Pygmalion; I was Frankenstein, and my monster had me by the throat. Frantically I fought back the tide of panic surging through me. At all costs I had to keep cool.

"Well, Polly," I said, forcing a smile, "you certainly have learned your fallacies."

"You're darn right," she said with a vigorous nod.

"And who taught them to you, Polly?"

"You did."

"That's right. So you do owe me something, don't you, my dear? If I hadn't come along you never would have learned about fallacies."

"Hypothesis Contrary to Fact," she said instantly.

I dashed perspiration from my brow. "Polly," I croaked, "you mustn't take all these things so literally. I mean this is just classroom stuff. You know that the things you learn in school don't have anything to do with life."

"Dicto Simpliciter," she said, wagging her finger at me playfully.

That did it. I leaped to my feet, bellowing like a bull. "Will you or will you not go steady with me?"

"I will not," she replied.

"Why not?" I demanded.

"Because this afternoon I promised Petey Burch that I would go steady with him."

I reeled back, overcome with the infamy of it. After he promised, after he made a deal, after he shook my hand! "The rat!" I shrieked, kicking up great chunks of turf. "You can't go with him, Polly. He's a liar. He's a cheat. He's a rat."

"Poisoning the Well," said Polly, "and stop shouting. I think shouting must be a fallacy too."

With an immense effort of will, I modulated my voice. "All right," I said. "You're a logician. Let's look at this thing logically. How could you choose Petey Burch over me? Look at me—a brilliant student, a tremendous intellectual, a man with an assured future. Look at Petey—a knothead, a jitterbug, a guy who'll never know where his next meal is coming from. Can you give me one logical reason why you should go steady with Petey Burch?"

"I certainly can," declared Polly. "He's got a raccoon coat."

Problems for Thought and Writing

1. What is your reaction to the "Author's Note" at the beginning? Is it too obviously signalling: "This author is trying to be funny"?

2. How does Shulman handle *point of view?* How would you characterize the *attitude* and *tone* of the narrator? Is he dead-panning? Is the narrator always speaking, or does he sometimes change places with the author?

3. Compare the use of stock attitudes, stock words, and stock postures in this story and their use by Stewart (page 125) and Thurber (page 120 and 210). Who wins?

4. Is any part of this story social satire?

5. Compare the logical fallacies the narrator taught Polly Espy with those taught by Robert Gorham Davis (page 77). Is Shulman accurate?

6. Do you agree with Polly that "shouting must be a fallacy too"?

~

EMOTIONAL MEANINGS * Robert H. Thouless

When we use a word in speech and writing, its most obvious purpose is to point to some thing or relation or property. This is the word's "meaning." We see a small four-footed animal on the road and call it a "dog," indicating that it is a member of the class of four-footed animals we call dogs. The word "dog" as we have used it there has a plain, straightforward, "objective" meaning. We have in no way gone beyond the requirements of exact scientific description.

Let us suppose also that one grandparent of the dog was a collie, another was an Irish terrier, another a fox terrier, and the fourth a bulldog. We can express these facts equally scientifically and objectively by saying that he is a dog of mixed breed. Still we have in no way gone beyond the requirements of exact scientific description.

* From *How to Think Straight.* Copyright, 1939, by Simon and Schuster, Inc. Reprinted by permission of Simon and Schuster, Inc.

Suppose, however, that we had called that same animal a "mongrel." The matter is more complicated. We have used a word which objectively means the same as "dog of mixed breed," but which also arouses in our hearers an emotional attitude of disapproval toward the particular dog. A word, therefore, can not only indicate an object, but can also suggest an emotional attitude toward it. Such suggestion of an emotional attitude does go beyond exact and scientific discussion because our approvals and disapprovals are individual —they belong to ourselves and not to the objects we approve or disapprove of. An animal which to the mind of its master is a faithful and noble dog of mixed ancestry may be a "mongrel" to his neighbor, whose chickens are chased by it.

Similarly, a Negro may be indicated objectively as a "colored man" or he may be indicated with strong emotional disapproval and contempt as a "nigger." The use of the latter word debases any discussion in which it is used below the level of impartial and objective argument.

Once we are on the lookout for this difference between "objective" and "emotional" meanings, we shall notice that words which carry more or less strong suggestions of emotional attitudes are very common and are ordinarily used in the discussion of such controversial questions as those of politics, morals, and religion. This is one reason why such controversies cannot yet be settled.

There is a well-known saying that the word "firm" can be declined as follows: I am *firm*, thou art *obstinate*, he is *pigheaded*. That is a simple illustration of what is meant. "Firm," "obstinate," and "pigheaded" all have the same objective meaning—that is, following one's own course of action and refusing to be influenced by other people's opinions. They have, however, different emotional meanings: "firm" has an emotional meaning of strong approval, "obstinate" of mild disapproval, "pigheaded" of strong disapproval. . . .

Such thinking in wartime may do much harm by leading humane people to condone cruelty. When the ordinarily liberal-minded Swinburne wrote a poem during the Boer War on the death of a British officer who had been blamed for the bad condition of the camps in which the Boer women and children were interned, he said:

> Nor heed we more than he what liars dare say
> Of mercy's holiest duties left undone
> Toward *whelps* and *dams* of *murderous* foes, whom none
> Save we had spared or feared to starve and slay.

Whelps and *dams* clearly mean in objective fact *children* and *wives*, with the added meaning of the emotional attitude adopted toward the females and young of wild beasts, while *murderous* means no more in objective fact than that our foes killed us when they could (as we also killed them), with the added emotional meaning of an attitude toward them which is our attitude to those who are guilty of murder.

The use of emotionally toned words is not, of course, always to be condemned. They are always harmful when we are trying to think clearly on a disputable point of fact. In poetry, on the other hand, they have a perfectly proper place, because in poetry (as in some kinds of prose) the arousing of suitable emotions is an important part of the purpose for which the words are used.

In "The Eve of St. Agnes," Keats has written:

> Full on this casement shone the wintry moon,
> And threw warm gules on Madeline's fair breast.

These are beautiful lines. Let us notice how much of their beauty follows from the proper choice of emotionally colored words and how completely it is lost if these words are replaced by neutral ones. The words with strikingly emotional meanings are *casement, gules, Madeline, fair,* and *breast. Casement* means simply a kind of window with emotional and romantic associations. *Gules* is the heraldic name for red, with the suggestion of romance which accompanies all heraldry. *Madeline* is simply a girl's name, but one calling out favorable emotions absent from a relatively plain and straightforward name. *Fair* simply means, in objective fact, that her skin was white or uncolored—a necessary condition for the colors of the window to show—but also *fair* implies warm emotional preference for an uncolored skin rather than one which is yellow, purple, black, or any of the other colors which skin might be. *Breast* has also similar emotional meanings, and the aim of scientific description might have been equally well attained if it had been replaced by such a neutral word as *chest*.

Let us now try the experiment of keeping these two lines in a metrical form, but replacing all the emotionally colored words by neutral ones, while making as few other changes as possible. We may write:

> *Full on this window shone the wintry moon,*
> *Making red marks on Jane's uncolored chest.*

No one will doubt that all of its poetic value has been knocked out of the passage by these changes. Yet the lines still mean the same in external fact; they still have the same objective meaning. It is only the emotional meaning which has been destroyed.

Now if Keats had been writing a scientific description for a text-book on physics instead of a poem, it would have been necessary for him to have used some such coldly objective terms as the ones into which we have just translated his lines. Such emotionally charged phrases as *warm gules* and *fair breast* would only have obscured the facts to which the scientist exactly but unbeautifully refers when he speaks of "the selective transmission of homogeneous light by pigmented glass."

The purpose of the present essay is to deal with the kind of problem in which cold and scientific thinking is required. Most of the practical problems of life are of this order. The fact that I shall abuse the use of emotional thinking in connection with such problems as tariffs, social ownership, revolution, and war does not mean that there is no place for emotional thinking. Poetry, romantic prose, and emotional oratory are all of inestimable value, but their place is not where responsible decisions must be made. The common (almost universal) use of emotional words in political thinking is as much out of place as would be a chemical or statistical formula in the middle of a poem. Real democracy will come only when the solution of national and international problems is carried out by scientific methods of thought, purged of all irrelevant emotion. Into the action which follows decision we can put all the emotion which we have refused to allow in our thinking. Let us think calmly and scientifically about war, and then actively oppose it with all the passion of which we are capable.

The growth of the exact thinking of modern science has been largely the result of its getting rid of all terms suggesting emotional attitudes and using only those which unemotionally indicate objective facts. It was not always so. The old alchemists called gold and silver "noble" metals, and thought that this emotionally colored word indicated something belonging to the metals themselves from which their properties could be deduced. Other metals were called "base." Although these terms have survived as convenient labels for the modern chemist, they carry none of their old emotional significance.

In popular biological discussions, on the other hand, such words are still used with their full emotional meaning, as when the "nobility" of man is contrasted with his alleged "base" origin. In this respect, popular biological discussion differs from that of the textbook and the laboratory, in which are used terms almost as devoid of emotional meaning as those of physics or chemistry.

Psychology is still younger in the ranks of the sciences, and the clearing away from it of emotional words has not gone very far. "Passion," "emotion," "sex" are all terms of our science which carry strong emotional meanings, so that it is difficult to discuss a controversial matter in psychology without using words which rouse strong emotions and confuse all issues. A beginning is being made. "Intelligence" was a subject on which it was difficult to think clearly because it carried so much emotional meaning. Now Professor Spearman has replaced it by what he calls "g" (or the "general factor"), which is a conception derived from the statistical analysis of a large collection of figures, and yet which is in its essence all that was really scientific in the old conception of intelligence. Some day a psychological genius will give us X or Z to replace the old emotional conception of sex, and we shall be able to discuss psychoanalysis as objectively as a mathematical physicist can discuss the quantum theory.

When we turn to politics and international questions, we are still further from straight scientific thinking. Such words as "Bolshevik," "Fascist," "reactionary," "revolutionary," "constitutional," "national honor," etc., are all words used in national and international political thinking which carry more of emotional than of any other meaning. So long as such words are the ordinary terms of rival politicians, how can we hope to think straight in national and international affairs? If a chemist doing an experiment depended on such thought processes as a nation uses in selecting its rulers or in deciding on peace or war with other nations, he would blow up his laboratory. This, however, would be a trivial disaster in comparison with what may result from emotional thinking in politics. Better have a hundred chemical laboratories blown up than the whole of civilization!

We must look forward to and try to help on the day when the thinking about political and international affairs will be as unemotional and as scientific as that about the properties of numbers or the atomic weights of elements. The spirit of impartial investigation of facts unswayed by irrelevant emotions has given us great advances in the sciences. Its triumphs will be even greater when it is applied to the most important affairs of life. We look forward to the day when we shall be able to discuss and settle such questions as Tariffs,

Public *vs.* Private Ownership, and Disarmament Treaties as success-fully as physicists have discussed and settled Einstein's theory of relativity.

Let us try to study a few more examples of the use of words with emotional meanings taken from various sources. Accounts of wars are rich sources of such material, so we are not surprised to find in a book on the French Commune the statement that large numbers of the regular troops were *assassinated* during the street fighting by the Communards, while a much larger number of the latter were *summarily executed* by the regulars. In order to reduce this to a state-ment of objective fact it is clear that the one word "killed" should be used in place both of *assassinated* and *summarily executed*. We have already noticed how such a choice of words with the same objective but opposite emotional meaning can be used to make us feel sym-pathetic to one and hostile to the other of two sides in warfare. During the Spanish Civil War, the supporters of the Government referred to themselves as the "Loyalists" and called Franco a "Rebel" or an "Insurgent." The supporters of Franco, on the other hand, called themselves "Nationalists" and referred to their opponents as "Reds." During the conflicts between Red and White forces in Russia and in China, our newspapers told us of the *atrocities* of the Bolshe-viks and the *wise severity* of the White commanders. Examination of the details (often possible only long afterwards) shows that the objective facts of an *atrocity* and of *wise severity* are much the same, and that they are not the kind of objective facts which will call out an emotion of approval in a humane person.

A similar choice of words will be noticed in political discussion. A fluent and forcible speech delivered by one of our own party is *eloquent*, a similar speech by one of the opposite party is *fanatical;* again two words with the same objective meaning but with the op-posite emotional meanings of approval and strong disapproval. The practical proposals of the opposition, moreover, are *panaceas*—a highly emotional word calling out the strongly disapproving emotions which we feel for those quack patent medicines which make extravagant claims. Those who show enthusiasm in support of proposals with which a speaker disagrees are *crackpots;* while those showing similar enthusiasm on his own side are called *sound.* If a politician wishes to attack some new proposal he has a battery of these and other words with emotional meanings at his disposal. He speaks of "this suggested *panacea* supported only by *fanatical crackpots*"; and the proposal is at once discredited in the minds of the majority of people, who like to think of themselves as moderate, distrustful of panaceas, and uninfluenced by windy eloquence. Also, we may notice that it has been discredited without the expenditure of any real thought, for of real objective argument there is none—only the manipulation of words calling out emotion.

It is not, however, only in warfare and politics that such words are used in order to influence opinion more easily than can be done by words embodying real thought. Art criticism is also a good source for this kind of material. Ruskin said of Whistler's Nocturnes: "I have heard and seen much of *Cockney impudence* before now, but never expected to hear a *coxcomb* ask two hundred guineas for *flinging a pot of paint in the public's face.*" As in earlier passages, I have italicized the words or phrases with strongly emotional meanings. Stripped of these and reduced to a statement of objective fact, the passage would have to be paraphrased in some such way as follows: "I have heard and seen much of the behavior of Londoners before now, but never expected to hear a painter ask two hundred guineas for painting a picture which seemed to me to have no meaning." Plainly not much is left of Ruskin's criticism after this operation has been performed on it.

As a last example, we may take a part of an attack made by a newspaper on a novel. This runs: "Its *vicious* plea for the acknowledgment and *condonation* of *sexual perversity*, and the grounds on which it is based, loosen the very *sheet anchor of conduct.*" This passage calls out such strong emotions of abhorrence that most readers will be content to condemn the novel without further inquiry. Yet the effect is gained entirely by the choice of words with emotional meanings. It happens to deal with a subject on which emotions are strong, so a dispassionate examination is all the more necessary. We note that a *plea* is simply an argument, plus a suggestion of a repugnance for the kind of argument used; that *condonation* is tolerance plus an emotional suggestion that such toleration is indefensible; that *sexual* means something in the life of love of which we disapprove, and that a *perversity* is an unusualness plus an emotional suggestion of abhorrence. The loosening of a *sheet anchor* is a metaphor implying change and suggesting to a landsman the emotion of fear, while *conduct* is simply behavior of which we approve.

So reduced to its bare bones of statement of objective fact (ignoring for a moment the special difficulties raised by the word *vicious*), the passage becomes: "Its argument for the acknowledgment and tolerance of unusualness in the life of love, and the grounds on which it is based, change the principles of behavior." This clearly is an important statement if it is true, but is not enough in itself to condemn the book, because undoubtedly our principles of behavior do need changing from time to time. We can only decide intelligently whether or not they need changing in the particular case under discussion, when we have made a dispassionate statement of what the proposed changes are and why they are defended. As in all other cases, discussion of the question with emotionally charged words obscures the problem and makes a sensible decision difficult or impossible.

The word *vicious* has some special difficulties of its own. It arouses emotions of disapproval, but there is no word with the same objective meaning which would not. If we call the book bad, corrupt, or evil, the same emotions would be aroused. So we cannot perform the simple operation of replacing *vicious* by an emotionally neutral word with the same objective meaning. Can we then leave it out altogether, on the ground that it has no objective meaning, but that it is used merely to arouse emotion?

Here we are up against a problem about which there has been much dispute. Some people consider that all such words as "good," "bad," "beautiful," "ugly," only indicate one's own emotional reactions toward actions or things and in no sense properties of the actions or things themselves. But when we see a man steal a penny from a child and we call his action "bad," we are in fact saying something meaningful about the action itself and not merely about our own feelings. As to what that something is we may leave the philosophers to dispute; it may only be that the man's action has subtracted from the total amount of human happiness. So to say a book is *vicious* is not the same kind of thing as contrasting the *slaughter* of regular troops by Communards with the *execution* of the Communards by regular soldiers. The statement that the book is *vicious* has a meaning which is not merely emotional, although, of course, the statement may not be true.

On the other hand, it is clearly not quite the same kind of meaning as a simple statement of outside fact such as "This is a book." Whether the book is good or bad is a real question, but it is a question peculiarly difficult to decide. Our own statement one way or the other is likely to be nothing but a reflection of our own personal prejudices and to have, therefore, no sort of scientific exactness. At the same time, such words certainly arouse strong emotions and should, there-

fore, be used sparingly in honest argument. The use of words implying moral judgments in the course of argument is very generally an
attempt to distort the hearers' view of the truth by arousing emotions.

If we are trying to decide a simple question of fact, such words
should be left out, because it is easier to settle one question at a time.
If a man is accused of poisoning his wife, the prosecuting attorney
should not say, "This *scoundrel* who hounded his wife to her grave."
The question to be decided is whether the man did poison his wife.
If he did, he is a "scoundrel" undoubtedly, but calling him a scoundrel
does not help to decide the question of fact. On the contrary, it
makes a correct decision more difficult by rousing emotions of hatred
for the accused in the minds of the jury. Another obvious objection
to the use of the word "scoundrel" before the man is convicted, which
puts it in the ranks of "crooked thinking," is that it "begs the question" or assumes what is to be proved. The man is only a scoundrel
if he is guilty, and yet the word has been used in the course of an
argument to prove that he is guilty.

These two objections can be urged against the word "vicious" in
the condemnation of a book quoted above. It calls up strong emotions making a just decision of the nature of the book difficult, and
it assumes exactly what the article professes to prove—that the book
is a bad one.

The aim of this essay has been to distinguish one kind of crooked
thinking, in the hope that those who recognize how their opinions
can be twisted away from the truth by the use of words with emotional meanings may be able to recognize this source of error and to
guard themselves against it. Those of its readers who have found
anything new to them in the ideas of this chapter should not, I suggest, be content simply to read the essay, but should try to do some
practical work on its subject matter. If you were studying botany,
you would not be content merely to read books on botany. If you
were, that would not carry you far in botanical knowledge. Instead
you would gather plants from the hedges and weeds from your garden, dissecting them, examining them with a microscope or magnify-
ing glass, and drawing them in your notebook. Psychology too should
be studied by practical methods. Emotional thinking (like most of
the other kinds of crooked thinking we shall be studying) is as common as a weed. It is to be found in the leading articles of newspapers, in the words of people carrying on discussions on political,
religious, or moral questions, and in the speeches made by public
men when these deal with controversial matters. In order to under-

stand it, we should collect specimens by putting them down on paper
and then we should dissect them. Current political and social controversy in the United States abounds in such words and phrases as
"crackpots," "economic royalists," "the abundant life," "bureaucracy"
—or, on the street level—"scabs," "finks," "nigger-lovers." The New
York *Herald Tribune* habitually referred to the child labor bill for
New York State as the "youth control bill"; the Hearst press dubbed
the New Deal the "Raw Deal"; Communists use the words "Trot-
zkyite" and "Fascist" to cover a multitude of sinners; Secretary Ickes
managed to get some powerful emotional undertones from Ferdinand
Lundberg's phrase, "America's Sixty Families."

) With these ideas and phrases in mind, it is not difficult to set forth
on a practical search for truth. I suggest that readers should copy
out controversial phrases from newspapers, books, or speeches which
contain emotionally colored words. Then they should underline all
the emotional words, afterwards rewriting the passages with the
emotional words replaced by neutral ones. Examine the passage then
in its new form in which it merely states objective facts without indicating the writer's emotional attitude toward them, and see whether
it is still good evidence for the proposition it is trying to prove. If it is,
the passage is a piece of straight thinking in which emotionally
colored words have been introduced merely as an ornament. If not,
it is crooked thinking, because the conclusion depends not on the
objective meaning of the passage but on the emotions roused by the
words.

When we condemn such a use of emotional words in writings and
speeches, we must remember that this is a symptom of a more deep-
seated evil—their prevalence in our own private, unexpressed thinking. Many of our highly colored political speakers whose speeches
stir us as we are stirred by romantic poetry show themselves unable
to think calmly and objectively on any subject. They have so accustomed themselves to think in emotionally toned words that they
can no longer think in any other way. They should have been poets
or professional orators, but certainly not statesmen.

It really does not matter much if we sometimes use emotional
words. We all do when we are trying to produce conviction. What
does matter is that we should not lose the power to think without
them. So a more important exercise than any we can perform on
written material is one we can perform on our own minds. When
we catch ourselves thinking in emotional phraseology, let us form a
habit of translating our thoughts into emotionally neutral words. So

we can guard ourselves from ever being so enslaved by emotional words and phrases that they prevent us from thinking objectively when we need to do so—that is, whenever we have to come to a decision on any debatable matter.

Problems for Thought and Writing

A key truth in Thouless' essay is that words not only specify objects but *at the same time* suggest and evoke emotional attitudes toward objects. In short, except in the strictest scientific description, it is impossible to say or write anything without conveying something of your own emotional attitude—and eliciting the reader's or listener's emotional response. His response to your words is always, partly, a response to the *attitude* your words convey. Consequently, many clever writers and speakers guide their words by what they know, or think they know, of their readers' likes and dislikes. Putting something in "a favorable light" is simply the process of evoking favorable associations for it in the reader's mind, and it is the basis of all *persuasion*. Mark Antony's funeral oration to the Roman citizens is one of the most brilliant examples in literature of the technique (see page 622). In the hands of the unscrupulous, of course, emotional meanings are manipulated to achieve a kind of verbal sleight of hand—to distort reality and to dupe the listener or reader. When President Eisenhower in 1953 refused to accept the North Korean terms for peace (for what seemed to him sound and fair reasons), the Soviet government called him a war-monger and a fascist. Moscow doubtless hoped that such words would turn the Russian people as well as the North Koreans more strongly against the United States.

1. Follow the news account of some controversial issue in your daily newspaper. Can you detect any systematic effort on the part of the paper to influence your attitude one way or the other by means of emotional diction?

2. Prepare a list of all emotionally charged words used by Fulton in "Happy Hunting for Red Front at Harvard U.," page 618.

3. Are emotional words ever justified in prose argument? If so, where and under what conditions? Identify every instance in Mandel's "Nobility and the United States," page 171, where the author uses such words as a weapon of attack. Do they undermine or discredit the objectivity of his argument? Do the same with Orwell (page 48), Milton (page 157), Mencken (page 66), or Whyte (page 217).

4. How successful or realistic do you think Thouless' call for rigidly scientific discussion (page 101) of international problems would be? Do you think the natives who were moved off the island of Bikini for the first atom bomb experiment were convinced that the bomb was more important than their homes and familiar surroundings?

5. Is *scientific*, as Thouless uses it, an emotionally weighted term?

6. What would be Archibald MacLeish's (page 665) probable reaction to Thouless' main thesis?

~

SENTIMENTALITY*   *Richard D. Altick*

Many situations in life are always fraught with emotion, no matter who participates in them—innocent childhood viewed by an adult, young love, betrayal, married happiness, pathetic accidents, poverty, old age, death. And they are the situations which form the basic material of literature; they include, indeed, most of the important things in life. Everybody wants to write about them; but, obviously, since they have been written about over and over, few people have anything new to say concerning them. Those who re-work the old themes often take refuge in sentimentality.

Sentimentality can be defined most simply as shallow and exaggerated emotion. Taking an emotional symbol or situation—home, mother, death of a pauper, return of a wanderer—the sentimentalist, perhaps from the most sincere of motives, extorts more feeling from it than a reasonable person would find there, and dwells upon it longer and more insistently than he should.

Furthermore, the sentimentalist, lacking fresh ideas, depends heavily upon the cliché in all its forms—upon the tried-and-true devices by which too many preceding writers have stirred their readers' feelings. But those images and phrases are now emotionally dehydrated; they have been used so often that they have lost their power to affect. And so the effect of sentimentality, to the reader who has a sense of fitness and freshness, is the opposite of what is intended. Depending upon the precise quality of the passage, the reader is either exasperated or amused. But he is not touched.

We can illustrate the nature of sentimentality by quoting two accounts dealing with the same material but differing radically in point of view. Not long ago a social worker, after visiting a "case" in a large eastern city, wrote a report from which the following excerpts are made, all proper names having been changed. The tone, whatever else it may be, is not sentimental:

The unfinished frame summer-kitchen addition to the dilapidated farmhouse Mrs. Denby occupies on the outskirts of Birchdale is a mute reminder

* From *Preface to Critical Reading*, Third Edition. By permission of Henry Holt and Company, Inc., Copyright 1956. [Title of selection chosen by editors.]

of the ambition Mr. Denby had entertained to remodel the property and make it more habitable: an ambition interrupted last autumn by his fatal three-month illness. He left his family in quite sorry straits. There are five children, the youngest only fourteen months old. They must live on their Mothers' Assistance Fund grant of $55 a month. Mrs. Denby, a no more than moderately intelligent woman, mingles a somewhat vulgar streak with strong Baptist religiosity. Her house is kept clean, but, with the exception of a shining new electric refrigerator in one corner of the kitchen, it is poorly furnished.

One of Mrs. Denby's elder sons was badly burnt in an accident some years ago and missed a year and a half of school. His sister, Elizabeth, is now living with Mr. Denby's relatives nearby, an arrangement which Mrs. Denby is willing to tolerate at least temporarily, although she has no truck with her numerous "in-laws."

Mr. Denby, the oldest of fifteen children, left school to go to work. He held various jobs, but none for long. He was constantly chasing the will o' the wisp of "more money," and as a result got nowhere. He was a notoriously poor provider, Mrs. Denby says, but despite this shortcoming her life with him was serene.

Their son George is said by his teachers to be retarded in his school work. He has not yet had an intelligence test, but his native ability seems possibly lower than average. He will have some difficulty in keeping up with his age-group.

Not long after the social worker's visit, the Denby house burned down, and one of the city newspapers ran the following story:

WIDOW SOBS AS FLAMES DESTROY ALL

A 38-year-old widow, mother of five children, poked aimlessly through the fire-blackened ruins of her little home at Center Road and Delaney Street yesterday and wept bitter tears of utter hopelessness.

"What are we to do?" Mrs. Hannah S. Denby sobbed. "The fire took everything except the clothes on our backs. It even burned my picture of my husband . . . and he died only six months ago.

And for Mrs. Denby, the loss of that picture seemed even harder to bear than the destruction of all but a few pieces of their furniture in the blaze which broke out Sunday afternoon shortly after the family had returned from church.

For her tow-headed, five-year-old daughter, Beth, the fire had meant another heart-rending loss, for her only doll and her doll coach were consumed by the flames.

And for 17-year-old Frank, now the man of the family, for 11-year-old James and seven-year-old George, the fire meant the end of the happiness they had just started to recapture in family life since the death of their father.

Only 16-month-old Robert was unaware of the feeling of family tragedy. He cooed gaily in his mother's arms.

For the time being the widow and her children have found a home with her sister. "But she is very ill," Mrs. Denby said, "and it is hardly fair for us to stay there. I wish I knew what we could do, where we could turn. Perhaps the good Lord will find a way. . . ."

Compare the two accounts, and you will have a good notion of the elements of sentimentality: the selection of detail to maintain a certain impression, whether wholly or partly false; the use of cliché symbols (e.g., the little girl and the burned doll coach); and the trite language itself ("bitter tears of utter hopelessness"). Do you think the writer of the newspaper account was sincerely moved by the Denbys' plight?

What is sentimental to one person may not be sentimental to another; it all depends upon how fine a sense of fitness the reader has. A reader who is ready to respond to any appeal to emotion, merely because it has something to do with babyhood or the first stirrings of pure young love, will not discriminate between the sentimental and the genuinely emotional. To him it is the subject that counts, not the treatment or the motives behind the treatment. But a more mature reader will instinctively reject an appeal which applies a pressure pump to his lachrymal glands. What do you think of this poem?

> She knelt upon her brother's grave,
> My little girl of six years old—
> He used to be so good and brave,
> The sweetest lamb of all our fold;
> He used to shout, he used to sing,
> Of all our tribe the little king—
> And so unto the turf her ear she laid,
> To hark if still in that dark place he play'd.
> No sound! no sound!
> Death's silence was profound;
> And horror crept
> Into her aching heart, and Dora wept.
> If this is as it ought to be,
> My God, I leave it unto thee.*

Do not think for a moment that we mean to depreciate the expression of emotion in literature. Our point is simply that writing which

---

* From *Collected Poems,* by T. E. Brown. By permission of the Macmillan Company, publishers.

expresses emotion in hackneyed and excessive terms not only is far inferior to writing which expresses that same emotion with dignity and restraint, but also can give us valuable warning that our generous and warm-hearted natures are about to be imposed upon.

Problems for Thought and Writing

I

1. Would you say that sentimentality results from *thinking* about something in a certain way, or merely from the way in which one *expresses* his thoughts? Fundamentally, is there any difference? What would Altick's answer be?

2. Since the American public at large seems to like sentimentality (e.g., the woman who likes to go to a "sad" movie because she enjoys having a "good cry" occasionally), isn't there some justification for the news story, "Widow Sobs as Flames Destroy All"?

3. Is sentimental writing *objective* writing? Can you perceive any parallel between the sentimentalist's selection and withholding of detail so as to create a certain impression, and the statistician's technique of sampling? Is sentimental writing dishonest?

4. Altick seems to be claiming that the sentimentalist says too much, and that good writing always leaves something *unsaid*. What, precisely, is the value of restraint?

5. Sentimentality has been defined as "emotion in excess of the fact." Would, then, literature of the "blood and guts" variety, dealing in excessive horror and violence, qualify as "sentimental"?

6. What other conventions, besides the ones Altick lists (page 109), does the sentimentalist characteristically follow? See the Introduction to "Argument and Persuasion," in Part II, page 539, for further discussion of sentimentality.

II

7. Read several stories from a few issues of one of the "slick" magazines (*The Saturday Evening Post, Redbook,* etc.) and write an essay discussing their qualities of style and tone. How are they written? What are the plots like? Do "types" of characters recur from story to story? Are the settings similar or radically different? Do the characters seem to exist for themselves or for the sake of the setting? What kind of endings do the stories have? What view of life, in general, do the stories endorse: critical, complacent, or unrealistic? Do the same with a group of Hollywood movies.

8. What devices of sentimentality do you detect in "How Love Came to General Grant" by Donald Ogden Stewart (page 125), or in the selection from Harold Bell Wright's novel (page 134), which Stewart's sketch parodies?

~

GETTING AT THE TRUTH * *Marchette Chute*

This is a rather presumptuous title for a biographer to use, since truth is a very large word. In the sense that it means the reality about a human being it is probably impossible for a biographer to achieve. In the sense that it means a reasonable presentation of all the available facts it is more nearly possible, but even this limited goal is harder to reach than it appears to be. A biographer needs to be both humble and cautious when he remembers the nature of the material he is working with, for a historical fact is rather like the flamingo that Alice in Wonderland tried to use as a croquet mallet. As soon as she got its neck nicely straightened out and was ready to hit the ball, it would turn and look at her with puzzled expression, and any biographer knows that what is called a "fact" has a way of doing the same.

Here is a small example. When I was writing my forthcoming biography, "Ben Jonson of Westminster," I wanted to give a paragraph or two to Sir Philip Sidney, who had a great influence on Jonson. No one thinks of Sidney without thinking of chivalry, and to underline the point I intended to use a story that Sir Fulke Greville told of him. Sidney died of gangrene, from a musket shot that shattered his thigh, and Greville says that Sidney failed to put on his leg armor while preparing for battle because the marshal of the camp was not wearing leg armor and Sidney was unwilling to do anything that would give him a special advantage.

The story is so characteristic both of Sidney himself and of the misplaced high-mindedness of late Renaissance chivalry that I wanted to use it, and since Sir Fulke Greville was one of Sidney's closest friends the information seemed to be reliable enough. But it is always well to check each piece of information as thoroughly as possible and so I consulted another account of Sidney written by a contemporary, this time a doctor who knew the family fairly well. The doctor, Thomas Moffet, mentioned the episode but he said that Sidney left off his leg armor because he was in a hurry.

The information was beginning to twist in my hand and could no

* From *The Saturday Review*, September 19, 1953. Reprinted by permission

longer be trusted. So I consulted still another contemporary who had mentioned the episode, to see which of the two he agreed with. This was Sir John Smythe, a military expert who brought out his book a few years after Sidney's death. Sir John was an old-fashioned conservative who advocated the use of heavy armor even on horseback, and he deplored the current craze for leaving off leg protection, "the imitating of which . . . cost that noble and worthy gentleman Sir Philip Sidney his life."

So here I was with three entirely different reasons why Sidney left off his leg armor, all advanced by careful writers who were contemporaries of his. The flamingo had a legitimate reason for looking around with a puzzled expression.

The only thing to do in a case like this is to examine the point of view of the three men who are supplying the conflicting evidence. Sir Fulke Greville was trying to prove a thesis: that his beloved friend had an extremely chivalric nature. Sir John Smythe also was trying to prove a thesis: that the advocates of light arming followed a theory that could lead to disaster. Only the doctor, Thomas Moffet, was not trying to prove a thesis. He was not using his own explanation to reinforce some point he wanted to make. He did not want anything except to set down on paper what he believed to be the facts; and since we do not have Sidney's own explanation of why he did not put on leg armor, the chances are that Dr. Moffet is the safest man to trust.

For Moffet was without desire. Nothing can so quickly blur and distort the facts as desire—the wish to use the facts for some purpose of your own—and nothing can so surely destroy the truth. As soon as the witness wants to prove something he is no longer impartial and his evidence is no longer to be trusted.

The only safe way to study contemporary testimony is to bear constantly in mind this possibility of prejudice and to put almost as much attention on the writer himself as on what he has written. For instance, Sir Anthony Weldon's description of the Court of King James is lively enough and often used as source material; but a note from the publisher admits that the pamphlet was issued as a warning to anyone who wished to "side with this bloody house" of Stuart. The publisher, at any rate, did not consider Weldon an impartial witness. At about the same time Arthur Wilson published his history of Great Britain, which contained an irresistibly vivid account of the agonized death of the Countess of Somerset. Wilson sounds reasonably impartial; but his patron was the Earl of Essex, who had good reason to hate that particular countess, and there is evidence that he invented the whole scene to gratify his patron.

Sometimes a writer will contradict what he has already written, and in that case the only thing to do is to investigate what has changed his point of view. For instance, in 1608 Captain John Smith issued a description of his capture by Powhatan, and he made it clear that the Indian chief had treated him with unwavering courtesy and hospitality. In 1624 the story was repeated in Smith's "General History of Virginia," but the writer's circumstances had changed. Smith needed money, "having a prince's mind imprisoned in a poor man's purse," and he wanted the book to be profitable. Powhatan's daughter, the princess Pocahontas, had recently been in the news, for her visit to England had aroused a great deal of interest among the sort of people that Smith hoped would buy his book. So Smith supplied a new version of the story, in which the once-hospitable Powhatan would have permitted the hero's brains to be dashed out if Pocahontas had not saved his life. It was the second story that achieved fame, and of course it may have been true. But it is impossible to trust it because the desire of the writer is so obviously involved; as Smith said in his prospectus, he needed money and hoped that the book would give "satisfaction."

It might seem that there was an easy way for a biographer to avoid the use of this kind of prejudiced testimony. All he has to do is to construct his biography from evidence that cannot be tampered with—from parish records, legal documents, bills, accounts, court records, and so on. Out of these solid gray blocks of impersonal evidence it should surely be possible to construct a road that will lead straight to the truth and that will never bend itself to the misleading curve of personal desire.

This might be so if the only problem involved were the reliability of the material. But there is another kind of desire that is much more subtle, much more pervasive, and much more dangerous than the occasional distortions of fact that contemporary writers may have permitted themselves to make; and this kind of desire can destroy the truth of a biography even if every individual fact in it is as solid and as uncompromising as rock. Even if the road is built of the best and most reliable materials it can still curve away from the truth because of this other desire that threatens it: the desire of the biographer himself.

A biographer is not a court record or a legal document. He is a human being, writing about another human being, and his own temperament, his own point of view, and his own frame of reference are unconsciously imposed upon the man he is writing about. Even if the biographer is free from Captain Smith's temptation—the need for making money—and wants to write nothing but the literal truth, he is still handicapped by the fact that there is no such thing as a completely objective human being.

An illustration of what can happen if the point of view is sufficiently strong is the curious conclusion that the nineteenth-century biographers reached about William Shakespeare. Shakespeare joined a company of London actors in 1594, was listed as an actor in 1598 and 1603, and was still listed as one of the "men actors" in the company in 1609. Shortly before he joined this company Shakespeare dedicated two narrative poems to the Earl of Southampton, and several years after Shakespeare died his collected plays were dedicated to the Earl of Pembroke. This was his only relationship with either of the two noblemen, and there is nothing to connect him with them during the fifteen years in which he belonged to the same acting company and during which he wrote nearly all his plays.

But here the desire of the biographers entered in. They had been reared in the strict code of nineteenth-century gentility and they accepted two ideas without question. One was that there are few things more important than an English lord; the other was that there are few things less important than a mere actor. They already knew the undeniable fact that Shakespeare was one of the greatest men who ever lived; and while they could not go quite so far as to claim him as an actual member of the nobility, it was clear to them that he must have been the treasured friend of both the Earl of Southampton and the Earl of Pembroke and that he must have written his plays either while basking in their exalted company or while he was roaming the green countryside by the waters of the river Avon. (It is another basic conviction of the English gentleman that there is nothing so inspiring as nature.) The notion that Shakespeare had spent all these years as the working member of a company of London actors was so abhorrent that it was never seriously considered. It could not be so; therefore it was not.

These biographers did their work well. When New South Wales built its beautiful memorial library to Shakespeare, it was the coat of arms of the Earl of Southampton that alternated with that of royalty in dignified splendor over the bookshelves. Shakespeare had been re-created in the image of desire, and desire will always ignore whatever is not relevant to its purpose. Because the English gentlemen did not like Shakespeare's background it was explained away as though it had never existed, and Shakespeare ceased to be an actor because so lowly a trade was not suited to so great a man.

All this is not to say that a biography should be lacking in a point of view. If it does not have a point of view it will be nothing more than a kind of expanded article for an encyclopedia—a string of facts arranged in chronological order with no claim to being a real biography at all. A biography must have a point of view and it must have a frame of reference. But it should be a point of view and a frame of reference implicit in the material itself and not imposed upon it.

It might seem that the ideal biographical system, if it could be achieved, would be to go through the years of research without feeling any kind of emotion. The biographer would be a kind of fact-finding machine and then suddenly, after his years of research, a kind of total vision would fall upon him and he would transcribe it in his best and most persuasive English for a waiting public. But research is fortunately not done by machinery, nor are visions likely to descend in that helpful manner. They are the product not only of many facts but also of much thinking, and it is only when the biographer begins to get emotional in his thinking that he ought to beware.

It is easy enough to make good resolutions in advance, but a biographer cannot altogether control his sense of excitement when the climax of his years of research draws near and he begins to see the pieces fall into place. Almost without his volition, A, B, and D fit together and start to form a pattern, and it is almost impossible for the biographer not to start searching for C. Something turns up that looks remarkably like C, and with a little trimming of the edges and the ignoring of one very slight discrepancy it will fill the place allotted for C magnificently.

It is at this point that the biographer ought to take a deep breath and sit on his hands until he has had time to calm down. He has no real, fundamental reason to believe that his discovery is C, except for the fact that he wants it to be. He is like a man looking for a missing piece in a difficult jigsaw puzzle, who has found one so nearly the right shape that he cannot resist the desire to jam it into place.

If the biographer had refused to be tempted by his supposed discovery of C and had gone on with his research, he might have found not only the connecting, illuminating fact he needed but much more besides. He is not going to look for it now. Desire has blocked the way. And by so much his biography will fall short of what might have been the truth.

It would not be accurate to say that a biographer should be wholly lacking in desire. Curiosity is a form of desire. So is the final wish to get the material down on paper in a form that will be fair to the reader's interest and worthy of the subject. But a subconscious desire to push the facts around is one of the most dangerous things a biographer can encounter, and all the more dangerous because it is so difficult to know when he is encountering it.

The reason Alice had so much trouble with her flamingo is that the average flamingo does not wish to be used as a croquet mallet. It has other purposes in view. The same thing is true of a fact, which can be just as self-willed as a flamingo and has its own kind of stubborn integrity. To try to force a series of facts into a previously desired arrangement is a form of misuse to which no self-respecting fact will willingly submit itself. The best and only way to treat it is to leave it alone and be willing to follow where it leads, rather than to press your own wishes upon it.

To put the whole thing into a single sentence: you will never succeed in getting at the truth if you think you know, ahead of time, what the truth ought to be.

Problems for Thought and Writing

I

One often hears the admonition that "honesty" and "objectivity" are admirable aims in writing and thinking. But here we are given some insight into the difficulty of achieving such aims—even with the best will in the world—and the tentative nature of even the most scrupulous and painstaking investigation. The problem of sifting evidence which Chute describes is not basically different from the problem faced by the scientist or logician. But there is one interesting difference: the materials Chute is handling are human materials—the testimony of human witnesses—instead of the relatively orderly testimony of the world of "nature." Humanistic evidence is more difficult to weigh than scientific; the humanistic investigator is in more danger of being deceived, has a harder time knowing when he has "got at" the truth. Because the problems of evidence discussed by Chute are similar to those every beginning writer meets, the editors feel that this essay is of particular value here.

1. Write an autobiographical sketch and weigh, as carefully as Chute did, such facts as these:

  a) What are or were my exact feelings toward my parents? (The stock and expected statement would be that you loved them, but the true statement is more concrete and explicit, and may reveal quite different emotions.)

  b) What were my *real* motives for coming to college? For the prestige of a degree? To avoid the shame of not going? To get a good job? To find a good husband? To become educated?

  c) What makes me tick? What do I really want and like (as apart from what others want and expect of me)?

2. Would Thouless (page 117) agree with Chute that the "ideal biographical system" would be "to go through the years of research without feeling any kind of emotion"? Would Thouless agree with Chute that this is impossible?

3. The man without "desire," without a vested interest, is, according to Chute, the most reliable witness. If that is true, would it not follow that the student who learns best is he who cares least about grades?

4. "A biography must have a point of view and it must have a frame of reference. But it should be a point of view and a frame of reference implicit in the material itself and not imposed upon it." This is an opinion shared by most English teachers and felt to apply to nearly all kinds of writing. Can you explain in detail why this kind of writing could never be sentimental?

5. Would you say Adams (page 260), Reed (page 276), or Fitzgerald (page 292) came closest to "getting at the truth" about themselves?

II

6. To what degree would the *style* of a piece of writing be affected by following the techniques Chute recommends? In answering this, one might compare Chute's method with that of, say, Mencken (page 66).

7. What role do concrete illustrations play in this essay? How does Chute's use of them demonstrate her intellectual principles?

8. Is Alice and her flamingo an irrelevancy in this essay or does it serve a useful purpose? Explain.

~

4 Humor and Satire

THE SECRET LIFE OF WALTER MITTY*

James Thurber

"We're going through!" The Commander's voice was like thin ice breaking. He wore his full-dress uniform, with the heavily braided white cap pulled down rakishly over one cold gray eye. "We can't make it, sir. It's spoiling for a hurricane, if you ask me." "I'm not asking you, Lieutenant Berg," said the Commander. "Throw on the power lights! Rev her up to 8,500! We're going through!" The pounding of the cylinders increased; ta-pocketa-pocketa-pocketa-*pocketa-pocketa*. The Commander stared at the ice forming on the pilot window. He walked over and twisted a row of complicated dials. "Switch on No. 8 auxiliary!" he shouted. "Switch on No. 8 auxiliary!" repeated Lieutenant Berg. "Full strength in No. 3 turret!" shouted the Commander. "Full strength in No. 3 turret!" The crew, bending to their various tasks in the huge, hurtling eight-engined Navy hydroplane, looked at each other and grinned. "The Old Man'll get us through," they said to one another. "The Old Man ain't afraid of Hell!" . . .

"Not so fast! You're driving too fast!" said Mrs. Mitty. "What are you driving so fast for?"

"Hmm?" said Walter Mitty. He looked at his wife, in the seat beside him, with shocked astonishment. She seemed grossly unfamiliar, like a strange woman who had yelled at him in a crowd. "You were up to fifty-five," she said. "You know I don't like to go more than forty. You were up to fifty-five." Walter Mitty drove on toward Waterbury in silence, the roaring of the SN202 through the worst storm in twenty years of Navy flying fading in the remote, intimate airways of his mind. "You're tensed up again," said Mrs. Mitty. "It's one of your days. I wish you'd let Dr. Renshaw look you over."

Walter Mitty stopped the car in front of the building where his
wife went to have her hair done. "Remember to get those overshoes
while I'm having my hair done," she said. "I don't need overshoes,"
said Mitty. She put her mirror back into her bag. "We've been all
through that," she said, getting out of the car. "You're not a young
man any longer." He raced the engine a little. "Why don't you
wear your gloves? Have you lost your gloves?" Walter Mitty reached
in a pocket and brought out the gloves. He put them on, but after
she had turned and gone into the building and he had driven on to
a red light, he took them off again. "Pick it up, brother!" snapped
a cop as the light changed, and Mitty hastily pulled on his gloves and
lurched ahead. He drove around the streets aimlessly for a time, and
then he drove past the hospital on his way to the parking lot.

. . . "It's the millionaire banker, Wellington McMillan," said the
pretty nurse. "Yes?" said Walter Mitty, removing his gloves slowly.
"Who has the case?" "Dr. Renshaw and Dr. Benbow, but there are
two specialists here, Dr. Remington from New York and Dr. Pritchard-Mitford from London. He flew over." A door opened down
a long, cool corridor and Dr. Renshaw came out. He looked distraught
and haggard. "Hello, Mitty," he said. "We're having the devil's own
time with McMillan, the millionaire banker and close personal friend
of Roosevelt. Obstreosis of the ductal tract. Tertiary. Wish you'd
take a look at him." "Glad to," said Mitty.

In the operating room there were whispered introductions: "Dr.
Remington, Dr. Mitty. Dr. Pritchard-Mitford, Dr. Mitty." "I've read
your book on streptothricosis," said Pritchard-Mitford, shaking hands.
"A brilliant performance, sir." "Thank you," said Walter Mitty.
"Didn't know you were in the States, Mitty," grumbled Remington.
"Coals to Newcastle, bringing Mitford and me up here for a tertiary."
"You are very kind," said Mitty. A huge, complicated machine, connected to the operating table, with many tubes and wires, began at
this moment to go pocketa-pocketa-pocketa. "The new anaesthetizer is
giving way!" shouted an interne. "There is no one in the East who
knows how to fix it!" "Quiet, man!" said Mitty, in a low, cool voice.
He sprang to the machine, which was now going pocketa-pocketa-
queep-pocketa-queep. He began fingering delicately a row of glistening dials. "Give me a fountain pen!" he snapped. Someone
handed him a fountain pen. He pulled a faulty piston out of the
machine and inserted the pen in its place. "That will hold for ten
minutes," he said. "Get on with the operation." A nurse hurried over
and whispered to Renshaw, and Mitty saw the man turn pale. "Core-

opsis has set in," said Renshaw nervously. "If you would take over,
Mitty?" Mitty looked at him and at the craven figure of Benbow, who
drank, and at the grave, uncertain faces of the two great specialists.
"If you wish," he said. They slipped a white gown on him; he adjusted a mask and drew on thin gloves; nurses handed him shining . . .

"Back it up, Mac! Look out for that Buick!" Walter Mitty jammed
on the brakes. "Wrong lane, Mac," said the parking-lot attendant,
looking at Mitty closely. "Gee. Yeh," muttered Mitty. He began
cautiously to back out of the lane marked "Exit Only." "Leave her
sit there," said the attendant. "I'll put her away." Mitty got out of
the car. "Hey, better leave the key." "Oh," said Mitty, handing the
man the ignition key. The attendant vaulted into the car, backed it
up with insolent skill, and put it where it belonged.

They're so damn cocky, thought Walter Mitty, walking along Main
Street; they think they know everything. Once he had tried to take
his chains off, outside New Milford, and he had got them wound
around the axles. A man had had to come out in a wrecking car
and unwind them, a young, grinning garageman. Since then Mrs.
Mitty always made him drive to a garage to have the chains taken
off. The next time, he thought, I'll wear my right arm in a sling;
they won't grin at me then. I'll have my right arm in a sling and
they'll see I couldn't possibly take the chains off myself. He kicked
at the slush on the sidewalk. "Overshoes," he said to himself, and
he began looking for a shoe store.

When he came out into the street again, with the overshoes in a
box under his arm, Walter Mitty began to wonder what the other
thing was his wife had told him to get. She had told him twice
before they set out from their house for Waterbury. In a way he
hated these weekly trips to town—he was always getting something
wrong. Kleenex, he thought, Squibb's, razor blades? No. Toothpaste, toothbrush, bicarbonate, carborundum, initiative and referen-
dum? He gave up. But she would remember it. "Where's the
what's-its-name?" she would ask. "Don't tell me you forgot the
what's-its-name." A newsboy went by shouting something about the
Waterbury trial.

. . . "Perhaps this will refresh your memory." The District Attorney suddenly thrust a heavy automatic at the quiet figure on the
witness stand. "Have you ever seen this before?" Walter Mitty took
the gun and examined it expertly. "This is my Webley-Vickers 50.80,"
he said calmly. An excited buzz ran around the courtroom. The
Judge rapped for order. "You are a crack shot with any sort of

firearms, I believe?" said the District Attorney, insinuatingly. "Objection!" shouted Mitty's attorney. "We have shown that the defendant could not have fired the shot. We have shown that he wore his right arm in a sling on the night of the fourteenth of July." Walter Mitty raised his hand briefly and the bickering attorneys were stilled. "With any known make of gun," he said evenly, "I could have killed Gregory Fitzhurst at three hundred feet *with my left hand*." Pandemonium broke loose in the courtroom. A woman's scream rose above the bedlam and suddenly a lovely, dark-haired girl was in Walter Mitty's arms. The District Attorney struck at her savagely. Without rising from his chair, Mitty let the man have it on the point of the chin. "You miserable cur!"

"Puppy biscuit," said Walter Mitty. He stopped walking and the buildings of Waterbury rose up out of the misty courtroom and surrounded him again. A woman who was passing laughed. "He said 'Puppy biscuit,'" she said to her companion. "That man said 'Puppy biscuit' to himself." Walter Mitty hurried on. He went into an A. & P., not the first one he came to but a smaller one farther up the street. "I want some biscuit for small, young dogs," he said to the clerk. "Any special brand, sir?" The greatest pistol shot in the world thought a moment. "It says 'Puppies Bark for It' on the box," said Walter Mitty.

His wife would be through at the hairdresser's in fifteen minutes, Mitty saw in looking at his watch, unless they had trouble drying it; sometimes they had trouble drying it. She didn't like to get to the hotel first; she would want him to be there waiting for her as usual. He found a big leather chair in the lobby, facing a window, and he put the overshoes and the puppy biscuit on the floor beside it. He picked up an old copy of *Liberty* and sank down into the chair. "Can Germany Conquer the World Through the Air?" Walter Mitty looked at the pictures of bombing planes and of ruined streets. . . . "The cannonading has got the wind up in young Raleigh, sir," said the sergeant. Captain Mitty looked up at him through tousled hair. "Get him to bed," he said wearily, "with the others. I'll fly alone." "But you can't, sir," said the sergeant anxiously. "It takes two men to handle that bomber and the Archies are pounding hell out of the air. Von Richtman's circus is between here and Saulier." "Somebody's got to get that ammunition dump," said Mitty. "I'm going over. Spot of brandy?" He poured a drink for the sergeant and one for himself. War thundered and whined around the dugout and battered at the door. There was a rending of wood, and splinters flew through the room. "A bit of a near thing," said Captain Mitty carelessly. "The box barrage is closing in," said the sergeant. "We only live once, Sergeant," said Mitty, with his faint, fleeting smile. "Or do we?" He poured another brandy and tossed it off. "I never see a man could hold his brandy like you, sir," said the sergeant. "Begging your pardon, sir." Captain Mitty stood up and strapped on his huge Webley-Vickers automatic. "It's forty kilometers through hell, sir," said the sergeant. Mitty finished one last brandy. "After all," he said softly, "what isn't?" The pounding of the cannon increased; there was the rat-tat-tatting of machine guns, and from somewhere came the menacing pocketa-pocketa-pocketa of the new flame-throwers. Walter Mitty walked to the door of the dugout humming "Auprès de Ma Blonde." He turned and waved to the sergeant. "Cheerio!" he said. . . .

Something struck his shoulder. "I've been looking all over this hotel for you," said Mrs. Mitty. "Why do you have to hide in this old chair? How did you expect me to find you?" "Things close in," said Walter Mitty vaguely. "What?" Mrs. Mitty said. "Did you get the what's-its-name? The puppy biscuit? What's in that box?" "Overshoes," said Mitty. "Couldn't you have put them on in the store?" "I was thinking," said Walter Mitty. "Does it ever occur to you that I am sometimes thinking?" She looked at him. "I'm going to take your temperature when I get you home," she said.

They went out through the revolving doors that made a faintly derisive whistling sound when you pushed them. It was two blocks to the parking lot. At the drugstore on the corner she said, "Wait here for me. I forgot something. I won't be a minute." She was more than a minute. Walter Mitty lighted a cigarette. It began to rain, rain with sleet in it. He stood up against the wall of the drugstore, smoking. . . . He put his shoulders back and his heels together. "To hell with the handkerchief," said Walter Mitty scornfully. He took one last drag on his cigarette and snapped it away. Then, with that faint, fleeting smile playing about his lips, he faced the firing squad; erect and motionless, proud and disdainful, Walter Mitty the Undefeated, inscrutable to the last.

Problems for Thought and Writing

1. On what values are Mitty's reveries based? (See J. H. Robinson, "Four Kinds of Thinking," page 461.) Do his notions of manhood and heroism correspond with your ideals?

2. Do we laugh *at* Mitty or sympathize with him? Is it possible to do both at the same time, or are we always in some way critical at the moment we laugh?

3. What "cliché situations" (as this term is defined by Richard Altick in "Sentimentality," page 109) does Thurber use to characterize Mitty? What is the effect of mentioning the fact that Dr. Benbow "drank"? Is this story in any sense sentimentalized? Why or why not?

4. Study the effect of that brief statement, "He raced the engine a little" (page 121). What would have been the effect had Thurber described Mitty's emotions rather than letting them show themselves in action?

5. Pride and humility, reverie and reality, courage and cowardice, manhood and mousehood, action and passivity, violence and domesticity—these are a few of the contrasts Thurber works into this story. How does he do so? Is irony thus achieved?

~

HOW LOVE CAME TO GENERAL GRANT*   *Donald Ogden Stewart*

IN THE MANNER OF HAROLD BELL WRIGHT

On a brisk winter evening in the winter of 1864 the palatial Fifth Avenue "palace" of Cornelius van der Griff was brilliantly lighted with many brilliant lights. Outside the imposing front entrance a small group of pedestrians had gathered to gape enviously at the invited guests of the "four hundred" who were beginning to arrive in elegant equipages, expensive ball dresses, and fashionable "swallowtails."

"Hully gee!" exclaimed little Frank, a crippled newsboy who was the only support of an aged mother, as a particularly sumptuous carriage drove up and a stylishly dressed lady of fifty-five or sixty stepped out, accompanied by a haughty society girl and an elderly gentleman in clerical dress. It was Mrs. Rhinelander, a social leader, and her daughter Geraldine, together with the Reverend Dr. Gedney, pastor of an exclusive Fifth Avenue church.

"What common-looking people," said Mrs. Rhinelander, surveying the crowd aristocratically with her lorgnette.

"Yes, aren't they?" replied the clergyman with a condescending glance which ill befit his clerical garb.

* From *A Parody Outline of History*, by Donald Ogden Stewart, copyright, 1921, by Doubleday and Company, Inc.

"I'm glad you don't have people like that *dans votre église*, Dr. Gedney," said young Geraldine, who thought it was "smart" to display her proficiency in the stylish French tongue. At this moment the door of the van der Griff residence was opened for them by an imposing footman in scarlet livery and they passed into the abode of the "elect."

"Hully gee!" repeated little Frank.

"What's going on tonight?" asked a newcomer.

"Gee—don't youse know?" answered the newsboy. "Dis is de van der Griffs' and tonight dey are givin' a swell dinner for General Grant. Dat lady wot just went in was old Mrs. Rhinelander. I seen her pitcher in de last *Harper's Weekly,* and dere was a story in de paper dis morning dat her daughter Geraldine was going to marry de general."

"That isn't so," broke in another. "It was just a rumor."

"Well, anyway," said Frank, "I wisht de general would hurry up and come—it's getting cold enough to freeze the tail off a brass monkey." The onlookers laughed merrily at his humorous reference to the frigid temperature, although many cast sympathetic looks at his thin, threadbare garments and registered a kindly thought for this brave boy who so philosophically accepted the buffets of fate.

"I bet this is him now," cried Frank, and all waited expectantly as a vehicle drove up. The cabman jumped off his box and held the carriage door open.

"Here you are, Miss Flowers," he said, touching his hat respectfully.

A silver peal of rippling laughter sounded from the interior of the carriage.

"Why, Jerry," came in velvet tones addressed to the coachman, "you mustn't be so formal just because I have come to New York to live. Call me Miss Ella, of course, just like you did when we lived out in Kansas," and with these words Miss Ella Flowers, for it was she, stepped out of the carriage.

A hush fell on the crowd as they caught sight of her face—a hush of silent tribute to the clear, sweet womanhood of that pure countenance. A young man on the edge of the crowd who was on the verge of becoming a drunkard burst into tears and walked rapidly away to join the nearest church. A pr-st---te who had been plying her nefarious trade on the avenue sank to her knees to pray for strength to go back to her aged parents on the farm. Another young man, catching sight of Ella's pure face, vowed to write home to his old mother and send her the money he had been expending in the city on drinks and dissipation.

And well might these city people be affected by the glimpse of the sweet, noble virtue which shone forth so radiantly in this Kansas girl's countenance. Although born in Jersey City, Ella had moved with her parents to the West at an early age, and she had grown up in the open country where a man's a man and women lead clean, sweet, womanly lives. Out in the pure air of God's green places and amid kindly, simple, big-hearted folks, little Ella had blossomed and thrived, the pride of the whole country, and as she had grown to womanhood there was many a masculine heart beat a little faster for her presence and many a manly blush of admiration came into the features of her admirers as she whirled gracefully with them in the innocent pleasure of a simple country dance. But on her eighteenth birthday, her parents had passed on to the Great Beyond and the heartbroken Ella had come east to live with Mrs. Montgomery, her aunt in Jersey City. This lady, being socially prominent in New York's "four hundred," was of course quite ambitious that her pretty little niece from the West should also enter society. For the last three months, therefore, Ella had been fêted at all the better-class homes in New York and Jersey City, and as Mrs. van der Griff, the Fifth Avenue social leader, was in the same set as Ella's aunt, it was only natural that when making out her list of guests for the dinner in honor of General Grant she should include the beautiful niece of her friend.

As Ella stepped from the carriage, her gaze fell upon little Frank, the crippled newsboy; and her eyes quickly filled with tears, for social success had not yet caused her to forget that "blessed are the weak." Taking out her purse, she gave Frank a silver dollar and a warm look of sympathy as she passed into the house.

"Gee, there went an angel," whispered the little cripple, and many who heard him silently echoed that thought in their hearts. Nor were they far from wrong.

But even an angel is not free from temptation, and by letting Ella go into society her aunt was exposing the girl to the whisperings of Satan—whisperings of things material rather than things spiritual. Many a girl just as pure as Ella has found her standards gradually lowered and her moral character slowly weakened by the contact with the so-called "refined" and "cultured" infidels one meets in fashionable society. Many a father and mother whose ambition has caused them to have their daughter go out in society have bitterly repented of that step as they watched the poor girl gradually succumbing to the temptation of the world. Let her who thinks it is "smart" to be in society consider that our brothels with their red plush curtains, their hardwood floors, and their luxurious appointments are filled largely with the wornout belles and debutantes of fashionable society.

The next minute a bugle call sounded down the street, and up drove a team of prancing grays. Two soldiers sprang down from the coachman's box and stood at rigid attention while the door of the carriage opened and out stepped General Ulysses S. Grant.

A murmur of admiration swept over the crowd at the sight of his manly inspiring features, in which the clean-cut virility of a life free from dissipation was accentuated by the neatly trimmed black beard. His erect military bearing—his neat, well-fitting uniform—but above all his frank, open face proclaimed him a man's man—a man among men. A cheer burst from the lips of the onlookers, and the brave but modest general lowered his eyes and blushed as he acknowledged their greeting.

"Men and women," he said, in a voice which, although low, one could see was accustomed to being obeyed, "I thank you for your cheers. It makes my heart rejoice to hear them, for I know you are not cheering me personally but only as one of the many men who are fighting for the cause of liberty and freedom, and for—" the general's voice broke a little, but he mastered his emotion and went on—"for the flag we all love."

At this he pulled from his pocket an American flag and held it up so that all could see. Cheer after cheer rent the air, and tears came to the general's eyes at this mark of devotion to the common cause.

"Wipe the d————d rebels off the face of the earth, G-d d———— 'em," shouted a too enthusiastic member of the crowd who, I fear, was a little the worse for drink. In an instant General Grant had stepped up to him and fixed upon him those fearless blue eyes.

"My man," said the general, "it hurts me to hear you give vent to these oaths, especially in the presence of ladies. Soldiers do not curse, and I think you would do well to follow their example."

The other lowered his head shamefacedly. "General," he said, "you're right and I apologize."

A smile lit up the general's handsome features, and he extended his hand to the other.

"Shake on it," he said simply, and as the crowd roared its approval of this speech the two men "shook."

Meanwhile within the van der Griff house all were agog with excitement in expectation of the arrival of the distinguished guest. Expensively dressed ladies fluttered here and there amid the elegant appointments; servants in stylish livery passed to and fro with trays of wine and other spirituous liquors.

At the sound of the cheering outside, the haughty Mrs. Rhinelander patted her daughter Geraldine nervously, and between mother and daughter passed a glance of understanding, for both felt that tonight, if ever, was Geraldine's opportunity to win the handsome and popular general.

The doorbell rang, and a hush fell over the chattering assemblage; then came the proud announcement from the doorman—"General Ulysses S. Grant"—and all the society belles crowded forward around the guest of honor.

It had been rumored that the general, being a soldier, was ignorant of social etiquette, but such proved to be far from the case. Indeed, he handled himself with such ease of manner that he captivated all, and for each and every young miss he had an apt phrase or a pretty compliment, greatly to their delight.

"Pleased to know you"—"Glad to shake the hand of such a pretty girl"—"What a nice little hand I wish I might hold it all evening"— with these and kindred pleasantries the general won the way into the graces of Mrs. van der Griff's fair guests, and many a female heart fluttered in her bosom as she gazed into the clear blue eyes of the soldier and listened to his well-chosen, tactful words.

"And how is the dear general this evening?"—this in the affected tone of old Mrs. Rhinelander as she forced her way through the crowd.

"Finer than silk," replied he, and he added solicitously: "I hope you have recovered from your lumbago, Mrs. Rhinelander."

"Oh, quite," answered she, "and here is Geraldine, General," and the ambitious mother pushed her daughter forward.

"*Comment vous portez-vous, mon Général?*" said Geraldine in French. "I hope we can have a nice *tête-à-tête* tonight," and she fawned upon her prey in a manner that would have sickened a less artificial gathering.

Were there not some amid all that fashionable throng in whom ideals of purity and true womanhood lived—some who cared enough for the sacredness of real love to cry upon this hollow mockery that was being used to ensnare the simple, honest soldier? There was only one, and she was at that moment entering the drawing room for the purpose of being presented to the general. Need I name her?

Ella, for it was she, had been upstairs busying herself with her toilet when General Grant had arrived, and she now hurried forward to pay her homage to the great soldier. And then, as she caught sight of his face, she stopped suddenly and a deep crimson blush spread over her features. She looked again, and then drew back behind a near-by portiere, her heart beating wildly.

Well did Ella remember where she had seen that countenance before, and as she stood there trembling the whole scene of her folly came back to her. It had happened in Kansas, just before her parents died, on one sunny May morning. She had gone for a walk; her footsteps had led her to the banks of a secluded lake where she often went when she wished to be alone. Many an afternoon had Ella dreamed idly away on this shore, but that day, for some reason, she had felt unusually full of life and not at all like dreaming. Obeying a thoughtless but innocent impulse, with no intention of evil, she had taken off her clothes and plunged thus n-k-d into the cool waters of the lake. After she had swum around a little she began to realize the extent of her folly and was hurriedly swimming toward the shore when a terrific cramp had seized her lower limbs, rendering them powerless. Her first impulse, to scream for help, was quickly checked with a deep blush, as she realized the consequences if a man should hear her call; for near by was an encampment of Union soldiers, none of whom she knew. The perplexed and helpless girl was in sore straits and was slowly sinking for the third time when a bearded stranger in soldier's uniform appeared on the bank and dove into the water. To her horror he swam rapidly toward her—but her shame was soon changed to joy when she realized that he was purposely keeping his eyes tight shut. With a few swift, powerful strokes he reached her side and, blushing deeply, took off his blue coat, fastened it around her, opened his eyes, and swam with her to the shore. Carrying her to where she had left her clothes, he stayed only long enough to assure himself that she had completely recovered the use of her limbs, and evidently to spare her further embarrassment, had vanished as quickly and as mysteriously as he had appeared.

Many a night after that had Ella lain awake thinking of the splendid features and the even more splendid conduct of this unknown knight who wore the uniform of the Union army. "How I love him," she would whisper to herself; "but how he must despise me!" she would cry, and her pillow was often wet with tears of shame and mortification at her folly.

It was shortly after this episode that her parents had taken sick and passed away. Ella had come east and had given up hope of ever seeing her rescuer again. You may imagine her feelings then when, on entering the drawing room at the van der Griffs', she discovered that the stranger who had so gallantly and tactfully rescued her from a watery grave was none other than General Ulysses S. Grant.

The poor girl was torn by a tumult of contrary emotions. Suppose he should remember her face. She blushed at the thought. And, besides, what chance had she to win such a great man's heart in competition with these society girls like Geraldine Rhinelander who had been "abroad" and spoke French?

At that moment one of the liveried servants approached the general with a trayful of filled wineglasses. So engrossed was the soldier hero in talking to Geraldine—or, rather, in listening to her alluring chatter—that he did not at first notice what was being offered him.

"Will you have a drink of champagne wine, General?" asked Mrs. van der Griff, who stood near.

The general raised his head and frowned as if he did not understand.

"Come, *mon Général*," cried Geraldine gayly, "we shall drink *à votre succès dans la guerre*," and the flighty girl raised a glass of wine on high.

Several of the guests crowded around, and all were about to drink to the general's health.

"Stop," cried General Grant, suddenly realizing what was being done; and something in the tone of his voice made everyone pause.

"Madam," said he, turning to Mrs. van der Griff, "am I to understand that there is liquor in those glasses?"

"Why, yes, General," said the hostess, smiling uneasily. "It is just a little champagne wine."

"Madam," said the general. "It may be 'just champagne wine' to you, but 'just champagne wine' has ruined many a poor fellow, and to me all alcoholic beverages are an abomination. I cannot consent, madam, to remain under your roof if they are to be served. I have never taken a drop—I have tried to stamp it out of the army, and I owe it to my soldiers to decline to be a guest at a house where wine and liquor are served."

An excited buzz of comment arose as the general delivered this ultimatum. A few there were who secretly approved his sentiments, but they were far too few in numbers, and constant indulgence in alcohol had weakened their wills so that they dared not stand forth. An angry flush appeared on the face of the hostess, for in society, "good form" is more important than courage and ideals, and by his frank statement General Grant had violently violated the canons of correct social etiquette.

"Very well, Mr. Grant," she said, stressing the "Mr.," "if that's the way you feel about it—"

"Stop," cried an unexpected voice, and to the amazement of all Ella Flowers stepped forward, her teeth clenched, her eyes blazing.

"Stop," she repeated. "He is right—the liquor evil is one of the worst curses of modern civilization, and if General Grant leaves so do I."

Mrs. van der Griff hesitated for an instant and then suddenly forced a smile.

"Why, Ella dear, of course General Grant is right," said she, for it was well known in financial circles that her husband, Mr. van der Griff, had recently borrowed heavily from Ella's uncle. "There will not be a drop of wine served tonight, and now, General, shall we go in to dinner? Will you be so kind as to lead the way with Miss Rhinelander?" The hostess had recovered her composure, and smiling sweetly at the guest of honor, gave orders to the servants to remove the wineglasses.

But General Grant did not hear her; he was looking at Ella Flowers. And as he gazed at the sweet beauty of her countenance he seemed to feel rising within him something which he had never felt before—something which made everything else seem petty and trivial. And as he looked into her eyes and she looked into his, he read her answer—the only answer true womanhood can make to clean, worthy manhood.

"Shall we go *à la salle-à-manger?*" sounded a voice in his ears, and Geraldine's sinuous arm was thrust through his.

General Grant took the proffered talon and gently removed it from him.

"Miss Rhinelander," he said firmly, "I am taking this young lady as my partner," and suiting the action to the word, he graciously extended his arm to Ella, who took it with a pretty blush.

It was General Grant's turn to blush when the other guests, with a few exceptions, applauded his choice loudly and made way enthusiastically as the handsome couple advanced to the brilliantly lighted dining room.

But although the hostess had provided the most costly of viands, I am afraid that the brave general did not fully appreciate them, for in his soul was the joy of a strong man who has found his mate and in his heart was the singing of the eternal song; "I love her—I love her—I love her!"

It was only too apparent to the other guests what had happened, and to their credit be it said that they heartily approved his choice, for Mrs. Rhinelander and her scheming daughter Geraldine had made countless enemies with their haughty manners, whereas the sweet simplicity of Ella Flowers had won her numerous friends. And all laughed merrily when General Grant, in his after-dinner speech, said "flowers" instead of "flour" when speaking of provisioning the army— a slip which caused both the general and Miss Flowers to blush furiously, greatly to the delight of the good-natured guests. "All the world loves a lover"—truer words were never penned.

After dinner, while the other men, according to the usages of best society, were filling the air of the dining room with the fumes of nicotine, the general, who did not use tobacco, excused himself— amid many sly winks from the other men—and wandered out into the conservatory.

There he found Ella.

"General," she began.

"Miss Flowers," said the strong man simply, "call me Ulysses."

And there let us leave them.

Problems for Thought and Writing

Stewart's piece is what is called *parody* or *burlesque*. The terms are closely allied in meaning. In writing they represent the attempt to ridicule by exaggerated imitation, as a *caricature* in drawing extends a nose here or a chin there to emphasize the defects suggested by nature. Stewart here attempts to ridicule the style of Harold Bell Wright (see selection on page 134) by placing an exaggerated focus on certain of its outstanding characteristics. In one sense, parody belongs to the larger classification of irony (see discussion on pp. 146-47), since it illuminates the discrepancy between the effect sought by the original writer and the actual effect produced upon the critical reader. Naturally, all readers are not critical readers, and many of us remain serenely unaware of the pathetic inadequacies of a piece of writing until some discerning critic points them out. The parodist is such a critic. He may, of course, be fair or unfair; but the talent he is exercising is an extremely effective weapon for deflating the confident postures of an adversary or for pricking the pride of the stupid, the affected, or the complacement among his fellows.

Read the selection from Harold Bell Wright and also Richard D. Altick's "Sentimentality" on page 109. Your first problem is to decide whether or not Stewart's parody is an *accurate and fair* one. A man might write a parody of the Bible in an effort to ridicule it, or of Lincoln's Gettysburg Address, but (unless his audience happened to be in an idol-smashing mood) no matter how clever his efforts, he would always risk offense. This kind of attack on something high or sacred usually goes by the name of *travesty,* parody's other face. It pulls down what is high or noble; it brings to the gutter what once was enthroned. Stewart, however, is giving dignity and importance to a style and view of life which, he assumes, all sensitive people would regard as pathetically lacking in dignity and importance. He is not directly *tearing down* the qualities of Wright's matter and style; he is *pretending to build them up.* This is the way of the parodist. Answer the following questions as a way of evaluating other specific qualities of Stewart's essay.

1. What *kind* of characters are present? Are they personalities or types? Do they impress you as persons who, unless we remind ourselves, seem to have a life outside their dramatic framework—the way Shakespeare's characters, for example, so often impress us?

2. What kind of language does everyone speak? Characterize it.

3. Why are certain ordinary words put in quotation marks? See "swallowtails" (page 125), "elect" (page 126), "smart" (page 128), and others.

4. Compare the printed spelling of "pr-st---te" on page 126 with the kind of moral censorship practiced by certain groups in the United States. Why does this make us laugh?

5. What kind of writing do the following phrases reflect? "A silver peal of rippling laughter," "buffets of fate," "a kindly thought," "clean, sweet, womanly lives." (See George Orwell, "Politics and the English Language," page 48, and Richard D. Altick, "Sentimentality," page 109.)

6. What minimum intelligence and knowledge did the author need to presuppose in his audience? What would be your opinion of someone who read this parody and did not think it funny (or did not know it was a parody)?

~

From THE WINNING OF BARBARA WORTH *   *Harold Bell Wright*

MISS BARBARA WORTH ARRIVES

Mrs. Worth, sitting on the wide veranda of her home after a lonely supper, lifted her eyes frequently from the work in her lap to look down the street. Perhaps it was unusual for a banker's wife to be darning her husband's socks; it may be, even, that bankers do not usually wear socks that have been darned. But Mrs. Worth was not sensible that her task was at all strange.

A group of dust-covered cow-boys, coming into town for an evening's pleasure, jogged past with loud laughter and soft-clinking spurs and bridle-chains. "There's Jefferson Worth's place," said one. "D'ye reckon he'll make good corralin' all the money there is in the world?"

Now and then a carriage, filled with well-to-do citizens out for an evening ride, drove slowly by. The people in the carriages always saluted Mrs. Worth and she returned their salutations with a prim little bow. But no one stopped to chat or to offer her a seat. In this, also, there was nothing strange to the woman on the porch of the big, empty house. Sometimes the people in the carriages, entertaining visiting friends, pointed to Jefferson Worth's house, with proper explanations, as they also called attention to the Pioneer Bank—Jefferson Worth's bank.

When dusk came and she could no longer see, Mrs. Worth laid aside her work and sat with folded hands, her face turned down the street. Inside the house the lights were not yet on; there was no need for them and she liked to sit in the dark.

The Indian servant woman came softly to the door. "Does the Senora wish anything?"

"No, thank you, Ynez; come and sit down."

Noiselessly the woman seated herself on the top step.

"It has been warm to-day, Ynez."

"Si, Senora."

"It is nearly three weeks since Mr. Worth left with Texas Joe for San Philipe, Ynez."

"Si, Senora."

"Do you know how far it is across the Desert to San Felipe?"

"Si, I think three—four day, maybe five, Senora."

"It will be very hot."

"Si, Senora. Las' year my sister's man—Jose—go for San Felipe. No much water. He no come back."

"Yes, I remember. What is it your people call The King's Basin Desert? The Hollow of God's Hand, isn't it?"

"Si, Senora. La Palma de la Mano de Dios."

"I wish they would come."

"He come pretty quick, I think. Mebbe so he not start when he think. Mebbe so what you call 'beesness' not let him come," said the Indian woman, soothingly.

"But Mr. Worth expected to be back two days ago and he is always on time, you know, Ynez."

"Si, Senora. But mebbe so this one time different."

"I do wish they would—Look, Ynez, look! There's some one stopping!"

A carriage was turning in toward the house.

"It is Senor Worth," said the Indian woman.

"Someone is with him, Ynez. They have a child."

As Jefferson Worth and the Seer came up the walk—the engineer carrying the little girl—Mrs. Worth rose unsteadily to her feet. "Run, quick, Ynez—quick! The lights!"

That night when the Seer, with everything possible done for his comfort, had retired, and the baby—bathed and fed—was sound asleep in a child's bed that Ynez had brought from an unused room in the banker's big house and placed in Mrs. Worth's own chamber, Jefferson Worth and his wife crept softly to the little girl's bedside. Silently they looked at the baby form under the snow-white coverlet and at the round, baby face, with the tumbled brown hair, on the pillow.

Mrs. Worth clasped her hands in eager longing as she whispered: "Oh, Jeff, can we keep her? Can we?"

Jefferson Worth answered in his careful manner: "Did you look for marks on her clothing?"

"There was nothing—not a letter even. And all that she can tell of her name is Barba. I'm sure she means Barbara." As she answered, Mrs. Worth searched her husband's face anxiously. Then she exclaimed: "Oh you do want her; you do!" and added wistfully: "Of course we must try to find her folks, but do you think it very wrong, Jeff, to wish—to wish that we never do? I feel as though she were sent to take the place of our own little girl. We need her so, Jeff. I need her so—and you—you will need her, when—" There was a day coming that the banker and his wife did not talk about. Since the birth and death of their one child, Mrs. Worth had been a hopeless invalid.

BARBARA AT THE AGE OF FIFTEEN

When they arrived at Barbara's home they found the Seer himself. The fifteen years had made no perceptible change in the general appearance of the engineer. His form was still strongly erect and vigorous, but his hair was a little gray, and to a close observer, his face in repose revealed a touch of sadness—that indescribable look of one who is beginning to feel less sure of himself, or rather who, from many disappointments, is beginning to question whether he will live to see his most cherished plans carried to completion—not because he has less faith in his visions, but because he has less hope that he will be able to make them clear to others.

When the evening meal was over the surveyor said good-by, for the expedition was to start in the morning and he had some work to do. When he was gone Barbara joined her father and the engineer on the porch. "Here they are," she said. "Haven't I kept them nicely for you?" She was holding toward the Seer a box of cigars.

"Indeed you have," returned the engineer in a pleased tone, helping himself to a cool, moist Havana. "You are a dear, good girl."

Jefferson Worth did not use tobacco, but it was an unwritten law of the household that the Seer, when he came, should always have his evening smoke on the porch and that Barbara should be the keeper of supplies. She liked to see her friend's strong face brought suddenly out of the dusk by the flare of the match and to watch the glow of the cigar end in the dark while they talked.

"And what do you think of your brother Abe, Barbara?" the big engineer asked when his cigar was going nicely. "Didn't he talk you nearly to death?"

The girl laughed. "I guess he didn't have a chance. I always do most of the talking, you know."

The Seer chuckled. "Abe told me once that most of the time he felt like an oyster and the rest of the time he was so mad at himself for being an oyster that he couldn't find words to do the subject justice."

"I think he is splendid!" retorted Barbara, enthusiastically.

"He is," returned the engineer earnestly. "I don't know of a man in the profession whom I would rely upon so wholly in work of a certain kind. You see Abe was born and raised in the wild, uncivilized parts of the country and he has a natural ability for his work that amounts almost to genius. With a knowledge of nature gained through his remarkable powers of observation and deduction, I doubt if Abe Lee to-day has an equal as what might be called a 'surveyor scout.' I believe he is made of iron. Hunger, cold, thirst, heat, wet, seem to make no impression on him. He can out-walk, out-work, out-last and out-guess any man I ever met. He has the instinct of a wild animal for finding his way and the coldest nerve I ever saw. His honesty and loyalty amount almost to fanaticism. But he is diffident and shy as a school girl and as sensitive as a bashful boy. I verily believe he knows more to-day about the great engineer-

ing projects in the West than nine-tenths of the school men but I've
seen him sit for an hour absolutely dumb, half scared to death,
listening to the cheap twaddle of some smart 'yellowlegs' with the
ink not dry yet on their diplomas. Put him in the field in charge of
a party of that same bunch, though, and he would be boss to the last
stake on the line or the last bite of grub in the outfit if he had to kill
half of them to do it. I guess you'll think I'm a bit enthusiastic about
my right hand man," he finished, with a short, apologetic laugh, "and
I am. It's because I know him."

He struck another match and Barbara saw his face for an instant.
As the match went out she drew a long breath. "I'm glad you said
that," she said softly. "I wanted you to. I'm sure he has earned it."

Then they talked of the Seer's new expedition that would start south
at daybreak, and it seemed to Barbara that the very air was electric
with the coming of a mighty age when the race would direct its
strength to the turning of millions of acres of desolate, barren waste
into productive farms and beautiful homes for the people.

At daybreak the girl was up to tell the Seer good-by. "I wish," she
said wistfully, as she stood with him a moment at the gate, "I wish it
was *my* Desert that you and Abe were going to survey."

The engineer smilingly answered: "Some day, perhaps, that, too,
will come."

"I know it will," she said simply.

And as she stood before him in all the beautiful strength of her
young womanhood, the Seer felt that sweet, mysterious power of her
personality—felt it with a father's loving pride. "I believe you do
know, Barbara," he said; "I believe you do."

ROMANCE COMES TO BARBARA

"Good morning, Mr. Holmes. How do you do?"

"Miss Worth!"

Had the engineer checked his horse so suddenly a few months before he would undoubtedly have gone over the animal's head. El
Capitan also stopped, while the man and the girl sat looking at each
other, Barbara smiling at the man's surprise.

"Is it really you?" asked Holmes at last, "or is it some new trick of
this confounded desert?" He rubbed his eyes. "I never saw a mirage
like this before and I don't think the heat has affected my brain." He
moved his horse closer. "Could you shake hands?"

Barbara held out her hand. "I assure you that I am very substantial," she laughed, "and I am here to stay, too."

"That's great! By George! it's good to see you," cried Holmes so heartily that the girl turned away her face and caused her horse to move ahead.

The engineer's horse, with a word from his rider, kept his place by El Capitan's side.

"It's very nice of you to say that but I didn't see you anywhere around last night when the stage arrived. Abe and Pat and Texas were there and this morning even Pablo came the first thing after breakfast."

Willard Holmes could not altogether hide his pleasure at her hinted rebuke. So she had thought of him—had looked for him—had missed him. "Indeed, you must forgive me. I did not know you were coming," he said and explained how his work took him away from Kingston much of the time.

"Of course, under those circumstances, I must forgive you," agreed Barbara, then added seriously: "I think I could forgive anyone who belonged to this desert work, anything, except one."

"And that?" He was watching her face. "What is it that you could not forgive?"

She returned his look steadily. "Don't you know?"

He drew a little back and she wondered at something in his voice and manner as he answered: "Yes, I know. You could never forgive one for being untrue to his work—for putting anything before the work itself."

"Yes," she returned, "that is it. I could never forgive one who did that."

"But how would you know? How could you judge?" he asked almost roughly. "Perhaps the very one whom you would call false to the work would, in reality, be doing the best thing for the work. I have noticed that, after all, those who have the loftiest ideals and the highest visions of man's duty to man and all that are seldom the ones who accomplish much of the actual work of the world. Look here, honestly now: how many of the people who are reclaiming this desert —I mean all of us—laborers, business men, ranchers, everybody who has come in here to do this work—how many of them do you think see a single thing beyond the dollars they have hoped to make on the venture? Whether it's the high wage paid by the Company, the big profits of the business man or the heavier crop of the rancher, it amounts to the same. And yet you would insist that they must not be governed by this desire for gain. So far as I can see, it is this same desire for gain that has driven men into doing every really great thing

that has ever been done. Look carefully into every great enterprise
that is of value to the world and you will find at the beginning of it
someone reaching for a dollar or its equivalent. Your father, for instance—"

Barbara threw out her hand protestingly. "Please don't, Mr. Holmes.
I know that what you say is every bit true. Father and I have gone
over it so many times. And yet I know, I *know* that what I feel is true
also. Oh, dear! what a muddle it is, isn't it? It seems so wrong to
spend one's life working for nothing but money. And yet all the really
good work in the world is done by those who don't work to do good
at all but for what they get out of it. I suppose now that you stayed
in the Desert all this past summer and worked so hard without any
vacation at all just for your salary."

"How did you know that I took no vacation?"

"Father told me. You seem to have made quite an impression on
my father. He has told me a great deal about you. But I want to
know—did you stay in the desert for money?"

Holmes wondered if she knew the danger that threatened the settlers because of the unsubstantial character of the Company's structures. "Perhaps," he said, "it was to save my professional reputation.
That would amount to the same thing, wouldn't it?"

Barbara laughed. "I don't think that your taking a vacation would
have lost you your reputation. That won't do, Mr. Chief Engineer."
For some reason Barbara seemed highly pleased at the turn the conversation had taken.

The man thought of those anxious days and nights at the intake,
when the safety of the success of the whole King's Basin project hung
on the whim of an uncertain river, but he did not explain to Barbara
nor did he tell her that a vacation would have made no difference in
his salary.

"I'll tell you why you stayed with the work in the Desert this summer, Mr. Holmes," she said, and in her voice was a note of pleased
triumph.

"Why?" he asked.

"Because you are learning the language of the country."

For an instant he was puzzled. Then he remembered the evening
he had said good-by. "Si, Senorita. I suppose one could not help
learning a little in La Palma de la Mano de Dios, could he?"

"Not if he had ancestors," came the answer.

Holmes flushed. "What a snob I must have seemed to you that

day," he said in deep disgust at the recollection of his first attempt to impress the western girl with the importance of his place in life.

"I don't think snob is just the word," she answered. "I didn't mind that ancestor business and all that one bit. In fact I think I rather enjoyed it. You were *such* a tenderfoot! But there was something else I did mind. Did you know that there was a time when I hated you with my whole heart?"

"Miss Worth!"

"It's so. I even promised myself that I would never speak to you again—never! Then I came after awhile to understand how foolish it was of me to blame you and father told me so much of your work here this summer that I became heartily ashamed of myself. I'm telling you now because, you see, I have come here to stay and to be, in a way, a tiny little part in this great work you are doing, and I feel that I ought to tell you so that we can start square again."

"But, Miss Worth, what in the world are you talking about?"

"I know it was foolish of me for you were not at all to blame. But I couldn't help it. It is all over though and we are square now—or will be when you have said that you forgive me."

"But I don't know what you mean. What on earth did I do?"

She looked straight at him. "Can't you even guess?"

"I haven't the ghost of an idea."

"Well, I'm glad you haven't," she declared, "even if it does make me appear so foolish. It was because the Seer was discharged and you were put in his place."

"But I—"

"Oh, I know all about it," she interrupted. "You didn't do it. You were not to blame. The Company did it because it was Good Business. It told you it was all over now. But please, I don't think we'd better talk about it only just for you to say that you forgive me. I had to tell you for that, you see."

Then the once carefully proper Willard Holmes did a thing that would have astonished his most intimate eastern friends beyond expression. Reining his horse close to El Capitan he held out his hand to Barbara.

"Shake, pard! You're the squarest girl I ever knew."

It was no flimsy, two-fingered ceremony, but a whole-hearted, whole-handed grip that made the man's blood move more quickly. Unconsciously, as he felt the warm strength in the touch of the girl's hand, he leaned toward her with quick eagerness. And Barbara, who was

looking straight into his face with the open frankness of one man to
another, started and drew back a little, turning her head aside.

Problems for Thought and Writing

1. If you have not already done so, study this selection in conjunction with
   Richard D. Altick's "Sentimentality," page 109. If Altick's essay has not
   been assigned, read it now, together with the "Problems for Thought and
   Writing" which follow it. Then read the selection preceding this one, which
   is a *parody* of it.

2. In Harold Bell Wright's books we are continually presented with certain
   simple contrasts: the Easterner *vs.* the Westerner, the rich man *vs.* the poor
   man, the trollop *vs.* the virgin, fancy dress *vs.* shabby clothes, clean hands *vs.*
   dirty hands, fancy talk *vs.* plain talk, complexity *vs.* simplicity, city *vs.*
   country, snobbery *vs.* humility, unblushing experience *vs.* blushing innocence.
   In every case, the first of these sets of contrasts gets the end of Wright's
   whip. Why should he pass such judgments? Is he appealing to any rooted
   American prejudices? In such emphasis is Wright exercising a formula for
   appealing to and stimulating our sentimentality?

3. Comment on the following words and expressions: "beautiful strength of her
   young womanhood," "the Seer," "father's loving pride," "the very air was
   electric with," "a whole-hearted, whole-handed grip," "shy as a school girl."

4. What significance do you find in Barbara's idealization of *work* and her contempt for "making money" as an end in itself?

5. Does this selection strike you as being funny, serious, boring, moralistic,
   dramatic, moving? What word can you find to describe it?

~

CONSTITUTIONAL
METAPHORS*   *Thomas Reed Powell*

Even before the eighteenth amendment, books about the United
States Constitution were apt to be pretty dry. They usually tell what
the Supreme Court says in a lot of cases and try to show how what
it says in one case will jibe all right with what it says in the other cases.
After the writers tell what happens in each case, then they try to
forget it and put to all the cases together and make up a set of rules to
show what the Supreme Court has been up to and what it is going to
do next. This is a very hard thing to do, and it is very hard to read
after it has been done. You have to think very hard all the time, and

* A review of James M. Beck's "The Constitution of the United States," from
The New Republic, February 11, 1925. Used by permission.

even then you get all mixed up. This kind of book makes you tired
because you have to try so hard to think, and so you usually stop trying to read it.

The new book which Mr. Beck has written about the Constitution is
a very different kind of book. You can read it without thinking. If
you have got tired trying to read the other kind of books, you will be
glad of the nice restful book that Mr. Beck has written. It runs along
like a story in a very interesting way. Most of the story is about how
the Constitution got made. This is really history, but it is written in
a very lively way like a novel, with a great many characters, almost
all male, and plenty of conversation and a very exciting plot. Many
of the chapters have names like those in a novel, such as "The Opening of the Battle," "The Crisis," "The Dawn," "Nearing the End,"
"The Curtain Falls," and others. Besides the story there are many
quotations from Shakespeare, Beethoven, Horace, Isaiah, Euripedes,
Beard, and other famous men. Many of these quotations are quite
old, but some of them seem fairly new. They help to make the book
a really high-class book. There is not much more to say about the
part of the book that tells how the Constitution got made, except that
it is fun and easy to read and seems pretty true to life.

The rest of the book is about what a good Constitution it is and
how bad it is to make changes in it. The main reason why it is so
good is because it was made by such good men. Mr. Beck says very
nice things about them. He calls them "a group of gentlemen of
substance and honor," and he thinks that "all apparently were inspired
by a fine spirit of self-effacement." They kept their ears a good way
from the ground, as gentlemen of substance and honor should, for Mr.
Beck says that "they represented the spirit of representative government at its best in avoiding the cowardice of time-servers and the low
cunning of demagogues." This means that they were the kind of men
who would do what they thought was best for all the people without
trying to find out what the people thought was best for themselves.
Some of the people in those days who were not gentlemen of substance
and honor had been trying to do very foolish things, and it was partly
to stop such foolishness that these good men came together to make
the Constitution.

It was this foolishness of the men who didn't make the Constitution
that made the men who made it make it such a good Constitution.
This was the second main reason why it is so good. It is what Mr.
Beck has in his mind when he speaks of "the anterior necessity of
those who had property interests to protect themselves against that

spirit of social revolt which we today call 'Bolshevism.'" If these men who made the Constitution had not been so full of their "fine spirit of self-effacement," they might not have seen so clearly what was the best thing to do. But they did. Mr. Beck says that it was because of the hard times that we got such a good Constitution. This was the third main reason. Of course the hard times couldn't give us a good Constitution all by themselves, but you can see how much they helped when you read Mr. Beck's book where it says:

It is therefore true that the Constitution was born of an economic travail, and that its merits were largely determined by the commercial necessities of the American people. It was largely the work of men of affairs; for most of the members of the Convention were influential, and, for the times, well-to-do professional and business men, who felt that, if their property interests were to be safeguarded and prosperity were to return after the panic of 1785, there must be, not merely freer commercial intercourse between the States, but also greater security to the rights of property against the disintegrating social tendencies, due to the distress among the masses, which, then as now, inevitably follows a depreciated currency.

I never knew what the Constitution really is until I read Mr. Beck's book. He says that "it is something more than a written formula of government—it is a great spirit. It is a high and noble assertion, and, indeed, vindication, of the morality of government." It is splendid to have a Constitution like that and to know, as Mr. Beck tells us, that "to the succeeding ages, the Constitution will be a flaming beacon." This is not all that it is, for Mr. Beck says also:

I have elsewhere likened the Constitution to a Gothic cathedral, like that of Rheims. Its foundations seem secure, even though some of its buttresses may be weakened and its statuary mutilated. Nevertheless it remains a noble and serviceable temple of Liberty and Justice. Let us hope that, with the present indifference of the masses to the Constitution and the spirit of innovation of this restless and impatient age, the time will not come that the Constitution will be as the Cathedral of Rheims when the author saw it in the summer of 1916. Rheims was a noble but pitiful ruin. Its high altar had been overthrown, and its glorious rose windows hopelessly shattered.

The high altar of the Constitution is the self-restraint which the American people of 1787 were wise enough to impose upon themselves and their posterity, and the rose windows are those great traditions of Liberty which we have gained at an infinite sacrifice of treasure and life from our English-speaking ancestry.

It helps us to know what the Constitution is if we know what it is not. It is a beacon and a Gothic cathedral, but it is not a rock and it is not a beach. Instead of these things, it is a floating dock. Mr. Beck puts it very beautifully when he says:

The Constitution is neither, on the one hand, a Gibraltar rock, which wholly resists the ceaseless washing of time and circumstance, nor is it, on the other hand, a sandy beach, which is slowly destroyed by the erosion of the waves. It is rather to be likened to a floating dock, which, while firmly attached to its moorings, and not therefore at the caprice of the waves, yet rises and falls with the tide of time and circumstance.

You might think that a Constitution which is all these wonderful things would be sure to last forever without any help from anything else. But this is not so. Mr. Beck says that it would not have lasted so long as it has if it had not been for the Supreme Court, which he says is "the balance wheel of the Constitution." He has a whole chapter which he calls "The Balance Wheel," and this chapter ends up by saying:

But always the Supreme Court stands as a great lighthouse, and even when the waves beat upon it with terrific violence (as in the Civil War, when it was shaken to its very foundation), yet after they have spent their fury, the great lamp of the Constitution—as that of another Pharos—illumines the troubled face of the waters with the benignant rays of those immutable principles of liberty and justice, which alone can make a nation free as well as strong.

It makes you see how marvelous the Supreme Court really is when it can be a balance wheel at the beginning of a chapter and a lighthouse at the end.

Even if you are not interested in the Constitution for its own sake, you will like to read what Mr. Beck says about it because he is such a lovely writer. He is the kind of writer who likes to write just for the sake of writing. He shows how he loves his work. He is not one of those writers who have to stop in their writing while they are making up their minds what to say. You can read him right along because he is so simple in his thoughts. He does not get you all mixed up the way so many writers do, but he brings up in your mind beautiful pictures of the Constitution as a temple and a beacon and a floating dock, and he lets you see the Supreme Court shining and balancing in a very wonderful way. I have read a great many books about the Constitu-

tion, but there is no other book that has given me just the same kind
of pleasure that this one has.

You will have a very happy feeling while you are reading Mr.
Beck's book, until you come to the last three chapters. Then you will
begin to feel sad. The ending is not a happy ending. It tells of
dangers that will hurt our country if we do not look out. It is not
enough to have a Gothic cathedral with a balance wheel. We must
all be wise and good men who will not make changes. This is like
so many books that have a moral lesson at the end. On his very last
page Mr. Beck tells us what we should do. He says that when the
Constitution came out of the safe in the State Department a few
years ago, "the ink, in which it had been engrossed nearly one hundred
and thirty-seven years ago, was found to have faded." He hopes that
this is not a bad sign. This is what he means when he says that "all
who believe in constitutional government must hope that this is not a
portentous symbol." Just hoping will not help any, and it would
not do any good to put fresh ink on top of the ink that is fading. We
must do something different from that. Mr. Beck tells us very plainly
what we should do when he says that "the American people must
write the compact, not with ink upon a parchment, but with 'letters
of living light'—to use Webster's phrase—upon their hearts." This
must be a very hard way to write, and I should think it would be a
good thing to write the ink letters as well as the light letters, because
the light might go out before the ink had all faded.

Problems for Thought and Writing

I

Powell is here writing *ironically*. He is letting us know, through an artistic
formula, that a discrepancy exists between a thing as it *is* and as it *ought to be*.
He pretends to praise Beck's book, but he praises it for the wrong reasons. And
his manner of writing clearly and humorously implies that the kind of individual
who *would* like such a book is a stupid person indeed. The style is that of an
adolescent who has barely mastered the English language or—dare we say it?—
of the freshman writer struggling to make captive in words an intellectual enthusiasm not yet ripe. The "inappropriateness" of this style is part of the critic's
design, and without this style the irony could not exist.

Irony as a *device of expression*, then, may be defined as the attempt to criticize or disparage something by pretending to like it, and to express that "liking"
in such a way that a reader or listener will know that the opposite is meant. If,
for example, you greet a downpour on a day you had planned to go picnicking
with the remark, "Isn't this a *lovely day!*" you will be giving voice to a simple
form of irony. And in conversation the irony is usually conveyed, or at least
intensified, by the inflection of the voice.

"The irony of fate," which involves the discrepancy between what we had expected or hoped for and the actual course or outcome of events, is not the same thing as an ironical *expression*. It is linked in its fundamental meaning to what has been described above, however, since irony in speaking and writing always involves a discrepancy between what is *said* and what is *meant*, or between the literal and implied meaning. Irony in its broadest philosophic sense, then, may be said always to concern itself with the discrepancy or conflict between appearance and reality, the relative and the absolute, the actual and the ideal. Specialized applications of the term, such as "dramatic irony," "Socratic irony," and the like may be approached and understood if that basic definition is kept in mind.

The ability to use irony when it is needed is part of any good writer's standard equipment. It goes without saying that this must be accompanied with the ability to determine where and when irony *is* needed or will be more useful than direct utterance. Rules can hardly be laid down, but we can perhaps characterize its proper use by analogy. Think of irony not as a war club or a cannon, but as a keen-edged dagger, particularly effective for close-in fighting. When you really want to be *devastating*, irony is your best weapon. It will demolish, where direct critical blows run the risk of glancing off an impervious or indifferent exterior.

Try your hand at an ironical essay on any subject. For example, if you live in a tiny dormitory room where, because of overcrowded conditions at college, you must share one closet with three roommates, you need look no farther for a subject. You can point out how handy it is to have your shoes and clothes mixed indiscriminately with theirs, because you frequently appear on campus in such interesting and unusual wardrobe combinations that you are well on your way to becoming a B.M.O.C. If the walls are thin and the sound of your neighbor's typewriter comes through half the night, don't lament that it keeps you awake. Point out that the regular, rhythmical beat of the keys lulls you comfortably to sleep. Or, if it *does* keep you awake sometimes, it's all to the good, because it keeps you up and at your own studies longer. And so on. Other possible subjects are listed below.

a) The comforts of attending football games in our stadium.
b) The easy art of skiing.
c) Simple instructions on how to do a one-and-one-half somersault, lay-out, and a half-twist from a high board.
d) A review of a movie.
e) A review of one of your textbooks.

II

1. Study the first paragraph carefully. Identify all the actual errors or improprieties in diction, sentence structure, and grammar. Why are they made?

2. How would you characterize the vocabulary of this review? Why does the author use the kinds of words he does? Is he posing? How?

3. How is the style of the review peculiarly fitted to an account of the quality of thought in the book? Do they—to use the author's inimitable prose—"jibe all right"?

~

A MODEST PROPOSAL*   *Jonathan Swift*

FOR PREVENTING THE CHILDREN OF IRELAND FROM BEING A BURDEN TO THEIR PARENTS OR COUNTRY

It is a melancholy object to those who walk through this great town or travel in the country, when they see the streets, the roads, and cabin-doors crowded with beggars of the female sex, followed by three, four, or six children, all in rags, and importuning every passenger for an alms. These mothers, instead of being able to work for their honest livelihood, are forced to employ all their time in strolling to beg sustenance for their helpless infants, who, as they grow up, either turn thieves for want of work, or leave their dear native country, to fight for the Pretender in Spain, or sell themselves to the Barbadoes.

I think it is agreed by all parties, that this prodigious number of children in the arms, or on the backs, or at the heels of their mothers, and frequently of their fathers, is in the present deplorable state of the kingdom a very great additional grievance; and therefore whoever could find out a fair, cheap, and easy method of making these children sound and useful members of the common-wealth, would deserve so well of the public as to have his statue set up for a preserver of the nation.

But my intention is very far from being confined to provide only for the children of professed beggars; it is of a much greater extent, and shall take in the whole number of infants at a certain age, who are born of parents in effect as little able to support them, as those who demand our charity in the streets.

As to my own part, having turned my thoughts, for many years, upon this important subject, and maturely weighed the several schemes of other projectors, I have always found them grossly mistaken in their computation. It is true, a child just dropt from its dam, may be supported by her milk for a solar year with little other nourishment, at most not above the value of two shillings, which the mother may certainly get, or the value in scraps, by her lawful occupation of begging; and it is exactly at one year old that I propose to provide

* 1729.

for them in such a manner, as, instead of being a charge upon their parents, or the parish, or wanting food and raiment for the rest of their lives, they shall, on the contrary, contribute to the feeding and partly to the clothing of many thousands.

There is likewise another great advantage in my scheme, that it will prevent those voluntary abortions, and that horrid practice of women murdering their bastard children, alas! too frequent among us—sacrificing the poor innocent babes, I doubt, more to avoid the expense than the shame—which would move tears and pity in the most savage and inhuman breast.

The number of souls in this kingdom being usually reckoned one million and a half, of these I calculate there may be about two hundred thousand couples whose wives are breeders; from which number I subtract thirty thousand couples, who are able to maintain their own children, although I apprehend there cannot be so many, under the present distresses of the kingdom; but this being granted, there will remain an hundred and seventy thousand breeders. I again subtract fifty thousand, for those women who miscarry, or whose children die by accident or disease within the year. There only remain an hundred and twenty thousand children of poor parents annually born: The question therefore is, How this number shall be reared, and provided for? which, as I have already said, under the present situation of affairs, is utterly impossible by all the methods hitherto proposed; for we can neither employ them in handicraft or agriculture; we neither build houses (I mean in the country) nor cultivate land: They can very seldom pick up a livelihood by stealing till they arrive at six years old, except where they are of towardly parts, although, I confess, they learn the rudiments much earlier; during which time they can however be properly looked upon only as probationers; as I have been informed by a principal gentleman in the county of Cavan, who protested to me, that he never knew above one or two instances under the age of six, even in a part of the kingdom so renowned for the quickest proficiency in that art.

I am assured by our merchants, that a boy or a girl before twelve years old, is no saleable commodity, and even when they come to this age, they will not yield above three pounds, or three pounds and half a crown at most, on the exchange; which cannot turn to account either to the parents or kingdom, the charge of nutriment and rags having been at least four times that value.

I shall now therefore humbly propose my own thoughts, which I hope will not be liable to the least objection.

I have been assured by a very knowing American of my acquaintance in London, that a young healthy child well nursed is at a year old a most delicious nourishing and wholesome food, whether stewed, roasted, baked, or boiled; and I make no doubt that it will equally serve in a fricassee, or a ragout.

I do therefore humbly offer it to publick consideration, that of the hundred and twenty thousand children, already computed, twenty thousand may be reserved for breed, whereof only one fourth part to be males; which is more than we allow to sheep, black cattle, or swine, and my reason is, that these children are seldom the fruits of marriage, a circumstance not much regarded by our savages; therefore, one male will be sufficient to serve four females. That the remaining hundred thousand may at a year old be offered in sale to the persons of quality and fortune, through the kingdom, always advising the mother to let them suck plentifully in the last month, so as to render them plump, and fat for a good table. A child will make two dishes at an entertainment for friends, and when the family dines alone, the fore or hind quarter will make a reasonable dish, and seasoned with a little pepper or salt will be very good boiled on the fourth day, especially in winter.

I have reckoned upon a medium, that a child just born will weigh 12 pounds, and in a solar year, if tolerably nursed, encreaseth to 28 pounds.

I grant this food will be somewhat dear, and therefore very proper for landlords, who, as they have already devoured most of the parents seem to have the best title to the children.

Infant's flesh will be in season throughout the year, but more plentiful in March, and a little before and after; for we are told by a grave author, an eminent French physician, that fish being a prolifick dyet, there are more children born in Roman Catholick countries about nine months after Lent, than at any other season; therefore reckoning a year after Lent, the markets will be more glutted than usual, because the number of popish infants, is at least three to one in this kingdom, and therefore it will have one other collateral advantage, by lessening the number of papists among us.

I have already computed the charge of nursing a beggar's child (in which list I reckon all cottagers, labourers, and four fifths of the farmers) to be about two shillings per annum, rags included; and I believe no gentleman would repine to give ten shillings for the carcass of a good fat child, which, as I have said will make four dishes of excellent nutritive meat, when he hath only some particular friend, or his own family to dine with him. Thus the squire will learn to be a good landlord, and grow popular among his tenants; the mother will have eight shillings neat profit, and be fit for work till she produces another child.

Those who are more thrifty (as I must confess the times require) may flay the carcass; the skin of which, artificially dressed, will make admirable gloves for ladies, and summer boots for fine gentlemen.

As to our city of Dublin, shambles may be appointed for this purpose, in the most convenient parts of it, and butchers we may be assured will not be wanting; although I rather recommend buying the children alive, and dressing them hot from the knife, as we do roasting pigs.

A very worthy person, a true lover of his country, and whose virtues I highly esteem, was lately pleased, in discoursing on this matter, to offer a refinement upon my scheme. He said, that many gentlemen of this kingdom, having of late destroyed their deer, he conceived that the want of venison might be well supplied by the bodies of young lads and maidens, not exceeding fourteen years of age, nor under twelve; so great a number of both sexes in every country being now ready to starve, for want of work and service: And these to be disposed of by their parents if alive, or otherwise by their nearest relations. But with due deference to so excellent a friend, and so deserving a patriot, I cannot be altogether in his sentiments; for as to the males, my American acquaintance assured me from frequent experience, that their flesh was generally tough and lean, like that of our schoolboys, by continual exercise, and their taste disagreeable, and to fatten them would not answer the charge. Then as to the females, it would, I think with humble submission, be a loss to the publick, because they soon would become breeders themselves: And besides it is not improbable that some scrupulous people might be apt to censure such a practice (although indeed very unjustly) as a little bordering upon cruelty, which, I confess, hath always been with me the strongest objection against any project, how well soever intended.

But in order to justify my friend, he confessed, that this expedient was put into his head by the famous Psalmanazar, a native of the island Formosa, who came from thence to London, above twenty years ago, and in conversation told my friend, that in his country when any young person happened to be put to death, the executioner sold the carcass to persons of quality, as a prime dainty, and that, in his time, the body of a plump girl of fifteen, who was crucified for an attempt to poison the Emperor, was sold to his Imperial Majesty's prime minister of state, and other great mandarins of the court, in joints from the gibbet, at four hundred crowns. Neither indeed can I deny, that if the same use were made of several plump young girls in this town, who, without one single groat to their fortunes, cannot stir abroad without a chair, and appear at a play-house and assemblies in foreign fineries which they never will pay for; the kingdom would not be the worse.

Some persons of a desponding spirit are in great concern about that vast number of poor people, who are aged, diseased, or maimed, and I have been desired to employ my thoughts what course may be taken, to ease the nation of so grievous an encumbrance. But I am not in the least pain upon that matter, because it is very well known, that they are every day dying, and rotting, by cold, and famine, and filth, and vermin, as fast as can be reasonably expected. And as to the younger labourers, they are now in almost as hopeful a condition. They cannot get work, and consequently pine away for want of nourishment, to a degree, that if at any time they are accidentally hired to common labour, they have not strength to perform it, and thus the country and themselves are happily delivered from the evils to come.

I have too long digressed, and therefore shall return to my subject. I think the advantages by the proposal which I have made are obvious and many, as well as of the highest importance.

For *first*, as I have already observed, it would greatly lessen the number of papists, with whom, we are yearly over-run, being the principal breeders of the nation, as well as our most dangerous enemies, and who stay at home on purpose with a design to deliver the kingdom to the Pretender, hoping to take their advantage by the absence of so many good Protestants, who have chosen rather to leave their country, than stay at home, and pay tithes against their conscience to an episcopal curate.

Secondly, the poorer tenants will have something valuable of their own which by law may be made liable to distress, and help to pay their landlord's rent, their corn and cattle being already seized, and money a thing unknown.

Thirdly, whereas the maintenance of an hundred thousand children, from two years old, and upwards, cannot be computed at less than ten shillings a piece per annum, the nation's stock will be thereby increased fifty thousand pounds per annum, besides the profit of a new dish, introduced to the tables of all gentlemen of fortune in the kingdom who have any refinement in taste, and the money will circulate among our selves, the goods being entirely of our own growth and manufacture.

Fourthly, the constant breeders, besides the gain of eight shillings sterling per annum, by the sale of their children, will be rid of the charge of maintaining them after the first year.

Fifthly, this food would likewise bring great custom to taverns, where the vintners will certainly be so prudent as to procure the best receipts for dressing it to perfection; and consequently have their houses frequented by all the fine gentlemen, who justly value themselves upon their knowledge in good eating; and a skilful cook, who understands how to oblige his guests, will contrive to make it as expensive as they please.

Sixthly, this would be a great inducement to marriage, which all wise nations have either encouraged by rewards, or enforced by laws and penalties. It would encrease the care and tenderness of mothers towards their children, when they were sure of a settlement for life to the poor babes, provided in some sort by the publick, to their annual profit instead of expence; we should soon see an honest emulation among the married women, which of them could bring the fattest child to the market. Men would become as fond of their wives during the time of their pregnancy, as they are now of their mares in foal, their cows in calf, or sows when they are ready to farrow, nor offer to beat or kick them (as is too frequent a practice) for fear of a miscarriage.

Many other advantages might be enumerated. For instance, the addition of some thousand carcasses in our exportation of barreled beef: the propagation of swine's flesh, and improvement in the art of making good bacon, so much wanted among us by the great destruction of pigs, too frequent at our tables, which are no way comparable in taste or magnificence to a well grown, fat yearling child, which roasted whole will make a considerable figure at a Lord Mayor's feast, or any other publick entertainment. But this, and many others, I omit, being studious of brevity.

Supposing that one thousand families in this city, would be constant customers for infant's flesh, besides others who might have it at merry meetings, particularly at weddings and christenings, I compute that Dublin would take off annually about twenty thousand carcasses, and the rest of the kingdom (where probably they will be sold somewhat cheaper) the remaining eighty thousand.

I can think of no one objection, that will possibly be raised against this proposal, unless it should be urged, that the number of people will be thereby much lessened in the kingdom. This I freely own, and 'twas indeed one principal design in offering it to the world. I desire the reader will observe, that I calculate my remedy for this one individual kingdom of Ireland, and for no other that ever was, is, or, I think, ever can be upon earth. Therefore let no man talk to me of other expedients: of taxing our absentees at five shilling a pound: of using neither cloths, nor household furniture, except what is of our own growth and manufacture: of utterly rejecting the materials and instruments that promote foreign luxury: of curing the expensiveness of pride, vanity, idleness, and gaming in our women: of introducing a vein of parsimony, prudence and temperance: of learning to love our country, wherein we differ even from Laplanders, and the inhabitants of Topinamboo: of quitting our animosities, and factions, nor act any longer like the Jews, who were murdering one another at the very moment their city was taken: of being a little cautious not to sell our country and consciences for nothing: of teaching landlords to have at least one degree of mercy towards their tenants. Lastly, of putting a spirit of honesty, industry, and skill into our shop-keepers, who, if a resolution could now be taken to buy only our native goods, would immediately unite to cheat and exact upon us in the price, the measure, and the goodness, nor could ever yet be brought to make one fair proposal of just dealing, though often and earnestly invited to it.

Therefore I repeat, let no man talk to me of these and the like expedients, till he hath at least some glimpse of hope, that there will ever be some hearty and sincere attempt to put them in practice.

But as to my self, having been wearied out for many years with offering vain, idle, visionary thoughts, and at length utterly despairing of success, I fortunately fell upon this proposal, which as it is wholly new, so it hath something solid and real, of no expense and little trouble, full in our own power, and whereby we can incur no danger in disobliging England. For this kind of commodity will not bear exportation, the flesh being of too tender a consistence, to admit a long continuance in salt, although perhaps I could name a country, which would be glad to eat up our whole nation without it.

After all, I am not so violently bent upon my own opinion, as to reject any offer, proposed by wise men, which shall be found equally innocent, cheap, easy, and effectual. But before something of that kind shall be advanced in contradiction to my scheme, and offering a better, I desire the author or authors, will be pleased maturely to consider two points. *First*, as things now stand, how they will be able to find food and raiment for a hundred thousand useless mouths and backs. And *Secondly*, there being a round million of creatures in human figure throughout this kingdom, whose whole subsistence put into a common stock would leave them in debt two millions of pounds sterling, adding those—who are beggars by profession, to the bulk of farmers, cottagers and labourers, with their wives and children, who are beggars in effect; I desire those politicians, who dislike my overture, and may perhaps be so bold to attempt an answer, that they will first ask the parents of these mortals, whether they would not at this day think it a great happiness to have been sold for food at a year old, in the manner I prescribe, and thereby have avoided such a perpetual scene of misfortunes as they have since gone through, by the oppression of landlords, the impossibility of paying rent without money or trade, the want of common sustenance, with neither house nor clothes to cover them from the inclemencies of the weather, and the most inevitable prospect of entailing the like, or greater miseries, upon their breed for ever.

I profess in the sincerity of my heart, that I have not the least personal interest in endeavouring to promote this necessary work, having no other motive than the publick good of my country, by advancing our trade, providing for infants, relieving the poor, and giving some pleasure to the rich. I have no children by which I can propose to get a single penny; the youngest being nine years old and my wife past child-bearing.

Problems for Thought and Writing

I

It has been said that "irony can go no further" than it does in this essay. Published in 1729, it was one of Swift's many attacks upon what he regarded as a deliberate policy of selfishness and injustice on the part of the British Parliament toward Ireland. As a piece of ironical attack, it is at once deceptively humble and savage in tone. If it were not irony, it would be intolerable. But the very intolerability of the "proposal," unbroken by any apologies, is what makes it so great. It is in every respect one of the classic examples of *sustained* irony, and it shows irony used for a far more serious purpose than in Powell's review of Beck's "The Constitution of the United States" (page 142). Yet the intent in each is fundamentally the same: to *destroy* the evil in the hope that it will be replaced by the good, to tear down faulty ideas and institutions in the hope that men may thereby be inspired to remodel them. Actually this is the aim of all *satire*: to ridicule the failings of mankind in the hope of reforming them. When satire becomes too angry, we speak of it as invective; too personal, as abuse. Obviously the satirist is always measuring people, ideas, and behavior against a norm or standard. And that standard has to be felt and accepted *as an ideal* by his readers; otherwise his satire is bound to be rejected. A communist satirizing

American society is not likely to get very far addressing an audience of Americans, for they would almost inevitably be hostile to communism to begin with. Likewise, it is *possible* for Powell to satirize Beck's style because most of us approve mature writing and recognize it when we see it. Therefore, we are equipped to understand and enjoy the ridiculing of a pompous style.

The questions below are designed to help you discover both similarities and differences between Powell and Swift.

1. In reviewing Beck's book, Powell put himself in the position of an imaginary reader who liked it. As a member of what group does Swift seem to be writing?

2. Does Swift regard the children as human beings or as a commodity? On the basis of your answer, what do you take to be his ultimate object of criticism?

3. Swift himself defined *satire* as an attack by ridicule upon the foibles of men with the hope of reforming them. Do you think that satire ever succeeds completely? Why or why not?

4. Full response to, and understanding of, Swift's irony is obviously dependent upon some familiarity with the historical conditions which occasioned it. Yet we still assume that it can be read with enjoyment and comprehension. What clues does Swift offer that he is actually writing ironically, clues that are immediately perceivable by readers in all periods of history?

5. In what sense may the irony be said to have been *doubled* at the end of the essay? Is the satirist satirizing his own benevolence?

6. Is there anything in the essay to suggest that Swift had a clear idea of the good with which he sought to replace the evils he castigates? Is it really necessary that he state that idea explicitly?

7. True comedy, it has been said, is always cruel to man. Powell is certainly cruel to Beck, and yet his review moves us to laughter. Does Swift's essay make you laugh? If so, is it the same kind of laughter you experienced in reading Powell? How would you distinguish between your responses?

II

8. Study the diction carefully. How often does Swift use the passive voice? Are there many long words? Does he seem to you to overwork prepositional phrases when adjectives would do just as well?

9. What profession do words such as the following connote: "price," "measure," "dealing," "per annum," "taxing," "absentees," "parsimony," "proposal"? The essay is crowded with them. What do they contribute to the total effect?

~

5 The Individual and Society

From AREOPAGITICA*   *John Milton*

I deny not but that it is of greatest concernment in the Church and Commonwealth to have a vigilant eye how books demean themselves as well as men; and thereafter to confine, imprison, and do sharpest justice on them as malefactors. For books are not absolutely dead things, but do contain a potency of life in them to be as active as that soul was whose progeny they are; nay, they do preserve as in a vial the purest efficacy and extraction of that living intellect that bred them. I know they are as lively, and as vigorously productive, as those fabulous dragon's teeth; and being sown up and down, may chance to spring up armed men. And yet, on the other hand, unless wariness be used, as good almost kill a man as kill a good book: who kills a man kills a reasonable creature, God's image; but he who destroys a good book, kills reason itself, kills the image of God, as it were, in the eye. Many a man lives a burden to the earth; but a good book is the precious life-blood of a master spirit, embalmed and treasured up on purpose to a life beyond life. 'Tis true, no age can restore a life, whereof perhaps there is no great loss; and revolutions of ages do not oft recover the loss of a rejected truth, for the want of which whole nations fare the worse. We should be wary, therefore, what persecution we raise against the living labors of public men, how we spill that seasoned life of man, preserved and stored up in books; since we see a kind of homicide may be thus committed, sometimes a martyrdom; and if it extend to the whole impression, a kind of massacre, whereof the execution ends not in the slaying of an elemental life, but strikes at that ethereal and fifth essence, the breath of reason itself, slays an immortality rather than a life. . . .

Good and evil we know in the field of this world grow up together almost inseparably; and the knowledge of good is so involved and

* 1664.

interwoven with the knowledge of evil, and in so many cunning resemblances hardly to be discerned, that those confused seeds which were imposed upon Psyche as an incessant labor to cull out, and sort asunder, were not more intermixed. It was from out the rind of one apple tasted, that the knowledge of good and evil, as two twins cleaving together, leaped forth into the world. And perhaps this is that doom which Adam fell into of knowing good and evil, that is to say, of knowing good by evil.

As therefore the state of man now is, what wisdom can there be to choose, what continence to forbear without the knowledge of evil? He that can apprehend and consider vice with all her baits and seeming pleasures, and yet abstain, and yet distinguish, and yet prefer that which is truly better, he is the true wayfaring Christian. I cannot praise a fugitive and cloistered virtue, unexercised and unbreathed, that never sallies out and sees her adversary, but slinks out of the race where that immortal garland is to be run for, not without dust and heat. Assuredly we bring not innocence into the world, we bring impurity much rather: that which purifies us is trial, and trial is by what is contrary. That virtue therefore which is but a youngling in the contemplation of evil, and knows not the utmost that vice promises to her followers, and rejects it, is but a blank virtue, not a pure; her whiteness is but an excremental whiteness; which was the reason why our sage and serious poet Spenser, whom I dare be known to think a better teacher than Scotus or Aquinas, describing true temperance under the person of Guion, brings him in with his palmer through the cave of Mammon and the bower of earthly bliss, that he might see and know, and yet abstain.

Since therefore, the knowledge and survey of vice is in this world so necessary to the constituting of human virtue, and the scanning of error to the confirmation of truth, how can we more safely, and with less danger, scout into the regions of sin and falsity, than by reading all manner of tractates and hearing all manner of reason? And this is the benefit which may be had of books promiscuously read. . . .

Problems for Thought and Writing

I

1. *Areopagitica* is probably the classic defense of intellectual freedom in the English language, and the principles here expressed were rooted deeply in the minds of the framers of our Constitution and in the culture which they established in the New World. Are there any signs in contemporary American life that these principles are being threatened? If so, what are they?

2. How "free" should speech and a free press be, in your opinion? Are censorship and "licensing acts" always, to some degree, necessary? Are the guardians of morals who watch over the productions of Hollywood, for example, performing a useful service?

3. Do you agree with Milton in the statement, ". . . as good almost kill a man as kill a good book"? Do you agree with his reasons for making this statement? Do you think Milton would have subscribed to the following modification of the statement, ". . . as good almost kill freedom as kill a [not necessarily "good"] book"? Obscenity and pornography, for example, are banned from the United States mails. Do you regard this as an unconstitutional limitation of individual freedom?

4. "I cannot praise a fugitive and cloistered virtue, unexercised and unbreathed, that never sallies out and sees her adversary, but slinks out of the race where that immortal garland is to be run for, not without dust and heat." In this famous passage Milton is, by implication, stating his conviction that the *truth* will be found only if we keep free and unblocked the media by which *all* men's efforts to discover it are expressed. Do you share his faith? Are you ready to guard with your life the right of your enemy to have his say? Is there, in your opinion, any tendency in the United States to put our "way of life," our "discovered truth" in quarantine?

II

5. Milton lived and wrote in the seventeenth century, and his style, even for that period, was a highly individualistic one. Compare his style with that of Thomas Jefferson (below) or Jonathan Swift (page 148) in the eighteenth century; with Matthew Arnold (page 422) or John Stuart Mill (page 378) in the nineteenth; or with C. S. Lewis (page 326) or Archibald MacLeish (page 665) in the twentieth. Write an essay describing its peculiar qualities.

6. Identify or define: progeny, efficacy, ethereal, essence, Psyche, dragon's teeth, cloistered, Spenser, Scotus, Aquinas, Mammon, tractates, promiscuously.

7. Write an essay on the "unbreathed virtue" of your teacher, congressman, parent, statesman.

~

DECLARATION OF INDEPENDENCE*   *Thomas Jefferson*

When, in the course of human events, it becomes necessary for one people to dissolve the political bands which have connected them with another, and to assume among the powers of the earth the separate and equal station to which the laws of nature and of nature's God entitle them, a decent respect to the opinions of mankind re-

* The unanimous declaration of the thirteen United States of America, in Congress, July 4, 1776.

quires that they should declare the causes which impel them to the separation.

We hold these truths to be self-evident: That all men are created equal; that they are endowed by their Creator with certain inalienable rights; that among these are life, liberty, and the pursuit of happiness. That, to secure these rights, governments are instituted among men, deriving their just powers from the consent of the governed; that, whenever any form of government becomes destructive of these ends, it is the right of the people to alter or to abolish it, and to institute a new government, laying its foundation on such principles, and organizing its powers in such form, as to them shall seem most likely to effect their safety and happiness. Prudence, indeed, will dictate that governments long established should not be changed for light and transient causes; and accordingly all experience hath shown that mankind are more disposed to suffer, while evils are sufferable, than to right themselves by abolishing the forms to which they are accustomed. But when a long train of abuses and usurpations, pursuing invariably the same object, evinces a design to reduce them under absolute despotism, it is their right, it is their duty, to throw off such government and to provide new guards for their future security. Such has been the patient suffering of these colonies, and such is now the necessity which constrains them to alter their former systems of government. The history of the present king of Great Britain is a history of repeated injuries and usurpations, all having in direct object the establishment of an absolute tyranny over these states. To prove this, let facts be submitted to a candid world.

He has refused his assent to laws the most wholesome and necessary for the public good.

He has forbidden his governors to pass laws of immediate and pressing importance, unless suspended in their operation till his assent should be obtained, and, when so suspended, he has utterly neglected to attend to them.

He has refused to pass other laws for the accommodation of large districts of people, unless those people would relinquish the right of representation in the legislature—a right inestimable to them and formidable to tyrants only.

He has called together legislative bodies, at places unusual, uncomfortable, and distant from the repository of their public records, for the sole purpose of fatiguing them into compliance with his measures.

He has dissolved representative houses repeatedly for opposing with manly firmness his invasions on the rights of the people.

He has refused for a long time after such dissolutions to cause others to be elected; whereby the legislative powers, incapable of annihilation, have returned to the people at large for their exercise: the state remaining in the mean time exposed to all the dangers of invasion from without, and convulsions within.

He has endeavored to prevent the population of these states; for that purpose obstructing the laws of naturalization of foreigners; refusing to pass others to encourage their migration hither, and raising the conditions of new appropriations of lands.

He has obstructed the administration of justice by refusing his assent to laws for establishing judiciary powers.

He has made judges dependent on his will alone for the tenure of their offices and the amount and payment of their salaries.

He has erected a multitude of new offices and sent hither swarms of officers to harass our people and eat out their substance.

He has kept among us, in times of peace, standing armies without the consent of our legislature.

He has affected to render the military independent of and superior to the civil power.

He has combined with others to subject us to a jurisdiction foreign to our constitution and unacknowledged by our laws; giving his assent to their acts of pretended legislation:

For quartering large bodies of armed troops among us:

For protecting them by a mock trial from punishment for any murders which they should commit on the inhabitants of these states:

For cutting off our trade with all parts of the world:

For imposing taxes on us without our consent:

For depriving us in many cases of the benefits of trial by jury:

For transporting us beyond seas to be tried for pretended offences:

For abolishing the free system of English laws in a neighbouring province, establishing therein an arbitrary government, and enlarging its boundaries so as to render it at once an example and fit instrument for introducing the same absolute rule into these colonies:

For taking away our charters, abolishing our most valuable laws, and altering fundamentally the forms of our governments:

For suspending our own legislature and declaring themselves invested with power to legislate for us in all cases whatsoever.

He has abdicated government here by declaring us out of his protection and waging war against us.

He has plundered our seas, ravaged our coasts, burnt our towns, and destroyed the lives of our people.

He is at this time transporting large armies of foreign mercenaries to complete the works of death, desolation and tyranny already begun with circumstances of cruelty and perfidy scarcely paralleled in the most barbarous ages and totally unworthy the head of a civilized nation.

He has constrained our fellow citizens taken captive on the high seas to bear arms against their country, to become the executioners of their friends and brethren, or to fall themselves by their hands.

He has excited domestic insurrection amongst us, and has endeavored to bring on the inhabitants of our frontiers the merciless Indian savages, whose known rule of warfare is an undistinguished destruction of all ages, sexes, and conditions.

In every stage of these oppressions we have petitioned for redress, in the most humble terms; our repeated petitions have been answered only by repeated injury. A prince whose character is thus marked by every act which may define a tyrant is unfit to be the ruler of a free people.

Nor have we been wanting in attention to our British brethren. We have warned them, from time to time, of attempts by their legislature to extend an unwarrantable jurisdiction over us. We have reminded them of the circumstances of our emigration and settlement here. We have appealed to their native justice and magnanimity; and we have conjured them by the ties of our common kindred, to disavow these usurpations, which would inevitably interrupt our connections and correspondence. They, too, have been deaf to the voice of justice and consanguinity. We must, therefore, acquiesce in the necessity which denounces our separation, and hold them, as we hold the rest of mankind, enemies in war; in peace, friends.

We, therefore, the representatives of the United States of America, in general congress assembled, appealing to the Supreme Judge of the World for the rectitude of our intentions, do, in the name and by the authority of the good people of these colonies, solemnly publish and declare that these united colonies are, and of right ought to be, free and independent states; that they are absolved from all allegiance to the British crown, and that all political connection between them and the state of Great Britain is, and ought to be, totally dissolved; and that as free and independent states they have full power to levy war, conclude peace, contract alliances, establish commerce, and to do all other acts and things which independent states may of right do. And for the support of this declaration, with a firm reliance on the protection of Divine Providence, we mutually pledge to each other our lives, our fortunes, and our sacred honor.

Problems for Thought and Writing

I

1. In paragraph one, the justification for assuming "separate and equal station" is based on "the laws of nature" and "nature's God." What do these terms mean? If the *Declaration* were written today, would the word "nature" be so conspicuous?

2. Are all men "created equal"? What is the testimony of psychology on this point? (For a careful study of this problem, examine a book by Henry A. Myers, *Are Men Equal?*)

3. If we no longer believe that men are "equal" in the sense Jefferson considered them to be, does it follow that our democracy is loosening at the foundations? How do you think Jefferson would react to Mandel's essay (page 171)?

4. Attempt to define "happiness" as Jefferson used the term.

II

5. What is the "tone" of the *Declaration*: negative, polite, hostile, truculent, challenging, suave? What term would you use to describe it?

6. Define: consanguinity, usurpations, inalienable, inestimable, candid world.

7. What qualities of style distinguish the *Declaration* as an eighteenth century document? What kind of argument is it? (See page 539.)

~

THE INDISPENSABLE
OPPOSITION *

Walter Lippmann

I

Were they pressed hard enough, most men would probably confess that political freedom—that is to say, the right to speak freely and to act in opposition—is a noble ideal rather than a practical necessity. As the case for freedom is generally put today, the argument lends itself to this feeling. It is made to appear that, whereas each man

* Reprinted by permission from *The Atlantic Monthly*, August, 1939. Copyright, 1939, The Atlantic Monthly Company.

claims his freedom as a matter of right, the freedom he accords to other men is a matter of toleration. Thus, the defense of freedom of opinion tends to rest not on its substantial, beneficial, and indispensable consequences, but on a somewhat eccentric, a rather vaguely benevolent, attachment to an abstraction.

It is all very well to say with Voltaire, 'I wholly disapprove of what you say, but will defend to the death your right to say it,' but as a matter of fact most men will not defend to the death the rights of other men: if they disapprove sufficiently what other men say, they will somehow suppress those men if they can.

So, if this is the best that can be said for liberty of opinion, that a man must tolerate his opponents because everyone has a 'right' to say what he pleases, then we shall find that liberty of opinion is a luxury, safe only in pleasant times when men can be tolerant because they are not deeply and vitally concerned.

Yet actually, as a matter of historic fact, there is a much stronger foundation for the great constitutional right of freedom of speech, and as a matter of practical human experience there is a much more compelling reason for cultivating the habits of free men. We take, it seems to me, a naïvely self-righteous view when we argue as if the right of our opponents to speak were something that we protect because we are magnanimous, noble, and unselfish. The compelling reason why, if liberty of opinion did not exist, we should have to invent it, why it will eventually have to be restored in all civilized countries where it is now suppressed, is that we must protect the right of our opponents to speak because we must hear what they have to say.

We miss the whole point when we imagine that we tolerate the freedom of our political opponents as we tolerate a howling baby next door, as we put up with the blasts from our neighbor's radio because we are too peaceable to heave a brick through the window. If this were all there is to freedom of opinion, that we are too good-natured or too timid to do anything about our opponents and our critics except to let them talk, it would be difficult to say whether we are tolerant because we are magnanimous or because we are lazy, because we have strong principles or because we lack serious convictions, whether we have the hospitality of an inquiring mind or the indifference of an empty mind. And so, if we truly wish to understand why freedom is necessary in a civilized society, we must begin by realizing that, because freedom of discussion improves our own opinions, the liberties of other men are our own vital necessity.

We are much closer to the essence of the matter, not when we quote Voltaire, but when we go to the doctor and pay him to ask us the most embarrassing questions and to prescribe the most disagreeable diet. When we pay the doctor to exercise complete freedom of speech about the cause and cure of our stomachache, we do not look upon ourselves as tolerant and magnanimous, and worthy to be admired by ourselves. We have enough common sense to know that if we threaten to put the doctor in jail because we do not like the diagnosis and the prescription it will be unpleasant for the doctor, to be sure, but equally unpleasant for our own stomachache. That is why even the most ferocious dictator would rather be treated by a doctor who was free to think and speak the truth than by his own Minister of Propaganda. For there is a point, the point at which things really matter, where the freedom of others is no longer a question of their right but of our own need.

The point at which we recognize this need is much higher in some men than in others. The totalitarian rulers think they do not need the freedom of an opposition: they exile, imprison, or shoot their opponents. We have concluded on the basis of practical experience, which goes back to Magna Carta and beyond, that we need the opposition. We pay the opposition salaries out of the public treasury.

In so far as the usual apology for freedom of speech ignores this experience, it becomes abstract and eccentric rather than concrete and human. The emphasis is generally put on the right to speak, as if all that mattered were that the doctor should be free to go out into the park and explain to the vacant air why I have a stomachache. Surely that is a miserable caricature of the great civic right which men have bled and died for. What really matters is that the doctor should tell *me* what ails me, that I should listen to him; that if I do not like what he says I should be free to call in another doctor; and that then the first doctor should have to listen to the second doctor; and that out of all the speaking and listening, the give-and-take of opinions, the truth should be arrived at.

This is the creative principle of freedom of speech, not that it is a system for the tolerating of error, but that it is a system for finding the truth. It may not produce the truth, or the whole truth all the time, or often, or in some cases ever. But if the truth can be found, there is no other system which will normally and habitually find so much truth. Until we have thoroughly understood this principle, we shall not know why we must value our liberty, or how we can protect and develop it.

II

Let us apply this principle to the system of public speech in a totalitarian state. We may, without any serious falsification, picture a condition of affairs in which the mass of the people are being addressed through one broadcasting system by one man and his chosen subordinates. The orators speak. The audience listens but cannot and dare not speak back. It is a system of one-way communication; the opinions of the rulers are broadcast outwardly to the mass of the people. But nothing comes back to the rulers from the people except the cheers; nothing returns in the way of knowledge of forgotten facts, hidden feelings, neglected truths, and practical suggestions.

But even a dictator cannot govern by his own one-way inspiration alone. In practice, therefore, the totalitarian rulers get back the reports of the secret police and of their party henchmen down among the crowd. If these reports are competent, the rulers may manage to remain in touch with public sentiment. Yet that is not enough to know what the audience feels. The rulers have also to make great decisions that have enormous consequences, and here their system provides virtually no help from the give-and-take of opinion in the nation. So they must either rely on their own intuition, which cannot be permanently and continually inspired, or, if they are intelligent despots, encourage their trusted advisers and their technicians to speak and debate freely in their presence.

On the walls of the houses of Italian peasants one may see inscribed in large letters the legend, 'Mussolini is always right.' But if that legend is taken seriously by Italian ambassadors, by the Italian General Staff, and by the Ministry of Finance, then all one can say is heaven help Mussolini, heaven help Italy, and the new Emperor of Ethiopia.

For at some point, even in a totalitarian state, it is indispensable that there should exist the freedom of opinion which causes opposing opinions to be debated. As time goes on, that is less and less easy under a despotism; critical discussion disappears as the internal opposition is liquidated in favor of men who think and feel alike. That is why the early successes of despots, of Napoleon I and of Napoleon III, have usually been followed by an irreparable mistake. For in listening only to his yes men—the others being in exile or in concentration camps, or terrified—the despot shuts himself off from the truth that no man can dispense with.

We know all this well enough when we contemplate the dictatorships. But when we try to picture our own system, by way of contrast, what picture do we have in our minds? It is, is it not, that anyone may stand up on his own soapbox and say anything he pleases,
like the individuals in Kipling's poem who sit each in his separate
star and draw the Thing as they see it for the God of Things as they
are. Kipling, perhaps, could do this, since he was a poet. But the
ordinary mortal isolated on his separate star will have an hallucina-
tion, and a citizenry declaiming from separate soapboxes will poison
the air with hot and nonsensical confusion.

If the democratic alternative to the totalitarian one-way broadcasts
is a row of separate soapboxes, then I submit that the alternative is
unworkable, is unreasonable, and is humanly unattractive. It is above
all a false alternative. It is not true that liberty has developed among
civilized men when anyone is free to set up a soapbox, is free to hire
a hall where he may expound his opinions to those who are willing to
listen. On the contrary, freedom of speech is established to achieve
its essential purpose only when different opinions are expounded in
the same hall to the same audience.

For, while the right to talk may be the beginning of freedom, the
necessity of listening is what makes the right important. Even in
Russia and Germany a man may still stand in an open field and speak
his mind. What matters is not the utterance of opinions. What matters is the confrontation of opinions in debate. No man can care profoundly that every fool should say what he likes. Nothing has been
accomplished if the wisest man proclaims his wisdom in the middle
of the Sahara Desert. This is the shadow. We have the substance of
liberty when the fool is compelled to listen to the wise man and learn;
when the wise man is compelled to take account of the fool, and to
instruct him; when the wise man can increase his wisdom by hearing
the judgment of his peers.

That is why civilized men must cherish liberty—as a means of promoting the discovery of truth. So we must not fix our whole attention
on the right of anyone to hire his own hall, to rent his own broadcasting station, to distribute his own pamphlets. These rights are incidental; and though they must be preserved, they can be preserved
only by regarding them as incidental, as auxiliary to the substance of
liberty that must be cherished and cultivated.

Freedom of speech is best conceived, therefore, by having in mind
the picture of a place like the American Congress, an assembly where
opposing views are represented, where ideas are not merely uttered

but debated, or the British Parliament, where men who are free to speak are also compelled to answer. We may picture the true condition of freedom as existing in a place like a court of law, where witnesses testify and are cross-examined, where the lawyer argues against the opposing lawyer before the same judge and in the presence of one jury. We may picture freedom as existing in a forum where the speaker must respond to questions; in a gathering of scientists where the data, the hypothesis, and the conclusion are submitted to men competent to judge them; in a reputable newspaper which not only will publish the opinions of those who disagree but will reëxamine its own opinion in the light of what they say.

Thus the essence of freedom of opinion is not in mere toleration as such, but in the debate which toleration provides: it is not in the venting of opinion, but in the confrontation of opinion. That this is the practical substance can readily be understood when we remember how differently we feel and act about the censorship and regulation of opinion purveyed by different media of communication. We find then that, in so far as the medium makes difficult the confrontation of opinion in debate, we are driven towards censorship and regulation.

There is, for example, the whispering campaign, the circulation of anonymous rumors by men who cannot be compelled to prove what they say. They put the utmost strain on our tolerance, and there are few who do not rejoice when the anonymous slanderer is caught, exposed, and punished. At a higher level there is the moving picture, a most powerful medium for conveying ideas, but a medium which does not permit debate. A moving picture cannot be answered effectively by another moving picture; in all free countries there is some censorship of the movies, and there would be more if the producers did not recognize their limitations by avoiding political controversy. There is then the radio. Here debate is difficult: it is not easy to make sure that the speaker is being answered in the presence of the same audience. Inevitably, there is some regulation of the radio.

When we reach the newspaper press, the opportunity for debate is so considerable that discontent cannot grow to the point where under normal conditions there is any disposition to regulate the press. But when newspapers abuse their power by injuring people who have no means of replying, a disposition to regulate the press appears. When we arrive at Congress we find that, because the membership of the House is so large, full debate is impracticable. So there are restrictive rules. On the other hand, in the Senate, where the conditions of full debate exist, there is almost absolute freedom of speech.

This shows us that the preservation and development of freedom of opinion are not only a matter of adhering to abstract legal rights, but also, and very urgently, a matter of organizing and arranging sufficient debate. Once we have a firm hold on the central principle, there are many practical conclusions to be drawn. We then realize that the defense of freedom of opinion consists primarily in perfecting the opportunity for an adequate give-and-take of opinion; it consists also in regulating the freedom of those revolutionists who cannot or will not permit or maintain debate when it does not suit their purposes.

We must insist that free oratory is only the beginning of free speech; it is not the end, but a means to an end. The end is to find the truth. The practical justification of civil liberty is not that self-expression is one of the rights of man. It is that the examination of opinion is one of the necessities of man. For experience tells us that it is only when freedom of opinion becomes the compulsion to debate that the seed which our fathers planted has produced its fruit. When that is understood, freedom will be cherished not because it is a vent for our opinions but because it is the surest method of correcting them.

The unexamined life, said Socrates, is unfit to be lived by man. This is the virtue of liberty, and the ground on which we may best justify our belief in it, that it tolerates error in order to serve the truth. When men are brought face to face with their opponents, forced to listen and learn and mend their ideas, they cease to be children and savages and begin to live like civilized men. Then only is freedom a reality, when men may voice their opinions because they must examine their opinions.

III

The only reason for dwelling on all this is that if we are to preserve democracy we must understand its principles. And the principle which distinguishes it from all other forms of government is that in a democracy the opposition not only is tolerated as constitutional but must be maintained because it is in fact indispensable.

The democratic system cannot be operated without effective opposition. For, in making the great experiment of governing people by consent rather than by coercion, it is not sufficient that the party in power should have a majority. It is just as necessary that the party in power should never outrage the minority. That means that it must listen to the minority and be moved by the criticisms of the minority.

That means that its measures must take account of the minority's objections, and that in administering measures it must remember that the minority may become the majority.

The opposition is indispensable. A good statesman, like any other sensible human being, always learns more from his opponents than from his fervent supporters. For his supporters will push him to disaster unless his opponents show him where the dangers are. So if he is wise he will often pray to be delivered from his friends, because they will ruin him. But, though it hurts, he ought also to pray never to be left without opponents; for they keep him on the path of reason and good sense.

The national unity of a free people depends upon a sufficiently even balance of political power to make it impracticable for the administration to be arbitrary and for the opposition to be revolutionary and irreconcilable. Where that balance no longer exists, democracy perishes. For unless all the citizens of a state are forced by circumstances to compromise, unless they feel that they can affect policy but that no one can wholly dominate it, unless by habit and necessity they have to give and take, freedom cannot be maintained.

Problems for Thought and Writing

I

1. The so-called "liberal" ideal is frequently criticized as empty of positive convictions, as a "going-away" process, a release of energies and an uncritical toleration with no substance of its own. How does Lippmann answer the charge against "mere" toleration?

2. What, specifically, according to Lippmann, is the *value* of permitting all men to speak their minds? Is the one who is permitted to speak the only one who benefits?

3. By what, would you say, is freedom limited? Ought a man in a free society be free to rent or not to rent houses to foreigners? In the housing shortage during and after World War II were landlords within their moral rights when they refused to rent apartments to families with children? Ought a man be free to refuse to hire aliens?

4. How successfully do you think the United States lives up to the democratic ideal outlined in the second paragraph of section III? Are most Americans tolerant of minority groups?

5. Lippmann says that the defense of freedom requires provision for "adequate give-and-take of opinion; it consists also in regulating the freedom of those revolutionists who cannot or will not permit or maintain debate when it does not suit their purposes" (page 169). How would you apply such a principle practically? How would you define a "subversive group"?

6. "What matters," writes Lippmann, "is the confrontation of opinions in debate." How much debate, open discussion, controversy, thrives on your campus?

How far, in this regard, is your college or university preparing you for active democratic citizenship?

II

7. Identify or define: Voltaire, Magna Carta, caricature, benevolent.

8. Lippmann has been a journalist most of his life. How would you characterize the diction of this essay?

9. For a terrifying fictional account of the kind of totalitarian state Lippmann imagines at the opening of section II, read George Orwell's novel, *1984*.

10. Outline and write a précis of the three main divisions of the essay. How firmly does it all hold together?

~

NOBILITY AND THE UNITED STATES*   *Oscar Mandel*

> You do not feel that in man there lives a spark of purer fire, which, when it is not fed, when it is not fanned, is covered by the ashes of daily cravings and indifference; yet, however late, it is almost never smothered.
>
> WILHELM MEISTER, *I, 14*

The want of a feeling for aristocracy, among the rich as well as the poor, among the intelligentsia and among artists, constitutes the most signal failure of the American spirit. To the death of this spirit we can attribute too the gradual recession of European culture or, to use the Europeans' unflattering term, its Americanization. The word "aristocracy" itself has been used in various familiar ways: to refer to a social or political caste, or, in a figurative and etymologically more dubious sense, to moral, intellectual or aesthetic excellence. But let us use the term as comprehensively as possible, intending not only moral and intellectual distinction, and not only aesthetic elevation, but also a distinct social group ideally embodying these qualities, and possessing in addition that much despised virtue known as manners, or good breeding. Thus the *feeling* for aristocracy is the desire for, or the picturing of, a harmonious nobility which expresses itself by moral, intellectual, aesthetic and social distinctiveness, and in that division of mankind known as class consciousness. This feeling is

* From *The American Scholar*, Spring, 1958. Used by permission.

traditionally the possession of an actual (and, of course, imperfect) aristocracy and of its intellectual allies.

Of course, the notion of class consciousness appears so odious in the United States (as it does in Russia) that its merit has come to be discussed as little as that of, say, the emancipation of the slaves. We tend to think of emancipation, and of our egalitarianism in general, as clear entries on the side of progress—as evils we have conquered. We even think that a system of social classes is incompatible with that form of love which we call humanitarianism. But social equality and the sense of human brotherhood are not, as a matter of fact, necessarily functions of each other; and surely in an age when equality has done nothing to disarm us of atomic bombs, flame throwers and guided missiles, it is permissible at least to re-examine our egalitarian assumptions.

The feeling for aristocracy is above all a hope. At no epoch in history did the thinking part of society believe that the political aristocracy had in fact realized this hope. Nevertheless, just as the ideals of chivalry could never be called useless, though they served mostly as guides or self-flattery, so the feeling for aristocracy (which, indeed, includes the ideal of chivalry) persisted from age to age, in different guises, not only as an overwhelming value but, in fact, as absolute necessity. Literature supported this feeling without hesitation and without afterthought. Perhaps literature created it. The feeling for aristocracy was too natural to be argued; it was one of those silent convictions or conditions of thought which Carlyle so wisely recommends—those which require no analyses and no defenses. It is the feeling we find in Vergil, in the romances of chivalry and all epics, in the Italian lyric, whether of Petrarch or of Poliziano, most sparklingly in Shakespeare's comedies, most clearly in the French neoclassical drama, and even, if we skip a little, in such places as Jane Austen's novels. We find it, I believe, in the dark Jacobean tragedies, and we find it in Goethe and in Tolstoy. But it begins to fade in the nineteenth century, and what is Baudelaire's dandyism, what is Mallarmé's hermeticism, what is that whole cult of the exquisite, from Gautier to Huysmans, and what is Yeats's magic-mongering, if not the feeling for aristocracy, too sick to walk in the traffic of the streets, taking refuge in closets, among coteries, reduced from a grand moral force to a tangential cult?

The feeling for aristocracy is above all a hope. If it had not been this, if Vergil, if Michelangelo, if Beethoven had not hoped, they would not have been memorable. All great, serious art, and much comic art, is idealizing art. What keeps it from being sentimental art, utopian art or fantasy is the cohesion of the true and the possible. As a matter of course, silently, writers of all epochs but ours have fused, within a single plot, within fourteen lines, within a single character, human truth with human possibility. Within Othello, within Desdemona, lie truth and possibility; humanity *might* be thus, while humanity *is* thus. Racine's Phèdre is bad but great; Iago is at least intelligent; Faust grandiose. Though never afraid of the truth, the great writers implicitly hoped, in that the very crimes and the very sorrows they portrayed belonged to those whose stature was enviable, worth emulating—to characters who represented to readers and spectators a perennial *ought*—in a word, to aristocrats. Even the good manners of French drama, even the mild decencies of *Cranford*, express this hope, this possibility of a harmonious nobility expressed by moral, intellectual, aesthetic and social distinctiveness.

Therefore, it is far from absurd to say that true art is moral. True art is the great indirect preacher. The absurdity is to say that art and morality spin in independent orbits. Where but in the idealization of man shall we seek the reason for the joy we feel in even the saddest work of art? Great art is everywhere human, and better than human. Those who believe that the feeling for aristocracy is a vacuous one may be right; but they cannot create great and serious art. Civilizations die when they have been forced to give up hope. The very essence of civilization is the hope, the energy, for betterment. (Hope is energy, and energy is hope.) And I do not speak of that invidious so-called progress which is marked by the prevalence of bathtubs and airplanes (though these are no impediments either), but again I mean the tendency toward aristocracy. Our literature has given up this hope. Worse, it elaborately belabors its bankruptcy. For the first time in its history, art has in fact become a mirror held up to nature rather than a challenge to nature. And what is left? We admire the modern novel; we cannot *love* it. I mean we do not feel the urge to keep it in our pockets and read it on all occasions, to fondle it, to memorize passages, to be tender with it. Can we say we read our violent novelists with *pleasure*, with *joyousness*? "This pleasure," says Montaigne, "consoles my old age and my solitude, it blunts the darts of all but the sharpest pains; to rid myself of an unpleasant thought, I run to my books." Fancy us running to Mr. Faulkner to rid ourselves of an unpleasant thought! No, we cannot *love* this literature (or this painting or this architecture—these antiseptic blocks of concrete and glass visibilized by livid fluorescent

light) because it has no hope; and it has not hope in that it wants
the feeling for aristocracy. Our most impressive art is that which
has abandoned mankind.

That individual works should be purely negative, that certain
authors should write of fools, criminals or dullards as though no other
life were possible on earth—all this is allowable. But if the thought
that we are "caught in the insoluble prison of being" (Wolfe's awkward phrase), in "the total animal soup of time" (Allen Ginsberg's
improvement)—if the thought that life is an *incurable* disease becomes
a kind of cultural premise, then our disease is a worse one even than
we think. Unhappily, the West—from Germany to California—has
lost its energy. Poetry, whose mood used to be imperative—

> At the round earths imagin'd corners, blow
> Your trumpets, Angells, and arise, arise
> From death, you numberlesse infinities
> Of soules—

has now declined into a sad indicative or a complete syntactical disintegration. Who, we ask, shall preach what ideals to whom? We
prefer the "slice of life," and affect not to remember that until recently
literature was moral, and often, indeed (shall we dare the word?)
patriotic. Who would create serious patriotic art in the West today
after the manner of Pindar, Vergil, Corneille or Tennyson? Who in
the West would require, as Wilhelm Meister does, that the theater
stand at the service of the state's economic enterprises? We know
better; not, God knows, without reason, we are disenchanted and dis-
gruntled. Therefore I make no brief for a new patriotic art (or even a
one-world art, concerning civil instead of international wars) or
optimistic art of any kind. Nor am I wishing a grand return to
Christian piety. We have had, it is true, a "religious revival," adorned
by some of our choicest spirits; but I doubt whether high-brow
Christianity has infused much hope even in these. Other hopes must
be found, without precluding pessimistic art. *The Duchess of Malfi* is
as terrible as *Light in August,* but its pessimism is not suicidal: the
Duchess is worth while; she is what humanity might be. But Faulkner, who has brought the Jacobean darkness to America, has wiped
out the Duchess, the image of hope. His aristocracy, unlike Webster's, lived in the irrecoverable past.

Of course, it would be an exaggeration to say that serious modern
literature is inevitably desperate. What matters is the cultural tendency, the intellectual norm. Yet even if we address ourselves to the

messages of respectable hope, the occasional affirmations, we can usually find a snake under that stone as well. Nine times out of ten we are invited to admire some primitive section of society or mindless behavior. These authors renounce civilization and intelligence even in their yea-saying. While music returns to the tom-tom, while painting adores Africa, while sociologists pore over the child and psychoanalysts finger the subconscious, the "affirmative" literary men invent a mystique of instinct, brute power, mindlessness, and seek out incoherent heroes in the corners and dead ends of civilization, among the depressed, the forgotten, the hapless innocent, the coarse, the elementary. In their books, civilization means decay, and they propose rebirth through the inchoate. Affirmation though this may be, it is actually treason to twenty-five centuries of hope in *cultivation*, in the rising of man above nature, in aristocracy. Our fashion now is to be entranced by aboriginal dancing, Aztec incantations, frenzied jazz and Congolese masks. I am far from denying the power and the permanence of the primitive: all is not danced in a gavotte, and man ought not to forget his origins, his mother the dark earth. But, as Baudelaire liked to say, man is at his best when he is, in a high sense, unnatural. If ever I hear a folk ballad superior to Schubert's "Raven," I shall join the backward rout. Meantime I am satisfied to count myself a member of a civilization which has discovered at any rate that a cow is better roasted than worshipped. We are not proud enough of the West.

In the graphic arts, the abandonment of mankind has consisted in the shift from men to shapes, from events to colors, from morality to geometry. The Expressionists, it is true, often launched more direct attacks on humanity, and to that extent remained "in the tradition"; but the more typical phenomenon of this century is the disintegration or elimination of the "human form divine," and, along with this, the death of the hope that lies at the bottom even of Rembrandt and Goya. Still, perhaps the most striking, because the most visible, area of dehumanization is in public architecture. Our great buildings are made for cubic men. Impressive as they are—and they are very impressive—they stand in their frigid glass, their white concrete, their icy chromium, like nerveless symbols of homelessness.

The feeling for aristocracy is transitive; it impinges on others and takes the natural form of more or less direct exhortation—

> O Florence! your sudden wealth and your upstart
> rabble, dissolute and overweening,
> already set you weeping in your heart!—

or else of that subtler idealization without actual program of which the Duchess of Malfi is an instance. But in our time, this feeling has become solipsistic. We have in this country a substantial minority of artists, scholars, teachers, scientists and unattached intellectuals who cultivate a quiet, private and sometimes embarrassed nobility. To many of these men and women the idea of their own superiority is actually painful, and they disguise it as far as they can in their speech, their dress, their manners. With a slangy style many of them seem to deprecate their own distinction and to apologize for it. They are careful not to proclaim their difference. Much less do they dream of exacting deference from their inferiors. In fact, words like "deference" and "nobility" are taking their departure from the common language. Writers and speakers use them "in a certain sense," or else they are cant.

Many American intellectuals live in a state of amiable schizophrenia: as liberals they refuse to believe that they are "any better than the next fellow," but as intellectuals they leave the populace alone, or they revile it while voting in its favor. If we except the few who are still trying to "elevate the masses," our true intellectuals live in a corner. They have ceased to exhort because they have lost their audience. Nobody wants them unless they can furnish an atomic bomb or a better television script. Just as under absolute monarchs the intellectuals conceal a part of themselves and are not in private quite what they seem in public, so in our democracy droves of the intelligent apply a lower faculty to the service of the masses, writing advertisements (for which they blush in private), composing scenarios and scripts (which they despise at cocktail parties), painting and drawing on salary (so they can earn enough money, they say, *really* to paint), inventing another toothpaste (while dreaming of research) or building a lavender ranch-type house (ridiculing their customers under their breaths). That which is noble in them they despair of practicing, or else they practice it in seclusion, "after hours," when no one is looking. Thus, while they are called upon to do char-work with their lower faculties, that portion of them which ought to exhort and lead mankind, that which makes for aristocracy, is secreted out of sight. The worse part of society is fed, nursed, amused and cuddled (for reasonable wages) by the better part. Consequently the people are leaderless and content to be so. They even contrive to elect Presidents they will not have to revere. As for that section of mankind called Society, which used to set a few external rules making for aristocracy, it has altogether withdrawn into discreet conformity, and if it carouses, does so unnoticed. The rich have turned into chameleons on the tree of democracy.

Traditionally, the three sources of the feeling for aristocracy were the political aristocracy itself (in spite of its *actual* turpitude), the church with its saints or prophets (in spite of *its* actual turpitude) and the artists. The artists were either employees of the political aristocracy or independent but willing allies. No one, I think, will deny that with a few exceptions, serious art has been, up to our own time, an aristocratic pursuit, by which I understand that it was supported by the effective aristocracy (which, as in Athens, might go under another name), and that it had the feeling for aristocracy. The Greek drama is no exception, for though it addressed itself to the population, like Elizabethan drama it was supported and protected by the rich. We usually ignore the fact that even the characters of serious literature were members of the political aristocracy. We blink and say that this was a social concession or that nobility of rank is a symbol, et cetera, et cetera. But these are lies: part of the feeling for aristocracy consists in the equation between nobility of position and nobility of mind. A virtuous President of the United States is something finer than a kindly John Doe. Democratic though we may be, we still shudder more at the death of the great than at the everyday casualties reported in the newspaper. The feeling for aristocracy is the hope or, if you will, the vision of a fusion of every nobility, including that of rank and breeding no less than that of morals and intellect. That is why, furthermore, the traditional hero is not only socially noble but also intelligent. Our own literature does not pay much attention to the intelligent. Zola—perhaps Flaubert—inaugurated the epoch of dumb protagonists, which Faulkner, with his rich gallery of morons and idiots, has brought to its morbid perfection. Abandoning the hero as a fable, much of our contemporary literature has made its theme that mud can't help being mud, that it is unhappy or dirty or ought to be made comfortable; but I propose that none of these subjects is fit concern for a whole nation of serious writers. Their *ultimate* concern ought not to be *l'homme moyen sensuel*, photographed, for zoological or political reasons, in all his unedifying stances. Though the task, as Dostoevsky and Conrad and Silone knew, is not an easy one, a transfiguration must be performed. These three authors wrested heroism from the human muck by dint of an agony of effort, falling a thousand times on the way. Flaubert (the protovillain in our piece) merely became a zoologist; Hemingway said *nada;* and Mr. Ginsberg, looking for innocence, howls.

I have spoken of the minority who practice a kind of nobility in private. Because privacy still exists, the cultural climate has been favorable to the one form of art which can be noble and private at the same time: lyric poetry. Sappho entertained her friends at banquets by singing her poems and pinching her lyre. Her relations with mankind at large were not relevant to the quality of her art. And the immortal themes persist. If the lyric poets too have retreated from mankind, it has never been their function to conquer it. In fact, the lonely cage today has made them sing more exquisitely than did the public Victorians. Where form is the final test of greatness, the abandonment of mankind is no impediment.

With the spread of democracy, the upper classes began by losing their political influence and ended by losing their cultural ascendancy. In the United States, Adams is succeeded by Jackson; in England, the gentry is reduced to that empty role of "barbarians," as Matthew Arnold calls them; and in the twentieth century, demos inherits the realm. It would be foolish to deplore this as a mere calamity. But the glories of democracy have been sung too often to require another chorus. Enough to remark that the upper classes bled and deserved to bleed for their failure to realize the vision of aristocracy presented to them (and at their own instance!) by artists, philosophers and churchmen. Now they have withdrawn; some remnants live out their pathetic uselessness in dark areas of Boston or in English country houses open to the public for a fee. The rich now, to paraphrase Milton, are but the poor writ large. They do not form a different class. They too, like their employees, are leaderless and have lost the ability to look upward or to demand from others an upward glance. They are not interested in aristocracy. In the nineteenth century, instead of affording through their fortunes the chance of creating an American architecture (not to mention the other arts), they translated Loire chateaux in North Carolina. For all their money, they could not emerge from the proletariat and turn themselves into a true aristocracy. They did attempt lavishness; but the twentieth century is too serious for golden spittoons, and has neither lavishness nor aristocracy. The vision of moral heroism, intellectual perfection and good breeding has been supplanted by the vision, or rather the virtual accomplishment, of prosperity and social justice. True, I have read American protests against "American materialism" by the hundreds. We are blessed with an uncommon number of professional recriminators against material goods and upholders of "the finer things of life." But aristocracy embraces material prosperity; human dignity is not a concept of subsistence-level societies; even Diogenes and St. Simeon Stylites required rich societies as foils for their exertions. The real question is, "Who has the wealth, and what does he do with it?" Let Lorenzo the Magnificent and let Voltaire keep their money. But he who can only buy several pink Cadillacs with it, or travel over the world sporting a necktie adorned with large pineapples, unacquainted with his own language and replacing courtesy by heartiness—that man has money but not wealth, and the best answer to him is the federal tax.

When the leaders of society disappeared, the artist hung in the air with his great sermon in his hands. He had always worked for an elite and had never really lost his faith in his patrons; nowhere else could he find fit receptacles for the moral exhortation which is great art. Perhaps he actually hoped that some day they might acquire from him his own feeling for aristocracy. In the first enthusiastic years of democracy, many artists simply readdressed their message and sent it to the new public, so that for a while there were some considerable artists trying a vision of brotherhood on the masses: Hugo in France, Dickens in England, Tolstoy in Russia, Whitman in America.

But as an artistic goal, inspiring or converting the masses was soon forgotten. Long before educators began to doubt the efficacy of mass education, artists gave up hoping. The masses, they found, had more urgent business going than nobility. The great movement of mankind was speeding toward the consummation of pink Cadillacs, and, as I have said, even the vocabulary of hope—"nobility," "virtue," "heroism," "breeding," "ceremony"—became all but archaic. Facts always breed their apologetics: since there is no one left to exhort, our fashionable theories of art have conveniently substituted form for content and declare (not fearing the stares of Aeschylus, Dante and Milton) that art should not and does not exhort, that it has nothing to do with moral persuasion. From the days of moral art, one sad vestige remains—proletarian art—which convinces us that the rich are unjust, without satisfying us that their victims are admirable.

It is an instructive paradox that, whereas Greece, with its slaves, and medieval Europe, with its cruelly rigid class-divisions, produced an art in which all the people, high or low, rich or poor, could delight, in our democracies art has split in two, the larger part consisting of true confessions and quiz programs for the masses, and the smaller part of *Finnegan's Wake* and the like for an aristocracy of practically nobody. To be sure, in all epochs there has been *some* division—e.g., a court literature of romances and a popular literature of fabliaux. But the division was less marked in these iniquitous societies (Chaucer wrote fabliaux, and Arthurian romances became popular property) and the best art, like Homer or religious sculpture, was held in common. But why does art tend to become unified in hierarchical societies and "dualized" in egalitarian ones? One answer may be that in hierarchical societies the masses have less power to demand art, and that, to the extent they are not utterly crushed, they are in the habit of looking up to their betters and of trying to emulate them. That the merchants, artisans and yeomen did not enjoy quite the same aspects of a given work of art as those enjoyed by the upper or the educated class, we may safely suppose; yet, in general, circumstances induced them to share in the common idiom. This is why we rightly think of the masses of another day as having had better taste than mankind does today. With democracy, of course, the liberated populace became itself the buyer of art, and imposed its taste freely, without troubling to consult an elite. Hence the split in art: the caterers to mass taste on the one side, and the "true" artists without allegiance on the other.

In this connection, let me say a word about contemporary Russian art. I have seen a little of their statuary and their painting in reproductions, like everyone else, but I know their literature only by hearsay. Assuming that this literature is actually of the class which extols the manufacture of extra tractors as a sublime human achievement, I should say that we are wrong to blame this misery on the fact that Russia is ruled by dictators. Seeing two evils, we naturally conclude that they must be organically linked, and so we flatter ourselves with the figment that "there is no art where there is no freedom." In reality, some dictatorships do annihilate thought and creation ("I draw my pistol when I hear the word culture," someone says in that infamous Nazi play *Schlageter*), but others cultivate, honor and even finance them. To go no further than the obvious, Caesar Augustus and Louis XIV stand out as abolishers of freedom and patrons of culture. And in the days of the Greeks an intellectual could usually escape the persecutions of democracy by removing himself to the tyrannies of Sicily or Macedonia. The real question is not that of freedom, but whether the intellectual can be genuinely loyal to the system—dogmatic, half-free or free—which prevails in his country. Medieval Catholicism did not allow substantial deviations, yet it commanded loyal support with the results in art and thought that we know. What ails Russian literature, therefore, is not so much a lack of freedom as a dedication to the ignoble by a dictatorship of proletarians over the proletariat.

With the disappearance of a political aristocracy, with the reduction of the church to a center of sociability and soothing homiletics, and with the quarantining of the artist and the theoretician, the leaderless plebeians (rich and poor alike) have dedicated themselves wholeheartedly to self-admiration. They do not seek models to imitate or a superior taste to emulate. True, we are not in a jungle. Occasionally we stumble on a modern house which is not shamed to dust by colonial architecture; occasionally the public patronizes a difficult and intelligent play. The trouble with the plebeians was never that they had low tastes or no morals, but that they jumbled good and bad together and could not distinguish. We know that they willingly clapperclawed Shakespeare's plays. They did as much for Lumpkin Ignoto's the next afternoon. The over-all effect of a landscape organized by the populace is unkemptness rather than uniform ugliness. The unkemptness is intellectual and moral as well as aesthetic. Much, for instance, could be said about the proliferation of bizarre Protestant sects—typical inventions of the unchecked popular imagination. Were and are not these sects *permitted* by the absence of a focus of leadership, everywhere respected even if not clearly understood? Superstition—all the ejaculations of vulgar prophets unaware of standards of thought—has given Christianity in the United States its uncouth diversity. Freed from the control of a superior caste, religion became intellectual bad taste.

The world does not live on correct taste, noble morality or even intellectual acuity, and I am not suggesting revolutions. This is merely an inquiry. If we ask an explanation for what ugliness we do discover in the life about us, we find it in the extinction of leadership, the loss of reverence, the muddling of hierarchy or, in short, the want of a feeling for aristocracy. Much has been written about our new suburbias, where flat boxes eye one another across barren hills stickled with telephone poles. Outside of the old residential centers, America is becoming a great slum equipped with social justice. Is cheap housing necessarily ugly? Not if popular taste is good. The residents of our slums think their houses beautiful. But these people are leaderless: no one with a feeling for aristocracy has been able to hold their attention and suggest models. They do not want, as the political aristocracy did, images of hope, images of a possible heroism, images of possible beauty shown to them. But if houses have been criticized, other blemishes have almost vanished from the consciousness of even the most atrabilious critics. Is it seemly that in a university the students should dress as though they were pausing between the digging of two ditches? In England they wear gowns; in many countries they still rise when their instructor enters the room. But when the populace becomes the country, there is no looking up. The word "snobbery" usually dismisses the subject. I recall the touching words Yeats wrote for his daughter:

> And may her bridegroom bring her to a house
> Where all's accustomed, ceremonious;
>
> .   .   .   .
>
> How but in custom and ceremony
> Are innocence and beauty born?

The feeling for aristocracy, which this great man possessed so inveterately, unites appropriate dress and moral congruity, courtesy and heroism. An elegant Elizabethan lyric is understood only by an elegant mind. We teach it, in our folly, as though all the crowds at football games could stomach it.

With mass education the universities ceased to be centers of moral or aesthetic leadership. The tentative advance of a few scholars suddenly met a trampling army of plebeian students, and those poor few who entertained the idea of standards and hierarchies submitted without more ado to the stampede, like Don Quixote under the hogs. Today our universities, manned by tangential intellectuals, produce either more tangential intellectuals or additions to the populace or caterers to the populace. Our language has gone the same way: it keeps growing—but so does a cancer. "Eats," says the sign of the roadside diner. Wherever we look, wherever we listen, we find the depredations of a populace left without standards, and desiring none. Occasionally an affable dictatorship—like that of Parisian designers— creates an oasis of good taste. For the rest—automobiles with fins, geometry passing for interior decoration, neon signs on churches— fashions and customs meander from bad to bad. Moral excellence declines as well, for we are content as a nation to have the inducements and opportunities for doing evil removed from us ("Retro, Satana!" is the motto of every bureaucracy) and think ourselves lucky that occasions for moral and physical heroism have been reduced by machinery to nearly none at all. In the vast organizations

of government, armed forces and business, decisions—the moral acts—
are made by boards, committees or faceless and undiscoverable employees "somewhere along the line." Bureaucracy cannot be blamed,
cajoled, exhorted or worshipped, as kings and even tyrants can. It is
all mouth, no ears and nearly no brain, and it superannuates moral
excellence, the virtue possible only to responsible individuals. In
many business offices all employees contribute weekly to a "gift
fund" which operates as an anonymous and automatic congratulator
or condoler of the sick, the wedded and the parturient, so that even
the minor exertions of generosity can be avoided. The instance is
trifling but worth recording.

What shall we say of endeavors to "elevate the people"? This
humane notion takes many forms. Mass education is one of them.
Another is the multiplication of symphony concerts. Most of our
cities have respectable museums and libraries. Ladies' groups sponsor a few chamber music recitals. Clubs discuss "great books." And
what else? The whole nation is a vast and ghostly museum and a
refuge for frightened or hungry Europeans. The good folk who
are "elevating the people" are no doubt inheriting this office from
the traditional occupation of conveying a feeling for aristocracy to
the elite. Now their subjects are the whole people. And the people
laugh at them, or else make a few pious motions. Then they return
to the television sets and the basketball games which so offend the
culture dispensers. The people act from a right instinct. They have,
in a sense, watched TV programs since Adam begot them, and no
one is going to disturb them now.

Where can the artist find a new elite willing to employ him?
Where will he find an audience to revive in him the desire to show
the life which might be? It would not matter if I knew, since these
social movements are neither impelled nor directed by pamphleteers.
But in any event, the alliance between the intellectuals and the
proletariat is over. This alliance (if we can call such a one-sided
affair an alliance) began about the time of the French and the Industrial Revolutions, and it was fed by an emotion which the eighteenth century practically invented: humanitarianism. The oppressed
masses found their vocal cords in the educated and humane men
and women who pitied them. Even those whose best solution consisted in the distribution of Bibles deserve our regard. In short, the
victory of the lower classes owes much to the work of the intellectuals, but the intellectuals earned few thanks in return. What
the thinking man earned was toleration: something less than apoth-

eosis. It is no exaggeration to say that the new public cashiered him. Now that the work of pity is done, he cannot take his mind off the great betrayal. But he is still a left-winger, by and large, still a Democrat or a Socialist or what-have-you, out of a kind of habit perhaps, forgetting that the poor coal miner, to whom he had reached his hand in the evil days, is richer than he and has quite forgotten him.

I propose we let the matter rest there. The time has come to stop sulking; we must twitch our mantles and try new pastures. The time has come to stop demanding "culture" of the masses and to stop reproving them for their "low tastes." Their tastes are normal. We resent them only because we expected too much: the more fools we. Horror or pity for the way of life of the majority, as expressed in novels and plays about human brutality, lust, greed and idiocy, is a product of disappointed idealism. If we could recall the artists of former ages, they would be astonished by the vehemence of our disgust. Even in Twain and Hardy we still find the common people as the natural subject of *humor* (though, indeed, we learn more truth about "plain folk" from *A Midsummer Night's Dream* and *Huckleberry Finn* than from a hundred solemn pieces of naturalism). To be sure, the serious approach to the masses was inevitable in the new civilization. The livelihood of the Renaissance artist did not, after all, depend on the masses, and one could be fond of a bumpkin who stayed more or less quietly in the place God had allotted him on earth. The Renaissance artist could afford his nonchalance. Yet, though time has changed us, this nonchalance is what we must regain. We need to forget our resentment, our sense of frustration over the uninspirable majority, and whatever sentimental expectations of a noble proletariat, viewing nothing but the classics on television sets, we may still be entertaining. The sooner we embrace once again the idea of hierarchy, the sooner we can send out emissaries toward a new elite fit to be addressed. Perhaps we can create this elite. Surely artists and all the "useless" thinkers are not condemned to write forever only to each other. We must find a deliverance from precious art on one side, and on the other side from those bitter and "depressing" novels which keep explaining, again and again, with never-ceasing and foolish despair, that the ignoble are ignoble. We must, above all, find *heroes* for our literature; we must return to the idealizing function of art.

We may wonder whether the vision of hope—that is to say, the feeling for aristocracy—is forever denied to the populace. Will there

ever be a time when all men and women share in the same intellectual and emotional life—when a new Chrétien de Troyes, a new
Spenser, a new Racine, a new Tolstoy reveal aspects of nobility to
the commonest among men? Whatever we may think of the future,
the time at any rate is not now. We have given the masses premature
titles to maturity, and our punishment has been despair.

Problems for Thought and Writing

I

1. Were you shocked by Mandel's open and unqualified endorsement of an
   aristocratic ideal? Did it seem un American or undemocratic to you? Would
   it have seemed so to Jefferson (page 150)?

2. Is Mandel's dissatisfaction with contemporary society essentially the same
   as that of Ortega y Gasset (page 188)?

3. Would Mandel, in your opinion, favor the "club system" as it is practiced
   at Princeton? (See "The Princeton Bicker," page 5.)

4. Is Mandel doing anything more than re-examining "our equalitarian assumptions"? Does he have any practical proposals? On a subject like this is it
   possible to have a "program"?

5. What does Mandel mean by saying that the feeling for aristocracy is above
   all a "hope"? Could that not be said of democracy as well?

6. Does Mandel seem to want the kind of society that produces *good art* more
   than the society that produces prosperous and contented citizens? Does the
   presence of good art, in your opinion, indicate the presence of a good society?

7. "For the first time in its history, art has in fact become a mirror held up to
   nature rather than a challenge to nature." Why does Mandel deplore this
   fact? Can you provide some evidence to back up or deny the assertion?
   What does Mandel mean by saying that Faulkner has "wiped out the
   Duchess"?

8. The modern admiration in some quarters for the primitive, the instinctual,
   the elementary, the subconscious is seen by Mandel as a kind of decadence.
   After reading Jung (page 333) and Barrett (page 348), do you agree with
   him?

9. Do you agree with Baudelaire that man is at his best when he is, in a high
   sense, "unnatural"?

10. "We have in this country a substantial minority of artists, scholars, teachers,
    scientists, and unattached intellectuals who cultivate a quiet, private and
    sometimes embarrassed nobility." Would Mandel, in your opinion, equate
    this class with the "Highbrows" described by Russell Lynes (page 477)?

11. Do you agree with Mandel that the American people are "leaderless" and
    "content to be so"?

12. Compare what Mandel and MacLeish (page 665) say about poetry and
    art. Would they come anywhere near agreement on other points? Which
    ones?

13. "Human dignity," writes Mandel, "is not a concept of subsistence-level societies." Would Mandel extend this premise and use it to support an aristocracy possessed of many virtues, but basically possessed of money? What is Mandel's distinction between wealth and money? How does he apply it?

14. Examine something in your environment which you regard as ugly. Can it be explained, as Mandel contends, by "the extinction of leadership, the loss of reverence, the muddling of hierarchy or, in short, the want of a feeling for aristocracy"?

15. Do you agree that "America is becoming a great slum equipped with social justice"?

16. Describe the antithesis between bureaucracy and heroism. Does Whyte (page 217) have anything to say on the point?

17. Explain what Mandel means by saying that "the alliance between the intellectuals and the proletariat is over."

II

18. Mandel has a swift and pungent style—clear, hard-hitting, emphatic. Point out specifically how he achieves these virtues. Are they achieved at the sacrifice of objectivity? Can his writing be compared with that of Mencken (page 66), for example?

19. Identify or define: etymologically, egalitarianism, Vergil, Goethe, Baudelaire, Mallarmé, hermeticism, Husymans, mongering, emulating, syntactical, *Light in August*, Jacobean, Webster, hapless, inchoate, Expressionists, solipsistic, schizophrenia, *l'homme moyen sensuel*, *Finnegan's Wake*, fabliaux, clapper-clawed, proliferation, ejaculation, atrabilious.

20. What is Mandel's principle of organization? Outline his essay. Compare it with Gilson's (page 635), another essay that covers a lot of ground. Which has a firmer hand on his mass of facts?

~

B. MAN AND THE MASS

THE UNKNOWN CITIZEN   *W. H. Auden*

(TO JS/07/M/378

THIS MARBLE MONUMENT

IS ERECTED BY THE STATE)

He was found by the Bureau of Statistics to be
One against whom there was no official complaint,
And all the reports on his conduct agree
That, in the modern sense of an old-fashioned word, he was a saint,
For in everything he did he served the Greater Community.
Except for the War till the day he retired

He worked in a factory and never got fired,
But satisfied his employers, Fudge Motors Inc.
Yet he wasn't a scab or odd in his views,
For his Union reports that he paid his dues,
(Our report on his Union shows it was sound)
And our Social Psychology workers found
That he was popular with his mates and liked a drink.
The Press are convinced that he bought a paper every day
And that his reactions to advertisements were normal in every way.
Policies taken out in his name prove that he was fully insured,
And his Health-card shows he was once in hospital but left it cured.
Both Producers Research and High-Grade Living declare
He was fully sensible to the advantages of the Installment Plan
And had everything necessary to the Modern Man,
A phonograph, a radio, a car and a frigidaire.
Our researchers into Public Opinion are content
That he held the proper opinions for the time of year;
When there was peace, he was for peace; when there was war, he
    went.
He was married and added five children to the population,
Which our Eugenist says was the right number for a parent of his
    generation,
And our teachers report that he never interfered with their education.
Was he free? Was he happy? The question is absurd:
Had anything been wrong, we should certainly have heard.

Problems for Thought and Writing

1. Why the designation *unknown* citizen, if, according to the poem, everything about him is known?
2. What is the dominant meter of the poem? What kinds of utterances in similar meter and tone does it remind you of? Read the poem aloud and try to say in what way the sound supports the sense.
3. Why does Auden capitalize the "Greater Community" in line 5?
4. In what sense are *irony* and *complacency* key words to an understanding of the poem?
5. Characterize the fictitious speaker, *i.e.* the person with the voice that speaks the poem, not the poet Auden. (See Gibson, page 70).
6. Compare the poem's tone, organization, and approach to its meaning with Swift's "A Modest Proposal" (page 148). What resemblances do you detect?
7. By what means other than that of the concept of the "mock reader" (see Gibson, page 70) does one know that the poem means precisely the reverse of what it says?

~

From THE REVOLT OF
THE MASSES*   *Ortega y Gasset*

What is he like, this mass-man who to-day dominates public life,
political and non-political, and why is he like it, that is, how has
he been produced?

It will be well to answer both questions together, for they throw
light on one another. The man who to-day is attempting to take
the lead in European existence is very different from the man who
directed the XIXth Century, but he was produced and prepared by
the XIXth Century. Any keen mind of the years 1820, 1850, and 1880
could by simple *a priori* reasoning, foresee the gravity of the present
historical situation, and in fact nothing is happening now which was
not foreseen a hundred years ago. "The masses are advancing,"
said Hegel in apocalyptic fashion. "Without some new spiritual influence, our age, which is a revolutionary age, will produce a catastrophe," was the pronouncement of Comte. "I see the flood-tide of
nihilism rising," shrieked Nietzsche from a crag of the Engadine. It
is false to say that history cannot be foretold. Numberless times
this has been done. If the future offered no opening to prophecy,
it could not be understood when fulfilled in the present and on the
point of falling back into the past. The idea that the historian is on
the reverse side a prophet, sums up the whole philosophy of history.
It is true that it is only possible to anticipate the general structure of
the future, but that is all that we in truth understand of the past or
of the present. Accordingly, if you want a good view of your own
age, look at it from far off. From what distance? The answer is
simple. Just far enough to prevent you seeing Cleopatra's nose.

What appearance did life present to that multitudinous man who
in ever-increasing abundance the XIXth Century kept producing?
To start with, an appearance of universal material ease. Never had
the average man been able to solve his economic problem with greater
facility. Whilst there was a proportionate decrease of great for-

* Reprinted from *The Revolt of the Masses* by Jose Ortega y Gasset. By permission of W. W. Norton & Company, Inc. Copyright 1932 by W. W. Norton &
Company, Inc.

tunes and life became harder for the individual worker, the middle classes found their economic horizon widened every day. Every day added a new luxury to their standard of life. Every day their position was more secure and more independent of another's will. What before would have been considered one of fortune's gifts, inspiring humble gratitude toward destiny, was converted into a right, not to be grateful for, but to be insisted on.

From 1900 on, the worker likewise begins to extend and assure his existence. Nevertheless, he has to struggle to obtain his end. He does not, like the middle class, find the benefit attentively served up to him by a society and a state which are a marvel of organization. To this ease and security of economic conditions are to be added the physical ones, comfort and public order. Life runs on smooth rails, and there is no likelihood of anything violent or dangerous breaking in on it. Such a free, untrammelled situation was bound to instil into the depths of such souls an idea of existence which might be expressed in the witty and penetrating phrase of an old country like ours: "Wide is Castile." That is to say, in all its primary and decisive aspects, life presented itself to the new man as *exempt from restrictions.* The realisation of this fact and of its importance becomes immediate when we remember that such a freedom of existence was entirely lacking to the common men of the past. On the contrary, for them life was burdensome destiny, economically and physically. From birth, existence meant to them an accumulation of impediments which they were obliged to suffer, without possible solution other than to adapt themselves to them, to settle down in the narrow space they left available.

But still more evident is the contrast of situations, if we pass from the material to the civil and moral. The average man, from the second half of the XIXth Century on, finds no social barriers raised against him. That is to say, that as regards the forms of public life he no longer finds himself from birth confronted with obstacles and limitations. There is nothing to force him to limit his existence. Here again, "Wide is Castile." There are no "estates" or "castes." There are no civil privileges. The ordinary man learns that all men are equal before the law.

Never in the course of history had man been placed in vital surroundings even remotely familiar to those set up by the conditions just mentioned. We are, in fact, confronted with a radical innovation in human destiny, implanted by the XIXth Century. A new stage has been mounted for human existence, new both in the physical and the social aspects. Three principles have made possible this new world: liberal democracy, scientific experiment, and industrialism. The two latter may be summed-up in one word: technicism. Not one of those principles was invented by the XIXth Century; they proceed from the two previous centuries. The glory of the XIXth Century lies not in their discovery, but in their implantation. No one but recognises that fact. But it is not sufficient to recognise it in the abstract, it is necessary to realise its inevitable consequences.

The XIXth Century was of its essence revolutionary. This aspect is not to be looked for in the scenes of the barricades, which are mere incidents, but in the fact that it placed the average man—the great social mass—in conditions of life radically opposed to those by which he had always been surrounded. It turned his public existence upside down. Revolution is not the uprising against pre-existing order, but the setting up of a new order contradictory to the traditional one. Hence there is no exaggeration in saying that the man who is the product of the XIXth Century is, for the effects of public life, a man apart from all other men. The XVIIIth-Century man differs, of course, from the XVIIth-Century man, and this one in turn from his fellow of the XVIth Century, but they are all related, similar, even identical in essentials when confronted with this new man. For the "common" man of all periods "life" had principally meant limitation, obligation, dependence; in a word, pressure. Say oppression, if you like, provided it be understood not only in the juridical and social sense, but also in the cosmic. For it is this latter which has never been lacking up to a hundred years ago, the date at which starts the practically limitless expansion of scientific technique—physical and administrative. Previously, even for the rich and powerful, the world was a place of poverty, difficulty and danger.[1]

The world which surrounds the new man from his birth does not compel him to limit himself in any fashion, it sets up no veto in opposition to him; on the contrary, it incites his appetite, which-in principle can increase indefinitely. Now it turns out—and this is most important—that this world of the XIXth and early XXth Centuries not only has the perfections and the completeness which it actually

[1] However rich an individual might be in relation to his fellows, as the world in its totality was poor, the sphere of conveniences and commodities with which his wealth furnished him was very limited. The life of the average man to-day is easier, more convenient and safer than that of the most powerful of another age. What difference does it make to him not to be richer than others if the world is richer and furnishes him with magnificent roads, railways, telegraphs, hotels, personal safety and aspirin?

possesses, but furthermore suggests to those who dwell in it the radical assurance that to-morrow it will be still richer, ampler, more perfect, as if it enjoyed a spontaneous, inexhaustible power of increase. Even to-day, in spite of some signs which are making a tiny breach in that sturdy faith, even to-day, there are few men who doubt that motorcars will in five years' time be more comfortable and cheaper than to-day. They believe in this as they believe that the sun will rise in the morning. The metaphor is an exact one. For, in fact, the common man, finding himself in a world so excellent, technically and socially, believes that it has been produced by nature, and never thinks of the personal efforts of highly-endowed individuals which the creation of this new world presupposed. Still less will he admit the notion that all these facilities still require the support of certain difficult human virtues, the least failure of which would cause the rapid disappearance of the whole magnificent edifice.

This leads us to note down in our psychological chart of the mass-man of to-day two fundamental traits: the free expansion of his vital desires, and therefore, of his personality; and his radical ingratitude towards all that has made possible the ease of his existence. These traits together make up the well-known psychology of the spoilt child. And in fact it would entail no error to use this psychology as a "sight" through which to observe the soul of the masses of to-day. Heir to an ample and generous past—generous both in ideals and in activities—the new commonalty has been spoiled by the world around it. To spoil means to put no limit on caprice, to give one the impression that everything is permitted to him and that he has no obligations. The young child exposed to this regime has no experience of its own limits. By reason of the removal of all external restraint, all clashing with other things, he comes actually to believe that he is the only one that exists, and gets used to not considering others, especially not considering them as superior to himself. This feeling of another's superiority could only be instilled into him by someone who, being stronger than he is, should force him to give up some desire, to restrict himself, to restrain himself. He would then have learned this fundamental discipline: "Here I end and here begins another more powerful than I am. In the world, apparently, there are two people: I myself and another superior to me." The ordinary man of past times was daily taught this elemental wisdom by the world about him, because it was a world so rudely organised, that catastrophes were frequent, and there was nothing in it certain, abundant, stable. But the new masses find themselves in the presence of a prospect full of possibilities, and furthermore, quite secure, with everything ready to their hands, independent of any previous efforts on their part, just as we find the sun in the heavens without our hoisting it up on our shoulders. No human being thanks another for the air he breathes, for no one has produced the air for him; it belongs to the sum-total of what "is there," of which we say "it is natural," because it never fails. And these spoiled masses are unintelligent enough to believe that the material and social organisation, placed at their disposition like the air, is of the same origin, since apparently it never fails them, and is almost as perfect as the natural scheme of things.

My thesis, therefore, is this: the very perfection with which the XIXth Century gave an organisation to certain orders of existence has caused the masses benefited thereby to consider it, not as an organised, but as a natural system. Thus is explained and defined the absurd state of mind revealed by these masses; they are only concerned with their own well-being, and at the same time they remain alien to the cause of that well-being. As they do not see, beyond the benefits of civilisation, marvels of invention and construction which can only be maintained by great effort and foresight, they imagine that their role is limited to demanding these benefits peremptorily, as if they were natural rights. In the disturbances caused by scarcity of food, the mob goes in search of bread, and the means it employs is generally to wreck the bakeries. This may serve as a symbol of the attitude adopted, on a greater and more complicated scale, by the masses of to-day towards the civilisation by which they are supported.

*   *   *

To start with, we are what our world invites us to be, and the basic features of our soul are impressed upon it by the form of its surroundings as in a mould. Naturally, for our life is no other than our relations with the world around. The general aspect which it presents to us will form the general aspect of our own life. It is for this reason that I stress so much the observation that the world into which the masses of to-day have been born displays features radically new to history. Whereas in past times life for the average man meant finding all around him difficulties, dangers, want, limitations of his destiny, dependence, the new world appears as a sphere of practically limitless possibilities, safe, and independent of anyone. Based on this primary and lasting impression, the mind of every contemporary man will be formed, just as previous minds were formed on the opposite impression. For that basic impression becomes an interior voice which ceaselessly utters certain words in the depths of each individual, and tenaciously suggests to him a definition of life which is, at the same time, a moral imperative. And if the traditional sentiment whispered: "To live is to feel oneself limited, and therefore to have to count with that which limits us," the newest voice shouts: "To live is to meet with no limitation whatever and, consequently, to abandon oneself calmly to one's self. Practically nothing is impossible, nothing is dangerous, and, in principle, nobody is superior to anybody." This basic experience completely modifies the traditional, persistent structure of the mass man. For the latter always felt himself, by his nature, confronted with material limitations and higher social powers. Such, in his eyes, was life. If he succeeded in improving his situation, if he climbed the social ladder, he attributed this to a piece of fortune which was favourable to him in particular. And if not to this, then to an enormous effort, of which he knew well what it had cost him. In both cases it was a question of an exception to the general character of life and the world; an exception which, as such, was due to some very special cause.

But the modern mass finds complete freedom as its natural, established condition, without any special cause for it. Nothing from outside incites it to recognise limits to itself and, consequently, to refer at all times to other authorities higher than itself. Until lately, the Chinese peasant believed that the welfare of his existence depended on the private virtues which the Emperor was pleased to possess. Therefore, his life was constantly related to this supreme authority on which it depended. *But the man we are now analysing accustoms himself not to appeal from his own to any authority outside him.* He is satisfied with himself exactly as he is. Ingenuously, without any need of being vain, as the most natural thing in the world, he will tend to consider and affirm as good everything he finds within himself: opinions, appetites, preferences, tastes. Why not, if, as we have seen, nothing and nobody force him to realise that he is a second-class man, subject to many limitations, incapable of creating or conserving that very organisation which gives his life the fullness and contentedness on which he bases this assertion of his personality?

The mass-man would never have accepted authority external to himself had not his surroundings violently forced him to do so. As to-day, his surroundings do not so force him, the everlasting mass-man, true to his character, ceases to appeal to other authority and feels himself lord of his own existence. On the contrary the select man, the excellent man is urged, by interior necessity, to appeal from himself to some standard beyond himself, superior to himself, whose service he freely accepts. Let us recall that at the start we distinguished the excellent man from the common man by saying that the former is the one who makes great demands on himself, and the latter the one who makes no demands on himself, but contents himself with what he is, and is delighted with himself.[2] Contrary to what is usually thought, it is the man of excellence, and not the common man who lives in essential servitude. Life has no savour for him unless he makes it consist in service to something transcendental. Hence he does not look upon the necessity of serving as an oppression. When, by chance, such necessity is lacking, he grows restless and invents some new standard, more difficult, more exigent, with which to coerce himself. This is life lived as a discipline—the noble life. Nobility is defined by the demands it makes on us—by obligations, not by rights. Noblesse oblige. "To live as one likes is plebeian; the noble man aspires to order and law" (Goethe). The privileges of nobility are not in their origin concessions or favours; on the contrary, they are conquests. And their maintenance supposes, in principle, that the privileged individual is capable of reconquering them, at any moment, if it were necessary, and anyone were to dispute them.[3] Private rights or *privileges* are not, then, passive possession and mere enjoyment, but they represent the standard attained by personal effort. On the other hand, common rights, such as those "of the man and the citizen," are passive property, pure usufruct and benefit, the generous gift of fate which every man finds before him, and which answers to no effort whatever, unless it be that of breathing and avoiding insanity. I would say, then, that an impersonal right is held, a personal one is upheld.

It is annoying to see the degeneration suffered in ordinary speech by a word so inspiring as "nobility." For, by coming to mean for many people hereditary "noble blood," it is changed into something similar to common rights, into a static, passive quality which is received and transmitted like something inert. But the strict sense, the *etymon* of the word nobility is essentially dynamic. Noble means

[2] That man is intellectually of the mass who, in face of any problem, is satisfied with thinking the first thing he finds in his head. On the contrary, the excellent man is he who contemns what he finds in his mind without previous effort, and only accepts as worthy of him what is still far above him and what requires a further effort in order to be reached.

[3] Vide *España Invertebrada* (1922), p. 156.

the "well known," that is, known by everyone, famous, he who has made himself known by excelling the anonymous mass. It implies an unusual effort as the cause of his fame. Noble, then, is equivalent to effortful, excellent. The nobility or frame of the son is pure benefit. The son is known because the father made himself famous. He is known by reflection, and in fact, hereditary nobility has an indirect character, it is mirrored light, lunar nobility, something derived from the dead. The only thing left to it of living, authentic, dynamic is the impulse it stirs in the descendant to maintain the level of effort reached by the ancestor. Always, even in this altered sense, *noblesse oblige*. The original noble lays an obligation on himself, the noble heir receives the obligation with his inheritance. But in any case there is a certain contradiction in the passing-on of nobility from the first noble to his successors. The Chinese, more logical, invert the order of transmission; it is not the father who ennobles the son, but the son who, by acquiring noble rank, communicates it to his forbears, by his personal efforts bringing fame to his humble stock. Hence, when granting degrees of nobility, they are graduated by the number of previous generations which are honoured; there are those who ennoble only their fathers, and those who stretch back their fame to the fifth or tenth grandparent. The ancestors live by reason of the actual man, whose nobility is effective, active—in a word: *is*, not *was*.[4]

"Nobility" does not appear as a formal expression until the Roman Empire, and then precisely in opposition to the hereditary nobles, then in decadence.

For me, then, nobility is synonymous with a life of effort, ever set on excelling oneself, in passing beyond what one is to what one sets up as a duty and an obligation. In this way the noble life stands opposed to the common or inert life, which reclines statically upon itself, condemned to perpetual immobility, unless an external force compels it to come out of itself. Hence we apply the term mass to this kind of man—not so much because of his multitude as because of his inertia.

As one advances in life, one realises more and more that the majority of men—and of women—are incapable of any other effort than that strictly imposed on them as a reaction to external compulsion.

[4] As in the foregoing it is only a matter of bringing the word "nobility" back to its original sense which excludes inheritance, this is not the place to study the fact that a "nobility of blood" makes its appearance so often in history. This question, then, is left untouched.

And for that reason, the few individuals we have come across who are capable of a spontaneous and joyous effort stand out isolated, monumentalised, so to speak, in our experience. These are the select men, the nobles, the only ones who are active and not merely reactive, for whom life is a perpetual striving, an incessant course of training. Training = *askesis*. These are the ascetics.[5] This apparent digression should not cause surprise. In order to define the actual mass-man, who is as much "mass" as ever, but who wishes to supplant the "excellent," it has been necessary to contrast him with the two pure forms which are mingled in him: the normal mass and the genuine noble or man of effort.

Now we can advance more rapidly, because we are now in possession of what, to my thinking, is the key—the psychological equation—of the human type dominant to-day. All that follows is a consequence, a corollary, of that root-structure, which may be summed up thus: the world as organised by the XIXth Century, when automatically producing a new man, has infused into him formidable appetites and powerful means of every kind for satisfying them. These include the economic, the physical (hygiene, average health higher than any preceding age), the civil and the technical (by which I mean the enormous quantity of partial knowledge and practical efficiency possessed by the average man to-day and lacking to him in the past). After having supplied him with all these powers, the XIXth Century has abandoned him to himself, and the average man, following his natural disposition, has withdrawn into himself. Hence, we are in presence of a mass stronger than that of any preceding period, but differing from the traditional type in that it remains, hermetically enclosed within itself, incapable of submitting to anything or anybody, believing itself self-sufficient—in a word, indocile.[6] If things go on as they are at present, it will be every day more noticeable in Europe—and by reflection, throughout the whole world—that the masses are incapable of submitting to direction of any kind. In the difficult times that are at hand for our continent, it is possible that, under a sudden affliction, they may for a moment have the good will to accept, in certain specially urgent matters, the direction of the superior minorities.

But even that good will will result in failure. For the basic texture

---

[5] Vide "El Origen deportivo del Estado," in *El Espectador*, VII, recently published.

[6] On the indocility of the masses, especially of the Spanish masses, I have already spoken in *España Invertebrada* (1922), and I refer the reader to what is there said.

of their soul is wrought of hermetism and indocility; they are from birth deficient in the faculty of giving attention to what is outside themselves, be it fact or person. They will wish to follow someone, and they will be unable. They will want to listen, and will discover they are deaf.

On the other hand, it is illusory to imagine that the mass-man of to-day, however superior his vital level may be compared with that of other times, will be able to control, by himself, the process of civilisation. I say process, and not progress. The simple process of preserving our present civilisation is supremely complex, and demands incalculably subtle powers. Ill-fitted to direct it is this average man who has learned to use much of the machinery of civilisation, but who is characterised by root-ignorance of the very principles of that civilisation.

I reiterate to the reader who has patiently followed me up to this point, the importance of not giving to the facts enunciated a primarily political significance. On the contrary, political activities, of all those in public life the most efficient and the most visible, are the final product of others more intimate, more impalpable. Hence, political indocility would not be so grave did it not proceed from a deeper, more decisive intellectual indocility. In consequence, until we have analysed this latter, the thesis of this essay will not stand out in its final clarity.

Problems for Thought and Writing

I

In the past few years many noted writers have emphasized the trend in modern life from individualism to mass behavior and conformity. In that list of writers are some famous names: Aldous Huxley, George Orwell, Lewis Mumford, David Riesman, W. H. Whyte, and scores of others. But the name that should head the list is Ortega y Gasset. He was not the first to note the phenomenon of mass culture, but he was the first to write a cogent, comprehensive book on the subject. The original Spanish edition of *The Revolt of the Masses* appeared in 1930, a compilation and distillation of many articles and lectures from earlier years. Although there are more up-to-date treatments of this problem, the editors have made a selection from this book because it is the classic statement. What others have been describing at such length in our own time, this prophetic philosopher saw in the '20's.

1. As you read this selection, do you feel that Ortega y Gasset is a snob? Are you offended at what seem to be his aristocratic assumptions? If so, consider another question: Are you offended at the mass man and his culture (which we all share)? If you are, then are you exempt from these same aristocratic assumptions? This is a major problem for the democratic man of our time.

How do you propose to solve it? (See Oscar Mandel, "Nobility and the United States," page 171, for one probing of this problem.)

2. The principles of the liberal-democratic world extolled and discussed by Milton, Jefferson, and Lippmann in the preceding section are obviously being threatened by the advent of the mass man and his culture. Yet the mass man and his culture grew from and were nurtured by that liberal-democratic tradition. From a noble revolutionary tradition we have descended—if Ortega is right—to a culture with the soul of a "spoiled child" (see page 191). If this is a valid conclusion, does it suggest that the liberal-democratic tradition was mistaken?

3. Do you regard your economic well-being and your freedom from class restrictions as "natural" or as "gifts" from your tradition and your forebears? See Ortega, page 195.

4. In the section beginning on page 192, does Ortega seem to be *favoring* suffering, restriction, submission to authority, as conditions of the healthy society?

5. Write an essay, in your own terms, distinguishing between the "excellent man" and the "common man." Do you agree with Goethe: "To live as one likes is plebeian; the noble man aspires to order and law"?

6. Compare Ortega's use of the word "nobility" with Mandel's (page 171). Do you agree with Ortega's definition? What is your own?

II

7. Are you content with Ortega's use of evidence? Test his practice against the principles laid down by Chute (page 113). Is his problem so different that those principles don't apply?

8. Define: *noblesse oblige,* anonymous, inertia, ascetic, plebeian, nihilism.

9. Can you detect any evidence that this is a translation? How does the writing differ from idiomatic modern English?

~

THE ILLUSION OF INDIVIDUALITY*

Erich Fromm

But what about ourselves? Is our own democracy threatened only by Fascism beyond the Atlantic or by the "fifth column" in our own ranks? If that were the case, the situation would be serious but not critical. But although foreign and internal threats of Fascism must be taken seriously, there is no greater mistake and no graver danger than not to see that in our own society we are faced with the same phenomenon that is fertile soil for the rise of Fascism anywhere: the insignificance and powerlessness of the individual.

This statement challenges the conventional belief that by freeing the individual from all external restraints modern democracy has achieved true individualism. We are proud that we are not subject to any external authority, that we are free to express our thoughts and feelings, and we take it for granted that this freedom almost automatically guarantees our individuality. *The right to express our thoughts,* however, *means something only if we are able to have thoughts of our own;* freedom from external authority is a lasting gain only if the inner psychological conditions are such that we are able to establish our own individuality. Have we achieved that aim, or are we at least approaching it? . . . In discussing the two aspects of freedom for modern man, we have pointed out the economic conditions that make for increasing isolation and powerlessness of the individual in our era; in discussing the psychological results we have shown that this powerlessness leads either to the kind of escape that we find in the authoritarian character, or else to a compulsive conforming in the process of which the isolated individual becomes an automaton, loses his self, and yet at the same time consciously conceives of himself as free and subject only to himself.

It is important to consider how our culture fosters this tendency to conform, even though there is space for only a few outstanding examples. The suppression of spontaneous feelings, and thereby of the development of genuine individuality, starts very early, as a matter of fact with the earliest training of a child. This is not to say that training must inevitably lead to suppression of spontaneity if the real aim of education is to further the inner independence and individuality of the child, its growth and integrity. The restrictions which such a kind of education may have to impose upon the growing child are only transitory measures that really support the process of growth and expansion. In our culture, however, education too often results in the elimination of spontaneity and in the substitution of original psychic acts by superimposed feelings, thoughts, and wishes. (By original I do not mean, let me repeat, that an idea has not been thought before by someone else, but that it originates in the individual, that it is the result of his own activity and in this sense is *his* thought.) To choose one illustration somewhat arbitrarily, one of the earliest suppressions of *feelings* concerns hostility and dislike. To start with, most children have a certain measure of hostility and rebelliousness as a result of their conflicts with a surrounding world that tends to block their expansiveness and to which, as the weaker opponent, they usually have to yield. It is one of the essential aims of the educational process to eliminate this antagonistic reaction. The methods are different; they vary from threats and punishments, which frighten the child, to the subtler methods of bribery or "explanations," which confuse the child and make him give up his hostility. The child starts with giving up the expression of his feeling and eventually gives up the very feeling itself. Together with that, he is taught to suppress the awareness of hostility and insincerity in others; sometimes this is not entirely easy, since children have a capacity for noticing such negative qualities in others without being so easily deceived by words as adults usually are. They still dislike somebody "for no good reason"—except the very good one that they feel the hostility, or insincerity, radiating from that person. This reaction is soon discouraged; it does not take long for the child to reach the "maturity" of the average adult and to lose the sense of discrimination between a decent person and a scoundrel, as long as the latter has not committed some flagrant act.

On the other hand, early in his education, the child is taught to have feelings that are not at all "his"; particularly is he taught to like people, to be uncritically friendly to them, and to smile. What education may not have accomplished is usually done by social pressure in later life. If you do not smile you are judged lacking in a "pleasing personality"—and you need to have a pleasing personality if you want to sell your services, whether as a waitress, a salesman, or a physician. Only those at the bottom of the social pyramid, who sell nothing but their physical labor, and those at the very top do not need to be particularly "pleasant." Friendliness, cheerfulness, and everything that a smile is supposed to express, become automatic responses which one turns on and off like an electric switch.[1]

To be sure, in many instances the person is aware of merely making a gesture; in most cases, however, he loses that awareness

---

[1] As one telling illustration of the commercialization of friendliness I should like to cite Fortune's report on "The Howard Johnson Restaurants." (Fortune, September, 1940, p. 96.) Johnson employs a force of "shoppers" who go from restaurant to restaurant to watch for lapses. "Since everything is cooked on the premises according to standard recipes and measurements issued by the home office, the inspector knows how large a portion of steak he should receive and how the vegetable should taste. He also knows how long it should take for the dinner to be served and he knows the exact degree of friendliness that should be shown by the hostess and the waitress."

and thereby the ability to discriminate between the pseudo feeling and spontaneous friendliness.

It is not only hostility that is directly suppressed and friendliness that is killed by superimposing its counterfeit. A wide range of spontaneous emotions are suppressed and replaced by pseudo feelings. Freud has taken one such suppression and put it in the center of his whole system, namely the suppression of sex. Although I believe that the discouragement of sexual joy is not the only important suppression of spontaneous reactions but one of many, certainly its importance is not to be underrated. Its results are obvious in cases of sexual inhibitions and also in those where sex assumes a compulsive quality and is consumed like liquor or a drug, which has no particular taste but makes you forget yourself. Regardless of the one or the other effect, their suppression, because of the intensity of sexual desires, not only affects the sexual sphere but also weakens the person's courage for spontaneous expression in all other spheres.

In our society emotions in general are discouraged. While there can be no doubt that any creative thinking—as well as any other creative activity—is inseparably linked with emotion, it has become an ideal to think and to live without emotions. To be "emotional" has become synonymous with being unsound or unbalanced. By the acceptance of this standard the individual has become greatly weakened; his thinking is impoverished and flattened. On the other hand, since emotions cannot be completely killed, they must have their existence totally apart from the intellectual side of the personality; the result is the cheap and insincere sentimentality with which movies and popular songs feed millions of emotion-starved customers.

There is one tabooed emotion that I want to mention in particular, because its suppression touches deeply on the roots of personality: the sense of tragedy. As we saw in an earlier chapter, the awareness of death and of the tragic aspect of life, whether dim or clear, is one of the basic characteristics of man. Each culture has its own way of coping with the problem of death. For those societies in which the process of individuation has progressed but little, the end of individual existence is less of a problem since the experience of individual existence itself is less developed. Death is not yet conceived as being basically different from life. Cultures in which we find a higher development of individuation have treated death according to their social and psychological structure. The Greeks put all emphasis on life and pictured death as nothing but a shadowy and dreary continuation of life. The Egyptians based their hopes on a belief in the indestructibility of the human body, at least of those whose power during life was indestructible. The Jews admitted the fact of death realistically and were able to reconcile themselves with the idea of the destruction of individual life by the vision of a state of happiness and justice ultimately to be reached by mankind in this world. Christianity has made death unreal and tried to comfort the unhappy individual by promises of a life after death. Our own era simply denies death and with it one fundamental aspect of life. Instead of allowing the awareness of death and suffering to become one of the strongest incentives for life, the basis for human solidarity, and an experience without which joy and enthusiasm lack intensity and depth, the individual is forced to repress it. But, as is always the case with repression, by being removed from sight the repressed elements do not cease to exist. Thus the fear of death lives an illegitimate existence among us. It remains alive in spite of the attempt to deny it, but being repressed it remains sterile. It is one source of the flatness of other experiences, of the restlessness pervading life, and it explains, I would venture to say, the exorbitant amount of money this nation pays for its funerals.

In the process of tabooing emotions modern psychiatry plays an ambiguous role. On the one hand its greatest representative, Freud, has broken through the fiction of the rational, purposeful character of the human mind and opened a path which allows a view into the abyss of human passions. On the other hand psychiatry, enriched by these very achievements of Freud, has made itself an instrument of the general trends in the manipulation of personality. Many psychiatrists, including psychoanalysts, have painted the picture of a "normal" personality which is never too sad, too angry, or too excited. They use words like "infantile" or "neurotic" to denounce traits or types of personalities that do not conform with the conventional pattern of a "normal" individual. This kind of influence is in a way more dangerous than the older and franker forms of name-calling. Then the individual knew at least that there was some person or some doctrine which criticized him and he could fight back. But who can fight back at "science"?

The same distortion happens to original *thinking* as happens to feelings and emotions. From the very start of education original thinking is discouraged and ready-made thoughts are put into people's heads. How this is done with young children is easy enough to see. They are filled with curiosity about the world, they want to grasp it physically as well as intellectually. They want to know the truth, since that is the safest way to orient themselves in a strange and powerful world. Instead, they are not taken seriously, and it does not matter whether this attitude takes the form of open disrespect or of the subtle condescension which is usual towards all who have no power (such as children, aged or sick people). Although this treatment by itself offers strong discouragement to independent thinking, there is a worse handicap: the insincerity—often unintentional—which is typical of the average adult's behavior toward a child. This insincerity consists partly in the fictitious picture of the world which the child is given. It is about as useful as instructions concerning life in the Arctic would be to someone who has asked how to prepare for an expedition to the Sahara Desert. Besides this general misrepresentation of the world there are the many specific lies that tend to conceal facts which, for various personal reasons, adults do not want children to know. From a bad temper, which is rationalized as justified dissatisfaction with the child's behavior, to concealment of the parents' sexual activities and their quarrels, the child is "not supposed to know" and his inquiries meet with hostile or polite discouragement.

The child thus prepared enters school and perhaps college. I want to mention briefly some of the educational methods used today which in effect further discourage original thinking. One is the emphasis on knowledge of facts, or I should rather say on information. The pathetic superstition prevails that by knowing more and more facts one arrives at knowledge of reality. Hundreds of scattered and unrelated facts are dumped into the heads of students; their time and energy are taken up by learning more and more facts so that there is little left for thinking. To be sure, thinking without a knowledge of facts remains empty and fictitious; but "information" alone can be just as much of an obstacle to thinking as the lack of it.

Another closely related way of discouraging original thinking is to regard all truth as relative.[2] Truth is made out to be a metaphysical concept, and if anyone speaks about wanting to discover the truth he is thought backward by the "progressive" thinkers of our age. Truth is declared to be an entirely subjective matter, almost

---

[2] Cf. to this whole problem Robert S. Lynd's *Knowledge for What?* Princeton University Press, Princeton, 1939. For its philosophical aspects cf. M. Horkheimer's *Zum Rationalismusstreit in der Gegenwärtigen Philosophie*, Zeitschrift für Sozialforschung, Vol. 3, 1934, Alcan, Paris.

a matter of taste. Scientific endeavor must be detached from subjective factors, and its aim is to look at the world without passion
and interest. The scientist has to approach facts with sterilized hands
as a surgeon approaches his patient. The result of this relativism,
which often presents itself by the name of empiricism or positivism
or which recommends itself by its concern for the correct usage of
words, is that thinking loses its essential stimulus—the wishes and
interests of the person who thinks; instead it becomes a machine to
register "facts." Actually, just as thinking in general has developed
out of the need for mastery of material life, so the quest for truth is
rooted in the interests and needs of individuals and social groups.
Without such interest the stimulus for seeking the truth would be
lacking. There are always groups whose interest is furthered by
truth, and their representatives have been the pioneers of human
thought; there are other groups whose interests are furthered by
concealing truth. Only in the latter case does interest prove harmful
to the cause of truth. The problem, therefore, is not that there is *an*
interest at stake, but *which kind* of interest is at stake. I might say
that inasmuch as there is some longing for the truth in every human
being, it is because every human being has some need for it.

This holds true in the first place with regard to a person's orientation in the outer world, and it holds especially true for the child.
As a child, every human being passes through a state of powerlessness,
and truth is one of the strongest weapons of those who have no power.
But the truth is in the individual's interest not only with regard to
his orientation in the outer world; his own strength depends to a
great extent on his knowing the truth about himself. Illusions about
oneself can become crutches useful to those who are not able to
walk alone; but they increase a person's weakness. The individual's
greatest strength is based on the maximum of integration of his personality, and that means also on the maximum of transparence to
himself. "Know thyself" is one of the fundamental commands that
aim at human strength and happiness.

In addition to the factors just mentioned there are others which
actively tend to confuse whatever is left of the capacity for original
thinking in the average adult. With regard to all basic questions
of individual and social life, with regard to psychological, economic,
political, and moral problems, a great sector of our culture has just
one function—to befog the issues. One kind of smoke-screen is the
assertion that the problems are too complicated for the average individual to grasp. On the contrary it would seem that many of the

basic issues of individual and social life are very simple, so simple, in fact, that everyone should be expected to understand them. To let them appear to be so enormously complicated that only a "specialist" can understand them, and he only in his own limited field, actually—and often intentionally—tends to discourage people from trusting their own capacity to think about those problems that really matter. The individual feels helplessly caught in a chaotic mass of data and with pathetic patience waits until the specialists have found out what to do and where to go.

The result of this kind of influence is a twofold one: one is a scepticism and cynicism towards everything which is said or printed, while the other is a childish belief in anything that a person is told with authority. This combination of cynicism and naïveté is very typical of the modern individual. Its essential result is to discourage him from doing his own thinking and deciding.

Another way of paralyzing the ability to think critically is the destruction of any kind of structuralized picture of the world. Facts lose the specific quality which they can have only as parts of a structuralized whole and retain merely an abstract, quantitative meaning; each fact is just *another* fact and all that matters is whether we know more or less. Radio, moving pictures, and newspapers have a devastating effect on this score. The announcement of the bombing of a city and the death of hundreds of people is shamelessly followed or interrupted by an advertisement for soap or wine. The same speaker with the same suggestive, ingratiating, and authoritative voice, which he has just used to impress you with the seriousness of the political situation, impresses now upon his audience the merits of the particular brand of soap which pays for the news broadcast. Newsreels let pictures of torpedoed ships be followed by those of a fashion show. Newspapers tell us the trite thoughts or breakfast habits of a debutante with the same space and seriousness they use for reporting events of scientific or artistic importance. Because of all this we cease to be genuinely related to what we hear. We cease to be excited, our emotions and our critical judgment become hampered, and eventually our attitude to what is going on in the world assumes a quality of flatness and indifference. In the name of "freedom" life loses all structure; it is composed of many little pieces, each separate from the other and lacking any sense as a whole. The individual is left alone with these pieces like a child with a puzzle; the difference, however, is that the child knows what a house is and therefore can recognize the parts of the house in the little pieces he is playing with, whereas the adult does not see the meaning of the "whole," the pieces of which come into his hands. He is bewildered and afraid and just goes on gazing at his little meaningless pieces.

What has been said about the lack of "originality" in feeling and thinking holds true also of the act of *willing*. To recognize this is particularly difficult; modern man seems, if anything, to have too many wishes and his only problem seems to be that, although he knows what he wants, he cannot have it. All our energy is spent for the purpose of getting what we want, and most people never question the premise of this activity: that they know their true wants. They do not stop to think whether the aims they are pursuing are something they themselves want. In school they want to have good marks, as adults they want to be more and more successful, to make more money, to have more prestige, to buy a better car, to go places, and so on. Yet when they do stop to think in the midst of all this frantic activity, this question may come to their minds: "If I do get this new job, if I get this better car, if I can take this trip—what then? What is the use of it all? Is it really I who wants all this? Am I not running after some goal which is supposed to make me happy and which eludes me as soon as I have reached it?" These questions, when they arise, are frightening, for they question the very basis on which man's whole activity is built, his knowledge of what he wants. People tend, therefore, to get rid as soon as possible of these disturbing thoughts. They feel that they have been bothered by these questions because they were tired or depressed—and they go on in the pursuit of the aims which they believe are their own.

Yet all this bespeaks a dim realization of the truth—the truth that modern man lives under the illusion that he knows what he wants, while he actually wants what he is *supposed* to want. In order to accept this it is necessary to realize that to know what one really wants is not comparatively easy, as most people think, but one of the most difficult problems any human being has to solve. It is a task we frantically try to avoid by accepting ready-made goals as though they were our own. Modern man is ready to take great risks when he tries to achieve the aims which are supposed to be "his"; but he is deeply afraid of taking the risk and the responsibility of giving himself his own aims. Intense activity is often mistaken for evidence of self-determined action, although we know that it may well be no more spontaneous than the behavior of an actor or a person hypnotized. When the general plot of the play is handed out, each actor can act vigorously the role he is assigned and even make up his lines and certain details of the action by himself. Yet he is only playing a role that has been handed over to him.

The particular difficulty in recognizing to what extent our wishes —and our thoughts and feelings as well—are not really our own but put into us from the outside, is closely linked up with the problem of authority and freedom. In the course of modern history the authority of the Church has been replaced by that of the State, that of the State by that of conscience, and in our era, the latter has been replaced by the anonymous authority of common sense and public opinion as instruments of conformity. Because we have freed ourselves of the older overt forms of authority, we do not see that we have become the prey of a new kind of authority. We have become automatons who live under the illusion of being self-willing individuals. This illusion helps the individual to remain unaware of his insecurity, but this is all the help such an illusion can give. Basically the self of the individual is weakened, so that he feels powerless and extremely insecure. He lives in a world to which he has lost genuine relatedness and in which everybody and everything has become instrumentalized, where he has become a part of the machine that his hands have built. He thinks, feels, and wills what he believes he is supposed to think, feel, and will; in this very process he loses his self upon which all genuine security of a free individual must be built.

The loss of the self has increased the necessity to conform, for it results in a profound doubt of one's own identity. If I am nothing but what I believe I am supposed to be—who am "I"? We have seen how the doubt about one's own self started with the breakdown of the medieval order in which the individual had had an unquestionable place in a fixed order. The identity of the individual has been a major problem of modern philosophy since Descartes. Today we take for granted that we are we. Yet the doubt about ourselves still exists, or has even grown. In his plays Pirandello has given expression to this feeling of modern man. He starts with the question: Who am I? What proof have I for my own identity other than the continuation of my physical self? His answer is not like Descartes' —the affirmation of the individual self—but its denial: I have no identity, there is no self excepting the one which is the reflex of what others expect me to be: I am "as you desire me."

This loss of identity then makes it still more imperative to conform; it means that one can be sure of oneself only if one lives up to the expectations of others. If we do not live up to this picture we not only risk disapproval and increased isolation, but we risk losing the identity of our personality, which means jeopardizing sanity.

By conforming with the expectations of others, by not being different, these doubts about one's own identity are silenced and a certain security is gained. However, the price paid is high. Giving up spontaneity and individuality results in a thwarting of life. Psychologically the automaton, while being alive biologically, is dead emotionally and mentally. While he goes through the motions of living, his life runs through his hands like sand. Behind a front of satisfaction and optimism modern man is deeply unhappy; as a matter of fact, he is on the verge of desperation. He desperately clings to the notion of individuality; he wants to be "different," and he has no greater recommendation of anything than that "it is different." We are informed of the individual name of the railroad clerk we buy our ticket from; handbags, playing cards, and portable radios are "personalized," by having the initials of the owner put on them. All this indicates the hunger for "difference" and yet these are almost the last vestiges of individuality that are left. Modern man is starved for life. But since, being an automaton, he cannot experience life in the sense of spontaneous activity he takes as surrogate any kind of excitement and thrill: the thrill of drinking, of sports, of vicariously living the excitements of fictitious persons on the screen.

What then is the meaning of freedom for modern man?

He has become free from the external bonds that would prevent him from doing and thinking as he sees fit. He would be free to act according to his own will, if he knew what he wanted, thought, and felt. But he does not know. He conforms to anonymous authorities and adopts a self which is not his. The more he does this, the more powerless he feels, the more is he forced to conform. In spite of a veneer of optimism and initiative, modern man is overcome by a profound feeling of powerlessness which makes him gaze toward approaching catastrophes as though he were paralyzed.

Looked at superficially, people appear to function well enough in economic and social life; yet it would be dangerous to overlook the deep-seated unhappiness behind that comforting veneer. If life loses its meaning because it is not lived, man becomes desperate. People do not die quietly from physical starvation; they do not die quietly from psychic starvation either. If we look only at the economic needs as far as the "normal" person is concerned, if we do not see the unconscious suffering of the average automatized person, then we fail to see the danger that threatens our culture from its human basis: the readiness to accept any ideology and any leader, if only he promises excitement and offers a political structure and symbols which allegedly give meaning and order to an individual's life. The despair of the human automaton is fertile soil for the political purposes of Fascism.

Problems for Thought and Writing

I

1. Do you agree with Fromm that contemporary American society is "fertile soil for the rise of Fascism"? If not, why not? If so, give examples other than those presented by Fromm in support of the thesis.
2. Observe Fromm's use of the words "repress" and "suppress" throughout the essay. Is he using them synonymously? If not, does he distinguish clearly between their meanings?
3. What does the author mean by "originality"?
4. Fromm deplores the way in which we are taught early in life not to trust or guide ourselves by our first impressions. What is the alternative? Does he offer any safeguards?
5. How would Fromm define "true" emotion as distinct from the "cheap and insincere sentimentality," i.e., "false" emotion, that he refers to on page 201?
6. Do you agree with Fromm that "Christianity has made death unreal and tried to comfort the unhappy individual by promises of a life after death" (page 202)? Is he guilty of oversimplification here? Is this a just or adequate representation of the Christian attitude toward death? Support your answer.
7. Can you think of other examples in contemporary society that will support the author's assertion that "Our own era simply denies death. . . ." (page 202)?
8. What is the fundamental *paradox* the author is seeking to point out in modern American society?
9. Fromm suggests that our elaborate funerals are a substitute for other forms of immortality. If you agree, how would you illustrate and defend the point? How would you refute it?
10. Does the cult of the "pleasing personality" that can be snapped on and off like a light switch tend to breed hypocrisy or friendliness? Does it discredit the expression of true emotion? See Richard Altick, "Sentimentality," page 109.

II

11. Define the following terms: pseudo-psychiatry, psychoanalysis, condescension, metaphysical, integration, automaton.
12. Analyze closely the paragraph, on pages 203-4, in which Fromm denies that all truth is relative. Is there any inconsistency between this position and his observation that the search for truth is rooted in self-interest?
13. Would you classify this selection as a closely reasoned, amply illustrated evaluation of a culture, or a series of angry blasts from a malcontent? Try outlining it before deciding.

∼

THE GREATEST MAN
IN THE WORLD*

James Thurber

Looking back on it now, from the vantage point of 1950, one can only marvel that it hadn't happened long before it did. The United States of America had been, ever since Kitty Hawk, blindly constructing the elaborate petard by which, sooner or later, it must be hoist. It was inevitable that some day there would come roaring out of the skies a national hero of insufficient intelligence, background, and character successfully to endure the mounting orgies of glory prepared for aviators who stayed up a long time or flew a great distance. Both Lindbergh and Byrd, fortunately for national decorum and international amity, had been gentlemen; so had our other famous aviators. They wore their laurels gracefully, withstood the awful weather of publicity, married excellent women, usually of fine family, and quietly retired to private life and the enjoyment of their varying fortunes. No untoward incidents, on a worldwide scale, marred the perfection of their conduct on the perilous heights of fame. The exception to the rule was, however, bound to occur and it did, in July, 1937, when Jack ("Pal") Smurch, erstwhile mechanic's helper in a small garage in Westfield, Iowa, flew a second-hand, single-motored Bresthaven Dragon-Fly III monoplane all the way around the world, without stopping.

Never before in the history of aviation had such a flight as Smurch's ever been dreamed of. No one had even taken seriously the weird floating auxiliary gas tanks, invention of the mad New Hampshire professor of astronomy, Dr. Charles Lewis Gresham, upon which Smurch placed full reliance. When the garage worker, a slightly built, surly, unprepossessing young man of twenty-two, appeared at Roosevelt Field in early July, 1937, slowly chewing a great quid of scrap tobacco, and announced, "Nobody ain't seen no flyin' yet," the newspapers touched briefly and satirically upon his projected twenty-five-thousand-mile flight. Aëronautical and automotive experts dismissed the idea curtly, implying that it was a hoax, a publicity stunt.

The rusty, battered, second-hand plane wouldn't go. The Gresham auxiliary tanks wouldn't work. It was simply a cheap joke.

Smurch, however, after calling on a girl in Brooklyn who worked in the flap-folding department of a large paper-box factory, a girl whom he later described as his "sweet patootie," climbed nonchalantly into his ridiculous plane at dawn of the memorable seventh of July, 1937, spit a curve of tobacco juice into the still air, and took off, carrying with him only a gallon of bootleg gin and six pounds of salami.

When the garage boy thundered out over the ocean the papers were forced to record, in all seriousness, that a mad, unknown young man—his name was variously misspelled—had actually set out upon a preposterous attempt to span the world in a rickety, one-engined contraption, trusting to the long-distance refuelling device of a crazy schoolmaster. When, nine days later, without having stopped once, the tiny plane appeared above San Francisco Bay, headed for New York, spluttering and choking, to be sure, but still magnificently and miraculously aloft, the headlines, which long since had crowded everything else off the front page—even the shooting of the Governor of Illinois by the Vileti gang—swelled to unprecedented size, and the news stories began to run to twenty-five and thirty columns. It was noticeable, however, that the accounts of the epoch-making flight touched rather lightly upon the aviator himself. This was not because facts about the hero as a man were too meagre, but because they were too complete.

Reporters, who had been rushed out to Iowa when Smurch's plane was first sighted over the little French coast town of Serly-le-Mer, to dig up the story of the great man's life, had promptly discovered that the story of his life could not be printed. His mother, a sullen short-order cook in a shack restaurant on the edge of a tourists' camping ground near Westfield, met all inquiries as to her son with an angry "Ah, the hell with him; I hope he drowns." His father appeared to be in jail somewhere for stealing spotlights and laprobes from tourists' automobiles; his young brother, a weak-minded lad, had but recently escaped from the Preston, Iowa, Reformatory and was already wanted in several Western towns for the theft of money-order blanks from post offices. These alarming discoveries were still piling up at the very time that Pal Smurch, the greatest hero of the twentieth century, blear-eyed, dead for sleep, half-starved, was piloting his crazy junk-heap high above the region in which the lamentable story of his private life was being unearthed, headed for New York and a greater glory than any man of his time had ever known.

The necessity for printing some account in the papers of the young man's career and personality had led to a remarkable predicament. It was of course impossible to reveal the facts, for a tremendous popular feeling in favor of the young hero had sprung up, like a grass fire, when he was halfway across Europe on his flight around the globe. He was, therefore, described as a modest chap, taciturn, blond, popular with his friends, popular with girls. The only available snapshot of Smurch, taken at the wheel of a phony automobile in a cheap photo studio at an amusement park, was touched up so that the little vulgarian looked quite handsome. His twisted leer was smoothed into a pleasant smile. The truth was, in this way, kept from the youth's ecstatic compatriots; they did not dream that the Smurch family was despised and feared by its neighbors in the obscure Iowa town, nor that the hero himself, because of numerous unsavory exploits, had come to be regarded in Westfield as a nuisance and a menace. He had, the reporters discovered, once knifed the principal of his high school—not mortally, to be sure, but he had knifed him; and on another occasion, surprised in the act of stealing an altarcloth from a church, he had bashed the sacristan over the head with a pot of Easter lilies; for each of these offenses he had served a sentence in the reformatory.

Inwardly, the authorities, both in New York and in Washington, prayed that an understanding Providence might, however awful such a thing seemed, bring disaster to the rusty, battered plane and its illustrious pilot, whose unheard-of flight had aroused the civilized world to hosannas of hysterical praise. The authorities were convinced that the character of the renowned aviator was such that the limelight of adulation was bound to reveal him to all the world as a congenital hooligan mentally and morally unequipped to cope with his own prodigious fame. "I trust," said the Secretary of State, at one of many secret Cabinet meetings called to consider the national dilemma, "I trust that his mother's prayer will be answered," by which he referred to Mrs. Emma Smurch's wish that her son might be drowned. It was, however, too late for that—Smurch had leaped the Atlantic and then the Pacific as if they were millponds. At three minutes after two o'clock on the afternoon of July 17, 1937, the garage boy brought his idiotic plane into Roosevelt Field for a perfect three-point landing.

It had, of course, been out of the question to arrange a modest little reception for the greatest flier in the history of the world. He was received at Roosevelt Field with such elaborate and pretentious ceremonies as rocked the world. Fortunately, however, the worn and spent hero promptly swooned, had to be removed bodily from his plane, and was spirited from the field without having opened his mouth once. Thus he did not jeopardize the dignity of this first reception, a reception illumined by the presence of the Secretaries of War and the Navy, Mayor Michael J. Moriarity of New York, the Premier of Canada, Governors Fanniman, Groves, McFeely, and Critchfield, and a brilliant array of European diplomats. Smurch did not, in fact, come to in time to take part in the gigantic hullabaloo arranged at City Hall for the next day. He was rushed to a secluded nursing home and confined to bed. It was nine days before he was able to get up, or to be more exact, before he was permitted to get up. Meanwhile the greatest minds in the country, in solemn assembly, had arranged a secret conference of city, state, and government officials, which Smurch was to attend for the purpose of being instructed in the ethics and behavior of heroism.

On the day that the little mechanic was finally allowed to get up and dress and, for the first time in two weeks, took a great chew of tobacco, he was permitted to receive the newspapermen—this by way of testing him out. Smurch did not wait for questions. "Youse guys," he said—and the *Times* man winced—"youse guys can tell the cock-eyed world dat I put it over on Lindbergh, see? Yeh—an' made an ass o' them two frogs." The "two frogs" was a reference to a pair of gallant French fliers who, in attempting a flight only halfway round the world, had, two weeks before, unhappily been lost at sea. The *Times* man was bold enough, at this point, to sketch out for Smurch the accepted formula for interviews in cases of this kind; he explained that there should be no arrogant statements belittling the achievements of other heroes, particularly heroes of foreign nations. "Ah, the hell with that," said Smurch. "I did it, see? I did it, an' I'm talkin' about it." And he did talk about it.

None of this extraordinary interview was, of course, printed. On the contrary, the newspapers, already under the disciplined direction of a secret directorate created for the occasion and composed of statesmen and editors, gave out to a panting and restless world that "Jacky," as he had been arbitrarily nicknamed, would consent to say only that he was very happy and that anyone could have done what

he did. "My achievement has been, I fear, slightly exaggerated," the
Times man's article had him protest, with a modest smile. These
newspaper stories were kept from the hero, a restriction which did
not serve to abate the rising malevolence of his temper. The situation was, indeed, extremely grave, for Pal Smurch was, as he kept
insisting, "rarin' to go." He could not much longer be kept from a
nation clamorous to lionize him. It was the most desperate crisis
the United States of America had faced since the sinking of the
Lusitania.

On the afternoon of the twenty-seventh of July, Smurch was spirited
away to a conference-room in which were gathered mayors, governors,
government officials, behaviorist psychologists, and editors. He gave
them each a limp, moist paw and a brief unlovely grin. "Hah ya?"
he said. When Smurch was seated, the Mayor of New York arose
and, with obvious pessimism, attempted to explain what he must say
and how he must act when presented to the world, ending his talk
with a high tribute to the hero's courage and integrity. The Mayor
was followed by Governor Fanniman of New York, who, after a
touching declaration of faith, introduced Cameron Spottiswood, Second Secretary of the American Embassy in Paris, the gentleman
selected to coach Smurch in the amenities of public ceremonies.
Sitting in a chair, with a soiled yellow tie in his hand and his shirt
open at the throat, unshaved, smoking a rolled cigarette, Jack Smurch
listened with a leer on his lips. "I get ya, I get ya," he cut in, nastily.
"Ya want me to ack like a softy, huh? Ya want me to ack like
that ―― ―― baby-faced Lindbergh, huh? Well, nuts to that,
see?" Everyone took in his breath sharply; it was a sigh and a hiss.
"Mr. Lindbergh," began a United States Senator, purple with rage,
"and Mr. Byrd—" Smurch, who was paring his nails with a jack-
knife, cut in again. "Byrd!" he exclaimed. "Aw fa God's sake, dat
big—" Somebody shut off his blasphemies with a sharp word. A
newcomer had entered the room. Everyone stood up, except Smurch,
who, still busy with his nails, did not even glance up. "Mr. Smurch,"
said someone sternly, "the President of the United States!" It had
been thought that the presence of the Chief Executive might have a
chastening effect upon the young hero, and the former had been,
thanks to the remarkable coöperation of the press, secretly brought
to the obscure conference-room.

A great, painful silence fell. Smurch looked up, waved a hand at
the President. "How ya comin'?" he asked, and began rolling a fresh

cigarette. The silence deepened. Someone coughed in a strained way. "Geez, it's hot, ain't it?" said Smurch. He loosened two more shirt buttons, revealing a hairy chest and the tattooed word "Sadie" enclosed in a stenciled heart. The great and important men in the room, faced by the most serious crisis in recent American history, exchanged worried frowns. Nobody seemed to know how to proceed. "Come awn, come awn," said Smurch. "Let's get the hell out of here! When do I start cuttin' in on de parties, huh? And what's they goin' to be *in* it?" He rubbed a thumb and forefinger together meaningly. "Money!" exclaimed a state senator, shocked, pale. "Yeh, money," said Pal, flipping his cigarette out of a window. "An' big money." He began rolling a fresh cigarette. "Big money," he repeated, frowning over the rice paper. He tilted back in his chair, and leered at each gentleman, separately, the leer of an animal that knows its power, the leer of a leopard loose in a bird-and-dog shop. "Aw fa God's sake, let's get some place where it's cooler," he said. "I been cooped up plenty for three weeks!"

Smurch stood up and walked over to an open window, where he stood staring down into the street, nine floors below. The faint shouting of newsboys floated up to him. He made out his name. "Hot dog!" he cried, grinning, ecstatic. He leaned out over the sill. "You tell 'em, babies!" he shouted down. "Hot diggity dog!" In the tense little knot of men standing behind him, a quick, mad impulse flared up. An unspoken word of appeal, of command, seemed to ring through the room. Yet it was deadly silent. Charles K. L. Brand, secretary to the Mayor of New York City, happened to be standing nearest Smurch; he looked inquiringly at the President of the United States. The President, pale, grim, nodded shortly. Brand, a tall, powerfully built man, once a tackle at Rutgers, stepped forward, seized the greatest man in the world by his left shoulder and the seat of his pants, and pushed him out the window.

"My God, he's fallen out the window!" cried a quick-witted editor.

"Get me out of here!" cried the President. Several men sprang to his side and he was hurriedly escorted out of a door toward a side-entrance of the building. The editor of the Associated Press took charge, being used to such things. Crisply he ordered certain men to leave, others to stay; quickly he outlined a story which all the papers were to agree on, sent two men to the street to handle that end of the tragedy, commanded a Senator to sob and two Congressmen to go to pieces nervously. In a word, he skillfully set the stage for the gigantic task that was to follow, the task of breaking to a grief-stricken world the sad story of the untimely, accidental death of its most illustrious and spectacular figure.

The funeral was, as you know, the most elaborate, the finest, the solemnest, and the saddest ever held in the United States of America. The monument in Arlington Cemetery, with its clean white shaft of marble and the simple device of a tiny plane carved on its base, is a place for pilgrims, in deep reverence, to visit. The nations of the world paid lofty tributes to little Jacky Smurch, America's greatest hero. At a given hour there were two minutes of silence throughout the nation. Even the inhabitants of the small, bewildered town of Westfield, Iowa, observed this touching ceremony; agents of the Department of Justice saw to that. One of them was especially assigned to stand grimly in the doorway of a little shack restaurant on the edge of the tourists' camping ground just outside the town. There, under his stern scrutiny, Mrs. Emma Smurch bowed her head above two hamburger steaks sizzling on her grill—bowed her head and turned away, so that the Secret Service man could not see the twisted, strangely familiar, leer on her lips.

Problems for Thought and Writing

1. Which of the following terms best describes the tone and character of this story: invective, irony, satire, travesty, sarcasm, burlesque, lampoon? See "Problems" sections after the essays in "Humor and Satire."

2. Why has this story been included by the editors in a section entitled "Man and the Mass"? What kinship does its theme have with those of Auden, Ortega, Fromm, or Whyte?

3. Explain why we laugh at the violent disposal of Smurch. Are we glad to be rid of him? Is it that we recognize the impossibility of such a solution? Are we just surprised? Are we really laughing at the officials and ignoring Smurch? Try to explore this complicated problem.

4. Suppose Smurch did not have the mother and background he did. Would he still be unacceptable as a hero?

5. What effect does the expression "quick-witted" have (page 215)?

6. What do you take to be the *purpose* of the story? Is it merely to amuse?

∼

THE NEW ILLITERACY* *William H. Whyte, Jr.*

We hear much about the reawakening interest in the humanities, the new appreciation of the generalness in the liberal arts, the growing dissatisfaction with overspecialization. Maybe so. But these signs are minute, I suggest, to those coming from the other direction. I offer the proposition that the trends that have been working against the humanities are likely to increase, not decrease, in the decade ahead.

I make the proposition because of a belief that the low estate of the humanities is intimately related with a philosophy of society that is coming to be the dominant cultural movement in the United States. The decline in English majors, the vocationalizing of college curriculums—these are no isolated phenomena; basically they are all of a piece with a great many other superficially different problems. They are the outward manifestations of a cohesive ideology, the effects of which can just as easily be traced in such disparate fields as advertising, popular magazine fiction, and life in suburbia.

Wherever it may be found and in whatever form the new illiteracy is nourished by several simple articles of faith. The essence of them is this: First, the individual exists only as a member of a group. He fulfils himself only as he works with others; of himself he is nothing. His tensions, his frustrations—these are penalties for his failure at adjustment, and they should, at all costs, be exercised. Ideally there should be no conflict between man and society, and the good world that we must strive for is one in which all are harmonious with one another and in which the measure of a man's activity is how well he contributes to that harmony. Above all else he must *get along*.

Now, is this simply a way of describing a point of view, a way of talking about uniformity? Not at all. To a degree people have always been conformists and always will be; what we are talking about is the open, articulate rationalization of conformity into something almost akin to a religion. For these tenets, these propositions are openly, indeed evangelistically, spoken, and they are being spoken more and more often. This is the heartland of the new illiteracy. In

* From *The Saturday Review*, November 21, 1953. Reprinted by permission.

each field—be it industry, education, advertising—leading thinkers of
the new illiteracy phrase the lesson with different vocabularies, all
varying in the degree of fatuousness but all in the central moral
united.

Let's take industry first. Its leaders all acknowledge, indeed
boast, a debt to science. For if it is true that adjustment to the system
is the desideratum then it follows that in proper methodology lies
salvation, and a good many social scientists who ought to know better
are busily at work dignifying this. They are not to be laughed away;
horrendous as their jargon may be, it is a sort of uniting force which
ennobles what so many people would like to hear. It is, to borrow
a word, a highly interdisciplinary vocabulary.

As an example of how this relationship can work let's take a look at
advertising for a moment. Advertising, as most of its more intelligent
practitioners freely concede, is badly written and lacks imagination.
What is the answer—more imagination, better writing?

Ah, but this is too simple. We are not dealing with the old verities,
we are told. We are dealing with mass communication. Let us not,
then, bother to study the lessons of the dead past. Ours is a scientific
problem; it is essentially the determination of consensus. So the need
is not for writers; the need is for technicians of mass communication,
technologists of semantics, men skilled in action research and scientific
measurement. There is, of course, one apparent drawback to polls
and surveys: they are based on what is already existent. They test
only what has been tried before; they cannot find out from people
whether they would like something new, something untried, for people cannot answer what they do not know. But no matter. A speaker
at a highly respectable conference at Columbia University explained
it this way: "The belief is still general that outstanding pieces of writing are produced under a mysterious force called inspiration. The
literary approach to writing, therefore, leads to a dead end. Science
offers a way through all these difficulties . . . The technologist must
sacrifice the possibility of superior communication in exchange for
certainty that his work will meet a commercial standard."

If this advice were cynical it wouldn't be so bad. The trouble is,
it isn't cynical. This is not mere counsel to lower your sights so you
can make more money; it is advice on how to help society, and the
moral is one a lot of people are glad to subscribe to. Nowadays if you
prostitute the language, if you assault the dignity of the individual—if
you strap a woman in a chair and place electrodes on her to chart her
reactions to advertising (as a recent picture in *Advertising Age*

demonstrated)—if you do these things you need feel no twinge of guilty conscience: you are getting the consensus. Soap operas? As a recent survey by the University of Chicago's Lloyd Warner demonstrated, these can be looked on as a service to society; illusory as their content may be, they help a large segment of our population adjust.

Let's look at another sector for a moment: the corporation. What cues are being offered? What has made for the emergence of the corporation as the dominant organization form in our society? It is due a great deal to the imagination and vigor of its past leaders. Will its future depend on these qualities too? A great many corporation people think so. A great many others, however, do not, and a *very* large proportion of the trainees coming in agree with them.

This is not the time to examine the way the human-relations philosophy has evolved since the famous experiments of Elton Mayo back in the Twenties. But it is fair to simplify to the extent of saying that what began as a healthy response to the needs of our increasingly complex organization is fast degenerating into something else. Today, as many interpret it, human relations means that the worker—whether he is in the shop or in the carpeted office—fulfils himself by making his peace with the system. It is the constant, he the variable. The most important thing in an organization is the maintenance of its equilibrium. Where is the spark to come from? From the sheer harmony of the group. To a degree these ideas are correct. For better or worse, we are living in an age of great organization. To express one's self in an organization one must be able to get along with other people. So be it. But how much—where do you draw the line?

I think a very clear case can be made that in far too many corporations, and in far too many of the courses that prepare men for the corporation, the emphasis on getting along has become almost deafening. Conversely, more and more the inner quality is deprecated. Let me give you an example. In connection with a study *Fortune* has just completed on junior executive training, we wrote 150 corporation presidents and asked them a very tough question. We asked the same question of 150 personnel directors. We acknowledged that any organization needs all kinds of people. But we did ask them this: if they *had* to choose, which of the following would they lean towards: (1) the adaptable administrator, skilled in managerial skills and concerned primarily with human relations and the techniques of making the corporation a smooth-working team; or (2) a man with strong personal convictions who is not shy about making decisions that will upset tested procedures and his colleagues.

The vote: the presidents split roughly fifty-fifty; the personnel men, three-to-one in favor of the administrator.

What was particularly interesting, however, were the comments that accompanied a great many of the letters favoring the team player. To paraphrase, they argued that, though imagination and vigor were often desirable, they were qualities that would be best relegated to staff positions. That is to say, the real leadership of the organization would not concern itself with new ideas except as a sort of neutral judge. The people who did concern themselves with them would be kept out of harm's way, sort of captive screwballs, whose qualities would be patronized when things got a bit dull around the shop. "We used to look primarily for brilliance," one president wrote us, "but now we don't care if you're a Phi Beta Kappa or a Tau Beta Phi. We want a well-rounded person who can handle well-rounded people."

We talked to a great many junior executives, and we were dismayed to find out how very thoroughly so many of them agreed. It is the extrovert qualities that they felt were important. "I'd sacrifice brilliance to human understanding every time," one told us. The things that set a man dreaming, the big questions that provoke his curiosity, the lone, individual speculation—no longer are these needed. We have now reached an age when they have become expendable. "All the basic creative work in engineering," one trainee told us, "has already been done. The only kind of research that counts is team research, directed at immediate, practical problems."

Not so long ago I saw a very interesting documentary film put out by the Monsanto Chemical Company. It was a pretty good film, but what did it have to say about Monsanto's research—much of which has been most imaginative? In one part of the picture you see five young men in white coats conferring around a microscope. The voice on the sound track rings out boldly, "No geniuses here. Just a bunch of good Americans working together."

What's wrong with genius? We asked a number of trainees how they thought a man like Steinmetz would fit in today. "I think we could straighten out his unfortunate characteristics."

Let me recapitulate a moment. There are three points that I am trying to document.

First, that the belief is growing that the health of our society depends upon increasing adjustment by the individual to the consensus of the group. Second, that this is not simply an unwitting yen for conformity, but a philosophy—a philosophy actively advocated by a sizable proportion of the leadership in each sector of our society. Third, and most important of all, these people are not pioneers; they are not a small band of revolutionaries working against the grain of our culture. Their doctrine is now orthodoxy.

To illustrate, let's take a look at the new suburbia for a moment. In the new package suburbs growing up outside our great cities we find a life so communal that they are strikingly like the Owenite and Fournier utopias of the early 1800's. To use a word the young suburbanites utter frequently, people in the rental courts and ranch-house superblocks learn to be "outgoing." Rarely does a person have to be alone; as a matter of fact, it is practically impossible. Every moment of the day there is a civic meeting of some kind: block parties, afternoon coffees, canasta, Stanley home parties.

A great deal of this is very healthy—a way of gaining roots in an increasingly transient life, a way of finding something meaningful to do. But some of the effects are not healthy: privacy has become clandestine. To be alone, to withdraw into one's self, to express urges not synonymous with the group's—when a person does these things (and everyone has the impulse) they tend to feel a little guilty about it. If suburbia has a neurosis it is the fear of being neurotic.

Well, now, just wait a minute, you might say—isn't this simply a temporary phenomenon; isn't this yen for consensus merely an expedient dictated by the kind of housing they find themselves in now?

A good way to answer the question is to have a look at their schools. Here, if nowhere else, the young suburbanites must declare their philosophy. It is they who have set up the schools, and they have spent much time and thought on their direction.

A pretty good example is the new high school in the package suburb of Park Forest, thirty-two miles south of Chicago. They are very proud of it; physically it is a spankingly modern, one-and-one-half-million-dollar plant. And they are proud of its curriculum as well as its plant.

The curriculum is by no means unique to Park Forest High—School Superintendent Eric Baber speaks very much like many superintendents elsewhere and his writings do not show unorthodoxy so much as a deep grasp of contemporary educational literature. The trouble with U.S. education, Baber has told the parents time and again, is that it is concentrated far too much on the intellectual aspect of education. Even teachers' colleges, he observes sadly, still require plane geometry for admission. Except for a small coterie, he asks, of what value to most people are the traditional academic disciplines? "The so-called 'bright student' is often one of the dumbest or least apt when he gets away from his textbooks and memory work," Baber told a teachers' workshop. "This is evidenced by the fact that many $20,000 to $100,000-a-year jobs in business, sales, sports, radio . . . are held by persons with I.Q.'s of less than ninety."

Baber is not actually against intelligence. He believes it should be channeled toward real-life, vocational needs more than to the academic requirements of the colleges.

Of the total of seventy subjects offered only one-half are in traditional academic subjects—and the latter, furthermore, are by no means ivory tower. Of seven offerings in English available to juniors and seniors the one concentrated on grammar, rhetoric, and composition is a one-semester "refresher course . . . for students who feel the need for additional preparation." Of more appeal to teen-agers, perhaps, will be the full-year courses in journalism and in speech, for which, in the "communication laboratory," facilities are available for practical things like radio and TV debating.

The seventy formal subject offerings by no means exhaust the life-adjustment curriculum. Today, Baber believes, the schools must assume more responsibility for the *total* growth of the child. Conceivably this could be left to other agencies—to the family or the church or society itself. Nevertheless, through such media as courses in family group living (twelfth-grade elective) and "doing" sessions in actual situations the school is going to tackle it. "They must have actual experiences in solving problems that have meaning for *them*," Baber says. "Ours is an age of group action."

On the premise of the school's philosophy the parents seem to be in accord with Baber and one another; if one wishes to quarrel with that philosophy he must quarrel with the people themselves. The educators may be in the vanguard, but at Park Forest they are bucking no trends. For what is it that parents want most emphasized by the school? They were asked just such a question, and when they wrote the answer in their own words one note was sounded more often than any other. The primary job of the high school should be to teach students how to be citizens to get along with other people.

It is in this attitude, I submit, that the real problem of the humanities lies, and we would do well not to underestimate its force.

If we are to halt the new illiteracy we must understand that it appeal, because it seems to answer some very vital contemporary needs. It *is* an age of great organization; ours *is* a society in which most persons work in collective units.

Furthermore, it is important to remember that the sensitivity to the group is not a reversal of our national character so much as an extension of it. The American genius has always lain in good part in our distrust of dogma, in our flexibility, in our urge for cooperative action. As long as 100 years ago Alexis de Tocqueville (no friend of conformity) was struck by this. "The more equal social conditions become," he wrote, "the more men display this reciprocal disposition to oblige each other."

But, having noted this, can we not then—*on their own ground*—carry the offensive against the scholars of this new illiteracy? Then it will not do for them to scoff at unbelievers as people homesick for a return to a closed society in which education is restricted to a small, aristocratic elite.

The real weakness of the new illiteracy is precisely the fact that it is not suited to the times. No man is an isle unto himself, to be sure, but how John Donne would writhe if he heard who was repeating it, and why. We have reason to be proud of how well we have been able to adapt to this age of great organizations, but certainly we must not so worship these virtues as to caricature them into defects. The great problems of bureaucracy—if they are to continue vigorously—are ideas and new thoughts, and, yes, conflict. It is wretched advice that the healthy system is one in which the individual feels no conflict. Every great advance has come about, and always will, because someone was frustrated by the status quo; because somebody exercised the skepticism, the questioning, and the kind of curiosity which, to borrow a phrase, blows the lid off everything.

It is time to put the technician of the new illiteracy in his place—and that's way, way down. He is fit only to be a lackey, not a leader. He can't conjure, he can't speculate, he can't dream; I imagine he has a terrible sense of humor.

And he lacks faith. For isn't that in a way what we are talking about? What is our democracy but a testament of faith in the individual? Faith not only in our fellow laymen, but faith in our own inner resources, in man's own ability to create and to dream.

The new illiteracy would have us suppose that the whole is greater than the sum of the parts, that the system itself has a wisdom beyond the reach of ordinary mortals. But this is not so. The individual can be greater than the group and his own imagination worth a thousand graphs and studies.

I

1. William H. Whyte, Jr. (1917-   ) is one of several leading social critics—including Ortega y Gasset, Erich Fromm, and David Riesman—who have been documenting our trend toward conformity and mass culture. This was one of many articles he wrote before the appearance of his important book, *The Organization Man* (1956), but it touches in brief space on some of the book's main issues.

   After reading Whyte's article, what do you think of the "well-adjusted" man or woman as an ideal? Do you think Whyte has his problem in focus?

2. Distinguish between ordinary conformity for social survival and peace, and "the open, articulate rationalization of conformity into something almost akin to a religion." Is Whyte describing conditions as you know them? Why does he refer to these conditions as "the new illiteracy"?

3. Why is "inspiration" at odds with the scientific processes of mass communications? Is freshman English at your college or university called "communications"? Do you see this as a portent or a problem?

4. Whyte suggests that "getting the consensus" has become not just a technique of research but a moral justification for all sorts of indignities. Explain. What is he disturbed at, basically?

5. Take these two sets of virtues: (1) cooperative, good teamworker, pleasant, gets along with others, popular, well-adjusted; and (2) brilliant, a genius, original, contemplative, imaginative, thoughtful. Which would you prefer a teacher to put after your name on a letter of recommendation?

6. Does your campus society scorn (or try to "help") the introvert, the "loner," the man preferring books to people? Has "privacy become clandestine" in your campus world?

7. Do you agree with Superintendent Eric Baber that intelligence should be channeled toward "real-life vocational needs more than to the academic requirements of the colleges"?

8. See John Donne's "Meditation," page 448. Compare his meaning ("no man is an island") with that of the supporters of "the new illiteracy."

9. When Whyte says that the "technician of the new illiteracy" "lacks faith," is he not obliquely saying that an important segment of American people no longer believe in the basic tenets of democracy? (See Jefferson, page 159.)

II

10. Define or identify: lackey, Alexis de Tocqueville, consensus, rhetoric, suburbia, tenets, evangelistically, desideratum, semantics, coterie.

11. Is Whyte's style journalistic, literary, historical? How can we characterize it?

~

6 People and Population

A. CULTURE AND LEBENSRAUM

THE INDIVIDUAL AND THE MASS*

Nicola Chiaromonte

If it is true that we live in a mass society, we must immediately admit one fact: there are some individuals who are more affected by it than others, but there are not, nor can there be, privileged persons. There cannot be, on the one hand, the anonymous and vulgar mass which lacks idealistic motives, and on the other a few individuals who succeed in keeping intact their nobility and the cult of the highest values. The mass and the few are inextricably mixed. At certain times we feel ourselves to be *individuals* endowed with feelings, needs, and spiritual demands which are not those of the anonymous crowd. And we speak of the mass situation in so far as we experience the confusion between, and the mutual involvement of, the anonymous and the personal. We feel a contrast between our individual beings and a social situation in which necessity, automatism, and collective servitude are especially refractory both to the individual's personal demands and to the "aristocratic values" which (at least at times) the individual seeks and by which he sometimes feels himself inspired.

What is a "mass situation"? Simplifying greatly, one can say that it is a social situation in which the experience of collective necessity is very strong. Before developing his famous analysis of the "revolt of the masses" Ortega y Gasset "places" the phenomenon of the "mass" by drawing the reader's attention to what he calls a "visual experience"—"the fact of agglomeration, of plenitude . . . The cities are full of inhabitants, the houses full of tenants, the hotels full of guests, the cafes full of customers, the parks full of strolling people, the wait-

* From *Dissent*, Spring, 1957, translated by Paul Alpers. Used by permission.

ing rooms of famous doctors full of patients, the theaters full of spectators, and the beaches full of bathers."

"What previously was, in general, no problem, now begins to be an everyday one, namely to *find room*," he observes. Now, if he had dwelt upon this experience of agglomeration, of the crowd, of *not finding room*, he would perhaps have led us to the heart of the "mass situation."

Even if we treat it in his terms, as extremely simple and commonplace, this experience is not, in the first place, purely "visual": it is also spiritual. It signifies for us the *essential* way in which the individual comes in contact with the life of others—or rather, of *everybody*. This becomes clear once we recognize it as a fact in the life of the individual consciousness, rather than as an external fact.

Not finding room is an agonizing experience. It means to feel oneself shut out, or at least to risk that; the others are already there, they occupy all, or almost all, the available space. To find room, an effort is necessary; one is obliged to make room for oneself. The struggle is not a struggle for life in general; on an astoundingly humble level, we must fight to occupy the little space which we need, which in some sense belongs to us, since we have the same right to it as others do. But no one guarantees it to us, apparently, since the simple presence of others in a crowd obstructs and prevents it. And it is also clear that the others have the same right as we do.

This experience does not occur merely on certain intermittent and rare occasions. It is regularly repeated in hundreds of instances, whenever, in fact, we come into contact with collective existence, instead of remaining in the circle of private relations between individuals. It is an absolutely typical and fundamental experience, more fundamental than the situations themselves in which we undergo it (work, search for material necessities, relations with bureaucratic machinery, participation in political life, amusements)—since one repeats substantially the same experience in each one of these instances.

Nor is this a purely physical fact (and even less is it completely "visual") concerning space and material necessities. It is enough to say, "finding room becomes a problem" to become aware that this implies a spiritual situation, and, precisely, a situation of preliminary hostility towards the others, those who take up the space and threaten not to let us have even the indispensable minimum of it. This hostility, on the other hand, is immediately contradicted by the evident fact that the others are not there to keep us from being ourselves, but because they are looking for what we are looking, and are equally hindered and impeded by the crowd. This hostility, then, is unreasonable and has no right to show itself. But to recognize this does not wipe out the feeling any more than it calms the anxiety to "find room": it only represses and muffles the feeling, which continues to lie, intact, at the bottom.

Furthermore, the experience of the crowd is not freely chosen. One is in a crowd on the street, on public conveyances, in a movie, in a stadium, not because one has decided to mix with the crowd, but because one cannot help it. One cannot avoid submitting to the numerous bondages of organization and bureaucracy which life in common imposes; one cannot escape even during leisure.

The situation which follows from this concerns everyone, the most refined intellectual as well as the most humble worker. Not even the economically privileged individual escapes. The way in which he enjoys his advantages depends, in fact, on the way in which others must seek to satisfy their needs.

Actually, it is always possible to avoid to some extent the material bondage imposed by collective life. But one cannot escape the predicament of collective living in its spiritual aspect.

Daily participation in "mass" life can seem occasional and transient —limited to certain moments and therefore analogous to the automatic way in which we obey the needs of the body. (Equating the needs of the body and relations with our fellows is in itself a serious fact!) But in any event, if instead of looking at these moments from the outside, as unimportant intervals of time, we try to think of them from the inside, as moments of life and of consciousness, these, let us say, passive moments will no longer seem so indifferent.

Immersed in the crowd, the individual feels himself a unit among many interchangeable units. And this, if you think about it, is already the beginning of a dissociation which does not stop here. In his family and the circle of his friends and acquaintances, the individual never feels himself a mere unit. Besides, it is all very well to think that once having left the crowd, one regains all one's individuality, whole and differentiated. But in the meanwhile, one has been aware of an elementary identity with the others which overcomes and wipes out every personal difference as well as every shade of individual thought.

It therefore seems legitimate to inquire whether he who leaves the crowd after feeling himself confused in it is, in truth, the same individual as before; whether he has the same ideas of himself and of his own ineffable quality as he had; whether indeed he has the right to retain such an idea and whether, by being too sure of it, he does not risk forming an idea of himself which is too favorable, too vaporous and idealistic.

This inquiry may seem idle. But when we reason as if the indistinct communication with others, imposed on us by our daily life, injures in no way our individuality or the quality of our "values," our reasoning implies an assumption which is not so simple: that those moments have no importance, are moments effectively indifferent. The trouble is that a great enough number of unimportant moments and indifferent acts gives us the precise image of the perfect *mass-man*—the man whose existence has a minimum of importance and who passively submits to this fact without even recognizing it.

Even on occasions of little weight (like those given as examples), the experience of the crowd is not limited to the feeling of anonymity. Indeed, to be precise, it is not we who feel anonymous in the crowd, it is the others who are anonymous to us. However, we know that the same thing happens to us in the eyes of others. In reality, no one is anonymous, but we all find ourselves in a situation of anonymity. It is because of this fact (given the very ordinary necessity which has brought us together) that we can speak of ourselves as all equal, as units that are undifferentiated and interchangeable.

My relations with my neighbor then assume a rather peculiar quality: the person next to me is a stranger and, at the same time, reflects at every point my own condition. Thus reflected by him, my condition is not the "human condition" in general, my "nature" is not the human nature of the novelists and philosophers, but, so to speak, *what is left over of it*. In that situation, I am reduced to the minimum and I know it—just as I know that a panic in the crowd would be enough to crush me.

II

One outlines in this fashion a rather wretched image of individual destiny; and one also begins to perceive what is effectively the relation between a mass situation and aristocratic values—a relation of externality and suspension.

This appears clearly enough when one realizes that communication between individuals in a crowd is reduced to conventional signs, or, in any event, to a very impoverished language. It is not that I cannot have a conversation with the next fellow. But it is as if I do not know him; as if I have in common with him only a humanity which is both very much reduced and rather general; as if, in addition, I know that my relation with him is purely occasional and transient. It is evident that there is no room for a genuine exchange of feelings and thoughts between us. One could indeed say that, given the situation in which we find ourselves, we can communicate only by remaining external to each other as much as possible. We can exchange only the most conventional words. The expression of complex ideas, subtle evaluations, the communication of delicate feelings must evidently be left for other occasions.

Ever since great cities have come into existence, we have been familiar with the image of next-door neighbors who meet every day without ever knowing each other, with the singular freedom and the grave solitude involved therein. The meaningless conversations consisting of commonplaces which people exchange when they meet have already been the subject of irony. We have a picture of human relations reduced to elementary proportions, to the point where their value is negative.

Similar images have been considered comic when opposed to the ideal fullness of authentic human expressions among beings who love each other or who have an ideal in common, a noble interest, a heroic destiny. We have naturally assumed that, while on the one hand there was the common people (the "mass") which got more and more common, there remained, on the other hand, in some circles or privileged classes (the youth, or the people, or the proletariat, or even the elite) the cult of authentic feelings and of "aristocratic values"—a human "nature" more or less intact.

We did not ask ourselves if that were possible: if one could in fact imagine a society in which spiritually privileged individuals (or groups, or classes) could exist with others who were subjected to an obscure commonness, without the quality of the one being influenced by the material and spiritual way of life of the others.

To think in this way was both grossly materialistic and irredeemably idealistic—materialistic because it was imagined that in a society relations between individuals could remain purely external, physical, economic, material; idealistic because it assumed the existence (at the bottom and on the fringes of the common conditions of existence) of a soul, a consciousness, that was impervious to the quality of the relations which could be established between individuals who live together in a determined social situation.

Given the existence on the fringes of the crowd, of an elite (or of a chosen class) what will be the relations between them? What, in other words, will be their common language? At the very least it will be a mixture of the selected and of the vulgar. In which case, the spiritual privilege of the elite has already been rather trimmed down. One can, of course, make the hypothesis of a radical withdrawal of the elite from the mass; or assert that, in the last analysis, the only possible relation between the two is that of violence. But the question of language will not be clarified. How will the elite make itself understood without adapting its language (that is, its values) to the mass?

The example used here, of the situation of the individual in a crowd, may seem frivolous. It only concerns, in fact, the most obvious aspect of the "mass situation."

One must, however, keep two things in mind. The first is that the nature of a society consists wholly in the manner of being together which it offers to the individuals who compose it—the way in which they *can* experience that fundamental bond which Aristotle calls *philia*. If in the society in which we live mass conditions and mass relationships predominate, this cannot fail to affect our vision of the world and of human relations; and thereby, the efficacy of aristocratic values in collective life.

In the second place, it is evident that the mass situation is not limited to daily and occasional relations of the individual with the crowd. The crowd is neither a prime fact nor an occasional phenomenon: it is the ultimate form, the form most evident and striking, of other facts that are more weighty and serious.

Still, when these general facts are enumerated in the usual way— working conditions, relations between the individual and the State, forms of technical and economic organization—one will still not have an image of the situation as it takes shape in the individual consciousness.

The collective demands from which the phenomenon of the "mass" is born are all prosaic: so prosaic that they appear indisputable and indisputably rational. It is an elementary rationality, which has the quality both of natural necessity and constriction from above. Thus, keeping to the obvious, it is natural and inevitable that, in the crowd on a subway, everyone has his share of discomfort. But no one, except perhaps technical specialists, could say whether that was inevitable in an absolute sense or "just"—whether one could not do something better. Indeed, since it is a question of material conditions, the "better" will always seem possible, but also doubtful, since the way of obtaining the "better" remains obscure. In daily experience, the mass situation is presented as an accomplished fact, that is neither just nor unjust; it is simply there. Its modes depend, of course, on the ability and good will of those in charge. But intrinsic in the very form of collective life is "necessity."

To live in a mass society means to automatically perform acts that are not free; doing what one does, not because it is natural, and not even because one considers it positively useful, but because one wishes to avoid the complications and bad results which would come (to oneself *and* to others) from acting differently. For the single individual this can be more or less painful. That is, the advantages which one derives from yielding to collective demands instead of resisting them can be more or less great. From the point of view of conscience, however, what matters is that one feels oneself subjected to an overpowering force which comes neither from a moral norm nor from the sum of individual demands, but simply from the fact of collective existence. It is an experience of disorder maintained by laws of iron.

It is natural that the individual in a crowd should count for what he has most externally in common with others. But this is also a grave constriction, because an individual can appear as a simple physical unit only when seen from outside. From *his* point of view, he cannot help feeling himself the free and mobile center of a network of vital relations which concern not only his fellows, but also the world as a whole and the meaning of his own existence. Now the conditions of mass society have this in common: the individual's own point of view is regularly driven down to the bottom. From this, along with the inevitable passivity, comes an experience of privation and of painful tension. Not having room also means not having room for the spirit.

Such a subjugation can be accepted as "natural." But it can never be "just" in the sense in which one says, for example, that among friends it is just that everything be shared equally. The difference is that, in this last case, even an unequal division could be just, provided that all agreed to it. In the case of the great number, even an arithmetically unexceptionable division is always imposed from outside: it can appear materially equal, but we can never be sure that it is justified.

Except when he recognizes common necessity, the individual who is part of a mass feels that every individual reaction (or attempted reaction) is affective; and the affective reactions are out of place there. What is normally required of us is a certain rationality of behavior—a certain *apathy*, at least in the sense of not brusquely opposing one's own demands to those of others. Even when a mass is carried along by "collective feeling," the characteristic fact is that the individual who lets himself be carried along can no longer distinguish his own feeling from those of the others, while the passion of all of them feeds his; he is completely subjected to the occasion. To escape, a violent wrench is required, a decision to separate himself from others, a desire to be *heretical*. Or else one must submit, adapt oneself, maneuver, manage things cleverly, and wait for the propitious occasion which permits everyone to have a little more space, ease, and freedom.

We are together because "we can't help it." This is the prime fact. No one can help it. Everyone knows that the other person is constrained by the same necessity which has compelled one's self. Here is, one could say, the normative fact of the "mass situation," its justification, and even the foundation of its humanity. Only if we recognize this necessity, this common subjection, does the other person impress himself on our consciousness as a "fellow man." Otherwise, the relation between individuals in a mass is material, external, and provisional, and the next fellow appears as a profoundly alien being, or even as an obstacle and an enemy; if he were removed our situation would be easier, we would be more comfortable, there would be *more room*.

In such a situation one is infinitely distant from any sense of security; everything is precarious. The individual next to me is nothing to me, and yet he is a man like me; his closeness weighs on me, but so does mine on him; contact with my fellows is inchoate and transitory, but I never cease being with them. In this way we experience a brutal sense of the ephemeral, material, dreary, overwhelming. *Oi Brotoi.* All is momentary, there is no durable meaning either in our acts or in our thoughts. We are mortal.

The condition of the individual in the mass is completely ambiguous and obscure: caused by all and willed by no one; inevitable and "natural," but unjustifiable and artificial; solitary and unanimous; essentially unstable and dangerous, but yet reassuring; loaded with violence and hostility, but yet fraternal. What is most ambiguous and obscure is the relation between the individual and his fellow. How does one treat him, and speak of him? *Who* is he—this being who is both an intimate and a stranger? It would be almost as easy to imagine what the first men were like in the dawn of time.

What can be the relation between such an experience and "aristocratic" demands?

This—to return to the commonplace examples which we have purposely chosen—is a little like asking oneself if it is possible to read

Kant in a packed train, or to practice epicurean wisdom in the middle of a mass of peasants on strike. Obviously not, and normally one would not even have such an idea. But why not? All you need is sufficient power of concentration and self-control. However, the question would be: If in similar situations, the individual could think and act so "aristocratically" would he conceivably communicate to his neighbor the fruits of his reflections, or persuade him to imitate his conduct? Obviously, we are dealing in absurdities.

Now, if one speaks of the relationship between the mass situation and spiritual and cultural "values," the first point to clear up is that of the language which is appropriate to the relationship, of the meanings which it allows to be communicated.

When one deals with a worker in a shop, or with an individual in a subway crowd, the mass situation is much more indifferent and, at the same time, much more rigid than any other social occasion. By its very nature, it admits both the Buddhist and the Christian, the humanist and the sectarian, the crudest and the most sensitive person; it is neutral as regards any distinction of race, color, or nationality; it is democratic in the extreme. But it is also exclusive, special, and demanding: obviously there is not a Christian way to work a lathe or a humanistic way of being on a train. The Christian, humanistic, or other "values" are reserved for different, more "suitable" occasions.

From the tolerance that is intrinsic in such a situation comes the optimistic attitude in looking at "modern times." Since the modern situation is presented as a simple state of fact, in itself neutral as to the more complex demands of the individual, one deduces that, whatever its imperfections and present evils, it is always possible to "christianize" them, let us say, or "humanize" them—to make them evolve towards the "better."

The pessimists, on the other hand, see in the simplicity and in the wretchedness of the mass a virulent and active negation of complex and "noble" demands. From the point of view of the uniqueness of the individual as from that of the universal quality of "values," the situation appears to them very nearly the worst possible.

The crucial fact, however, escapes both optimists and pessimists. To speak of "values" regarding a concrete situation means to speak of modes of being, not of ideal pure relations. Now, it is as modes of being that Christian or humanistic "values" are found to be suspended, reduced to suitable proportions (that is, to some form of private cult), and therefore inoperative. Optimism seems groundless. But if one speaks of "values" in a purely spiritual sense, then, certainly, no state of fact can contradict them. On the plane of discourse, "values" remain eternally valid, for one can validly talk about them in any situation. It would be absurd to maintain that a given social situation hinders liberty of thought or the possibility, for the individual, of behaving honestly and delicately to the man next to him. What a factual condition can hinder is the natural translation of thoughts into acts; or that an individual's noble behavior represents not a private and exceptional fact, but a norm to which all *ought* to conform.

The intellectuals' pessimism refers to the discursive efficacy of moral and cultural "values" on the mass. But actually the crisis concerns more fundamental facts.

III

The individual, in his work, in politics, in the circumstances of social life, may submit to acting in a given way because "he can't help it." In behaving this way, however, he does not deny that it would be better to be able to do what he does with the conviction of doing something good and useful. But he feels forced to put aside the question of good and evil. Naturally, if the necessity to which he submitted seemed to be in absolute contradiction to his firm religious or moral convictions, he would not act as he does; he would have compunctions about doing wrong and his situation would change. But what one does because one cannot do otherwise does not appear as a moral choice, does not openly contradict any "value." Indeed, such an action is characterized by rationality, in the sense in which one considers it rational for the individual to submit to circumstances independent of his will. Thus, it hardly seems reasonable for a worker to oppose the technical demands of the factory on the grounds of conscience; or for a citizen to claim the privilege of individual liberty as against bondage to the collective organization. Such ties do not appear bad in themselves, just as being crushed in a mob does not seem degrading in itself. There is no reason to be opposed to them.

And yet the situation is obscure and troubling.

The question of doing right or wrong, whatever sense it has, is present and disturbing just because it is avoided, or better, repressed. The ambiguous character of the situation is revealed by the fact that there seems to be no reason at all to oppose it. But neither does one accept it. There are, instead, many reasons to submit to it. But they are reasons of convenience, more than of conscience. Conscience (in the sense of willing assent to what one does) is suspended.

This experience of suspension, of obscurity, of doubt, is the severe test to which the modern situation puts "values"—not only traditional beliefs, but the idea itself that it is necessary to believe in something, and that the difference between believing in what one does and *what one is*, and not believing in them, is a real difference.

For this reason the mass situation is a morally extreme one. In sum, it is what we mean by nihilism: to live by setting aside the question of whether what one does day by day has any meaning, to know that one sets aside the question, and to recognize, at the same time, that this does not change the course of events.

The course of events, in fact, does not change. But existence is deprived of meaning when it is reduced to a long series of obligatory and indifferent acts. It is stripped of value, not so much with respect to the "values" of culture and of tradition (which can always be in some way maintained and cultivated privately), but in itself. Existence is literally "unbelievable," and an unbelievable existence means an existence which drags on in a state of continual bad faith.

In order for this to happen, it is necessary—it is important to insist upon this—that material or, at any rate "objective," conditions be bad. It is enough for the individual to find himself in an ambiguous situation respecting his own action, to do what he does without conviction —to act without violating any deeply felt belief, but also without clearly observing one.

IV

One can at this point return to what, according to Ortega y Gasset, distinguishes the mentality of the mass-man: the fact that "to have an idea does not mean to have reasons for having it."

If one assumes that such a man thinks capriciously; that, good reasons being clear to him because they are written in the heaven of intelligible Ideas, he arbitrarily chooses, *against* them, the idea which suits him; and that then, even knowing the place of truth, he "does not care in the least to be in the right," then, certainly, his will appears as wicked as it is obstinate.

But such an assumption is not legitimate. Such a man, granted that he exists, would be an intellectual sophist, not a mass man.

Even according to Ortega y Gasset's definition, the *mass man*, the "man in the street," *homo communis*, is not someone who refuses to give reasons or does not care about being in the right: he has not reasons to give and, as for being in the right, he *cannot* care about it. He has only the ideas that his situation provides—no more than that. In a situation in which the most obvious reasons are reasons of fact and of necessity, he can receive only conventional, stereotyped ideas. These ideas are not false; rather, they are neither false nor true. The mass man has literally lost true reasons. This is the only fact which explains how, in the modern situation, the "aristocratic values" have, in their turn, "lost power."

In what sense, then, may one say that the intellectual is superior to the man of the masses? In no sense. The intellectual can distinguish himself from the mass only by his greater consciousness of their common situation. But he can show this consciousness in only one way—by speaking the truth without presuming that he is the sole owner of it. As a matter of fact, the question is not majority and minority, the mob and the elite. *The mass situation involves everybody.* The necessity of daily relations, which not even the most privileged can avoid, makes us all part of the mass; we are all forced to use the current language, especially those who strongly desire to communicate with their fellows and to address the community as such.

The language of the mass, based as it is on ready-made notions, consists of cut and dried formulas in which words have a fixed value, purely indicative and only slightly expressive. The most obvious example is the language of propaganda, advertising, and what are called, not by chance, "media of mass communication." Such a tongue resembles the language of cybernetics which the experts themselves call a dead language—incapable of transmitting information about *new facts.* The simple mixing of such a conventional language with the more or less authentic language of private life and of significant exchanges between individuals creates a situation without precedent.

So that the situation of the intellectual, or of the Platonic philosopher who, having returned to the cave, seeks to communicate to his fellows the truths which he has glimpsed, is paradoxical. The language of the street is ineluctable; no one has created it, but everybody is forced to use it. To the extent to which he preserves some freedom, however, the intellectual cannot accept a situation and the language it involves simply because "he cannot help it." But, on the other hand, he cannot ignore a state of things and a language to which, since he is only an individual among others, he yields like the others. If he wishes to talk to others, he is obliged to use their language. No matter how refined, sensitive, and aware he may be, he can define his ideas only in relation to the ideas of the mass; even if it is to oppose them. This already sets him in bondage. On the other hand, if he truly seeks lost reasons and truths, if he wishes to communicate meanings and not merely to use formulas, if he feels himself the more or less worthy heir of a tradition, the intellectual must wish to be free. But he knows one thing for certain: he exists and works in a situation in which he himself has only an equivocal and doubtful relation to tradition, to the "aristocratic values," to reasons and intelligible truths. This is an extreme situation.

The situation is extreme not so much as regards culture as its *raison d'être*, which is truth lived and participated in. Culture, in fact, is the ground not of truth, but of the search for it. Truth appears only in lived experience, in feeling oneself in harmony with the nature of things and the world. And common truth is found and lived in common; it is a vital harmony which no idea or cultural form, no single individual, can ever really express, much less create.

Truth—like man himself—does not merely need to be left at liberty, not to be oppressed; above all, it must be freely sought and desired. Now, to the extent to which the individual's experience of his social existence is an experience of non-truth and of non-free acts, he does not seek the truth: he wants ready-made ideas, quickly reassuring; he seeks, not freedom, but the organization of a force capable of assuring the satisfaction of his needs. Of truth, as of liberty, the individual feels only the privation, and only when he is face to face with himself —in the lack of reason and of sense which he discovers in his existence.

So corrupt a situation does not change by virtue of pure ideas, nor by violence, but uniquely, "according to the order of Time," through our suffering the common lot in common, seeking to understand it.

And the fact remains that we do not leave the cave in a mass, but only one by one.

Problems for Thought and Writing

I

1. The first paragraph of this article clearly takes issue with an assumption of Ortega y Gasset (see page 188). Do you accept Chiaromonte's qualification?

2. The problem of "finding room" in a mass-dominated world and culture is not just spatial ("visual") but is also a spiritual problem. Compare that problem in the world Adams (page 260) or Stegner (page 255) describe with that in the world sketched by Ortega (page 188) or Mowrer (page 238).

3. Write an essay on your personal need for spiritual *lebensraum*. Have you felt this need sharply? Is your society providing more or less of it?

4. To what extent are democratic-liberal values dependent on mere *space* to move around in? As America fills up and loses its frontier is it likely (or inevitable?) that the land of the free will become the land of the controlled and conditioned?

5. What does Chiaromonte mean by a "situation of anonymity"? How is this associated with democratic equality? What are some of the implications of this condition for modern life?

6. How would Mandel (page 171) reply to Chiaromonte's doubts about the possibility of aristocratic values in a mass society?

7. What does Chiaromonte mean by referrring to the crowd as the "ultimate form" of the mass situation in which we live?

8. On page 231 Chiaromonte remarks: "From the point of view of conscience . . . what matters is that one feels oneself subjected to an overpowering force which comes neither from a moral norm nor from the sum of individual demands, but simply from the fact of collective existence." Why should "conscience" enter into the question of "space"? Relate the author's point to your own experience.

9. Find some illustrations in your campus society of the "language of the mass." Do you think Chiaromonte is exaggerating the persistence of it?

10. "Culture . . . is the ground not of truth, but of the search for it." (Page 237.) What is the meaning of this statement?

11. What does the "cave" in the last line refer to? Explain its relevance here.

II

12. Would you say that this essay is as economical as it might be?

13. Define: ineluctable, paradoxical, cybernetics, *homo communis*, inchoate, efficacy, humanistic, discursive, ephemeral, agglomeration, plentitude, refractory.

14. This is a difficult essay. Make a one-sentence statement of its main point. Then write one-sentence statements of the main point in each paragraph. With this preparation, write a *digest* of the piece that is one-half the present length. Have you improved on it?

~

SAWDUST, SEAWEED, AND SYNTHETICS*   *Edgar Ansel Mowrer*

The Hazards of Crowding

A great-grandfather of mine left Central Illinois as "too darned civilized" when he failed to sight a deer on his own birthday. Another close relative finds my house in the New Hampshire woods "too lonely," although the nearest neighbor is less than a quarter of a mile away! Even under ideal conditions there are always some people

* From *The Saturday Review*, December 8, 1956. Reprinted by permission.

who will think the world is too crowded. In a scientific sense, however, it is important to ask: How many people are too many?

To begin with, any humane or logical blueprint of an optimum earth must allow for varying degrees of human density, from the 137 people per acre in Manhattan (87,680 per square mile) to the utter emptiness of Antarctica.

The earth's present density (forty-two per square mile of land) still permits almost everybody able to travel to find somewhat the sort of environment that means the most. But not for long—not at the present rate of human increase. Java suffers from no less than 1,000 souls per square mile. There a drive through the so-called countryside resembles, for the number of people encountered, the U.S. seacoast between Miami Beach and Fort Lauderdale, Florida—an unending suburb! And the eastern seaboard of the United States, taken as a single area, already counts 180 to the square mile, over three times the national average.

Thanks to her readiness to accept the Lord's living bounty our country is confounding the population "experts" of the Twenties and Thirties who dolefully predicted a stationary or diminishing American population. In fact, a great change has come over American society. The average young American woman, according to Betsy Talbot Blackwell, editor of *Mademoiselle*, "follows the current trend of marrying in her late teens or early twenties, and raising as many children as the good Lord gives her." The American people have increased no less than 31 million in the past twenty years. Two and eight-tenths millions joined the throng in 1955, and each successive sunrise (as of October 1956) sees 7,200 more citizens than the previous dawn.

Certainly these child-eager American young women, taken together, seem to have reversed what demographers thought was a one-way street, namely, the so-called Demographic Transition. This was the breakthrough from an original situation as a high birth-rate, high death-rate country to a low birth-rate, low death-rate country. It was thought to occur whenever a population reached a certain standard of living. Instead, an American birth-rate that from 1935 to 1945 was about 20 per 1,000 has since the end of World War II stayed around 25 per 1,000. The United States is setting a new pattern: middle birth-rate with low death-rate. As a result future estimates have been drastically revised upward. One demographer predicts a U.S. population of 193,400,000 for 1975 and no less than 320 million for the year 2000! Although population forecasting is obviously more of an art than a science present calculations might well turn out to be correct.

For the American reversal of the prewar trend, if it continues, is something new—a rising living standard provoking more rather than less conception.

Anyhow, for two-thirds of the world's population births are still running close to the physiological maximum. Costa Rica (1952) chalked up no less a birth-rate than 54.6 per 1,000 inhabitants. India is another example. India's population, thanks to a high death-rate, remained virtually stable for two or three thousand years prior to 1850 —and the country was well fed and prosperous. Since the British cut the death-rate the number of Indians has zoomed skyward with no promise of relief. Ceylon's population is growing by 3 per cent a year! Before Perry Japan had a stable population. Since that gentleman "opened" it the Japanese have multiplied like weeds. Under American occupation after World War II they grew almost visibly— and still do. Some have calculated that the world's people will by the year 2106 have reached 20 billion.

Nature's explosive fecundity is as awesome as the power of the atom. A well-fed amoeba will double in an hour. Given adequate food and favorable circumstances it could by the sixth day have produced enough amoebas to exceed the weight of the entire earth! One type of plant louse breeds so quickly that if all its progeny survived the lice would in ten generations weigh as much as 500 million stout men (Huxley). If every codfish egg became adult and reproduced, within six years the Atlantic Ocean would be a solid mass of cod. Certain protozoa might, theoretically, fill *all known space* in a few years.

Human beings cannot quite keep up but some try hard. The Hutterites of the USA and Canada have increased by some nineteen times in the last seventy years. At the present rate they would in 250 years more equal the present population of the United States. The original 6,000 French settlers of Canada have multiplied no less than 700 times in a little over 300 years. Let present death rates sink further—as seems likely if mankind avoids a major atomic war—and there seem no *a priori* limits on the number of people except those of available food and other primary resources.

Already the vehemence of our growth threatens with extinction many other forms of organic life. A contemporary zoologist, N. J. Berrill, believes that the earth produces roughly the same amount of life at all times. It follows that when one organic element, in this case the human race, starts roaring its expansive way across the earth's surface other elements fade and die out. Hence, the present growing "prevalence of people" must—Berrill holds—seem to all other life *like a cancer whose strange cells multiply without restraint, ruthlessly demanding the nourishment that all the body has need of.*" And he concludes that sooner or later the body (or the community) is starved of support and perishes.

As a whole Americans are still barely aware of any problem. Our tradition is one of limitless spaces to be filled, limitless resources to be developed. Businessmen are purring over the flood of new customers. Even trained economists look upon the torrent of new babies primarily in terms of the ever-expanding market. The spectacle of suburbs mushrooming out over once pastoral landscapes around our cities may at some point cause a reconsideration. But in proportion to other countries ours is still only moderately populated. As against less than one acre of cultivated land per person in most parts of the earth, our own ratio, though down to just over two acres per head, is still sufficient to flood the country with unconsumed food which the Government lets rot rather than sell, give, or throw away. Botanist Karl Sax states that even "with present agricultural techniques, the United States and Canada could provide ample food for a population of 200 million and a subsistence diet for nearly 1 billion." So Americans need not yet fear hunger. Not so a country like India. There—according to chemist Harrison Brown—nine-tenths of the *total labor* is already devoted to obtaining food. Unless the birth rate falls sharply no improvement seems conceivable.

Such rapid human increase has started a first-class controversy among experts, both recognized and self-proclaimed. Obviously, unlimited reproduction must *at some point*—unless offset by a growing death rate—lead to starvation. The dispute is about the location of that point.

Viewers-with-alarm (who go back to the Church father Tertullian) see the limit as fairly close at hand. And anyhow, even if we do not soon run out of food we are—they believe—rapidly using up many other essential resources (including cheap water) whose exhaustion or decline would shortly force us back into a purely agricultural condition. On the other hand, specialists of equal prestige regard natural growth as a sign of laudable virility which will correct itself before it becomes dangerous.

The argument—with the specialists so divided—is as confusing as all-important. Nonetheless, if a layman may presume, it seems largely irrelevant to the real question. The demographers are mostly overlooking the essential point. This is not what is the earth's *maximum,* but what is its *optimum* population? *At what density are human beings most able to live the Good Life?* If by stepping up the fertility of our women we can provide more favorable surroundings for their children, well and good. If, on the other hand, further urbanization and suburbanization will prevent the fullest individual development of which people are capable then it is time to slow down.

It is surprising how few population students seem to have centered their investigation upon this point. Even the promising title "Ideal Size for Our Population" (*New York Times* Magazine, May 1, 1955), by the sociologist Kingsley Davis, is deceptive. Mr. Davis at one point writes bravely:

"Some (person) will, as I do, see certain disadvantages in an ever larger number of people—disadvantages which do not concern tangibles such as food and housing but rather the intangible but nonetheless treasured aspects of life." But then he spoils the effect: "These may seem *trivial* considerations and *in a way they are*." (My italics.)

Personal freedom, nature, beauty, privacy, solitude, variety, savor—trivial? Surely Mr. Davis would admit that all are essential components of valid human living even at the present dubious level.

It is, or should be, perfectly obvious that the greater the crowding, the larger the number of people in proportion to diminishing natural resources, the more the authorities will be obliged to curtail their liberties, not because they are necessarily opposed to freedom but because they must do so if living is to be made endurable for any of them. The result could well be the hive, or world-wide welfare state, which looks after the material needs of all its citizens while strictly controlling their actions; in short, a kind of benevolent "Nineteen Eighty-four" where Big Brother is looking at each person just about every minute.

Now the drive for freedom, we know, is not only anchored in the freeman's soul, it is a part of his biological nature. The reaction against constraint is one of the earliest and deepest to appear in higher animals. It will hardly disappear in man, or if it does seems bound to reappear later. Constraint and an overdense population are inseparable.

What of that close relationship between man and the rest of nature which crowding is already tending to distort? How far can mankind lose contact with both the organic substratum and the macrocosmic framework of his life and prosper spiritually?

Many individuals have little or no desire for natural surroundings.

Nature—except human nature—leaves them unmoved. Some have nonetheless been greatly creative.

Yet how many more human creators have felt just the other way! Poets of all times and places, most painters and sculptors, the majority of great writers, many abstract thinkers, the greatest scientists have avowed an intimate need of nature. In some of them the thirst for natural things, for the full sky, landscapes, trees, flowers, wild animals, the tang of the autumn wind, the tumbling seas and tranquil lakes, has been an obsession. They have truly fed upon nature in all its aspects. The implication is clear that severed from nature man's imagination and inquiring mind would diminish, perhaps wither utterly.

How long could a rashly multiplying mankind continue to find enough beauty? So far in history people seem to have derived beauty chiefly from two things—nature, primitive or cultivated, and the nature-inspired products of man's own mind and hands. Where would they seek it if a growing population should cover most of the earth with utilitarian devices—and desecrate the remainder in the process?

To be sure, modern expressionistic, abstract, and functional art claims to supply the thirsting soul with all that previous generations got from *natural* content, *natural* expression, and *natural* ornament. Architects not only justify their banal (not to say primitive) designs but glorify them on the theory that "function determines form" and that a successfully embodied "function" has a beauty of its own superior to the "illustrative" or "ornamental" designs of the past.

To what extent are these claims fulfilled? Opinions differ widely. Where the evidence is still inconclusive one can but express a personal conviction. I literally grew up in a generation of writers and artists frantically striving to free themselves from naturalistic form and conscious meaning. And I conclude that wherever and whenever man no longer has a full natural environment on which to feed his sense of beauty he will succumb to dreariness. Think of today's slums and slagheaps, garbage dumps, and polluted rivers. Consider our ruined landscapes, commercially exploited U.S. highways, all the monotonous Levittowns. How avoid the conclusion that too many people and sufficient beauty—natural or man-made—seem incompatible?

What of the diminishing privacy that accompanies crowding? Privacy is freedom from observation, disturbance, and interference, whether with thoughts, emotions, or acts. It is privately that people receive their most powerful and original impulses. But who—today—

wants privacy? Certainly not the "integration-minded" American teachers who rate pupil conformity and popularity above ability to learn or express. Not those millions who instinctively flock together like sparrows when there is plenty of room elsewhere.

Perhaps the need for privacy begins only with individuals of a certain kind. And perhaps even among them only those understand its value who have seen what life without it can become—the awful promiscuity of the boat-dwellers on the Pearl River at Canton, China; or crowded Calcutta on a summer night during the monsoon; or Russian workers packed four families in a room and unable to open the window lest they freeze! Even without these sights many Americans who passed some time in crowded military camps in wartime learned how essential some privacy can become to happiness. Certainly without it the creative portion of mankind would find it more difficult to achieve that concentration essential to maximum mental creativity.

Solitude is something else. One can—with sufficient will power—find solitude in a crowd, in a suburban rose garden, or indoors in a great city, windows closed and doors barred. Some great minds have done so. But surely that solitude is best where the possibility of being alone is coupled with privacy, silence, and the exciting quality of remoteness which only untouched nature seems to possess. Certain supreme beauties move us more the further away from cities they lie— the empty starlit sky, the glint of moonlight on a lake, towering mountains. Clearly for the few drawn to contemplation and the search for truth, who are the teachers of the race, a world with no remaining wilderness would be poor indeed.

Needs differ, even among animals—as any dog lover can testify. Any good society must provide for varying preferences—for crowd-warmth as well as for freedom, nature, natural beauty, privacy, and solitude. But if we say that an optimum population for this planet is one that can most fully enjoy the *savor* of life we have to admit that savor is hard to define. It includes all sorts of things—freedom, nature, spaciousness, the sense of adventure—and a certain smacking of the lips. It can even (at least for me) be *symbolized* by one type of available food.

It is here that the demographers reveal their appalling inhumanity. Solemnly they calculate the amount of nourishment necessary to fill even more billions of bellies. Looking at the maximum nourishment obtainable, some are already counting on wood pulp and algae. Through tens of millions of acres of forests or algae "farms" in the sea and floating islands whose inhabitants would cut down their physical activities so as to need a minimum of calories, the earth, they reason—might conceivably nourish no less than 200 billion creatures—though whether they could any longer at that point be called human I cannot say. Some masterminds go further. A British physicist, J. D. Bernal, has suggested solving the food problem by synthesizing an edible something from coal, limestone, and air. (This has, I believe, been done and I would wish Communists like Bernal no worse than having to live on it.) On such a basis, zoologist Berrill acidly comments, there might develop "a population so universally dense that there would be sitting room only." Yet if maximum multiplication is a man's aim (or fate) here is a promising approach.

It inspires a less promising conclusion: Raising as many children as the good Lord sends may—short of catastrophe—at some point require everyone to live upon *sawdust, seaweed,* and/or *synthetics.* Provided one cared to live at all. Personally I should not. Suffering we can stand if we must. But not the tedium of a savorless existence.

Sir Charles Darwin insists that man, like any other organism, will regularly reproduce right up to the starvation limit. Some people have always been hungry. Some are hungry today. Some always will be hungry. Nothing that man does can change it. Perhaps not. But if man's will cannot limit the size of his family how can Sir Charles know that his statement is anything but a conditioned reflex, empty of either truth or falsehood? Determinism anywhere makes argument useless. Besides, other distinguished specialists believe that mankind can control its numbers if it puts its mind to it.

One other objection to limiting population deserves more consideration. It runs that by limiting the number of human beings we would actually worsen the race by limiting the occurrence of superior men and women. If—one may reason—"teachers of the human race" occur in anything like a regular proportion, then the more people, the more outstanding individuals on earth at any time and the faster civilization will grow.

What little we know about the frequency of greatness does not sustain this view. Observed evidence is all the other way. Athens, Alexandria, Florence, Cordova, medieval Paris—these seem to have brought forth genius in all fields far more thickly than modern New York or London, not to speak of Canton or Calcutta. Renaissance Italy, Germany, France, Britain, and the Low Countries, Persia at one period—with relatively few inhabitants—appear to have been proportionately richer in high-quality individuals than today's teeming supernations. A serious investigation of population density and human quality might well indicate an optimum size to cities as well as an optimum human density. Such an investigation would be difficult. And maintaining the optimum, once it was found, even harder. After all, in our own times two countries, Ireland and Sweden, have kept their numbers under control with admirable results.

One ingenious way to control population has been stated by an inhabitant of Lin Yutang's imaginary island of Thainos: "Very simple. We have a system of proportionate taxation. The larger the family the higher the tax. That stops it, all right."

Difficult to enact and enforce? Perhaps. But compare it with an alternative remedy currently proposed. Dr. Fritz Zwicky suggests that those who find the earth too crowded simply bomb large pieces out of frigid planets like Jupiter, Saturn, and Neptune, create out of the material salvaged a hundred new planets with climates and motions like the earth's, and go live on them. He even offers, given ten years and enough money, to build an interplanetary ship. Which is more utopian: to call upon people to limit the number of their offspring or to rearrange the Solar System?

Until the advent of nuclear weapons it could be argued that no Great Power, however desirous of promoting the quality rather than the quantity of its citizens, dare do so lest it be militarily overwhelmed by a conceivably inferior but more numerous enemy. But the H-bombs seem to have become the "equalizers" of nations much as the six-shooter was that of individuals. Certainly they have made it unlikely that man can surmount the next half-century without a holocaust that would solve the population problem for some time unless he establishes some sort of supernational authority. On this account the threat of multiplication to where "the earth is covered with a writhing mass of human beings much as a dead cow is covered with a writhing mass of maggots" is presumably just a poetic nightmare. Yet the dilemma of some not-too-distant future is real enough—an increasingly dreary, shrinking life for ever more people, or an ever nobler, broader life for a limited number. There is no escape. So maybe the average American young woman had better start helping God to keep human quality up by some limitation on human numbers.

Problems for Thought and Writing

I

1. What, in your opinion, is the relationship between population overcrowding and democratic (or Christian) values? Is it possible to love your neighbor

if you never have any privacy? Is individualism possible if people crowd
the earth like maggots?

2. Cutting of the death rate by the British in India has proved to be something
of a national disaster. Was, then, the humanitarianism that prompted the
development wrong? Can you propose a solution to this grim paradox?

3. Should we thank God for fecundity or fear it as a curse?

4. The main question, according to Mowrer, is: "At what density are human
beings most able to live the Good Life?" Assume that we know that "density"
figure: what measures should we take to preserve it? And what would be
our definition of the "Good Life"? Would it include individual freedom?

5. Why do businessmen generally exult at a rise in population? Does a flood
of babies necessarily mean better times?

6. Why does "the hive" allow few personal liberties? Define the "hive" as it
can exist in human society.

7. What leads Mowrer to comment on "the awful promiscuity of the boat-
dwellers on the Pearl River at Canton, China"? Do we have anything approxi-
mating that in American cities?

8. With overcrowding we have less personal freedom, privacy, solitude, less
variety and less natural beauty. How, in your opinion, should we stop this
overpopulation? By birth control, atom bombs, prayer, increased death rate,
increased infant mortality, tax on large families, compulsory sterilization?
What objections will be raised to some of these solutions?

9. Do you agree with Mowrer's suggested solution: "So maybe the average
American young woman had better start helping God to keep human quality
up by some limitation on human numbers"?

II

10. Compare the theme and organization of this article with that of Whyte
(page 217). Both were published in *The Saturday Review*. If they both
are typical of the magazine, what can you say about the magazine's editorial
policy and general character?

11. Write a theme entitled "The Ethics of Space."

~

MEN OR MORONS? *   *Earnest A. Hooton*

OBSOLESCENCE OF NATURAL SELECTION

The obsolescence of natural selection is largely due to humanitarianism and to the efficacy of modern medical science. It is obvious that
the most skillful and successful medical practice could have little
effect for good or for evil upon the population, as long as it was
restricted to those few who could afford the luxury of high fees.

* From *Apes, Men, and Morons*, by Earnest A. Hooton. Copyright 1937 by
G. P. Putnam's Sons. Published by G. P. Putnam's Sons. Used by permission.

When, however, there arose enlightened leaders among men who taught the nobility, not only of casting out devils, but also of healing the sick, making whole the lame, and causing the blind to see, the doctor began to yearn to be the savior of all mankind. This did no harm at all, as long as his miracles were imaginary and his nostrums continued to waft his patients to the Elysian Fields. But when he really began to succeed, Pandora's box was open.

Studies of the individual age composition of ancient and primitive skeletal populations indicate that an increase of longevity is a marked phenomenon of modern civilized life. Statistics of infant mortality show that the constitutional inferiors of today stand a much better chance of surviving to adult years, and of reproducing their kind, than they have presumably enjoyed at any previous time. Again, modern advances in sanitation and in the knowledge of communicable diseases have done much to control the epidemics which periodically have decimated the populations of times past. What are the consequences of such preservation and prolongation of human life?

In the first place the effect must be to increase proportionally that section of the population which is helpless because young, and also that section which is relatively helpless because old. Both increases place additional burdens upon the family and the state. The economically depressed, who seem always the most prolific, have larger numbers of offspring who must be fed, clothed, and educated, and probably more surviving children of inferior bodily and mental endowment. Familial care and earnings must be distributed among a greater number of less fit young. There follows the tendency to dissipate the family resources upon the inferior offspring and to neglect those who are better fitted in individual hereditary endowment to cope with the world. The major portion of parental energy is exerted upon the effort to make the best of bad reproductive jobs. Instead of saving the bacon, we misdirect our hog-raising efforts to the futile task of attempting to make silk purses of the animal's ears. The more active and able-bodied children are left to fend for themselves—an abandonment which for many of them leads to delinquency.

At the other end of the curve we have the increase of the population of advanced age. Let us consider the effect of the continued activity of these elders. It is perhaps most clearly manifested in the modern gerontocracy, or the rule of old men. One of the most constant characteristics of old age is an inability to recognize its own obsolescence and an unwillingness to relinquish its direction of the life of family and state. The dominion of senility in the family increases the conflict between generations, since three instead of two are involved, and must be one of the factors tending toward familial disruption. In the political and economic world, it means that those who have attained the seniority requisite for leadership are likely to be a generation behind their times in thought, relatively impervious to the advance of ideas, and completely unsympathetic with the world of the middle-aged and the juvenile which they dominate.

Add to this the fact that these elderly potentates perform their public functions in a personal aura of corporeal and mental disintegration, being indeed not immortal, but subject not only to ordinary human ailments but also to those of old age. I have said on a previous occasion that it is impossible to estimate, for example, to what extent the miseries of nations may have been enhanced by the vagaries of the enlarged prostates of their senile rulers, or by the climacteric mental disturbances of the latters' wives. If indeed we are to tolerate the sway of those debilitated by age, it would seem necessary at least to make some appraisal of the extent to which their functions are impaired by disease, in order that our entire public policy may not be moribund. For those who retire from active life with the onset of senility, there remains public care in the form of old age pensions and homes for the aged, or alternatively, retirement to the family chimney corner.

Now I am not arguing in favor either of a policy of infanticide or of senicide. I am merely calling attention to the fact that the benevolent and efficient labors of modern medicine are raising new and grave population problems. I may here state what I believe to be the anthropological view of pathology. Man is a made-over and makeshift organism, the end product of many adaptations and unsatisfactory compromises between heredity and environment. Early in the life of the average individual, various working parts of his organism begin to weaken under the attack of infections or through sheer constitutional inferiority, but, in some way or other, functions are partially maintained, and the animal goes limping along through life, aided by the crutches of medical science and sustained by that brutal tenacity of life which seems to be an inheritance from lower evolutionary stages. By some saturnine gift of nature the reproductive system of the human animal continues to function when the nervous system is completely disintegrated, the alimentary and excretory systems thoroughly disorganized, and virtually the entire organism is in a state of morbidity. By superskillful tinkering and patching, life and activity are maintained, and the animal continues to exercise one of its strongest instincts and to produce more and more of worse and worse offspring.

EDUCATION AND ETHICS

The pathway of degressive human evolution, like hell, is paved with good intentions—medical, educational, and ethical. The fallacy of social ethics lies, I think, in the assumption that all human life is inherently good and worthy of preservation, and that by a process of environmental tinkering, fools may be transmuted into sages, criminals into saints, and politicians into statesmen. Surely this conception is nothing but a secularized belief in conversion and personal salvation. The clergyman of yesterday is the unfrocked sociologist of today.

When are we to realize that a great proportion of mankind continues to be as stupid, unteachable, bloodthirsty, predatory, and savage as we are wont to imagine that maligned and regrettably extinct precursor—Neanderthal man? Is it because the precepts of Christianity have not been sufficiently disseminated, or because the blessings of plumbing and mechanical transport have been too narrowly restricted, or because there are still a few persons who lack the degree of Bachelor of Arts? I think it is because no little of the human germ plasm is poisonous slime, and we have not had the intelligence and the courage to attempt to find out anything about human heredity. We have imagined universal education, mutual understanding, and improvement of the social environment to be the ingredients with which we can concoct the human millennium; we have mixed them up and stirred them in, and turned out a horrible mess. There must be something the matter with our basic element—man himself.

It is not yet too late to begin the studies of human inheritance which are essential for man's wise and efficient control of his own evolution. Such studies should begin with genetic researches upon the gross anatomy and general physiology of the human animal, his pathology, his psychology and mental capacity, and should proceed ultimately to his sociability—or fitness to function in human society. Of course environment is important, but we cannot exercise an intelligent control of environment without a fundamental knowledge of the range and restrictions of hereditary variations.

THE BANNER OF EQUALITY

When Mr. Midshipman Easy was called to account for a serious breach of naval discipline, he replied that it was "all zeal," and when requested to explain why he had flown the silk petticoat of a señorita from the masthead of a prize of war, he stated that "it was the banner of equality and the rights of man." We have adopted this easyish philosophy without its saving grace of humor; we have been plunging zealously ahead under a banner of equality and the rights of man, which turns out to be less significant than the señorita's lingerie.

It might well have been said to Luke: "Thou art the physician, and hast the keys of life and death," for that precisely is the responsibility of the medical profession, of which dental science is not the least important division. In medical science lies the only practicable control of human evolution and of biological progress. Medical science must cease to regard its function as primarily curative and preventive. It must rid itself of the obsession that its chief responsibility is to the individual rather than to society. It must allocate to itself the function of discovering how the human animal may be improved as a biological organism. The future of mankind does not depend upon political or economic theory, nor yet upon measures of social amelioration, but upon the production of better minds in sounder bodies. . . .

The Changing Psychological Status of Man

The survival of the organically unsound and the perpetuation of their constitutional ailments are tolerable only if the lowering of physique is unaccompanied by mental deterioration. Civilized man endeavors to persuade himself that his intelligence improves and his mental health remains unimpaired no matter how enfeebled his body has become. He has tried to believe that mental vigor and high ideals of conduct flourish in an organic environment of pathology and degeneration.

The cumulative tradition of civilization has handed down innumerable inventions and devices for facilitating existence. The individual can maintain life and perpetuate his kind with a minimum of physical effort and with little or no exercise of intelligence. We have become parasites upon the cultural achievements of the past and upon the inventive benefactions of a few creative contemporaries. The stimuli for a full utilization of the hereditary endowment of mental equipment have diminished, since the latter is no longer essential for survival. Loss of function atrophies the intelligence as surely as disuse withers muscles and shrinks bones.

The last century has witnessed in certain advanced nations the application of a system of ethics and a practice of sociology which, on the behavioristic side, may be called humanitarianism and which, in its institutional aspect, is termed democracy. Both theory and practice are the outgrowths of the highest ideals of human conduct. There is little doubt that the optimum human society is realized under this régime, provided that its members are possessed individually of high intelligence and are habituated to a reciprocity of altruistic conduct. However, excessive altruism and indiscriminate humanitarianism are impracticable because they reduce the intelligence of the population. The noblest manifestation of human science is the extension of medical care to all classes of the population. The finest exemplifications of man's unselfishness are charity toward the weak and the helpless and forbearance for the wrongdoer. Now it is impossible to disregard the fact that the preservation of the biologically unfit lowers the physical level of the population. It is not commonly known, however, that intelligence declines with organic deterioration, and it is convenient to deny this psycho-physical parallelism, since its implications are exceedingly unpleasant. I have spent ten cheerless years in studying the relation of physique to intelligence and to economic and educational status, in the inmates of American penitentiaries, jails, and insane asylums. Every jot and tittle of the vast mass of evidence which I have analyzed indicates that inferior biological status is inextricably associated with diminished intelligence, and that the combination of the two is mainly responsible for economic inadequacy and antisocial conduct. Dismiss crime, if you like, as a pathological by-product of society. Disregard the findings I have stated without submitting my proof. Deny the logic of the contention that weak minds are found in weak bodies. Nevertheless, if you will but pause to survey the state of our society, you must join in my cry, "What must we do to be saved?"

The howl of the Roman mob, *"Panem et circenses!"* (bread and the circus) is re-echoing ominously through this nation. However, neither emotion nor rhetoric will alleviate the situation, and let him who will put his trust in such sops to Cerberus as bonuses, old age pensions, and legislation for social security. We must either do some biological housecleaning or delude ourselves with the futile hope that a government of the unfit, for the unfit, and by the unfit will not perish from the earth.

REMEDIES

Now it seems to me perfectly clear that what we must do, in some way or other, is to encourage a sit-down reproductive strike of the busy breeders among the morons, criminals, and social ineffectuals of our population. Probably compulsory sterilization alone would serve in the case of the insane and the mentally deficient, but it is very difficult to enforce such a measure in a democracy, unless it has been preceded by an educational campaign which has reached all of the teachable and socially-minded individuals of the electorate. Probably the only effective method of obtaining the desired result would be to establish in our secondary schools and colleges courses of applied human biology which would disseminate knowledge of the facts of heredity and of the relation of man's organism to his behavior. Of course science really knows as yet comparatively little about human genetics, and is quite incapable of enunciating directions for breeding geniuses. But it is wholly competent to suggest measures which would prevent the birth of the majority of our imbeciles and morons. The young ought to be brought to an early realization that their success in life and their value to society depend not only upon occupational skill and character, but also upon an understanding that their reproductive function must be exercised in accordance with their individual capacities and limitations. We must inculcate into the rising generation a code of biological ethics.

The only valid reason for trying to improve the biological status of man is that he be made a better animal—more honest, more unselfish, more decent and considerate in his human relations. I think that a biological purge is the essential prerequisite for a social and a spiritual salvation. Let us temper mercy with justice and dispense charity with intelligence. We must stop trying to cure malignant biological growths with patent sociological nostrums. The emergency demands a surgical operation.

Problems for Thought and Writing

I

1. In Ortega (page 188), Chiaromonte (page 225), and Mowrer (page 238) we have met various treatments of the problem of the mass vs. human excellence, the anonymous and automatized crowd vs. the free and moral individual. Hooton concentrates his attention on the moral and mental deterioration that accompanies physical deterioration—and what we can do about it. His recommendation is a radical one: "I think that a biological purge is the essential prerequisite for a social and a spiritual salvation." In short, if we are to have excellence we must control breeding.

   a) Would Mandel (page 171) agree with Hooton's implied definition of "excellence"?

   b) Is Hooton basically concerned with the *quantity* of people or their *quality?* Does he want to get rid of people or improve them? Would he have written this piece if we weren't living in an overpopulated world? Compare his motives for writing with those of Mowrer (page 238).

   c) Is it a fair conclusion from Hooton's words that those destroying our elbow-room are also destroying our opportunity to live as free men, and that those most responsible for destroying elbow-room are, in the main, the heavy breeders, humanitarians, and medical practitioners? If this conclusion is true, what is any patriot's obvious duty?

2. "The clergyman of yesterday is the unfrocked sociologist of today." Is Hooton being facetious here or is there validity in his remark? Can you provide other illustrations of the same point?

3. Is it a "scientific" conclusion to state that the increase in old age will increase "the conflict between generations"?

4. Do you feel that the right to breed is an inalienable right and that it is an impiety even to recommend curbing or interfering with it? Would the problem have even occurred to Jefferson at the time he wrote the *Declaration of Independence* (page 159)? Why or why not?

5. "We have imagined universal education, mutual understanding, and improvement of the social environment to be the ingredients with which we can concoct the human millennium. . . ." (Page 250.) Another way of saying much the same thing is that we have placed our faith in *love*. But one product of love is children, and one product of children (in mass quantities) is the destruction of most of the things that make civilized living possible: freedom, space, living-room, individuality—love itself. Does love, then, have a built-in antithesis? Is it not entirely desirable as a moral condition? See Fromm, page 505.

6. Hooton's main appeal is for "a code of biological ethics." Is that the proper concern for a biologist? As a scientist, is not his province that of "fact" alone? Or are the domains of "fact" and "ethics" connected?

II

7. Compare the prose style of this essay with that of Mencken (page 66). Do they use the same techniques?

8. Define: senility, genocide, gerontocracy, senicide, infanticide, potentates, pathology, atrophy, altruism, nostrums.

9. Is this objective, "scientific" writing or is it persuasive, "propagandistic"?

10. Compare the use of the word "inheritance" by Hooton and Ortega (page 188).

~

THE MAKING OF PATHS* *Wallace Stegner*

On the Saskatchewan homestead that we located in 1915 there was at first absolutely nothing. I remember it as it originally was, for my brother and I, aged eight and six, accompanied my father when he went out to make the first "improvements." Our land lay exactly on the international border; the four-foot iron post jutting from the prairie just where our wagon tract met the section-line trail to Hydro, Montana, marked not only the otherwise invisible distinction between Canada and the United States but the division between our land and all other, anywhere.

There were few other marks to show which three hundred and twenty acres of that empty plain were ours. The land spread as flat as if it had been graded, except where, halfway to our western line, a shallow, nearly imperceptible coulee began, feeling its way, turning and turning again, baffled and blocked, a watercourse so nearly a slough that the spring runoff had hardly any flow at all, its water not so much flowing as pushed by the thaw behind it and having to go somewhere, until it passed our land and turned south, and near the line found another lost coulee, which carried in most seasons some water—not enough to run but enough to seep, and with holes that gave sanctuary to a few minnows and suckers. That was Coteau Creek, a part of the Milk-Missouri watershed. In good seasons we sometimes got a swim of sorts in its holes; in dry years we hauled water from it in barrels, stealing from the minnows to serve ourselves and our stock. Between it and our house we wore, during the four or five summers we spent vainly trying to make a wheat farm there, one of our private wagon tracks.

Coteau Creek was a landmark and sometimes a hazard. Once my father, gunning our old Model T across one of its fords, hit something and broke an axle. Next day he walked forty miles into Chinook, Montana, leaving me with a homesteader family, and the day after that he brought back the axle on his back and installed it himself after the homesteader's team had hauled the Ford out of the creek bed. I remember that square, high car, with its yellow spoke wheels

* From *The Making of Paths* by Wallace Stegner. First published in *The New Yorker*. © 1958 The New Yorker Magazine, Inc.

and its brass bracing rods from windshield to mudguards and its four-eared brass radiator cap. It stuck up black and foreign, a wanderer from another planet, on the flats by Coteau Creek, while my father, redfaced and sweating, crawled in and out under the jacked-up rear end and I squatted in the car's shade and played what games I could with pebbles and a blue robin's egg. We sat there on the plain, something the earth refused to swallow, right in the middle of everything and with the prairie as empty as nightmare clear to the line where hot earth met hot sky. I saw the sun flash off brass, a heliograph winking off a message into space, calling attention to us, saying "Look, look!"

Because that was the essential feeling of the country for me—the sense of being foreign and noticeable, of sticking out—I did not at first feel even safe, much less that I was taking charge of and making my own a parcel of the world. I moped for the town on the Whitemud River, forty miles north, where we lived in winter, where all my friends were, where my mother was waiting until we got a shelter built on the homestead. Out here we did not belong to the earth as the prairie dogs and burrowing owls and picket-pin gophers and weasels and badgers and coyotes did, or to the sky as the hawks did, or to any combination as meadow larks and robins and sparrows did. Our shack, covered with tar paper, was an ugly rectangle on the face of the prairie, and not even the low roof, rounded like the roof of a railroad car to give the wind less grip on it, could bind it into the horizontal world.

Before we got the shack built, we lived in a tent, which the night wind constantly threatened to blow away, flapping the canvas and straining the ropes and pulling the pegs from the gravel. And when, just as we were unloading the lumber for the shack, a funnel-shaped cloud appeared in the south, moving against a background of gray-black shot with lightning-forks, and even while the sun still shone on us, the air grew tense and metallic to breathe, and the light like a reflection from brass glowed around us, and high above, pure and untroubled, the zenith was blue—then indeed exposure was like paralysis or panic, and we looked at the strangely still tent, bronzed in the yellow air, and felt the air shiver and saw a dart of wind move like a lizard across the dust and vanish again. My father rushed us to the three shallow square holes, arranged in a triangle, with the iron section stake at their apex, that marked the corner of our land, and with ropes he lashed us to the stake and made us cower down

in the holes. They were no more than a foot deep; they could in no
sense be called a shelter. Over their edge our eyes, level with the
plain, looked southward and saw nothing between us and the ominous
funnel except gopher mounds, the still unshaken grass. Across the
coulee a gopher sat up, erect as the picket pin from which he took
his name.

Then the grass stirred; it was as if gooseflesh prickled suddenly on
the prairie's skin. The gopher disappeared as if some friend below
had reached up and yanked him into his burrow. Even while we
were realizing it, the yellow air darkened, and then all the brown
and yellow went out of it and it was blue-black. The wind began
to pluck at the shirts on our backs, the hair on our heads was
wrenched, the air was full of dust. From the third hole my father,
glaring over the shallow rim, yelled to my brother and me to keep
down, and with a fierce rush rain trampled our backs, and the curly
buffalo grass at the level of my squinted eyes was strained out straight
and whistling. I popped my head into my arms and fitted my body
to the earth. To give the wind more than my flat back, I felt, would
be sure destruction, for that was a wind, and that was a country, that
hated a foreign and vertical thing.

The cyclone missed us; we got only its lashing edge. We came up
cautiously from our muddy burrows and saw the clearing world and
smelled the air, washed and rinsed of all its sultry oppressiveness. I
for one felt better about being who I was, but for a good many weeks
I watched the sky with suspicion; exposed as we were, it could jump
on us like a leopard from a tree. And I know I was disappointed in
the shack my father swiftly put together on our arid flat. A soddy that
poked its low brow no higher than the tailings of a gopher's burrow
would have suited me better. The bond with the earth that all the
footed and winged creatures felt in that country was quite as valid
for me.

And that was why I so loved the trails and paths we made; they
were ceremonial, an insistence not only that we had a right to be in
sight on those prairies but that we owned a piece of them and controlled it. In a country practically without landmarks, as that part
of Saskatchewan was, it might have been assumed that any road
would comfort the soul. But I don't recall feeling anything special
about the graded road that led us three-quarters of the forty miles
of our annual June pilgrimage from town to homestead, or for the
wiggling tracks that turned off it to the homesteads of others. It was
our own trail, lightly worn, its ruts a slightly fresher green where old

cured grass had been rubbed away, that lifted my heart; it took off across the prairie like an extension of myself. Our own wheels had made it; broad, iron-shod wagon wheels first, then narrow democrat wheels that cut through the mat of grass and scored the earth until it blew and washed and started a rut, then finally the wheels of the Ford.

By the time we turned off it, the road we had followed from town had itself dwindled to a pair of ruts, but it never quite disappeared; it simply divided into branches like ours. I do not know why the last miles, across buffalo grass and burnouts, past a shack or two abandoned by the homesteaders who had built them, across Coteau Creek, and on westward until the ruts passed through our gate in our fence and stopped before our house, should always have excited me so, unless it was that the trail was a thing we had exclusively created and that it led to a place we had exclusively built. Those tracks demonstrated our existence as triumphantly as an Indian is demonstrated by his handprint painted in ochre on a cliff wall. Not so idiotically as the stranded Ford, this trail and the shack and chicken house and privy at its end said, "See? We are here." Thus, in a sense, was "located" a homestead.

More satisfying than the wagon trail, even, because more intimately and privately made, were the paths that our daily living wore in the prairie. I loved the horses for poking along the pasture fence looking for a way out, because that habit very soon wore a plain path all around inside the barbed wire. Whenever I had to go and catch them for something, I went out of my way to walk in it, partly because the path was easier on my bare feet but more because I wanted to contribute my feet to the wearing process. I scuffed and kicked at clods and persistent grass clumps, and twisted my weight on incipient weeds and flowers, willing that the trail around the inside of our pasture should be beaten dusty and plain, a worn border to our inheritance.

It was the same with the path to the woodpile and the privy. In June, when we reached the homestead, that would be nearly overgrown, the faintest sort of radius line within the fireguard. But our feet quickly wore it anew, though there were only the four of us, and though other members of the family, less addicted to paths than I, often frustrated and irritated me by cutting across from the wrong corner of the house, or detouring past the fence-post pile to get a handful of cedar bark for kindling, and so neglecting their plain duty to the highway. It was an unspeakable satisfaction to me when after a few weeks I could rise in the flat morning light that came across the prairie in one thrust, like a train rushing down a track, and see the beaten footpath, leading gray and dusty between grass and cactus and the little orange flowers of the false mallow that we called wild geranium, until it ended, its purpose served, at the hooked privy door.

Wearing any such path in the earth's rind is an intimate act, an act like love, and it is denied to the dweller in cities. He lacks the proper mana for it, he is out of touch. Once, on Fifty-eighth Street in New York, I saw an apartment dweller walking his captive deer on a leash. They had not the pleasure of leaving a single footprint, and the sound of the thin little hoofs on concrete seemed as melancholy to me as, at the moment, the sound of my own.

Problems for Thought and Writing

This piece is included partly because it is a sensitive and competent piece of writing, partly because it adds a meditative footnote to any discussion of "People and Populations." As our world becomes more and more filled with people, as frontiers disappear, as crowds overtake individuals, the world of value that Wallace Stegner knew as a boy in Saskatchewan becomes a receding memory. In reading Chiaromonte, Mowrer, and Hooton (pages 225, 238, 247) we should not become so involved in the intellectual and technical aspects of the over-population problem that we forget its purely emotional side. What a sad loss when and if our world no longer affords a man the chance to make his own path! Stegner has not undervalued his own rare experience. "Wearing any such path in the earth's rind is an intimate act, an act like love, and it is denied to the dweller in cities."

1. Imagine that a modern suburban housing tract were built on the site of Stegner's old homesteading claim. Compare the paths made by small boys in that community with those Stegner made.

2. Are Stegner's details simply objective? Consider: "we . . . saw a dart of wind move like a lizard . . . ," "that was a country that hated a foreign and vertical thing," "then narrow democratic wheels that cut through the mat of grass. . . ."

3. Is there anything sentimental about this piece? Is nostalgia exploited to excess? Is a dead past romantically glorified? Be specific in answering. (See Altick, page 109.)

~

B. SOME GENERATIONS OF MEN

QUINCY (1838–1848) *   Henry Adams

Under the shadow of Boston State House, turning its back on the house of John Hancock, the little passage called Hancock Avenue runs, or ran, from Beacon Street, skirting the State House grounds, to Mount Vernon Street, on the summit of Beacon Hill; and there, in the third house below Mount Vernon Place, February 16, 1838, a child was born, and christened later by his uncle, the minister of the First Church after the tenets of Boston Unitarianism, as Henry Brooks Adams.

Had he been born in Jerusalem under the shadow of the Temple and circumcised in the Synagogue by his uncle the high priest, under the name of Israel Cohen, he would scarcely have been more distinctly branded, and not much more heavily handicapped in the races of the coming century, in running for such stakes as the century was to offer; but, on the other hand, the ordinary traveller, who does not enter the field of racing, finds advantage in being, so to speak, ticketed through life, with the safeguards of an old, established traffic. Safeguards are often irksome, but sometimes convenient, and if one needs them at all, one is apt to need them badly. A hundred years earlier, such safeguards as his would have secured any young man's success; and although in 1838 their value was not very great compared with what they would have had in 1738, yet the mere accident of starting a twentieth-century career from a nest of associations so colonial— so troglodytic—as the First Church, the Boston State House, Beacon Hill, John Hancock and John Adams, Mount Vernon Street and Quincy, all crowding on ten pounds of unconscious babyhood, was so queer as to offer a subject of curious speculation to the baby long after he had witnessed the solution. What could become of such a child of the seventeenth and eighteenth centuries, when he should wake up to find himself required to play the game of the twentieth? Had he been consulted, would he have cared to play the game at all, holding such cards as he held, and suspecting that the game was to

* From Henry Adams, *The Education of Henry Adams* (Boston: Houghton Mifflin Company, 1946).

be one of which neither he nor any one else back to the beginning of time knew the rules or the risks or the stakes? He was not consulted and was not responsible, but had he been taken into the confidence of his parents, he would certainly have told them to change nothing as far as concerned him. He would have been astounded by his own luck. Probably no child, born in the year, held better cards than he. Whether life was an honest game of chance, or whether the cards were marked and forced, he could not refuse to play his excellent hand. He could never make the usual plea of irresponsibility. He accepted the situation as though he had been a party to it, and under the same circumstances would do it again, the more readily for knowing the exact values. To his life as a whole he was a consenting, contracting party and partner from the moment he was born to the moment he died. Only with that understanding—as a consciously assenting member in full partnership with the society of his age—had his education an interest to himself or to others.

As it happened, he never got to the point of playing the game at all; he lost himself in the study of it, watching the errors of the players; but this is the only interest in the story, which otherwise has no moral and little incident. A story of education—seventy years of it—the practical value remains to the end in doubt, like other values about which men have disputed since the birth of Cain and Abel; but the practical value of the universe has never been stated in dollars. Although every one cannot be a Gargantua-Napoleon-Bismarck and walk off with the great bells of Notre Dame, every one must bear his own universe, and most persons are moderately interested in learning how their neighbors have managed to carry theirs.

This problem of education, started in 1838, went on for three years, while the baby grew, like other babies, unconsciously, as a vegetable, the outside world working as it never had worked before, to get his new universe ready for him. Often in old age he puzzled over the question whether, on the doctrine of chances, he was at liberty to accept himself or his world as an accident. No such accident had ever happened before in human experience. For him, alone, the old universe was thrown into the ash-heap and a new one created. He and his eighteenth-century, troglodytic Boston were suddenly cut apart—separated forever—in act if not in sentiment, by the opening of the Boston and Albany Railroad; the appearance of the first Cunard steamers in the bay; and the telegraphic messages which carried from Baltimore to Washington the news that Henry Clay and James K. Polk were nominated for the Presidency. This was in May, 1844; he

was six years old; his new world was ready for use, and only fragments of the old met his eyes.

Of all this that was being done to complicate his education, he knew
only the color of yellow. He first found himself sitting on a yellow
kitchen floor in strong sunlight. He was three years old when he took
this earliest step in education; a lesson of color. The second followed
soon; a lesson of taste. On December 3, 1841, he developed scarlet
fever. For several days he was as good as dead, reviving only under
the careful nursing of his family. When he began to recover strength,
about January 1, 1842, his hunger must have been stronger than any
other pleasure or pain, for while in after life he retained not the faintest recollection of his illness, he remembered quite clearly his aunt
entering the sick-room bearing in her hand a saucer with a baked
apple.

The order of impressions retained by memory might naturally be
that of color and taste, although one would rather suppose that the
sense of pain would be first to educate. In fact, the third recollection
of the child was that of discomfort. The moment he could be removed, he was bundled up in blankets and carried from the little
house in Hancock Avenue to a larger one which his parents were to
occupy for the rest of their lives in the neighboring Mount Vernon
Street. The season was mid-winter, January 10, 1842, and he never
forgot his acute distress for want of air under his blankets, or the
noises of moving furniture.

As a means of variation from a normal type, sickness in childhood
ought to have a certain value not to be classed under any fitness or
unfitness of natural selection; and especially scarlet fever affected
boys seriously, both physically and in character, though they might
through life puzzle themselves to decide whether it had fitted or
unfitted them for success; but this fever of Henry Adams took greater
and greater importance in his eyes, from the point of view of education, the longer he lived. At first, the effect was physical. He fell
behind his brothers two or three inches in height, and proportionally
in bone and weight. His character and processes of mind seemed to
share in this fining-down process of scale. He was not good in a fight,
and his nerves were more delicate than boys' nerves ought to be.
He exaggerated these weaknesses as he grew older. The habit of
doubt; of distrusting his own judgment and of totally rejecting the
judgment of the world; the tendency to regard every question as
open; the hesitation to act except as a choice of evils; the shirking of
responsibility; the love of line, form, quality; the horror of ennui; the

passion for companionship and the antipathy to society—all these are
well-known qualities of New England character in no way peculiar to
individuals but in this instance they seemed to be stimulated by the
fever, and Henry Adams could never make up his mind whether, on
the whole, the change of character was morbid or healthy, good or
bad for his purpose. His brothers were the type; he was the variation.

As far as the boy knew, the sickness did not affect him at all, and he
grew up in excellent health, bodily and mental, taking life as it was
given; accepting its local standards without a difficulty, and enjoying
much of it as keenly as any other boy of his age. He seemed to himself quite normal, and his companions seemed always to think him so.
Whatever was peculiar about him was education, not character, and
came to him, directly and indirectly, as the result of that eighteenth-
century inheritance which he took with his name.

The atmosphere of education in which he lived was colonial, revolutionary, almost Cromwellian, as though he were steeped, from his
greatest grandmother's birth, in the odor of political crime. Resistance
to something was the law of New England nature; the boy looked
out on the world with the instinct of resistance; for numberless
generations his predecessors had viewed the world chiefly as a thing
to be reformed, filled with evil forces to be abolished, and they saw
no reason to suppose that they had wholly succeeded in the abolition;
the duty was unchanged. That duty implied not only resistance to
evil, but hatred of it. Boys naturally look on all force as an enemy,
and generally find it so, but the New Englander, whether boy or man,
in his long struggle with a stingy or hostile universe, had learned
also to love the pleasure of hating; his joys were few.

Politics, as a practice, whatever its professions, had always been
the systematic organization of hatreds, and Massachusetts politics
had been as harsh as the climate. The chief charm of New England
was harshness of contrasts and extremes of sensibility—a cold that
froze the blood, and a heat that boiled it—so that the pleasure of
hating—one's self if no better victim offered—was not its rarest amusement; but the charm was a true and natural child of the soil, not a
cultivated weed of the ancients. The violence of the contrast was
real and made the strongest motive of education. The double exterior nature gave life its relative values. Winter and summer, cold
and heat, town and country, force and freedom, marked two modes
of life and thought, balanced like lobes of the brain. Town was
winter confinement, school, rule, discipline; straight, gloomy streets,
piled with six feet of snow in the middle; frosts that made the snow

sing under wheels or runners; thaws when the streets became dangerous to cross; society of uncles, aunts, and cousins who expected children to behave themselves, and who were not always gratified; above
all else, winter represented the desire to escape and go free. Town
was restraint, law, unity. Country, only seven miles away, was liberty, diversity, outlawry, the endless delight of mere sense impressions given by nature for nothing, and breathed by boys without
knowing it.

Boys are wild animals, rich in the treasures of sense, but the New
England boy had a wider range of emotions than boys of more equable
climates. He felt his nature crudely, as it was meant. To the boy
Henry Adams, summer was drunken. Among senses, smell was the
strongest—smell of hot pine-woods and sweet-fern in the scorching
summer noon; of new-mown hay; of ploughed earth; of box hedges;
of peaches, lilacs, syringas; of stables, barns, cowyards; of salt water
and low tide on the marshes; nothing came amiss. Next to smell
came taste, and the children knew the taste of everything they saw
or touched; from pennyroyal and flagroot to the shell of a pignut and
the letters of a spelling-book—the taste of A-B, AB, suddenly revived
on the boy's tongue sixty years afterwards. Light, line, and color
as sensual pleasures, came later and were as crude as the rest. The
New England light is glare, and the atmosphere harshens color. The
boy was a full man before he ever knew what was meant by atmosphere; his idea of pleasure in light was the blaze of a New England sun. His idea of color was a peony, with the dew of early
morning on its petals. The intense blue of the sea, as he saw it a
mile or two away, from the Quincy hills; the cumuli in a June afternoon sky; the strong reds and greens and purples of colored prints
and children's picture-books, as the American colors then ran; these
were ideals. The opposites or antipathies, were the cold grays of
November evenings, and the thick, muddy thaws of Boston winter.
With such standards, the Bostonian could not but develop a double
nature. Life was a double thing. After a January blizzard, the boy
who could look with pleasure into the violent snow-glare of the cold
white sunshine, with its intense light and shade, scarcely knew what
was meant by tone. He could reach it only by education.

Winter and summer, then, were two hostile lives, and bred two
separate natures. Winter was always the effort to live; summer was
tropical license. Whether the children rolled in the grass, or waded
in the brook, or swam in the salt ocean, or sailed in the bay, or fished
for smelts in the creeks, or netted minnows in the salt-marshes, or

took to the pine-woods and the granite quarries, or chased muskrats
and hunted snapping-turtles in the swamps, or mushrooms or nuts
on the autumn hills, summer and country were always sensual living,
while winter was always compulsory learning. Summer was the
multiplicity of nature; winter was school.

The bearing of the two seasons on the education of Henry Adams
was no fancy; it was the most decisive force he ever knew; it ran
through life, and made the division between its perplexing, warring,
irreconcilable problems, irreducible opposites, with growing emphasis to the last year of study. From earliest childhood the boy was
accustomed to feel that, for him, life was double. Winter and summer, town and country, law and liberty, were hostile, and the man
who pretended they were not, was in his eyes a schoolmaster—that is,
a man employed to tell lies to little boys. Though Quincy was but
two hours' walk from Beacon Hill, it belonged in a different world.
For two hundred years, every Adams, from father to son, had lived
within sight of State Street, and sometimes had lived in it, yet none
had ever taken kindly to the town, or been taken kindly by it. The
boy inherited his double nature. He knew as yet nothing about his
great-grandfather, who had died a dozen years before his own birth:
he took for granted that any great-grandfather of his must have
always been good, and his enemies wicked; but he divined his great-
grandfather's character from his own. Never for a moment did he
connect the two ideas of Boston and John Adams; they were separate
and antagonistic; the idea of John Adams went with Quincy. He
knew his grandfather John Quincy Adams only as an old man of
seventy-five or eighty who was friendly and gentle with him, but
except that he heard his grandfather always called "the President,"
and his grandmother "the Madam," he had no reason to suppose that
his Adams grandfather differed in character from his Brooks grandfather who was equally kind and benevolent. He liked the Adams
side best, but for no other reason than that it reminded him of the
country, the summer, and the absence of restraint. Yet he felt also
that Quincy was in a way inferior to Boston, and that socially Boston
looked down on Quincy. The reason was clear enough even to a
five-year old child. Quincy had no Boston style. Little enough style
had either; a simpler manner of life and thought could hardly exist,
short of cave-dwelling. The flint-and-steel with which his grandfather Adams used to light his own fires in the early morning was
still on the mantelpiece of his study. The idea of a livery or even a
dress for servants, or of an evening toilette, was next to blasphemy.

Bathrooms, water-supplies, lighting, heating, and the whole array of domestic comforts, were unknown to Quincy. Boston had already a bathroom, a water-supply, a furnace, and gas. The superiority of Boston was evident, but a child liked it no better for that.

The magnificence of his grandfather Brooks's house in Pearl Street or South Street has long ago disappeared, but perhaps his country house at Medford may still remain to show what impressed the mind of a boy in 1845 with the idea of city splendor. The President's place at Quincy was the larger and older and far the more interesting of the two; but a boy felt at once its inferiority in fashion. It showed plainly enough its want of wealth. It smacked of colonial age, but not of Boston style or plush curtains. To the end of his life he never quite overcame the prejudice thus drawn in with his childish breath. He never could compel himself to care for nineteenth-century style. He was never able to adopt it, any more than his father or grandfather or great-grandfather had done. Not that he felt it as particularly hostile, for he reconciled himself to much that was worse; but because, for some remote reason, he was born an eighteenth-century child. The old house at Quincy was eighteenth century. What style it had was in its Queen Anne mahogany panels and its Louis Seize chairs and sofas. The panels belonged to an old colonial Vassall who built the house; the furniture had been brought back from Paris in 1789 or 1801 or 1817, along with porcelain and books and much else of old diplomatic remnants; and neither of the two eighteenth-century styles—neither English Queen Anne nor French Louis Seize— was comfortable for a boy, or for any one else. The dark mahogany had been painted white to suit daily life in winter gloom. Nothing seemed to favor, for a child's objects, the older forms. On the contrary, most boys, as well as grown-up people, preferred the new, with good reason, and the child felt himself distinctly at a disadvantage for the taste.

Nor had personal preference any share in his bias. The Brooks grandfather was as amiable and as sympathetic as the Adams grandfather. Both were born in 1767, and both died in 1848. Both were kind to children, and both belonged rather to the eighteenth than to the nineteenth centuries. The child knew no difference between them except that one was associated with winter and the other with summer; one with Boston, the other with Quincy. Even with Medford, the association was hardly easier. Once as a very young boy he was taken to pass a few days with his grandfather Brooks under charge of his aunt, but became so violently homesick that within twenty-four hours he was brought back in disgrace. Yet he could not remember ever being seriously homesick again.

The attachment to Quincy was not altogether sentimental or wholly sympathetic. Quincy was not a bed of thornless roses. Even there the curse of Cain set its mark. There as elsewhere a cruel universe combined to crush a child. As though three or four vigorous brothers and sisters, with the best will, were not enough to crush any child, every one else conspired towards an education which he hated. From cradle to grave this problem of running order through chaos, direction through space, discipline through freedom, unity through multiplicity, has always been, and must always be, the task of education, as it is the moral of religion, philosophy, science, art, politics, and economy; but a boy's will is his life, and he dies when it is broken, as the colt dies in harness, taking a new nature in becoming tame. Rarely has the boy felt kindly towards his tamers. Between him and his master has always been war. Henry Adams never knew a boy of his generation to like a master, and the task of remaining on friendly terms with one's own family, in such a relation, was never easy.

All the more singular it seemed afterwards to him that his first serious contact with the President should have been a struggle of will, in which the old man almost necessarily defeated the boy, but instead of leaving, as usual in such defeats, a lifelong sting, left rather an impression of as fair treatment as could be expected from a natural enemy. The boy met seldom with such restraint. He could not have been much more than six years old at the time—seven at the utmost— and his mother had taken him to Quincy for a long stay with the President during the summer. What became of the rest of the family he quite forgot; but he distinctly remembered standing at the house door one summer morning in a passionate outburst of rebellion against going to school. Naturally his mother was the immediate victim of his rage; that is what mothers are for, and boys also; but in this case the boy had his mother at unfair disadvantage, for she was a guest, and had no means of enforcing obedience. Henry showed a certain tactical ability by refusing to start, and he met all efforts at compulsion by successful, though too vehement protest. He was in fair way to win, and was holding his own, with sufficient energy, at the bottom of the long staircase which led up to the door of the President's library, when the door opened, and the old man slowly came down. Putting on his hat, he took the boy's hand without a word, and walked with him, paralyzed with awe, up the road to the town. After the first moments of consternation at this interference in a domestic dispute, the boy reflected that an old gentleman close on eighty would never trouble himself to walk near a mile on a hot summer morning over a shadeless road to take a boy to school, and that it would be strange if a lad imbued with the passion of freedom could not find a corner to dodge around, somewhere before reaching the school door. Then and always, the boy insisted that this reasoning justified his apparent submission; but the old man did not stop, and the boy saw all his strategical points turned, one after another, until he found himself seated inside the school, and obviously the centre of curious if not malevolent criticism. Not till then did the President release his hand and depart.

The point was that this act, contrary to the inalienable rights of boys, and nullifying the social compact, ought to have made him dislike his grandfather for life. He could not recall that it had this effect even for a moment. With a certain maturity of mind, the child must have recognized that the President, though a tool of tyranny, had done his disreputable work with a certain intelligence. He had shown no temper, no irritation, no personal feeling, and had made no display of force. Above all, he had held his tongue. During their long walk he had said nothing; he had uttered no syllable of revolting cant about the duty of obedience and the wickedness of resistance to law, he had shown no concern in the matter; hardly even a consciousness of the boy's existence. Probably his mind at that moment was actually troubling itself little about his grandson's iniquities, and much about the iniquities of President Polk, but the boy could scarcely at that age feel the whole satisfaction of thinking that President Polk was to be the vicarious victim of his own sins, and he gave his grandfather credit for intelligent silence. For this forbearance he felt instinctive respect. He admitted force as a form of right; he admitted even temper, under protest; but the seeds of a moral education would at that moment have fallen on the stoniest soil in Quincy, which is, as every one knows, the stoniest glacial and tidal drift known in any Puritan land.

Neither party to this momentary disagreement can have felt rancor, for during these three or four summers the old President's relations with the boy were friendly and almost intimate. Whether his older brothers and sisters were still more favored he failed to remember, but he was himself admitted to a sort of familiarity which, when in his turn he had reached old age, rather shocked him, for it must have sometimes tried the President's patience. He hung about the library; handled the books; deranged the papers; ransacked the drawers; searched the old purses and pocketbooks for foreign coins; drew the swordcane; snapped the travelling-pistols; upset everything in the corners, and penetrated the President's dressing-closet where a row of tumblers, inverted on the shelf, covered caterpillars which were supposed to become moths or butterflies, but never did. The Madam bore with fortitude the loss of the tumblers which her husband purloined for these hatcheries; but she made protest when he carried off her best cut-glass bowls to plant with acorns or peachstones that he might see the roots grow; but which, she said, he commonly forgot like the caterpillars.

At that time the President rode the hobby of tree-culture, and some fine old trees should still remain to witness it, unless they have been improved off the ground, but his was a restless mind, and although he took his hobbies seriously and would have been annoyed had his grandchild asked whether he was bored like an English duke, he probably cared more for the processes than for the results, so that his grandson was saddened by the sight and smell of peaches and pears, the best of their kind, which he brought up from the garden to rot on his shelves for seed. With the inherited virtues of his Puritan ancestors, the little boy Henry conscientiously brought up to him in his study the finest peaches he found in the garden, and ate only the less perfect. Naturally he ate more by way of compensation, but the act showed that he bore no grudge. As for his grandfather, it is even possible that he may have felt a certain self-reproach for his temporary rôle of schoolmaster seeing that his own career did not offer proof of the worldly advantages of docile obedience—for there still exists somewhere a little volume of critically edited Nursery Rhymes with the boy's name in full written in the President's trembling hand on the fly-leaf. Of course there was also the Bible, given to each child at birth, with the proper inscription in the President's hand on the fly-leaf; while their grandfather Brooks supplied the silver mugs.

So many Bibles and silver mugs had to be supplied, that a new house, or cottage, was built to hold them. It was "on the hill," five minutes' walk above "the old house," with a far view eastward over Quincy Bay, and northward over Boston. Till his twelfth year, the child passed his summers there, and his pleasures of childhood mostly centered in it. Of education he had as yet little to complain. Country schools were not very serious. Nothing stuck to the mind except home impressions, and the sharpest were those of kindred children; but as influences that warped a mind, none compared with the mere effect of the back of the President's bald head, as he sat in his pew on Sundays, in line with that of President Quincy, who, though some ten years younger, seemed to children about the same age. Before railways entered the New England town, every parish church showed half-a-dozen of these leading citizens, with gray hair, who sat on the main aisle in the best pews, and had sat there, or in some equivalent dignity, since the time of St. Augustine, if not since the glacial epoch. It was unusual for boys to sit behind a President grandfather, and to read over his head the tablet in memory of a President great-grandfather, who had "pledged his life, his fortune, and his sacred honor" to secure the independence of his country and so forth; but boys naturally supposed, without much reasoning, that other boys had the equivalent of President grandfathers, and that churches would always go on, with the bald-headed leading citizens on the main aisle, and Presidents or their equivalents on the walls. The Irish gardener once said to the child: "You'll be thinkin' you'll be President too!" The casualty of the remark made so strong an impression on his mind that he never forgot it. He could not remember ever to have thought on the subject; to him, that there should be a doubt of his being President was a new idea. What had been would continue to be. He doubted neither about Presidents nor about Churches, and no one suggested at that time a doubt whether a system of society which had lasted since Adam would outlast one Adams more.

The Madam was a little more remote than the President, but more decorative. She stayed much in her own room with the Dutch tiles, looking out on her garden with the box walks, and seemed a fragile creature to a boy who sometimes brought her a note or a message, and took distinct pleasure in looking at her delicate face under what seemed to him very becoming caps. He liked her refined figure; her gentle voice and manner; her vague effect of not belonging there, but to Washington or to Europe, like her furniture, and writing-desk with little glass doors above and little eighteenth-century volumes in old binding, labeled "Peregrine Pickle" or "Tom Jones" or "Hannah More." Try as she might, the Madam could never be Bostonian, and it was her cross in life, but to the boy it was her charm. Even at that age, he felt drawn to it. The Madam's life had been in truth far from Boston. She was born in London in 1775, daughter of Joshua Johnson, an American merchant, brother of Governor Thomas Johnson of Maryland; and Catherine Nuth, of an English family in London. Driven from England by the Revolutionary War, Joshua Johnson took his family to Nantes, where they remained till the peace.

The girl Louisa Catherine was nearly ten years old when brought back to London, and her sense of nationality must have been confused; but the influence of the Johnsons and the services of Joshua obtained for him from President Washington the appointment of Consul in London on the organization of the Government in 1790. In 1794 President Washington appointed John Quincy Adams Minister to The Hague. He was twenty-seven years old when he returned to London, and found the Consul's house a very agreeable haunt. Louisa was then twenty.

At that time, and long afterwards, the Consul's house, far more than the Minister's, was the centre of contact for travelling Americans, either official or other. The Legation was a shifting point, between 1785 and 1815; but the Consulate, far down in the City, near the Tower, was convenient and inviting; so inviting that it proved fatal to young Adams. Louisa was charming, like a Romney portrait, but among her many charms that of being a New England woman was not one. The defect was serious. Her future mother-in-law, Abigail, a famous New England woman whose authority over her turbulent husband, the second President, was hardly so great as that which she exercised over her son, the sixth to be, was troubled by the fear that Louisa might not be made of stuff stern enough, or brought up in conditions severe enough, to suit a New England climate, or to make an efficient wife for her paragon son, and Abigail was right on that point, as on most others where sound judgment was involved; but sound judgment is sometimes a source of weakness rather than of force, and John Quincy already had reason to think that his mother held sound judgments on the subject of daughters-in-law which human nature, since the fall of Eve, made Adams helpless to realize. Being three thousand miles away from his mother, and equally far in love, he married Louisa in London, July 26, 1797, and took her to Berlin to be the head of the United States Legation. During three or four exciting years, the young bride lived in Berlin; whether she was happy or not, whether she was content or not, whether she was socially successful or not, her descendants did not surely know; but in any case she could by no chance have become educated there for a life in Quincy or Boston. In 1801 the overthrow of the Federalist Party drove her and her husband to America, and she became at last a member of the Quincy household, but by that time her children needed all her attention, and she remained there with occasional winters in Boston and Washington, till 1809. Her husband was made Senator in 1803, and in 1809 was appointed Minister to Russia. She went with him to St. Petersburg, taking her baby, Charles Francis, born in 1807; but broken-hearted at having to leave her two older boys behind. The life at St. Petersburg was hardly gay for her; they were far too poor to shine in that extravagant society; but she survived it, though her little girl baby did not, and in the winter of 1814-15, alone with the boy of seven years old, crossed Europe from St. Petersburg to Paris, in her travelling-carriage, passing through the armies, and reaching Paris in the *Cent Jours* after Napoleon's return from Elba. Her husband next went to England as Minister, and she was for two years at the Court of the Regent. In 1817 her husband came home to be Secretary of State, and she lived for eight years in F Street, doing her work of entertainer for President Monroe's administration. Next she lived four miserable years in the White House. When that chapter was closed in 1829, she had earned the right to be tired and delicate, but she still had fifteen years to serve as wife of a Member of the House, after her husband went back to Congress in 1833. Then it was that the little Henry, her grandson, first remembered her, from 1843 to 1848, sitting in her panelled room, at breakfast, with her heavy silver teapot and sugar-bowl and cream-jug, which still exist somewhere as an heirloom of the modern safety-vault. By that time she was seventy years old or more, and thoroughly weary of being beaten about a stormy world. To the boy she seemed singularly peaceful, a vision of silver gray, presiding over her old President and her Queen Anne mahogany; an exotic, like her Sèvres china; an object of deference to every one, and of great affection to her son Charles; but hardly more Bostonian than she had been fifty years before, on her wedding-day, in the shadow of the Tower of London.

Such a figure was even less fitted than that of her old husband, the President, to impress on a boy's mind, the standards of the coming century. She was Louis Seize, like the furniture. The boy knew nothing of her interior life, which had been, as the venerable Abigail, long since at peace, foresaw, one of severe stress and little pure satisfaction. He never dreamed that from her might come some of those doubts and self-questionings, those hesitations, those rebellions against law and discipline, which marked more than one of her descendants; but he might even then have felt some vague instinctive suspicion that he was to inherit from her the seeds of the primal sin, the fall from grace, the curse of Abel, that he was not of pure New England stock, but half exotic. As a child of Quincy he was not a true Bostonian, but even as a child of Quincy he inherited a quarter taint of Maryland blood. Charles Francis, half Marylander by birth, had hardly seen Boston till he was ten years old, when his parents left him there at school in 1817, and he never forgot the experience. He was to be nearly as old as his mother had been in 1845, before he quite accepted Boston, or Boston quite accepted him.

A boy who began his education in these surroundings, with physical strength inferior to that of his brothers, and with a certain delicacy of mind and bone, ought rightly to have felt at home in the eighteenth century and should, in proper self-respect, have rebelled against the standards of the nineteenth. The atmosphere of his first ten years must have been very like that of his grandfather at the same age, from 1767 till 1776, barring the battle of Bunker Hill, and even as late as 1846, the battle of Bunker Hill remained actual. The tone of Boston society was colonial. The true Bostonian always knelt in self-abasement before the majesty of English standards; far from concealing it as a weakness, he was proud of it as his strength. The eighteenth century ruled society long after 1850. Perhaps the boy began to shake it off rather earlier than most of his mates.

Indeed this prehistoric stage of education ended rather abruptly with his tenth year. One winter morning he was conscious of a certain confusion in the house in Mount Vernon Street, and gathered, from such words as he could catch, that the President, who happened to be then staying there, on his way to Washington, had fallen and hurt himself. Then he heard the word paralysis. After that day he came to associate the word with the figure of his grandfather, in a tall-backed, invalid armchair, on one side of the spare bedroom fireplace, and one of his old friends, Dr. Parkman or P. P. F. Degrand, on the other side, both dozing.

The end of this first, or ancestral and Revolutionary, chapter came on February 21, 1848—and the month of February brought life and death as a family habit—when the eighteenth century, as an actual and living companion, vanished. If the scene on the floor of the House, when the old President fell, struck the still simple-minded American public with a sensation unusually dramatic, its effect on a ten-year-old boy, whose boy-life was fading away with the life of his grandfather, could not be slight. One had to pay for Revolutionary patriots; grandfathers and grandmothers; Presidents; diplomats; Queen Anne mahogany and Louis Seize chairs, as well as for Stuart portraits. Such things warp young life. Americans commonly believed that they ruined it, and perhaps the practical common-sense of the American mind judged right. Many a boy might be ruined by much less than the emotions of the funeral service in the Quincy church, with its surroundings of national respect and family pride. By another dramatic chance it happened that the clergyman of the parish, Dr. Lunt, was an unusual pulpit orator, the ideal of a somewhat austere intellectual type, such as the school of Buckminster and Channing inherited from the old Congregational clergy. His extraordinarily refined appearance, his dignity of manner, his deeply cadenced voice, his remarkable English and his fine appreciation, gave to the funeral service a character that left an overwhelming impression on the boy's mind. He was to see many great functions—funerals and festivals—in after-life, till his only thought was to see no more, but he never again witnessed anything nearly so impressive to him as the last services at Quincy over the body of one President and the ashes of another.

The effect of the Quincy service was deepened by the official ceremony which afterwards took place in Faneuil Hall, when the boy was taken to hear his uncle, Edward Everett, deliver a Eulogy. Like all Mr. Everett's orations, it was an admirable piece of oratory, such as only an admirable orator and scholar could create; too good for a ten-year-old boy to appreciate at its value; but already the boy knew that the dead President could not be in it, and had even learned why he would have been out of place there; for knowledge was beginning to come fast. The shadow of the War of 1812 still hung over State Street; the shadow of the Civil War to come had already begun to darken Faneuil Hall. No rhetoric could have reconciled Mr. Everett's audience to his subject. How could he say there, to an assemblage of Bostonians in the heart of mercantile Boston, that the only distinctive mark of all the Adamses, since old Sam Adams's father a hundred and fifty years before, had been their inherited quarrel with State Street, which had again and again broken out into riot, bloodshed, personal feuds, foreign and civil war, wholesale banishments and confiscations, until the history of Florence was hardly more turbulent than that of Boston? How could he whisper the word Hartford Convention before the men who had made it? What would have been said had he suggested the chance of Secession and Civil War?

Thus already, at ten years old, the boy found himself standing face to face with a dilemma that might have puzzled an early Christian. What was he?—where was he going? Even then he felt that something was wrong, but he concluded that it must be Boston. Quincy had always been right, for Quincy represented a moral principle—

the principle of resistance to Boston. His Adams ancestors must have been right, since they were always hostile to State Street. If State Street was wrong, Quincy must be right! Turn the dilemma as he pleased, he still came back on the eighteenth century and the law of Resistance; of Truth; of Duty, and of Freedom. He was a ten-year-old priest and politician. He could under no circumstances have guessed what the next fifty years had in store, and no one could teach him; but sometimes, in his old age, he wondered—and could never decide—whether the most clear and certain knowledge would have helped him. Supposing he had seen a New York stock-list of 1900, and had studied the statistics of railways, telegraphs, coal, and steel—would he have quitted his eighteenth-century, his ancestral prejudices, his abstract ideals, his semi-clerical training, and the rest, in order to perform an expiatory pilgrimage to State Street, and ask for the fatted calf of his grandfather Brooks and a clerkship in the Suffolk Bank?

Sixty years afterwards he was still unable to make up his mind. Each course had its advantages, but the material advantages, looking back, seemed to lie wholly in State Street.

Problems for Thought and Writing

I

1. This is the first chapter of Adams' book *The Education of Henry Adams.* That book has been described by Louis Kronenberger as "a perfectly conscious study of frustration and deflected purpose; of the failure of a superior man to find the right place, or any tolerable place, in a civilization growing ever more corrupt, rapacious, and vulgar." In what ways is this chapter a purposeful beginning for such a book?

2. "To his life as a whole he was a consenting, contracting party and partner from the moment he was born to the moment he died." This condition is almost exactly opposite to what Chiaromonte declares (page 225) is possible or available to modern mass man. To what extent can you share Adams' feeling? To what extent do you feel you have been a "contracting party" to your life or to what extent merely *pushed around* by it? Hard as this may be to measure, it is an illuminating question to ask.

3. Kronenberger writes: "Adams self-consciously sought to channel his experiences and to convert them into education." Is this, in any sense, a confession of failure—of failure to *act?* What evidence does Adams give you?

4. In saying that the New Englander learned "to love the pleasure of hating," Adams is obviously not just describing his early life but trying to *explain* it. Resistance, hatred, opposition—these were some of the *shaping* forces that gave his life form. Compare the conditions of his life with those of the modern world described by Leslie Fiedler (page 298), Ortega y Gasset (page 188) and Chiaromonte (page 225). Put your own life in its *essential* setting and

make an attempt to explain it. Or compare and contrast the conditions of your life with those of Adams.

5. "From earliest childhood the boy was accustomed to feel that, for him, life was double." (page 265) Note the use of contrast in this essay as an organizational and thematic device. Winter and summer, Boston and Quincy —the two seasons, the two places—how are they symbolic of his life?

6. "From cradle to grave this problem of running order through chaos, direction through space, discipline through freedom, unity through multiplicity, has always been, and must always be, the task of education. . . ." Would it have occurred to you to describe the task of education in these terms? Why or why not?

7. What does Adams mean by speaking of himself as belonging to the eighteenth century?

II

8. Examine Adams' use of concrete detail for effect. Consider his description of the "sensual pleasures" of summer. Is this lushness compatible with his "Puritan" temperament?

9. Identify or define: the social compact, cant, purloined, expiatory, troglodytic.

10. Study the sentence rhythms of this essay. How do they add to the meaning and effect of the whole?

11. Do you find Adams' use of the third person a happy or awkward device?

12. Who is the "mock reader" of this piece? (See Gibson, page 375.)

~

ALMOST THIRTY * John Reed

In the spring of 1917, when he wrote the following essay, John Reed felt little of the self-confidence that had carried him so buoyantly through the preceding decade. A serious operation—the removal of his left kidney—had been followed by the termination of his three years' employment by the *Metropolitan Magazine*, with whose editors he had quarreled over their war policy. The eminent position he had created for himself by his articles on Mexico, the World War, and American labor struggles was crumbling. And at the same time the thing he had dreaded ever since August, 1914, had happened: the United States had been drawn into the war. All this gave him the sense, so strongly revealed in the essay, that an era of his life had ended, and led him to attempt the task of personal understanding and evaluation.

---

* From *The New Republic*, April 15 and 29, 1936. Used by permission.

Precisely why the essay was not published I do not know. It remained with Reed's papers until these were turned over by Louise Bryant to the Harvard Alumni John Reed Committee, by whose permission it is now printed. If it had appeared when it was written, what would chiefly have surprised one group of readers, those who still thought of him as a playboy, was Reed's seriousness. What would have surprised another group was the note of uncertainty, almost of despair. The truth is that Reed, on the one hand, had always been more reflective and somewhat less sure of himself than his conduct indicated and, on the other, was even at this time by no means so inhibited in action by his doubts as a reader of the essay might be led to suppose, for all his energies were engaged in the struggle to prevent the declaration of war and, later, to mitigate the effects of militarism.

Yet Reed's skepticism was real enough, and its focal point is apparent: as a result of the collapse of the revolutionary movement in the war, he had lost his confidence in the working class. This is important, because, soon after "Almost Thirty" was finished, Reed went to Russia. No reader of *Ten Days That Shook the World* can doubt that the triumph of the revolution had overwhelming personal significance for Reed. Why this was so, "Almost Thirty" makes clear.

—GRANVILLE HICKS

I am twenty-nine years old, and I know that this is the end of a part of my life, the end of youth. Sometimes it seems to me the end of the world's youth too; certainly the great war has done something to us all. But it is also the beginning of a new phase of life; and the world we live in is so full of swift change and color and meaning that I can hardly keep from imagining the splendid and terrible possibilities of the time to come. The last ten years I've gone up and down the earth drinking in experience, fighting and loving, seeing and hearing and testing things. I've traveled all over Europe, and to the borders of the East, and down in Mexico, having adventures; seeing men killed and broken, victorious and laughing, men with visions and men with a sense of humor. I've watched civilization change and broaden and sweeten in my lifetime; and I've watched it wither and crumble in the red blast of war. And war I have seen, too, in the trenches, with the armies. I'm not quite sick of seeing yet, but soon I will be—I know that. My future life will not be what it has been. And so I want to stop a minute, and look back, and get my bearings. A great deal of my boyhood was illness and physical weakness, and I was never really well until my sixteenth year. The beginning of my remembered life was a turmoil of imaginings—formless perceptions of beauty, which broke forth in voluminous verses, sensations of fear, of tenderness, of pain. Then came a period of intense emotion, in which I endowed certain girls with the attributes of Guinevere and had a vision of Galahad and the Sangraal in the sky over the school football field; a furious energy drove me to all kinds of bodily and mental exercise, without any particular direction—except that I felt sure I was going to be a great poet and novelist. After that I was increasingly active and restless, more ambitious of place and power, less exalted, scattering myself in a hundred different directions; life became a beloved moving picture, thought about only in brilliant flashes, conceived as emotion and sensation. And now, almost thirty, some of that old superabundant vitality is gone, and with it the all-sufficient joy of mere living. A good many of my beliefs have got twisted by the great war. I am weakened by a serious operation. Some things I think I have settled, but in other ways I am back where I started—a turmoil of imaginings.

I must find myself again. Some men seem to get their direction early, to grow naturally and with little change to the thing they are to be. I have no idea what I shall be or do one month from now. Whenever I have tried to become some one thing, I have failed; it is only by drifting with the wind that I have found myself and plunged joyously into a new role. I have discovered that I am only happy when I'm working hard at something I like. I never stuck long at anything I didn't like, and now I couldn't if I wanted to; on the other hand, there are very few things I don't get some fun out of, if only the novelty of experience. I love people, except the well-fed smug, and am interested in all new things and all the beautiful old things they do. I love beauty and chance and change, but less now in the external world and more in my mind. I suppose I'll always be a romanticist.

From the very beginning my excitable imagination fed on fantasy. I still remember my grandfather's house, where I was born—a lordly gray mansion modeled on a French château, with its immense park, its formal gardens, lawns, stables, greenhouses and glass grape arbor, the tame deer among the trees. All that remains to me of my grandfather is his majestic height, his long slim fingers, and the polished courtesy of his manners. He had come around the Horn in a sailing ship when the west coast was the wild frontier, made his pile, and lived with Russian lavishness. Portland was less than thirty years

old, a little town carved out of the Oregon forests, with streets deep
in mud, and the wilderness coming down close around it. Through
this my grandfather drove his blooded horses to his smart carriages,
imported from the east—and from Europe—with liveried coachmen
and footmen on the box. The lawn terrace below the house was surrounded on three sides by great fir trees, up whose sides ran gas pipes
grown over with bark; on summer evenings canvas was laid on the
turf, and people danced, illuminated by flaming jets of gas which
seemed to spout from the trees. There was something fantastic in all
that.

Then we were poor, living in a little house down in the town, with
a crowd of gay young people around my gay young father and mother.
My head was full of fairy stories and tales of giants, witches, and
dragons, and I invented a monster called Hormuz who lived in the
woods behind the town and devoured little children—with which I
terrified the small boys and girls of the neighborhood and incidentally
myself. Almost all the servants in those days were Chinese, who
stayed for years, at last getting to be almost members of the family.
They brought ghosts and superstitions into the house, and the tang
of bloody feuds among themselves, idols and foods and drinks,
strange customs and ceremonies; half affectionate, half contemptuous,
wholly independent, and withal outlandish, they have left me a memory of pigtails and gongs and fluttering red paper. And there was my
uncle, a romantic figure who played at coffee planting in Central
America, mixed in revolutions, and sometimes blew in, tanned and
bearded and speaking "spiggoty" like a mestizo. Once the tale ran
that he had helped to lead a revolution that captured Guatemala for
a few brief days, and was made secretary of state; the first thing he
did was to appropriate the funds of the national treasury to give a
grand state ball, and then he declared war on the German Empire—
because he had flunked his German course in college. Later he went
out to the Philippines as a volunteer in the Spanish War—and the tale
of how he was made king of Guam is still told with shouts of mirth by
the veterans of the Second Oregon.

My mother, who has always encouraged me in the things I wanted
to do, taught me to read. I don't know when that was, but I remember the orgy of books I plunged into. History was my passion,
kings strutting about and the armored ranks of men-at-arms clashing
forward in close ranks against a hail of cloth-yard shafts; but I was
equally enamored of Mark Twain, and Bill Nye, and Blackmore's
Lorna Doone, and Webster's Unabridged Dictionary, and the *Arabian*

Nights, and *The Tales of the Round Table.* What I didn't understand, my imagination interpreted. At the age of nine I began to write a Comic History of the United States—after Bill Nye—and I think it was then I made up my mind to be a writer.

About that time we moved to an apartment hotel, and I went to school. Those first few years of school stimulated my ambition to learn, but since then the curricula of schools and colleges have meant little for me. I've always been an indifferent student, to say the least, except when some subject like elementary chemistry, or English poetry, or composition caught my imagination—or the personality of some great teacher, like Professor Copeland of Harvard. Why should I have been interested in the stupid education of our time? We take young soaring imaginations, consumed with curiosity about the life they see all around, and feed them with dead technique: the flawless purity of Washington, Lincoln's humdrum chivalry, our dull and virtuous history and England's honest glory; Addison's graceful style as an essayist, Goldsmith celebrating the rural clergy of the eighteenth century, Dr. Johnson at his most vapid, and George Eliot's *Silas Marner;* Macaulay, and the sonorous oratings of Edmund Burke; and in Latin, Caesar's Gallic guidebook and Cicero's mouthings about Roman politics. And the teachers! Men and women—usually women —whose chief qualification is that they can plow steadily through a dull round of dates, acts, half-truths, and rules for style, without questioning, without interpreting, and without seeing how ridiculously unlike the world their teachings are. I have forgotten most of it, forced on me before I was ready; what I do know came mostly from books I had the curiosity to read outside school hours. And many fine things I have had to force myself to explore again, because school once spoiled them for me.

But in going to school I first entered the world of my fellows, and the social experience meant more and more to me until it almost crowded out the study side altogether. I can still see the school playground full of running and shouting and clamoring boys, and feel as I felt then when they stopped here and there to look at me, a new boy, with curious and insolent eyes. I was small, though, and not very well, and at the beginning I didn't mix much with them. . . . But after school was out there were great doings, which were too exciting to keep out of. The town was divided into districts, ruled over by gangs of boys in a constant state of fierce warfare. I belonged to the Fourteenth Street gang, whose chief was a tall, curly-headed Irish boy who lived across the street—he is now a policeman. My best friend could make sounds like a bugle, and he was trumpeter. Standing in the middle of the street he would blow, and in a minute boys would come swarming to him, tearing up lawns and making mudballs as they came. Then we'd go running and shouting up the hill to give battle to the Montgomery Street gang or beat off their attack. . . . And there were the wooded hills behind the town, where Indians and bears and outlaws might be lurking to be trailed by our scouts and Robin Hoods.

Both my mother's parents and my father came from upper New York state, and when I was ten years old my mother and my brother and I went east to visit them. We spent a summer month at Plymouth, Massachusetts, visited New York (I still remember the awful summer heat, the vermin in our boardinghouse, and the steam engines on the Elevated), and were in Washington when the *Maine* blew up and the first volunteers left for the Spanish War.

Then I was back in Portland, in a new house, settling into the life of school and play. We had a theater in our attic, where we acted our own plays, and we built scenic railways in the yard and log cabins in the woods back of town. I had a number of highly colored schemes for getting adventure and wealth at the same time. For instance, I once began to dig a tunnel from our house to school, about a mile away; we were going to steal two sheep and hide them in the tunnel, and these two sheep were going to have children, and so on, until a large flock had gathered—then we'd sell them. My brother and I had a pony, and we went on camping trips back in the woods, and sailing and swimming and camping up the Willamette River. I began to write poetry, too, and read voraciously everything I could get hold of, from Edwin Arnold's *Light of Asia* and Marie Corelli to Scott and Stevenson and Sir Thomas Malory.

But with all this I wasn't entirely happy. I was often ill. Outside of a few friends, I wasn't a success with the boys. I hadn't strength or fight enough to be good at athletics—except swimming, which I have always loved; and I was a good deal of a physical coward. I would sneak out over the back fence to avoid boys who were "laying" for me or who I thought were "laying" for me. Sometimes I fought, when I couldn't help myself, and sometimes even won; but I preferred to be called a coward than fight. I hated pain. My imagination conjured up horrible things that would happen to me, and I simply ran away. One time, when I was on the editorial board of the school paper, a boy I was afraid of warned me not to publish a joking paragraph I had written about him—and I didn't. . . . My way to school lay through a sort of slum district called Goose Hollow, peopled with brutal Irish boys, many of whom grew up to be prizefighters and baseball stars. I was literally frightened out of my senses when I went through Goose Hollow. Once a Goose Hollowite made me promise to give him a nickel if he didn't hit me, and walked up to my house with me while I got it for him. . . . The strange thing was that when I was cornered and fought, even a licking wasn't a hundredth as bad as I thought it would be; but I never learned anything from that—the next time I ran away just the same and suffered the most ghastly pangs of fear.

I wasn't much good at the things other boys were, and their codes of honor and conduct didn't hold me. They felt it, too, and had a sort of good-natured contempt for me. I was neither one thing nor the other, neither altogether coward nor brave, neither manly nor sissified, neither ashamed nor unashamed. I think that is why my impression of my boyhood is an unhappy one, and why I have so few close friends in Portland, and why I don't want ever again to live there.

It must have disappointed my father that I was like that, though he never said much about it. He was a great fighter, one of the first of the little band of political insurgents who were afterward, as the Progressive party, to give expression to the new social conscience of the American middle class. His terrible slashing wit, his fine scorn of stupidity and cowardice and littleness, made him many enemies, who never dared attack him to his face but fought him secretly and were glad when he died. As United States marshal under Roosevelt, it was he who, with Francis J. Heney and Lincoln Steffens, smashed the Oregon land fraud ring, which was a brave thing to do in Oregon then. I remember him and Heney in the marshal's office guying William J. Burns, the detective on the case, for his Hawkshaw make-up and his ridiculous melodramatics. In 1910 a man came around to browbeat my father into contributing to the Republican campaign fund, and he kicked the collector down the courthouse stairs—and was removed from the marshalship by President Taft. Afterward he ran for Congress, but lost out by a slim margin, mainly because he came east to see me graduate from college instead of stumping the state.

When I was sixteen I went east to a New Jersey boarding school and then to Harvard College and afterward to Europe for a year's travel, and my brother followed me through college. We never knew until later how much our mother and father denied themselves that we might go and how he poured out his life that we might live like rich men's sons. He and mother always gave us more than we asked, in freedom and understanding as well as material things. And on the day my brother graduated from college he broke under the terrible effort and died a few weeks later. It has always seemed to me bitter irony that he couldn't have lived to see my little success. He was always more like a wise, kind friend than a father.

Boarding school, I think, meant more to me than anything in my boyhood. Among these strange boys I came as a stranger, and I soon found out that they were willing to accept me at my own value. I was in fine health. The ordered life of the community interested me; I was impressed by its traditional customs and dignities, school patriotism, and the sense of a long settled and established civilization, so different from the raw, pretentious West. My stories and verses were published in the school paper; I played football and ran the quarter mile with very good average success; I had a fight or two and stuck it out. There were perilous adventures, too, when a few of us stole down the fire escapes at night and went to country dances, slipping back to bed in the dormitory at dawn. With the school social butterflies, I "fussed" girls in the town and was not laughed at. Busy, happy, with lots of friends, I expanded into self-confidence. So without trying I found myself, and since then I have never been very much afraid of men.

In 1906 I went up to Harvard almost alone, knowing hardly a soul in the university. My college class entered over seven hundred strong, and for the first three months it seemed to me, going around to lectures and meetings, as if every one of the seven hundred had friends but me. I was thrilled with the immensity of Harvard, its infinite opportunities, its august history and traditions—but desperately lonely. I didn't know which way to turn, how to meet people. Fellows passed me in the Yard, shouting gayly to one another; I saw parties off to Boston, Saturday night, whooping and yelling on the back platform of the street car, and they passed hilariously singing under my window in the early dawn. Athletes and musicians and writers and statesmen were emerging from the ranks of the class. The freshman clubs were forming.

And I was out of it all. I "went out" for the college papers and tried to make the freshman crew, even staying in Cambridge vacations to go down to the empty boathouse and plug away at the machines —and was the last man kicked off the squad before they went to New London. I got to know many fellows to nod to and a very few intimately, but most of my friends were whirled off and up into prominence and came to see me no more. One of them said he'd room with me sophomore year—but he was tipped off that I wasn't "the right sort" and openly drew away from me. And I, too, hurt a boy who was my friend. He was a Jew, a shy, rather melancholy person. We were always together, we two outsiders. I became irritated and morbid about it—it seemed I would never be part of the rich splendor of college life with him around—so I drew away from him. . . . It hurt him very much, and it taught me better. Since then he has forgiven it and done wonderful things for me, and we are friends.

My second year was better. I was elected an editor of two of the papers and knew more fellows. The fortunate and splendid youths, the aristocrats who filled the clubs and dominated college society, didn't seem so attractive. In two open contests, the trial for editor of the college daily paper and that for assistant manager of the varsity crew, I qualified easily for election; but the aristocrats blackballed me. However, that mattered less. During my freshman year I used to *pray* to be liked, to have friends, to be popular with the crowd. Now I had friends, plenty of them; and I have found that when I am working hard at something I love, friends come without my trying, and stay; and fear goes, and that sense of being lost which is so horrible.

From that time on I never felt out of it. I was never popular with the aristocrats; I was never elected to any clubs but one, and that one largely because of a dearth of members who could write lyrics for the annual show. But I was on the papers, was elected president of the Cosmopolitan Club, where forty-three nationalities met, became manager of the musical clubs, captain of the water-polo team, and an officer in many undergraduate activities. As song leader of the cheering section, I had the supreme blissful sensation of swaying two thousand voices in great crashing choruses during the big football games. The more I met the college aristocrats, the more their cold, cruel stupidity repelled me. I began to pity them for their lack of imagination and the narrowness of their glittering lives—clubs, athletics, society. College is like the world; outside there is the same class of people, dull and sated and blind.

Harvard University under President Eliot was unique. Individualism was carried to the point where a man who came for a good time could get through and graduate without having learned anything, but on the other hand, anyone could find there anything he wanted from all the world's store of learning. The undergraduates were practically free from control; they could live pretty much where they pleased and do as they pleased—so long as they attended lectures. There was no attempt made by the authorities to weld the student body together or to enforce any kind of uniformity. Some men came with allowances of fifteen thousand dollars a year pocket money, with automobiles and servants, living in gorgeous suites in palatial apartment houses; others in the same class starved in attic bedrooms.

All sorts of strange characters, of every race and mind, poets, philosophers, cranks of every twist, were in our class. The very hugeness of it prevented any one man from knowing more than a few of his classmates, though I managed to make the acquaintance of about five hundred of them. The aristocrats controlled the places of pride and power, except when a democratic revolution, such as occurred in my senior year, swept them off their feet; but they were so exclusive that most of the real life went on outside their ranks—and all the intellectual life of the student body. So many fine men were outside the charmed circle that, unlike most colleges, there was no disgrace in not being a club man. What is known as college spirit was not very powerful; no odium attached to those who didn't go to football games and cheer. There was talk of the world, and daring thought, and intellectual insurgency; heresy has always been a Harvard and a New England tradition. Students themselves criticized the faculty for not educating them, attacked the sacred institution of intercollegiate athletics, sneered at undergraduate clubs so holy that no one dared mention their names. No matter what you were or what you did—at Harvard you could find your kind. It wasn't a breeder for masses of mediocrely educated young men equipped with business psychology; out of each class came a few creative minds, a few scholars, a few gentlemen with insolent manners, and a ruck of nobodies. . . . Things have changed now. I liked Harvard better then.

Toward the end of my college course two influences came into my life which had a good deal to do with shaping me. One was contact with Professor Copeland, who, under the pretense of teaching English composition, has stimulated generations of men to find color and strength and beauty in books and in the world and to express it again. The other was what I call, for lack of a better name, the manifestation of the modern spirit. Some men, notably Walter Lippmann, had been reading and thinking and talking about politics and economics, not as dry theoretical studies, but as live forces acting on the world, on the university even. They formed the Socialist Club to study and discuss all modern social and economic theories and began to experiment with the community in which they lived.

Under their stimulus the college political clubs, which had formerly been quadrennial mushroom growths for the purpose of drinking beer, parading, and burning red fire, took on a new significance. The club drew up a platform for the Socialist party in the city elections. It had social legislation introduced into the Massachusetts Legislature. Its members wrote articles in the college papers challenging undergraduate ideals and muckraked the university for not paying its servants living wages and so forth. Out of the agitation sprang the Harvard Men's League for Women's Suffrage, the Single Tax Club, an anarchist group. The faculty was petitioned for a course in socialism. Prominent radicals were invited to Cambridge to lecture. An open forum was started, to debate college matters and the issues of the day. The result of this movement, upon the undergraduate world, was potent. All over the place radicals sprang up, in music, painting, poetry, and the theater. The more serious college papers took a socialistic or at least progressive tinge. Of course all this made no ostensible difference in the look of Harvard society, and probably the clubmen and the athletes who represented us to the world never even heard of it. But it made me and many others realize that there was something going on in the dull outside world more thrilling than college activities and turned our attention to the writings of men like H. G. Wells and Graham Wallas, wrenching us away from the Oscar Wildean dilettantism that had possessed undergraduate littérateurs for generations.

After college Waldo Peirce and I went abroad as "bull-pushers" on a cattle boat for a year's happy-go-lucky wandering. Waldo rebelled at the smells and the ship's company and jumped overboard off Boston Light, swimming back to shore and later taking the *Lusitania* to Liverpool; meanwhile I was arrested for his murder, clapped in irons, and brought before an Admiralty court at Manchester, where Waldo turned up in the nick of time. I tramped down across England alone, working on farms and sleeping in haymows, meeting Peirce in London again. Then we hoofed it to Dover and tried to stow away on a Channel steamer for France—and got arrested in Calais, of course. Separating, we went through northern France on foot, to Rouen and Paris, and started on a wild automobile trip through Touraine to the Spanish border and across; and I proceeded into Spain alone, having adventures. I spent the winter in Paris, with excursions around the country, letting it soak in. Then I came home to America to settle down and make my living.

Lincoln Steffens recommended me for a job on the *American Maga-*

zine, where I stayed three years, reading manuscripts and writing stories and verses. More than any other man Lincoln Steffens has influenced my mind. I met him first while I was at Harvard, where he came loving youth, full of understanding, with the breath of the world clinging to him. I was afraid of him then—afraid of his wisdom, his seriousness, and we didn't talk. But when I came back from France I told him what I had seen and done, and he asked me what I wanted to do. I said I didn't know, except that I wanted to write. Steffens looked at me with that lovely smile: "You can do anything you want to," he said; and I believed him. Since then I have gone to him with my difficulties and troubles, and he has always listened while I solved them myself in the warmth of his understanding. Being with Steffens is to me like flashes of clear light; it is as if I see him, and myself, and the world, with new eyes. I tell him what I see and think, and it comes back to me beautiful, full of meaning. He does not judge or advise—he simply makes everything clear. There are two men who give me confidence in myself, who make me want to work and to do nothing unworthy—Copeland and Steffens.

New York was an enchanted city to me. It was on an infinitely grander scale than Harvard. Everything was to be found there—it satisfied me utterly. I wandered about the streets, from the soaring imperial towers of downtown, along the East River docks, smelling of spices and the clipper ships of the past, through the swarming East Side—alien towns within towns—where the smoky flare of miles of clamorous pushcarts made a splendor of shabby streets; coming upon sudden shrill markets, dripping blood and fish scales in the light of torches, the big Jewish women bawling their wares under the roaring great bridges; thrilling to the ebb and flow of human tides sweeping to work and back, west and east, south and north. I knew Chinatown, and Little Italy, and the quarter of the Syrians; the marionette theater, Sharkey's and McSorley's saloons, the Bowery lodginghouses and the places where the tramps gathered in winter; the Haymarket, the German Village, and all the dives of the Tenderloin. I spent all one summer night on top of a pier of the Williamsburg Bridge; I slept another night in a basket of squid in the Fulton Market, where the red and green and gold sea things glisten in the blue light of the sputtering arcs. The girls that walk the streets were friends of mine, and the drunken sailors off ships newcome from the world's end, and the Spanish longshoremen down on West Street.

I found wonderful obscure restaurants where the foods of the whole world could be found. I knew how to get dope; where to go to hire a man to kill an enemy; what to do to get into gambling rooms and secret dance halls. I knew well the parks and the streets of palaces, the theaters and hotels, the ugly growth of the city spreading like a disease, the decrepit places whence life was ebbing, and the squares and streets where an old, beautiful, leisurely existence was drowned in the mounting roar of the slums. I knew Washington Square and the artists and writers, the near-Bohemians, the radicals. I went to gangsters' balls at Tammany Hall, on excursions of the Tim Sullivan Association, to Coney Island on hot summer nights. . . . Within a block of my house was all the adventure of the world; within a mile was every foreign country.

In New York I first loved, and I first wrote of the things I saw, with a fierce joy of creation—and knew at last that I could write. There I got my first perceptions of the life of my time. The city and its people were an open book to me; everything had its story, dramatic, full of ironic tragedy and terrible humor. There I first saw that reality transcended all the fine poetic inventions of fastidiousness and mediaevalism. I was not happy or well long, away from New York— I am not now, for that matter; but I cannot live continually in its heart any more. In the city I have no time for much but sensation and experience, but now I want some time of quiet and leisure for thought, so I can extract from the richness of my life something beautiful and strong. I am living now in the country, within an hour of town, so I can go down occasionally and plunge into the sea of people, the roaring and the lights—and then come back here to write of it, in the quiet hills, in sunshine and clean wind.

During this time I read a good deal of radical literature, attended meetings of all sorts, met socialists, anarchists, single-taxers, labor leaders, and besides, all the hairsplitting Utopians and petty doctrine-mongers who cling to skirts of Change. They interested me, so many different human types; and the livingness of theories which could dominate men and women captived my imagination. On the whole, ideas alone didn't mean much to me. I had to see. In my rambles about the city I couldn't help but observe the ugliness of poverty and all its train of evil, the cruel inequality between rich people who had too many motor cars and poor people who didn't have enough to eat. It didn't come to me from books that the workers produced all the wealth of the world, which went to those who did not earn it.

The Lawrence strike of the textile workers had just ended, and the I.W.W. dominated the social and industrial horizon like a portent of the rising of the oppressed. That strike brought home to me hard the knowledge that the manufacturers get all they can out of labor, pay as little as they must, and permit the existence of great masses of the miserable unemployed in order to keep wages down; that the forces of the state are on the side of property against the propertyless. Our Socialist party seemed to me duller than religion and almost as little in touch with labor. The Paterson strike broke out. I met Bill Haywood, Gurley Flynn, Tresca, and the other leaders; they attracted me. I liked their understanding of the workers, their revolutionary thought, the boldness of their dream, the way immense crowds of people took fire and came alive under their leadership. Here was drama, change, democracy on the march made visible—a war of the people. I went to Paterson to watch it, was mistaken for a striker while walking the public street, beaten by the police, and jailed without any charge. In the jail I talked with exultant men who had blithely defied the lawless brutality of the city government and gone to prison laughing and singing. There were horrors in that jail, too; men and boys shut up for months without trial, men going mad and dying, bestial cruelty and disease and filth—and all for the poor. When I came out I helped to organize the pageant of the Paterson strike, in Madison Square Garden, New York—drilling a thousand men and women in Paterson and bringing them across New Jersey to act out, before an immensely moved audience of twenty thousand people, the wretchedness of their lives and the glory of their revolt.

Since then I have seen and reported many strikes, most of them desperate struggles for the bare necessaries of life; and all I have witnessed only confirms my first idea of the class struggle and its inevitability. I wish with all my heart that the proletariat would rise and take their rights—I don't see how else they will get them. Political relief is so slow to come, and year by year the opportunities of peaceful protest and lawful action are curtailed. But I am not sure any more that the working class is capable of revolution, peaceful or otherwise; the workers are so divided and bitterly hostile to each other, so badly led, so blind to their class interest. The war has been a terrible shatterer of faith in economic and political idealism. And yet I cannot give up the idea that out of democracy will be born the new world—richer, braver, freer, more beautiful. As for me, I don't know what I can do to help—I don't know yet. All I know is that my happiness is built on the misery of other people, that I eat because others go hungry, that I am clothed when other people go almost naked through the frozen cities in winter; and that fact poisons me, disturbs my serenity, makes me write propaganda when I would rather play—though not so much as it once did.

I quit my job to work on the pageant, and when it was all over I went to pieces nervously, and friends took me abroad for the summer. The strike was starved and lost, the men went back to work dispirited and disillusioned, and the leaders, too, broke down under the long strain of the fight. The I.W.W. itself seemed smashed—indeed it has never recovered its old prestige. I got diphtheria in Italy and came back to New York weak and despondent. For six months I did almost nothing. And then, though the interest of Lincoln Steffens, the *Metropolitan Magazine* asked me to go to Mexico as war correspondent, and I knew that I must do it.

Villa had just captured Chihuahua when I got to the border, and was getting ready to move on Torreón. I made straight for Chihuahua and there got a chance to accompany an American mining man down into the mountains of Durango. Hearing that an old half bandit, half general was moving to the front, I cut loose and joined him, riding with a wild troop of Mexican cavalry two weeks across the desert, seeing battle at close range, in which my companions were defeated and killed, and fleeing for my life across the desert. I joined Villa then in his march on Torreón and was in at the fall of that stronghold.

Altogether I was four months with the Constitutionalist armies in Mexico. When I first crossed the border, deadliest fear gripped me. I was afraid of death, of mutilation, of a strange land and strange people whose speech and thought I did not know. But a terrible curiosity urged me on; I felt I *had to know* how I would act under fire, how I would get along with these primitive folks at war. And I discovered that bullets are not very terrifying, that the fear of death is not such a great thing, and that the Mexicans are wonderfully congenial. That four months of riding hundreds of miles across the blazing plains, sleeping on the ground with the hombres, dancing and carousing in looted haciendas all night after an all-day ride, being with them intimately in play, in battle, was perhaps the most satisfactory period of my life. I made good with these wild fighting men and with myself. I loved them, and I loved the life. I found myself again. I wrote better than I have ever written.

Then came the European war, to which I went as correspondent, spending a year and a half traveling in all the belligerent countries and on the front of five nations in battle. In Europe I found none of the spontaneity, none of the idealism, of the Mexican revolution. It was a war of the workshops, and the trenches were factories turning out ruin—ruin of the spirit as well as of the body, the real and only death. Everything had halted but the engines of hate and destruction. European life, that flashed so many vital facets, ran in one channel, and runs in it now. There seems to me little to choose between the sides; both are horrible to me. The whole great war is to me just a stoppage of the life and ferment of human evolution. I am waiting, waiting for it all to end, for life to resume, so I can find my work.

In thinking it over, I find little in my thirty years that I can hold to. I haven't any God and don't want one; faith is only another word for finding oneself. In my life as in most lives, I guess, love plays a tremendous part. I've had love affairs, passionate happiness, wretched maladjustments; hurt deeply and been deeply hurt. But at last I have found my friend and lover, thrilling and satisfying, closer to me than anyone has ever been. And now I don't care what comes.

Problems for Thought and Writing

I

1. Would you say that Reed is, essentially, evaluating his life or boasting about it? Is he, in your opinion, acquiring maturity or only more experiences? Do you think he identifies excitement with "life"? These are separate questions but can be capsuled in one: how much of a *man* do you think Reed is?

2. Do you think it is natural for every young man or woman to undergo the experience of "finding himself"? Do you think, say, an English aristocrat of the 18th century would have been much troubled by the problem? Is experience for the sake of experience in any sense a modern phenomenon? If you think it is, what are your reasons?

3. Compare Reed's opinions of his teachers with Mencken's (page 66). Would you say the two men had similar personalities? Would you call them both "revolutionaries"?

4. Do you think it was hard for Reed to confess his cowardice? Why or why not?

5. Compare and contrast the character of your college campus with the Harvard Reed knew about 1907 (described on pages 283-86). How, do you suppose, will your start in life be different?

6. Would you say that the average undergraduate today is more blasé, less romantic, than Reed was? If so, why?

7. Do you find Reed's radicalism convincing? Do you feel that it was rooted in conviction and principle or that it was just an aspect of Reed's need to be in the thick of things?

8. Does Reed's interest in the "livingness of theories which could dominate men and women" set him apart in any way from the prevailing ambitions and interests of the present younger generation? Is the generation of the 1960's much concerned about theories of any kind? Why or why not?

9. Do you envy Reed his world and experiences? Why or why not? Be specific.

10. A student said to one of the editors recently: "Every young man deserves his war!" This was spoken out of the sense that there was no opportunity for heroism in the "peaceful" world of the cold war, and that the generation of World War II had really been lucky. Do you think every generation desires to have some suffering to boast about? Is this desire likely to create the suffering? How do you react to the student's remark?

II

11. Identify or define: Mark Twain, Bill Nye, *Lorna Doone*, Addison, Goldsmith, George Eliot, Macaulay, Edmund Burke, *The Light of Asia*, Marie Corelli, Sir Thomas Malory.

12. What *tone* does Reed assume in his essay? Would you say he is ever sentimental?

13. Reed's style is journalistic and Adams' may be called historical. What are the distinguishing marks between the two?

~

THE CRACK-UP*   *F. Scott Fitzgerald*

February, 1936

Of course all life is a process of breaking down, but the blows that do the dramatic side of the work—the big sudden blows that come, or seem to come, from outside—the ones you remember and blame things on and, in moments of weakness, tell your friends about, don't show their effect all at once. There is another sort of blow that comes from within—that you don't feel until it's too late to do anything about it, until you realize with finality that in some regard you will never be as good a man again. The first sort of breakage seems to happen quick—the second kind happens almost without your knowing it but is realized suddenly indeed.

Before I go on with this short history, let me make a general observation—the test of a first-rate intelligence is the ability to hold two opposed ideas in the mind at the same time, and still retain the ability to function. One should, for example, be able to see that things are hopeless and yet be determined to make them otherwise. This philosophy fitted on to my early adult life, when I saw the improbable, the implausible, often the "impossible," come true. Life was some-

* From F. Scott Fitzgerald, *The Crack-Up*, edited by Edmund Wilson. Copyright 1945 by New Directions. Reprinted by permission of New Directions.

thing you dominated if you were any good. Life yielded easily to intelligence and effort, or to what proportion could be mustered of both. It seemed a romantic business to be a successful literary man —you were not ever going to be as famous as a movie star but what note you had was probably longer-lived—you were never going to have the power of a man of strong political or religious convictions but you were certainly more independent. Of course within the practice of your trade you were forever unsatisfied—but I, for one, would not have chosen any other.

As the twenties passed, with my own twenties marching a little ahead of them, my two juvenile regrets—at not being big enough (or good enough) to play football in college, and at not getting overseas during the war—resolved themselves into childish waking dreams of imaginary heroism that were good enough to go to sleep on in restless nights. The big problems of life seemed to solve themselves, and if the business of fixing them was difficult, it made one too tired to think of more general problems.

Life, ten years ago, was largely a personal matter. I must hold in balance the sense of the futility of effort and the sense of the necessity to struggle; the conviction of the inevitability of failure and still the determination to "succeed"—and, more than these, the contradiction between the dead hand of the past and the high intentions of the future. If I could do this through the common ills—domestic, professional and personal—then the ego would continue as an arrow shot from nothingness with such force that only gravity would bring it to earth at last.

For seventeen years, with a year of deliberate loafing and resting out in the center—things went on like that, with a new chore only a nice prospect for the next day. I was living hard, too, but: "Up to forty-nine it'll be all right," I said. "I can count on that. For a man who's lived as I have, that's all you could ask."

—And then, ten years this side of forty-nine, I suddenly realized that I had prematurely cracked.

II

Now a man can crack in many ways—can crack in the head—in which case the power of decision is taken from you by others! or in the body, when one can but submit to the white hospital world; or in the nerves. William Seabrook in an unsympathetic book tells, with some pride and a movie ending, of how he became a public charge. What led to his alcoholism or was bound up with it, was a collapse of his nervous system. Though the present writer was not so entangled—having at the time not tasted so much as a glass of beer for six months—it was his nervous reflexes that were giving way—too much anger and too many tears.

Moreover, to go back to my thesis that life has a varying offensive, the realization of having cracked was not simultaneous with a blow, but with a reprieve.

Not long before, I had sat in the office of a great doctor and listened to a grave sentence. With what, in retrospect, seems some equanimity, I had gone on about my affairs in the city where I was then living, not caring much, not thinking how much had been left undone, or what would become of this and that responsibility, like people do in books; I was well insured and anyhow I had been only a mediocre caretaker of most of the things left in my hands, even of my talent.

But I had a strong sudden instinct that I must be alone. I didn't want to see any people at all. I had seen so many people all my life —I was an average mixer, but more than average in a tendency to identify myself, my ideas, my destiny, with those of all classes that I came in contact with. I was always saving or being saved—in a single morning I would go through the emotions ascribable to Wellington at Waterloo. I lived in a world of inscrutable hostilities and inalienable friends and supporters.

But now I wanted to be absolutely alone and so arranged a certain insulation from ordinary cares.

It was not an unhappy time. I went away and there were fewer people. I found I was good-and-tired. I could lie around and was glad to, sleeping or dozing sometimes twenty hours a day and in the intervals trying resolutely not to think—instead I made lists—made lists and tore them up, hundreds of lists: of cavalry leaders and football players and cities, and popular tunes and pitchers, and happy times, and hobbies and houses lived in and how many suits since I left the army and how many pairs of shoes (I didn't count the suit I bought in Sorrento that shrunk, nor the pumps and dress shirt and collar that I carried around for years and never wore, because the pumps got damp and grainy and the shirt and collar got yellow and starch-rotted). And lists of women I'd liked, and of the times I had let myself be snubbed by people who had not been my betters in character or ability.

—And then suddenly, surprisingly, I got better.

—And cracked like an old plate as soon as I heard the news.

That is the real end of this story. What was to be done about it

will have to rest in what used to be called the "womb of time."
Suffice it to say that after about an hour of solitary pillow-hugging,
I began to realize that for two years my life had been drawing on
resources that I did not possess, that I had been mortgaging myself
physically and spiritually up to the hilt. What was the small gift of
life given back in comparison to that?—when there had once been a
pride of direction and a confidence in enduring independence.

I realized that in those two years, in order to preserve something
—an inner hush maybe, maybe not—I had weaned myself from all
the things I used to love—that every act of life from the morning
tooth-brush to the friend at dinner had become an effort. I saw that
for a long time I had not liked people and things, but only followed
the rickety old pretense of liking. I saw that even my love for those
closest to me was become only an attempt to love, that my casual
relations—with an editor, a tobacco seller, the child of a friend, were
only what I remembered I *should* do, from other days. All in the
same month I became bitter about such things as the sound of the
radio, the advertisements in the magazines, the screech of tracks,
the dead silence of the country—contemptuous at human softness,
immediately (if secretively) quarrelsome toward hardness—hating the
night when I couldn't sleep and hating the day because it went
toward night. I slept on the heart side now because I knew that the
sooner I could tire that out, even a little, the sooner would come that
blessed hour of nightmare which, like a catharsis, would enable me
to better meet the new day.

There were certain spots, certain faces I could look at. Like most
Middle Westerners, I have never had any but the vaguest race prejudices—I always had a secret yen for the lovely Scandinavian blondes
who sat on porches in St. Paul but hadn't emerged enough economically to be part of what was then society. They were too nice to be
"chickens" and too quickly off the farmlands to seize a place in the
sun, but I remember going round blocks to catch a single glimpse of
shining hair—the bright shock of a girl I'd never know. This is urban,
unpopular talk. It strays afield from the fact that in these latter days
I couldn't stand the sight of Celts, English, Politicians, Strangers,
Virginians, Negroes (light or dark), Hunting People, or retail clerks,
and middlemen in general, all writers (I avoided writers very carefully because they can perpetuate trouble as no one else can)—and
all the classes as classes and most of them as members of their class . . .

Trying to cling to something, I like doctors and girl children up to
the age of about thirteen and well-brought-up boy children from

about eight years old on. I could have peace and happiness with
these few categories of people. I forgot to add that I liked old men
—men over seventy, sometimes over sixty if their faces looked seasoned. I like Katharine Hepburn's face on the screen, no matter
what was said about her pretentiousness, and Miriam Hopkins' face,
and old friends if I only saw them once a year and could remember
their ghosts.

All rather inhuman and undernourished, isn't it? Well, that, children, is the true sign of cracking up.

It is not a pretty picture. Inevitably it was carted here and there
within its frame and exposed to various critics. One of them can only
be described as a person whose life makes other people's lives seem
like death—even this time when she was cast in the usually unap-
pealing role of Job's comforter. In spite of the fact that this story
is over, let me append our conversation as a sort of postscript:

"Instead of being so sorry for yourself, listen—" she said. (She
always says "Listen," because she thinks while she talks—*really*
thinks.) So she said: "Listen, suppose this wasn't a crack in you—
suppose it was a crack in the Grand Canyon."

"The crack's in me," I said heroically.

"Listen! The world only exists in your eyes—your conception of it.
You can make it as big or as small as you want to. And you're trying
to be a little puny individual. By God, if I ever cracked, I'd try to
make the world crack with me. Listen! The world only exists
through your apprehension of it, and so it's much better to say that
it's not you that's cracked—it's the Grand Canyon."

"Baby et up all her Spinoza?"

"I don't know anything about Spinoza. I know—" She spoke, then,
of old woes of her own, that seemed, in the telling, to have been
more dolorous than mine, and how she had met them, over-ridden
them, beaten them.

I felt a certain reaction to what she said, but I am a slow-thinking
man, and it occurred to me simultaneously that of all natural forces,
vitality is the incommunicable one. In days when juice came into
one as an article without duty, one tried to distribute it—but always
without success; to further mix metaphors, vitality never "takes." You
have it or you haven't it, like health or brown eyes or honor or a
baritone voice. I might have asked some of it from her, neatly
wrapped and ready for home cooking and digestion, but I could
never have got it—not if I'd waited around for a thousand hours with
the tin cup of self-pity. I could walk from her door, holding myself

very carefully like cracked crockery, and go away into the world of bitterness, where I was making a home with such materials as are found there—and quote to myself after I left her door:

"*Ye are the salt of the earth. But if the salt hath lost its savour, wherewith shall it be salted?*"
Matthew 5:13.

Problems for Thought and Writing

I

If Reed's life (page 276) was a romantic pursuit of adventures and heroic causes, Fitzgerald's was a pursuit of pleasure—until, that is, pleasure turned to satiety and suffering. Fitzgerald is the artistic historian of the great binge known as the jazz age—and of its economic, physical, and emotional collapse. *The Crack-Up* is his record (collected by Edmund Wilson) of that collapse as he personally faced it in the morning-after of the thirties. In Reed we can see a symbol of the social idealisms of the pre-War and early post-War era (Reed died in 1920), and in Fitzgerald a symbol of the irreverence and irresponsibility of the twenties, an age no longer accessible to idealisms. But such a comparison would be too pat. They were both representatives (and victims) of their ages, but Fitzgerald was far more than a playboy. *The Great Gatsby* and *Tender is the Night* are two of the most sensitive and accomplished novels to record that age's experience. *The Crack-Up*, with the same art and without sentimentality or self-pity, records the end of the party. The failure, as Fitzgerald recounts it, becomes almost noble, almost tragic.

1. Continue the comparison and contrast between Reed and Fitzgerald. Consult Chute's "Getting at the Truth" (page 113) as a precaution against oversimplifications or distortions.

2. "The test of a first-rate intelligence is the ability to hold two opposed ideas in the mind at the same time, and still retain the ability to function." Do you agree with this generalization? Test it.

3. Precisely how did Fitzgerald recognize that he had "cracked"? Does it seem psychologically convincing to you? Why or why not?

4. Fitzgerald describes the nature of his crack-up in terms of an inability to love, increase in his racial prejudices, growth of bitterness, etc. Why did he fear the appearance of these symptoms? What was *horrible* about them?

5. Write your own essay on the theme: "Of all natural forces, vitality is the incommunicable one."

6. What do you suppose Fitzgerald meant by writing: "Life, ten years ago, was largely a personal matter"?

II

7. Does the fact that Fitzgerald's style is that of a novelist affect to any important degree *what* he says, the nature of his insights? Does it allow him access to aspects of experience denied to Adams, for example? To Reed?

8. Do Fitzgerald's sentences seem a little loose, a little "careless"? Are they in fact, or do they just seem that way? Are they ever ungrammatical?

9. Does Fitzgerald make much use of imagery in this piece? Do you regard the following as effective: "Then the ego would continue as an arrow shot from nothingness with such force that only gravity would bring it to earth at last"?

~

THE UN-ANGRY YOUNG MEN*

Leslie A. Fiedler

AMERICA'S POST-WAR GENERATION

"Be careful what you wish for in your youth," says an aphorism of Goethe's by which I have long been haunted, "for you will get it in your middle-age." It is a terrifying thought, but at forty I feel capable of amending it into one still more terrifying: "Be careful what you wish for in your youth," my new version runs, "for *the young* will get it in your middle-age." Since what I wished for when I was young was maturity and an end to innocence, in short, middle-age itself, I thought I was playing it safe; and, anyhow, I always added under my breath, like Augustine praying to be delivered from the lusts of the flesh: "Not yet, dear God, not *yet!*" First violence and despair, the flirtation with failure and the commitment to radical politics; then all the savour of slow disenchantment; and only at long last the acceptance of responsibility and accommodation—this was the pattern I imagined and approximately lived, the pattern of many of us to whom the Great Depression seemed perversely enough our Great Good Time; and the Spanish Civil War, to which most of us did not even go, *our* war.

Only the other day, someone now just past thirty recounted to me a childhood memory: his mother knocking her head against a refrigerator door, over and over, until his sullen and blustering older brother had promised he would not go to Spain after all. That older brother has become, only too aptly, a millionaire; but it was a long haul from the kitchen in Brooklyn to his present office in Toledo or South Bend or wherever. God knows the "not yet!" we prayed under our breath was answered. We have notoriously had the most pro-

* From *Encounter*, January, 1958. Used by permission.

longed youth on record: a youth wished on us by our predecessors of the 1920's, who could conceive of no greater good, and from which we must recover as from a wasting disease. To the younger generation now defining itself, I am grateful for at least one thing—it has lifted from me the burden of being young, under which I had begun to feel myself ageing without dignity, like some fading beauty obliged to pretend her wrinkles do not exist. No one will, I hope, ever again refer to my fortyish contemporaries (now busy deploring the *much* younger young) as "young novelists," "young critics," "young intellectuals." We may now proceed to become grandfathers in peace.

To be sure, none of us will ever be as old as those who are now around thirty, just as none of us were ever as young as, say, Scott Fitzgerald; for the new young in America are mature with the maturity we dreamed. We ended their innocence before they knew they possessed it; and they passed directly from gradeschool to middle-age with a copy of *Partisan Review* or *Kenyon Review* as a passport —their only youth our youth, which is to say, the mythical youth of the '30's.

My own high-school age son, reliving for the third or fourth time the attitudes I first remember noticing in the freshman classes I taught just before World War II, complains sometimes that my generation has robbed his of the possibilities of revolt. He sees clearly enough that for him the revolutionary gesture would be an empty piece of mimicry, incongruous in a world which has found there is no apocalypse and that contemporary society threatens not exclusion and failure but acceptance and success. What he does not yet perceive is the even more crippling fact that, by anticipation, my generation has robbed his of new possibilities even of accommodation, of accommodation as a revolt against revolt. The single new slogan available to his generation is the pitiful plea: "Get off my back!" Yet it is they who should be on ours!

To me the most appalling aspect of the writing of the post-war generation in America, as of its life-style, is its familiarity. I will not conventionally deplore (though to deplore at all has become now the conventional form of our relationship) their sterility in art—their obsession with criticism. Each does what he can; and construing a poem by John Crowe Ransom, though it may not be as good as writing it, is considerably better than biting your finger-nails. Frankly, I like criticism; and I find myself nodding with approval from time to time over an attractively-written essay by a younger critic, perhaps some piece of high-handed abuse, only to wake with a start to the realisation that my approval is *self*-approval; that the ideas and attitudes are much like my own or those of my contemporaries, unearned intellectual income.

The young who should be hard at work, fatuously but profitably attacking us, spend a good deal of their time discreetly amending, expanding, analysing, and dissecting—when they are not simply cribbing from us. They fatuously attack chiefly themselves—and I fall into their trap, adding my voice to that of the schoolteacher telling them that they no longer read, or to that of the camp-director assuring them that they do not even make casual, summertime love with the vigour of the generations before them. How dull they are! Which is to say: How dull *we* are without our pasts; how banal our dissent from dissent without the living memory of a commitment to dissent.

The young are able to share our essential experiences only vicariously; neither the Great Depression which begins our youth nor the Second World War which ends it are to them more than class-room history. Yet our reaction to both they not only live again, but live *by*. How soon they grow comfortable (not rich, of course, but secure on a level that does not even have the baleful fascination of really cashing in) on echoes of echoes of the attitudes of the '30's or earlier.

The generations of the 1920's and the '30's existed for the imagination, as well as for the census-taker, because they had their own myths of themselves, their own books, their own programmes, their own journals. The young to-day do not even have a magazine. What, say, the *Hound and Horn* was for the '20's, what *Partisan Review* (even briefly the *New Masses*) for the '30's, is represented for the '50's by nothing at all—or worse. The most substantial and successful of recent literary quarterlies is the *Hudson Review*, a genteel, prematurely middle-aged version of the *Kenyon Review*, edited by younger men endowed with a solemnity before literature almost indistinguishable from *rigor mortis*, but sustained by contributions from older men not yet so close to death. The only "new" political journal is *Dissent*, edited chiefly by ageing radicals unwilling to leave the Garden of the '30's, and representing nostalgia at the point where it fades into academicism. The situation is superficially not unlike that in England, where two of the most recent journals, ENCOUNTER and the *London Magazine,* are presided over by two of the chief surviving representatives of the '30's, Stephen Spender and John Lehmann. In England, however, where there is considerable evidence of liveliness among the young, this seems to be more a matter of the failure of finances than of spiritual resources.

The new generation in the United States has found no new journal, because it has found no new voice and no new themes. I do not mean that there are no younger writers who are interesting and no books worth reading; I do mean that by and large there is no coherent body of new fiction or poetry which indicates a direction or creates a strikingly new image of the new age. The Angry Young Men of Britain have managed, whatever their shortcomings, to project themselves and their dilemma in such figures as Kingsley Amis's Lucky Jim; for the nearest equivalent our new young must look to a middle-aged New Yorker regular, J. D. Salinger. The recent Nation symposium on the college student agrees that the one novel they feel is truly theirs is Salinger's Catcher in the Rye; and I myself have seen several imitations of that book in prep-school literary magazines, some quite frankly labelled, "Holden Caulfield in Baltimore," "Holden Caulfield in Philadelphia," etc. Yet whatever the merit of Salinger's novel as a work of art or of Holden as an archetypal figure, the disturbing fact is that he is the creation of a man past thirty-five; and that he was first created in a story in Good Housekeeping, which took place before World War II. The same dark-haired, tall, lost, young man, broken loose from school and heading for a breakdown, travelled then through Europe as he travelled later through New York; he has only grown a little younger with the passage of fifteen or sixteen years, having been a college student at the moment of his birth and having become a secondary schoolboy in his reincarnation. He is not, in any case, a creation of the latest young—only, like so much else, a creation for them, an inheritance.

Having no new matter, the young need no new medium; the older quarterlies are open to them (and one can even earn academic credit toward promotion by publishing in former anti-academic journals like Partisan Review), as are the back pages of such weeklies as the New Republic and the Nation; the New Yorker itself is not unfriendly, and if one has the proper tone and themes, he is more than welcome in Mademoiselle and Harper's Bazaar. The latter, swollen with ads for ladies' lingerie and jewellery, pay extremely well, as do such recently founded, but not new, publications as Playboy, Nugget, etc. Such "men's magazines," which have become the favourite reading matter of male college students, particularly in private Eastern universities, are attempts to be what *Esquire* was in the early '30's, a happily commercial combination of semi-pornographic art and serious fiction. The coloured photograph has reached a point of technical excellence which makes *Playboy*'s nude "Playmate of the Month" more lush and convincing than all her predecessors; but no writers have been turned up so far to match *Esquire*'s Hemingway and Faulkner, so that few readers are tempted to read much beyond the description of how the photographers persuaded the "Playmate" to pose. It is, of course, doubtful that most of *Playboy*'s subscribers ever find out what the quality of its stories are; as the editors of *Harper's Bazaar* assume that their readers will seldom get past the ads, so the editors of the men's magazines assume that theirs will never get past the pin-ups. Printing stories amounts more to subsidising writers than really publishing them.

It is all, as Trotsky once remarked of quite another problem, like hitting one's head against an open door. When a young poet does appear (as one has recently in California), who bucks current fashion enough to choose William Carlos Williams rather than Wallace Stevens as a master, and gets himself censored—at this point *Life* magazine moves in with cameras; and he becomes merely another feature, lost somewhere between a contest for girl baton-twirlers and a spread on intercontinental ballistic weapons. Opportunities are distressingly plentiful everywhere—not only for publication and publicity, but for study and travel. Scholarships and fellowships abound; the great Foundations are eager to invest in the young, to send them to school or Europe or Asia or up and down America. Whatever the imagination can conceive, there is plenty of money to achieve; and when the imagination withers away before the limitless possibilities, money beings to usurp its function. Half of the academic young (and a higher and higher percentage of talented youth goes into academic life) are engaged in the kind of project that can be contrived only by a bureaucracy driven half-mad by money which increases faster than it is spent.

In a fantastic way, all the traditional strategies of the intellectual for evading the pressures of his world are transformed into subsidised programmes. Expatriation (renamed, of course, the Prix de Rome or Year-after-Year Abroad) is financed with the same even-handed munificence that sponsors a scholarly study of population pressures or right-left asymmetry in the atom. Only one goal becomes increasingly difficult—perhaps impossible: failure. Only one satisfaction is forbidden: violence.

From childhood on, the new young have been supervised by parents and teachers, influenced at one remove or another by Freud and the universal pacifism which attacked the American middle-class after the First World War, and deeply troubled over whether their charges should be allowed to play with toy bazookas, read the horrors of Grimm or of the latest comic book. Some have been forbidden all these, some allowed only therapeutic doses; on the whole, however, American society seems to have decided to let children and adolescents indulge vicariously in massive bouts of aggressiveness and terror. On the screen, in popular literature, on television and radio, these are permitted—with the tacit understanding: *this is all!*

Foreign observers find it easy to see the mythology of violence on which our children are raised: the crash of fist into jaw, the crumpling of bullet-riddled bodies, the bright red gobbets of blood. What they often miss is the anxiety which hedges that mythology about, the sense in which what is fostered with one hand is forbidden with the other: the PTA (Parent Teacher Association) meetings that discuss censorship; the testifying psychologists hinting darkly of evil to come; the popular guides for new mothers which advocate expurgating from the child's life all mention of disaster and death. This is the first of the contradictions which have conditioned our young.

Even more critical is the one which arises from the fact that the present generation is perhaps the first in the United States born into an era of social peace. Since our beginnings, violence has been the very pattern of American life: a continent violently appropriated, a national life created in revolution and defined in the midst of Indian warfare, the degrading brutality of slavery, and the conflict between competing national groups. Even after the closing of the frontier, the Civil War, and the end of mass immigration, violence persisted in America, not as the threat of war but as the shape of everyday life. World War I brought to our people for the first time the shocking vision (still at long distance) of violence as a threat imposed from outside on an entire nation. This left behind a further complicating factor: a heritage of compulsory pacifism for the young, and a pattern for the war-novel based on that pacifism which in almost forty years no novelist has managed to recast.

The imagination of the '20's lived off that remembered feast of terror as well as a mythology of murder and night-time pursuit bred by Prohibition. The '30's subsisted on the social violence always present in our life but exacerbated by the Great Depression: the death of Sacco and Vanzetti set the tone before the period had properly begun, and was succeeded by images of Pinkertons and smashed picket lines, Gastonia and Paterson and South Chicago; of Bonus Marchers and hostile troops; of the quieter terror of despair in the bread-lines and among the unemployed selling apples. The Civil War in Spain was a first climax; and the Second World War, with its guilt-ridden atomic conclusion, the end of all. At this point, the imagination faltered before the bureaucratisation of terror—not merely its immensity, but the dispersal of personal responsibility. Before Dachau, before Hiroshima, older perceptions of horror failed; and the older responses of sentimentality and righteous indignation (how hard it is to remember the furore over the Fascists' amateur bombing of Guernica) were revealed as impotent. Yet for the majority of Americans still, war remained something remote, something belonging "overseas"; and to many, though an occasion for suffering abroad, it proved an occasion for prosperity at home.

For our younger generations, The Second World War is a dim childhood recollection, reinforced by facts learned in the classroom from a teacher who seemed, perhaps, incomprehensibly and unforgivably "shook" by it all. The oldest of the newer young went off to that war in time for peace; the armed forces to them meant schools and post-war billets, chances for culture-mongering, sightseeing, or black-marketeering, depending on their tastes. The Spanish War, of course, scarcely exists for them at all. I can remember as early as 1941 overhearing one college girl complaining to another (they were studying, no doubt, for an exam in "Spanish Civilisation"): "Franco? Franco? I can never remember what *side* he was on!" Even the conflict in Korea, presumably *their* war, touched directly only a relative few; and the reactions even of those few were so set in the older G.I. pattern of cynicism and compulsory griping, that they were able to leave no record of it for the imagination.

Since Korea, we have lived under the Eisenhower dispensation in a kind of social truce. The sort of labour violence that made the typical street scene of my childhood (the mass picket-line, the striker clubbed, the scab kicked in the groin) is by and large out of sight and even of existence. In the South, to be sure, recent events have stirred up again riots and bombing; but even there events are strangely limited in their consequences. What looks like the beginnings of civil war ends with an irate citizen getting his hand cut by a bayonet; and meanwhile, concealed for a little beneath the upsurge of brutality, the long-term change proceeds: the lynching of negroes reaches the

point of vanishing completely and a negro singer becomes a leading
matinée idol of the whole nation. Outside of the South, certainly,
the young must produce their own violence—with autos or knives or
brickbats—if they are to have it at all.

The latest concern with the depredations of juvenile delinquents
is sharpened, I think, because their outbreaks seem so isolated on a
generally peaceful scene. I do not intend to say that violence has
disappeared utterly from our lives; the daily newspaper is there to
remind us it has not, but it has ebbed away. Never has the violence
of the young seemed so non-functional, so *theoretical,* as it were—
so sought after for its own sake. Most of the traditional motives for
violence are gone: defending the frontier, making the world safe for
democracy, teaching the Jew or Dago or Nigger his place, demonstrating against War and Fascism; the young have lost their faith in all
the ancient excuses for violence; they have only a vestigial hunger
for it for its own sake. It may have been in part self-deceit when
my own generation hung Hitler in effigy, tore off its silk stockings and
underpants to hurl into anti-Japanese bonfires—or rioted in the streets
against the cops: crying all the while that these were blows for the
cause of humanity. We felt at least the *need* to pretend, to invest
our aggression in a sanctioned cause; and our actions were congruous
with our world.

The young now, however, inhabit a world where their truer movies
are not, like those of the '30's, black-and-white images of violent
action, but grey ones of suffocating inaction. Compare, say, *I Was
a Fugitive from a Chain Gang* with *Marty,* in the latter of which
nothing much happens at all, and violence has shrunk to a dream
dreamed over the latest adventures of Mike Hammer, best-selling
Private Eye. The function which Mickey Spillane performs for the
semi-literate, the books of Hemingway and Faulkner and Nathanael
West perform for the more informed and subtle young. They provide,
that is to say, images of violence, in which the intellectual new
young can find satisfaction.

Incapable of actual politics, the intellectual young sometimes find
it possible to commit themselves to politics-once-removed: to a kind
of ghostly anti-Fascism, or the rewarmed dream of the New Deal as
embodied by Adlai Stevenson. A few—progressively fewer and fewer,
I suspect—of the very young and bright (the sort of boy or girl, say,
who goes through the New York public school system in an ac-
celerated programme and graduates from a Special High School at
fifteen) even manage to repeat the Communist experience, circulating

official petitions against the Bomb and singing the pseudo-folk songs
with which that Movement keeps alive its own sentimental version
of the New Deal:

> *Was at Franklin Roosevelt's side*
> *Just a while afore he died,*
> *Said, "One world must come out of World War II"—*
> *Yankee, Russian, White, or Tan—*
> *Lord, a man is just a man. . . .*
> *We're all brothers and we're only*
> *Passing through!*

It is the ghostliest manifestation of all; but outside of such tiny
groups, few of the young so utterly inhabit the past. Yet the sensibility of all who read has been conditioned by the literature of the
'30's, bereft now of political meaning but based on violence and
postulated on the expectation of failure. Their dreams are possessed
by images that their society cannot fulfil. In a world rent by violence,
and plagued by disaster, America remains strangely immune at home.
Only the newspaper headlines grow shriller, though they cannot
disturb Ike's round of golf and the sense of security which it represents
for the people to whom that game is a necessary symbol.

   It seems impossible for the young to identify themselves with some
distant cause. The sides are no longer so neatly defined, allegiances
no longer so naïvely given. The daily newspaper falls from hands
that clutch the latest reprinting of Orwell's *Homage to Catalonia*,
which provides, in a way, a ready-made disillusionment applicable
to any cause. The dream of violence and the fact of security; the
dream of failure and the fact of success—here is the centre of our
new comedy; but it is not yet written, for no one seems to stand at
the proper vantage point.
   The trouble is that there are at the moment no new social groups
out of which a truly new generation can emerge. The '20's marked
a climax in the breakthrough of provincial writers, of the displacement of New York and Boston by the mid-West as the source of
imagery and thematic material in fiction and poetry; such books as
Fitzgerald's *The Great Gatsby* and Hemingway's *In Our Time* complete the process begun by *An American Tragedy* and *Main Street*
and *Winesburg Ohio*. The '30's saw the inruption of urban Jews
(the final blow in the smashing of the Anglo-Saxon domination of
American culture) and the establishment of their pattern of struggle

and accommodation as essential American themes. This pattern has remained, in diluted form, sovereign to this day. First rebellion; then a pleasant university job, teaching the young in turn to rebel (only vicariously, after a while); these then move on to their own jobs teaching the still younger how to. . . . There is no end.

Just as the second generation intellectuals in New York were moving from dispossession to possession, wave after wave of young Southerners were, as the '30's wore on, emerging from their areas of deprivation. They clutched not Marx in one hand and a "proletarian novel" in the other; but a volume of neo-metaphysical poetry in one and of "close" criticism in the other—only to disappear into the colleges to the North, still crying the slogans of Agrarianism to their students, who were, alas, only interested in John Donne.

The first pity of the contemporary situation is that the relationship of the new young to the generations just before them is that of pupil to teacher, their common ground the school-room. No longer is the young writer, bored in college, able to set up against the teacher who bores him the image of some lonely poet slumped over his empty Pernod glass in a Parisian café. The lonely poet *is* the teacher, and if he is momentarily in Paris (or Athens or Rome), he is there to give a series of lectures under the auspices of the State Department. On the other hand, we who are teachers no longer have the privilege of seeing before us alien minds with destinies quite different from our own, chafing to be free as we would wish them to be free, but as we cannot, of course, *teach* them to be. Not only are the new young our students; they are our younger brothers, our nephews, the children of our best friends, following behind us, and distinguishable from our shadows only when they, dutifully and perfunctorily, raise an occasional cry of protest against us.

How committed they are in advance to academic life or the salons of upper bohemia or suburban peace! Ever more young men arise out of a world gone prosperous to the core, and head for the places which we before them have already occupied, mapped, and cleared for comfortable living.

In this respect, the situation of our new young is completely different from that of their opposite numbers in England. The young British writer has the inestimable advantage of representing a new class on its way into a controlling position in the culture of his country. He is able to define himself against the class he replaces: against the ideal of "Bloomsbury," which is to say, against a blend of homosexual sensibility, upper-class aloofness, liberal politics, and avant-garde literary devices. When he is boorish rather than well-behaved, rudely angry rather than ironically amused, when he is philistine rather than arty—even when he merely writes badly, he can feel he is performing a service for literature, liberating it from the tyranny of a taste based on a world of wealth and leisure which has become quite unreal. His books are, indeed, about the comedy of his relationship to the writers of the '30's (who are not only a generation but a class away from him) and he finds it easy enough to reject them.

He is not in any case excoriating (merely in order to be as nasty in his own way as they were, and are, in theirs) predecessors who are scarcely different from himself. The British writer in Swansea or Reading is a long way from Oxford and Cambridge, and merely to report what life is like in such places is to have found a new and fertile subject matter. American writers are, however, at least two generations deep in their Swanseas and Readings—in Bloomington (Indiana) or Madison (Wisconsin) or Moscow (Idaho). The baby-sitter moving, soiled diaper in hand, across a declassed and blighted landscape is no longer for us a sufficient muse; and our own tradition of strategic bad writing goes back as far as Melville.

Even the main sub-divisions within our new generation are second-hand, reflections of the older ones between New Yorker and South-erner, urbanite and agrarian (theoretical now, since the two are likely to be teaching in the small mid-Western town), sociologue and new critic, contributor to *Partisan Review* or *Kenyon Review*. Long since, our Augustan peace has blurred those once bitter distinctions. This is an age of interfaith tolerance, after all; and only an occasional challenge to a duel disturbs the truce that finds Philip Rahv and Allen Tate presiding over the same school for training young critics, who may, indeed, bypass the traditions of both masters and be translated directly into the back pages of the *New Yorker*.

It is, however, worth distinguishing still the major sub-groups within the new generations. First, the New York academics, who represent the latest form of status-striving among descendants of East European immigrants. In the first generation, there was a simple-hearted drive to found fortunes in woollens, ladies' underwear, junk—no matter; in the second, an impulse to enter the (still financially rewarding) respectability of the public professions of law and medicine; in the third, an urge to find a place in publishing and the

universities, to become writers and intellectuals. In my own generation, there are notorious cases of men with no taste (much less any
love) for literature becoming critics out of sheer bafflement. Never
have so many natural operators and minor machiavellians pushed so
eagerly and with less reason into the academy. The old tragedy of
the poet forced into manufacturing paper bags becomes the new
comedy of the proto-tycoon lecturing on the imagery of Wallace
Stevens.

The New York intellectual in academia is typically a product of
Columbia (though he may also have gone to some large, mid-Western
university to get away from home), a student of Lionel Trilling, who
has received his finishing touches at the Kenyon School of Letters,
or one of the British Universities (preferably Downing College at
Cambridge) or the Harvard Graduate School. Nurtured on critical
dialectics and trained in "close reading" by the New Critics, he (a
little ostentatiously) handles a body of learning appalling in scope.
This learning is deep and real, though such writers do not carry it
lightly; and they are never, therefore, guilty of gross lapses like those
of the more sketchily informed younger British writers—like Kingsley
Amis, for instance, who is able to refer quite blandly in an American
publication to Faulkner's lack of humour.

In addition to contributing to a vast, communal, talmudic com-
mentary on the literary canon defined in the '20's and '30's—Melville,
Faulkner, Stevens, etc. such intellectuals normally occupy themselves
with problems of "Popular Culture" or the "Mass Arts." Indeed,
there is a sense in which this is their special subject; though here,
too, they are likely to follow the lead of such a writer of the '30's as
Dwight Macdonald. Among writers of this breed, such a concern is
in part an inverted snobbism, a resistance to culture-mongering, which
leads them to prefer a standard Hollywood Western to an "Art Film,"
and boxing to ballet. It is also, however, a kind of vestigial anti-
bourgeois politics: a protest against the vulgarisation of life in a
commercial society; and finally, it is a professional protest against a
world which will sponsor and support them, but which will not look
up from the latest copy of *Life* to read their works or those they
admire.

Yet they are, after all, members of the first generations to have
grown up under the full impact of triumphant mass culture; and it is
their interest in this subject which connects the New York intellectuals with their British contemporaries (who, however different
in other respects, share a concern with jazz, say, and science fiction—

a sense that these give direct evidence of their new situation), and even with their less literate confrères, right down to the current highschooler. The first cultural snobbism of the very newest young tends to be based on taste in jazz. "Do you dig Bird?" that is to say, "Do you like the music of Charlie Parker?" is a question that separates those in the know from those who are "nowhere"; and beyond the "Bird" there are ever-retreating horizons of Modern or Progressive Jazz. "It's a way of life," I remember hearing a young drummer in Missoula, Montana, explain quite solemnly to a graduate student, who had asked him why, if he read books (he was an admirer of Norman Mailer) he also blew jazz. "A way of life." I suppose it is also a way of life to the high school kids I used to watch this past summer in Washington Square Park in New York, their shirts un-buttoned to the waist and a pair of bongo-drums between their knees.

Expectedly enough, the nearest thing to a spokesman for the very new young is (or rather was briefly over the past couple of years—in and around New York) Jean Shepard, a disc-jockey with some training in psychology, who used to lecture his listeners on the perils of conformism when he was not spinning records or singing a commercial which began:

> Nedicks, shmeedicks,
> Double deedix,
> Pipkins all agree . . .

Under his guidance, highly disorganised meetings (he preferred to call them "mills") were held in some Eastern colleges, at which he spoke endlessly, while the audience clambered around the hall, mak-ing a racket and turning off and on the lights. He finally gathered together his "Night People," those who listened to his programme after midnight, in a kind of public demonstration at which several hundred kids were supposed to fly four-inch kites to express their contempt for everything ("Go fly a kite!"). Quite appropriately, on the appointed day, the wind failed to blow, and the Night People trickled off sullenly.

The situation in American Popular Culture is, at the moment, a thoroughly absurd one. On its own level, it has never been in a duller or less promising condition. Movie houses close down or play to smaller and smaller audiences—more and more, just the young; though in my own town this year for the first time in history there was no appreciable jump in box-office receipts when college began.

Popular music is in so dismal a state that the disc-jockeys, to fill their time, have to play a larger and larger proportion of revivals of old hit tunes; Broadway subsists on importations and revivals and especially the rewriting of its own dramatic repertoire as musical comedies. Everywhere Popular Culture begins to live parasitically on its own past (the rôle of old movies on T.V. is too well known to need more than a bare reference). On the other hand, everyone, and not least the highbrows, wants to *read* about popular culture. There have been two recent books anthologising the mass of new writing on the subject, and one of them is at the moment being distributed as a bonus by a large Book Club. The study of popular culture threatens itself to become a branch of popular culture.

The interest of the urban academics in the "mass arts" is matched in intensity by that of the radicals-once-removed, who may, indeed, sit side by side with them (they are more distinct ideally than in action) in a New York University or Harvard classroom. Such belated or symbolic revolutionaries, the youngsters who insist on reliving step by step the political past of the '30's, may have become (if they are old enough) Trotskyites in 1945 or 46, and certainly now subscribe to *Dissent*, approving especially the articles blasting Lionel Trilling or David Riesman, who are portrayed as arch-defenders of the *status quo*, and to whom they are bound by spasms of filial rejection. They cannot, however, in rôle or function distinguish themselves from their colleagues who admire Riesman and Trilling and subscribe to ENCOUNTER. They, too, sit behind desks in the offices of Rinehart or Doubleday; they, too, teach at Columbia or Minnesota or Brandeis University; and the Ford Foundation is only too delighted to subsidise what their politics has largely become: the writing of histories of the radical past. Needless to say, their youth, too, comes at second-hand.

If on his Left, the urban intellectual finds a *Dissent*-er; on his Right (this time, say, in R. P. Blackmur's class in The School of Letters or at a lecture in Cambridge by F. R. Leavis), he may find a writer for the *Hudson Review:* a limp, Hugh Kenner-ish admirer of Ezra Pound or Wyndham Lewis, dreaming that all their manly spite and vigour are his own; and writing careful exegeses of the *Cantos*, in which he conceals certain bitter political comments for the initiated. It is a figure like Yvor Winters that he is likely to emulate, finding in him a moral ferocity not incompatible with a Christian gentleman's version of taste. Such a young intellectual sometimes imagines a pure politics of the literary Right, which would make clear to anyone with real sensibility how a love of the best in art and a dignified McCarthyism can go hand in hand. It is these Right-wing purists who like to think of themselves as the new radicals, isolated and despised by liberals with hardening arteries and professorships; but they, too, are welcome among the "celebrities" on Mike Wallace's T.V. interview programme; for they, too, are still fighting in terms of a concept of Right and Left antiquated enough to seem undisturbing in any parlour.

Beyond all these groups (and within them) are the homosexuals, the staunchest party of all. Indeed, one feels sometimes that homosexuality is the purest and truest protest of the latest generation, not a burden merely, an affliction to be borne, but a politics to be flaunted. Certainly, there is a logic to their identification of their sensibility with that of the artist in a country like America, where an undue interest in the arts is likely to bring on a boy the stigma of being a "sissy." Unlike England, America has no long tradition of allowing the homosexual to tyrannise over literary taste, nor indeed a tradition of fiction asserting (behind the most perfunctory of disguises) homosexual responses to experience as the cultivated norm. The sort of thing which would seem in Britain dull and routine, trapped in a world of platitudes as old as Oscar Wilde, strikes an American reader as comparatively fresh. The earliest work of Truman Capote—or more strikingly of Carson McCullers—as well as such a recent novel as James Baldwin's *Giovanni's Room*, seem in our context to be conquests of new areas of feeling, an opening up. On the stage and in the movies, a similar break-through occurs on the middle-brow level; the young men with bare chests (all looking like Marlon Brando) and the middle-aged slatterns who assault their purity (all looking like Anna Magnani) become standard not only on Broadway but in movie houses in the remotest mountain town; while such films as *Picnic* propose to the American woman the homosexual's ideal of the handsome young man as her own. Leopold and Loeb are suddenly exhumed from comparative obscurity to be made the centre of two recent novels and one current play.

Implicit in the whole trend is a certain impatience with the customary taboos and restraints; and particularly in its highbrow manifestations the celebrations of homosexual sensibility implies a rejection of the ideal of the monogamous family and of men who are men (i.e., Gary Cooper). It is, perhaps, more than that, too: the last possible protest against bourgeois security and the home in the suburbs in a world where adultery is old hat. But they come so fast, the new homosexuals, queen treading on queen: and we are so ready for them, so eager to prove our own emancipation by understanding and accepting. It is the same old trap, though more elegantly upholstered. For each group there is its fitting and proper mode of accommodation; this one usually finds publication in the pages of *Harper's Bazaar*, *Mademoiselle*, and *Vogue*. Indeed, such publication is their passport into an upper bohemia, where good manners are appreciated and high style is savoured, a world of chic, eager to read the latest effete exploitation of the Faulknerian scene and the Faulknerian themes of dissolution and infertility.

What is finally most distressing about all this is not that the devices of the young are so dismal and unfruitful, but that they are not even theirs. If I draw as dark a picture as legitimate distortion can make of their plight, it is not to blame them but to blame us who have dreamed them—and have taught them the dream as they sat before us in class. I would not rob them of free will and the possibility of guilt—but *they* must blame themselves. It is depressing enough to look in the mirror the young hold up to nature and see a host of little Trillings and Riesmans; more horrible yet to think of an endless proliferation of James Burnhams and Arthur Millers; and the mind falters at the thought of catching sight of something one fears is intended to be oneself. Enough, dear friends, and students, enough!

Yet it does not matter really—for so long as the imagination lives, every plight is potentially the stuff of a vision that will transcend it by capturing it. It is not generations, thank God, that write books or come to understanding; it is men. The generations are what the books are about, what the understanding comes to terms with. At the moment, one has the sense of young writers at a loss for a subject: poets all technique and no theme; novelists desperately contriving factitious subjects because they need somehow to keep writing books. But the subject is there: the comedy of themselves in their passionate and absurd relationship to us. When a young writer arises who can treat this matter in all its fresh absurdity, we will be done with symposia on the Younger Generation, with self-recrimination and sullen defensiveness and abuse. And I (I fondly hope) will be leaning from a window to cheer him on and to shake down on his head the torn scraps of all surviving copies of this article.

Problems for Thought and Writing

I

1. This essay really discusses *two* generations: the author's generation of the Depression and World War II, and that of the present. As members of the "younger" generation, do you agree with Fiedler's criticism that you have no "voice" and no "theme" but "grow comfortable on echoes of echoes of the attitudes of the '30's or earlier"?

2. What does Fiedler mean by the statement: "To be sure, none of us will ever be as old as those who are now around thirty, just as none of us were ever as young as, say, Scott Fitzgerald. . . ."

3. How can contemporary society "threaten not exclusion and failure but acceptance and success"? How can one be "threatened" by success?

4. Is Fiedler justified in saying that the only proper work of the younger generation should be in "fatuously but profitably attacking" the older? Is it fair to damn the younger generation simply because its members happen to respect and need the experience of the older?

5. "Half of the academic young . . . are engaged in the kind of project that can be contrived only by a bureaucracy driven half-mad by money which increases faster than it is spent." Is this, in your opinion, a true statement? Do you think it is supposed to be taken seriously?

6. "Never has the violence of the young seemed so non-functional, so *theoretical,* as it were—so sought after for its own sake." Does Fiedler seem to make a *value* out of violence? Is he assuming that a generation deprived of opportunities for it is somehow spiritually or psychologically impoverished?

7. Would you say that Fiedler's article is, at base, nothing but another statement of the plight of modern man in mass society—a society without unique values or causes, a people without anything to believe in or fight for? Compare Fiedler's assertions with those of Chiaromonte's article (from *Dissent*), page 225.

II

8. Consider the statement: "The most substantial and successful of recent literary quarterlies is the *Hudson Review*, a genteel, prematurely middle-aged version of the *Kenyon Review*, edited by younger men endowed with a solemnity before literature indistinguishable from *rigor mortis*, but sustained by contributions from older men not yet so close to death." Is this objective criticism or satire?

9. Do you think that Fiedler is trying so hard to write cleverly that he is willing at times to sacrifice accuracy to wit? Is this better to do, in your opinion, than to write dully? Support your opinion with *specific* arguments.

10. Identify Lionel Trilling, David Riesman, James Burnham, Arthur Miller, Truman Capote, Yvor Winters, Ezra Pound, Wyndham Lewis.

~

7 Knowledge and Belief

RELIGION AS AN OBJECTIVE PROBLEM*

Julian Huxley

Religion, like any other subject, can be treated as an objective problem, and studied by the method of science. The first step is to make a list of the ideas and practices associated with different religions—gods and demons, sacrifice, prayer, belief in a future life, taboos and moral rules in this life. This, however, is but a first step. It is like making a collection of animals and plants, or a catalogue of minerals or other substances, with their properties and uses. Science always begins in this way, but it cannot stop at this level: it inevitably seeks to penetrate deeper and to make an analysis.

This analysis may take two directions. It may seek for a further understanding of religion as it now exists, or it may adopt the historical method and search for an explanation of the present in the past.

With regard to the historical approach, it is clear that religion, like other social activities, evolves. Further, its evolution is determined by two main kinds of factors. One is its own emotional and intellectual momentum, its inner logic: the other is the influence of the material and social conditions of the period. As an example of the first, take the tendency from polytheism towards monotheism: granted the theistic premise, this tendency seems almost inevitably to declare itself in the course of time. As examples of the second, we have the fact of propitiatory sacrifice related to helplessness in face of external nature.

The comparative evolutionary study of religion brings out two or three main points. For instance, we have the original prevalence of magical ideas, and their application first to the practical activities of communal existence such as food-getting and war, and only later to the problems of personal salvation: and these in their turn come

* Reprinted from *Man Stands Alone* by Julian Huxley, by permission of Harper & Brothers. Copyright 1941 by Julian Huxley.

gradually to be dominated more by moral ideas and less by magic. In
the sphere of theology we have the early prevalence of rambling myth,
and its gradual crystallization into a fully-rationalized system. In
this domain too we see an interesting evolution from an early stage in
which certain objects, acts, and persons are supposed to be imbued
with an impersonal sacred influence or *mana,* and a later stage at
which this sacred influence is pushed back a stage and attributed to
supernatural beings behind objects.

Finally, there is the important fact that religious beliefs and practices have a very strong time-lag—a high degree of hysteresis, if you
prefer a physical metaphor.

We next have to ask ourselves what is the result of our other type
of analysis of the nature of religion. In the most general terms, it is
that religion is the product of a certain type of interaction between
man and his environment. It always involves an emotional component—the sense of sacredness. It always involves a more than
intellectual belief—a sense of compulsive rightness. It is always
concerned with human destiny, and with a way of life. It always
brings the human being into some sort of felt relation with powers or
agencies outside his personal self. It always involves some sort of
escape from inner conflict. These different components may be very
unequally developed, but they are always present.

Pushing the analysis a stage further, religion is seen as an attempt
to come to terms with the irrational forces that affect man—some
cosmic, some social, some personal. These terms may be terms of
capitulation or of victory, of compromise or of escape. Here once
more there is immense variety.

A very important further point is this—that there is no single function of religion. We may class religious functions by their external
points of reference or by their internal origins. Externally, the first
religious function is to place man in a satisfactory emotional relation
with his non-human environment, regarded as outer destiny or fate.
The second is to do the same for his social environment; the third, to
do the same for his personal actions.

Looked at from the point of view of internal origin, the matter is
much more complicated. One very important religious function is
that of rationalization—giving coherent explanations in rational terms
for acts and feelings which arise from instinctive and therefore
irrational sources. Another is that which we have already mentioned,
the desire for unity. These two between them provide the theological
side of religions.

More fundamental—since they provide the raw materials on which the rationalizing and unifying urges act—are the purely emotional components. These fall under two main heads—the functions arising from conflict or reaction between the self and the outer world, and those arising from conflict or reaction between parts of the self.

Among the former we may mention the need to escape from frustration and limitations; and the need for enhancement of the actual, the gilding of the imperfect. At length we come to relations between parts of the self, which are the most potent of all in generating religious reactions. Here we must take account of several basic facts of the human mind. First there is the inevitability of conflict—a necessary consequence of man's mental make-up. Then there is the illimitable nature of desire and aspiration. Analogous to this last, but in the intellectual instead of the emotional sphere, is man's concept-forming activity, which inevitably gives rise to abstract terms like justice, truth, and beauty. These, being abstract, are empty; but illimitable desire perennially fills them with its imaginations. Then there is the fact of childhood repression, with its consequences, only now beginning to be realized by the world, of a burden of (often unconscious) guilt. Closely linked with this is the obsession of certitude. The mechanism of repression is an all-or-none mechanism: and the conscious accompaniment of such a mechanism is a subjective sense of certitude.

Another very important function is to provide something which is felt as eternal and unchanging (even though in reality it may merely be long-range and slow-changing) over against the limitations and changes of ordinary existence.

But I must not spend too much time on mere analysis. The next question is whether the scientific approach can throw any light on the present crisis in religion and its possible future solution.

The particular situation that confronts the religion of Western civilization is this. The concept of God has reached the limits of its usefulness: it cannot evolve further. Supernatural powers were created by man to carry the burden of religion. From diffuse magic *mana* to personal spirits; from spirits to gods; from gods to God—so crudely speaking, the evolution has gone. The particular phase of that evolution which concerns us is that of gods. In one period of our Western civilization the gods were necessary fictions, useful hypotheses by which to live.

But the gods are only necessary or useful in a certain phase of evolution. For gods to be of value to man, three things are necessary.

The disasters of the outer world must still be sufficiently uncomprehended and uncontrolled to be mysteriously alarming. Or else the
beastliness and hopelessness of common life must be such as to
preclude any pinning of faith to the improvement in this world: then
God can, and social life cannot, provide the necessary escape-mecha-
nism. The belief in magical power must still be current, even if it be
in a refined or sublimated form. And the analytic exploration of his
own mind by man must not be so advanced that he can no longer
project and personify the unconscious forces of his Super-ego and his
Id as beings external to himself.

The advance of natural science, logic, and psychology have brought
us to a stage at which God is no longer a useful hypothesis. Natural
science has pushed God into an ever greater remoteness, until his
function as ruler and dictator disappears and he becomes a mere first
cause or vague general principle. The realization that magic is a
false principle, and that control is to be achieved by science and its
application, has removed the meaning from sacrificial ritual and
petitionary prayer. The analysis of the human mind, with the discovery of its powers of projection and wish-fulfilment, its hidden sub-
consciousness and realized repressions, makes it unnecessary to believe
that conversion and the like are due to any external spiritual power
and unscientific to ascribe inner certitude to guidance by God.

And theological logic, inevitably tending to unify and to universal-
ize its ideas of the Divine, has resulted in a monotheism which is
self-contradictory and incomprehensible, and in some respects of less
practical value than the polytheism which it replaced.

If you grant theism of any sort, the logical outcome is monotheism.
But why theism at all? Why a belief in supernatural beings who
stand in some relation to human destiny and human aspirations?
Theistic belief depends on man's projection of his own ideas and
feelings into nature: it is a personification of non-personal phenomena.
Personification is God's major premise. But it is a mere assumption,
and one which, while serviceable enough in earlier times, is now seen
not only to be unwarranted, but to raise more difficulties than it solves.
Religion, to continue as an element of first-rate importance in the life
of the community, must drop the idea of God or at least relegate it to
a subordinate position, as has happened to the magical element in the
past. God, equally with gods, angels, demons, spirits, and other small
spiritual fry, is a human product, arising inevitably from a certain
kind of ignorance and a certain degree of helplessness with regard to
man's external environment.

With the substitution of knowledge for ignorance in this field, and the growth of control, both actually achieved and realized by thought as possible, God is simply fading away, as the Devil has faded before him, and the pantheons of the ancient world, and the nymphs and the local spirits.

> Peor and Baalim
> Forsake their temples dim . . .

Milton wrote of the fading of all the pagan gods; and Milton's God too is joining them in limbo. God has become more remote and more incomprehensible, and, most important of all, of less practical use to men and women who want guidance and consolation in living their lives. A faint trace of God, half metaphysical and half magic, still broods over our world, like the smile of a cosmic Cheshire Cat. But the growth of psychological knowledge will rub even that from the universe.

However—and this is vital—the fading of God does not mean the end of religion. God's disappearance is in the strictest sense of the word a theological process: and while theologies change, the religious impulses which gave them birth persist.

The disappearance of God means a recasting of religion, and a recasting of a fundamental sort. It means the shouldering by man of ultimate responsibilities which he had previously pushed off on to God.

What are these responsibilities which man must now assume? First, responsibility for carrying on in face of the world's mystery and his own ignorance. In previous ages that burden was shifted on to divine inscrutability: "God moves in a mysterious way." . . . Now we lay it to the account of our own ignorance, and face the possibility that ignorance of ultimates may, through the limitations of our nature, be permanent.

Next, responsibility for the long-range control of destiny. That we can no longer shift on to God the Ruler. Much that theistic religion left to divine guidance remains out of our hands: but our knowledge gives us power of controlling our fate and that of the planet we inhabit, within wide limits. In a phrase, we are the trustees of the evolutionary process and, like all trustees, responsible for our trust.

Thirdly and most urgently, responsibility for the immediate health and happiness of the species, for the enhancement of life on this earth, now and in the immediate future. Poverty, slavery, ill-health, social misery, democracy, kingship, this or that economic or political system

—they do not inhere inevitably in a divinely appointed order of things: they are phenomena to be understood and controlled in accordance with our desire, just as much as the phenomena of chemistry or electricity.

Finally, there is the question of the immediate future of religion. Can science make any prophecy or offer any guidance in regard to this? I think that within limits, it can. In the first place, by analysing the reasons for the breakdown of the traditional supernatural religious systems of the West, it can point out that, unless the trend of history is reversed, the breakdown is an irremediable one. For it is due to the increase of our knowledge and control, the decrease of our ignorance and fear, in relation to man's external environment—machinery, crop-production, physical and chemical invention, floods, disease-germs—and unless science and technology disappear in a new Dark Age, this will persist.

The collapse of supernaturalist theology has been accompanied by the collapse, first of supernatural moral sanctions, and then of any absolute basis for morals. This too must be regarded as a process which, in the event of the continuance of civilization, is irreversible.

We can, however, go further. We have seen that the breakdown of traditional religion has been brought about by the growth of man's knowledge and control over his environment. But biologists distinguish between the external and the internal environment. Our blood provides our tissues with an internal environment regulated to a nicety both as regards its temperature and its chemical constitution, whereas the blood of a sea-urchin affords no such constancy. The organization of an ants' nest provides for the species an internal environment of a social nature. And in contrast with the rapid increase of man's knowledge of and control over his external environment, there has been little or no corresponding progress as regards the internal environment of his species. This is equally true in regard to the structure of society which provides the social environment for the individual and the race, and for the complex of feelings and ideas which provide the psychological environment in which the personal life of the individual is bathed.

These two aspects of man's internal environment of course interact and at points indeed unite—witness the field of social psychology: but for the most part they can be best considered from two very different angles—on the one side from the angle of economics, politics, law and sociology, on the other from the angle of psychological science. Not only have we as yet no adequate scientific knowledge or control over these phenomena, but our absence of control is causing widespread bewilderment. The common man to-day is distressed not only over his own sufferings, but at the spectacle of the helplessness of those in responsible positions in face of the maladjustments of the world's economic and political machinery.

In this field the fear of the uncomprehended, banished elsewhere, has once more entered human life. The fear is all the more deadly because the forces feared are of man's own making. No longer can we blame the gods. The modern Prometheus has chained himself to the rock, and himself fostered the vulture which now gnaws his vitals: his last satisfaction, of defying the Olympian tyrant, is gone.

The distress and the bewilderment are experienced as yet mainly in the more tangible realm of social and economic organization: the mental stresses and distortions arising from the social maladjustment remain for the time being in the background of public consciousness.

With the aid of our analysis of the nature and functions of religion, we can accordingly make certain definite assertions as to its future. The prophesy of science about the future of religion is that the religious impulses will become progressively more concerned with the organization of society—which, in the immediate future, will mean the organization of society on the basis of the nation or the regional group of nations.

The process, of course, has already begun. Many observers have commented on the religious elements in Russian communism—the fanaticism, the insistence on orthodoxy, the violent "theological" disputes, the "worship" of Lenin, the spirit of self-dedication, the persecutions, the common enthusiasm, the puritan element, the mass-emotions, the censorship. A very similar set of events is to be seen in Nazi Germany. In that country, of especial interest to the scientist and the student of comparative religion are such phenomena as the falsification of history and anthropological theory in the interest of a theory of the State and of the Germanic race which serves as the necessary "theological" rationalization of the emotions underlying the Nazi movement, and the dragooning of the Protestant churches to fit them into the Nazi scheme of things. The modern persecution of the Jews, which has its real basis in economic and social dislike, is justified on the basis of this new religiously-felt Germanism, just as the medieval persecutions of the Jews, which equally sprang from economic and social dislike, was justified on the basis of Christianity.

These are the first gropings of the human mind after a social embodiment of the religious impulse. They are as crude and in some respects as nasty as its first gropings, millennia previously, after a theistic embodiment of religion. The beast-headed gods and goddesses of those earlier times, the human sacrifice, the loss of self-criticism in the flood of emotional certitude, the sinister power of a privileged hierarchy, the justification of self and the vilification of critics and the violence toward opponents—these and other primitive phenomena of early God-religion have their counterparts in today's dawn of social religion. And the general unrest and the widespread preoccupation with emotionally-based group movements such as Fascism and Communism, is in many ways comparable with the religious unrest that swept the Mediterranean world in the centuries just before and after the beginning of the Christian Era.

To achieve some real understanding and control of the forces and processes operating in human societies is the next great task for science; and the applications of scientific discovery in this field will have as their goal what we may call the Socialized State. The religious impulse, itself one of the social forces to be more fully comprehended and controlled, will increasingly find its outlet in the promotion of the ideals of the Socialized State.

Exactly how all this will happen no one can say—whether the religious impulse will again crystallize into a definite religious system with its own organization, or will find its outlets within the bounds of other organizations, as it does for instance in the Communist party in Russia. We can, however, on the basis of the past history of religion, make a further prophecy. We can be reasonably sure that the inner momentum of logic and moral feelings, combined with the outer momentum derived from increasing comprehension and control, will lead to an improvement in the expression of this socialized religion comparable to the progress of theistic religion from its crude beginnings toward developed monotheism.

Accordingly, we can prophesy that in the long run the nationalistic element in socialized religion will be subordinated or adjusted to the internationalist: that the persecution of minorities will give place to toleration; that the subtler intellectual and moral virtues will find a place and will gradually oust the cruder from their present pre-eminence in the religiously-conceived social organism.

We can also assert with fair assurance that this process of improvement will be a slow one, and accompanied by much violence and suffering.

Finally we can make the prophecy that part of this process will come about through interaction between two expressions of the religious spirit—one which strives to identify itself with the Socialized State, and the other which reacts against the limitations thus imposed and strives to assert and uphold values that are felt to be more permanent and more universal. The cruder and more violent is the socialized religion, the more will it encourage such reactions. Already in Nazi Germany such a reaction has taken place among certain elements of the Protestant churches, who feel that their principles embody something higher, more lasting, and more general than anything, however intense, which is at the basis of a nationalist and racialist conception of social aims.

This is the one domain in which traditional religion, with its universalist monotheism, will in the near future have a real advantage over socialized religion, which for some time will inevitably be bound up with nationalist states.

It is probable, however, that a universalist Humanism (and probably Communism too) will soon become a strong rival of the old theistic systems in this field. It is also probable that with the growth of intolerant socialized feelings, both in Communistic and Fascist societies, the pioneers of such a Humanism will be those most exposed to religious persecution, but also those who will be doing most for their form of socialized religion and for religious progress in general.

One final prophecy, and I have done. It seems evident that as the religious impulse comes to create these new outlets of expression, whether by way of the Socialized State or by way of Humanism, it will be increasingly confronted by psychological problems—as indeed will the Socialized State itself. Men will realize that economic and social planning will not solve their problems so long as ignorance and absence of control obtain in regard to their own minds. Psychological science will then come into its own, with social psychology as its dominant branch. And this will mean a new understanding of religious phenomena, and new possibilities of integrating them with the life of the community.

To sum up, I would say first that the so-called "conflict between science and religion" has been a conflict between one aspect of science and one aspect of religion. These aspects have both been concerned with man's relation to his *external* environment. The systems of religion which are in danger of collapse grew out of man's ignorance and helplessness in face of external nature; the aspect of science which is endangering those religious systems is that which has provided knowledge and control in this same domain.

In the near future, the religious impulse will find its main outlet in relation to the internal environment of the human species—social, economic, and psychological—for it is the forces of this internal environment that are now causing distress and bewilderment and are being felt as Destiny to be propitiated or otherwise manipulated. Meanwhile science will find its main scope for new endeavour in this same field, since it is here that our ignorance and our lack of control are now most glaring.

There will again be a race between the effects of ignorance and those of knowledge; but with several new features. For one thing the growth of science in the new field will this time not lag by many centuries behind that of the new modes of religious expression; and for another, the facts concerning the religious impulse and its expression will themselves fall within the scope of the new scientific drive. The probable result will be that in the Socialized State the relation between religion and science will gradually cease to be one of conflict and will become one of co-operation. Science will be called on to advise what expressions of the religious impulse are intellectually permissible and socially desirable, if that impulse is to be properly integrated with other human activities and harnessed to take its share in pulling the chariot of man's destiny along the path of progress.

Problems for Thought and Writing

I

1. "Religion," says Huxley, "like other social activities, evolves." Is religion merely a "social activity" in your estimation? Do all of its elements actually "evolve"?

2. In what sense does religion "always involve some sort of escape from inner conflict"? From another point of view, may it not be said that religion frequently intensifies inner conflict?

3. Do you accept Huxley's use of the word "rationalization" on page 316? Is so-called rational or systematic theology "rationalization" as James Harvey Robinson would define the term (see page 461)?

4. Into what two main divisions does Huxley classify the "emotional components" of religion? Does it strike you as a sufficiently comprehensive and convincing classification?

5. Are abstract terms by nature and definition "empty," as Huxley argues on page 317? Is "justice," for example, the product only of desire and imagination?

6. This essay purports to examine religion as an *objective* problem, or in other words to look at religion objectively. To look at something objectively means to take account of *all* the facts of reality, and to exclude none that may be so designated. How objective, on the whole, would you say Huxley has been?

7. Huxley says that "God is no longer a useful *hypothesis*." Has religion traditionally regarded God as a hypothesis? If so, give examples. If not, distinguish precisely between its view and Huxley's.

8. St. Augustine based one of his proofs for the existence of God on the assumption that a universe intelligible to a human mind must have been fashioned by a greater, but nevertheless similar, mind. Would Huxley accept such reasoning? Why or why not? Study carefully the paragraph on pages 318-319 in which he discusses "theism."

9. Compare Huxley's analysis of knowledge as a means for controlling nature with C. S. Lewis' attempt to prove that man's conquest of nature actually means nature's conquest of man ("The Abolition of Man," page 326). See also the arguments of Etienne Gilson (page 635) and W. T. Stace (page 640).

10. What are the dangers involved in regarding "socialized religion," e.g., Fascism, Communism, as "stages" in an inevitable and inexorable evolutionary process?

11. "In the near future," says Huxley, "the religious impulse will find its main outlet in relation to the internal environment of the human species. . . ." Would it then be religion?

II

12. In any kind of expository writing, "asserting" must be accompanied by a corresponding and related amount of "supporting." Do you think Huxley fulfills this requirement?

13. How would you characterize the *tone* of this selection. Is it closer to T. H. Huxley (page 556) or to Matthew Arnold (page 566)? Is it humble or proud?

14. Evaluate as objectively as you can Huxley's arguments in support of his statement that "The concept of God has reached the limits of usefulness."

15. Someone once remarked that Julian Huxley had all of the attitudes of objectivity, but none of the reality. Do you agree? Why or why not?

∼

THE ABOLITION OF MAN *   C. S. Lewis

*It came burning hot into my mind, whatever he said and however
he flattered, when he got me home to his house, he would sell me
for a slave.*

                                                                BUNYAN

'Man's conquest of Nature' is an expression often used to describe
the progress of applied science. 'Man has Nature whacked' said
someone to a friend of mine not long ago. In their context the words
had a certain tragic beauty, for the speaker was dying of tuberculosis.
'No matter,' he said, 'I know I'm one of the casualties. Of course
there are casualties on the winning as well as on the losing side. But
that doesn't alter the fact that it is winning.' I have chosen this story
as my point of departure in order to make it clear that I do not wish
to disparage all that is really beneficial in the process described as
'Man's conquest,' much less all the real devotion and self-sacrifice that
has gone to make it possible. But having done so I must proceed to
analyse this conception a little more closely. In what sense is Man the
possessor of increasing power over Nature?

Let us consider three typical examples: the aeroplane, the wireless, and the contraceptive. In a civilized community, in peacetime,
anyone who can pay for them may use these things. But it cannot
strictly be said that when he does so he is exercising his own proper
or individual power over Nature. If I pay you to carry me, I am
not therefore myself a strong man. Any or all of the three things I
have mentioned can be withheld from some men by other men—by
those who sell, or those who allow the sale, or those who own the
sources of production, or those who make the goods. What we call
Man's power is, in reality, a power possessed by some men which
they may, or may not, allow other men to profit by. Again, as regards
the powers manifested in the aeroplane or the wireless, Man is as
much the patient or subject as the possessor, since he is the target both
for bombs and for propaganda. And as regards contraceptives, there
is a paradoxical, negative sense in which all possible future generations are the patients or subjects of a power wielded by those already

* From *The Abolition of Man*, by C. S. Lewis. Copyright 1947. Reprinted
by permission of The Macmillan Company, publishers.

alive. By contraception simply, they are denied existence; by contraception used as a means of selective breeding, they are, without their concurring voice, made to be what one generation, for its own reasons, may choose to prefer. From this point of view, what we call Man's power over Nature turns out to be a power exercised by some men over other men with Nature as its instrument.

It is, of course, a commonplace to complain that men have hitherto used badly, and against their fellows, the powers that science has given them. But that is not the point I am trying to make. I am not speaking of particular corruptions and abuses which an increase of moral virtue would cure: I am considering what the thing called 'Man's power over Nature' must always and essentially be. No doubt, the picture could be modified by public ownership of raw materials and factories and public control of scientific research. But unless we have a world state this will still mean the power of one nation over others. And even within the world state or the nation it will mean (in principle) the power of majorities over minorities, and (in the concrete) of a government over the people. And all long-term exercises of power, especially in breeding, must mean the power of earlier generations over later ones.

The latter point is not always sufficiently emphasized, because those who write on social matters have not yet learned to imitate the physicists by always including Time among the dimensions. In order to understand fully what Man's power over Nature, and therefore the power of some men over other men, really means, we must picture the race extended in time from the date of its emergence to that of its extinction. Each generation exercises power over its successors: and each, in so far as it modifies the environment bequeathed to it and rebels against tradition, resists and limits the power of its predecessors. This modifies the picture which is sometimes painted of a progressive emancipation from tradition and a progressive control of natural processes resulting in a continual increase of human power. In reality, of course, if any one age really attains, by eugenics and scientific education, the power to make its descendants what it pleases, all men who live after it are the patients of that power. They are weaker, not stronger: for though we may have put wonderful machines in their hands we have pre-ordained how they are to use them. And if, as is almost certain, the age which had thus attained maximum power over posterity were also the age most emancipated from tradition, it would be engaged in reducing the power of its predecessors almost as drastically as that of its successors. And we must also remember that, quite apart from this, the later a generation comes—the nearer it lives to that date at which the species becomes extinct—the less power it will have in the forward direction, because its subjects will be so few. There is therefore no question of a power vested in the race as a whole steadily growing as long as the race survives. The last men, far from being the heirs of power, will be of all men most subject to the dead hand of the great planners and conditioners and will themselves exercise least power upon the future. The real picture is that of one dominant age—let us suppose the hundredth century A.D.—which resists all previous ages most successfully and dominates all subsequent ages most irresistibly, and thus is the real master of the human species. But even within this master generation (itself an infinitesimal minority of the species) the power will be exercised by a minority smaller still. Man's conquest of Nature, if the dreams of some scientific planners are realized, means the rule of a few hundreds of men over billions upon billions of men. There neither is nor can be any simple increase of power on Man's side. Each new power won *by* man is a power *over* man as well. Each advance leaves him weaker as well as stronger. In every victory, besides being the general who triumphs, he is also the prisoner who follows the triumphal car.

I am not yet considering whether the total result of such ambivalent victories is a good thing or a bad. I am only making clear what Man's conquest of Nature really means and especially that final stage in the conquest, which, perhaps, is not far off. The final stage is come when Man by eugenics, by pre-natal conditioning, and by an education and propaganda based on a perfect applied psychology, has obtained full control over himself. *Human* nature will be the last part of Nature to surrender to Man. The battle will then be won. We shall have 'taken the thread of life out of the hand of Clotho' and be henceforth free to make our species whatever we wish it to be. The battle will indeed be won. But who, precisely, will have won it?

For the power of Man to make himself what he pleases means, as we have seen, the power of some men to make other men what *they* please. In all ages, no doubt, nurture and instruction have, in some sense, attempted to exercise this power. But the situation to which we must look forward will be novel in two respects. In the first place, the power will be enormously increased. Hitherto the plans of educationalists have achieved very little of what they attempted and indeed, when we read them—how Plato would have every infant 'a bastard nursed in a bureau,' and Elyot would have the boy see no men before the age of seven and, after that, no women,[1] and how Locke wants children to have leaky shoes and no turn for poetry[2]—we may well thank the beneficent obstinacy of real mothers, real nurses, and (above all) real children for preserving the human race in such sanity as it still possesses. But the man-moulders of the new age will be armed with the powers of an omnicompetent state and an irresistible scientific technique: we shall get at last a race of conditioners who really can cut out all posterity in what shape they please. The second difference is even more important. In the older systems both the kind of man the teachers wished to produce and their motives for producing him were prescribed by the *Tao* [†]—a norm to which the teachers themselves were subject and from which they claimed no liberty to depart. They did not cut men to some pattern they had chosen. They handed on what they had received: they initiated the young neophyte into the mystery of humanity which over-arched him and them alike. It was but old birds teaching young birds to fly. This will be changed. Values are now mere natural phenomena. Judgements of value are to be produced in the pupil as part of the conditioning. Whatever *Tao* there is will be the product, not the motive, of education. The conditioners have been emancipated from all that. It is one more part of Nature which they have conquered. The ultimate springs of human action are no longer, for them, something given. They have surrendered—like electricity: it is the function of the Conditioners to control, not to obey them. They know how to *produce* conscience and decide what kind of conscience they will produce. They themselves are outside, above. For we are assuming the last

---

[1] *The Boke Named the Governour*, I, iv: 'Al men except physitions only shulde be excluded and kepte out of the norisery.' I, vi: 'After that a childe is come to seuen yeres of age . . . the most sure counsaille is to withdrawe him from all company of women.'

[2] *Some Thoughts concerning Education*, §7: 'I will also advise his *Feet to be wash'd* every Day in cold Water, and to have his Shoes so thin that they might leak and *let in Water*, whenever he comes near it.' §174: 'If he have a poetick vein, 'tis to me the strangest thing in the World that the Father should desire or suffer it to be cherished or improved. Methinks the Parents should labour to have it stifled and suppressed as much as may be.' Yet Locke is one of our most sensible writers on education.

[† A Chinese word meaning, literally, "the way." Lewis uses it throughout the book from which this selection is taken to refer to the doctrine that there are certain absolute values in the universe, absolutes of moral right and wrong no less than of mathematical truth and falsehood, and that these truths are "built into" the universe as we experience it, not just mental inventions.]

stage of Man's struggle with Nature. The final victory has been won. Human nature has been conquered—and, of course, has conquered, in whatever sense those words may now bear.

The Conditioners, then, are to choose what kind of artificial *Tao* they will, for their own good reasons, produce in the Human race. They are the motivators, the creators of motives. But how are they going to be motivated themselves? For a time, perhaps, by survivals, within their own minds, of the old 'natural' *Tao*. Thus at first they may look upon themselves as servants and guardians of humanity and conceive that they have a 'duty' to do it 'good.' But it is only by confusion that they can remain in this state. They recognize the concept of duty as the result of certain processes which they can now control. Their victory has consisted precisely in emerging from the state in which they were acted upon by those processes to the state in which they use them as tools. One of the things they now have to decide is whether they will, or will not, so condition the rest of us that we can go on having the old idea of duty and the old re-actions to it. How can duty help them to decide that? Duty itself is up for trial: it cannot also be the judge. And 'good' fares no better. They know quite well how to produce a dozen different conceptions of good in us. The question is which, if any, they should produce. No conception of good can help them to decide. It is absurd to fix on one of the things they are comparing and make it the standard of comparison.

To some it will appear that I am inventing a factitious difficulty for my Conditioners. Other, more simple-minded, critics may ask 'Why should you suppose they will be such bad men?' But I am not sup-posing them to be bad men. They are, rather, not men (in the old sense) at all. They are, if you like, men who have sacrificed their own share in traditional humanity in order to devote themselves to the task of deciding what 'Humanity' shall henceforth mean. 'Good' and 'bad,' applied to them, are words without content: for it is from them that the content of these words is henceforward to be derived. Nor is their difficulty factitious. We might suppose that it was pos-sible to say 'After all, most of us want more or less the same things— food and drink and sexual intercourse, amusement, art, science, and the longest possible life for individuals and for the species. Let them simply say, This is what we happen to like, and go on to condition men in the way most likely to produce it. Where's the trouble?' But this will not answer. In the first place, it is false that we all really like the same things. But even if we did, what motive is to impel the Conditioners to scorn delights and live laborious days in order that we, and posterity, may have what we like? Their duty? But that is only the *Tao*, which they may decide to impose on us, but which cannot be valid for them. If they accept it, then they are no longer the makers of conscience but still its subjects, and their final conquest over Nature has not really happened. The preservation of the species? But why should the species be preserved? One of the questions before them is whether this feeling for posterity (they know well how it is produced) shall be continued or not. However far they go back, or down, they can find no ground to stand on. Every motive they try to act on becomes at once a *petitio*. It is not that they are bad men. They are not men at all. Stepping outside the *Tao*, they have stepped into the void. Nor are their subjects necessarily unhappy men. They are not men at all: they are artefacts. Man's final conquest has proved to be the abolition of Man.

Yet the Conditioners will act. When I said just now that all motives fail them, I should have said all motives except one. All motives that claim any validity other than that of their felt emotional weight at a given moment have failed them. Everything except the *sic volo, sic jubeo* has been explained away. But what never claimed objectivity cannot be destroyed by subjectivism. The impulse to scratch when I itch or to pull to pieces when I am inquisitive is immune from the solvent which is fatal to my justice, or honour, or care for posterity. When all that says 'it is good' has been debunked, what says 'I want' remains. It cannot be exploded or 'seen through' because it never had any pretensions. The Conditioners, therefore, must come to be motivated simply by their own pleasure. I am not here speaking of the corrupting influence of power nor expressing the fear that under it our Conditioners will degenerate. The very words *corrupt* and *degenerate* imply a doctrine of value and are therefore meaningless in this context. My point is that those who stand outside all judgements of value cannot have any ground for preferring one of their own impulses to another except the emotional strength of that impulse. We may legitimately hope that among the impulses which arise in minds thus emptied of all 'rational' or 'spiritual' motives, some will be benevolent. I am very doubtful myself whether the benevolent impulses, stripped of that preference and encouragement which the *Tao* teaches us to give them and left to their merely natural strength and frequency as psychological events, will have much influence. I am very doubtful whether history shows us one example of a man who, having stepped outside traditional morality and attained power, has used that power benevolently. I am inclined to think that the Conditioners will hate the conditioned. Though regarding as an illusion the artificial conscience which they produce in us their subjects, they will yet perceive that it creates in us an illusion of meaning for our lives which compares favourably with the futility of their own: and they will envy us as eunuchs envy men. But I do not insist on this, for it is mere conjecture. What is not conjecture is that our hope even of a 'conditioned' happiness rests on what is ordinarily called 'chance'—the chance that benevolent impulses may on the whole predominate in our Conditioners. For without the judgement 'Benevolence is good'—that is, without re-entering the *Tao*—they can have no ground for promoting or stabilizing their benevolent impulses rather than any others. By the logic of their position they must just take their impulses as they come, from chance. And Chance here means Nature. It is from heredity, digestion, the weather, and the association of ideas, that the motives of the Conditioners will spring. Their extreme rationalism, by 'seeing through' all 'rational' motives, leaves them creatures of wholly irrational behaviour. If you will not obey the *Tao*, or else commit suicide, obedience to impulse (and therefore, in the long run, to mere 'nature') is the only course left open.

At the moment, then, of Man's victory over Nature, we find the whole human race subjected to some individual men, and those individuals subjected to that in themselves which is purely 'natural'—to their irrational impulses. Nature, untrammelled by values, rules the Conditioners and, through them, all humanity. Man's conquest of Nature turns out, in the moment of its consummation, to be Nature's conquest of Man. Every victory we seemed to win has led us, step by step, to this conclusion. All Nature's apparent reverses have been but tactical withdrawals. We thought we were beating her back when she was luring us on. What looked to us like hands held up in surrender was really the opening of arms to enfold us for ever. If the fully planned and conditioned world (with its *Tao* a mere product of the planning) comes into existence, Nature will be troubled no more by the restive species that rose in revolt against her so many millions of years ago, will be vexed no longer by its chatter of truth and mercy and beauty and happiness. *Ferum victorem cepit:* and if the eugenics are efficient enough there will be no second revolt, but all sunk beneath the Conditioners, and the Conditioners beneath her, till the moon falls or the sun grows cold.

Problems for Thought and Writing

I

1. Do Lewis' opening examples *prove* his conclusion at the end of the second paragraph, that "Man's power over Nature turns out to be a power exercised by some men over other men with Nature as its instrument"?

2. How would Lewis regard vocational aptitude tests?

3. Do men today commonly assume, as Lewis asserts ironically on page 329, that "Values are now mere natural phenomena"? Would Julian Huxley (page 315) so assume?

4. Do you agree with the author's assumption on pages 330-31 that any judgment of comparison attests the existence of an absolute standard, against which the objects or ideas compared are being measured? (See Introduction to "Evaluation," page 629.)

II

5. Identify or define: infinitesimal, Clotho, ambivalent, factitious, *petitio*, artefact, *sic volo, sic jubeo,* eunuch, untrammelled, *ferum victorem cepit.*

6. Does the style Lewis adopts offer an additional clue to his total meaning and purpose? Does he write in what we ordinarily think of as a "philosophical" style? (See discussions after selections by Thomas Reed Powell and Jonathan Swift under "Humor and Satire.")

7. Would you call Lewis' analysis more or less *objective* than Julian Huxley's? Remember that to be objective means to admit all the facts of reality and to exclude none.

8. In what way does Lewis illustrate an "analogical" mode of argument? Are his analogies convincing? Do they invariably prove his thesis? (See Introductions to "Comparison and Contrast," page 418, and "Argument and Persuasion," (page 539.)

~

THE UNDISCOVERED SELF * Carl G. Jung

For more than fifty years we have known, or could have known, that there is an unconscious as a counterbalance to consciousness. Medical psychology has furnished all the necessary empirical and experimental proofs of this. There is an unconscious psychic reality which demonstrably influences consciousness and its contents. All

* From *The Atlantic Monthly*, November, 1957. Copyright 1957, 1958, by C. G. Jung. This essay was written as a result of conversations between Carleton Smith, Director of the National Arts Foundation, and Dr. Jung, and was later expanded in book form in *The Undiscovered Self* (Boston: Little Brown & Co., Inc., 1958).

this is known, but no practical conclusions have been drawn from it. We still go on thinking and acting as before, as if we were *simplex* and not *duplex*. Accordingly we imagine ourselves to be innocuous, reasonable, and humane. We do not think of distrusting our motives or of asking ourselves how the inner man feels about the things we do in the outside world. But actually it is frivolous, superficial, and unreasonable of us, as well as psychically unhygienic, to overlook the reaction and viewpoint of the unconscious.

One can regard one's stomach or heart as unimportant and worthy of contempt, but that does not prevent overeating or overexertion from having consequences that affect the whole man. Yet we think that psychic mistakes and their consequences can be got rid of with mere words, for "psychic" means less than air to most people. All the same, nobody can deny that without the psyche there would be no world at all and still less a human world. Virtually everything depends on the human soul and its functions. It should be worthy of all the attention we can give it, especially today, when everyone admits that the weal or woe of the future will be decided neither by the attacks of wild animals nor by natural catastrophes nor by the danger of world-wide epidemics but simply by the psychic changes in man.

It needs only an almost imperceptible disturbance of equilibrium in a few of our rulers' heads to plunge the world into blood, fire, and radioactivity. The technical means necessary for this are present on both sides. And certain conscious deliberations, uncontrolled by any inner opponent, can be indulged in all too easily, as we have seen already from the example of one "leader." The consciousness of modern man still clings so much to outward objects that he makes them exclusively responsible, as if it were on them that the decision depended. That the psychic state of certain individuals could emancipate itself for once from the behavior of objects is something that is considered far too little, although irrationalities of this sort are observed every day and can happen to everyone.

The forlornness of consciousness in our world is due primarily to the loss of instinct, and the reason for this lies in the development of the human mind over the past aeon. The more power man had over nature the more his knowledge and skill went to his head and the deeper became his contempt for the merely natural and accidental, for that which is irrationally given—including the objective psyche, which is all that consciousness is not.

In contrast to the subjectivism of the conscious mind, the unconscious is objective, manifesting itself mainly in the form of contrary feelings, fantasies, emotions, impulses, and dreams, none of which one makes oneself but which come upon one objectively. Even today psychology is still for the most part the science of conscious contents, measured as far as possible by collective standards. The individual psyche became a mere accident, a "random" phenomenon, while the unconscious, which can only manifest itself in the real, "irrationally given" human being, was ignored altogether. This was not the result of carelessness or of lack of knowledge, but of downright resistance to the mere possibility of there being a second psychic authority besides the ego. It seems a positive menace to the ego that its monarchy could be doubted. The religious person, on the other hand, is accustomed to the thought of not being sole master in his own house. He believes that God, and not he himself, decides in the end. But how many of us would dare to let the will of God decide, and which of us would not feel embarrassed if he had to say how far the decision came from God himself?

The religious person, so far as one can judge, stands directly under the influence of the reaction from the unconscious. As a rule he calls this the operation of *conscience*. But since the same psychic background produces reactions other than moral ones, the believer is measuring his conscience by the traditional ethical standard and thus by a collective value, in which endeavor he is assiduously supported by his Church. So long as the individual can hold fast to his traditional beliefs, and the circumstances of his time do not demand stronger emphasis on individual autonomy, he can rest content with the situation. But the situation is radically altered when the worldly-minded man who is oriented to external factors and has lost his religious beliefs appears en masse, as is the case today. The believer is then forced into the defensive and must catechize himself on the foundation of his beliefs. He is no longer sustained by the tremendous suggestive power of the *consensus omnium*, and is keenly aware of the weakening of the Church and the precariousness of its dogmatic assumptions.

To counter this the Church recommends more faith, as if this gift of grace depended on man's good will and pleasure. The seat of faith, however, is not consciousness but spontaneous religious experience, which brings man's faith into immediate relation with God.

Here we must ask: Have I any religious experience and immediate relation to God, and hence that certainty which will keep me, as an individual, from dissolving in the crowd?

To this question there is a positive answer only when the individual is willing to fulfill the demands of rigorous self-examination and self-knowledge. If he follows through his intention, he will not only discover some important truths about himself, but will also have gained a psychological advantage: he will have succeeded in deeming himself worthy of serious attention and sympathetic interest. He will have set his hand to a declaration of his own human dignity and taken the first step toward the foundations of his consciousness—that is, toward the unconscious, the only accessible source of religious experience.

This is certainly not to say that what we call the unconscious is identical with God or is set up in his place. It is the medium from which the religious experience seems to flow. As to what the further cause of such an experience may be, the answer to this lies beyond the range of human knowledge. Knowledge of God is a transcendental problem.

The religious person enjoys a great advantage when it comes to answering the crucial question that hangs over our time like a threat: he has a clear idea of the way his subjective existence is grounded in his relation to "God." I put the word "God" in quotes in order to indicate that we are dealing with an anthropomorphic idea whose dynamism and symbolism are filtered through the medium of the unconscious psyche. Anyone who wants to can at least draw near the source of such experiences, no matter whether he believes in God or not. Without this approach it is only in rare cases that we witness those miraculous conversions of which Paul's Damascus experience is the prototype.

That religious experiences exist no longer needs proof. But it will always remain doubtful whether what metaphysics and theology call God and the gods is the real ground of these experiences. The question is idle, actually, and answers itself by reason of the subjectively overwhelming numinosity of the experience. Anyone who has had it is *seized* by it and therefore not in a position to indulge in fruitless metaphysical or epistemological speculations. Absolute certainty brings its own evidence and has no need of anthropomorphic proofs.

In view of the general ignorance of and bias against psychology it must be accounted a misfortune that the one experience which makes sense of individual existence should seem to have its origin in a medium that is certain to catch everybody's prejudices. Once more the doubt is heard: "What good can come out of Nazareth?" The unconscious, if not regarded outright as a sort of refuse bin underneath the conscious mind, is at any rate supposed to be of "merely animal nature." In reality, however, and by definition it is of uncertain extent and constitution, so that over- or under-valuation of it is groundless and can be dismissed as mere prejudice. At all events such judgments sound very queer in the mouths of Christians whose Lord was himself born on the straw of a stable, among the domestic animals. It would have been more to the taste of the multitude if he had got himself born in a temple. In the same way, the worldly-minded mass man looks for the numinous experience in the mass meeting, which provides an infinitely more imposing background than the individual soul. Even Church Christians share this pernicious delusion.

Psychology's insistence on the importance of unconscious processes for religious experience is extremely unpopular, no less with the Right than with the Left. For the former the deciding factor is the historical revelation that came to man from outside; to the latter this is sheer nonsense, and man has no religious function at all, except belief in the party doctrine, when suddenly the most intense faith is called for. On top of this, the various creeds assert quite different things, and each of them claims to possess the absolute truth. Yet today we live in a unitary world where distances are reckoned by hours and no longer by weeks and months. Exotic races have ceased to be peep shows in ethnological museums. They have become our neighbors, and what was yesterday the prerogative of the ethnologist is today a political, social, and psychological problem. Already the ideological spheres begin to touch, to interpenetrate, and the time may not be so far off when the question of mutual understanding in this field will become acute.

To make oneself understood is certainly impossible without far-reaching comprehension of the other's viewpoint. The insight needed for this will have repercussions on both sides. History will undoubtedly pass over those who feel it is their vocation to resist this inevitable development, however desirable and psychologically necessary it may be to cling to what is essential and good in our own tradition. Despite all the differences, the unity of mankind will assert itself irresistibly. On this card Marxist doctrine has staked its life, while the West hopes to get through with technology and economic aid. Communism has not overlooked the enormous importance of the

ideological element and the universality of basic principles. The
nations of the Far East share this ideological weakness with us and are
just as vulnerable as we are.

The underestimation of the psychological factor is likely to take
bitter revenge. It is therefore high time we caught up with ourselves
in this matter. For the present this must remain a pious wish, because
self-knowledge, in addition to being highly unpopular, seems to be
unpleasantly idealistic, reeks of morality, and is preoccupied with the
psychological shadow, which is denied whenever possible or at least
not spoken of. The task that faces our age is indeed almost insuper-
ably difficult. It makes the highest demands on our responsibility if
we are not to be guilty of another *trahison des clercs*. It addresses
itself to those guiding and influential personalities who have the
necessary intelligence to understand the situation our world is in.

One might expect them to consult their consciences. But since it is
not only a matter of intellectual understanding but of moral conclusions, there is unfortunately no cause for optimism. Nature, as
we know, is not so lavish with her boons that she joins to a high
intelligence the gifts of the heart also. As a rule, where one is present
the other is lacking, and where one capacity is present to perfection
it is generally at the cost of all the others. The discrepancy between
intellect and feeling, which get in each other's way at the best of
times, is a particularly painful chapter in the history of the human
psyche.

There is no sense in formulating the task that our age has forced
upon us as a moral demand. We can, at best, merely make the
psychological world situation so clear that it can be seen even by the
myopic, and give utterance to words and ideas which even the hard
of hearing can hear. We may hope for men of understanding and
men of good will, and must therefore not grow weary of reiterating
those thoughts and insights which are needed. Finally, even the
truth can spread and not only the popular lie.

With these words I should like to draw the reader's attention to the
main difficulty he has to face. The horror which the dictator states
have of late brought upon mankind is nothing less than the culmination of all those atrocities of which our ancestors made themselves
guilty in the not so distant past. Quite apart from the barbarities and
blood baths perpetrated by the Christian nations among themselves
throughout European history, the European has also to answer for
all the crimes he has committed against the dark-skinned peoples dur-

ing the process of colonization. In this respect the white man carries a very heavy burden indeed. It shows us a picture of the common human shadow that could hardly be painted in blacker colors. The evil that comes to light in man and which undoubtedly dwells within him is of gigantic proportions, so that for the Church to talk of original sin and to trace it back to Adam's relatively innocent slip-up with Eve is almost a euphemism. The case is far graver and is grossly under-estimated.

Since it is universally believed that man *is* merely what his con-sciousness knows of itself, he regards himself as harmless and so adds stupidity to iniquity. He does not deny that terrible things have happened and still go on happening, but it is always the others who do them. And when such deeds belong to the recent or remote past, they quickly and conveniently sink into the sea of forgetfulness, and that state of chronic woolly-mindedness returns which we describe as "normality."

In shocking contrast to this is the fact that nothing has finally dis-appeared and nothing has been made good. The evil, the guilt, the profound unease of conscience, the obscure misgiving, are there before our eyes, if only we would see. Man has done these things; I am a man who has his share of human nature; therefore I am guilty with the rest and bear unaltered and indelibly within me the capacity and the inclination to do them again at any time. Even if, juristically speaking, we were not accessories to the crime, we are always, thanks to our human nature, potential criminals. In reality we merely lacked a suitable opportunity to be drawn into the infernal melee. None of us stands outside humanity's black collective shadow. Whether the crime lies many generations back or happens today, it remains the symptom of a disposition that is always and everywhere present—and one would therefore do well to possess some "imagination in evil," for only the fool can permanently neglect the conditions of his own nature. In fact, this negligence is the best means of making him an instrument of evil. Harmlessness and naïveté are as little helpful as it would be for a cholera patient and those in his vicinity to remain un-conscious of the contagiousness of the disease. On the contrary, they lead to projection of the unrecognized evil into the "other." This strengthens the opponent's position in the most effective way, because the projection carries the *fear* which we involuntarily and secretly feel for our own evil over to the other side and considerably increases the formidableness of his threat.

What is even worse, our lack of insight deprives us of the *capacity to deal with evil.* Here, of course, we come up against one of the main prejudices of the Christian tradition, and one that is a great stumbling block to our policies. We should, so we are told, eschew evil and if possible neither touch nor mention it. For evil is also the thing of ill omen, that which is tabooed and feared. This apotropaic attitude toward evil, and the apparent circumventing of it, flatter the primitive tendency in us to shut our eyes to evil and drive it over some frontier or other, like the Old Testament scapegoat, which was supposed to carry the evil into the wilderness.

But if one can no longer avoid the realization that evil, without man's ever having chosen it, is lodged in human nature itself, then it bestrides the psychological stage as the equal and opposite partner of good. This realization leads straight to a psychological dualism, already unconsciously prefigured in the political world-schism and in the even more unconscious dissociation in modern man himself. The dualism does not come from this realization; rather, we are in a split condition to begin with. It would be an insufferable thought that we had to take personal responsibility for so much guiltiness. We therefore prefer to localize the evil with individual criminals or groups of criminals, while washing our hands in innocence and ignoring the general proclivity to evil.

This sanctimoniousness cannot be kept up in the long run, because the evil, as experience shows, lies in man—unless, in accordance with the Christian view, one is willing to postulate a metaphysical principle of evil. The great advantage of this view is that it exonerates man's conscience of too heavy a responsibility and fobs it off on the Devil, in correct psychological appreciation of the fact that man is much more the victim of his psychic constitution than its inventor. Considering that the evil of our day puts everything that has ever agonized mankind in the deepest shade, one must ask oneself how it is that, for all our progress in the administration of justice, in medicine, and in technics, for all our concern for life and health, monstrous engines of destruction have been invented which could easily exterminate the human race.

No one will maintain that the atomic physicists are a pack of criminals because it is to their efforts that we owe that peculiar flower of human ingenuity, the hydrogen bomb. The vast amount of intellectual work that went into the development of nuclear physics was put forth by men who devoted themselves to their task with the greatest exertions and self-sacrifice and whose moral achievement could just as easily have earned them the merit of inventing something useful and beneficial to humanity. But even though the first step along the road to a momentous invention may be the outcome of a conscious decision, here as everywhere the spontaneous idea—the hunch or intuition—plays an important part. In other words, the unconscious collaborates too and often makes decisive contributions.

So it is not the conscious effort alone that is responsible for the result; somewhere or other the unconscious, with its barely discernible goals and intentions, has its finger in the pie. If it puts a weapon in your hand, it is aiming at some kind of violence. Knowledge of the truth is the foremost goal of science, and if in pursuit of the longing for light we stumble upon an immense danger, then one has the impression more of fatality than of premeditation. It is not that present-day man is capable of greater evil than the man of antiquity or the primitive. He merely has incomparably more effective means with which to realize his proclivity to evil. As his consciousness has broadened and differentiated, so his normal nature has lagged behind. That is the great problem before us today. *Reason alone does not suffice.*

In theory, it lies within the power of reason to desist from experiments of such hellish scope as nuclear fission if only because of their dangerousness. But fear of the evil which one does not see in one's own bosom, but always expects in somebody else's, checks reason every time, although one knows that the use of this weapon means the certain end of our present human world. The fear of universal destruction may spare us the worst, yet the possibility of it will nevertheless hang over us like a dark cloud so long as no bridge is found across the world-wide psychic and political split—a bridge as certain as the existence of the hydrogen bomb. If a world-wide consciousness could arise that all division and all fission is due to the splitting of opposites in the psyche, then one would really know where to attack. But if even the smallest and most personal stirrings of the individual soul—so insignificant in themselves—remain as unconscious and unrecognized as they have done hitherto, they will go on accumulating and produce mass groupings and mass movements which cannot be subjected to reasonable control or manipulated to a good end. All direct efforts to do so are no more than shadow boxing, the most infatuated by illusion being the gladiators themselves.

The deciding factor lies with the individual man, who knows no answer to his dualism. This abyss has suddenly yawned open before him with the latest events in world history, after mankind had lived for many centuries in the comfortable belief that a unitary God had created man in his own image, as a little unity. Even today people are largely unconscious of the fact that every individual is a cell in the structure of various international organisms and is therefore causally implicated in their conflicts. He knows that as an individual being he is more or less meaningless and feels himself the victim of uncontrollable forces, but on the other hand he harbors within himself a dangerous shadow and opponent who is involved as an invisible helper in the dark machinations of the political monster.

It is in the nature of political bodies always to see the evil in the opposite group, just as the individual has an ineradicable tendency to get rid of everything he does not know and does not want to know about himself by foisting it off on somebody else. Nothing has a more divisive and alienating effect upon society than this moral complacency and lack of responsibility, and nothing promotes understanding and *rapprochement* more than the mutual withdrawal of projections. This necessary corrective requires self-criticism, for one cannot just tell the other person to withdraw them. He does not recognize them for what they are, any more than one does oneself. We can recognize our prejudices and illusions only when, from a broader psychological knowledge of ourselves and others, we are prepared to doubt the absolute rightness of our assumptions and compare them carefully and conscientiously with the objective facts.

Funnily enough, "self-criticism" is an idea much in vogue in Marxist countries; but there it is subordinated to ideological considerations and must serve the state, and not truth and justice in men's dealings with one another. The mass state has no intention of promoting mutual understanding and the relationship of man to man; it strives rather for atomization, for the psychic isolation of the individual. The more unrelated individuals are, the more consolidated the state becomes, and vice versa.

There can be no doubt that in the democracies too the distance between man and man is much greater than is conducive to public welfare or beneficial to our psychic needs. True, all sorts of attempts are being made to level out glaring social contrasts by appealing to people's idealism, enthusiasm, and ethical conscience; but, characteristically, one forgets to apply the necessary self-criticism, to answer the question: *Who* is making the idealistic demand? Is it, perchance, someone who jumps over his own shadow in order to hurl himself avidly on an idealistic program that promises him a welcome alibi? How much respectability and apparent morality is there, cloaking with deceptive colors a very different world of darkness? One would first like to be assured that the man who talks of ideals is himself ideal, so that his words and deeds *are* more than they *seem*.

To be ideal is impossible, and remains therefore an unfulfilled postulate. Since we usually have keen noses in this respect, most of the idealisms that are preached and paraded before us sound rather hollow and only become acceptable when their opposite is openly admitted to. Without this counterweight the ideal goes beyond our human capacity, becomes incredible because of its humorlessness, and degenerates into bluff, albeit a well-meant one. Bluff is an illegitimate way of overpowering and suppressing people, and leads to no good.

Recognition of the shadow, on the other hand, leads to the modesty we need in order to acknowledge imperfection. And it is just this conscious recognition and consideration that are needed wherever a human relationship is to be established. A human relationship is not based on differentiation and perfection, for these only emphasize the differences or call forth the exact opposite; it is based rather on imperfection, on what is weak, helpless, and in need of support—the very ground and motive of dependence. The perfect has no need of the other, but weakness has, for it seeks support and does not confront its partner with anything that might force him into an inferior position and even humiliate him. This humiliation may happen only too easily where idealism plays too prominent a role.

Reflections of this kind should not be taken as superfluous sentimentalities. The question of human relationship and of the inner cohesion of our society is an urgent one in view of the atomization of the pent-up mass man, whose personal relationships are undermined by general mistrust. Wherever justice is uncertain and police-spying and terror are at work, human beings fall into isolation, which of course is the aim and purpose of the dictator state, since it is based on the greatest possible accumulation of depotentiated social units.

To counter this danger, the free society needs a bond of an affective nature, a principle of a kind like *caritas*, the Christian love of your neighbor. But it is just this love for one's fellow man that suffers most of all from the lack of understanding wrought by projection. It would therefore be very much to the interest of the free society to give some thought to the question of human relationship from the psychological point of view, for in this resides its real cohesion and consequently its strength. Where love stops, power begins, and violence, and terror.

These reflections are not intended as an appeal to idealism, but only to heighten the consciousness of the psychological situation. I do not know which is weaker: idealism or the insight of the public. I only know that it needs time to bring about psychic changes that have any prospect of enduring. Insight that dawns slowly seems to me to have more lasting effects than a fitful idealism which is unlikely to hold out for long.

What our age thinks of as the "shadow" and inferior part of the psyche contains more than something merely negative. The very fact that through self-knowledge—that is, by exploring our own souls—we come upon the instincts and their world of imagery should throw some light on the powers slumbering in the psyche, of which we are seldom aware so long as all goes well. They are potentialities of the greatest dynamism, and it depends entirely on the preparedness and attitude of the conscious mind whether the irruption of these forces and the images and ideas associated with them will tend toward construction or catastrophe.

The psychologist seems to be the only person who knows from experience how precarious is the psychic preparedness of modern man, for he is the only one who sees himself compelled to seek out in man's nature those helpful forces and ideas which ever and again have enabled the individual to find the right way through darkness and danger. For this exacting work the psychologist requires all his patience; he may not rely on any traditional "oughts" and "musts," leaving the other person to make all the effort and contenting himself with the easy role of adviser and admonisher. Everyone knows the futility of preaching about things that are desirable, yet the general helplessness in this situation is so great, and the need so dire, that one prefers to repeat the old mistake instead of racking one's brains over a subjective problem. Besides, it is always a question of treating one single individual only and not ten thousand, where the trouble one takes would be worth while, though one knows well enough that nothing has happened at all unless the individual changes.

The effect on *all* individuals, which one would like to see realized, may not set in for hundreds of years, for the spiritual transformation of mankind follows the slow tread of the centuries and cannot be hurried or held up by any rational process of reflection, let alone brought to fruition in one generation. What does lie within our reach, however, is the change in individuals who have, or create, an opportunity to influence others of like mind in their circle of acquaintance. I do not mean by persuading or preaching—I am thinking rather of the well-known fact that anyone who has insight into his own actions, and has thus found access to the unconscious, involuntarily exercises an influence on his environment. The deepening and broadening of his consciousness produces the kind of effect which the primitives call "mana." It is an unintentional influence on the unconscious of others, a sort of unconscious prestige, and its effect lasts only so long as it is not disturbed by conscious intention.

Nor is the striving for self-knowledge altogether without prospects, since there exists a factor which, though completely disregarded, meets our expectations halfway. This is the unconscious *Zeitgeist*. It compensates the attitude of the conscious mind and anticipates changes to come. An excellent example of this is modern art: though seeming to deal with aesthetic problems, it is really performing a work of psychological education on the public by breaking down and destroying their previous aesthetic views of what is beautiful in form and meaningful in content. The pleasingness of the artistic product is replaced by chill abstractions of the most subjective nature, which brusquely slam the door on the naïve and romantic delight in the senses and their obligatory love for the object. This tells us, in plain and universal language, that the prophetic spirit of art has turned away from the old object-relationship and toward the—for the time being—dark chaos of subjectivisms.

Certainly art, so far as we can judge it, has not yet discovered in this darkness what it is that holds all men together and could give expression to their psychic wholeness. Since reflection seems to be needed for this purpose, it may be that such discoveries are reserved for other fields of endeavor. Great art till now has always derived its fruitfulness from the myth, from the unconscious process of symbolization which continues through the ages and, as the primordial manifestation of the human spirit, will continue to be the root of all creation in the future. The development of modern art with its seemingly nihilistic trend toward disintegration must be understood as the symptom and symbol of a mood of world destruction and world renewal that has set its mark on our age. This mood makes itself felt everywhere, politically, socially, and philosophically. We are living in what the Greeks called the "right time" for a metamorphosis of the gods—that is, of the fundamental principles and symbols. This peculiarity of our time, which is certainly not of our conscious choosing, is the expression of the unconscious man within us who is changing. Coming generations will have to take account of this momentous transformation if humanity is not to destroy itself through the might of its own technology and science.

As at the beginning of the Christian aeon, so again today we are faced with the problem of the moral backwardness which has not kept pace with our scientific, technical, and social developments. So much is at stake and so much depends on the psychological constitution of modern man. Is he capable of resisting the temptation to use his power for the purpose of staging a world conflagration? Is he conscious of the path he is treading, and what the conclusions are that must be drawn from the present world situation and his own psychic situation? Does he know that he is on the point of losing the life-preserving myth of the inner man which Christianity has treasured up for him? Does he realize what lies in store should this catastrophe ever befall him? Is he even capable of realizing that this would be a catastrophe at all? And finally, does the individual know that *he* is the makeweight that tips the scales?

Happiness and contentment, equability of soul and meaningfulness of life—these can be experienced only by the individual and not by a state, which on the one hand is nothing but a convention of independent individuals among themselves and, on the other, continually threatens to hypertrophy and suppress the individual. The psychiatrist is one of those who know most about the conditions of the soul's welfare upon which so infinitely much depends in the social sum. The social and political circumstances of the time are certainly of considerable significance, but their importance for the weal or woe of the individual has been boundlessly overestimated insofar as they are taken for the sole deciding factors.

In this respect all our social goals commit the error of overlooking the psychology of the person for whom they are intended, and—very often—of promoting only his illusions.

I hope, therefore, that a psychiatrist who in the course of a long life has devoted himself to the causes and consequences of psychic disorders may be permitted to express his opinion, in all the modesty enjoined upon him as an individual, about the questions raised by the world situation today. I am neither spurred on by excessive optimism nor in love with high ideals, but am merely concerned with the fate of the individual human being—that infinitesimal unit on whom a world depends, and in whom, if we read the meaning of the Christian message aright, even God seeks his goal.

Problems for Thought and Writing

I

1. Jung refers to the unconscious mind as "objective" and the conscious as "subjective." Explain what he means by the terms. Is this usage the one you are accustomed to or expect?

2. Is not Jung making an argument for *irrationality* and its forces? Do you think the social consequences of his advice would be beneficial or harmful?

3. "Have I any religious experience and immediate relation to God, and hence that certainty which will keep me, as an individual, from dissolving in the crowd?" If a man or woman had a positive answer to Jung's question, would he or would he not be exempt from the dangers expressed by Chiaromonte (page 225)? What do you think Chiaromonte would say? Would Fromm agree with Jung here? (See page 198.)

4. "The forlornness of consciousness in our world is due primarily to the loss of instinct . . ." What does Jung mean by this statement? Do you feel it is valid or an exaggeration?

5. "But it will always remain doubtful," writes Jung, "whether what metaphysics and theology call God and the gods is the real ground of these experiences. The question is idle, actually . . ." Is the question an "idle" one to you? Are you willing to accept the fact of religious *experience* as a psychological fact and ignore the question of theological *fact*?

6. After mentioning the heavy crimes of man against man perpetrated by Europeans in the past and present, Jung remarks: "In this respect the white man carries a very heavy burden indeed." Explain the obvious irony in the statement. Are we, as Americans, exempt from this guilt or the feeling of it? One critic (Reinhold Niebuhr) has called it the "irony" of our history that we are so obviously involved in the world's crimes and yet think of ourselves as a people with clean hands. Do you think of yourself (as individual and as American) as "involved" in the crimes of the concentration camps or exempt from them? Do you feel "guilty" about Hiroshima and Nagasaki? How would Jung explain your answer?

7. What, in Jung's terms, is original sin? What does it mean to the orthodox Christian? Do you or do you not believe in its existence? If you do, define it.

8. "But fear of the evil which one does not see in one's own bosom, but always expects in somebody else's, checks reason every time." To what degree does that statement explain the tensions of the cold war, of the development of nuclear weapons, of their use in World War II? How, in your opinion, can we mend the "world-wide psychic split"? What is Jung's recommendation?

9. What does Jung mean by "the mutual withdrawal of projections"?

10. Is the condition of "atomization," the "psychic isolation of the individual" promoted only by conditions in Marxist countries, or does it also exist in the West? Read Chiaromonte (page 225) and Whyte (page 217).

11. A "human relationship," says Jung, is not based on the ideal, on perfection, but on imperfection, on "what is weak, helpless, and in need of support. . . ." Explain what Jung means. Would this be equally true of a relationship with God or what is called God in human experience?

12. Jung writes of the "spiritual transformation of mankind" as if it were a sure thing—simply very far distant in the future. In your opinion, can that spiritual transformation take place unless we solve the problem of burgeoning populations and provide physical as well as psychic *lebensraum*? See Mowrer (page 238) and Hooton (page 247) in this volume.

13. "Great art till now has always derived its fruitfulness from the myth, from the unconscious process of symbolization which continues through the ages and, as the primordial manifestation of the human spirit, will continue to be the root of all creation in the future." This statement encompasses one of Jung's basic beliefs—the belief in the *collective unconscious*, the racial memory which persists today and is manifested in certain symbolic or archetypal forms. This problem is too complex for investigation here, but a good starter is to ask: What does Jung mean by myth?

II

14. Identify or define: apotropaic, hypertrophy, subjective, dynamism, numinous, euphemism, *rapprochement*.

15. Would you call this article an *argument* or a *piece of exposition*?

16. Jung, known as the founder of analytical psychology, is a Swiss. Can you detect anything "foreign" or unidiomatic about his writing?

~

ZEN[1] FOR THE WEST*   *William Barrett*

I

Zen Buddhism presents a surface so bizarre and irrational, yet so colorful and striking, that some Westerners who approach it for the first time fail to make sense of it, while others, attracted by this surface, take it up in a purely frivolous and superficial spirit. Either response would be unfortunate. The fact is that Zen, as Dr. Suzuki demonstrates, is an essential expression of Buddhism, and Buddhism is one of the most tremendous spiritual achievements in human history—an achievement which we Westerners probably have not yet fully grasped. We have to remember how recent it is that we have

[1] Zen from Japanese *zazen*, to sit and meditate, a translation of the Chinese *ch'an*, which in turn was the translation of the Indian *Dhyana* (meditation). Thus Zen begins as a particular sect of Buddhism, an essentially meditative one, but in its development it radically transforms the traditional Buddhist discipline of meditation: the dualism between meditation and activity is abolished.

* From *Essays in Zen Buddhism*, by William Barrett. Copyright © 1956 by William Barrett. Reprinted by permission of Doubleday & Company, Inc.

sought out any knowledge of the East. Only a century separates us from Schopenhauer, the first Western philosopher who attempted a sympathetic interpretation of Buddhism, a brilliant and sensational misunderstanding on the basis of meagre translations. Since then great strides have been made in Oriental studies, but a curiously paradoxical provincialism still haunts the West: the civilization which has battered its way into every corner of the globe has been very tardy in examining its own prejudices by the wisdom of the non-Western peoples. Even today when the slogan "One World!" is an incessant theme of Sunday journalism and television, we tend to interpret it in a purely Western sense to mean merely that the whole planet is now bound together in the net of modern technology and communications. That the phrase may imply a necessity for coming to terms with our Eastern opposite and brother, seems to pass publicly unnoticed. There are many signs, however, that this tide must turn.

I consider it a great stroke of personal good fortune to have stumbled (and quite by chance) upon the writings of D. T. Suzuki years ago. I emphasize the word "personal" here because I am not a professional Orientalist and my interest in Suzuki's writings has been what it is simply because these writings shed light upon problems in my own life—one proof that Zen does have a much needed message for Westerners. There are now a good many books available on Buddhism, but what makes Suzuki unique—and unique not only among writers on Buddhism but among contemporary religious writers generally—is that he starts from the assumption that Buddhism is a living thing that began some 2500 years ago with Gotama's experience of enlightenment, has been developing ever since, and is still alive and growing. Hence the extraordinary freshness and vitality of his writings, so that if you go on from them to other books on Buddhism you will find that these latter take on a life from him that they themselves would never have initially for the Westerner. Suzuki has steeped himself thoroughly in Chinese Buddhism, and the practical and concrete Chinese spirit probably provides an introduction to Buddhism more congenial to the Westerner than the soaring metaphysical imagination of the Indians. One picture is worth a thousand words, as the old Chinese saying has it, and this Chinese genius for the concrete may never have been better realized than in the anecdotes, paradoxes, poems of the Zen masters. Westerners usually think that the religious and philosophic thought of China is summed up in the two names of Lao-tsu and Confucius; Suzuki shows us that some of the great figures of Chinese Buddhism were at least the equal of these two. And if his writings did nothing else, they would still be important for giving us knowledge of this great chapter of Buddhist history that had been virtually unknown to us hitherto.

But do these ancient Oriental masters have anything to say to us who belong to the present-day West? Very much so, I think; and the reason is that we Westerners have only recently come to face certain realities of life with which the Oriental has been living for centuries. This is a large claim, and requires some itemized documentation.

What we call the Western tradition is formed by two major influences, Hebraic and Greek, and both these influences are profoundly dualistic in spirit. That is, they divide reality into two parts and set one part off against the other. The Hebrew makes his division on religious and moral grounds: God absolutely transcends the world, is absolutely separate from it; hence there follow the dualisms of God and creature, the Law and the erring members, spirit and flesh. The Greek, on the other hand, divides reality along intellectual lines. Plato, who virtually founded Western philosophy single-handed— Whitehead has remarked that 2500 years of Western philosophy is but a series of footnotes to Plato—absolutely cleaves reality into the world of the intellect and the world of the senses. The great achievement of the Greeks was to define the ideal of rationality for man; but in doing so, Plato and Aristotle not only made reason the highest and most valued function, they also went so far as to make it the very center of our personal identity. The Orientals never succumbed to this latter error; favoring intuition over reason, they grasped intuitively a center of the personality which held in unity the warring opposites of reason and unreason, intellect and senses, morality and nature. So far as we are Westerners, we inherit these dualisms, they are part of us: an irrationally nagging conscience from the Hebrews, an excessively dividing rational mind from the Greeks. Yet the experience of modern culture, in the most diverse fields, makes them less and less acceptable.

Medieval Christianity still lives in the rational world of the Greeks. The universe of St. Thomas Aquinas is the same bandbox universe of Aristotle, a tight tiny tidy rational whole, where all is in apple-pie order, and everything occupies its logical and meaningful place in the absolute hierarchy of Being. When we turn from such humanized universes to Indian thought, we are at first staggered by the vision of vast spaces, endless aeons of time, universe upon universe, against which man looks very small and meaningless; then we realize these are the spaces and times of modern astronomy, and the Indian idea is therefore closer to us. The distinguished Protestant theologian Paul Tillich has described the essential experience of modern man as an encounter with "meaninglessness": lost in the vastness of the universe, man begins to think that his own existence and that of the universe are "meaningless." The God of Theism, says Tillich echoing Nietzsche, is dead, and Western man must find a God beyond the God of Theism: the God offered us by rational theology is no longer acceptable. From the point of view of the medieval Catholic (and many still survive) the very premises of Buddhist thinking would look "meaningless"; they are also more difficult and grim, but they look much closer to what we moderns may have to swallow.

In science itself, modern developments have combined to make our inherited rationalism more shaky. Physics and mathematics, the two most advanced of Western sciences, have in our time become paradoxical: that is, arrived at the state where they breed paradoxes for reason itself. One hundred fifty years ago the philosopher Kant attempted to show that there were ineluctable limits to reason, but the Western mind, positivistic to the core, could be expected to take such a conclusion seriously only when it showed up in science itself. Well, science in this century has at last caught up with Kant: almost simultaneously Heisenberg in physics, and Godel in mathematics, have shown ineluctable limits to human reason. Heisenberg's Principle of Indeterminacy shows essential limits to our ability to know and predict physical states of affairs, and opens up to us the glimpse of a nature irrational and chaotic at bottom. Godel's results would seem to have even more far-reaching consequences when one reflects that in the Western tradition, from the Pythagoreans and Plato onward, mathematics has inspired the most absolute claims of rationalism. Now it turns out that even in his most precise science—in the province where his reason had seemed omnipotent—man cannot escape his essential finitude: every system of mathematics that he constructs is doomed to incompleteness. Mathematics is like a ship in mid-ocean that has sprung leaks (paradoxes) which have been temporarily plugged, but our reason can never guarantee that the ship will not spring other leaks. That this human insecurity should manifest itself in what had hitherto been the very citadel of reason, mathematics, marks a new turn in Western thinking. The next step would be to recognize the essentially paradoxical nature of reason itself.

This step has been taken by some modern philosophers. The most original and influential philosopher now alive on the European continent is the German Existentialist Martin Heidegger. A German friend of Heidegger told me that one day when he visited Heidegger he found him reading one of Suzuki's books; "If I understand this man correctly," Heidegger remarked, "this is what I have been trying to say in all my writings." This remark may be the slightly exaggerated enthusiasm of a man under the impact of a book in which he recognizes some of his own thoughts; certainly Heidegger's philosophy in its tone and temper and sources is Western to its core, and there is much in him that is not in Zen, but also very much more in Zen that is not in Heidegger; and yet the points of correspondence between the two, despite their disparate sources, are startling enough. For what, after all, is Heidegger's final message but that Western philosophy is a great error, the result of the dichotomizing intellect that has cut man off from unity with Being itself and from his own Being. This error begins (in Plato) with locating truth in the intellect; the world of nature thereby becomes a realm of objects set over against the mind, eventually objects to be manipulated by scientific and practical calculation. Twenty-five hundred years of Western metaphysics move from Plato's intellectualism to Nietzsche's Will to Power, and concurrently man does become in fact the technological master of the whole planet; but the conquest of nature merely estranges him from Being itself and from his own Being and delivers him over to an ever ascending, ever more frantic will to power. "Divide and conquer" might thus be said to be the motto which Western man has adopted toward Being itself; but this of course is the counsel of power not of wisdom. Heidegger repeatedly tells us that this tradition of the West has come to the end of its cycle; and as he says this, one can only gather that he himself has already stepped beyond that tradition. Into the tradition of the Orient? I should say at least that he has come pretty close to Zen.

If these happenings in science and philosophy indicate changed ways of thinking in the West, our modern art would seem to indicate very new ways of feeling. Whatever may be said on the thorny subject of modern art, the one fact that is clear is that to the artistic conservative it represents a scandal and a break with the tradition. Our modern art presents a surface so irrational, bizarre, and shocking that it must be considered a break with the older more rational canons of Western art. That Western painters and sculptors in this century have gone outside their tradition to nourish themselves with the art of the rest of the world—Oriental, African, Melanesian—signifies that what we knew as *the* tradition is no longer able to nourish its most creative members; its confining mould has broken, under pressures from within. Our painting has detached itself from three-dimensional space, the arena of Western man's power and mobility; detached itself from the object, the supreme fixation of Western man's extroversion; and it has become subjective, contrary to the whole tenor of our Western life. Is all this merely malaise and revolt, or prophecy of a different spirit to come? In the past, new styles in painting have often been thus prophetic. In the art of literature, of course, the writer can be vocal about the new and revolutionary thing, and we find a novelist like D. H. Lawrence preaching against the bloodless rationalism of his culture. Lawrence urged the necessity of something he called "mindlessness," of becoming "mindless," if the meddlesome and self-conscious intellect were not in the end to cut off Western man irreparably from nature and even the possibility of real sexual union. Oddly enough, this "mindlessness" of Lawrence is a groping intuition after the doctrine of "no-mind" which Zen Buddhism had elaborated a thousand years before. (See Chapter 7.) Unlike Lawrence, however, the Zen masters developed this doctrine without falling into primitivism and the worship of the blood. In Lawrence's behalf it must be remembered that his culture gave him no help at all on these matters, and he had to grope in the dark pretty much on his own. And to change to one final literary example that involves no preaching or thesis whatsoever: the most considerable work of prose in English in this century is probably James Joyce's *Ulysses,* and this is so profoundly Oriental a book that the psychologist C. G. Jung recommended it as a long-needed bible for the white-skinned peoples. Joyce shattered the aesthetic of the Georgians that would divide reality into a compartment of the Beautiful forever separate from the opposite compartments of the Ugly or Sordid. *Ulysses,* like the Oriental mind, succeeds in holding the opposites together: light and dark, beautiful and ugly, sublime and banal. The spiritual premise of this work is an acceptance of life that no dualism—whether puritanical or aesthetic—could ever possibly embrace.

Admittedly, all these happenings I have cited—from science, philosophy, art—make up a very selective list; this list could be expanded greatly; nevertheless even as it stands, these instances make up a body of "coincidence" so formidable that they must make us pause. When events run parallel this way, when they occur so densely together in time and in such diverse fields, they can no longer be considered as mere meaningless "coincidence" but as very meaningful symptoms; in this case symptoms that the West in its own depths begins to experience new things, begins in fact to experience its own opposite. In this new climate a concern with something like Zen Buddhism can no longer be taxed as idle exoticism, for it has to do with the practical daily bread of the spirit.

The really somber paradox about all these changes is that they have happened in the deep and high parts of our culture, while in the areas in between everything goes on as usual. Despite the discoveries of its artists, philosophers, theoretical scientists, the West, in its public and external life at any rate, is just as Western as ever, if not more so. Gadgets and traffic accumulate, the American way of life (or else the Russian) spreads all over the globe, the techniques for externalizing life become year by year more slick and clever. All of which may only show what a creature of contradictions Western man has become. And now that at last his technology has put in his hands the hydrogen bomb, this fragmented creature has the power to blow himself and his planet to bits. Plain common sense would seem to advise that he turn to look inward a little.

II

None of the above considerations has to do with Zen itself. Or rather—to put it abruptly as Zen likes to do—Zen has nothing at all to do with them. They deal with the complicated abstractions of the intellect—philosophy, culture, science, and the rest—and what Zen seeks above all is the concrete and the simple that lie beyond the snarled tangles of intellectualization. Zen *is* the concrete itself. Zen eschews abstractions, or uses them only to get beyond them. Even when Zen declares against abstractions, it has to put the matter concretely: thus when the great Master Tokusan has his enlightenment, he does not merely say in pallid fashion that concepts are not enough; no, he burns all his philosophic texts, declaring, "All our understanding of the abstractions of philosophy is like a single hair in the vastness of space." Let the Western reader fasten upon this image and he will find it harder to miss the point. Or when another Master remarks on the difficulty of solving one of the Zen questions—which is equivalent to answering the riddle of existence itself—he does not merely say that it is difficult or so very very difficult that it is well-nigh impossible, but this: "It is like a mosquito trying to bite into an iron bull." The image lives because the image suggests the meaning beyond conceptualization.

Now it is just this concreteness of expression, this extraordinary profusion of images and examples, that can make Zen most helpful to the Westerner, who in fact derives from a more highly abstract culture. But it would be a mistake for the Western reader to imagine that these are merely so many literary devices or adornments adopted by the Zen masters. On the contrary, the language of Zen is of the essence, the manner of expression is one with the matter. Zen expresses itself concretely because Zen is above all interested in facts not theories, in realities and not those pallid counters for reality which we know as concepts. "Fact" may suggest to the Western mind something merely quantitative or statistical—therefore also a lifeless and abstract thing. Zen wants, rather, the facts as living and concrete. In this sense, Zen might be described as Radical Intuitionism—if the Westerner wishes a handle by which to lay hold of it. This does not mean that it is merely a philosophy of intuition like Bergson's, though it agrees with Bergson that the conceptualizing intellect does not reach reality; rather, it is radical intuition in the act itself. Radical Intuitionism means that Zen holds that thinking and sensing live, move, and have their being within the vital medium of intuition. We see with the two eyes only insofar as we are also seeing (though we may not know it) with the third eye—the eye of intuition. Hence, any sensory facts will do for Zen provided they serve to awaken the third eye, and we encounter in the Zen writings the most extraordinary incidents of illumination in connection with the most humble objects. In the end all language is pointing: we use language to point beyond language, beyond concepts to the concrete. The monk asks the Master, "How may I enter in the Way?", and the Master, pointing to the mountain spring, responds, "Do you hear the sound of that torrent? There you may enter." Another time Master and monk are walking upon the mountain, and the Master asks, "Do you smell the mountain laurel?" "Yes." "There, I have held nothing back from you."

In its emphasis upon the living fact over the mere idea, Zen is true to the essential teaching of Buddha. Buddha cared very little for the philosophers; there were said to be already some 63 schools in existence in his time, and he had occasion to observe from their wrangling how imprisoned in the labyrinths of the intellect the human spirit can become. Thus Zen itself is not a philosophy (the Western reader must be warned here), though there lie behind it some of the great

philosophies of Mahayana Buddhism. Though Buddha began by opposing the philosophers, nevertheless in the course of its history
Buddhism evolved one of the greatest and most profound philosophies
ever created. Is this a contradiction of the original spirit of the
founder? No; for Buddhist philosophy is activated by an altogether
different purpose from that of Western philosophy: Buddhism takes
up philosophy only as a device to save the philosopher from his con-
ceptual prison; its philosophy is, as it were, a non-philosophy, a philosophy to undo philosophy. A comparison of the mind of Buddha and
Plato—probably the greatest intellects of East and West—may make us
understand how sharply East and West diverge on this crucial point.
For Plato philosophy is a discipline that leads us from the lower to the
higher world, from the world of the senses to the world of ideas, to
leave us abiding in this latter world as much as is humanly possible;
for the Buddhist, philosophy should lead us beyond the intellect back
into the one real world that was always there in its undivided wholeness. Zen presupposes this view of philosophy, but goes beyond the
mere restatement of it to make actual use of it in its practical and concrete Chinese fashion.

This passion for the living fact accounts for that quality in the Zen
masters which must seem most amazing to the Westerner: their supreme matter-of-factness. "What is the Tao (the way, the truth)?"
asks the disciple. "Your everyday mind," replies the Master; and he
goes on to amplify: "When I am hungry, I eat; when tired, I sleep."
The disciple is puzzled, and asks whether this is not what everybody
else does too. No, the Master replies; most people are never wholly
in what they are doing; when eating, they may be absent-mindedly
preoccupied with a thousand different fantasies; when sleeping, they
are not sleeping. The supreme mark of the thoroughly integrated man
is to be without a divided mind. This matter-of-fact spirit of Zen is
expressed in another paradoxical statement: "Before you have studied
Zen, mountains are mountains and rivers are rivers; while you are
studying it, mountains are no longer mountains and rivers no longer
rivers; but once you have had Enlightenment, mountains are once
again mountains and rivers are rivers." The stories of their arduous
struggles for Enlightenment teach us that this matter-of-fact spirit of
the Zen masters is not a thing easily come by: they are indeed awesome figures who have crossed the mountains and rivers, floods and
fires of the spirit in order to come back sole and whole to the most
banal things of daily life. The nearest thing to this, so far as I know,
that the West has produced is Kierkegaard's wonderful comparison of

the Knight of Resignation and the Knight of Faith: the former all fidgets and romanticism, aspiring after the infinite but never at home with the finite, while the Knight of Faith sits so solidly in his existence that from without he looks as prosaic and matter-of-fact as a tax-collector. But this ideal of being in direct and unmediated relation to ordinary reality was something that poor Kierkegaard, who waged a feverish lifelong struggle against the mediating and devouring power of his intelligence, could only aspire after but never realize.

In this striving for an unmediated relation to reality, as well as in its doctrine of an enlightenment (satori) that goes beyond reason, Zen would seem to be a form of Mysticism. But Zen is not mysticism as the West understands mysticism. The mystic, as defined by William James in *Varieties of Religious Experience* (James did not know about Zen), is one who pierces the veil of the natural or sensuous world in order to experience direct union with the higher reality. This formula holds for most of the great Western mystics from Plotinus onward, but it would not hold of Zen, which would reject this kind of mysticism as dualistic through and through, since it divides reality into lower and higher worlds. For Zen, higher and lower are one world; and in the records of Zen enlightenment which Suzuki sets before us there does not seem to occur anywhere the blurring of consciousness, the trancelike or semi-hallucinated state, which you will find among Western mystics. Even where it seems to move closest to mysticism, Zen remains supremely matter-of-fact. Nor is Zen to be confused with anything like pantheism, even though the Zen writings abound in statements that the Buddha-nature is to be found everywhere, in the dried up dirt-scraper, the cypress tree in the courtyard, etc. etc. Pantheism involves a division between the God who penetrates nature and nature itself as the phenomenal garment of God. But this too is a dualism that Zen leaves behind.

Neither a philosophy, then, in the Western sense, nor a mysticism, not Pantheism and not Theism, Zen might seem to the reader at this point so much a matter of subtlety and nuance as to be devoid of all practical value. On the contrary; for the greatest contemporary tribute to the practicality of Zen comes not from philosophers or artists, but from two prominent *practicing* psychiatrists, C. G. Jung and Karen Horney, who became passionately interested in Zen for its therapeutic possibilities. Jung has written about Zen, and before her death Karen Horney visited Japan to observe the life of a Zen monastery at first hand. What attracted Jung to Zen was its remarkable pursuit of psychological wholeness. Horney saw something similar, but in terms of her own psychology: namely, the search for self-realization without either the false image of an idealized self ("We are saved such as we are," says the Zen master), or without the resigned and dependent clinging to external props like family, social group, or church (after his enlightenment the disciple slaps the Master Obaku's face, remarking "There is not, after all, very much in the Buddhism of Obaku," and the master is pleased, for the disciple shows he can now stand on his own two feet). Certainly the Zen masters, as we read of them in Suzuki's pages give us the powerful impression of fully individuated individuals, carved out of one whole and solid block. What is most incredible to the Westerner is that this demand for the individuation of the disciple should be made by a *religion!* Western religions have always been willing to settle for less, very much less, from the believer —his filial obedience or docility, let him be a miserable psychological fragment otherwise. The reason is that Western religion has always placed the weight of emphasis upon the religious object outside the individual—God beyond the world, the Mosaic Law, the Church, the divine personality of Jesus. One can hardly imagine a Western religion producing a saying like the Zen Master's to his monks, "When you utter the name of Buddha, wash your mouth out." Zen is individualistic, and so iconoclastic and antinomian in its individualism that it will seem irreverent to many Westerners; but this is only because Zen wishes to strip the individual naked in order to return him to himself: in the end he cannot lean even upon the image of Buddha. Here precisely is the aspect of Zen Buddhism which is the greatest challenge to Western religions, and which needs to be studied most by us Westerners; for the march of our own history, as the great world of medieval religious images recedes ever further from our grasp and an increasingly secularized society engulfs us, has stripped Western man naked and left no rocklike security anywhere to lean upon. Here there looms before the frightened eyes of the Westerner what Buddhism calls the Great Emptiness; but if he does not run away in fear, this great void may bloom with all manner of miracles, and heaven and earth, in consort once again, engender effortlessly all their ancient marvels.

Problems for Thought and Writing

I

1. The Western tradition is, writes Barrett, "profoundly dualistic" in spirit. For glimpses of various aspects of that dualistic spirit see the pieces in this

volume by Plato (page 450), Arnold (page 422), Santayana (page 437), and Jung (page 333). Do you think it inevitable that a civilization view reality in terms of right *vs.* wrong, God *vs.* creature, spirit *vs.* flesh, etc.? What would Jung say of the dangers of so doing?

2. Zen Buddhism, in various forms, has lately attracted a number of followers in the West. Can you think of any plausible reasons for this attraction? Are we as a culture tending less and less to view reality dualistically?

3. Both Barrett and Jung lament the loss of *intuition* in modern man—the displacement of it by reason. Is the problem here that man is so *reasonable* or that he thinks he *ought* to be?

4. The essential experience of modern man, in the words of Paul Tillich, is an encounter with "meaninglessness." That feeling can arise from a sense of the vastness of the universe and the consequent smallness of man; but could it not also arise from a sense of the smallness of the universe, the lack of space dealt with in Chiaromonte (page 225) and Mowrer (page 238). Do you feel this, in any way, to have been your "essential experience"?

5. What evidence does Barrett cite in support of the basic *irrationality* of man? Does this surprise you? Disturb you? Do you think man's irrationality might be manipulated for the public good as effectively or perhaps even more effectively than his rationality? See Jung (page 333).

6. What does Barrett mean by the "paradoxical" nature of reason?

7. In what basic regard does the thought of the Existentialist Martin Heidegger correspond with that of Zen?

8. "The result of man's technological mastery of nature," writes Barrett, "merely estranges him from Being itself and from his own Being and delivers him over to an ever ascending ever more frantic will to power." What does Barrett mean by "Being" and "his own Being"?

9. In what ways do the views of Jung and Barrett on modern art correspond? (See Jung, page 333.)

10. After quoting the Zen statement about the difficulty of the riddle of existence —"It is like a mosquito trying to bite into an iron bull"—Barrett remarks: "The image lives because the image suggests the meaning beyond conceptualization." What does Barrett's statement mean? Is there a meaning *beyond* conceptualization? Or is Barrett merely saying that the image is so good that conceptualization is unnecessary?

11. What is the essential difference between Plato and Buddha as Barrett describes it?

12. What was the attraction of Zen for Carl Jung and psychiatrist Karen Horney? In what ways, according to Barrett, does Zen demand much more from the believer than Western religions?

II

13. Study the organization and paragraph structure of this essay. Compare it with that of Gilson (page 635).

14. Since Schopenhauer's interpretation of Buddhism, writes Barrett, we have made great strides in Oriental studies, but—note these words—"a curiously paradoxical provincialism still haunts the West: the civilization which has battered its way into every corner of the globe has been very tardy in ex-

amining its own prejudices by the wisdom of the non-Western peoples."
Evaluate that statement (and others like it) in the critical terms provided
by Gibson (page 70). Who is the "mock reader" here?

15. Identify or define: bizarre, enlightenment, metaphysical, paradox, ineluctable,
positivistic, dichotomizing, canons, D. H. Lawrence, *Ulysses*, the Georgians,
labyrinths.

16. Concreteness is a virtue constantly drummed into the ears of the beginning
writer by English teachers. Is their notion of concreteness usually the same
as that practiced by Zen? Are the reasons for recommending it the same?
Explain—*concretely*—the difference.

PART II

THE ORGANIZATION OF THOUGHT

PART II

The Organization of Thought

INTRODUCTION

In the following sections will be found discussions of (1) Definition and Description, (2) Comparison and Contrast, (3) Classification and Division, (4) Process and Narrative, (5) Argument and
Persuasion, and (6) Evaluation, followed by pieces illustrating
these modes of thought and organization. The first four of these
categories deal with problems of exposition—how something can
be explained, ordered, clarified. The last two sections deal with
two important intellectual processes that employ, among other
things, these expository techniques.

The editors' Introductions to each of the above main sections
should be carefully noted. The rationale of the second part of
this book—and its usefulness—rests on an understanding of these
rhetorical modes and the ways in which they can serve as the vehicles and the very hosts of thought. For these rhetorical problems are not merely ways of writing: they are ways in which the
mind may be used to order, verify, and clarify the evidence that
comes to it. "Form in writing," says M. Cocteau, "must be the
form of the mind. Not a way of saying things, but of thinking
them." Studying the rhetorical patterns that follow will help form
the mind that would impress its form in good writing.

Definition and Description

Anyone who has spent a day with a three-year-old knows something about the problems of definition.

"What's that furry thing down there?"

"That's a caterpillar."

"What's that long thing you're wearing?"

"That's a necktie."

"What's that black thing up there?"

"That's a ventilator."

"What's that red thing going around?"

"That's a wheel."

The child is engaged here in one of the simplest and most elemental forms of defining: the process of *naming*. By putting tags on things, the child feels a little more at home in a strange world, a little less threatened by its mysteries. Of course, naming caterpillars, neckties, ventilators, and wheels doesn't, as Hayakawa reminds us (page 458), tell us much about them. But the child doesn't want to know much about them. What he wants to know is how he *relates* to them. It is essential, therefore, that they have *identities*—that they can be separated off from other "furry" things, "long" things, "black" things, or "red things going around." By so identifying them the child gives features to the blur of reality, and acquires the comfort of knowing that the next time a certain kind of furry thing humps into his life, he can call it by a familiar and friendly name, "caterpillar."

But giving names to things is not, obviously, all there is to defining. To name a girl "Joan" is not to say much about her appearance, personality, character, race, or religious affiliation. And if we told our three-year-old that the "furry" thing was a wombat, he would have been just as satisfied. A definition is more than a label; it is a statement about an identity, a description and analysis of what lies behind a name (or word).

Before investigating a few conventional ways of defining, we need to recognize some of the intellectual difficulties involved in the subject. We use and make definitions every day, but philosophers and logicians are far from agreement as to what we really do when we define.

An ancient difficulty, for example, is the controversy between the nominalists and realists. When we define, are we defining *words* or the *realities* the words represent? In either case, of course, we use words. But does the matter end with words? The nominalist, along with the modern dictionary maker, would say yes: the words by which things are known are assigned by man, and they can be defined by other words invented and assigned by man. The realist would say no: when we define a chair we do more than collect the words naming those attributes we associate with chairs; instead our words refer to some ideal entity, "chair," which transcends both language and time. "Chair" would be there whether we were or not, whether we verbalized or not, whether we perceived or not.

The problem becomes clearer (and more difficult) when we refer to abstract entities or moral qualities such as "courage" or "honor." Whether "honor" is a word or a reality was a question Falstaff wrestled with on the battlefield near Shrewsbury:

> Well, 't is no matter; honour pricks me on. Yea, but how if honour prick me off when I come on? How then? Can honour set to a leg? No. Or an arm? No. Or take away the grief of a wound? No. Honour hath no skill in surgery, then? No. What is honour? A word. What is in that word honour? What is that honour? Air; a trim reckoning! Who hath it? He that died o' Wednesday. Doth he feel it? No. Doth he hear it? No. 'T is insensible, then? Yea, to the dead. But will it not live with the living? No. Why? Detraction will not suffer it. Therefore I'll none of it. Honour is a mere scutcheon: and so ends my catechism.
>
> (Shakespeare, *The First Part of Henry the Fourth*, Act V, Scene I.)

Falstaff, in order to rationalize his own cowardice, found it convenient to be a nominalist. But in more philosophic terms the problem is this: when we seek the meaning of "honor" are we (1) seeking all the ways in which the word "honor" is used by men, or (2) seeking some ideal entity, *honor*, which is assumed to have a real existence? The realist, for example, would probably say that the *beauty* of a beautiful statue was as much in existence were the statue buried or exposed to human eyes. The nominalist would say no: "beauty" must be apprehended to be known; it is a word we give to certain human *experiences*.

But what about a mathematical concept like "apogee"—that point in the orbit of the moon (or other heavenly body) most distant from the earth? A term like "apogee" is, by definition, already ideal, final. Mathematics, as we shall observe later (page 550), is a *deductive* system, and a means by which, within the terms of that system, we can achieve certainty. An ancient or medieval realist would of course claim that mathematics leads us to final truth, that the system itself was immutably and irrevocably true. Most modern mathematicians make no such claim. So with a term like "apogee" it is absurd to distinguish between the realistic and nominalistic definition. The definition is a stipulated one (see page 374); apogee is a concept which exists because man made it exist; the words that define it are its very body.

Obviously, such questions take us deeply into metaphysical, logical, epistemological problems which we can scarcely touch on here. But it is important to realize that definition—the statement about what something *is* —is one of the knottiest questions in human thought. If we learn to be somewhat self-conscious about the definitions we use or make, we can learn a great deal about the assumptions on which we operate our lives. Assume that we agree with Milton (in *Lycidas*) that "*Fame* is no plant that grows on mortal soil." This is, of course, a loose and metaphorical definition, but the meaning is clear enough. Another way of putting it is that the no-toriety, the publicity, the praise which men receive from other men are not the ingredients of "fame." We can, of course, use the term, describe its attributes, list famous men—but this, to the realist, is not enough. He would say, with Milton, that there has to be a final model, an *ideal*. And he might add that without the possibility of such an ideal, life would be meaningless and not worth living. The nominalist, on the other hand, is more "scientific," more *inductive* (see pag 547). He insists that defini-tion (and, by implication, truth) be derived from experience, from empirical discovery. But no man is *either* inductive *or* deductive in all his thinking, and no man is *either* pure nominalist or realist. But there is little doubt that our world today tends to be nominalistic. Few of us would try to de-fine "democracy" by relating the political institutions and processes of the United States with some ideal entity, some nonworldly absolute, called "democracy." Most of us feel, rather, that a word means what human beings in their *experience* have come to think it means. And that is per-haps particularly the case with words like "justice" and "truth" and "good" and "evil." Values that once were absolute are now put to the vote. Is this relativism dangerous? Some of the authors in this volume—particularly Gilson (page 635), Stace (page 640) and Mandel (page 171)—fear it deeply.

But actually modern thought has redefined reality in such radical ways that the terms "nominalist" and "realist" seem hardly applicable any longer. An observed "fact" of today's physics, for example, is that certain particles in the atomic nucleus move from one place to another without crossing the intervening distance. Is that fact, so manifestly nonlogical, something *real?* Again, a group of modern grammarians known as structural linguists have pointed out that words are products of cultural growth and reflect cultural attitudes. When we say that a word "stands for" (is a "symbol" of) a cer-tain reality, we are not just saying that *this* (word) equals *that* (reality); we are saying that this race or people or nation happen to look at their experi-ence in this way. Some Indian tribes, for example, use no nouns in their language. There are no "things" or "substantives" in their way of looking at the world, for to them everything is verb, everything is in motion. Ben-jamin Whorf, an eminent structural linguist, asks us in one of his books to reconsider our use of the noun "sky." "Sky," after all, is not a noun or a *thing*, but a kind of verb, a continuum made up of atmospheric molecules, light waves, electrical particles—things in motion. Our conventional ways of defining, inherited from the Greeks, divide the world up into classes, little packaged categories. It is convenient to analyze reality in this way, but we should remember that most of our experience does not come in parcels but as a unity, a continuous interrelationship.

In our daily lives, however, we aren't usually so subtle. If I am a manufacturer and need a new gear to be made in the shop, I expect that my definition of the new gear (the blueprint) will result in something predictable, something substantive, something classifiable. If I am a biologist naming a butterfly, it is hardly enough to define that animal by placing it in the great continuum called "life." Ultimately it may be true that both the gear and the butterfly are simply forms of energy (since "matter" in the old sense no longer exists) and not significantly different at all. Perhaps those words "gear" and "butterfly" are even blinding us to the true conformations of the "reality" before us rather than describing them. But in the crude business of getting along in the world—working and eating and waging hot and cold wars—we must accept more naïve definitions.

We have called definition a statement about a thing's identity, a description and analysis of what lies behind a name (or words). To come to some agreement about what words mean is crucial, and any argument lacking in such agreement is futile (see "Argument and Persuasion," page 539). In 1950, for example, the North and South Koreans each called the other side the "aggressor." An impartial United Nations commission investigated and declared the North Koreans to be, in fact, the "aggressors," and that settled the truth of the matter for most Westerners. But the problem was not simply that of a lie *versus* a non-lie; the problem was one of coming to agreement about what words mean. The North Koreans were not members of the United Nations, so the "impartiality" of that body looked like prejudice to them. But that men *can* come to agreement, *can* meet on common ground, is a presumption upon which all civilization rests. If a judge were to consult his imagination rather than the common law for a definition of "theft" or "first-degree murder," we should have no safety under the law at all. If a physician were to use "measles" to describe all visible diseases he would be a menace. But such intellectual malpractice is far from unknown, and Lewis Carroll reminded us of some of its dangers in *Through the Looking Glass*.

"I don't know what you mean by 'glory,'" Alice said.

Humpty-Dumpty smiled contemptuously. "Of course you don't— till I tell you. I meant 'there's a nice knock-down argument for you!'"

"But 'glory' doesn't mean 'a nice knock-down argument,'" Alice objected.

"When *I* use a word," Humpty Dumpty said in rather a scornful tone, "it means just what I choose it to mean—neither more nor less."

"The question is," said Alice, "whether you *can* make words mean so many different things."

"The question is," said Humpty Dumpty, "which is to be master—that's all."

Alice was too much puzzled to say anything; so after a minute Humpty Dumpty began again. "They've a temper, some of them—particularly verbs: they're the proudest—adjectives you can do anything with, but not verbs—however, *I* can manage the whole lot of them! Impenetrability! That's what *I* say!"

"Would you tell me please," said Alice, "what that means?"

"Now you talk like a reasonable child," said Humpty Dumpty, looking very much pleased. "I meant by 'impenetrability' that we've had enough of that subject, and it would be just as well if you'd mention what you mean to do next, as I suppose you don't mean to stop here all the rest of your life."

"That's a great deal to make one word mean," Alice said, in a thoughtful tone.

"When I make a word do a lot of work like that," said Humpty Dumpty, "I always pay it extra."

"Oh!" said Alice.

By no means are definitions always objective statements; they can also be the carriers of passion and prejudice, opinion and conviction. Take the case of a man at a lunch counter who shoves his cup back toward the waiter with the words: "I ordered a cup of *coffee!*" "That's what you got," the waiter replies. "That's not what *I* call coffee!" is the rejoinder. Superficially the argument is about a statement of *fact;* but actually it is an argument about *value.* Or take the argument Milton used in justifying the beheading of Charles I. A king can be defined as a man with such attributes as courage, virtue, nobility, generosity, wisdom, self-control. Did Charles I possess them? No. Therefore, he was no king, and was not exempt from being treated as any other man—even as a common criminal. Here again the question seems to involve only matters of fact, but actually that definition of "king" was a value judgment with profound implications. A comic definition such as: "Man is an animal split half the way up who walks on the split end," does not fool anybody, for it is obviously partial, it obviously leaves much out of account. Its objectivity is patently specious. But take this serious definition: "Love is the investment of the libido in an object of erotic attraction." The psychologist who wrote that was not trying to be funny, yet it is almost as partial as the comic definition above. (The jargon of science leaves us all with sober faces, even when, perhaps, we should be splitting our sides.) That may be a *useful* definition, but it is certainly not *complete:* anyone who has been in love would have great difficulty equating his experience with that statement (consider Erich Fromm's extended definition of love, page 505). What we put in and what we leave out of a definition will reflect to some degree what we *want* in and out; it will reflect our particular way of looking at what we see, and our particular motives in making the definition in the first place.

In a practical sense, all we normally want in a definition is a statement that so limits and modifies a word (and the reality we assume it represents) that it will never be confused with any other word in the same language. A definition can be written in one sentence or occupy an entire essay or book. But in either case we want it to *limit* and hence to *order* a meaning so that it won't be confused with other meanings.

How can this be done?

LOGICAL DEFINITION

A traditional way of limiting and ordering a meaning is that propounded by Aristotle: a subject is explained by placing it in a general class and then by differentiating it from all other members of that class. Take this definition of a chair.

> A chair is an article of furniture, with or without arms, designed to seat one person.

That is a logical, *sentence* definition, and its parts are designated by special names: "chair" is the *term,* "is" is the *copula,* "article of furniture" is the *class* (or *genus*), and all the limiting words or phrases following are the *differentiae*—the characteristics setting chairs apart from sofas, stools, settees, benches, or other articles or furniture upon which people may sit.

Is that a good definition? Test it by seeing if you can substitute any other word for the *term.* If you can, then obviously you must add some qualification to the *differentiae.* Again, if it is a good definition, the sentence ought to be reversible; the subject ought to be convertible into the predicate. In this case convertibility is clearly possible. But what about such a definition as this: "A dictionary is a book"? We cannot say, "A book is a dictionary," so, though the statement may be true, it is not a *definition.* To be a definition the class *book* must be qualified and limited in many ways.

> A dictionary [*term*] is [*copula*] a book [*class*] containing the words of one or more languages, or a selection of those words, usually arranged in alphabetical order, and followed by explanations of their meanings, etymology, pronunciation, parts of speech, and other information [*differentiae*].

Does this stand up? Let us apply our two tests. Is there anything else in existence that might be substituted for the word "dictionary" here? What about a biographical dictionary, a book containing information about men instead of words? Clearly we must amend our *differentiae* with at least this qualification. Then what about convertibility? Can we turn the sentence around and say that a book, so qualified, is a dictionary? The definition seems to pass that test.

Two other matters must be noted in framing a logical, sentence definition. The *class* must be larger than the *term* and must include it, but it must not be *too* large. For example, to put "dictionary" in the class *thing* or *object* would be to let it rattle around too loosely.

Again, one must be careful to put the *class* in the same part of speech as the *term*. To say "a circle is *when* you have an infinite number of points equidistant from a center" is not to define. A noun cannot be equated with an adverb.

INFORMAL AND EXTENDED DEFINITIONS

Writing sentence definitions is more of an exercise in logic than in rhetoric. They are the bare bones of a meaning, and permit none of those connotative details that enrich a meaning and relate it to what, in most cases, has been our actual experience with it. What definition of water as H_2O can correspond with our personal knowledge of water: the lake in the summer, the feeling of thirst, the sound of water drawing for the bath, water boiling over in the car radiator? These informal elements, the connotative as well as denotative qualities inhering in a meaning, are often what give a definition its essential significance and interest. Let us, for example, take Wordsworth's statement: "The child is father of the man." Logically, the sentence is a poor definition. Children cannot be fathers. But imaginatively it is a most illuminating definition and shocks us into an awareness of a fact that we might know, but which we have doubtless never thought of in just that way: that a man's character is a bequest from his own childhood, that what he was as a child has "fathered" what he became as a man. A whole essay could be written about this one sentence, and that essay would be an informal definition. It could limit and control a meaning that was simply too unusual, too personal, too poetic for handling by logical means. But that is not to say it is less true.

An extended definition is simply a definition taking up a considerable amount of space and going into a considerable amount of detail. It may take the form of an essay in which the *differentiae* are explained and illustrated systematically and thoroughly, or it may—as in most informal definitions—follow no clear logical pattern at all. But most definitions worthy of the name are extended, for most items of reality are, the closer we get to them, full of such rich variousness and complexity that no single sentence can more than hint at what they *are*.

All of the essays following are extended definitions. But nearly all of them could, after careful analysis, be seen as sentence definitions in which the *differentiae* have received detailed and extensive treatment. Haldane, for example, defines the adjective "hard" both in terms of naïve human ex-

perience and of scientific measurement, but the logic of his essay could—
with some hard work—be distilled into the capsule of a sentence definition.
The same is true of the essays by John Stuart Mill and Morton Cronin. But
what of the sketch by Sally Carrighar? Here we have a piece far beyond
either the purposes or the capacities of the formal worker in meanings. It
is the work of an artist and, strictly speaking, it is not a definition at all.
But nonetheless Sally Carrighar is showing us something as she believes
it really "is," and she, no less than the logical or scientific definer, builds her
"definition" on the carefully observed and examined *details* of her subject.
To be sure, she makes an "inductive leap"—or rather "dive"—that takes her
far into the world of imagination; but, scientists remind us, it is just that
disciplined joining of fact with fancy which characterizes the greatest scientific minds and leads to our most important discoveries. In telling us how
a trout sees its world, the author has defined a "point of view," she has
added another dimension to our awareness of life. To define such things
is a quite different task from defining tables and chairs, and a much more
difficult one. But it would be a fundamental mistake to think that defining
is a mere matter of logic. For the final definition we all must make is: What
does life mean? Surely, imagination, sympathy, insight, and faith will be
as much needed in that task as logical analysis.

But whether a definition is in sentence form or extended, formal or informal, logical or imaginative (or a potpourri of the lot), certain techniques
for developing and controlling that definition are almost always useful.
Here are a few of them.

(1) *Description.* Draw a picture, verbally or graphically, to show us
what the term-to-be-defined looks like, feels like, tastes like, smells like,
and/or sounds like. If you are defining something intangible or abstract, see if you can suggestively describe it by use of a metaphor
(see pages 412-20).

(2) *Comparison and Contrast.* This is an essential element in nearly
all definitions. In defining "day" it is useful to discuss "night." In
defining "democracy" it may help to discuss "totalitarianism," its near
opposite. See "Comparison and Contrast," page 418.

(3) *Derivation.* Where did something come from? What are its
roots? One of the commonest uses of derivation consists in tracing
the linguistic history, or etymology, of words. If, for example, you
know that "education" derives partly from the Latin *educere,* to lead
forth, you know something about the aims of education.

(4) *Enumeration.* Often the mere listing of qualities inhering in a
subject is a way of defining it. In biology, for example, we define the
class *Mammalia* by listing all those characteristics which distinguish
mammals from other vertebrates. Or if you can truthfully and honestly
make any statement with the words "all" or "most" or "a majority," then
you have made an important and useful defining statement. Such a
statement may be called an enumeration.

(5) *Sampling.* If you are trying to define a large or elusive entity,

like the mood of a crowd or the political temper of a nation, the best—perhaps the only—way to do so is to get a representative "sample" of that mood or temper. Public opinion polls do such defining constantly, but the technique is used by scholars and scientists as well—wherever, in fact, we need some assessment of the *probability* of an event.

(6) *Classification and Process.* These rhetorical modes are also useful methods of limiting and controlling a meaning. See the essays on these subjects in this volume (page 455 and page 494).

The Uses of Definition

But these *techniques* of definition cannot be separated from the *uses* to which definition is put. The *way* to define is inseparable from *what* is being defined.

You will not, for example, use the same procedures in defining an *intangible* like "gravity" or an *abstraction* like "justice" as you will in defining a *concrete object*, like "airplane." Airplanes are made by man and can be weighed, measured, disassembled, touched. But "gravity" can be known only by its *effects*. So in defining "gravity" you must collect circumstantial rather than existential evidence; you know your quarry by its tracks. The two kinds of evidence are similarly gathered, but acquiring sound circumstantial evidence is more exacting. You use it not just to "describe" an entity, you use it to "prove" its existence—just as the footprints, the broken window, and the missing silver "prove" the existence of a burglar. Nobody saw the burglar just as nobody has directly apprehended gravity, but the context of evidence can be great enough (if carefully collected and analyzed) to constitute scientific or legal or other "proof."

Even more difficult is defining abstractions—concepts which, though based on fact and experience, exist primarily as *ideas*. You can't do up "justice" in a plastic bag and you can't measure its effects with scientific instruments (not even with lie detectors). You must get its meaning by probing the history and mind of man. What has justice meant to men in the past? Is capital punishment just or unjust? Is justice really obtainable under human law? Did God treat Adam justly? Is it valid to regard men as innocent until proven guilty? We must ask questions of this nature in defining the words. Probably no definitive answer is possible, but to engage in such pursuits is an important responsibility of the educated man. Abstractions, after all, are hosts to some of our highest values. If "truth," "beauty," "freedom," "nobility," "courage," "happiness," "peace," are to be vital terms and not dead clichés, then they must be redefined in the consciousness and imagination of each new generation.

But definitions are put to other uses than those touched on above, and we should briefly note a few of them. Some definitions are used in (1) an *investigative* way, to seek out truth, some in (2) a *descriptive* way, to describe current or past usage of a word or idea, and some in (3) a *prescriptive* way, to prescribe or stipulate a meaning.

A definition of the first sort might be the geometrical axiom, "the shortest distance between two points is a straight line," or the physical law that "energy is equal to the mass times the velocity of light squared" ($e = mc^2$). These are statements of truths or presumed truths made in order to aid inquiry into further truth. When they are shown to be useless or wrong they are abandoned or qualified—as the "Law of Conservation of Matter" was ousted by the law stated above.

A definition of the second sort might serve to establish an historical meaning, such as the derivation and current meaning of a word—and of course the realities symbolized by it. Subjects amenable to this kind of definition are seldom as precisely measurable as those in the first category, but that does not mean they are less important. If, for example, you attempted to define the origins and development of the dramatic concept of "tragedy," you would have a subject fitting here. And you would certainly begin with a consideration of Aristotle's famous definition:

> Tragedy . . . is an imitation of an action that is serious, complete, and of a certain magnitude; in language embellished with each kind of artistic ornament, the several kinds being found in separate parts of the play; in the form of action, not of narrative; through pity and fear effecting the proper purgation of these emotions.

A prescriptive definition stipulates a meaning; it is an expression of the *will* of the definer. The children dividing up sides—"You be the cops, and I'll be the robbers!"—are stipulating meanings. God stipulated meanings in the first chapter of *Genesis:*

> And God said, 'Let there be light': and there was light. And God saw the light, that it was good: and God divided the light from the darkness. And God called the light Day, and the darkness he called Night.

That divine prescription has stood the test of time pretty well, though sometimes men amuse themselves by calling white black and black white. Sometimes, too, men as earnest as Humpty Dumpty are as arbitrary in stipulating that "glory" (or its equivalent) means "a nice knockdown argument." Hitler defined a Jew as someone with any amount, no matter how small, of Jewish "blood." Why not say, with the same logic, that anyone was a German who possessed any amount of German blood? Hitler, like Humpty Dumpty, was not interested in logic but in power. And sovereign nations around the tables of summit conferences are often as willful and capricious in defining such things as "peace," "democracy," and "free elections." That those with the power to prescribe meanings must be amenable to some higher court of reason was the burden of much of George Orwell's writing. (His writing is sampled in this volume on page 48.) In *Animal Farm*, Orwell makes unmistakably clear what can happen to democratic principles when pigs get the power and use it to stipulate what things **mean:**

All Animals Are Equal
But Some Animals Are More Equal Than Others

And in Orwell's novel, *1984*, the Humpty Dumpties did even better than that. Here were the slogans of the masters of Doublethink:

War Is Peace
Freedom Is Slavery
Ignorance Is Strength

Obviously, part of the task of keeping definitions in our civilization clear and pure is to keep a firm democratic rein on those with the power, or craving the power, to stipulate meanings.

Words connote as well as denote, sound as well as mean, provoke as well as prove, confuse as well as explain. Words, in short, are creatures like the people who made them: contradictory, passionate, lazy, intelligent. It is the definer's job to discipline them as best he can. He may not march to truth with that army, but he will get an instructive look at the human condition.

~

UMPIRE* *Walker Gibson*

Everyone knows he's blind as a bat.
Besides, it's tricky to decide,
As ball meets mitt with a loud splat,
Whether it curved an inch outside
Or just an inch the other way
For a called strike. But anyway,
Nobody thinks that just because
Instead he calls that close one ball,
That that was what it really *was*.
(The pitcher doesn't agree at all.)

His eyes are weak, his vision's blurred,
He can't tell a strike from a barn door—
And yet we have to take his word.
The pitch that was something else before
(And *there's* the mystery no one knows)
Has gotten to be a ball by now,

* From Walker Gibson, *The Reckless Spenders* (Bloomington, Ind.: University of Indiana Press, 1954).

Or got to be called ball, anyhow.
All this explains why, I suppose,
People like to watch baseball games,
Where Things are not confused with Names.

Problems for Thought and Writing

1. When the Umpire "defines" a strike and the crowd yells no, there is a dispute about whether a certain *name* belongs with a certain *reality*. That is the essential problem of definition. Read the introductory essay on "Definition" (page 365) and examine the theme of this poem in terms of the realist *vs.* nominalist controversy there discussed.

2. Explain the punch line of the poem.

3. Define "ball" as the Umpire defines it and as the crowd defines it. Evaluate the two definitions in an attempt to find the true definition.

~

WHAT "HARD" MEANS*   *J. B. S. Haldane*

In the last article I wrote about the way in which ordinary words change their meaning as they are used in science and technology, taking as an example the word "hot." All adjectives start as descriptions of qualities. They end up as descriptions of quantities, if they are taken over by science. A word like "big" or "long" is entirely relative. A mile is a long swim but a short walk, because an ordinary man often walks a mile, but seldom swims a mile. A man is large compared to a cat, and small compared to an elephant, and so on. This sort of contradiction does not trouble anyone but philosophers, because we are accustomed to measure lengths, and we all know what a foot or a mile means.

But we are in much greater difficulties with some other common adjectives such as "hard." Of course we use the word metaphorically, as when we talk of a hard question, meaning one which is difficult to answer, or hard X-rays, meaning rays which penetrate easily through matter. But I want to deal with the word in its ordinary sense, as when we say that iron is harder than butter. Everyone will agree that this is true. But it is not so easy to decide which of two pieces

---

* From J. B. S. Haldane, *A Banned Broadcast and Other Essays* (London: Chatto and Windus, Ltd., 1946).

of iron is harder, and as a matter of fact there may be no definite answer to the question. When we come to accurate measurement, we find that the word "hard" has dozens of slightly different meanings.

The most usual test of hardness in steels is that of Brinell. A very hard steel ball of 10 millimetres diameter is pressed onto a steel plate for 30 seconds with a load of 3 tons. The hardness number decreases with the depth of the indentation.

Another test of hardness which generally agrees pretty well with the Brinell test is the weight which must be put on a diamond point in order that it should just produce a visible scratch when pulled sideways. But as soon as we use moving bodies to measure hardness things become very complicated. For example at a relative speed of 30 feet per second a disc of "soft" iron was cut by a steel tool; at 100 feet per second the disc cut the tool itself, and at 300 feet per second the disc cut quartz. In the same way hardness varies with temperature.

If we compare an ordinary hardened carbon tool steel and a high-speed tool steel at ordinary temperatures, the former is probably a little harder by the Brinell test. But at a dull red heat the high-speed steel is still hard, while the ordinary tool steel is about as soft as is copper at room temperature . . .

Hardness is also used as a measure of the amount of wear which a material will stand. But here again the details are very important. We may want to test how a metal stands up to rolling friction without lubricant. This is essential in tests of rails, and wheels of railway vehicles. Or we may want to know how a metal stands up to sliding abrasion, either with or without a film of oil. One steel may stand up better to rolling friction, and another to sliding friction. Here their differences in hardness probably depend on the fact that metals sliding over one another actually melt at the point of contact, so their properties at high temperatures become important.

Within a century or less we shall probably be able to calculate the various kinds of hardness with great exactitude from a knowledge of the forces between atoms. At present we can only do so very roughly. Probably the physicists of the future will be able to specify the different kinds of hardness very completely in terms of a few numbers.

It would be possible to deal in the same way with the meanings of various words such as toughness, elasticity, and brittleness, which are applied to solids. None of these can be expressed by a single number.

The properties of liquids are a good deal simpler than those of solids, and the properties of gases are simpler still, though anyone concerned with the design of aeroplanes finds even gases quite complicated enough. And when we come to such a property of material systems as life, the complications are of course vastly greater. Scientists are reproached because they cannot say in simple terms what life is. It is easy enough to point out differences between a dog or a cabbage and a stone or a machine. It is much harder to draw the line when we get down to the agents of smallpox and other diseases, which behave in some ways as if alive and in others as if dead. But if anyone reproaches science because it cannot yet give a complete account of life, it is a fair reply to ask him what he means by hardness, and how he would tell if one thing is harder than another.

Problems for Thought and Writing

1. How would you frame a sentence definition of "hard" on the basis of Haldane's essay?

2. Toward the end of his definition Haldane writes, "It is much harder to draw the line when we get down to the agents of smallpox and other diseases. . . ." Is the word "harder" as used in this sentence part of Haldane's definition? Is its omission justified?

3. What controlling and ordering techniques are most obvious in Haldane's definition?

4. Define an adjective. Do you agree with Haldane when he writes, "All adjectives start as descriptions of qualities. They end up as descriptions of quantities, if they are taken over by science"? Can any adjective be defined without taking into account its quantitative aspects? Is there any fundamental difference between an "aesthetic" definition and a "scientific" one?

~

ON LIBERTY*   *John Stuart Mill*

The subject of this Essay is not the so-called Liberty of the Will, so unfortunately opposed to the misnamed doctrine of Philosophical Necessity; but Civil, or Social Liberty: the nature and limits of the power which can be legitimately exercised by society over the individual. A question seldom stated, and hardly ever discussed, in general terms, but which profoundly influences the practical controversies of the age by its latent presence, and is likely soon to make itself recognized as the vital question of the future. It is so far from being

* From *On Liberty*, 1859.

new, that, in a certain sense, it has divided mankind, almost from the remotest ages; but in the stage of progress into which the more civilized portions of the species have now entered, it presents itself under new conditions, and requires a different and more fundamental treatment.

The struggle between Liberty and Authority is the most conspicuous feature in the portions of history with which we are earliest familiar, particularly in that of Greece, Rome, and England. But in old times this contest was between subjects, or some classes of subjects, and the government. By liberty, was meant protection against the tyranny of the political rulers. The rulers were conceived (except in some of the popular governments of Greece) as in a necessarily antagonistic position to the people whom they ruled. They consisted of a governing One, or a governing tribe or caste, who derived their authority from inheritance or conquest; who, at all events, did not hold it at the pleasure of the governed, and whose supremacy men did not venture, perhaps did not desire, to contest, whatever precautions might be taken against its oppressive exercise. Their power was regarded as necessary, but also as highly dangerous; as a weapon which they would attempt to use against their subjects, no less than against external enemies. To prevent the weaker members of the community from being preyed upon by innumerable vultures, it was needful that there should be an animal of prey stronger than the rest, commissioned to keep them down. But as the king of the vultures would be no less bent upon preying on the flock than any of the minor harpies, it was indispensable to be in a perpetual attitude of defence against his beak and claws. The aim, therefore, of patriots, was to set limits to the power which the ruler should be suffered to exercise over the community; and this limitation was what they meant by liberty. It was attempted in two ways. First, by obtaining a recognition of certain immunities, called political liberties or rights, which it was to be regarded as a breach of duty in the ruler to infringe, and which, if he did infringe, specific resistance, or general rebellion, was held to be justifiable. A second, and generally a later expedient, was the establishment of constitutional checks; by which the consent of the community, or of a body of some sort supposed to represent its interests, was made a necessary condition to some of the more important acts of the governing power. To the first of these modes of limitation, the ruling power, in most European countries, was compelled, more or less, to submit. It was not so with the second; and to attain this, or when already in some degree possessed, to attain it more completely, became everywhere the principal object of the lovers of liberty. And so long as mankind were content to combat one enemy by another, and to be ruled by a master, on condition of being guaranteed more or less efficaciously against his tyranny, they did not carry their aspirations beyond this point.

A time, however, came, in the progress of human affairs, when men ceased to think it a necessity of nature that their governors should be an independent power, opposed in interest to themselves. It appeared to them much better that the various magistrates of the State should be their tenants or delegates, revocable at their pleasure. In that way alone, it seemed, could they have complete security that the powers of government would never be abused to their disadvantage. By degrees, this new demand for elective and temporary rulers became the prominent object of the exertions of the popular party, wherever any such party existed; and superseded, to a considerable extent, the previous efforts to limit the power of rulers. As the struggle proceeded for making the ruling power emanate from the periodical choice of the ruled, some persons began to think that too much importance had been attached to the limitation of the power itself. *That* (it might seem) was a resource against rulers whose interests were habitually opposed to those of the people. What was now wanted was, that the rulers should be identified with the people; that their interest and will should be the interest and will of the nation. The nation did not need to be protected against its own will. There was no fear of its tyrannizing over itself. Let the rulers be effectually responsible to it, promptly removable by it, and it could afford to trust them with power of which it could itself dictate the use to be made. Their power was but the nation's own power, concentrated, and in a form convenient for exercise. This mode of thought, or rather perhaps of feeling, was common among the last generation of European liberalism, in the Continental section of which, it still apparently predominates. Those who admit any limit to what a government may do, except in the case of such governments as they think ought not to exist, stand out as brilliant exceptions among the political thinkers of the Continent. A similar tone of sentiment might by this time have been prevalent in our own country, if the circumstances which for a time encouraged it had continued unaltered.

But, in political and philosophical theories, as well as in persons, success discloses faults and infirmities which failure might have concealed from observation. The notion, that the people have no need to limit their power over themselves, might seem axiomatic, when popular government was a thing only dreamed about, or read of as having existed at some distant period of the past. Neither was that notion necessarily disturbed by such temporary aberrations as those of the French Revolution, the worst of which were the work of an usurping few, and which, in any case, belonged, not to the permanent working of popular institutions, but to a sudden and convulsive outbreak against monarchical and aristocratic despotism. In time, however, a democratic republic [1] came to occupy a large portion of the earth's surface, and made itself felt as one of the most powerful members of the community of nations; and elective and responsible government became subject to the observations and criticisms which wait upon a great existing fact. It was now perceived that such phrases as 'self-government,' and 'the power of the people over themselves,' do not express the true state of the case. The 'people' who exercise the power, are not always the same people with those over whom it is exercised; and the self-government spoken of, is not the government of each by himself, but of each by all the rest. The will of the people, moreover, practically means, the will of the most numerous or the most active *part* of the people; the majority, or those who succeed in making themselves accepted as the majority: the people, consequently, *may* desire to oppress a part of their number; and precautions are as much needed against this, as against any other abuse of power. The limitation, therefore, of the power of government over individuals, loses none of its importance when the holders of power are regularly accountable to the community, that is, to the strongest party therein. This view of things, recommending itself equally to the intelligence of thinkers and to the inclination of those important classes in European society to whose real or supposed interests democracy is adverse, has had no difficulty in establishing itself; and in political speculations 'the tyranny of the majority' is now generally included among the evils against which society requires to be on its guard.

Like other tyrannies, the tyranny of the majority was at first, and is still vulgarly, held in dread, chiefly as operating through the acts of the public authorities. But reflecting persons perceived that when society is itself the tyrant—society collectively, over the separate individuals who compose it—its means of tyrannizing are not restricted to the acts which it may do by the hands of its political functionaries. Society can and does execute its own mandates: and if it issues wrong

[1 The United States.]

mandates instead of right, or any mandates at all in things with which it ought not to meddle, it practises a social tyranny more formidable than many kinds of political oppression, since, though not usually upheld by such extreme penalties, it leaves fewer means of escape, penetrating much more deeply into the details of life, and enslaving the soul itself. Protection, therefore, against the tyranny of the magistrate is not enough; there needs protection also against the tyranny of the prevailing opinion and feeling; against the tendency of society to impose, by other means than civil penalties, its own ideas and practices as rules of conduct on those who dissent from them; to fetter the development, and, if possible, prevent the formation, of any individuality not in harmony with its ways, and compel all characters to fashion themselves upon the model of its own. There is a limit to the legitimate interference of collective opinion with individual independence; and to find that limit, and maintain it against encroachment, is as indispensable to a good condition of human affairs, as protection against political despotism.

But though this proposition is not likely to be contested in general terms, the practical question, where to place the limit—how to make the fitting adjustment between individual independence and social control—is a subject on which nearly everything remains to be done. All that makes existence valuable to any one, depends on the enforcement of restraints upon the actions of other people. Some rules of conduct, therefore, must be imposed, by law in the first place, and by opinion on many things which are not fit subjects for the operation of law. What these rules should be, is the principal question in human affairs; but if we except a few of the most obvious cases, it is one of those which least progress has been made in resolving. No two ages, and scarcely any two countries, have decided it alike; and the decision of one age or country is a wonder to another. Yet the people of any given age and country no more suspect any difficulty in it, than if it were a subject on which mankind had always been agreed. The rules which obtain among themselves appear to them self-evident and self-justifying. This all but universal illusion is one of the examples of the magical influence of custom, which is not only, as the proverb says, a second nature, but is continually mistaken for the first. The effect of custom, in preventing any misgiving respecting the rules of conduct which mankind impose on one another, is all the more complete because the subject is one on which it is not generally considered necessary that reasons should be given, either by one person to others, or by each to himself. People are accustomed to

believe, and have been encouraged in the belief by some who aspire
to the character of philosophers, that their feelings, on subjects of
this nature, are better than reasons, and render reasons unnecessary.
The practical principle which guides them to their opinions on the
regulation of human conduct, is the feeling in each person's mind
that everybody should be required to act as he, and those with whom
he sympathizes, would like them to act. No one, indeed, acknowledges to himself that his standard of judgment is his own liking;
but an opinion on a point of conduct, not supported by reasons, can
only count as one person's preference; and if the reasons, when given,
are a mere appeal to a similar preference felt by other people, it is
still only many people's liking instead of one. To an ordinary man,
however, his own preference, thus supported, is not only a perfectly
satisfactory reason, but the only one he generally has for any of his
notions of morality, taste, or propriety, which are not expressly written
in his religious creed; and his chief guide in the interpretation even
of that. Men's opinions, accordingly, on what is laudable or blame-
able, are affected by all the multifarious causes which influence their
wishes in regard to the conduct of others, and which are as numerous
as those which determine their wishes on any other subject. Sometimes their reason—at other times their prejudices or superstitions:
often their social affections, not seldom their antisocial ones, their
envy or jealousy, their arrogance or contemptuousness: but most
commonly, their desires or fears for themselves—their legitimate or
illegitimate self-interest. Wherever there is an ascendant class, a large
portion of the morality of the country emanates from its class interests,
and its feelings of class superiority. The morality between Spartans
and Helots, between planters and negroes, between princes and
subjects, between nobles and roturiers, between men and women,
has been for the most part the creation of these class interests and
feelings: and the sentiments thus generated, react in turn upon the
moral feelings of the members of the ascendant class, in their relations
among themselves. Where, on the other hand, a class, formerly
ascendant, has lost its ascendancy, or where its ascendancy is unpopular, the prevailing moral sentiments frequently bear the impress
of an impatient dislike of superiority. Another grand determining
principle of the rules of conduct, both in act and forbearance, which
have been enforced by law or opinion, has been the servility of
mankind towards the supposed preferences or aversions of their temporal masters, or of their gods. This servility, though essentially
selfish, is not hypocrisy; it gives rise to perfectly genuine sentiments

of abhorrence; it made men burn magicians and heretics. Among so many baser influences, the general and obvious interests of society have of course had a share, and a large one, in the direction of the moral sentiments: less, however, as a matter of reason, and on their own account, than as a consequence of the sympathies and antipathies which grew out of them: and sympathies and antipathies which had little or nothing to do with the interests of society, have made themselves felt in the establishment of moralities with quite as great force.

The likings and dislikings of society, or of some powerful portion of it, are thus the main thing which has practically determined the rules laid down for general observance, under the penalties of law or opinion. And in general, those who have been in advance of society in thought and feeling, have left this condition of things unassailed in principle, however they may have come into conflict with it in some of its details. They have occupied themselves rather in inquiring what things society ought to like or dislike, than in questioning whether its likings or dislikings should be a law to individuals. They preferred endeavoring to alter the feelings of mankind on the particular points on which they were themselves heretical, rather than make common cause in defence of freedom, with heretics generally. The only case in which the higher ground has been taken on principle and maintained with consistency, by any but an individual here and there, is that of religious belief: a case instructive in many ways, and not least so as forming a most striking instance of the fallibility of what is called the moral sense: for the *odium theologicum*, in a sincere bigot, is one of the most unequivocal cases of moral feeling. Those who first broke the yoke of what called itself the Universal Church, were in general as little willing to permit difference of religious opinion as that church itself. But when the heat of the conflict was over, without giving a complete victory to any party, and each church or sect was reduced to limit its hopes to retaining possession of the ground it already occupied; minorities, seeing that they had no chance of becoming majorities, were under the necessity of pleading to those whom they could not convert, for permission to differ. It is accordingly on this battle-field, almost solely, that the rights of the individual against society have been asserted on broad grounds of principle, and the claim of society to exercise authority over dissentients openly controverted. The great writers to whom the world owes what religious liberty it possesses, have mostly asserted freedom of conscience as an indefeasible right, and denied absolutely that a human being is accountable to others for his religious belief. Yet so natural to mankind is intolerance in whatever they really care about, that religious freedom has hardly anywhere been practically realized, except where religious indifference, which dislikes to have its peace disturbed by theological quarrels, has added its weight to the scale. In the minds of almost all religious persons, even in the most tolerant countries, the duty of toleration is admitted with tacit reserves. One person will bear with dissent in matters of church government, but not of dogma; another can tolerate everybody, short of a Papist or an Unitarian; another, every one who believes in revealed religion; a few extend their charity a little further, but stop at the belief in a God and in a future state. Wherever the sentiment of the majority is still genuine and intense, it is found to have abated little of its claim to be obeyed.

In England, from the peculiar circumstances of our political history, though the yoke of opinion is perhaps heavier, that of law is lighter, than in most other countries of Europe; and there is considerable jealousy of direct interference, by the legislative or the executive power, with private conduct; not so much from any just regard for the independence of the individual, as from the still subsisting habit of looking on the government as representing an opposite interest to the public. The majority have not yet learnt to feel the power of the government their power, or its opinions their opinions. When they do so, individual liberty will probably be as much exposed to invasion from the government, as it already is from public opinion. But, as yet, there is a considerable amount of feeling ready to be called forth against any attempt of the law to control individuals in things in which they have not hitherto been accustomed to be controlled by it; and this with very little discrimination as to whether the matter is, or is not, within the legitimate sphere of legal control; insomuch that the feeling, highly salutary on the whole, is perhaps quite as often misplaced as well grounded in the particular instances of its application. There is, in fact, no recognized principle by which the propriety or impropriety of government interference is customarily tested. People decide according to their personal preferences. Some, whenever they see any good to be done, or evil to be remedied, would willingly instigate the government to undertake the business; while others prefer to bear almost any amount of social evil, rather than add one to the departments of human interests amenable to governmental control. And men range themselves on one or the other side in any particular case, according to this general direction of their sentiments; or according to the degree of interests which they feel in the particular thing which it is proposed that the government should do; or according to the belief they entertain that the government would, or would not, do it in the manner they prefer; but very rarely on account of any opinion to which they consistently adhere, as to what things are fit to be done by a government. And it seems to me that, in consequence of this absence of rule or principle, one side is at present as often wrong as the other; the interference of government is, with about equal frequency, improperly invoked and improperly condemned.

The object of this Essay is to assert one very simple principle, as entitled to govern absolutely the dealings of society with the individual in the way of compulsion and control, whether the means used be physical force in the form of legal penalties, or the moral coercion of public opinion. That principle is, that the sole end for which mankind are warranted, individually or collectively, in interfering with the liberty of action of any of their number, is self-protection. That the only purpose for which power can be rightfully exercised over any member of a civilized community, against his will, is to prevent harm to others. His own good, either physical or moral, is not a sufficient warrant. He cannot rightfully be compelled to do or forbear because it will be better for him to do so, because it will make him happier, because, in the opinions of others, to do so would be wise, or even right. These are good reasons for remonstrating with him, or reasoning with him, or persuading him, or entreating him, but not for compelling him, or visiting him with any evil, in case he do otherwise. To justify that, the conduct from which it is desired to deter him must be calculated to produce evil to some one else. The only part of the conduct of any one, for which he is amenable to society, is that which concerns others. In the part which merely concerns himself, his independence is, of right, absolute. Over himself, over his own body and mind, the individual is sovereign.

It is, perhaps, hardly necessary to say that this doctrine is meant to apply only to human beings in the maturity of their faculties. We are not speaking of children, or of young persons below the age which the law may fix as that of manhood or womanhood. Those who are still in a state to require being taken care of by others, must be protected against their own actions as well as against external injury. For the same reason, we may leave out of consideration those backward states of society in which the race itself may be considered as in its nonage. The early difficulties in the way of spontaneous progress are so great, that there is seldom any choice of means for overcoming them; and a ruler full of the spirit of improvement is warranted in the use of any expedients that will attain an end, perhaps otherwise unattainable. Despotism is a legitimate mode of government in dealing with barbarians, provided the end be their improvement, and the means justified by actually effecting that end. Liberty, as a principle, has no application to any state of things anterior to the time when mankind have become capable of being improved by free and equal discussion. Until then, there is nothing for them but implicit obedience to an Akbar or a Charlemagne, if they are so fortunate as to find one. But as soon as mankind have attained the capacity of being guided to their own improvement by conviction or persuasion (a period long since reached in all nations with whom we need here concern ourselves), compulsion, either in the direct form or in that of pains and penalties for non-compliance, is no longer admissible as a means to their own good, and justifiable only for the security of others.

It is proper to state that I forego any advantage which could be derived to my argument from the idea of abstract right, as a thing independent of utility. I regard utility as the ultimate appeal on all ethical questions; but it must be utility in the largest sense, grounded on the permanent interests of man as a progressive being. Those interests, I contend, authorize the subjection of individual spontaneity to external control, only in respect to those actions of each, which concern the interest of other people. If any one does an act hurtful to others there is a *primâ facie* case for punishing him, by law, or, where legal penalties are not safely applicable, by general disapprobation. There are also many positive acts for the benefit of others, which he may rightfully be compelled to perform; such as, to give evidence in a court of justice; to bear his fair share in the common defence, or in any other joint work necessary to the interest of the society of which he enjoys the protection; and to perform certain acts of individual beneficence, such as saving a fellow creature's life, or interposing to protect the defenceless against ill-usage, things which whenever it is obviously a man's duty to do, he may rightfully be made responsible to society for not doing. A person may cause evil to others not only by his actions but by his inaction, and in either case he is justly accountable to them for the injury. The latter case, it is true, requires a much more cautious exercise of compulsion than the former. To make any one answerable for doing evil to others, is the rule; to make him answerable for not preventing evil, is, comparatively speaking, the exception. Yet there are many cases clear enough and grave enough to justify that exception. In all things which regard the external relations of the individual, he is *de jure* amenable to those whose interests are concerned, and if need be, to society as their protector. There are often good reasons for not holding him to the responsibility; but these reasons must arise from the special expediences of the case: either because it is a kind of case in which he is on the whole likely to act better, when left to his own discretion, than when controlled in any way in which society have it in their power to control him; or because the attempt to exercise control would produce other evils, greater than those which it would prevent. When such reasons as these preclude the enforcement of responsibility, the conscience of the agent himself should step into the vacant judgment-seat, and protect those interests of others which have no external protection; judging himself all the more rigidly, because the case does not admit of his being made accountable to the judgment of his fellow-creatures.

But there is a sphere of action in which society, as distinguished from the individual, has, if any, only an indirect interest; comprehending all that portion of a person's life and conduct which affects only himself, or, if it also affects others, only with their free, voluntary, and undeceived consent and participation. When I say only himself, I mean directly, and in the first instance: for whatever affects himself, may affect others *through* himself; and the objection which may be grounded on this contingency, will receive consideration in the sequel. This, then, is the appropriate region of human liberty. It comprises, first, the inward domain of consciousness; demanding liberty of conscience, in the most comprehensive sense; liberty of thought and feeling; absolute freedom of opinion and sentiment on all subjects, practical or speculative, scientific, moral, or theological. The liberty of expressing and publishing opinions may seem to fall under a different principle, since it belongs to that part of the conduct of an individual which concerns other people; but, being almost of as much importance as the liberty of thought itself, and resting in great part on the same reasons, is practically inseparable from it. Secondly, the principle requires liberty of tastes and pursuits; of framing the plan of our life to suit our own character; of doing as we like, subject to such consequences as may follow; without impediment from our fellow-creatures, so long as what we do does not harm them, even though they should think our conduct foolish, perverse, or wrong. Thirdly, from this liberty of each individual, follows the liberty, within the same limits, of combination among individuals; freedom to unite, for any purpose not involving harm to others: the persons combining being supposed to be of full age, and not forced or deceived.

No society in which these liberties are not, on the whole, respected, is free, whatever may be its form of government; and none is completely free in which they do not exist absolute and unqualified. The only freedom which deserves the name, is that of pursuing our own good in our own way, so long as we do not attempt to deprive others of theirs, or impede their efforts to obtain it. Each is the proper guardian of his own health, whether bodily, or mental and spiritual. Mankind are greater gainers by suffering each other to live as seems good to themselves, than by compelling each to live as seems good to the rest.

Though this doctrine is anything but new, and, to some persons, may have the air of a truism, there is no doctrine which stands more directly opposed to the general tendency of existing opinion and practice. Society has expended fully as much effort in the attempt (according to its lights) to compel people to conform to its notions of personal, as of social excellence. The ancient commonwealths thought themselves entitled to practise, and the ancient philosophers countenanced, the regulation of every part of private conduct by public authority, on the ground that the State had a deep interest in the whole bodily and mental discipline of every one of its citizens; a mode of thinking which may have been admissible in small republics surrounded by powerful enemies, in constant peril of being subverted by foreign attack or internal commotion, and to which even a short interval of relaxed energy and self-command might so easily be fatal, that they could not afford to wait for the salutary permanent effects of freedom. In the modern world, the greater size of political communities, and above all, the separation between the spiritual and temporal authority (which placed the direction of men's consciences in other hands than those which controlled their worldly affairs), prevented so great an interference by law in the details of private life; but the engines of moral repression have been wielded more strenuously against divergence from the reigning opinion in self-regarding, than even in social matters; religion, the most powerful of the elements which have entered into the formation of moral feeling, having almost always been governed either by the ambition of a hierarchy, seeking control over every department of human conduct, or by the spirit of Puritanism. And some of those modern reformers who have placed themselves in strongest opposition to the religions of the past, have been noway behind either churches or sects in their assertion of the right of spiritual domination: M. Comte,[2] in particular, whose social system, as unfolded in his *Traité de Politique Positive*, aims at establishing (though by moral more than by legal appliances) a despotism of society over the individual, surpassing anything contemplated in the political ideal of the most rigid disciplinarian among the ancient philosophers.

Apart from the peculiar tenets of individual thinkers, there is also in the world at large an increasing inclination to stretch unduly the powers of society over the individual, both by the force of opinion and even by that of legislation: and as the tendency of all the changes taking place in the world is to strengthen society, and diminish the power of the individual, this encroachment is not one of the evils which tend spontaneously to disappear, but, on the contrary, to grow more and more formidable. The disposition of mankind, whether as rulers or as fellow-citizens, to impose their own opinions and inclinations as a rule of conduct on others, is so energetically supported by some of the best and by some of the worst feelings incident to human nature, that it is hardly ever kept under restraint by anything but want of power; and as the power is not declining, but growing, unless a strong barrier of moral conviction can be raised against the mischief, we must expect, in the present circumstances of the world, to see it increase. . . .

Problems for Thought and Writing

I

1. Much of Mill's definition of "liberty" is based on a tracing of its history. In its earliest stages, he writes, liberty "meant protection against the tyranny of the political rulers." Is liberty still conceived of in these terms? What are the stages in the development of the idea as Mill delineates them? Can you cite specific historical events which would support or refute Mill's generalizations?

2. Does it seem "axiomatic" to you that "people have no need to limit their power over themselves"? Did history, according to Mill, show this notion to be valid?

3. How does Mill distinguish between "society" as a "tyrant" and "the tyranny of the majority"? Which kind of tyranny does he regard as the more fearful? Why? Do you accept the validity of his distinction?

4. What, to Mill, is the "limit to the legitimate interference of collective opinion with individual independence"?

[2 A French philosopher (1798–1857) and founder of the positivist philosophy.]

5. According to Mill, "custom" operates strongly to convince a people of the rightness and inviolability of their rules of conduct. Do you see any parallel between this habit and the habit of rationalizing? (See J. H. Robinson, "Four Kinds of Thinking," page 461.)

6. Do you think men's opinions are likely to be "reasonable" if, as Mill says, they are most commonly inspired by "self-interest"?

7. Would you call Mill an "absolutist" or a "relativist" in his ethical thinking? What does he say about morality emanating from "class interests"?

8. Do you think it is necessary that religious "tolerance" be accompanied by a degree of religious "indifference"?

9. Do you think Mill makes a good case for his main principle, ". . . that the sole end for which mankind are warranted, individually or collectively, in interfering with the liberty of action of any of their number, is self-protection"? Do you think he defines "self-protection" precisely enough?

10. In Mill's summation of the qualities manifested by a "free" society do you detect any that are noticeably absent or threatened in American society today? Do you, for example, agree that "absolute freedom of opinion and sentiment on all subjects . . ." is a requisite for a "free" society?

11. Mill's final paragraph has struck many readers as being brilliantly prophetic. Do you agree with him that "a strong barrier of moral conviction" is a sufficient safeguard against the power of the state? Why is the power of society growing and that of the individual declining? See essays in the section, "The Individual and Society," (page 157).

II

12. Define *odium theologicum, primâ facie, de jure.*

13. Mill was one of the most brilliant political thinkers of nineteenth-century England and the most enlightened proponent of the Utilitarian philosophy. But he was no armchair philosopher. For a number of years he was a member of Parliament from Westminster, and he became noted not only for his progressive thinking but also for his powers as a speaker. In this essay do you detect an "oratorical" tone to his writing? How would you distinguish between an "oratorical" or "rhetorical" manner of writing and a "scientific" or "businesslike" manner of writing?

14. This is a tightly reasoned essay and demands close reading and study for full comprehension. In order to see the close relationships between its parts, try to make a brief paraphrase of each paragraph. Then read over your paraphrases. Have you pin-pointed Mill's essential theme?

15. Study the structure of the first sentences in each of Mill's paragraphs. What transitional devices are apparent in them? Are they effective?

~

THE AMERICAN
INTELLECTUAL*
Morton Cronin

One of Emerson's complaints when he wrote "The American Scholar" was that his country had not yet developed a sizeable body of intellectuals. That complaint is seldom heard any more. Nowadays the grievance which spokesmen for this group express most often is not that America lacks intellectuals, but that she does not love them, that in fact she rejects them and refuses to listen to their counsel on any important subject.

Whether America has actually jilted its intellectuals or not, it is undoubtedly true that many of them believe that she has. They often describe their characteristic symptom as a feeling of *alienation*. That word is so romantic, not to say exotic, and vibrates, cello-like, with such beautifully tragic overtones that it is almost enough in itself to win an argument. But when a feeling of repudiation flourishes in a nonintellectual, it generally receives a chillingly clinical designation: *persecution complex*. Which is the fairer term depends, of course, on the facts of the matter. Is it true that the American intellectual is rejected and considered of no account in his society? I am going to suggest that it is not true. Father Bruckberger told part of the story when he made the simple observation that it is the intellectuals who have rejected America (*Harper's*, February, 1956). But they have done more than that. They have grown dissatisfied with the role of the intellectual. It is they, not America, who have become anti-intellectual.

WHAT IS AN INTELLECTUAL?

The object of our scrutiny pleads for definition. What is an intellectual? I shall define him as *properly* an individual who has elected as his primary duty and pleasure in life the activity of thinking in a Socratic way about moral problems, whether these be social or individual. He explores such problems consciously, articulately, and candidly, first by asking factual questions, then by asking moral questions, finally by suggesting action which seems appropriate in the

* From the *AAUP Bulletin*, Summer, 1958. Used by permission.

light of the factual and moral information which he has elicited. His function is analogous to that of a judge, who must first ascertain the facts, then the law, and in the end must accept the obligation of revealing in as obvious a manner as possible the course of reasoning which led him to his decision.

This definition excludes many individuals who are usually referred to as intellectuals—the average scientist, for one. I have excluded him because, while his accomplishments may contribute to the solution of moral problems, he has not been charged, either by society or by himself, with the task of accosting any but the factual aspects of those problems. Like other human beings, he encounters moral issues even in the every-day performance of his routine duties—he is not supposed to cook his experiments, manufacture evidence, or doctor his reports. But his primary task is not to think about the moral code which governs his activity, any more than a businessman is expected to dedicate his energies to an exploration of business ethics. During most of his waking life he will take his code for granted, as the businessman takes his ethics.

The definition also excludes the majority of teachers, even on the college level, despite the fact that teaching has traditionally been the method whereby many intellectuals earn their living. The intellectual bent of most teachers is only slightly above the average for the population as a whole. They may teach very well, and more than earn their salaries, but most of them bring little or no independent reflection to bear on human problems which involve moral judgment. This description even fits the majority of eminent, and justly eminent, scholars. Being learned in some branch of human knowledge is one thing; living in "public and illustrious thoughts," as Emerson would say, is something else.

The definition also excludes creative writers and artists, as such. They make an indispensable contribution to moral life, but it is not a Socratic contribution. They must dramatize and embellish their argument, and this necessity introduces many supra-realistic and extra-logical elements. In fact, an artist is well within his rights if he departs this world more or less completely—in music and modern painting this is the rule rather than the exception—and creates something in the realm of pure art which does not answer at all to the moral or sociological world in the ordinary sense.

The role of the intellectual must also be distinguished from that of the politician. The latter shares with the intellectual a preoccupation with moral problems, but he is not free to range where he wishes in the inspection of man's estate and to consider human problems on whatever level of abstractness or concreteness he desires. Furthermore, his duties prevent him from developing that candor which is indispensable in the intellectual. One of his principal obligations is to compose differences and this obligation will often generate prudential reasons for not stating the whole truth as he sees it. He may think very well, and after the Socratic manner, but if he consistently reveals the full nature of his thinking he will become a bad politician, and eventually no politician at all.

Finally, the definition separates the intellectual from the saint, the prophet, and the revolutionary. These last make the mightiest of all contributions to moral life. If any individual human beings can be said to create or discover moral values for an entire people, they are the ones who do it. But, once again, the character of their main activity cannot be called Socratic. Their typical utterances are short, sententious, and authoritative. What makes men saints, prophets, or revolutionaries is not so much their plans for mankind as it is their determination to inaugurate those plans. Convinced that they have found the truth, they concentrate—rightly, for them—on living it and making it prevail, in the course of which they do not seek the dialectical opposition which the Socratic thinker requires. Their characteristic tendency is to fight their battle with slogans and vivid affirmations which briskly summarize their thought and experience.

Precisely where, then, can one lay hold of intellectuals? Well, they can be detected in any occupation, although in some occupations you will have to conduct a long day's hunt in order to bag one. Some teachers are intellectuals. Also some journalists. Even some editors. Some clergymen. Most theologians, I suspect, although I never met one. Some lawyers, usually young ones with time on their hands or old ones on the federal bench. Very few doctors nowadays, for obvious reasons. Some college presidents, theoretically, but I cannot remember any in my time, except Hutchins and one other whose name would not mean anything to you. An occasional businessman, so help me. Some women, no doubt. Even longshoremen contribute their portion to this category, as Eric Hoffer proves.

But in no case will a man's trade or profession necessarily mark him as an intellectual. That status is only achieved by the cultivation of three characteristics, none of which has anything in particular to do with the classifications used in employment offices.

First of all, an intellectual is interested in moral problems as they concern the generality of people, not just as they concern himself, his relatives, and his close associates. The problems with which he himself is afflicted will influence the direction of his thinking, but his thinking does not stop with whatever *modus vivendi* he works out between the world and himself. Briefly, he considers general problems, seeks general solutions, and contributes to the public philosophy.

Secondly, his views are fully articulated. He is a conscious thinker. He collects evidence, weighs and sifts it, and exhibits a developed capacity for separating the true from the false. He does not mind disclosing his premises and explaining his terms. He does not disdain exceptions and qualifications, nor shrink from ironies and paradoxes. His mode of discourse, in short, is at the opposite extreme from the gnomic utterance of the intuitive thinker.

His third and most important characteristic is his willingness— indeed, his eagerness—to subject his views to critical discussion. If he is a good example of his type he will glow with health and good humor in an argument. He stalks truth in the dialectic maze the way some men maneuver for love in the labyrinth of romance. Yet his object is not to score debating points. For him the pursuit of truth must be cooperative, as well as dialectic, and all the pleasure vanishes when that pursuit turns into a mere contest of wills with his interlocutor. It is easy for him to say "I don't know," and he is impressed when his own questions evoke that reply.

From what I have said concerning the occupational habitat of intellectuals, it naturally follows that, despite their absorption in what is more or less public business, they do not always occupy a public stage. Indeed, as I conceive the species, most of them do not. When the circumstances of their lives invite publication, some portion of their reflections will usually appear in print. And a few, like Walter Lippmann, Reinhold Niebuhr, and Sidney Hook, will become really public figures. But the type is not determined by the size of its audience. An intellectual's audience may consist of only a small circle of friends—no congregation, no band of students even—and he will still perform the intellectual's function as truly and authentically as his famous brothers.

WHAT GOOD IS AN INTELLECTUAL?

The term *intellectual* is one of those words which are both honorific and pejorative. Among those who deserve it, there are men who shrink from it, men who feel ennobled by it, and men in whom both of these reactions are in sweet conflict. This is about as it should be, for there will always be bad as well as good intellectuals.

But that is not the worst of it. Even in the hands of the best of intellectuals, the Socratic method of arriving at moral judgments may, like any other method known on this planet, guide men to hell as well as to heaven. An intellectual may study the available facts with matchless care, press home the most intelligent questions, develop his argument from start to finish with unapproachable logic, square his recommendation of policy with the best moral values which either his culture or inspiration can provide—and still when all is said and done, he is only guessing. The ultimate result is determined by Mr. X. (I do not want to offend the American intellectual by using any three-letter word.) Some things are so well known that they are hard to remember—the fact, for instance, that what justifies the intellectual process of reaching moral decisions is not that it is unerring but only that it presumably increases the percentage of lucky bets.

The uneasiness which afflicts the position which intellectuals occupy in society also results from the fact that no preparation of any formal character, no ritual of initiation, no conjunction of the planets at time of birth must necessarily precede the practice of their vocation. Like politics or teaching English, anyone can try his hand at it, and proof of his incapacity will never be as conclusive as if he tried to splash about in theoretical physics. He can always scream that having studied with Whitehead and knowing where to put the commas are not what make the philosopher. And he will be right. The occasional forays of irregulars into intellectual analysis will commonly strike more telling blows than campaigns prepared by gouty professionals.

But the status of the intellectual wavers for still another reason. The Socratic technique, even when judged by its own standards, cannot be brought to the purity and finish that, say, chiropractic technique can be brought to. There are no pure intellectuals, and there will always be some in whom their function has been so pitifully corrupted by immoderate zeal or unconscious commitments that the best they can offer is excellent logic marching superbly towards the wrong conclusion, with only one more day of history necessary for all the world to see its falseness. And there is no remedy for these aberrations. The sensitivity to moral and human values which keeps the intellectual process from being an empty exercise in formal logic is also the thing which makes the intellectual susceptible to those loyalties which compel him to suppress facts, ignore considerations, and substitute harrumphing indignation for thoughtful candor.

Finally, any assessment of the value of an intellectual must reckon with the circumstance that the apparatus for distilling moral truth and manufacturing social policy does not enjoy a monopoly. Other contrivances compete with his for this business, some of which are called intuition, spontaneous insight, susceptibility to revelation, and unconscious reasoning. These devices represent the free play of intelligence, and owe their share of success to the fact that human affairs will sometimes yield in a flash their true nature to the moral entrepreneur whose formal equipment does not rear up between him and reality. Another operation in this market consists in invoking precedent and tradition whenever possible, thus offering both the intuitive and the intellectual products which have been turned out in the past. This mode of supplying the demand for moral ideas pleases more customers than all the others combined. And then there is the artist's practice, which appeals to those who like precision work. It often unites in varying and unpredictable proportions all the other processes, including the intellectual's, but receives its most distinctive character from its concern for esthetic or stylistic values. And this concern, rarely separable in representational art and literature from a concern for moral truth, is perhaps what gives the artist that right combination of engagement and perspective which the intellectual also needs but too often lacks.

Our protagonist, in short, is never infallible, he is never perfectly intellectual, and his system is only one of several for arriving at acceptable decisions. I have dwelt on the limitations of the intellectual mode because its typical American proponent careens towards the assumption that brains and good intentions can accomplish anything. With no embarrassment whatever, he will declare his *faith* in human reason. *Faith* is the right word, but it is odd that he should use it when we remember his deprecation of it in other contexts.

On the other hand, we cannot dispense with any method which experience has demonstrated will increase our chances of success in reaching for moral truth. The intellectual possesses such a method. Popes must have theologians, as well as models of piety and stout bishops. Kings need privy councilors, wise in policy and deft in expressing it, along with patriot-heroes and capable ministers. And a healthy society requires independent intellectuals, men who work for neither Pope nor King, as well as solid citizens and good providers.

Every organized segment of church, state, and private life stands to benefit whenever the nonintellectual's resort to custom, intuition, or esthetic inspiration is checked and supplemented by the Socratic explorations which are the individuals' particular business. But the intellectual activity which concerns us most in this discussion is that

which private individuals carry on for the benefit of the public philosophy. Other things being equal, they are the intellectuals *par
excellence*, for they can achieve a maximum of independence and
candor. The interests of the state, of the church, and of private
groups of all sorts, as interpreted by their official servants, including
the intellectuals among them, have an ineradicable tendency to separate from the interests of the generality. It is the free intellectuals
who constitute *society's* Kitchen Cabinet or Brain Trust, and help
these servants keep their attention focused on the big picture.

Finally, the value of an article is determined, as economists may,
by its scarcity as well as its utility. A good intellectual is hard to
find, and even a not-so-good one is, like a so-so husband, not always
obtainable when you want one. We know how to contrive as many
corporation lawyers and baby specialists as we need, but formulas
for making intellectuals are only rumors.

How Should an Intellectual Behave in Society?

Now that we have said what an intellectual is and have suggested
both the limitations and the usefulness of his *modus operandi*, we
can consider the question of his proper relations with the rest of
society. And in doing this we shall come more often to what is wrong
with American intellectuals.

Like other individuals who perform special functions, the intellectual requires some special privileges. As everyone knows, the most
important of these is the right, not only to subject established views
to a more poignant examination than is customary among most of his
fellow citizens, but to state the results of his examination in a public
manner without provoking the social and economic pressures with
which society usually protects its established code.

Contrary to what one often hears, freedom for intellectuals—among
professors it is called academic freedom—is special. It is as special
as the scientist's right to practice vivisection or the judge's right to
render a binding judgment. Where it differs from these rights is in
the fact that everyone shares in it to some extent, and no one's share,
including the intellectual's, is easy to measure. *But the intellectual's
share is always larger than that of the average citizen.*

Many American intellectuals delight in suggesting that *everyone*
should be free to express whatever opinions he wishes without any
contraction of his social or economic opportunities. When this suggestion is not the cool product of intellectual demagoguery, it is

simply the result of a naive conception of how societies are necessarily organized.

It should not be necessary to repeat that no freedom, intellectual or otherwise, is ever absolute for anyone. Furthermore, the activity of most people inevitably commits them to programs of cooperative endeavor whose ideological basis can be *widely* reconsidered only at infrequent intervals. Societies are not founded on questions; they are founded on answers, however spurious, and can accommodate only a limited number of individuals whose regular business is to challenge those answers. There are people who concede that cohesion is an indispensable attribute of a viable society but would deny society the mechanisms by which it achieves cohesion—a fatuity akin to the one which dominates those men who urge their government to negotiate international agreements but to forego as an indelicacy any effective means of enforcement.

Now, it may be that a given population as a whole should be freer than it is to express opinions. But no matter how free it becomes in this respect, its intellectuals—if it has any—must be freer. This may be undemocratic, as the scientist's special right or the judge's may be, but without these special rights we can have no scientists, judges, or intellectuals.

I must now recite the killjoy lesson that exceptional privileges usually entail exceptional obligations. The intellectual's most important obligation consists in maintaining a greater degree of independence, integrity, and candor in his relations with the world than can be reasonably expected of most men. His primary duty is to tell the whole truth as he sees it, in detail as well as in general. His primary duty is not to make that truth prevail. In fact, if he slips too deeply into the tactical maneuvers of social action, especially those which require close organizational ties, he will, like a judge who wades in politics, evoke the suspicion that he can no longer be trusted with his special prerogative. And this suspicion will be justified by the common experience of mankind. For when an individual becomes profoundly involved in a program of political action, he usually cannot be counted on to make a fair assessment of opposing programs. Such involvement on the part of an intellectual will be enough to establish the presumption that he has stopped being an intellectual and can now with propriety be treated as factionalists treat one another.

No one can say for certain just when the line is crossed which

separates the domain of the intellectual from that of the party man.
There can be no Hatch Act for intellectuals. Furthermore, the location of the line will vary with historical circumstances and with the
temperament of the individual concerned. But it is important for
practical as well as theoretical purposes to acknowledge that the line
always exists and that reasonable men can at least identify those
instances in which it has been grievously overstepped.

It has been a long time since an apartment in the ivory tower was
a fashionable residence for an American intellectual. In so far as
this desertion of the old neighborhood has reduced a preoccupation
with trivialities, as exemplified in much of the study formerly lavished
on classical languages, its results have been admirable. But to the
extent that it has obliterated the necessary distinction between intellectuals and their fellow citizens, its results have not been admirable.
This distinction cannot be erased, even in the name of democracy,
without the emaciation of intellectuals, and eventually of democracy
too. The unromantic fact is that an intellectual should, when he
purports to function as an intellectual, occupy a position which is
somewhat remote from the urgencies and envelopments of political
life. On the other hand, his reflections will not be worth much if
he has had no experience of such intimacies. And his aim in life
is not to achieve the impartiality of the wife in Lincoln's story who
exclaimed, "Go it husband, go it bear." But when an intellectual
practices his vocation he must draw back from his experience and
maximize the tranquility with which he brings that experience to the
study of human problems. He must even listen seriously to whatever
the bear has to say for himself. It may be that this necessity is one
of the sources of error in the Socratic method. When enough people
in a society have acquired a fierce taste for hot loyalty and pungent
discipline, the intellectual whose mouth does not water for these
sensations may lose touch with social reality. If he does lose touch,
events will sweep past him and he will be left spinning like a top.
But so be it. It is his occupational hazard. Even under favorable
conditions his method will not always work.

No one can define with exactness that blend of thought and feeling,
of detachment and engagement, which yields the best intellectual
results. But the presence of too much feeling is easy to detect, and
it is characteristic of the person who passes for an intellectual in
America. The test is a simple one: How does he respond to opposition? How eager is he to venture his opinions in free and dispassionate debate? More often than not, he is an individual who, like

any orthodox citizen, confines his ideological activity to singing hymns of faith with like-minded individuals. He accuses America of being anti-intellectual, but his own consciously-held conception of his proper role has extinguished an essential difference between the intellectual and his countrymen—for he is proud of his emotion, cultivates it on principle, and protects it from any Socratic challenge. His image of the complete intellectual is a person who (1) sympathizes intensely on the right side of current social and political questions—the right side usually being the liberal or leftist side; (2) associates more or less exclusively, even in his professional life if he can manage it, with other correct-thinking persons; (3) supplements this activity with an interest in literature, art, and folk music.

This image obviously owes something to the Marxist revolutionary, whose example, however discredited, still influences the American intellectual, if only because, like a woman between marriages, he has not yet reorganized his imaginative life around a figure of superior power. But, disturbed rather than inspired by memories of his first love, he does not participate in any revolutionary activity, which would detonate his pent-up sympathies and sweeten his disposition. Nor, if he is typical, does he express his urgencies in conventional American politics, for, despite his characteristic concern for the masses, he is curiously snobbish. He does not like the masses, he just wants to be their champion. But how? He might write on social questions, of course, but the average American intellectual—I refer now to the one whose circumstances in life would make such activity natural—the one in the academic world, for instance—is singularly unproductive in this respect. The example of Thorstein Veblen does not stir him. He does not have the patience. It is hard to write if emotion has crystallized your thoughts into a series of slogans. You discover that they can all be put in one paragraph. You discover something worse. That paragraph has already been written. The result is that the American intellectual from whom one would normally expect a public contribution characteristically stands between thought and action and howls like a donkey in tension between two bales of hay.

The second rule of behavior for the intellectual, comparable in importance to the one which limits his partisan involvement in affairs, is that he cannot demand that society love him without reservation. A certain hostility is part of the tribute paid to distinction. Intellectuals are not alone in provoking it. Businessmen, lawyers, doctors, public officials, army officers, clergymen, even people who are just

good-looking or quick-witted—all who impinge with any force upon
their fellow men receive a measure of resentment. The distrust which
intellectuals generate is not only natural but, provided always that
it does not turn morbid, it is also desirable. It is a necessary defense
of the population against an elite group which, being human as well
as elite, is subject to error, presumption, and impatience, and is no
more to be followed blindly than are priests or politicians. The
country protects itself against Wall Street bankers in the same way;
so much so, in fact, that a public statement in actual praise of them
is almost unheard of. This natural hostility towards the intellectual,
together with his own need to maintain an intellectual's distance,
means that he need never give up all claim to that lovely word
alienation.

But the typical American intellectual asserts that the feeling which
exists between him and his society is neither normal nor desirable.
He claims that America is not both pro- and anti-intellectual, but
that it is just anti-intellectual. It is hard to reply specifically to this
charge, because it is usually stated as an axiom. What are the facts?
If I may be a witness, I must testify that on those occasions when
I have been taken for an intellectual, for no other reason than that I
taught in a college, I have often received such touching deference
and respect that I have had to go out of my way in order to put at
ease those men in other walks of life. Whoever observes alumni
attending their class reunions will notice a wistful hope in some of
the meatiest faces that their old professors, baggy clothes and all,
will pay some attention to them.

It is true that many intellectuals, especially in the teaching profession, do not make as much money as individuals of comparable ability
in other occupations. But neither do army officers and clergymen,
even when they become generals and bishops. Is America abnormally
anti-military and anti-religious? Indeed, intellectuals often sigh that
America is too fond of the military and too soft towards religion. The
arguments for putting more money in the pockets of intellectuals are
just, but America's resistance to those arguments does not prove that
she is peculiarly anti-intellectual. It has been a rare period in the
history of any country when being an intellectual was a paying
proposition. Wealth is accumulated by people who address themselves to that objective in life. When intellectuals do this—many who
enter the communication industries, for instance—they stand a better
chance of collecting a fortune than many a businessman. But traditionally most intellectuals, like scientists, professional soldiers, and

ecclesiastics, array themselves for other battles. They give up money, but in return they receive an opportunity to modify in a conscious way, wearing the while no man's livery, the ideology of their society, in so far as it is given to human beings to achieve such free and conscious modifications. If they prize this opportunity, the rest of the world will admire, respect, and envy them, including their shiny pants and twisted neckties. The intellectual who feels too bitter about his difficulties in acquiring a house with three bedrooms, two baths, and a knotty-pine den has succumbed to the values of those segments of his society whose influence he most deplores. If the American intellectual, despite these considerations, persists in his feeling of persecution, we may eventually witness his miserable demise à la *Death of a Salesman,* for there is no essential difference between his insistence and Willy Loman's that he be well liked.

Rule number three: Without impairing his vocation of reporting the truth as he sees it, an intellectual does well to retain a decent measure of tolerance for the prejudices of his society, however dismal. He should strive, at least in the normal course of his activity, to offer his solutions without anguish or indignation, for he should realize even more than other men how the emergence of unappreciated or unforeseen facts may make him wish that he had stayed in bed. Certain moral truths may be eternal, but they only achieve this status enclouded in general terms, where they can hover serenely, like Buddha's smile, above the sweaty problems of human application, their radiance providing inspiration rather than specific guidance. He is a schoolboy intellectual who does not acknowledge that in the human world good and evil have such an affinity for one another that, after the manner of women in a polygamous society, the fair one will sometimes yield only to the man who also weds her ugly sisters. As other men, an intellectual is obliged to do the best he can, but a knowledge that that best is never certain to accomplish its aim is as desirable in an intellectual as it is in nonintellectuals. The mulishness of his countrymen may, for all he can definitely know, save him from having to witness one of his brilliant mistakes grinding into action.

Finally, the business of being an intellectual requires some sophistication about the nature of culture, in the anthropological sense of that word. Good or bad, the traditions men receive from their predecessors distinguish them from animals. It is literally true that nauseous traditions would be better than none, for traditions of any sort are proof that man's development is not confined to what he can learn in a single lifetime. But the extent to which he can change his customs in any one generation without inviting disaster has its limits, regardless of how desirable, abstractly considered, such changes might be. An intellectual must, like a good psychiatrist, resign himself to the fact that a solution which the patient cannot accept without undue resistance is no solution. His failure to do so gives him the character of an intellectual trifler and rightfully provokes contempt on the part of politicians and others who, in their own way, achieve maturity by respecting the limitations of their culture.

PLACATORY REMARKS

Like other human beings, the American intellectual would rather be admired than analyzed. Instead of pressing him further, I shall just add some protestations in order to demonstrate that I am bent on a mere lover's quarrel and not a crime of passion.

I would not give the impression that the intellectual should possess no firm convictions. He may possess as many of them as his study of events has brought him to. What makes him an intellectual in this respect, and sets him apart from other intelligent people with firm convictions, is only his matador's readiness to confront the hour of truth and risk his convictions with grace, style, and regularity.

Nor does this conception of the intellectual dehumanize him. Lawyers subdue their righteous impulses in arguing a case, regardless of how convinced they are that the opposition exhibits the grossest effrontery in contesting the matter. Are lawyers inhuman? Medical students learn to cut on human bodies without grievous distress. This takes some learning, but it does not result in many students becoming ghouls. I doubt that we need worry about stunting the intellectual's emotional life. No one is suggesting that he make love, raise a family, tender mortgage payments, and receive traffic tickets without emotion. However professional his search for truth in his capacity as an intellectual, the rest of his life will give him many opportunities to scream his head off like a normal human being.

Finally, an intellectual has a right to stop being an intellectual at any time. His changing his role may result in glorious consequences, as when many gifted individuals abandoned the schoolroom and the study before and during the American Revolution. The point is simply that when an intellectual goes all-out for politics, he cannot retain that special privilege which rightfully protects him as an independent thinker. When present-day activists who submit to party discipline are caught in the intellectual henhouse, their usual defense is to flap their arms indignantly, scratch up the dust, and cackle to the best of their ability that nobody's here but us chickens. But these activists are not intellectuals as I perceive the species. They may have been at one time, and they may become intellectuals again. But as long as they remain under orders, their freedom signed over to higher authority, they must expect to be treated as nonintellectuals treat one another in conflict, without extra consideration for their social and economic well-being. I doubt that Nathan Hale complimented the British on their dexterity with rope, but there is no record that he wailed bitterly that this was a fine way to treat a college man.

Problems for Thought and Writing

I

1. Is Morton Cronin *stipulating* a meaning here or merely refining a traditional definition? See "Definition and Description," page 305.

2. How many of the techniques for limiting a meaning which were outlined in the introductory discussion to this section are evident here?

3. What, in your opinion, was Cronin's *motive* for writing this article? Was he merely trying to write a good definition or did he want to *use* that definition for some further purpose?

4. Why can an artist not qualify as an intellectual? Is Cronin *degrading* artists by this exclusion? If we feel so, is it because we have prejudged the meaning of "intellectual," and read in emotional values that Cronin did not put there?

5. What are the three characteristics by which the status of "intellectual" is achieved? Would Nevins and Josephson (page 580) qualify?

6. "The sensitivity to moral and human values which keeps the intellectual process from being an empty exercise in formal logic is also the thing which makes the intellectual susceptible to those loyalties which compel him to suppress facts, ignore considerations, and substitute harrumphing indignation for thoughtful candor." If guilty of such trespasses is he still, by Cronin's definition, an intellectual?

7. The intellectual *par excellence*, says Cronin, is the private individual whose Socratic explorations are carried on for the benefit of the "public philosophy." What is meant by "public philosophy" here?

8. "Societies are not founded on questions; they are founded on answers. . . ." Explain what Cronin means. Do you agree?

9. The distinction between intellectuals and their fellow citizens cannot be erased, says Cronin, "without the emaciation of intellectuals, and eventually of democracy too." To what degree would Mandel (page 171) in your opinion agree with this statement?

10. In what way is the American intellectual, according to Cronin, affected by leftist and Marxist ideology?

11. Is Cronin himself, in your opinion, pro- or anti-intellectual? What evidence can you find to suggest that he is not impartial?

II

12. Is this essay a good definition? Why or why not?

13. What evidences of wit do you find? Do they tend to increase or decrease your respect for Cronin's intelligence?

14. Is this an argument as well as a definition? If you think so, what is the thesis of the argument?

15. How does the problem of definition here differ—if at all—from that faced by Lynes (page 477)?

16. Could this piece have been improved by being shortened? Where would you recommend cutting?

~

THE CUTTHROAT TROUT*   *Sally Carrighar*

Only a sharpened, seeing look in the Trout's eyes proved that he had wakened. No shift of the eyes had flashed their crystalline shine. The wrongness of some sound had roused him. He peered from his nook along the west shore of the pond. Was there a glisten of wet fur in the polished darkness? Or did he see the pale clouds hung in the water, moonlight, which had turned to luminous froth the bubbles clinging to the underwater plants?

His shelter was a groove among the sticks of the beaver house. He was holding himself as still as the sticks, so quiet in their tangle that a slippery ooze had grown upon them. His breathing lightened until the water drained through his gills with no perceptible beat, no pulse to send its circular waves out through the pond, revealing that he lay at the center of them.

From the edge of the Beaver's sunken pile of aspen boughs a string of small globes, faintly silver, smoked to the top. Some animal must have touched a branch and rubbed out air that was held within its fur. The water swayed; the creature had begun to swim. Its stroke was not familiar to the Trout, not one of the rhythms that he knew as harmless or a threat. It had more pulse than the Beaver's paddling or the striding of a moose. It was rougher than the swim-

* Reprinted from *One Day at Teton Marsh* by Sally Carrighar, by permission of Alfred A. Knopf, Inc. Copyright 1946, 1947, by Sally Carrighar.

ming of a fish and heavier than a muskrat's sculling. At first the Trout must steady himself with his fins to keep from being slapped against the sticks. But the underwater waves diminished. The last of them struck the shores and clattered back, a liquid echo. The only motion in the pond then was its regular mottling flow, a current from the brook to the beaver dam.

The surging had torn the film of sleep from a thousand little minds. After it ceased, constrained breaths made the pond seem lifeless. But hunger was a danger too. It rose above the fear of the animals, one by one—of the smallest first. Soon the twinkling prowls of the mayfly nymphs, the quick strokes of the water-boatmen, and the foraging of even tinier creatures mingled in a hum like that of insects in the air, but louder. The lightest sounds were wave-beats in the pond. To the Trout's ears came the twanging of minute activity.

Night was nearly over. The Trout knew by the brightening of the water, by his hunger, and the stiffness in his muscles. He saw the webs of the pelican start to push the bird's breast over the top of the pond. Its wing-tips dipped in the water, the webs were shoveling back with greater vigor, the breast was shrinking upward. Only the kick of the feet now broke the surface. When the bird was gone, the fin on the Trout's back stood a little higher, and a ripple scalloped from its front edge to the rear.

The Beaver swam to the entrance of the house and climbed in onto the floor. His angry voice came through the wall. He was driving from his bed the muskrat he allowed to share his home. The feet of a mother moose and her calf had waded off the bank. They dragged their splashes down the shore to a patch of horsetail. The big soft muffles plunged beneath the surface, closed around the plants and pulled them dripping from the water. Even yet the Trout would not risk showing himself. He was the wariest of all the animals in the pond.

Besides the stranger's threat, a more familiar danger kept him hiding. Three times a day the Osprey dived in the pond for fish. The Trout's good time-sense held him under cover when its strike was due: at dawn, as soon as the hawk could see its prey; at noon; and at sunset, with the first receding wave of light. Most mornings the Trout went out for an early swim, returning to his nook before he would be visible from the air; but not on this day.

His wait was an exquisite balancing of instincts. Hunger was sufficient reason to start forth, and the pond's flow was a stimulation. The current, passing through the walls of the beaver house, divided around the Trout. All night its touch had slid along his skin, from nose to tail, as though he ceaselessly swam forward. Now he was awake to feel the fine strokes down his sides—the touch of moving water; only the sight of moving prey could be more quickening to a trout. But he submitted to the quieting urge. He stayed in his groove, with ears and lateral lines both listening for the hawk.

The fluffs of moonlight disappeared in a tremulous green shine. No wind rocked the surface now, but the Trout could see the current draining toward the dam. It was a checkered wavering, unhurried and unaltering. Daylight reached the bottom, where the water's ripples had been fixed in sandy silt.

Directly over him the Trout could look into the air. His view was circular, and small; his own length would have spanned it. Beyond that opening the surface was an opaque silver cover, stretching to the shores. Reflected in it were the floor of the pond, the swimming animals, and the underwater plants. The Trout could see the lustrous belly of a leopard frog spring past. He also saw, in the mirror spread above, the frog's bronze, spotted back. The pond was a shallow layer of the world, with a ceiling on which its life was repeated upside-down.

Upon the surface crashed a huge light-feathered breast. Claws reached and speared a bullhead. A brown throat, then a beak and head came through the top of the pond, and wings and tail. A shower of bubbles scattered downward as the long wings lowered in a sweep. The wings began to lift the Osprey. A final thrashing took him out of the surface, leaving the reverberations of his dive.

The wariness of the Trout released its check. He floated from his groove. He still seemed motionless, as if the current had dislodged him. Slowly his fins commenced a ribbonlike stroke. His tail pressed gently on the water, left and right.

Freeing his entire strength in a tail-thrust then, he was across the pond. A spinning turn, and, energy closely held, he slanted toward the bottom silt—the touch, and a spasm of upward speed had flung him into the dangerous dazzling air.

A slicing dive back deep in the pond, a glimpse of another trout, and he whipped in its pursuit. But just before his teeth would have nicked its tail, he whirled, and the trout ahead whirled too, in perfect unison.

He cut forward in the channel of the current, throwing his tail from side to side as he tried to find in his own speed some full outlet for his strength. The water of the pond would give him nowhere more than a mild and yielding pressure. He was a native cutthroat of the Snake, a turbulent swift river, but the placid pond and the little brook that fed it were the only home that he had known. In early summer of the year the beavers built the pond, his parents had come up the brook to spawn. The new dam trapped them and their offspring. The river poured along the east side of the marsh, so near that the Trout could feel its deep vibration. He had not seen it, but his spirit cried for its stronger flow, its more combative force.

Yet idle swimming could be pleasant. He glided to the backwash past the brook, toward food not scented, seen, or heard, but certain to appear. Sculled by his tail, he wove through bare elastic water-lily stalks, beneath a cover of translucent leaves. He was at rest in motion, fins outspread to ride the smooth support, his slippery skin quick-sliding through the wetness. But he stiffened, shot ahead, bent nose to tail, kicked back the tail in a sharp return, perhaps to savor the grace of a body incapable of awkwardness in an element incapable of angles: beautiful play.

He saw a streaming like fine grasses drawn by the current—dace! With a forward spring he snatched a minnow at the side of the school. Alarm flashed through them all, and the leaders swung to flee into the brook. The milling of the others would have made each one available to the Trout, but he swerved away.

He'd seen a pair of reedy, jointed legs, seeming to be rooted in the silt, but still, not quivering as reeds would in the flow of the pond. The dace swam toward them. The dace had left the safety of the shallows because a harmless moose was splashing there. The Trout had captured one, and now the great blue heron certainly would catch another. But would not catch the Trout! Already he was far beyond the stab of the bird's beak.

Near the shore the water swished with the feet of ducks. A quick look: no mergansers' feet, with paddle-toes for diving, there among the webs of mallards, pintails, and of baldpates. The Trout swam under them. He need not dread an enemy's unexpected dive here while the feet were moving the ducks about in search of food, while they were easy, pushing webfuls of water back and folding in and drawing forward; not while one foot hung, a pivot, and the other swung an oval breast; or both of a duck's webs splashed at the surface, holding him bill-down. As long as no fear tensed the feet, the Trout felt safe.

The long stripe on a pintail's neck shone white as it lowered the bird's head, swanlike, to the bottom. But swiftly it was pulled above the surface. Now all the feet were quiet, spread from the feathered bellies, ready for a leap. The Trout, alert, poised in midwater.

He did not know what animal had frightened the ducks. While they continued their wary wait, the white keel of the pelican dipped through the surface, slid ahead, and, checked by its wide webs, glided to a stop. The Trout streamed off, away from the watchful ducks, and gradually forgot their warning.

When he was a young fish, nearly every animal he saw seemed hungry for him. One by one then he outgrew the threat of frogs, kingfishers, snakes, and larger trout. He learned the tricks of human fishermen. Minks and mergansers chased him still but could not capture him. No other creature in the pond was quite so swift. And he almost was too heavy to be carried by an osprey. Soon the Trout might reach security that few wild creatures know, unless the alien of the early morning proved a danger.

Every instinct whispers some command; for him the loudest command was always, *live*. He listened for it, always deferred his other urges to it. Survival was so strong an impulse in him that the most involuntary workings of his body helped him hide. The pale sheen on his belly matched the cover of the pond, to an eye below. One watching from across the surface might confuse the iridescence of his scales with scales of sunlight on the ripples. The black spots spattered on his skin disguised his shape when seen from any angle. To a mate or rival he might show two crimson gashes on his throat, but usually he folded them beneath his jaws.

When his alarm had quieted, he started to the beaver house. First he passed a bank of sedges. In summer when their shade was green, the Trout had turned to emerald here. This autumn day the grass was tawny, and its color, focused in his eyes, had caused the grains of yellow in his skin to scatter out and tint him olive. If the inborn guardian in his tissues could arrange it, he would live. Yet other animals also had ingenious aids, some useful in attack.

He circled the island on the dam, now moving through a tunnel of grasses, bent with the tips of the blades awash. The sun was laying gold bars over him. He moved with a little flourish, for it seemed that he was really safe. Beyond the far side of the island a floating log pressed down the top of the pond. He started under—and was circled with a crash.

Escape! Escape to a nook in the dam! He split the water and was there. Wheeling, he shot in the hole and flung out his fins to check him. The water bulged in after him, as the one who chased him surged to a stop outside.

He had not seen what creature dived from the log. But his dash to the shelter, finished between heartbeats, was long enough to tell him that the other gained. Gained! Did panic echo, now, from days when the rush of most pursuers swept upon him like a wave?

His refuge was a space in the roots of a cottonwood, a dead tree anchoring the dam. Through interwoven fibers he could see his enemy, an animal he did not know, the Otter. The creature darted around the root-maze, trying to peer in. His eyes would show in one place, reaching for the Trout. A drive with a quick foot and the brown-furred face would push into another hole. Eagerly it was weaving forward, cocked ears sharp as claws.

The Otter found a looser tangle, which his paws began to tear. The water was tainted with the scent of his excitement, acrid in the nostrils of the Trout. Close beside the Trout's face now a lean webbed paw had grasped a root. The claws were scratching as the toes kept tightening in convulsive grips. The Otter tried to burrow through, but the tangle held. Should the Trout attempt to reach the sturdier beaver house? No longer was there safety in a flight. He tensed his tail for a great thrust; yet he hesitated.

As suddenly then as if the Otter had seen a more accessible fish, he drew back out of the roots. He swam away with a vertical sculling, so that each roll took him to the top. The pulses in the water matched the surging that had stirred the pond at dawn.

The water beat for some time with his strokes and other creatures' startled movements. When the Trout could feel the light quick overlap of wavelets nearly spent, he knew that the Otter had gone to the far end of the pond. Then he could have fled to the beaver house, but he was waiting for the Osprey's midday dive. His new fear had not blurred his sense of the older menace.

The Osprey's perch was in the tree whose roots now hid him. He could not see the hawk, but when the spread wings glided from the upper boughs, they came into his air-view. He watched, as he never had from the beaver house, the way the Osprey hovered high above his victim, and how he plunged, so slanting his dive that he dropped from behind an unsuspecting fish. The Trout could recognize the jolting of the pond, the splashing as the Osprey struggled from the water, the sudden quiet, and widening of the echoes. The hawk returned in his air-view, carrying a mountain sucker to his branch. After he ate the fish, he flew back down to clean his claws. The Trout could see them across the pond, thin hooks that cut the surface, trailing silvered sacs of air.

At last the water near the cottonwood roots sucked up, a motion meaning that some heavy animal was climbing out. A gust of drops fell onto the surface, as the creature shuddered the moisture from its fur. Feet ran over the top of the dam. As they passed the base of the tree, a sift of dirt fell through the roots and briefly stuck to the mucous coating on the skin of the Trout.

The pond was all in motion, for the wind had risen. The wind had stirred the marsh for several days, with short lulls. The Trout sensed that it brought a change of season. He could even taste the proof of summer's end, as dust, seeds, crumbling leaves and bark washed through the pond.

Bright-edged shadows of the waves were racing over the bottom silt. They swept across the underwater plants and seemed to shake them. The surface layer of the pond was blowing to the upper end of the backwash. There the water turned below, to sweep back down along the bottom. Against the dam this flowing sheet rolled up. It pressed beneath the Trout's fins as a breeze will lift against the wings of a bird.

Whenever the wind would strain the top of the rigid dead tree, he could feel a pulling in the roots. Suddenly they began to writhe, to tear. The Trout was out of the maze and back in the beaver house as if the water had parted for him.

The Osprey's tree, upturned by the wind, fell into the pond. Billows met rebounding billows, whirls and eddies struggled, surges rocked the Trout. Gradually the violence quieted. Through a cloud of mud he dimly saw that the trunk of the tree was under the surface, propped up from the bottom on its boughs.

He settled himself to feel the current's long touch on his sides. But what disturbing change was this: the water's stroking soon was regular, yet took a new course—not from his nose to tail but downward now. The water's pressure was becoming lighter and its color rosier. The top of the pond was falling.

Inherited memories warned him that the change was ominous. But he did not leave his shelter, for it seemed that a greater danger threatened him outside: the Otter had returned. Sometimes the

Trout could hear him in the water, sometimes out along the narrowing shores. The Trout would not be caught through panic. He lay in his nook and watched the surface drop.

Only when it reached the nook itself did he nose outside. Feeling the Otter's surging near, he turned down to a refuge lower in the wall. The top of the pond descended on him there. The water, draining off the bank beside the house, was roily, so that he could not see where he would go. But he entered it and let its motion guide him.

The currents were not flowing in familiar paths. They all converged in a powerful new suction. Since the roots of the cottonwood tree had been interwoven with the dam, its fall had torn apart the beaver's masonry of mud and sticks. The whole marsh seemed to be swirling toward the gap and plunging through it.

The Trout turned back. He would escape to the brook. He sensed that he must leave the doomed pond and would seek the water's source, as the other fish had done. He could not reach it. While he, the one most wary, stayed in the house to escape the Otter, the pond had shrunk below the mouth of the brook. The only water now connecting them was a thin sheet crinkling over a pebble bar.

Gone, lost above the surface, were the undercut banks of roots, the grassy tunnels, brush, and other shoreline hideaways. The Trout returned to the lower end of the pond. He glided with his fins streamlined in the depressions in his sides, and with so slight a sculling that he might be trying to make smoothness hide him. As he approached the dam, he saw the Otter. Dodging up the bottom toward the island, he slipped beneath the log, which drifted now with one end resting on the silt.

The Otter was walking on the pond floor, moving with a swing from his shoulders to his high arched rump. He somersaulted to the surface for a breath; then looped and tumbled through the water. He straightened toward the hole in the dam. The fluent column of his body merged with the strands of the current, and he vanished.

The surface soon was shattered by a splash. The Otter was back. He had climbed up over the dam, beside the gap. He dived in, disappeared through the break, and again returned. A plunge, a joining with the water's sweep, and a swift ride: he had found a game.

The Trout was holding down his top fin, tense with fear. He spread it, and it struck the under side of the log. And yet his belly touched the silt. The log was the pond's last refuge, but the water soon would leave it.

Nothing in the Trout's experience could help him. He only could give himself to the urge that so intensely pressed to have him live. He waited until the Otter had dived and once more swung out through the hold. Leaving the log with a jet of speed, the Trout had reached the gap. A gushing force took hold of him. It hurled him through the break. Too quick for thought he dodged the wreckage of the dam. He leapt to pass the brink of the fall and dropped in the foam beneath. The cascade lightened, slowed, and he found himself in a shallow creek-bed, moving over cobblestones.

His high emotion quickened his choice of route: to the left, through streamers of emerald algae; right, along a slit between the stones; here a turn to miss a piece of driftwood, there to pass a boulder. The air was seldom far above his topmost fin. Sometimes he drew a breath of it, and it seared his gills with dryness. Avoiding one by one the unfamiliar hazards, he progressed.

His lateral lines were jarred by a new sound, a tremendous, heavy pouring. He swam around a bend in the creek and slid across a bar. And there a torrent plunged upon him, water more swift than any he had known. He was in the river, the violent tumult of the Snake.

It nearly overwhelmed him, but he found a milder flow along the bank. A curve there held a pool as in a shell. The pool was covered by a sweeper, a willow with its caught debris. The Trout discovered the refuge, entered it, and spiraled down into the cool green quiet.

Through the afternoon he stayed there, gaining back his poise and fitting his spirit to the strange new shape of his life. Most of the time he hung in the water, motionless, but now and then a ripple ran through his fins, and he chopped his breaths as with excitement. When the first gray wave of dusk washed over the pool, he rose to the top.

He swam along the bank, where small ripples pattered into crevices among the roots. The motion of the water here was light and peaceful like the pond's. Turning out, he met a crisper current, stimulating as the pond had never been. An even greater challenge growled from the center of the river, from grinding rocks that yielded to the push of water irresistibly strong. The Trout began to slant his strokes into the torrent. With a leap he sprang to the very heart of its taut pressure. Enormous weight bore down upon him, but he gripped it, driving his way against it with exultant power.

To fight! To fight the turbulent flow! To sharpen his nerves on its chill; to cut quick arcs through the weaving water; to throw so much force into his muscles' swing that they could drive him upstream, past the rocks beneath, with the whole flood pounding toward him; to fling himself out into the air and see the river under him, a river wider than the pond, wide for his play—all this, the heritage of a trout, he knew now for the first time.

He faced the flood and, sculling exactly at the current's pace, remained above the same stone. Swirling past were many insects, blown in the river. He stayed to take a cricket only, for exhilaration sang in his nerves. He leapt—

But stopped, caught. Talons had stabbed into his flesh, were now locked through it. They were holding him in the center of a splash. A feathered throat was lowering before his eyes. Wings were sweeping down at the sides, enclosing him. The Osprey, forgotten in his conquest of the river, had made its sunset dive.

His torn nerves stung the Trout to action. The claws were powerful that bound him, but his thrashing bent their grip. They almost rigidly resisted, but they did bend. They were a pressure, like the river's force—to fight!

His instinct focused on one urge, to get himself in deeper water. Arching his body downward, he furiously tried to scull from side to side. The hawk's wings beat, attempting to lift his own weight and the Trout's. The wings and the driving paddle of the Trout's tail pulled against each other. So far the Trout had not been able to drag the bird down, but he held him under the surface of the water.

The river was aiding the fish. For the Osprey was growing desperate for a breath. At first the spines on the pads of his feet had pierced the skin of the Trout. They pressed their hold no longer. And the Trout could feel the talons in his flesh release their clutch. The hawk was trying to withdraw them, but their curving points were caught securely.

The bird and fish were swirling downstream. They jolted to a stop, snagged by the willow sweeper. The water's force was beating at them. It poured through the Osprey's feathers. The push of the wings was weakening. They suddenly relaxed, awash in the flow. And the claws were limp.

The Trout had fought another pressure, his exhaustion. When the straining of the talons ceased, he too relaxed. For long enough to gather a little strength, he waited. Then he began an intermittent thrashing. With bursts of effort he tried to jerk himself away. One by one the claws worked out, some slipping loose but more of them tearing through his sides. Finally a twist of his body sent him forward, free.

He turned down under the willow, lower and lower in the dark pool. With his flesh so cut, his lateral lines no longer clearly caught the echo of his motions, thus to guide him. He was careful, therefore, not to swim against the bottom. His chin touched, and he sank upon a stone. The stone was smooth, and soft with slime-coat algae. Soon he had drifted over on his side. His eyes were dull and his fins closed. His consciousness sank lower.

The Trout had been so stimulated by the river that he had ignored his innate caution. But now he was listening again to instinct, not to the water's roar. As he lay and waited for his strength to seep back into him, no creature could have been more passive, none more acquiescent.

The water's cold had numbed the anguish in his severed nerves. It would draw his wounds together. Already it had put in winter sluggishness the parasites that possibly would enter his exposed flesh. And gradually, as he rested, the cold became a tonic to his temper. Cold was as sharpening to him as the warm sun is to insects. By midnight he was swimming experimentally around the bottom. He circled higher. The Osprey was gone from the willow sweeper. The Trout moved out of the pool.

He found a backwash near the bank and held himself on the edge, where a smooth flow passed. Moonlight, falling on the surface, showed that a drift of small debris was swirling by. Drowned insects should be in it. His eye discovered a bright bit up ahead. He swayed forward. His mouth opened, touched it, and it broke with a singing snap. More came floating toward him—little round stars. Some winked out. He let the others pass.

But here was what he liked, a mayfly. Earlier in the day the year's last swarm had left the river for their brief erotic life. Now their delicate spent bodies would be nourishment for the Trout. Many others came his way. After his hunger had been satisfied, he took one more, and shot it out of his mouth for the chance of catching it again, of biting it in two and tossing out and snapping up the pieces.

Now he was not shaped like a smooth wedge, for the cover of one gill was hanging loose, and his sides were ragged. And so his balance in the turns of the water was not perfect. His fins were spread, all needed to aid his sculling tail. Yet the fins were rippling with an easy motion, easy as a creature can be only when it feels that more of living is ahead.

The winter, when a trout is quiet, would be long enough for his wounds to heal, and for his nerves to sharpen. Soon the last migrating Osprey would be gone, but would come back. And otters might be hunting here. The Trout must learn the dangers of this flood, and learn to be wary even while he was exhilarated by it. He would. The wisdom of instinct, as of intelligence, can be disregarded, and it also can be drawn upon.

By the time he would be ready to try his strength once more against the river, the Snake would be a slapping, dodging, driving, wild spring torrent.

Problems for Thought and Writing

I

1. This essay obviously gives us a picture of "nature" as it really is, not as a sentimentalist would have it be. In a sense, then, it may be called "realistic" writing. But it is just as surely imaginative writing. What makes it so? Would you classify it as a sample of "scientific" writing? Why or why not?

2. What is the point of view from which the essay is written? Why would the effect and *authenticity* of the account of the trout's daily habits have been lost if it had been written from any other point of view?

3. How conscious are you of the presence of the *author* as you read this selection? What is the advantage?

4. Read Richard Altick on "Sentimentality" (page 109) and evaluate this essay according to his standards.

II

5. In any good piece of writing, the style should support and enforce the meaning. That is to say, in the broadest sense "style" is not something grafted on to a bare trunk of meaning for purposes of decoration. Its purpose is not to "make pretty," but to "make clear"; it is built in, not added on. In what ways does the author's style here fit the things and events described?

6. Observe that there is hardly a single *transition* or *connective* in the entire essay. Why? How do the structure, length, and arrangement of sentences contribute to vividness?

7. Compare the balance between style and sense in this selection with what you find in Carson's "The Gray Beginnings" (page 526). Do you perceive any similarity of technique? What other qualities do the two essays have in common? Are their points of view the same?

~

2 Comparison and Contrast

What we call the Western tradition is formed by two major influences, Hebraic and Greek, and both these influences are profoundly dualistic in spirit. That is, they divide reality into two parts and set one part off against the other. The Hebrew makes his division on religious and moral grounds. . . . The Greek, on the other hand, divides reality along intellectual lines. . . . So far as we are Westerners, we inherit these dualisms, they are part of us: an irrationally nagging conscience from the Hebrews, an excessively dividing rational mind from the Greeks. Yet the experience of modern culture, in the most diverse fields, makes them less and less acceptable.

In that statement William Barrett (page 350) suggests why comparing and contrasting is one of our persistent intellectual habits. And Matthew Arnold, in "Hebraism and Hellenism" (page 422), develops the same thesis. The Hebrews divided reality into contending forces of good and evil; the Greeks divided it into mind against body. A consequence is that in the ethical and intellectual life of Western man, it is almost instinctive to deal with *both sides* of a question; to ask if something is *good or bad;* to query if an argument is *emotional* or *reasonable.* Either/or, this and that, high and low, past and present, back and forth, light and dark, conscious and subconscious—all these conceptions and habits of thought are second nature to us, and they require that we constantly draw *distinctions, compare and contrast,* set one thing off against another. Joseph Wood Krutch (page 440) sought some unity that would link the "colloid" and the "crystal," but his conclusion was: "the ultimate All is not one thing, but two."

It is, of course, too simple to say that we got all our dualistic habits from the Hebrews and Greeks. But it is true that in some cultures—the Indian, for example—the emphasis is not on the duality of life but on its unity, not on *this and that* but on *this-and-that.* The Hindu sees his universe as basically undifferentiated; the Westerner, with his penchant for scientific analysis, sees his as an arena for opposing and contending forces.

But the philosophical aspects of the problem are not our main concern. We only mention them because, in reading the explanations which follow, the reader should know that the techniques so confidently described rest on a whole lot of philosophic and moral assumptions which may or may not be true. One of those assumptions (derived from Aristotle) is that reality can be divided into *classes*. But many modern physicists, mathematicians, logicians, structural linguists, analytic psychologists, and others would call that description of reality false. That is not to say they would refuse to put things in classes for the sake of convenience, but they would deny any confidence in the necessary *reality* of those classes.

But in its daily work and play the West assumes, with Aristotle, the existence of classes. Doing the same, we can then see comparison and contrast, along with other rhetorical techniques, as an aspect of *class analysis*. In definition we differentiate a term from other members of its class; in classification we analyze and divide a class into its parts; in comparison and contrast we explore for likenesses or unlikenesses between two or more members of the same class. More specifically, we can define comparison as the process of showing likenesses or similarities between two (or more) members of the same class, and contrast as the process of showing the unlikenesses or differences between two (or more) members of the same class. These processes, as you may remember (see "Definition," page 370), are also involved in the process of formal defining, for they are useful ways of fencing in the *differentiae*.

But what is a class and why must comparisons and contrasts be *limited* to *members of the same class?* The first question is complicated and could take us far afield. For convenience let us say that a class is any category larger than the terms to be compared and/or contrasted into which they both fit. But the rule that a true comparison or contrast is limited to *members of the same class* has some importance. Right off we can think of examples where it seems to be violated. Shakespeare wrote:

> Shall I compare thee to a summer's day?
> Thou art more lovely and more temperate . . .

And we commonly hear such statements as "He's sour as a lemon" or "She's sly as a fox." These are not, properly speaking, comparisons at all. They are *analogies*. Men and women fall under the class *man*, not under plants or animals; and Shakespeare's lady is not obviously in the class *time*—or whatever class we decide "day" belongs in. Shakespeare is not *comparing* his lady with "day," he is simply drawing an analogy between *certain aspects* of a summer's day and *certain aspects* of a young lady's beauty. In a comparison (or contrast) we would be forced to think of mosquitoes and thunderstorms and prickly heat—of *all* that a summer's day denotes and connotes. But in an analogy we are selective: we compare only the beauty of the day with the beauty of the girl—a point of likeness between things essentially dissimilar. It is, so to speak, an imaginative, not a logical, comparison.

Common rhetorical vehicles (or "figures of speech") for comparisons, contrasts, and analogies alike are: *similes, metaphors, symbols*. A simile is a comparison or analogy using the words "like" or "as."

It is a beauteous evening, calm and free,
The holy time is quiet as a Nun
Breathless with adoration. . . .

A metaphor differs from a simile only in the fact that the word "as" or "like" is omitted. Instead of saying, "His will was like iron," the metaphor says, "He had an iron will." Metaphor involves a statement that something *is* something else, a narrowing of the identification. Take this statement:

The ship *plowed* the seas.

This could be translated into a simile: "The ship went through the seas *as* a plow goes through the earth." To say the ship actually *plowed* the seas is, strictly speaking, false. But there is no good reason why the verb "to plow" must be confined to the noun that inspired it. Pulling words from one context into another, linking meanings that can be known imaginatively but not logically, catching the sense of the unknown in the prism of the known, vitalizing language by cross-insemination—all these and more are functions of metaphor.

A *symbol* is both simpler and more complex. Essentially it is a concrete object to which some abstract or emotional meaning is attached—as the cross *stands for* Christianity or the flag for one's country. A symbol is the *sign* of a meaning. Thus all words are symbols—and even, in a sense, all the complex structures we can make out of words. But a symbol does not literally compare: a country is not *like* its flag, for example. Relative to metaphors and similes,, symbols are arbitrary—but they also tend to become more fixed in our memory and experience and thus have great power in evoking emotional responses.

Closely related to symbol, yet more than a "figure of speech," is *allegory*. Plato's "Allegory of the Cave" (page 450), for example, is a tale or parable in which all the characters and all the main props are symbols of something else. Thus the cave is our world, the shadows are what mere humans take to be reality, the chains are the human condition, the dark and the light are ignorance and knowledge, the sun is the light of truth, and so on. The sun is not literally *like* truth, but we can fix it with that meaning. By doing so we can relate the concrete and the abstract; we can, if we accept all the symbols, tell a tale and tell the truth at the same time. So reading an allegory is the process of reading a series of connected analogies.

These are the forms comparison, contrast, and analogy usually take. But we should not forget that these three are possible ways of *judging* as well as ways of *ordering*. When Joseph Wood Krutch compares and contrasts the colloid and the crystal (page 440) he has no axe ot grind, no vested interest in one or the other, yet it is instinctive in him—as in most of us—to *try* to resolve the dichotomy, to bring both sides together or to choose one over the other. The facts won't let him pull this off, much as he would like to. But the facts didn't bother G. Lowes Dickinson very much. In "Red-bloods and 'Mollycoddles'" comparison and contrast is clearly used as a kind of pseudo-scientific vehicle for the expression of a prejudice. The balancing scales are there, but they are subtly weighted. Dickinson, obviously, is a "mollycoddle" and likes it, and wants you to like it. In "Hebraism and Hellenism" Arnold clearly wants more Hellenism in the world—though he is fair (and personally committed) to both sides. Santayana, himself an apostate Catholic, is remarkably objective in comparing and contrasting the Protestant and Catholic "leaving" church. The reader himself must choose his side, for it seems as if Santayana has not prejudged in the slightest. But, on rereading, is that quite true? Is there not a subtle indication of the author's taste—though we know he will leave you to yours?

These are all—with the possible exception of Krutch—technically true comparisons and contrasts. But when we come to Plato (page 450) and Donne (page 448)—allegory and analogy—we see value judgments imbedded in the very structure of the writing. "No man is an island," writes Donne. Obviously not, the literal reader might reply. But we interpret the metaphor to read: No man is detached from other men, as an island is from the mainland. Well, so what? Is that just a fact and nothing more? Obviously not. There is the all-important overtone: But a lot of men *think* they can live detached lives. I, John Donne, am telling them that they are grossly mistaken, that they have added up reality all wrong, that they do not know their own nature or that of others. So the analogy is a sermon. And Plato's "Allegory" serves a similar didactic purpose.

Clearly these devices can be potent instruments of persuasion, and it is important to know that that potency can be used dangerously as well as constructively. Robert Gorham Davis, in "Logical Fallacies" (page 77), discussed the dangers of "false analogy." In criticizing representative democracy, Thomas Carlyle asked, in effect: How can you run a ship if you change captains every time you meet a critical situation? The question to ask, as Davis reminds us, is whether there is any real or basic similarity between a ship and a government? Does a captain have the same duties as a prime minister? Is his task more or less complicated? Does he usually face the same urgency in making decisions? Is the purpose of a ship's voyage comparable to that of a political administration? These are just a few of the questions that might be asked. Obviously the analogy is shaky. But take this recent statement by a news commentator: "Getting rid of communism is like getting rid of malaria: you don't get anywhere by swatting mosquitoes, you have to go after their breeding places." By this analogy he was trying to point out that communism is an *idea;* that it takes root where there are conditions of poverty, ignorance, and disease; and that it could not be effectively dealt with by seeking out individual communists or by military force. Is this a true analogy? Our answer must depend, of course, on our knowledge of communism (and of malaria mosquitoes!), but it seems on the face of it both valid and unusually perceptive. Its validity, however, should not blind us to the fact that it is more than a factual statement. It is not just an objective description but a value judgment, a call to action. Whether analogy is a good or evil instrument depends entirely on the honesty and intelligence of the user, and no set of simple rules will tell us how to judge.

In our culture, where divisiveness seems almost as natural as life itself, it is inevitable that we should (officially) prefer good to evil, light to darkness, health to disease, heaven to hell, wealth to poverty, love to hate, ourselves to the enemy. It is not quite so inevitable that we should prefer the country to the city, dogs to cats, wine to beer, sex to literature, or Picasso to Proust. But the habit of drawing such comparisons and making such distinctions is very much with us. For we are dualistic by inheritance, and so long as we accept that legacy, we shall draw comparisons and contrasts and analogues: sometimes because we want things to remain apart and sometimes—let us hope—because we want to bring them together.

~

HEBRAISM AND HELLENISM*   *Matthew Arnold*

The final aim of both Hellenism and Hebraism, as of all great spiritual disciplines, is no doubt the same: man's perfection, or salvation. The very language which they both of them use in schooling us to reach this aim is often identical. Even when their language indicates by variation—sometimes a broad variation, often a but slight and subtle variation—the different courses of thought which are uppermost in each discipline, even then the unity of the final end and aim is still apparent. To employ the actual words of that discipline with which we ourselves are all of us most familiar, and the words of which, therefore, come most home to us, that final end and aim is "that we might be partakers of the divine nature." These are the words of a Hebrew apostle; but of Hellenism and Hebraism alike this is, I say, the aim. When the two are confronted, as they very often are confronted, it is nearly always with what I may call a rhetorical purpose: the speaker's whole design is to exalt and enthrone one of the two, and he uses the other only as a foil and to enable him

* From *Culture and Anarchy* (1869).

the better to give effect to his purpose. Obviously, with us, it is usually Hellenism which is thus reduced to minister to the triumph of Hebraism. There is a sermon on Greece and the Greek spirit by a man never to be mentioned without interest and respect, Frederick Robertson, in which this rhetorical use of Greece and the Greek spirit, and the inadequate exhibition of them necessarily consequent upon this, is almost ludicrous, and would be censurable if it were not to be explained by the exigencies of a sermon. On the other hand, Heinrich Heine and other writers of his sort give us the spectacle of the tables completely turned, and of Hebraism brought in just as a foil and contrast to Hellenism and to make the superiority of Hellenism more manifest. In both these cases there is injustice and misrepresentation. The aim and end of both Hebraism and Hellenism is, as I have said, one and the same, and this aim and end is august and admirable.

Still, they pursue this aim by very different courses. The uppermost idea with Hellenism is to see things as they really are; the uppermost idea with Hebraism is conduct and obedience. Nothing can do away with this ineffaceable difference. The Greek quarrel with the body and its desires is that they hinder right thinking; the Hebrew quarrel with them is that they hinder right acting. "He that keepeth the law, happy is he"; "Blessed is the man that feareth the Eternal, that delighteth greatly in His commandments";—that is the Hebrew notion of felicity; and, pursued with passion and tenacity, this notion would not let the Hebrew rest till, as is well known, he had at last got out of the law a network of prescriptions to enwrap his whole life, to govern every moment of it, every impulse, every action. The Greek notion of felicity, on the other hand, is perfectly conveyed in these words of a great French moralist: "*C'est le bonheur des hommes*"—when? when they abhor that which is evil? no;—when they exercise themselves in the law of the Lord day and night? no;— when they die daily? no;—when they walk about the New Jerusalem with palms in their hands? no;—but when they think aright, when their thought hits: "*quand ils pensent juste.*" At the bottom of both the Greek and the Hebrew notion is the desire, native in man, for reason and the will of God, the feeling after the universal order— in a word, the love of God. But while Hebraism seizes upon certain plain, capital intimations of the universal order, and rivets itself, one may say, with unequaled grandeur of earnestness and intensity on the study and observance of them, the bent of Hellenism is to follow, with flexible activity, the whole play of the universal order, to be apprehensive of missing any part of it, of sacrificing one part to another, to slip away from resting in this or that intimation of it, however capital. An unclouded clearness of mind, an unimpeded play of thought, is what this bent drives at. The governing idea of Hellenism is *spontaneity of consciousness;* that of Hebraism, *strictness of conscience.*

Christianity changed nothing in this essential bent of Hebraism to set doing above knowing. Self-conquest, self-devotion, the following not our own individual will but the will of God, *obedience,* is the fundamental idea of this form, also, of the discipline to which we have attached the general name of Hebraism. Only, as the old law and the network of prescriptions with which it enveloped human life were evidently a motive-power not driving and searching enough to produce the result aimed at—patient continuance in well-doing, self-conquest—Christianity substituted for them boundless devotion to that inspiring and affecting pattern of self-conquest offered by Jesus Christ; and by the new motive-power, of which the essence was this, though the love and admiration of Christian churches have for centuries been employed in verifying, amplifying, and adorning the plain description of it, Christianity, as St. Paul truly says, "establishes the law," and, in the strength of the ampler power which she has thus supplied to fulfil it, has accomplished the miracles, which we all see, of her history.

So long as we do not forget that both Hellenism and Hebraism are profound and admirable manifestations of man's life, tendencies, and powers, and that both of them aim at a like final result, we can hardly insist too strongly on the divergence of line and of operation with which they proceed. It is a divergence so great that it most truly, as the prophet Zechariah says, "has raised up thy sons, O Zion, against thy sons, O Greece!" The difference whether it is by doing or by knowing that we set most store, and the practical consequences which follow from this difference, leave their mark on all the history of our race and of its development. Language may be abundantly quoted from both Hellenism and Hebraism to make it seem that one follows the same current as the other towards the same goal. They are, truly, borne towards the same goal; but the currents which bear them are infinitely different. It is true, Solomon will praise knowing: "Understanding is a well-spring of life unto him that hath it." And in the New Testament, again, Jesus Christ is a "light," and "truth makes us free." It is true, Aristotle will undervalue knowing: "In what concerns virtue," says he, "three things are necessary—knowledge, deliberate will, and perseverance; but whereas the two last are all-important, the first is a matter of little importance." It is true that with the same impatience with which St. James enjoins a man to be not a forgetful hearer but a *doer of the word,* Epictetus exhorts us to *do* what we have demonstrated to ourselves we ought to do; or he taunts us with futility, for being armed at all points to prove that lying is wrong, yet all the time continuing to lie. It is true, Plato, in words which are almost the words of the New Testament or the *Imitation,* calls life a learning to die. But underneath the superficial agreement the fundamental divergence still subsists. The "understanding" of Solomon is "the walking in the way of the commandments"; this is "the way of peace," and it is of this that blessedness comes. In the New Testament, the truth which gives us the peace of God and makes us free is the love of Christ constraining us to crucify, as he did, and with a like purpose of moral regeneration, the flesh with its affections and lusts, and thus establishing, as we have seen, the law. The moral virtues, on the other hand, are with Aristotle but the porch and access to the intellectual, and with these last is blessedness. That partaking of the divine life, which both Hellenism and Hebraism, as we have said, fix as their crowning aim, Plato expressly denies to the man of practical virtue merely, of self-conquest with any other motive than that of perfect intellectual vision. He reserves it for the lover of pure knowledge, of seeing things as they really are—the φιλομαθής.

Both Hellenism and Hebraism arise out of the wants of human nature, and address themselves to satisfying those wants. But their methods are so different, they lay stress on such different points, and call into being by their respective disciplines such different activities, that the face which human nature presents when it passes from the hands of one of them to those of the other is no longer the same. To get rid of one's ignorance, to see things as they are, and by seeing them as they are to see them in their beauty, is the simple and attractive ideal which Hellenism holds out before human nature; and from the simplicity and charm of this ideal, Hellenism, and human life in the hands of Hellenism, is invested with a kind of aërial ease, clearness, and radiancy; they are full of what we call sweetness and light. Difficulties are kept out of view, and the beauty and rationalness of the ideal have all our thoughts. "The best man is he who most tries to perfect himself, and the happiest man is he who most feels that he *is* perfecting himself"—this account of the matter by Socrates, the true Socrates of the *Memorabilia,* has some-

thing so simple, spontaneous, and unsophisticated about it that it
seems to fill us with clearness and hope when we hear it. But there
is a saying which I have heard attributed to Mr. Carlyle about Socrates—a very happy saying, whether it is really Mr. Carlyle's or not—
which excellently marks the essential point in which Hebraism differs
from Hellenism. "Socrates," this saying goes, "is terribly *at ease
in Zion.*" Hebraism—and here is the source of its wonderful strength
—has always been severely pre-occupied with an awful sense of the
impossibility of being at ease in Zion; of the difficulties which oppose
themselves to man's pursuit or attainment of that perfection of which
Socrates talks so hopefully, and, as from this point of view one might
almost say, so glibly. It is all very well to talk of getting rid of one's
ignorance, of seeing things in their reality, seeing them in their
beauty; but how is this to be done when there is something which
thwarts and spoils all our efforts?

This something is *sin;* and the space which sin fills in Hebraism,
as compared with Hellenism, is indeed prodigious. This obstacle
to perfection fills the whole scene, and perfection appears remote
and rising away from earth, in the background. Under the name
of sin, the difficulties of knowing oneself and conquering oneself
which impede man's passage to perfection become, for Hebraism,
a positive, active entity hostile to man, a mysterious power which
I heard Dr. Pusey the other day, in one of his impressive sermons,
compare to a hideous hunchback seated on our shoulders, and which
it is the main business of our lives to hate and oppose. The discipline
of the Old Testament may be summed up as a discipline teaching
us to abhor and flee from sin; the discipline of the New Testament,
as a discipline teaching us to die to it. As Hellenism speaks of thinking clearly, seeing things in their essence and beauty, as a grand and
precious feat for man to achieve, so Hebraism speaks of becoming
conscious of sin, of awakening to a sense of sin, as a feat of this kind.
It is obvious to what wide divergence these differing tendencies, actively followed, must lead. As one passes and repasses from Hellenism to Hebraism, from Plato to St. Paul, one feels inclined to rub
one's eyes and ask oneself whether man is indeed a gentle and simple
being, showing the traces of a noble and divine nature, or an unhappy
chained captive, laboring with groanings that cannot be uttered to
free himself from the body of this death.

Apparently it was the Hellenic conception of human nature which
was unsound, for the world could not live by it. Absolutely to call
it unsound, however, is to fall into the common error of its Hebraizing

enemies; but it was unsound at that particular moment of man's development, it was premature. The indispensable basis of conduct
and self-control, the platform upon which alone the perfection aimed
at by Greece can come into bloom, was not to be reached by our
race so easily; centuries of probation and discipline were needed
to bring us to it. Therefore the bright promise of Hellenism faded,
and Hebraism ruled the world. Then was seen that astonishing
spectacle, so well marked by the often-quoted words of the prophet
Zechariah, when men of all languages and nations took hold of the
skirt of him that was a Jew, saying, "We will go with you, for we have
heard that God is with you." And the Hebraism which thus received
and ruled a world all gone out of the way, and altogether become
unprofitable, was and could not but be the later, the more spiritual,
the more attractive development of Hebraism. It was Christianity;
that is to say, Hebraism aiming at self-conquest and rescue from the
thrall of vile affections, not by obedience to the letter of a law, but
by conformity to the image of a self-sacrificing example. To a world
stricken with moral enervation Christianity offered its spectacle of an
inspired self-sacrifice; to men who refused themselves nothing, it
showed one who refused himself everything;—"my Savior banished
joy!" says George Herbert. When the *alma Venus,* the life-giving
and joy-giving power of nature, so fondly cherished by the pagan
world, could not save her followers from self-dissatisfaction and
ennui, the severe words of the apostle came bracingly and refresh-
ingly: "Let no man deceive you with vain words, for because of these
things cometh the wrath of God upon the children of disobedience."
Through age after age and generation after generation, our race, or
all that part of our race which was most living and progressive, was
baptized into a death; and endeavored, by suffering in the flesh, to
cease from sin. Of this endeavor, the animating labors and afflictions
of early Christianity, the touching asceticism of medieval Christianity,
are the great historical manifestations. Literary monuments of it,
each in its own way incomparable, remain in the *Epistles* of St. Paul,
in St. Augustine's *Confessions,* and in the two original and simplest
books of the *Imitation.*

Of two disciplines laying their main stress, the one on clear intelligence, the other on firm obedience; the one on comprehensively
knowing the grounds of one's duty, the other on diligently practicing
it; the one on taking all possible care (to use Bishop Wilson's words
again) that the light we have be not darkness, the other that according to the best light we have we diligently walk, the priority naturally

belongs to that discipline which braces all man's moral powers and founds for him an indispensable basis of character. And, therefore, it is justly said of the Jewish people, who were charged with setting powerfully forth that side of the divine order to which the words "conscience" and "self-conquest" point, that they were "entrusted with the oracles of God"; as it is justly said of Christianity, which followed Judaïsm and which set forth this side with a much deeper effectiveness and a much wider influence, that the wisdom of the old pagan world was foolishness compared to it. No words of devotion and admiration can be too strong to render thanks to these beneficent forces which have so borne forward humanity in its appointed work of coming to the knowledge and possession of itself; above all, in those great moments when their action was the wholesomest and the most necessary.

But the evolution of these forces, separately and in themselves, is not the whole evolution of humanity, their single history is not the whole history of man; whereas their admirers are always apt to make it stand for the whole history. Hebraism and Hellenism are, neither of them, the *law* of human development, as their admirers are prone to make them; they are, each of them, *contributions* to human development, august contributions, invaluable contributions, and each showing itself to us more august, more invaluable, more preponderant over the other, according to the moment in which we take them and the relation in which we stand to them. The nations of our modern world, children of that immense and salutary movement which broke up the pagan world, inevitably stand to Hellenism in a relation which dwarfs it and to Hebraism in a relation which magnifies it. They are inevitably prone to take Hebraism as the law of human development, and not as simply a contribution to it, however precious. And yet the lesson must perforce be learned, that the human spirit is wider than the most priceless of the forces which bear it onward, and that to the whole development of man Hebraism itself is, like Hellenism, but a contribution.

Perhaps we may help ourselves to see this clearer by an illustration drawn from the treatment of a single great idea which has profoundly engaged the human spirit, and has given it eminent opportunities for showing its nobleness and energy. It surely must be perceived that the idea of immortality, as this idea rises in its generality before the human spirit, is something grander, truer, and more satisfying than it is in the particular forms by which St. Paul, in the famous fifteenth chapter of the *Epistle to the Corinthians,* and Plato, in the *Phaedo,* endeavor to develop and establish it. Surely we cannot but feel that the argumentation with which the Hebrew apostle goes about to expound this great idea is, after all, confused and inconclusive; and that the reasoning, drawn from analogies of likeness and equality, which is employed upon it by the Greek philosopher, is over-subtle and sterile. Above and beyond the inadequate solutions which Hebraism and Hellenism here attempt, extends the immense and august problem itself, and the human spirit which gave birth to it. And this single illustration may suggest to us how the same thing happens in other cases also.

But meanwhile, by alternations of Hebraism and Hellenism, of a man's intellectual and moral impulses, of the effort to see things as they really are and the effort to win peace by self-conquest, the human spirit proceeds; and each of these two forces has its appointed hours of culmination and seasons of rule. As the great movement of Christianity was a triumph of Hebraism and man's moral impulses, so the great movement which goes by the name of the Renascence was an uprising and reinstatement of man's intellectual impulses and of Hellenism. We in England, the devoted children of Protestantism, chiefly know the Renascence by its subordinate and secondary side of the Reformation. The Reformation has been often called a Hebraizing revival, a return to the ardor and sincereness of primitive Christianity. No one, however, can study the development of Protestantism and of Protestant churches without feeling that into the Reformation too—Hebraizing child of the Renascence, and offspring of its fervor rather than its intelligence, as it undoubtedly was —the subtle Hellenic leaven of the Renascence found its way, and that the exact respective parts, in the Reformation, of Hebraism and of Hellenism are not easy to separate. But what we may with truth say is that all which Protestantism was to itself clearly conscious of, all which it succeeded in clearly setting forth in words, had the characters of Hebraism rather than of Hellenism. The Reformation was strong in that it was an earnest return to the Bible and to doing from the heart the will of God as there written. It was weak in that it never consciously grasped or applied the central idea of the Renascence—the Hellenic idea of pursuing, in all lines of activity, the law and science, to use Plato's words, of things as they really are. Whatever direct superiority, therefore, Protestantism had over Catholicism was a moral superiority, a superiority arising out of its greater sincerity and earnestness—at the moment of its apparition, at any rate—in dealing with the heart and conscience. Its pretensions to an intellectual superiority are in general quite illusory. For Hellenism, for the thinking side in man as distinguished from the acting side, the attitude of mind of Protestantism towards the Bible in no respect differs from the attitude of mind of Catholicism towards the Church. The mental habit of him who imagines that Balaam's ass spoke in no respect differs from the mental habit of him who imagines that a Madonna of wood or stone winked; and the one, who says that God's Church makes him believe what he believes, and the other, who says that God's Word makes him believe what he believes, are for the philosopher perfectly alike in not really and truly knowing, when they say "God's Church" and "God's Word," what it is they say or whereof they affirm.

In the sixteenth century, therefore, Hellenism reëntered the world, and again stood in presence of Hebraism—a Hebraism renewed and purged. Now, it has not been enough observed, how, in the seventeenth century, a fate befell Hellenism in some respects analogous to that which befell it at the commencement of our era. The Renascence, that great reawakening of Hellenism, that irresistible return of humanity to nature and to seeing things as they are, which in art, in literature, and in physics produced such splendid fruits, had, like the anterior Hellenism of the pagan world, a side of moral weakness and of relaxation or insensibility of the moral fiber, which in Italy showed itself with the most startling plainness, but which in France, England, and other countries was very apparent too. Again this loss of spiritual balance, this exclusive preponderance given to man's perceiving and knowing side, this unnatural defect of his feeling and acting side, provoked a reaction. Let us trace that reaction where it most nearly concerns us.

Science has now made visible to everybody the great and pregnant elements of difference which lie in race, and in how signal a manner they make the genius and history of an Indo-European people vary from those of a Semitic people. Hellenism is of Indo-European growth, Hebraism is of Semitic growth; and we English, a nation of Indo-European stock, seem to belong naturally to the movement of Hellenism. But nothing more strongly marks the essential unity of man than the affinities we can perceive, in this point or that, between members of one family of peoples and members of another. And no affinity of this kind is more strongly marked than that likeness in the strength and prominence of the moral fiber, which, notwithstanding immense elements of difference, knits in some special sort the genius and history of us English, and our American descendants across the

Atlantic, to the genius and history of the Hebrew people. Puritanism, which has been so great a power in the English nation, and in the strongest part of the English nation, was originally the reaction in the seventeenth century of the conscience and moral sense of our race against the moral indifference and lax rule of conduct which in the sixteenth century came in with the Renascence. It was a reaction of Hebraism against Hellenism; and it powerfully manifested itself, as was natural, in a people with much of what we call a Hebraizing turn, with a signal affinity for the bent which was the master-bent of Hebrew life. Eminently Indo-European by its *humor,* by the power it shows, through this gift, of imaginatively acknowledging the multiform aspects of the problem of life and of thus getting itself unfixed from its own over-certainty, of smiling at its own over-tenacity, our race has yet (and a great part of its strength lies here), in matters of practical life and moral conduct, a strong share of the assuredness, the tenacity, the intensity of the Hebrews. This turn manifested itself in Puritanism, and has had a great part in shaping our history for the last two hundred years. Undoubtedly it checked and changed amongst us that movement of the Renascence which we see producing in the reign of Elizabeth such wonderful fruits. Undoubtedly it stopped the prominent rule and direct development of that order of ideas which we call by the name of Hellenism, and gave the first rank to a different order of ideas. Apparently, too, as we said of the former defeat of Hellenism, if Hellenism was defeated this shows that Hellenism was imperfect and that its ascendancy at that moment would not have been for the world's good.

Yet there is a very important difference between the defeat inflicted on Hellenism by Christianity eighteen hundred years ago, and the check given to the Renascence by Puritanism. The greatness of the difference is well measured by the difference in force, beauty, significance, and usefulness between primitive Christianity and Protestantism. Eighteen hundred years ago it was altogether the hour of Hebraism. Primitive Christianity was legitimately and truly the ascendant force in the world at that time, and the way of mankind's progress lay through its full development. Another hour in man's development began in the fifteenth century, and the main road of his progress then lay for a time through Hellenism. Puritanism was no longer the central current of the world's progress; it was a side stream crossing the central current and checking it. The cross and the check may have been necessary and salutary, but that does not do away with the essential difference between the main stream of man's advance and a cross or side stream. For more than two hundred years the main stream of man's advance has moved towards knowing himself and the world, seeing things as they are, spontaneity of consciousness; the main impulse of a great part, and that the strongest part, of our nation has been towards strictness of conscience. They have made the secondary the principal at the wrong moment, and the principal they have at the wrong moment treated as secondary. This contravention of the natural order has produced, as such contravention always must produce, a certain confusion and false movement, of which we are now beginning to feel, in almost every direction, the inconvenience. In all directions our habitual causes of action seem to be losing efficaciousness, credit, and control, both with others and even with ourselves. Everywhere we see the beginnings of confusion, and we want a clue to some sound order and authority. This we can only get by going back upon the actual instincts and forces which rule our life, seeing them as they really are, connecting them with other instincts and forces, and enlarging our whole view and rule of life.

Problems for Thought and Writing

I

1. What, in your opinion, is Arnold's purpose in drawing this distinction between Hellenism and Hebraism? How would you define the two terms? Is his criticism as applicable to modern American society as it was to English society in 1869?

2. Elaborate upon and deepen Arnold's distinction between "spontaneity of consciousness" and "strictness of conscience" (page 424). Would you, as an individual, rather be "in good taste" or "morally right" in any given situation? Does the determination of this question indicate in any significant ways the bent of your own character?

3. What is the meaning of Thomas Carlyle's statement, "Socrates is terribly *at ease in Zion*" (page 426)?

4. In what sense was the Protestant Reformation a "Hebraizing revival"?

5. Do you think Arnold is on solid ground when he attributes certain attitudes, like those included in Hebraism and Hellenism, to the "genius" of certain races?

6. In what sense does Arnold regard the idea of "sin" as an impediment to perfection?

7. In what ways today is this ancient dualism being destroyed or altered? Read Barrett (page 348) and Jung (page 333) on this subject.

II

8. Identify or define: Dr. Pusey, rhetorical, ludicrous, felicity, Zechariah, Epictetus, regeneration, "Sweetness and Light," entity, salutary, anterior, Semitic, efficaciousness.

9. Compare Arnold's use of *balance* in his sentences with that of Dickinson, below. Is either writer defeated by his stylistic instrument? Is there anything dated about this technique?

~

RED-BLOODS AND ''MOLLYCODDLES''*
G. Lowes Dickinson

I am staying at a pleasant place in New Hampshire. The country is hilly and wooded, like a larger and wilder Surrey, and through it flows what, to an Englishman, seems a large river, the Connecticut. Charming villas are dotted about, well designed and secluded, in pretty gardens. I mention this because, in my experience of America, it is unique. Almost everywhere the houses stare blankly at one another and at the public roads, ugly, unsheltered, and unashamed, as much as to say, "Every one is welcome to see what goes on here. We court publicity. See how we eat, drink, and sleep. Our private life is the property of the American people." It was not, however, to describe the country that I began this letter, but to elaborate a generalisation developed by my host and myself as a kind of self-protection against the gospel of "strenuousness."

We have divided men into Red-bloods and Mollycoddles. "A Red-blood man" is a phrase which explains itself, "Mollycoddle" is its opposite. We have adopted it from a famous speech of Mr. Roosevelt, and redeemed it—perverted it, if you will—to other uses. A few examples will make the notion clear. Shakspere's Henry V is a typical Red-blood; so was Bismarck; so was Palmerston; so is almost any business man. On the other hand, typical Mollycoddles were Socrates, Voltaire, and Shelley. The terms, you will observe, are comprehensive, and the types very broad. Generally speaking, men of action are Red-bloods. Not but what the Mollycoddle may act,

* From *Appearances* by G. Lowes Dickinson. Reprinted by permission of George Allen & Unwin, Ltd., London.

and act efficiently. But, if so, he acts from principle, not from the instinct of action. The Red-blood, on the other hand, acts as the stone falls, and does indiscriminately anything that comes to hand. It is thus that he carries on the business of the world. He steps without reflection into the first place offered him and goes to work like a machine. The ideals and standards of his family, his class, his city, his country, and his age, he swallows as naturally as he swallows food and drink. He is therefore always "in the swim"; and he is bound to "arrive," because he has set before himself the attainable. You will find him everywhere, in all the prominent positions. In a military age he is a soldier, in a commercial age a business man. He hates his enemies, and he may love his friends; but he does not require friends to love. A wife and children he does require, for the instinct to propagate the race is as strong in him as all other instincts. His domestic life, however, is not always happy; for he can seldom understand his wife. This is part of his general incapacity to understand any point of view but his own. He is incapable of an idea and contemptuous of a principle. He is the Samson, the blind force, dearest to Nature of her children. He neither looks back nor looks ahead. He lives in present action. And when he can no longer act, he loses his reason for existence. The Red-blood is happiest if he dies in the prime of life; otherwise, he may easily end with suicide. For he has no inner life; and when the outer life fails, he can only fail with it. The instinct that animated him being dead, he dies too. Nature, who has blown through him, blows elsewhere. His stops are dumb; he is dead wood on the shore.

The Mollycoddle, on the other hand, is all inner life. He may indeed act, as I said, but he acts, so to speak, by accident; just as the Red-blood may reflect, but reflects by accident. The Mollycoddle in action is the Crank: it is he who accomplishes reforms; who abolished slavery, for example, and revolutionised prisons and lunatic asylums. Still, primarily, the Mollycoddle is a critic, not a man of action. He challenges all standards and all facts. If an institution is established, that is a reason why he will not accept it; if an idea is current, that is a reason why he should repudiate it. He questions everything, including life and the universe. And for that reason Nature hates him. On the Red-blood she heaps her favours; she gives him a good digestion, a clear complexion, and sound nerves. But to the Mollycoddle she apportions dyspepsia and black bile. In the universe and in society the Mollycoddle is "out of it" as inevitably as the Red-blood is "in it." At school he is a "smug" or a

"swat," while the Red-blood is captain of the Eleven. At college, he
is an "intellectual," while the Red-blood is in the "best set." In the
world, he courts failure while the Red-blood achieves success. The
Red-blood sees nothing; but the Mollycoddle sees through everything. The Red-blood joins societies; the Mollycoddle is a non-
joiner. Individualist of individualists, he can only stand alone, while
the Red-blood requires the support of a crowd. The Mollycoddle
engenders ideas, and the Red-blood exploits them. The Mollycoddle
discovers, and the Red-blood invents. The whole structure of civilisation rests on foundations laid by Mollycoddles; but all the building
is done by Red-bloods. The Red-blood despises the Mollycoddle;
but, in the long run, he does what the Mollycoddle tells him. The
Mollycoddle also despises the Red-blood, but he cannot do without
him. Each thinks he is master of the other, and, in a sense, each is
right. In his lifetime the Mollycoddle may be the slave of the Red-
blood; but after his death, he is his master, though the Red-blood
know it not.

Nations, like men, may be classified roughly as Red-blood and
Mollycoddle. To the latter class belong clearly the ancient Greeks,
the Italians, the French, and probably the Russians; to the former the
Romans, the Germans, and the English. But the Red-blood nation
par excellence is the American; so that, in comparison with them,
Europe as a whole might almost be called Mollycoddle. This characteristic of Americans is reflected in the predominant physical type—
the great jaw and chin, the huge teeth and predatory mouth; in their
speech, where beauty and distinction are sacrificed to force; in their
need to live and feel and act in masses. To be born a Mollycoddle
in America is to be born to a hard fate. You must either emigrate or
succumb. This, at least, hitherto has been the alternative practised.
Whether a Mollycoddle will ever be produced strong enough to
breathe the American atmosphere and live, is a crucial question for
the future. It is the question whether America will ever be civilised.
For civilisation, you will have perceived, depends on a just balance
of Red-bloods and Mollycoddles. Without the Red-blood there would
be no life at all, no stuff, so to speak, for the Mollycoddle to work
upon; without the Mollycoddle, the stuff would remain shapeless and
chaotic. The Red-blood is the matter, the Mollycoddle the form;
the Red-blood the dough, the Mollycoddle the yeast. On these two
poles turns the orb of human society. And if, at this point, you
choose to say that poles are points and have no dimensions, that
strictly neither the Mollycoddle nor the Red-blood exist, and that

real men contain elements of both mixed in different proportions, I have no quarrel with you except such as one has with the man who states the obvious. I am satisfied to have distinguished the ideal extremes between which the Actual vibrates. The detailed application of the conception I must leave to more patient researchers.

One point more before I close. This Dichotomy, so far as I can see, applies only to man. Woman appears to be a kind of hybrid. Regarded as a creature of instinct, she resembles the Red-blood, and it is to him that she is first attracted. The hero of her youth is the athlete, the soldier, the successful man of business; and this predilection of hers accounts for much of human history, and in particular for the maintenance of the military spirit. On the other hand, as a creature capable of and craving sympathy, she has affinities with the Mollycoddle. This dual nature is the tragedy of her life. The Red-blood awakens her passion, but cannot satisfy it. He wins her by his virility, but cannot retain her by his perception. Hence the fact, noted by a cynic, that it is the Mollycoddle who cuckolds the Red-blood. For the woman, married to the Red-blood, discovers too late that she is to him only a trophy, a scalp. He hangs her up in the hall, and goes about his business. Then comes the Mollycoddle, divining all, possessing and offering all. And if the Red-blood is an American, and the Mollycoddle an European, then the situation is tense indeed. For the American Red-blood despises woman in his heart as profoundly as he respects her in outer observance. He despises her because of the Mollycoddle he divines in her. Therefore he never understands her; and that is why European Mollycoddles carry off American women before the very eyes of the exasperated Red-blood. "Am I not clean?" he cries. "Am I not healthy? Am I not athletic and efficient?" He is, but it does not help him, except with young girls. He may win the body, but he cannot win the soul. Can it be true then that most women would like two husbands, one Red-blood, the other Mollycoddle, one to be father of their children, the other to be the companion of their souls? Women alone can answer; and, for the first time in history, they are beginning to be articulate.

Problems for Thought and Writing

I

1. This essay was included in this volume for two main reasons: (1) it is a good example of comparison and contrast and (2) it is an excellent example of

either/or thinking. Is Dickinson giving us an objective comparison and contrast or is he passing a value judgment, expressing a prejudice? In his own estimation, do you suppose he is a Red-blood or a Mollycoddle? Where is prejudice evident?

2. What are some of the dangers of either/or thinking? Does a comparison and contrast have to resolve itself into such a dualistic form as this essay displays? Why or why not?

3. Dickinson claims that he is presenting two "ideal extremes." Is this a valid procedure? Could not one claim that neither "ideal" really exists? Then how could the "Actual" (page 436) *vibrate* between them? Consult Barrett on dualism (page 348).

4. Dickinson admits that he writes in generalizations, but can this admission exempt him from the charge of oversimplification and exaggeration? What, in this regard, do you think of his attempt to classify nations as Red-blood or Mollycoddle? Is there, for example, a "predominant physical type" of American?

5. Do you think Dickinson knows much about women? Why or why not?

6. Would Admiral Nelson qualify for Dickinson's list of Red-bloods? If so, how do you suppose Dickinson would account for his great success with Lady Hamilton?

7. What does Dickinson mean in writing that women are "beginning to be articulate"? (It should be noted that the essay was written in 1913.)

II

8. What evidence is there that this essay was written by an Englishman in 1913? Study the style as well as the matter.

9. Who is the "mock reader" of this essay? (See Gibson, page 70.)

10. Can you specify any instance or instances where the rhetorical *form* of Dickinson's essay seemed to trick or lure him into making false or ridiculous statements? What about the remark: "Can it be true then that most women would like two husbands, one Red-blood, the other Mollycoddle, one to be the father of their children, the other to be the companion of their souls?"

~

LEAVING CHURCH *   *George Santayana*

Protestant faith does not vanish into the sunlight as Catholic faith does, but leaves a shadowy ghost haunting the night of the soul. Faith, in the two cases, was not faith in the same sense; for the Catholic it was belief in a report or an argument: for the Protestant it was confidence in an allegiance. When Catholics leave the

* Reprinted from *Soliloquies in England and Later Soliloquies,* by George Santayana, published by Charles Scribner's Sons.

church they do so by the south door, into the glare of the market-place, where their eye is at once attracted by the wares displayed in the booths, by the flower-stalls with their bright awnings, by the fountain with its baroque Tritons blowing the spray into the air, and the children laughing and playing round it, by the concourse of townspeople and strangers, and by the soldiers, perhaps, marching past; and if they cast a look back at the church at all, it is only to admire its antique architecture, that crumbling filigree of stone so poetically surviving in its incongruous setting. It is astonishing some-times with what contempt, with what a complete absence of under-standing, unbelievers in Catholic countries look back on their religion. For one cultivated mind that sees in that religion a monument to his racial genius, a heritage of poetry and art almost as precious as the classical heritage, which indeed it incorporated in a hybrid form, there are twenty ignorant radicals who pass it by apologetically, as they might the broken toys or dusty schoolbooks of childhood. Their political animosity, legitimate in itself, blinds their imagination, and renders them even politically foolish; because in their injustice to human nature and to their national history they discredit their own cause, and provoke reaction.

Protestants, on the contrary, leave the church by the north door, into the damp solitude of a green churchyard, amid yews and weep-ing willows and overgrown mounds and fallen illegible gravestones. They feel a terrible chill; the few weedy flowers that may struggle through that long grass do not console them; it was far brighter and warmer and more decent inside. The church—boring as the platitudes and insincerities were which you listened to there for hours—was an edifice, something protective, social, and human; whereas here, in this vague unhomely wilderness, nothing seems to await you but discouragement and melancholy. Better the church than the mad-house. And yet the Protestant can hardly go back, as the Catholic does easily on occasion, out of habit, or fatigue, or disappointment in life, or metaphysical delusion, or the emotional weakness of the death-bed. No, the Protestant is more in earnest, he carries his prob-lem and his religion within him. In his very desolation he will find God. This has often been a cause of wonder to me: the Protestant pious economy is so repressive and morose and the Catholic so charitable and pagan, that I should have expected the Catholic sometimes to sigh a little for his Virgin and his saints, and the Protestant to shout for joy at having got rid of his God. But the trouble is that the poor Protestant can't get rid of his God; for his

idea of God is a vague symbol that stands not essentially, as with
the Catholic, for a particular legendary or theological personage, but
rather for that unfathomable influence which, if it does not make for
righteousness, at least has so far made for existence and has imposed
it upon us; so that go through what doors you will and discard what
dogmas you choose, God will confront you still whichever way you
may turn. In this sense the enlightened Catholic, too, in leaving
the church, has merely rediscovered God, finding him now not in the
church alone, but in the church only as an expression of human fancy,
and in human life itself only as in one out of a myriad forms of
natural existence. But the Protestant is less clear in his gropings,
the atmosphere of his inner man is more charged with vapours, and
it takes longer for the light dubiously to break through; and often
in his wintry day the sun sets without shining.

Problems for Thought and Writing

I

1. As an essay of comparison and contrast, this reflection is obviously highly
compressed, and relies almost exclusively upon *metaphor* and *suggestion*. It
will, of course, suggest different things to different readers, for no two experiences of religion are alike, even within the same sect. It was probably that
fact which caused the author to use such a high degree of suggestion in his
writing. A metaphor, however, is meaningful only if we can determine
what it stands for. Santayana's entire sketch is an extended and varied metaphor that seems to stand only for the title, "Leaving Church," and that is
itself a suggestive phrase, capable of many interpretations. What, precisely,
do you take to be the *subject* of comparison and contrast?

2. What, exactly, do the following antitheses mean to you: (a) the north door
vs. the south door; (b) "belief in a report or an argument" *vs.* "confidence
in an allegiance"; (c) the glaring market-place *vs.* the "damp solitude of a
green churchyard"; (d) God as a "vague symbol" and "unfathomable influence" *vs.* God as a "particular legendary or theological personage"?

3. Does Santayana in any way betray his sympathy for one or the other of the
two faiths he is comparing?

II

4. It is easy, in writing comparison or contrast, to be so rhythm-bound by the
sense of balance, so committed to seeing only *two* sides of an issue, that the
writing obscures rather than illuminates the complexities and nuances of a
subject. Was that the case here with Santayana? Why or why not?

5. Is suggestive writing, designed to evoke in us an associative response, necessarily *obscure*? Can you find any examples of obscurity in this selection?

~

THE COLLOID AND THE CRYSTAL*

Joseph Wood Krutch

The first real snow was soon followed by a second. Over the radio the weatherman talked lengthily about cold masses and warm masses, about what was moving out to sea and what wasn't. Did Benjamin Franklin, I wondered, know what he was starting when it first occurred to him to trace by correspondence the course of storms? From my stationary position the most reasonable explanation seemed to be simply that winter had not quite liked the looks of the landscape as she first made it up. She was changing her sheets.

Another forty-eight hours brought one of those nights ideal for frosting the panes. When I came down to breakfast, two of the windows were almost opaque and the others were etched with graceful, fernlike sprays of ice which looked rather like the impressions left in rocks by some of the antediluvian plants, and they were almost as beautiful as anything which the living can achieve. Nothing else which has never lived looks so much as though it were actually informed with life.

I resisted, I am proud to say, the almost universal impulse to scratch my initials into one of the surfaces. The effect, I knew, would not be an improvement. But so, of course, do those less virtuous than I. That indeed is precisely why they scratch. The impulse to mar and to destroy is as ancient and almost as nearly universal as the impulse to create. The one is an easier way than the other of demonstrating power. Why else should anyone not hungry prefer a dead rabbit to a live one? Not even those horrible Dutch painters of bloody still—or shall we say stilled?—lifs can have really believed that their subjects were more beautiful dead.

Indoors it so happened that a Christmas cactus had chosen this moment to bloom. Its lush blossoms, fuchsia-shaped but pure red rather than magenta, hung at the drooping ends of strange thick stems and outlined themselves in blood against the glistening back-

ground of the frosty pane—jungle flower against frostflower; the warm
beauty that breathes and lives and dies competing with the cold
beauty that burgeons, not because it wants to, but merely because
it is obeying the laws of physics which require that crystals shall take
the shape they have always taken since the world began. The effect
of red flower against white tracery was almost too theatrical, not
quite in good taste perhaps. My eye recoiled in shock and sought
through a clear area of the glass the more normal out-of-doors.

On the snow-capped summit of my bird-feeder a chickadee pecked
at the new-fallen snow and swallowed a few of the flakes which
serve him in lieu of the water he sometimes sadly lacks when there
is nothing except ice too solid to be picked at. A downy woodpecker was hammering at a lump of suet and at the coconut full of
peanut butter. One nuthatch was dining while the mate waited his
—or was it her?—turn. The woodpecker announces the fact that he
is a male by the bright red spot on the back of his neck, but to me,
at least, the sexes of the nuthatch are indistinguishable. I shall never
know whether it is the male or the female who eats first. And that is
a pity. If I knew, I could say, like the Ugly Duchess, "and the moral
of that is . . ."

But I soon realized that at the moment the frosted windows were
what interested me most—especially the fact that there is no other
natural phenomenon in which the lifeless mocks so closely the living.
One might almost think that the frostflower had got the idea from
the leaf and the branch if one did not know how inconceivably more
ancient the first is. No wonder that enthusiastic biologists in the
nineteenth century, anxious to conclude that there was no qualitative
difference between life and chemical processes, tried to believe that
the crystal furnished the link, that its growth was actually the same
as the growth of a living organism. But excusable though the fancy
was, no one, I think, believes anything of the sort today. Protoplasm
is a colloid and the colloids are fundamentally different from the
crystalline substances. Instead of crystallizing they jell, and life in
its simplest known form is a shapeless blob of rebellious jelly rather
than a crystal eternally obeying the most ancient law.

No man ever saw a dinosaur. The last of these giant reptiles was
dead eons before the most dubious halfman surveyed the world about
him. Not even the dinosaurs ever cast their dim eyes upon many of
the still earlier creatures which preceded them. Life changes so
rapidly that its later phases know nothing of those which preceded
them. But the frostflower is older than the dinosaur, older than the

protozoan, older no doubt than the enzyme or the ferment. Yet it is precisely what it has always been. Millions of years before there were any eyes to see it, millions of years before any life existed, it grew in its own special way, crystallized along its preordained lines of cleavage, stretched out its pseudo-branches and pseudo-leaves. It was beautiful before beauty itself existed.

We find it difficult to conceive a world except in terms of purpose, of will, or of intention. At the thought of the something without beginning and presumably without end, of something which is, nevertheless, regular though blind, and organized without any end in view, the mind reels. Constituted as we are it is easier to conceive how the slime floating upon the waters might become in time *homo sapiens* than it is to imagine how so complex a thing as a crystal could have always been and can always remain just what it is— complicated and perfect but without any meaning, even for itself. How can the lifeless even obey a law?

To a mathematical physicist I once confessed somewhat shame-facedly that I had never been able to understand how inanimate nature managed to follow so invariably and so promptly her own laws. If I flip a coin across a table, it will come to rest at a certain point. But before it stops at just that point, many factors must be taken into consideration. There is the question of the strength of the initial impulse, of the exact amount of resistance offered by the friction of that particular table top, and of the density of the air at the moment. It would take a physicist a long time to work out the problem and he could achieve only an approximation at that. Yet presumably the coin will stop exactly where it should. Some very rapid calculations have to be made before it can do so, and they are, presumably, always accurate.

And then, just as I was blushing at what I suppose he must regard as my folly, the mathematician came to my rescue by informing me that Laplace had been puzzled by exactly the same fact. "Nature laughs at the difficulties of integration," he remarked—and by "integration" he meant, of course, the mathematician's word for the process involved when a man solves one of the differential equations to which he has reduced the laws of motion.

When my Christmas cactus blooms so theatrically a few inches in front of the frost-covered pane, it also is obeying laws but obeying them much less rigidly and in a different way. It blooms at about Christmastime because it has got into the habit of doing so, because, one is tempted to say, it wants to. As a matter of fact it was, this

year, not a Christmas cactus but a New Year's cactus, and because of
this unpredictability I would like to call it "he," not "it." His flowers
assume their accustomed shape and take on their accustomed color.
But not as the frostflowers follow their predestined pattern. Like
me, the cactus has a history which stretches back over a long past
full of changes and developments. He has not always been merely
obeying fixed laws. He has resisted and rebelled; he has attempted
novelties, passed through many phases. Like all living things he has
had a will of his own. He has made laws, not merely obeyed them.

"Life," so the platitudinarian is fond of saying, "is strange." But
from our standpoint it is not really so strange as those things which
have no life and yet nevertheless move in their predestined orbits and
"act" though they do not "behave." At the very least one ought to
say that if life is strange there is nothing about it more strange than
the fact that it has its being in a universe so astonishingly shared on
the one hand by "things" and on the other by "creatures," that man
himself is both a "thing" which obeys the laws of chemistry or
physics and a "creature" who to some extent defies them. No other
contrast, certainly not the contrast between the human being and the
animal, or the animal and the plant, or even the spirit and the body,
is so tremendous as this contrast between what lives and what
does not.

To think of the lifeless as merely inert, to make the contrast merely
in terms of a negative, is to miss the real strangeness. Not the shapeless stone which seems to be merely waiting to be acted upon but
the snowflake or the frostflower is the true representative of the lifeless universe as opposed to ours. They represent plainly, as the stone
does not, the fixed and perfect system of organization which includes
the sun and its planets, includes therefore this earth itself, but against
which life has set up its seemingly puny opposition. Order and
obedience are the primary characteristics of that which is not alive.
The snowflake eternally obeys its one and only law: "Be thou six
pointed"; the planets their one and only: "Travel thou in an ellipse."
The astronomer can tell where the North Star will be ten thousand
years hence; the botanist cannot tell where the dandelion will bloom
tomorrow.

Life is rebellious and anarchial, always testing the supposed im-
mutability of the rules which the nonliving changelessly accepts.
Because the snowflake goes on doing as it was told, its story up to
the end of time was finished when it first assumed the form which
it has kept ever since. But the story of every living thing is still in

the telling. It may hope and it may try. Moreover, though it may succeed or fail, it will certainly change. No form of frostflower ever became extinct. Such, if you like, is its glory. But such also is the fact which makes it alien. It may melt but it cannot die.

If I wanted to contemplate what is to me the deepest of all mysteries, I should choose as my object lesson a snowflake under a lens and an amoeba under the microscope. To a detached observer—if one can possibly imagine any observer who *could* be detached when faced with such an ultimate choice—the snowflake would certainly seem the "higher" of the two. Against its intricate glistening perfection one would have to place a shapeless, slightly turbid glob, perpetually oozing out in this direction or that but not suggesting so strongly as the snowflake does, intelligence and plan. Crystal and colloid, the chemist would call them, but what an inconceivable contrast those neutral terms imply! Like the star, the snowflake seems to declare the glory of God, while the promise of the amoeba, given only perhaps to itself, seems only contemptible. But its jelly holds, nevertheless, not only its promise but ours also, while the snowflake represents some achievement which we cannot possibly share. After the passage of billions of years, one can see and be aware of the other, but the relationship can never be reciprocal. Even after these billions of years no aggregate of colloids can be as beautiful as the crystal always was, but it can know, as the crystal cannot, what beauty is.

Even to admire too much or too exclusively the alien kind of beauty is dangerous. Much as I love and am moved by the grand, inanimate forms of nature, I am always shocked and a little frightened by those of her professed lovers to whom landscape is the most important thing, and to whom landscape is merely a matter of forms and colors. If they see or are moved by an animal or flower, it is to them merely a matter of a picturesque completion and their fellow creatures are no more than decorative details. But without some continuous awareness of the two great realms of the inanimate and the animate there can be no love of nature as I understand it, and what is worse, there must be a sort of disloyalty to our cause, to us who are colloid, not crystal. The pantheist who feels the oneness of all living things, I can understand; perhaps indeed he and I are in essential agreement. But the ultimate All is not one thing, but two. And because the alien half is in its way as proud and confident and successful as our half, its fundamental difference may not be disregarded with impunity. Of us and all we stand for, the enemy is not so much death as the not-living, or rather that great system which succeeds without ever having had the need to be alive. The frost-flower is not merely a wonder; it is also a threat and a warning. How admirable, it seems to say, not living can be! What triumphs mere immutable law can achieve!

Some of Charles Peirce's strange speculations about the possibility that "natural law" is not law at all but merely a set of habits fixed more firmly than any habits we know anything about in ourselves or in the animals suggest the possibility that the snowflake was not, after all, always inanimate, that it merely surrendered at some time impossibly remote the life which once achieved its perfect organization. Yet even if we can imagine such a thing to be true, it serves only to warn us all the more strongly against the possibility that what we call the living might in the end succumb also to the seduction of the immutably fixed.

No student of the anthill has ever failed to be astonished either into admiration or horror by what is sometimes called the perfection of its society. Though even the anthill can change its ways, though even ant individuals—ridiculous as the conjunction of the two words may seem—can sometimes make choices, the perfection of the techniques, the regularity of the habits almost suggests the possibility that the insect is on its way back to inanition, that, vast as the difference still is, an anthill crystallizes somewhat as a snowflake does. But not even the anthill, nothing else indeed in the whole known universe is so perfectly planned as one of these same snowflakes. Would, then, the ultimately planned society be, like the anthill, one in which no one makes plans, any more than a snowflake does? From the cradle in which it is not really born to the grave where it is only a little deader than it always was, the ant-citizen follows a plan to the making of which he no longer contributes anything.

Perhaps we men represent the ultimate to which the rebellion, begun so long ago in some amoeba-like jelly, can go. And perhaps the inanimate is beginning the slow process of subduing us again. Certainly the psychologist and the philosopher are tending more and more to think of us as creatures who obey laws rather than as creatures of will and responsibility. We are, they say, "conditioned" by this or by that. Even the greatest heroes are studied on the assumption that they can be "accounted for" by something outside themselves. They are, it is explained, "the product of forces." All the emphasis is placed, not upon that power to resist and rebel which we were once supposed to have, but upon the "influences" which "formed us."

Men are made by society, not society by men. History as well as character "obeys laws." In their view, we crystallize in obedience to some dictate from without instead of moving in conformity with something within.

And so my eye goes questioningly back to the frosted pane. While I slept the graceful pseudo-fronds crept across the glass, assuming, as life itself does, an intricate organization. "Why live," they seem to say, "when we can be beautiful, complicated, and orderly without the uncertainty and effort required of a living thing? Once we were all that was. Perhaps some day we shall be all that is. Why not join us?"

Last summer no clod or no stone would have been heard if it had asked such a question. The hundreds of things which walked and sang, the millions which crawled and twined were all having their day. What was dead seemed to exist only in order that the living might live upon it. The plants were busy turning the inorganic into green life and the animals were busy turning that green into red. When we moved, we walked mostly upon grass. Our pre-eminence was unchallenged.

On this winter day nothing seems so successful as the frostflower. It thrives on the very thing which has driven some of us indoors or underground and which has been fatal to many. It is having now its hour of triumph, as we before had ours. Like the cactus flower itself, I am a hothouse plant. Even my cats gaze dreamily out of the window at a universe which is no longer theirs.

How are we to resist, if resist we can? This house into which I have withdrawn is merely an expedient and it serves only my mere physical existence. What mental or spiritual convictions, what will to maintain to my own kind of existence can I assert? For me it is not enough merely to say, as I do say, that I shall resist the invitation to submerge myself into a crystalline society and to stop planning in order that I may be planned for. Neither is it enough to go further, as I do go, and to insist that the most important thing about a man is not that part of him which is "the product of forces" but that part, however small it may be, which enables him to become something other than what the most accomplished sociologist, working in conjunction with the most accomplished psychologist, could predict that he would be.

I need, so I am told, a faith, something outside myself to which I can be loyal. And with that I agree, in my own way. I am on what I call "our side," and I know, though vaguely, what I think that is. Wordsworth's God had his dwelling in the light of setting suns. But the God who dwells there seems to me most probably the God of the atom, the star, and the crystal. Mine, if I have one, reveals Himself in another class of phenomena. He makes the grass green and the blood red.

Problems for Thought and Writing

I

1. "The impulse to mar and destroy is as ancient and nearly as universal as the impulse to create." From this statement and the whole essay would you say that Krutch would basically agree with Barrett (page 348) and Fromm (page 198) and Jung (page 333) in maintaining that good and evil, creativeness and destructiveness, love and hate are not separate but inseparably linked in man's essential being? The purpose of this essay is to delineate a dualism: but is Krutch's final aim to show a basic division or a basic unity? What does he mean by, "the ultimate All is not one thing, but two"?

2. "It was beautiful before beauty itself existed," writes Krutch of the crystal. What philosophic attitude toward nature and reality does that remark betray? See Definition, page 365.

3. Which seemed more strange when Krutch got through, the plant or the frostflower? How did he achieve this effect?

4. "No other contrast, certainly not the contrast between the human being and the animal, or the animal and the plant, or even the spirit and the body, is so tremendous as this contrast between what lives and what does not." What does "tremendous" mean here? Is Krutch writing as a scientist?

5. "Order and obedience are the primary characteristics of that which is not alive . . ." Can that be regarded as a moral parable as well as a scientific fact? If so, apply it. Could it be applied to "spiritually dead" people and societies?

6. Why for Krutch can there be no love of nature without "some continuous awareness of the two great realms of the inanimate and the animate"? Why does he refer to the "not-living" as the "enemy"? The enemy in what battle?

7. Compare the "ant-citizen" and the "mass man" as described by Chiaromonte page 225), Ortega y Gasset (page 188) and Fromm (page 198).

8. Krutch is worried about the tendency of modern thought to see man as the product of forces rather than a self-willing force himself. In the tentative comparison he draws between this apparent loss of will and the crystal's "order and obedience" is he (1) suggesting a *causal* relationship between two evolutionary processes or (2) criticizing some tendencies in modern thought or (3) just developing a kind of artistic fantasy from the comparison? Who, here, is his "mock reader"? (See Gibson, page 70).

II

9. Is the tone of this essay in any way or place sentimental?

10. Identify or define: protoplasm, protozoan, pseudo, platitudinarian, fronds.

11. Is the *purpose* of this essay to preach a sermon or describe a natural phenomenon?

12. What, in your opinion, are the rhetorical advantages of the comparison–contrast technique?

~

NO MAN IS AN ISLAND*   *John Donne*

Perchance he for whom this bell tolls may be so ill, as that he
knows not it tolls for him; and perchance I may think myself so
much better than I am, as that they who are about me, and see my
state, may have caused it to toll for me, and I know not that. The
church is Catholic, universal, so are all her actions; all that she does
belongs to all. When she baptizes a child, that action concerns me;
for that child is thereby connected to that body which is my head too,
and ingrafted into that body whereof I am a member. And when
she buries a man, that action concerns me: all mankind is of one
author, and is one volume; when one man dies, one chapter is not
torn out of the book, but translated into a better language; and every
chapter must be so translated; God employs several translators; some
pieces are translated by age, some by sickness, some by war, some by
justice; but God's hand is in every translation, and his hand shall
bind up all our scattered leaves again for that library where every
book shall lie open to one another. As therefore the bell that rings
to a sermon calls not upon the preacher only, but upon the congregation to come, so this bell calls us all; but how much more me,
who am brought so near the door by this sickness. There was a
contention as far as a suit (in which both poetry and dignity, religion
and estimation, were mingled), which of the religious orders should
ring to prayers first in the morning; and it was determined, that they
should ring first that rose earliest. If we understand aright the dignity
of this bell that tolls for our evening prayer, we would be glad to
make it ours by rising early, in that application, that it might be ours
as well as his, whose indeed it is. The bell doth toll for him that
thinks it doth; and though it intermit again, yet from that minute
that that occasion wrought upon him, he is united to God. Who
casts not up his eye to the sun when it rises? but who takes off his
eye from a comet when that breaks out? Who bends not his ear to
any bell which upon any occasion rings? but who can remove it from
that bell which is passing a piece of himself out of this world? No
man is an island, entire of itself; every man is a piece of the continent,
a part of the main. If a clod be washed away by the sea, Europe is

* Meditation XVII, from *Devotions upon Emergent Occasions* (1624).

the less, as well as if a promontory were, as well as if a manor of thy friend's or of thine own were: any man's death diminishes me, because I am involved in mankind, and therefore never send to know for whom the bell tolls; it tolls for thee. Neither can we call this a begging of misery, or a borrowing of misery, as though we were not miserable enough of ourselves, but must fetch in more from the next house, in taking upon us the misery of our neighbors. Truly it were an excusable covetousness if we did, for affliction is a treasure, and scarce any man hath enough of it. No man hath affliction enough that is not matured and ripened by it, and made fit for God by that affliction. If a man carry treasure in bullion, or in a wedge of gold, and have none coined into current money, his treasure will not defray him as he travels. Tribulation is treasure in the nature of it, but it is not current money in the use of it, except we get nearer and nearer our home, heaven, by it. Another man may be sick too, and sick to death, and this affliction may lie in his bowels, as gold in a mine, and be of no use to him; but this bell, that tolls me of his affliction, digs out and applies that gold to me: if by this consideration of another's danger I take mine own into contemplation, and so secure myself, by making my recourse to my God, who is our only security.

Problems for Thought and Writing

John Donne (1572-1631), one of the great poets and preachers of the English Renaissance, displays in this famous devotional Meditation not only a magnificent command of prose, but an example of intelligent and imaginative use of *analogy*. As the introduction to this section points out, analogy is unlike a true comparison in that the things compared do not belong to the same class. What is gained by saying, "No man is an island, entire of itself; every man is a piece of the continent, a part of the main," over saying: "All men are physically and spiritually interdependent"? Obviously analogy adds a poetic dimension to a comparison— and quite as obviously it makes a statement not just of fact but of value. Argument by analogy can, as Davis points out (page 81), be employed unscrupulously and illicitly, but employed honestly and sensitively it can be one of the most effective means not only of describing truth but of seeking it out. For the fact is that no men, no societies, no aspects of nature are "islands," uninvolved one in the other; this is one reason why the techniques of comparison, contrast, and especially analogy are important: they are the techniques which bridge islands and link us to the main.

1. Compare the use Donne makes of the "island" analogy and the use made of it by some modern advocates of cooperation and "togetherness" as reported by William H. Whyte (page 217).
2. Would you call the "book" analogy as effective as the "island" one? Why or why not?
3. Translate the "book" analogy, give us its literal meaning. What has been lost by so doing?

4. What is the meaning of "The bell doth toll for him that thinks it doth"?

5. What does Donne mean by saying that "affliction is a treasure"? Would you call that statement a metaphor? Why? Is a metaphor the same thing as an analogy? How is the "treasure" image developed?

6. Can you name any literary or patriotic uses to which the main theme of this Meditation has been put?

7. Write a parody of the Meditation. Keep the style but change the meaning. (See the discussion of parody following "How Love Came to General Grant," page 133.)

~

THE ALLEGORY OF THE CAVE*   *Plato*

Next, said I, here is a parable to illustrate the degrees in which our nature may be enlightened or unenlightened. Imagine the condition of men living in a sort of cavernous chamber underground, with an entrance open to the light and a long passage all down the cave.[1] Here they have been from childhood, chained by the leg and also by the neck, so that they cannot move and can see only what is in front of them, because the chains will not let them turn their heads. At some distance higher up is the light of a fire burning behind them; and between the prisoners and the fire is a track [2] with a parapet built along it, like the screen at a puppet-show, which hides the performers while they show their puppets over the top.

I see, said he.

Now behind this parapet imagine persons carrying along various artificial objects, including figures of men and animals in wood or stone or other materials, which project above the parapet. Naturally, some of these persons will be talking, others silent.[3]

* From *The Republic*, translated by Francis MacDonald Cornford (Oxford: The Clarendon Press, 1941).

[1] The *length* of the "way in" (*eisodos*) to the chamber where the prisoners sit is an essential feature, explaining why no daylight reaches them.

[2] The track crosses the passage into the cave at right angles, and is *above* the parapet built along it.

[3] A modern Plato would compare his Cave to an underground cinema, where the audience watch the play of shadows thrown by the film passing before a light at their backs. The film itself is only an image of "real" things and events in the world outside the cinema. For the film Plato has to substitute the clumsier apparatus of a procession of artificial objects carried on their heads by persons who are merely part of the machinery, providing for the movement of the objects and the sounds whose echo the prisoners hear. The parapet prevents these persons' shadows from being cast on the wall of the Cave.

It is a strange picture, he said, and a strange sort of prisoners.

Like ourselves, I replied; for in the first place prisoners so confined would have seen nothing of themselves or of one another, except the shadows thrown by the fire-light on the wall of the Cave facing them, would they?

Not if all their lives they had been prevented from moving their heads.

And they would have seen as little of the objects carried past.

Of course.

Now, if they could talk to one another, would they not suppose that their words referred only to those passing shadows which they saw? [4]

Necessarily.

And suppose their prison had an echo from the wall facing them? When one of the people crossing behind them spoke, they could only suppose that the sound came from the shadow passing before their eyes.

No doubt.

In every way, then, such prisoners would recognize as reality nothing but the shadows of those artificial objects. [5]

Inevitably.

Now consider what would happen if their release from the chains and the healing of their unwisdom should come about in this way. Suppose one of them set free and forced suddenly to stand up, turn his head, and walk with eyes lifted to the light; all these movements would be painful, and he would be too dazzled to make out the objects whose shadows he had been used to see. What do you think he would say, if someone told him that what he had formerly seen was meaningless illusion, but now, being somewhat nearer to reality and turned towards more real objects, he was getting a truer view? Suppose further that he were shown the various objects being carried by and were made to say, in reply to questions, what each of them was. Would he not be perplexed and believe the objects now shown him to be not so real as what he formerly saw?

Yes, not nearly so real.

And if he were forced to look at the fire-light itself, would not his eyes ache, so that he would try to escape and turn back to the things which he could see distinctly, convinced that they really were clearer than these other objects now being shown to him?

[4] Adam's text and interpretation. The prisoners, having seen nothing but shadows, cannot think their words refer to the objects carried past behind their backs. For them shadows (images) are the only realities.

[5] The state of mind called *eikasia* in the previous chapter.

Yes.

And suppose someone were to drag him away forcibly up the steep and rugged ascent and not let him go until he had hauled him out into the sunlight, would he not suffer pain and vexation at such treatment, and, when he had come out into the light, find his eyes so full of its radiance that he could not see a single one of the things that he was now told were real?

Certainly he would not see them all at once.

He would need, then, to grow accustomed before he could see things in that upper world. At first it would be easiest to make out shadows, and then the images of men and things reflected in water, and later on the things themselves. After that, it would be easier to watch the heavenly bodies and the sky itself by night, looking at the light of the moon and stars rather than the Sun and the Sun's light in the day-time.

Yes, surely.

Last of all, he would be able to look at the Sun and contemplate its nature, not as it appears when reflected in water or any alien medium, but as it is in itself in its own domain.

No doubt.

And now he would begin to draw the conclusion that it is the Sun that produces the seasons and the course of the year and controls everything in the visible world, and moreover is in a way the cause of all that he and his companions used to see.

Clearly he would come at last to that conclusion.

Then if he called to mind his fellow prisoners and what passed for wisdom in his former dwelling-place, he would surely think himself happy in the change and be sorry for them. They may have had a practice of honouring and commending one another, with prizes for the man who had the keenest eye for the passing shadows and the best memory for the order in which they followed or accompanied one another, so that he could make a good guess as to which was going to come next.[6] Would our released prisoner be likely to covet those prizes or to envy the men exalted to honour and power in the Cave? Would he not feel like Homer's Achilles, that he would far sooner "be on earth as a hired servant in the house of a landless

---

[6] The empirical politician, with no philosophic insight, but only a "knack of remembering what usually happens" (*Gorg.* 501 A). He has *eikasia* = conjecture as to what is likely (*eikos*).

man"[7] or endure anything rather than go back to his old beliefs and
live in the old way?

Yes, he would prefer any fate to such a life.

Now imagine what would happen if he went down again to take
his former seat in the Cave. Coming suddenly out of the sunlight,
his eyes would be filled with darkness. He might be required once
more to deliver his opinion on those shadows, in competition with the
prisoners who had never been released, while his eyesight was still
dim and unsteady; and it might take some time to become used to
the darkness. They would laugh at him and say that he had gone up
only to come back with his sight ruined; it was worth no one's while
even to attempt the ascent. If they could lay hands on the man who
was trying to set them free and lead them up, they would kill him.[8]

Yes, they would.

Every feature in this parable, my dear Glaucon, is meant to fit our
earlier analysis. The prison dwelling corresponds to the region revealed to us through the sense of sight, and the fire-light within it to
the power of the Sun. The ascent to see the things in the upper world
you may take as standing for the upward journey of the soul into the
region of the intelligible; then you will be in possession of what I
surmise, since that is what you wish to be told. Heaven knows
whether it is true; but this, at any rate, is how it appears to me. In
the world of knowledge, the last thing to be perceived and only with
great difficulty is the essential Form of Goodness. Once it is perceived, the conclusion must follow that, for all things, this is the cause
of whatever is right and good; in the visible world it gives birth to
light and to the lord of light, while it is itself sovereign in the
intelligible world and the parent of intelligence and truth. Without
having had a vision of this Form no one can act with wisdom, either
in his own life or in matters of state.

Problems for Thought and Writing

This is one of the most famous analogies in our Western tradition, and is one
of the classic illustrations of the nature of reality as Plato (and most of the Western World) historically has conceived it. The basic assumption is that reality is
dualistic, that the world we apprehend with our senses is a "shadow" world, and
that the "real" world is elsewhere—the Platonic world of "ideas." This basic

[7] This verse, being spoken by the ghost of Achilles, suggests that the Cave is
comparable with Hades.
[8] An allusion to the fate of Socrates.

notion—that the worlds of appearance and reality, body and mind, the actual and ideal, are distinct—so permeates much of our everyday thinking that we are scarcely conscious of its dominating influence. It is an assumption at the root of all irony (see page 146); it is involved in most of our judgments of right and wrong, beauty and ugliness; it has made possible in our thought such concepts as perfection, infinity, eternity, the absolute; it has governed the shape of most of our religious and some of our scientific thinking; it has led us to put reason over intuition as the source of truth. Alfred North Whitehead has remarked that 2500 years of Western philosophy is but a series of footnotes to Plato. Today, with the advent of Analytic Psychology (see Jung, page 333) and Structural Linguistics (see introductory discussion in "Definition and Description," page 365) and a growing interest in Oriental thought and religions (see Barrett, page 348), some seekers for truth are beginning to define reality in other ways. But still the dualistic habit is dominant. Joseph Wood Krutch, craving to find unity between the colloid and the crystal, was driven to conclude: "But the ultimate ALL is not one thing, but two."

1. Compare and contrast "reality" as it is described in "The Allegory of the Cave" with "reality" as Jung (page 333) and Barrett (page 348) hope the West will come to regard it.

2. What is an allegory? How does it differ, if at all, from an analogy? How does it differ from a metaphor? A simile?

3. What if someone were to take issue with Plato and say, "But man's life on earth isn't at all like being chained in a cave! A cave is dark all the time, the earth is only dark half the time. We don't have to look just one way, but are free to walk around and explore and leave when we want to. The analogy is purely imaginary and arbitrary and it doesn't fit the true conditions at all!" Is there any way of answering such an objection?

4. Would you say that the Theory of Evolution was an *allegory* about human existence in much the same way Plato's myth of the cave was?

5. "In the world of knowledge, the last thing to be perceived and only with great difficulty is the essential Form of Goodness." Study this statement and the others following until the end of the piece. Do you agree with every step of Plato's logic? Is logic in fact the real instrument of his argument?

6. The last sentence in the "Allegory" could be translated: "Without having had a vision of Absolute Justice no one on this earth can act justly." Do you agree with it in this form? (See this problem as it is dealt with in "Definition and Description," page 365.)

7. What is the meaning of the pain experienced by the man who goes into the light for the first time?

~

3 Classification and Division

Two friends met after a long absence. Their conversation went like this:

MIKE: How are you, Joe?
JOE: Lousy. I think I'm getting ulcers.
MIKE: What's wrong?
JOE: My job is driving me nuts!
MIKE: What do you do?
JOE: Work in a fruit store—in the *lemon* department. All day I stand in front of three bins and sort lemons. I put the big lemons in one bin, the little lemons in another bin, and the rotten lemons in a third bin.
MIKE: Sounds like a snap to me.
JOE: Snap, hell! All day: decisions, decisions, decisions!

Joe's nervous complaints, reminiscent of those of the business executive, are at least partly attributable to his distaste for problems of classification. Making decisions can, of course, prove more taxing for some people than for others; but those of us who one morning have had to face anything from a pile of undifferentiated lemons to a desk littered with a month's accumulation of back work have known the particular kind of decision involved here—analyzing the raw materials of a problem and deciding how those materials should be divided and sorted.

Classification, like comparison and contrast, is a form of *class analysis*. It involves one of two procedures: (1) the division of a whole, according to some reasonable scheme, into the classes that make it up, or (2) the placing of a subject into the class and ultimately into the whole of which it is a part. Joe, facing his lemons, was engaged in the first process—commonly called "division." A zoologist trying to identify a new specimen might illustrate the second: he first places it in the largest and most obvious category to which it belongs, the phylum; then, in descending order, he identifies its class, order, family, genus, species, and—if possible—variety. By so classifying the specimen he has identified it in relation to the world in which it exists. The first process classifies upward, so to speak, and the second downward.

But both processes finally assume, if we accept ancient premises, that reality is orderly, that it can be classified. Of course Joe's problem above was purely arbitrary, and man-made. Assume instead, though, that he was not Joe but Socrates, and assume that he was trying to classify not lemons,

455

but all the forms of political government. In Plato's *Republic* we get one
(rather unsuccessful) result of this effort. Political states can be classified
in hierarchical order, from highest to lowest (or *vice versa*), and it can be
demonstrated how one derives from the next. Furthermore, since states
are like men (being made of up men), it is possible to find an equivalence
in human character for each form of political organization. The result,
much oversimplified, may be summed up as follows:

FORM	DESCRIPTION	HUMAN EQUIVALENT
(1) Aristocracy	Government by the best	The just and good man
(2) Timarchy	Government by the honorable	The proud man
(3) Oligarchy	Government by the rich	The covetous man
(4) Democracy	Government by the people	The free (undisciplined) man
(5) Tyranny	Government by one man	The despotic man

If a modern worker, equipped with electronic calculator and tabulated
statistical data, went to work on a similar problem in the modern world,
he could indeed produce a result: he could demonstrate that certain kinds
of government exist and that they have certain characteristics. But would
he feel justified in ranking them in order of importance and in comparing
them with human characteristics? Not likely, if he prided himself on his
scientific impartiality and "objectivity." Was Plato, then, not being "objective"? In his own terms, he was. He assumed he was describing "reality," not just as it was by accident at a moment of human history but as
it was in nature immutably. All things—governments, animals, people,
social classes, plants—had a certain rank in a vertical hierarchy of value.
Likewise all things could be compared and contrasted horizontally: the
philosopher-king was to the state what the head was to the body, what
man was to the animals. This was the way it was in *nature*, in the very
structure of reality. So classification in the hands of men like Plato (and
Aristotle even more), who could make sweeping assumptions about both
the *description* and the *valuation* of reality, was a very different thing from
what it normally is in the hands of a modern classifier, running facts, statistics, and other "tabulated data" through the secular intelligence of an
IBM machine.

The problem of knowing whether classifications are "real"—*i.e.*, really in
nature—or only arbitrary is essentially the problem, raised in "Definition
and Description," (page 365), of "nominalism" *vs.* "realism." This ancient
problem is still with us, though increasingly we are formulating it in different terms. But in taxonomy—a branch of botany and zoology dealing
with classification—one of the most basic metaphysical questions is still un-
answered: are the zoologist's and botanist's classifications really *in nature*
or are they only *man-given* distinctions?

But in ordinary work-a-day life we are not normally concerned with these ultimate questions. The chemist knows, for example, that the classification of elements into the Periodic Table is not, strictly speaking, the way things *are*. It is a description of reality as it *appears*—and is thus very useful—but he now knows that the elements, rather than being immutably distinct, are all composed of energy in various combinations and can, under certain conditions, alter their very identity. Likewise the librarian, working with that brilliant invention known as the Dewey Decimal System of classification, is not concerned whether or not a book has been previously registered in some ultimate card-catalogue. He isn't interested in the "truth" of the classification; he only cares that it "works." Nor does the modern sociologist—in describing and distinguishing the qualities of our upper class, upper-middle class, middle-middle, lower-middle, upper-lower, and lower class—care about the *metaphysical* validity of his results. The question, he doubtless would say, is irrelevant and silly.

Nonetheless we should be aware that classifying is often more than an objective, disinterested appraisal of facts. In classifying books we are not likely to find evidence of prejudice or partiality—unless we met the unlikely case of some wild librarian putting *The Philosophy of Nietzsche* under "Comedy and Humor" or the Bible under "Pornography." But usually the classifier, especially if his materials deal with human beings or are not easily measured, passes a value judgment in the very act of classifying. Russell Lynes, for example, in "Highbrow, Lowbrow, Middlebrow" (page 477), gives the name "middlebrow" to a segment of our population and then includes in it "the cultural do-gooders." The diction itself weights the case, and it is unlikely that many of Lynes's readers would cherish the category "middlebrow" for themselves. Likewise with Edmund Wilson's classification of American presidents. He puts Eisenhower in a group which "neither knows about professional politics nor understands the problems of government . . ." He puts Truman in a group of which the type "is a product of his party machine, in which he has had his whole existence and which circumscribes his whole ambition." These classifications may be true or false: the point is, they are *value judgments* as well as divisions of a whole. And in classifying "four kinds of thinking," to take another example, James Harvey Robinson clearly directs us to see that "rationalizing" is an inferior use to which we often put our brains.

It is quite as valid, of course, to classify things into bad-better-best as it is into this-this-this. But like all devices for shaping meaning, classification can be employed for unscrupulous as well as honest purposes. There is no easy test. The best one, as always, is an active intelligence and imagination, a respect for evidence, and a knowledge of logic.

~

GIVING THINGS NAMES*   *S. I. Hayakawa*

The figure below shows eight objects, let us say animals, four large and four small, a different four with round heads and another four with square heads, and still another four with curly tails and another four with straight tails. These animals, let us say, are scampering about your village, but since at first they are of no importance to you, you ignore them. You do not even give them a name.

One day, however, you discover that the little ones eat up your grain, while the big ones do not. A differentiation sets itself up, and, abstracting the common characteristics of A, B, C, and D, you decide to call these gogo; E, F, G, and H you decide to call gigi. You chase away the gogo, but leave the gigi alone. Your neighbor, however, has had a different experience; he finds that those with square heads bite, while those with round heads do not. Abstracting the common characteristics of B, D, F, and H, he calls them daba, and A, C, E, and G he calls dobo. Still another neighbor discovers, on the other hand, that those with curly tails kill snakes, while those with straight tails do not. He differentiates them, abstracting still another set of common characteristics: A, B, E, and F are busa, while C, D, G, and H are busana.

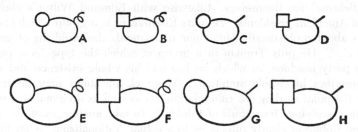

Now imagine that the three of you are together when E runs by. You say, "There goes the gigi"; your first neighbor says, "There goes the dobo"; your other neighbor says, "There goes the busa." Here immediately a great controversy arises. What is it really, a gigi, a dobo, or a busa? What is its right name? You are quarreling violently when along comes a fourth person from another village who calls it a muglock, an edible animal, as opposed to uglock, an inedible animal—which doesn't help matters a bit.

* From *Language In Thought and Action* by S. I. Hayakawa, copyright, 1941, 1949, by Harcourt, Brace and Company, Inc.

Of course, the question, "What is it really? What is its right name?" is a nonsense question. By a nonsense question is meant one that is not capable of being answered. Things can have "right names" only if there is a necessary connection between symbols and things symbolized, and we have seen that there is not. That is to say, in the light of your interest in protecting your grain, it may be necessary for you to distinguish the animal E as a gigi; your neighbor, who doesn't like to be bitten, finds it practical to distinguish it as a dobo; your other neighbor, who likes to see snakes killed, distinguishes it as a busa. What we call things and where we draw the line between one class of things and another depend upon the interests we have and the purposes of the classification. For example, animals are classified in one way by the meat industry, in a different way by the leather industry, in another different way by the fur industry, and in a still different way by the biologist. None of these classifications is any more final than any of the others; each of them is useful for its purpose.

This holds, of course, regarding everything we perceive. A table "is" a table to us, because we can understand its relationship to our conduct and interests; we eat at it, work on it, lay things on it. But to a person living in a culture where no tables are used, it may be a very big stool, a small platform, or a meaningless structure. If our culture and upbringing were different, that is to say, our world would not even look the same to us.

Many of us, for example, cannot distinguish between pickerel, pike, salmon, smelts, perch, croppies, halibut, and mackerel; we say that they are "just fish, and I don't like fish." To a seafood connoisseur, however, these distinctions are real, since they mean the difference to him between one kind of good meal, a very different kind of good meal, or a poor meal. To a zoologist, even finer distinctions become of great importance, since he has other and more general ends in view. When we hear the statement then, "This fish is a specimen of the pompano, Trachinotus carolinus," we accept this as being "true," even if we don't care, not because that is its "right name," but because that is how it is classified in the most complete and most general system of classification which people most deeply interested in fish have evolved.

When we name something, then, we are classifying. The individual object or event we are naming, of course, has no name and belongs to no class until we put it in one. To illustrate again, suppose that we were to give the extensional meaning of the word "Korean." We would have to point to all "Koreans" living at a particular moment and say, "The word 'Korean' denotes at the present moment these persons: A_1, A_2, A_3, . . . A_n." Now, let us say, a child, whom we shall designate as Z, is born among these "Koreans." The extensional meaning of the word "Korean," determined prior to the existence of Z, does not include Z. Z is a new individual belonging to no classification, since all classifications were made without taking Z into account. Why, then, is Z also a "Korean"? Because we say so. And, saying so—fixing the classification—we have determined to a considerable extent future attitudes toward Z. For example, Z will always have certain rights in Korea; he will always be regarded in other nations as an "alien" and will be subject to laws applicable to "aliens."

In matters of "race" and "nationality," the way in which classifications work is especially apparent. For example, the present writer is by "race" a "Japanese," by "nationality" a "Canadian," but, his friends say, "essentially" an "American," since he thinks, talks, behaves, and dresses much like other Americans. Because he is "Japanese," he is excluded by law from becoming a citizen of the United States; because he is "Canadian," he has certain rights in all parts of the British Empire; because he is "American," he gets along with his friends and teaches in an American institution of higher learning without any noticeable special difficulties. Are these classifications "real"? Of course they are, and the effect that each of them has upon what he may and may not do constitutes their "reality."

There was, again, the story some years ago of the immigrant baby whose parents were "Czechs" and eligible to enter the United States by quota. The child, however, because it was born on what happened to be a "British" ship, was a "British subject." The quota for Britishers was full for that year, with the result that the newborn infant was regarded by immigration authorities as "not admissible to the United States." How they straightened out this matter, the writer does not know. The reader can multiply instances of this kind at will. When, to take another example, is a person a "Negro"? By the definition accepted in the United States, any person with even a small amount of "Negro blood"—that is, whose parents or ancestors were classified as "Negroes"—is a "Negro." It would be exactly as justifiable to say that any person with even a small amount of "white blood" is "white." Why do they say one rather than the other? Because the former system of classification suits the convenience of those making the classification.

There are few complexities about classifications at the level of dogs and cats, knives and forks, cigarettes and candy, but when it comes to classifications at high levels of abstraction, for example, those describing conduct, social institutions, philosophical and moral problems, serious difficulties occur. When one person kills another, is it an act of murder, an act of temporary insanity, an act of homicide, an accident, or an act of heroism? As soon as the process of classification is completed, our attitudes and our conduct are to a considerable degree determined. We hang the murderer, we lock up the insane man, we free the victim of circumstances, we pin a medal on the hero.

Problems for Thought and Writing

I

1. Why does Hayakawa in his illustration call "What is its right name?" a nonsense question?
2. Is the classification of races and nationalities by the U. S. immigration authorities a case of rationalization? (See J. H. Robinson, "Four Kinds of Thinking," page 461.)
3. How does a classification differ from a definition? Are we not in both cases "giving things names"?
4. As an exercise, classify the essays in this section according to some standard of division—according to style, subject matter, human interest, intelligence, etc. Do so with any other group of essays in either part of the volume.

II

5. Compare the number of relatively simple and complex sentences in this selection. Hayakawa has for years been active in various semantic groups dedicated to the simplification and clarification of English usage. Is his style a model of what you would call "lucidity"?
6. Would you characterize Hayakawa's approach as a rigorously "scientific" one? Why or why not?

~

FOUR KINDS OF THINKING*

James Harvey Robinson

We do not think enough about thinking, and much of our confusion is the result of current illusions in regard to it. Let us forget for the moment any impressions we may have derived from the philosophers, and see what seems to happen in ourselves. The first thing that we notice is that our thought moves with such incredible rapidity that

*Reprinted from *The Mind in the Making*, by James Harvey Robinson, by permission of Harper & Brothers. Copyright 1921, by Harper & Brothers; copyright, 1949, by Bankers Trust Co.

it is almost impossible to arrest any specimen of it long enough to
have a look at it. When we are offered a penny for our thoughts we
always find that we have recently had so many things in mind that
we can easily make a selection which will not compromise us too
nakedly. On inspection we shall find that even if we are not downright ashamed of a great part of our spontaneous thinking it is far
too intimate, personal, ignoble or trivial to permit us to reveal more
than a small part of it. I believe this must be true of everyone. We
do not, of course, know what goes on in other people's heads. They
tell us very little and we tell them very little. The spigot of speech,
rarely fully opened, could never emit more than driblets of the ever
renewed hogshead of thought—*noch grösser wie's Heidelberger Fass.*
We find it hard to believe that other people's thoughts are as silly as
our own, but they probably are.

We all appear to ourselves to be thinking all the time during our
waking hours, and most of us are aware that we go on thinking
while we are asleep, even more foolishly than when awake. When
uninterrupted by some practical issue we are engaged in what is now
known as a *reverie.* This is our spontaneous and favorite kind of
thinking. We allow our ideas to take their own course and this
course is determined by our hopes and fears, our spontaneous desires,
their fulfillment or frustration; by our likes and dislikes, our loves
and hates and resentments. There is nothing else anything like so
interesting to ourselves as ourselves. All thought that is not more
or less laboriously controlled and directed will inevitably circle about
the beloved Ego. It is amusing and pathetic to observe this tendency
in ourselves and in others. We learn politely and generously to
overlook this truth, but if we dare to think of it, it blazes forth like
the noontide sun.

The reverie or "free association of ideas" has of late become the
subject of scientific research. While investigators are not yet agreed
on the results, or at least on the proper interpretation to be given to
them, there can be no doubt that our reveries form the chief index
to our fundamental character. They are a reflection of our nature
as modified by often hidden and forgotten experiences. We need
not go into the matter further here, for it is only necessary to observe
that the reverie is at all times a potent and in many cases an omnipotent rival to every other kind of thinking. It doubtless influences
all our speculations in its persistent tendency to self-magnification
and self-justification, which are its chief preoccupations, but it is the
last thing to make directly or indirectly for honest increase of knowl-

edge.[1] Philosophers usually talk as if such thinking did not exist or were in some way negligible. This is what makes their speculations so unreal and often worthless.

The reverie, as any of us can see for himself, is frequently broken and interrupted by the necessity of a second kind of thinking. We have to make practical decisions. Shall we write a letter or no? Shall we take the subway or a bus? Shall we have dinner at seven or half-past? Shall we buy U. S. Rubber or a Liberty Bond? Decisions are easily distinguishable from the free flow of the reverie. Sometimes they demand a good deal of careful pondering and the recollection of pertinent facts; often, however, they are made impulsively. They are a more difficult and laborious thing than the reverie, and we resent having to "make up our mind" when we are tired, or absorbed in a congenial reverie. Weighing a decision, it should be noted, does not necessarily add anything to our knowledge, although we may, of course, seek further information before making it.

A third kind of thinking is stimulated when any one questions our belief and opinions. We sometimes find ourselves changing our minds without any resistance or heavy emotion, but if we are told that we are wrong we resent the imputation and harden our hearts. We are incredibly heedless in the formation of our beliefs, but find ourselves filled with an illicit passion for them when anyone proposes to rob us of their companionship. It is obviously not the ideas themselves that are dear to us, but our self-esteem, which is threatened. We are by nature stubbornly pledged to defend our own from attack, whether it be our person, our family, our property, or our opinion. A United States Senator once remarked to a friend of mine that God Almighty could not make him change his mind on our Latin-America policy. We may surrender, but rarely confess ourselves vanquished. In the intellectual world at least peace is without victory.

Few of us take the pains to study the origin of our cherished

---

[1] The poet-clergyman, John Donne, who lived in the time of James I, has given a beautifully honest picture of the doings of a saint's mind: "I throw myself down in my chamber and call in and invite God and His angels thither, and when they are there I neglect God and His angels for the noise of a fly, for the rattling of a coach, for the whining of a door. I talk on in the same posture of praying, eyes lifted up, knees bowed down, as though I prayed to God, and if God or His angels should ask me when I thought last of God in that prayer I cannot tell. Sometimes I find that I had forgot what I was about, but when I began to forget it I cannot tell. A memory of yesterday's pleasures, a fear of tomorrow's dangers, a straw under my knee, a noise in mine ear, a light in mine eye, an anything, a nothing, a fancy, a chimera in my brain troubles me in my prayer."—Quoted by Robert Lynd, *The Art of Letters*, pp. 46-47.

convictions; indeed, we have a natural repugnance to so doing. We like to continue to believe what we have been accustomed to accept as true, and the resentment aroused when doubt is cast upon any of our assumptions leads us to seek every manner of excuse for clinging to them. *The result is that most of our so-called reasoning consists in finding arguments for going on believing as we already do.*

I remember years ago attending a public dinner to which the Governor of the state was bidden. The chairman explained that His Excellency could not be present for certain "good" reasons; what the "real" reasons were the presiding officer said he would leave us to conjecture. This distinction between "good" and "real" reasons is one of the most clarifying and essential in the whole realm of thought. We can readily give what seem to us "good" reasons for being a Catholic or a Mason, a Republican or a Democrat, an adherent or opponent of the League of Nations. But the "real" reasons are usually on a quite different plane. Of course the importance of this distinction is popularly, if somewhat obscurely, recognized. The Baptist missionary is ready enough to see that the Buddhist is not such because his doctrines would bear careful inspection, but because he happened to be born in a Buddhist family in Tokyo. But it would be treason to his faith to acknowledge that his own partiality for certain doctrines is due to the fact that his mother was a member of the First Baptist church of Oak Ridge. A savage can give all sorts of reasons for his belief that it is dangerous to step on a man's shadow, and a newspaper editor can advance plenty of arguments against the Bolsheviki. But neither of them may realize why he happens to be defending his particular opinion.

The "real" reasons for our beliefs are concealed from ourselves as well as from others. As we grow up we simply adopt the ideas presented to us in regard to such matters as religion, family relations, property, business, our country, and the state. We unconsciously absorb them from our environment. They are persistently whispered in our ear by the group in which we happen to live. Moreover, as Mr. Trotter has pointed out, these judgments, being the product of suggestion and not of reasoning, have the quality of perfect obviousness, so that to question them

. . . is to the believer to carry skepticism to an insane degree, and will be met by contempt, disapproval, or condemnation, according to the nature of the belief in question. When, therefore, we find ourselves entertaining an opinion about the basis of which there is a quality of feeling which tells us that to inquire into it would be absurd, obviously unnecessary, unprofitable, undesirable, bad form, or wicked, we may know that that opinion is a non-rational one, and probably, therefore, founded upon inadequate evidence.[2]

Opinions, on the other hand, which are the result of experience or of honest reasoning do not have this quality of "primary certitude." I remember when as a youth I heard a group of business men discussing the question of the immortality of the soul, I was outraged by the sentiment of doubt expressed by one of the party. As I look back now I see that I had at the time no interest in the matter, and certainly no least argument to urge in favor of the belief in which I had been reared. But neither my personal indifference to the issue, nor the fact that I had previously given it no attention, served to prevent an angry resentment when I heard *my* ideas questioned.

This spontaneous and loyal support of our preconceptions—this process of finding "good" reasons to justify our routine beliefs—is known to modern psychologists as "rationalizing"—clearly only a new name for a very ancient thing. Our "good" reasons ordinarily have no value in promoting honest enlightenment, because, no matter how solemnly they may be marshaled, they are at bottom the result of personal preference or prejudice, and not of an honest desire to seek or accept new knowledge.

In our reveries we are frequently engaged in self-justification, for we cannot bear to think ourselves wrong, and yet have constant illustrations of our weaknesses and mistakes. So we spend much time finding fault with circumstances and the conduct of others, and shifting on to them with great ingenuity the onus of our own failures and disappointments. *Rationalizing is the self-exculpation which occurs when we feel ourselves, or our group, accused of misapprehension or error.*

The little word *my* is the most important one in all human affairs, and properly to reckon with it is the beginning of wisdom. It has the same force whether it is *my* dinner, *my* dog, and *my* house, or *my* faith, *my* country, and *my* God. We not only resent the imputation that our watch is wrong, or our car shabby, but that our conception of the canals of Mars, of the pronunciation of "Epictetus," of the medicinal value of salicine, or the date of Sargon I, is subject to revision.

Philosophers, scholars, and men of science exhibit a common sensitiveness in all decisions in which their *amour propre* is involved.

[2] *Instincts of the Herd*, p. 44.

Thousands of argumentative works have been written to vent a grudge. However stately their reasoning, it may be nothing but rationalizing, stimulated by the most commonplace of all motives. A history of philosophy and theology could be written in terms of grouches, wounded pride, and aversions, and it would be far more instructive than the usual treatments of these themes. Sometimes, under Providence, the lowly impulse of resentment leads to great achievements. Milton wrote his treatise on divorce as a result of his troubles with his seventeen-year-old wife, and when he was accused of being the leading spirit in a new sect, the Divorcers, he wrote his noble *Areopagitica* to prove his right to say what he thought fit, and incidentally to establish the advantage of a free press in the promotion of Truth.

All mankind, high and low, thinks in all the ways which have been described. The reverie goes on all the time not only in the mind of the mill hand and the Broadway flapper, but equally in weighty judges and godly bishops. It has gone on in all the philosophers, scientists, poets, and theologians that have ever lived. Aristotle's most abstruse speculations were doubtless tempered by highly irrelevant reflections. He is reported to have had very thin legs and small eyes, for which he doubtless had to find excuses, and he was wont to indulge in very conspicuous dress and rings and was accustomed to arrange his hair carefully.[3] Diogenes the Cynic exhibited the impudence of a touchy soul. His tub was his distinction. Tennyson in beginning his "Maud" could not forget his chagrin over losing his patrimony years before as the result of an unhappy investment in the Patent Decorative Carving Company. These facts are not recalled here as a gratuitous disparagement of the truly great, but to insure a full realization of the tremendous competition which all really exacting thought has to face, even in the minds of the most highly endowed mortals.

And now the astonishing and perturbing suspicion emerges that perhaps almost all that had passed for social science, political economy, politics, and ethics in the past may be brushed aside by future generations as mainly rationalizing. John Dewey has already reached this conclusion in regard to philosophy.[4] Veblen[5] and other writers have revealed the various unperceived presuppositions of the traditional political economy, and now comes an Italian sociologist, Vilfredo

[3] Diogenes Laertius, book v.
[4] *Reconstruction in Philosophy.*
[5] *The Place of Science in Modern Civilization.*

Pareto, who, in his huge treatise on general sociology, devotes hundreds of pages to substantiating a similar thesis affecting all the social sciences.[6] This conclusion may be ranked by students of a hundred years hence as one of the several great discoveries of our age. It is by no means fully worked out, and it is so opposed to nature that it will be very slowly accepted by the great mass of those who consider themselves thoughtful. As a historical student I am personally fully reconciled to this newer view. Indeed, it seems to me inevitable that just as the various sciences of nature were, before the opening of the seventeenth century, largely masses of rationalizations to suit the religious sentiments of the period, so the social sciences have continued even to our own day to be rationalizations of uncritically accepted beliefs and customs.

It will become apparent as we proceed that the fact that an idea is ancient and that it has been widely received is no argument in its favor, but should immediately suggest the necessity of carefully testing it as a probable instance of rationalization.

This brings us to another kind of thought which can fairly easily be distinguished from the three kinds described above. It has not the usual qualities of the reverie, for it does not hover about our personal complacencies and humiliations. It is not made up of the homely decisions forced upon us by everyday needs, when we review our little stock of existing information, consult our conventional preferences and obligations, and make a choice of action. It is not the defense of our own cherished beliefs and prejudices just because they are our own—mere plausible excuses for remaining of the same mind. On the contrary, it is that peculiar species of thought which leads us to *change* our mind.

It is this kind of thought that has raised man from his pristine, subsavage ignorance and squalor to the degree of knowledge and comfort which he now possesses. On his capacity to continue and greatly extend this kind of thinking depends his chance of groping his way out of the plight in which the most civilized peoples of the world now find themselves. In the past this type of thinking has been called Reason. But so many misapprehensions have grown up around the word that some of us have become suspicious of it. I

[6] *Traité de Sociologie Générale, passim.* The author's term *"derivations"* seems to be his precise way of expressing what we have called the "good" reasons, and his *"residus"* correspond to the "real" reasons. He well says, *"L'homme éprouve le besoin de raisonner, et en outre d'étendre un voile sur ses instincts et sur ses sentiments"*—hence, rationalization. (P. 788.) His aim is to reduce sociology to the "real" reasons. (P. 791.)

suggest, therefore, that we substitute a recent name and speak of "creative thought" rather than of Reason. *For this kind of meditation begets knowledge, and knowledge is really creative inasmuch as it makes things look different from what they seemed before and may indeed work for their reconstruction.*

In certain moods some of us realize that we are observing things or making reflections with a seeming disregard of our personal preoccupations. We are not preening or defending ourselves; we are not faced by the necessity of any practical decision, nor are we apologizing for believing this or that. We are just wondering and looking and mayhap seeing what we never perceived before.

Curiosity is as clear and definite as any of our urges. We wonder what is in a sealed telegram or in a letter in which some one else is absorbed, or what is being said in the telephone booth or in low conversation. This inquisitiveness is vastly stimulated by jealousy, suspicion, or any hint that we ourselves are directly or indirectly involved. But there appears to be a fair amount of personal interest in other people's affairs even when they do not concern us except as a mystery to be unraveled or a tale to be told. The reports of a divorce suit will have "news value" for many weeks. They constitute a story, like a novel or play or moving picture. This is not an example of pure curiosity, however, since we readily identify ourselves with others, and their joys and despair then become our own.

We also take note of, or "observe," as Sherlock Holmes says, things which have nothing to do with our personal interests and make no personal appeal either direct or by way of sympathy. This is what Veblen so well calls "idle curiosity." And it is usually idle enough. Some of us when we face the line of people opposite us in a subway train impulsively consider them in detail and engage in rapid inferences and form theories in regard to them. On entering a room there are those who will perceive at a glance the degree of preciousness of the rugs, the character of the pictures, and the personality revealed by the books. But there are many, it would seem, who are so absorbed in their personal reverie or in some definite purpose that they have no bright-eyed energy for idle curiosity. The tendency to miscellaneous observation we come by honestly enough, for we note it in many of our animal relatives.

Veblen, however, uses the term "idle curiosity" somewhat ironically, as is his wont. It is idle only to those who fail to realize that it may be a very rare and indispensable thing from which almost all distinguished human achievement proceeds, since it may lead to systematic examination and seeking for things hitherto undiscovered. For research is but diligent search which enjoys the high flavor of primitive hunting. Occasionally and fitfully idle curiosity thus leads to creative thought, which alters and broadens our own views and aspirations and may in turn, under highly favorable circumstances, affect the views and lives of others, even for generations to follow. An example or two will make this unique human process clear.

Galileo was a thoughtful youth and doubtless carried on a rich and varied reverie. He had artistic ability and might have turned out to be a musician or painter. When he had dwelt among the monks at Valambrosa he had been tempted to lead the life of a religious. As a boy he busied himself with toy machines and he inherited a fondness for mathematics. All these facts are of record. We may safely assume also that, along with many other subjects of contemplation, the Pisan maidens found a vivid place in his thoughts.

One day when seventeen years old he wandered into the cathedral of his native town. In the midst of his reverie he looked up at the lamps hanging by long chains from the high ceiling of the church. Then something very difficult to explain occurred. He found himself no longer thinking of the building, worshippers, or the services; of his artistic or religious interest; of his reluctance to become a physician as his father wished. He forgot the question of a career and even the *graziosissime donne*. As he watched the swinging lamps he was suddenly wondering if mayhap their oscillations, whether long or short, did not occupy the same time. Then he tested this hypothesis by counting his pulse, for that was the only timepiece he had with him.

This observation, however remarkable in itself, was not enough to produce a really creative thought. Others may have noticed the same thing and yet nothing came of it. Most of our observations have no assignable results. Galileo may have seen that the warts on a peasant's face formed a perfect isosceles triangle, or he may have noticed with boyish glee that just as the officiating priest was uttering the solemn words, *ecce agnus Dei*, a fly lit on the end of his nose. To be really creative, ideas have to be worked up and then "put over," so that they become a part of man's social heritage. The highly accurate pendulum clock was one of the later results of Galileo's discovery. He himself was led to reconsider and successfully to refute the old notions of falling bodies. It remained for Newton to prove that the moon was falling, and presumably all the heavenly bodies. This quite upset all the consecrated views of the heavens as managed by angelic engineers. The universality of the laws of gravitation stimulated the attempt to seek other and equally important natural laws and cast grave doubts on the miracles in which mankind had hitherto believed. In short, those who dared to include in their thought the discoveries of Galileo and his successors found themselves in a new earth surrounded by new heavens.

On the 28th of October, 1831, two hundred and fifty years after Galileo had noticed the isochronous vibrations of the lamps, creative thought and its currency had so far increased that Faraday was wondering what would happen if he mounted a disk of copper between the poles of a horseshoe magnet. As the disk revolved, an electric current was produced. This would doubtless have seemed the idlest kind of experiment to the stanch business men of the time who, it happened, were just then denouncing the child-labor bills in their anxiety to avail themselves to the full of the results of earlier idle curiosity. But should the dynamos and motors which have come into being as the outcome of Faraday's experiment be stopped this evening, the business man of to-day, agitated over labor troubles, might, as he trudged home past lines of "dead" cars, through dark streets to an unlighted house, engage a little creative thought of his own and perceive that he and his laborers would have no modern factories and mines to quarrel about if it had not been for the strange, practical effects of the idle curiosity of scientists, inventors, and engineers.

The examples of creative intelligence given above belong to the realm of modern scientific achievement, which furnishes the most striking instances of the effects of scrupulous, objective thinking. But there are, of course, other great realms in which the recording and embodiment of acute observation and insight have wrought themselves into the higher life of man. The great poets and dramatists and our modern story-tellers have found themselves engaged in productive reveries, noting and artistically presenting their discoveries for the delight and instruction of those who have the ability to appreciate them.

The process by which a fresh and original poem or drama comes into being is doubtless analogous to that which originates and elaborates so-called scientific discoveries; but there is clearly a temperamental difference. The genesis and advance of painting, sculpture, and music offer still other problems. We really as yet know shockingly little about these matters, and indeed very few people have the least curiosity about them.[7] Nevertheless, creative intelligence in its various forms and activities is what makes man. Were it not for its slow, painful, and constantly discouraged operations through the ages man would be no more than a species of primate living on seeds, fruit, roots, and uncooked flesh, and wandering naked through the woods and over the plains like a chimpanzee.

The origin and progress and future promotion of civilization are ill understood and misconceived. These should be made the chief theme of education, but much hard work is necessary before we can reconstruct our ideas of man and his capacities and free ourselves from innumerable persistent misapprehensions. There have been obstructionists in all times, not merely the lethargic masses, but the moralists, the rationalizing theologians, and most of the philosophers, all busily if unconsciously engaged in ratifying existing ignorance and mistakes and discouraging creative thought. Naturally, those who reassure us seem worthy of honor and respect. Equally naturally, those who puzzle us with disturbing criticisms and invite us to change our ways are objects of suspicion and readily discredited. Our personal discontent does not ordinarily extend to any critical questioning of the general situation in which we find ourselves. In every age the prevailing conditions of civilization have appeared quite natural and inevitable to those who grew up in them. The cow asks no questions as to how it happens to have a dry stall and a supply of hay. The kitten laps its warm milk from a china saucer, without knowing anything about porcelain; the dog nestles in the corner of a divan with no sense of obligation to the inventors of upholstery and the manufacturers of down pillows. So we humans accept our breakfasts, our trains and telephones and orchestras and movies, our national Constitution, our moral code and standards of manners, with the simplicity and innocence of a pet rabbit. We have absolutely inexhaustible capacities for appropriating what others do for us with no thought of a "thank you." We do not feel called upon to make any least contribution to the merry game ourselves. Indeed, we are usually quite unaware that a game is being played at all.

[7] Recently a re-examination of creative thought has begun as a result of new knowledge which discredits many of the notions formerly held about "reason." See, for example, *Creative Intelligence,* by a group of American philosophic thinkers; John Dewey, *Essays in Experimental Logic* (both pretty hard books); and Veblen, *The Place of Science in Modern Civilization.* Easier than these and very stimulating are Dewey, *Reconstruction in Philosophy,* and Woodworth, *Dynamic Psychology.*

We have now examined the various classes of thinking which we can readily observe in ourselves and which we have plenty of reasons to believe go on, and always have been going on, in our fellow-men. We can sometimes get quite pure and sparkling examples of all four kinds, but commonly they are so confused and intermingled in our reverie as not to be readily distinguishable. The reverie is a reflection of our longings, exultations, and complacencies, our fears, suspicions, and disappointments. We are chiefly engaged in struggling to maintain our self-respect and in asserting that supremacy which we all crave and which seems to us our natural prerogative. It is not strange, but rather quite inevitable, that our beliefs about what is true and false, good and bad, right and wrong, should be mixed up with the reverie and be influenced by the same considerations which determine its character and course. We resent criticisms of our views exactly as we do of anything else connected with ourselves. Our notions of life and its ideals seem to us to be *our own* and as such necessarily true and right, to be defended at all costs.

We very rarely consider, however, the process by which we gained our convictions. If we did so, we could hardly fail to see that there was usually little ground for our confidence in them. Here and there, in this department of knowledge or that, some one of us might make a fair claim to have taken some trouble to get correct ideas of, let us say, the situation in Russia, the sources of our food supply, the origin of the Constitution, the revision of the tariff, the policy of the Holy Roman Apostolic Church, modern business organization, trade unions, birth control, socialism, the League of Nations, the excess-profits tax, preparedness, advertising in its social bearings; but only a very exceptional person would be entitled to opinions on all of even these few matters. And yet most of us have opinions on all these, and on many other questions of equal importance, of which we may know even less. We feel compelled, as self-respecting persons, to take sides when they come up for discussion. We even surprise ourselves by our omniscience. Without taking thought we see in a flash that it is most righteous and expedient to discourage birth control by legislative enactment, or that one who decries intervention in Mexico is clearly wrong, or that big advertising is essential to big business and that big business is the pride of the lands. As godlike beings, why should we not rejoice in our omniscience?

It is clear, in any case, that our convictions on important matters are not the result of knowledge or critical thought, nor, it may be added, are they often dictated by supposed self-interest. Most of them are *pure prejudices* in the proper sense of that word. We do not form them ourselves. They are the whispering of "the voice of the herd." We have in the last analysis no responsibility for them and need assume none. They are not really our own ideas, but those of others no more well informed or inspired than ourselves, who have got them in the same careless and humiliating manner as we. It should be our pride to revise our ideas and not to adhere to what passes for respectable opinion, for such opinion can frequently be shown to be not respectable at all. We should, in view of the considerations that have been mentioned, resent our supine credulity. As an English writer has remarked:

If we feared the entertaining of an unverifiable opinion with the warmth with which we fear using the wrong implement at the dinner table, if the thought of holding a prejudice disgusted us as does a foul disease, then the dangers of man's suggestibility would be turned into advantages.[8]

The purpose of this essay is to set forth briefly the way in which the notions of the herd have been accumulated. This seems to me the best, easiest, and least invidious educational device for cultivating a proper distrust for the older notions on which we still continue to rely.

The "real" reasons, which explain how it is we happen to hold a particular belief, are chiefly historical. Our most important opinions—those, for example, having to do with traditional, religious, and moral convictions, property rights, patriotism, national honor, the state, and indeed all the assumed foundations of society—are, as I have already suggested, rarely the result of reasoned consideration, but of unthinking absorption from the social environment in which we live. Consequently, they have about them a quality of "elemental certitude," and we especially resent doubt or criticism cast upon them. So long, however, as we revere the whisperings of the herd, we are obviously unable to examine them dispassionately and to consider to what extent they are suited to the novel conditions and social exigencies in which we find ourselves to-day.

The "real" reasons for our beliefs, by making clear their origins and history, can do much to dissipate this emotional blockade and rid us of our prejudices and preconceptions. Once this is done and we come critically to examine our traditional beliefs, we may well find some of them sustained by experience and honest reasoning, while others must be revised to meet new conditions and our more

---

[8] Trotter, *op. cit.*, p. 45. The first part of this little volume is excellent.

extended knowledge. But only after we have undertaken such a critical examination in the light of experience and modern knowledge, freed from any feeling of "primary certitude," can we claim that the "good" are also the "real" reasons for our opinions.

I do not flatter myself that this general show-up of man's thought through the ages will cure myself or others of carelessness in adopting ideas, or of unseemly heat in defending them just because we have adopted them. But if the considerations which I propose to recall are really incorporated into our thinking and are permitted to establish our general outlook on human affairs, they will do much to relieve the imaginary obligation we feel in regard to traditional sentiments and ideals. Few of us are capable of engaging in creative thought, but some of us can at least come to distinguish it from other and inferior kinds of thought and accord to it the esteem that it merits as the greatest treasure of the past and the only hope of the future.

Problems for Thought and Writing

I

1. What are the main classifications of thinking as Robinson sees them? Can you think of other groupings which would be equally valid?

2. If our thinking moves with such "incredible rapidity" that "it is almost impossible to arrest any specimen of it long enough to have a look at it," how can a man ever "know himself"? What would Etienne Gilson say (page 635)? Carl Jung (page 333)? William Barrett (page 348)?

3. Why should "self-magnification and self-justification" be the "persistent tendency" of reveries? Are they? Are most people like Thurber's Walter Mitty (see page 120)?

4. How does the making of decisions differ from reverie?

5. What is rationalizing? What is Robinson's distinction between "good" and "real" reasons? Do any of the other authors you have read in this volume seem in their analysis of individual and social behavior to be applying this distinction? Consider Chute (page 113), and Fromm (page 198).

6. "And now the astonishing and perturbing suspicion emerges that perhaps almost all that had passed for social science, political economy, politics, and ethics in the past may be brushed aside by future generations as mainly rationalizing" (page 466). Evaluate this "suspicion"—or part of it—by examining a specific instance of past social science, politics, etc., for evidence of rationalization.

7. Do you feel that most religious beliefs are, in whole or in part, rationalizations? How would Robinson stand on this question?

8. What forms does *reasoning* take in Robinson's classifications? Does this category seem to you clearly distinct from the others?

II

9. Identify or define: *amour propre*, gratuitous, disparagement, John Dewey, Veblen, Vilfredo Pareto, invidious, "primary certitude," preoccupation.

10. Examine your most cherished conviction (or prejudice) for evidences of rationalization.

11. Is Robinson's essay well organized? Is there any confusion in his main divisions? Outline the essay.

~

TYPES OF AMERICAN PRESIDENTS*
Edmund Wilson

Our presidents have run in sequences, and since the middle of the nineteenth century, they have tended to be classifiable under three main types. You have, first, the public-spirited idealist who may or may not be a good politician, but who knows American history, understands the importance and the meaning of the United States in the larger world, and assumes the responsibility of maintaining our unique role. The first seven American presidents necessarily belonged to this type, and we have had several men of this caliber since, though only at irregular intervals: Lincoln, Theodore Roosevelt, Woodrow Wilson, Franklin Roosevelt. All four of these gave everything they had—Lincoln, Wilson, and Franklin Roosevelt their lives—worthily to represent the United States of America, to preside over, direct, and take part in the next act of the republican drama.

An administration on this high level is likely, however, to be followed by a slump, with an inferior type of man in office: the small party politician—the Warren G. Harding or Harry S. Truman. This type has but little conception of what the other kind of president has been up to. He is a product of his party machine, in which he has had his whole existence and which circumscribes his whole ambition. It has been for him not only his profession, but also his college, his church, and his club; it has even become somehow his country. He puts old party pals in office, and when, as invariably happens—Teapot

* From Edmund Wilson, *A Piece of My Mind: Reflections at Sixty* (New York: Farrar, Straus & Cudahy, 1956).

Dome, the Pauley appointment, General Vaughn and his colleagues—
the latter get into trouble for trafficking in public property or taking
presents from industrial interests, the president of this stripe has no
thought except to protect them. For him, party loyalty is everything.
Virtue, in the school he has been to, means constancy in sticking by
one's team-mates, and it is doubtful whether President Truman ever
really understood, in Pauley's case, what people were complaining
about when they objected that a lobbyist for the oil companies ought
not to be made Undersecretary of the Navy. A president of this kind
inhabits so different a world from the man of high civic conscience
that the outlook and the language of the latter are hardly intelligible
to him, and Truman, succeeding Roosevelt, would be touching in his
failure to connect with his chief if he had not preserved all the smugness of the sound and successful party man.

A third type, clearly defined, is the man who neither knows about
professional politics nor understands the problems of government, but
has arrived at a position of eminence through achievement in some
quite different field: Grant, Hoover, Eisenhower. These three—two
generals and an engineer—were put in by the Republican interests
for the reason that they combined being popular heroes whom the
public could be made to accept with an ignorance both of politics and
of economics. They can be depended upon not to obstruct the
designs of big business, and one of the features of their administra-
tions is the extreme naïveté they are likely to show in inviting big
business to take possession. Grant nominated as his Secretary of the
Treasury Alexander Stewart, a dry-goods millionaire, and was surprised to learn of the law which debarred this office to merchants.
In the same way, President Eisenhower selected as Secretary of
Defense Charles E. Wilson, the president of General Motors, and
was equally surprised to learn that a man with large industrial interests was not eligible for this post. This was also, it would seem, news
to Wilson, who announced that no alarm need be felt, since "for
years" he had "thought that what was good for our country was good
for General Motors and vice versa"; but he was obliged to go through
the forms of getting rid of his General Motors stock.

There is, also, perhaps, a fourth category of presidents which stands
out less sharply than the other three: the kind of "borderline case"
represented by Grover Cleveland and William Howard Taft. Such
men stand also for the status quo, but they bring to public office
special qualities of training and integrity.

Problems for Thought and Writing

1. Are the three categories—idealist, politician, hero—in which Wilson places the presidents of the last hundred years the only available categories? What might be some others?

2. Is this classification scientifically objective—the result of "analysis"—or is it a value judgment in which emotion and private feeling is evident? Is the presence of opinion and feeling by itself any sign that Wilson is not being objective?

3. In what ways can a classification like this be used as a device of persuasion? Does the fact that both Truman and Eisenhower fall in pejorative categories even, so to speak, the score between them? Or is there subtle and persuasive weighting here?

~

HIGHBROW, LOWBROW, MIDDLEBROW *

Russell Lynes

I

My wife's grandmother, the wife of a distinguished lawyer, once declined to dine with the Cartiers of jewelry fame because they were, as she put it "in trade." Life for grandmother was relatively simple where social distinctions were concerned, but while there are still a few people who think and act much as she did, the passage of time has eliminated a great deal of that particular kind of snobbishness from American society. We are replacing it with another kind. The old structure of the upper class, the middle class, and the lower class is on the wane. It isn't wealth or family that makes prestige these days. It's high thinking.

Our heroes now are not the Carnegies or the Morgans but the intellectuals—the atomic scientists, the cultural historians, the writers, the commentators, the thinkers of global thoughts who, we assume for lack of another faith, know better than anyone else how we should cope with what we call with new resonance our national destiny. What we want are oracles, and the best substitutes we can find are the intellectuals. Einstein makes headlines as Milliken never did. Toynbee's popularity is to be reckoned with as Spengler's never was.

* From *Harper's Magazine*, February, 1949. Copyright 1949 by Russell Lynes. By permission of the author.

Even Calvert whiskey has selected as Men of Distinction more artists, architects, writers, and commentators than it has industrialists or financiers. What we are headed for is a sort of social structure in which the highbrows are the elite, the middlebrows are the bourgeoisie, and the lowbrows are *hoi polloi.*

For the time being this is perhaps largely an urban phenomenon, and the true middlebrow may readily be mistaken in the small community for a genuine highbrow, but the pattern is emerging with increasing clarity, and the new distinctions do not seem to be based either on money or on breeding. Some lowbrows are as rich as Billy Rose, and as flamboyant, some as poor as Rosie O'Grady and as modest. Some middlebrows run industries; some run the women's auxiliary of the Second Baptist Church. Some highbrows eat caviar with their Proust; some eat hamburger when they can afford it. It is true that most highbrows are in the ill-paid professions, notably the academic, and that most middlebrows are at least reasonably well off. Only the lowbrows can be found in about equal percentages at all financial levels. There may be a time, of course, when the highbrows will be paid in accordance with their own estimate of their worth, but that is not likely to happen in any form of society in which creature comforts are in greater demand than intellectual uplift. Like poets they will have to be content mostly with prestige. The middlebrows are influential today, but neither the highbrows nor the lowbrows like them; and if we ever have intellectual totalitarianism, it may well be the lowbrows and the highbrows who will run things, and the middlebrows who will be exiled in boxcars to a collecting point probably in the vicinity of Independence, Missouri.

While this social shift is still in its early stages, and the dividing lines are still indistinct and the species not yet frozen, let us assume a rather lofty position, examine the principal categories, with their subdivisions and splinter groups, and see where we ourselves are likely to fetch up in the new order.

II

The highbrows come first. Edgar Wallace, who was certainly not a highbrow himself, was asked by a newspaper reporter in Hollywood some years ago to define one. "What is a highbrow?" he said. "A highbrow is a man who has found something more interesting than women."

Presumably at some time in every man's life there are things he finds more interesting than women; alcohol, for example, or the

World Series. Mr. Wallace has only partially defined the highbrow. Brander Matthews came closer when he said that "a highbrow is a person educated beyond his intelligence," and A. P. Herbert came closest of all when he wrote that "a highbrow is the kind of person who looks at a sausage and thinks of Picasso."

It is this association of culture with every aspect of daily life, from the design of his razor to the shape of the bottle that holds his sleeping pills, that distinguishes the highbrow from the middle-brow or the lowbrow. Spiritually and intellectually the highbrow inhabits a precinct well up the slopes of Parnassus, and his view of the cultural scene is from above. His vision pinpoints certain lakes and quarries upon which his special affections are concentrated—a perturbed lake called Rilke or a deserted quarry called Kierkegaard —but he believes that he sees them, as he sees the functional design of his razor, always in relation to the broader cultural scene. There is a certain air of omniscience about the highbrow, though that air is in many cases the thin variety encountered on the tops of high mountains from which the view is extensive but the details are lost.

You cannot tell a man that he is a lowbrow any more than you can tell a woman that her clothes are in bad taste, but a highbrow does not mind being called a highbrow. He has worked hard, read widely, traveled far, and listened attentively in order to satisfy his curiosity and establish his squatters' rights in this little corner of intellectualism, and he does not care who knows it. And this is true of both kinds of highbrow—the militant, or crusader, type and the passive, or dilettante, type. These types in general live happily to-gether; the militant highbrow carries the torch of culture, the passive highbrow reads by its light.

The carrier of the torch makes a profession of being a highbrow and lives by his calling. He is most frequently found in university and college towns, a member of the liberal-arts faculty, teaching languages (ancient or modern), the fine arts, or literature. His spare time is often devoted to editing a magazine which is read mainly by other highbrows, ambitious undergraduates, and the editors of middlebrow publications in search of talent. When he writes for the magazine himself (or for another "little" magazine) it is usually criticism or criticism of criticism. He leaves the writing of fiction and poetry to others more bent on creation than on what has been created, for the highbrow is primarily a critic and not an artist—a taster, not a cook. He is often more interested in where the arts have been, and where they are going, than in the objects themselves.

He is devoted to the proposition that the arts must be pigeon-holed, and that their trends should be plotted, or as W. H. Auden puts it—

> Our Intellectual marines,
> Landing in Little Magazines,
> Capture a trend.

This gravitation of the highbrows to the universities is fairly recent. In the twenties, when the little magazines were devoted to publishing experimental writing rather than criticism of exhumed experimental writing, the highbrows flocked to Paris, New York, and Chicago. The *transatlantic review, transition,* and the *Little Review* of the lower-case era of literature, were all published in Paris; BROOM was published in New York; *Poetry* was (and still is) published in Chicago. The principal little magazines now, with the exception of *Partisan Review,* a New York product but written mostly by academics, are published in the colleges—the *Kenyon Review,* the *Sewanee Review,* the *Virginia Quarterly,* and so on—and their flavor reflects this. But this does not mean that highbrows do not prefer the centers in which cultural activities are the most varied and active, and these are still London, Paris, New York, and more recently Rome. Especially in the fine arts, the highbrow has a chance to make a living in the metropolis where museums are centered and where art is bought and sold as well as created. This is also true of commercial publishing, in which many highbrows find suitable, if not congenial, refuge.

But no matter where they may make their homes, all highbrows live in a world which they believe is inhabited almost entirely by Philistines—those who through viciousness or smugness or the worship of materialism gnaw away at the foundations of culture. And the highbrow sees as his real enemy the middlebrow, whom he regards as a pretentious and frivolous man or woman who uses culture to satisfy social or business ambitions; who, to quote Clement Greenberg in *Partisan Review,* is busy "devaluating the precious, infecting the healthy, corrupting the honest, and stultifying the wise."

It takes a man who feels strongly to use such harsh words, but the militant highbrow has no patience with his enemies. He is a serious man who will not tolerate frivolity where the arts are concerned. It is part of his function as a highbrow to protect the arts from the culture-mongers, and he spits venom at those he suspects of selling the Muses short.

The fact that nowadays everyone has access to culture through schools and colleges, through the press, radio, and museums, disturbs him deeply; for it tends to blur the distinctions between those who are serious and those who are frivolous. "Culturally what we have," writes William Phillips in *Horizon*, "is a democratic free-for-all in which every individual, being as good as every other one, has the right to question any form of intellectual authority." To this Mr. Greenberg adds, "It becomes increasingly difficult to tell who is serious and who not."

The highbrow does not like to be confused, nor does he like to have his authority questioned, except by other highbrows of whose seriousness he is certain. The result is precisely what you would expect: the highbrows believe in, and would establish, an intellectual elite, "a fluid body of intellectuals . . . whose accepted role in society is to perpetuate traditional ideas and values and to create new ones." Such an elite would like to see the middlebrow eliminated, for it regards him as the undesirable element in our, and anybody else's, culture.

"It must be obvious to anyone that the volume and social weight of middlebrow culture," Mr. Greenberg writes, "borne along as it has been by the great recent increase in the American middle class, have multiplied at least tenfold in the past three decades. This culture presents a more serious threat to the genuine article than the old-time pulp dime novel, Tin Pan Alley, *Schund* variety ever has or will. Unlike the latter, which has its social limits clearly marked out for it, middlebrow culture attacks distinctions as such and insinuates itself everywhere. . . . Insidiousness is of its essence, and in recent years its avenues of penetration have become infinitely more difficult to detect and block."

By no means all highbrows are so intolerant or so desperate as this, or so ambitious for authority. Many of them, the passive ones, are merely consumers totally indifferent to the middlebrows or supercilious about them. Others without a great deal of hope but in ardent good faith expend themselves in endeavor to widen the circle of those who can enjoy the arts in their purest forms. Many museums, colleges, and publishing houses are at least partly staffed by highbrows who exert a more than half-hearted effort to make the arts exciting and important to the public. But they are aware that most of their labors are wasted. In his heart of hearts nearly every highbrow believes with Ortega y Gasset that "the average citizen [is] a creature incapable of receiving the sacrament of art, blind and deaf to pure beauty." When, for example, the Metropolitan Museum planned to expand its facilities a few years ago, an art dealer who can clearly be classified as a highbrow remarked: "All this means is less art for more people."

There are also many highbrows who are not concerned in the least with the arts or with literature, and who do not fret themselves about the upstart state of middlebrow culture. These are the specialized highbrows who toil in the remote corners of science and history, of philology and mathematics. They are concerned with their investigations of fruit-flies or Elizabethan taxation or whatever it may be, and they do not talk about them, as the dilettante always talks of the arts, to the first person they can latch onto at a cocktail party. When not in their laboratories or the library, they are often as not thoroughly middlebrow in their attitudes and tastes.

The real highbrow's way of life is as intellectualized as his way of thinking, and as carefully plotted. He is likely to be either extremely self-conscious about his physical surroundings and creature comforts or else sublimely, and rather ostentatiously, indifferent to them. If he affects the former attitude, he will within the limits of his income surround himself with works of art. If he cannot afford paintings he buys drawings. Color reproductions, except as casual reminders tucked in the frame of a mirror or thrown down on a table, are beneath him. The facsimile is no substitute in his mind for the genuine, and he would rather have a slight sketch by a master, Braque or Picasso or even Jackson Pollock, than a fully-realized canvas by an artist he considers not quite first-rate. Drawings by his friends he hangs in the bathroom. His furniture, if it is modern, consists of identifiable pieces by Aalto, or Breuer, or Mies van der Rohe, or Eames; it does not come from department stores. If he finds modern unsympathetic, he will tend to use Biedermaier or the more "entertaining" varieties of Victorian, which he collects piece by piece with an eye to the slightly eccentric. If he has antiques, you may be sure they are not maple; the cult of "early American" is offensive to him.

The food that he serves will be planned with the greatest care, either very simple (a perfect French omelette made with sweet butter) or elaborate recipes from *Wine and Food* magazine published in London and edited by André Simon. If he cannot afford a pound of butter with every guinea fowl, he will in all probability resort to the casserole, and peasant cookery with the sparer parts of animals and birds seasoned meticulously with herbs that he gets from a little importer in the wholesale district. His wine is more likely to be a "perfectly adequate little red wine" for eighty-nine cents a half-gallon than an imported French vintage. (Anybody with good advice can buy French wines, but the discovery of a good domestic bottle shows perception and educated taste.) He wouldn't dream of washing his salad bowl. His collection of phonograph records is likely to bulk large at the ends and sag in the middle —a predominance of Bach-and-before at one end and Stravinsky, Schönberg, Bartok, and New Orleans jazz at the other. The nineteenth century is represented, perhaps, by Beethoven quartets and late sonatas, and some French "art songs" recorded by Maggie Teyte. His radio, if he has one, is turned on rarely; he wouldn't have a television set in the house.

The highbrow who disregards his creature comforts does it with a will. He lives with whatever furniture happens to come his way in a disorganized conglomeration of Victorian, department store, and Mexican bits and pieces. He takes care of his books in that he knows where each one is no matter in what disorder they may appear. Every other detail of domestic life he leaves to his wife, of whose taste he is largely unaware, and he eats what she gives him without comment. If he is a bachelor, he eats in a cafeteria or drugstore or diner and sometimes spills soup on the open pages of his book. He is oblivious to the man who sits down opposite him, and if Edgar Wallace is right, to the woman who shares his table. He is not a man without passions, but they have their place. Dress is a matter of indifference to him.

The highbrows about whom I have been writing are mainly consumers and not creators—editors, critics, and dilettantes. The creative artists who are generally considered highbrows—such men as T. S. Eliot, E. M. Forster, Picasso, and Stravinsky—seem to me to fall in another category, that of the professional man who, while he may be concerned with communicating with a limited (and perhaps largely highbrow) audience, is primarily a doer and not a done-by. When Eliot or Forster or Picasso or Stravinsky sits down at his worktable, I do not know whether he says to himself, "I am going to create Art," but I very much doubt if that is what is in his mind. He is concerned rather with the communication of ideas within the frame of a poem, a novel, a painting, or a ballet suite, and if it turns out to be art (which many think it frequently does) that is to him a by-product of creation, an extra dividend of craftsmanship, intelligence, and sensibility. But when this happens he is taken up by the highbrow consumer and made much of. In fact he may become, whether he likes it or not, a vested interest, and his reputation will be every bit as carefully guarded by the highbrows as a hundred shares of Standard Oil of New Jersey by the middlebrows. He will be sold—at a par decided upon by the highbrows—to the middlebrows, who are natural gamblers in the commodities of culture.

In a sense it is this determination of par that is the particular contribution of the highbrow. Others may quarrel with his evaluations, but the fact remains that unless there were a relatively small group of self-appointed intellectuals who took it upon themselves to ransack the studios of artists, devour the manuscripts of promising writers, and listen at the keyholes of young composers, many talented men and women might pass unnoticed and our culture be the poorer. Their noncommercial attitude toward discovery of talent is useful, though they have an obsession with the evils of the monetary temptations with which America strews the artist's path. They stand as a wavering bulwark against the enticements of Hollywood and the advertising agencies, and they are saddened by the writers and painters who have set out to be serious men, as Hemingway did, and then become popular by being taken up by the middlebrows. They even go so far as to say that a story published in *Partisan Review* is a better story than if it were published in the *New Yorker* or *Harper's Bazaar*, for the reason that "what we have is at once a general raising and lowering of the level, for with the blurring of distinctions new writing tends to become more and more serious and intellectual and less and less bold and extreme. . . ."

This attitude, which is the attitude of the purist, is valuable. The ground in which the arts grow stays fertile only when it is fought over by both artists and consumers, and the phalanx of highbrows in the field, a somewhat impenetrable square of warriors, can be counted on to keep the fray alive.

III

The highbrow's friend is the lowbrow. The highbrow enjoys and respects the lowbrow's art—jazz for instance—which he is likely to call a spontaneous expression of folk culture. The lowbrow is not interested, as the middlebrow is, in pre-empting any of the highbrow's function or in any way threatening to blur the lines between the serious and the frivolous. In fact he is almost completely oblivious of the highbrow unless he happens to be taken up by him—as many jazz musicians, primitive painters, and ballad writers have been—and then he is likely to be flattered, a little suspicious, and somewhat amused. A creative lowbrow like the jazz musician is a prominent citizen in his own world, and the fact that he is taken up by the highbrows has very little effect on his social standing therein. He is tolerant of the highbrow, whom he regards as somewhat odd and out-of-place in a world in which people do things and enjoy them without analyzing why or worrying about their cultural implications.

The lowbrow doesn't give a hang about art *qua* art. He knows what he likes, and he doesn't care why he likes it—which implies that all children are lowbrows. The word "beautiful," which has long since ceased to mean anything to the highbrow, is a perfectly good word to the lowbrow. Beautiful blues, beautiful sunsets, beautiful women, all things that do something to a man inside without passing through the mind, associations without allusions, illusions without implications. The arts created by the lowbrow are made in the expression of immediate pleasure or grief, like most forms of jazz; or of usefulness, like the manufacturing of a tool or a piece of machinery or even a bridge across the Hudson. The form, to use a highbrow phrase, follows the function. When the lowbrow arts follow this formula (which they don't always do), then the highbrow finds much in them to admire, and he calls it the vernacular. When, however, the lowbrow arts get mixed up with middlebrow ideas of culture, then the highbrow turns away in disgust. Look, for example, at what happened to the circus, a traditional form of lowbrow art. They got in Norman Bel Geddes to fancy it up, and now its special flavor of authenticity is gone—all wrapped up in pink middlebrow sequins. This is not to say that the lowbrow doesn't like it just as much as he ever did. It is the highbrow who is pained.

Part of the highbrow's admiration for the lowbrow stems from the lowbrow's indifference to art. This makes it possible for the highbrow to blame whatever he doesn't like about lowbrow taste on the middlebrow. If the lowbrow reads the comics, the highbrow understands; he is frequently a connoisseur of the comics himself. But if he likes grade-B double features, the highbrow blames that on the corrupting influence of the middlebrow moneybags of Hollywood. If he participates in give-away quiz programs, it is because the radio polsters have decided that the average mental age of the listening audience is thirteen, and that radio is venal for taking advantage of the adolescent.

The lowbrow consumer, whether he is an engineer of bridges or a bus driver, wants to be comfortable and to enjoy himself without having to worry about whether he has good taste or not. It doesn't make any difference to him that a chair is a bad Grand Rapids copy of an eighteenth-century *fauteuil* as long as he's happy when he sits down in it. He doesn't care whether the movies are art, or the radio improving, so long as he has fun while he is giving them his attention and getting a fair return of pleasure from his investment. It wouldn't occur to him to tell a novelist what kind of book he should write, or a movie director what kind of movie to make. If he doesn't like a book he ignores it; if he doesn't like a movie he says so, whether it is a "Blondie" show or "Henry V." If he likes jive or square-dancing, he doesn't worry about whether they are fashionable or not. If other people like the ballet, that's all right with him, so long as he doesn't have to go himself. In general the lowbrow attitude toward the arts is live and let live. Lowbrows are not Philistines. One has to know enough about the arts to argue about them with highbrows to be a Philistine.

IV

The popular press, and also much of the unpopular press, is run by the middlebrows, and it is against them that the highbrow inveighs.

"The true battle," Virginia Woolf wrote in an unmailed letter to the *New Statesman*, ". . . lies not between highbrow and lowbrow, but between highbrows and lowbrows joined together in blood brotherhood against the bloodless and pernicious pest who comes between."

The pests divide themselves into two groups: the Upper Middlebrows and the Lower Middlebrows. It is the upper middlebrows who are the principal purveyors of highbrow ideas and the lower middlebrows who are the principal consumers of what the upper middlebrows pass along to them.

Many publishers, for example, are upper middlebrows—as are most educators, museum directors, movie producers, art dealers, lecturers, and the editors of most magazines which combine national circulation with an adult vocabulary. These are the men and women who devote themselves professionally to the dissemination of ideas and cultural artifacts and, not in the least incidentally, make a living along the way. They are the cultural do-gooders, and they see their mission clearly and pursue it with determination. Some of them are disappointed highbrows; some of them try to work both sides of the street; nearly all of them straddle the fence between highbrow and middlebrow and enjoy their equivocal position.

The conscientious publisher, for instance, believes in the importance of literature and the dignity of publishing as a profession. He spends a large part of his time on books that will not yield him a decent return on his investment. He searches out writers of promise; he pores over the "little" magazines (or pays other people to); he leafs through hundreds and hundreds of pages of manuscript. He advises writers, encourages them, coaxes them to do their best work; he even advances them money. But he is not able to be a publisher at all (unless he is willing to put his personal fortune at the disposal of financially naïve muses) if he does not publish to make money. In order to publish slender volumes of poetry he must also publish fat volumes of historical romance, and in order to encourage the first novel of a promising young writer he must sell tens of thousands of copies of a book by an old hand who grinds out one best seller a year. He must take the measure of popular taste and cater to it at the same time that he tries to create a taste for new talent. If he is a successful publisher he makes money, lives comfortably, patronizes the other arts, serves on museum boards and committees for the Prevention of This and the Preservation of That, contributes to the symphony, and occasionally buys pictures by contemporary painters.

The highbrow suspects that the publisher does not pace his book-lined office contriving ways to serve the muses and that these same muses have to wait their turn in line until the balance sheet has been served. He believes that the publisher is really happy only when he can sell a couple of hundred thousand copies of a novel about a hussy with a horse-whip or a book on how to look forty when forty-five. To the highbrow he is a tool to be cultivated and used, but not to be trusted.

The museum director is in much the same position, caught between the muses and the masses. If he doesn't make a constant effort to swell the door-count, his middlebrow trustees want to know why he isn't serving the community; if he does, the high-brows want to know why he is pandering to popular taste and not minding his main business—the service of scholarship and the support of artists currently certified to be "serious." Educators are in the same position, bound to be concerned with mass education often at the expense of the potential scholar, and editors of all magazines except those supported by private angels or cultural institutions know that they must not only enlighten but entertain if they are to have enough readers to pay the bills. To the highbrow this can lead to nothing but compromise and mediocrity.

The upper-middlebrow consumer takes his culture seriously, as seriously as his job allows, for he is gainfully employed. In his leisure hours he reads Toynbee or Sartre or Osbert Sitwell's serialized memoirs. He goes to museum openings and to the theater and he keeps up on the foreign films. He buys pictures, sometimes old masters if he can afford them, sometimes contemporary works. He has a few etchings and lithographs, and he is not above an occasional color reproduction of a Van Gogh or a Cézanne. Writers and painters are his friends and dine at his house; if, however, his own son were to express an interest in being an artist, he would be dismayed ("so few artists ever really pull it off")—though he would keep a stiff upper lip and hope the boy would learn better before it was too late. His house is tastefully decorated, sometimes in the very latest mode, a model of the modern architect's dream of functionalism, in which case he can discourse on the theory of the open plan and the derivations of the international style with the zest and uncertain vocabulary of a convert. If his house is "traditional" in character, he will not put up with Grand Rapids copies of old pieces; he will have authentic ones, and will settle for Victorian if he cannot afford Empire. He, or his wife, will ransack second-hand shops for entertaining bibelots and lamps or a piece of Brussels carpet for the bedroom. He never refers to curtains as "drapes." He talks about television as potentially a new art form, and he listens to the Saturday afternoon opera broadcasts. His library contains a few of the more respectable current best sellers which he reads out of "curiosity" rather than interest. (Membership in any sort of book club he considers beneath him.) There are a few shelves of first editions, some of them autographed by friends who have dined at his house, some of them things (like a presentation copy of *Jurgen*) that he "just happened to pick up" and a sampling of American and British poets. There is also a shelf of paper-bound French novels— most of them by nineteenth-century writers. The magazines on his table span the areas from *Time* and the *New Yorker* to *Harper's* and the *Atlantic,* with an occasional copy of the *Yale* and *Partisan Reviews,* and the *Art News.*

From this it can be seen that he supports the highbrows—buys some of the books they recommend and an occasional picture they have looked upon with favor—and contributes to organized efforts to promote the arts both by serving on boards and shelling out money. In general he is modest about expressing his opinion on cultural matters in the presence of highbrows but takes a slightly lordly tone when he is talking to other middlebrows. If he discovers a "little" painter or poet the chances are excellent that the man has already been discovered and promoted by a highbrow or by an upper-middlebrow entrepreneur (art dealer or publisher). Once in a while he will take a flyer on an unknown artist, and hang his picture inconspicuously in the bedroom. He takes his function as a patron of the arts seriously, but he does it for the pleasure it gives him to be part of the cultural scene. If he does it for "money, fame, power, or prestige," as Virginia Woolf says he does, these motives are so obscured by a general sense of well-being and well-meaning that he would be shocked and surprised to be accused of venality.

V

If the upper middlebrow is unsure of his own tastes, but firm in his belief that taste is extremely important, the lower middlebrow is his counterpart. The lower middlebrow ardently believes that he knows what he likes, and yet his taste is constantly susceptible to the pressures that put him in knickerbockers one year and rust-colored slacks the next. Actually he is unsure about almost everything, especially about what he likes. This may explain his pronouncements on taste, which he considers an effete and questionable virtue, and his resentment of the arts; but it may also explain his strength.

When America and Americans are characterized by foreigners and highbrows, the middlebrows are likely to emerge as the dominant group in our society—a dreadful mass of insensible backslappers, given to sentimentality as a prime virtue, the willing victims of slogans and the whims of the bosses, both political and economic. The picture painted by middlebrow exploiters of the middlebrow, such as the advertisers of nationally advertised brands, is strikingly similar to that painted by the highbrow; their attitudes and motives are quite different (the highbrow paints with a snarl, the advertiser with a gleam), but they both make the middlebrow out to be much the same kind of creature. The villain of the highbrow and the hero of the advertisers is envisaged as "the typical American family"— happy little women, happy little children, all spotless or sticky in the jam pot, framed against dimity curtains in the windows or decalcomania flowers on the cupboard doors. Lower-middlebrowism is a world pictured without tragedy, a world of new two-door sedans and Bendix washers, and reproductions of hunting prints over the living-room mantel. It is a world in which the ingenuity and patience of the housewife are equaled only by the fidelity of her husband and his love of home, pipe, and radio. It is a world that smells of soap. But it is a world of ambition as well, the constant striving for a better way of life—better furniture, bigger refrigerators, more books in the bookcase, more evenings at the movies. To the advertisers this is Americanism; to the highbrows this is the dead weight around the neck of progress, the gag in the mouth of art.

The lower middlebrows are not like this, of course, and unlike the highbrows and the upper middlebrows, whose numbers are tiny by comparison, they are hard to pin down. They live everywhere, rubbing elbows with lowbrows in apartment houses like vast beehives, in row houses all alike from the outside except for the planting, in large houses at the ends of gravel driveways, in big cities, in medium cities and suburbs, and in small towns, from Boston to San Francisco, from Seattle to Jacksonville. They are the members of the book clubs who read difficult books along with racy and innocuous ones that are sent along by Messrs. Fadiman, Canby, Beecroft *et al.* They are the course-takers who swell the enrollments of adult education classes in everything from "The Technique of the Short Story" to "Child Care." They are the people who go to hear the lecturers that swarm out from New York lecture bureaus with tales of travel on the Dark Continent and panaceas for saving the world from a fate worse than capitalism. They eat in tea shoppes and hold barbecues in their backyards. They are hell-bent on improving their minds as well as their fortunes. They decorate their homes under the careful guidance of *Good Housekeeping* and the *Ladies' Home Journal,* or, if they are well off, of *House and Garden,* and are subject to fads in furniture so long as these don't depart too radically from the traditional and the safe, from the copy of Colonial and the reproduction of Sheraton. In matters of taste, the lower-middlebrow world is largely dominated by women. They select the furniture, buy the fabrics, pick out the wallpapers, the pictures, the books, the china. Except in the selection of his personal apparel and the car, it is almost *infra dig* for a man to have taste; it is not considered quite manly for the male to express opinions about things which come under the category of "artistic."

Nonetheless, as a member of the school board or the hospital board he decides which design shall be accepted when a new building goes up. The lower middlebrows are the organizers of the community fund, the members of the legislature, the park commissioners. They pay their taxes and they demand services in return. There are millions of them, conscientious stabilizers of society, slow to change, slow to panic. But they are not as predictable as either the highbrows or the bosses, political or economic, think they are. They can be led, they can be seduced, but they cannot be pushed around.

VI

Highbrow, lowbrow, upper middlebrow, and lower middlebrow —the lines between them are sometimes indistinct, as the lines between upper class, lower class, and middle class have always been in our traditionally fluid society. But gradually they are finding their own levels and confining themselves more and more to the company of their own kind. You will not find a highbrow willingly attending a Simon & Schuster cocktail party any more than you will find an upper middlebrow at a Rotary Club luncheon or an Elks' picnic.

The highbrows would like, of course, to eliminate the middlebrows and devise a society that would approximate an intellectual feudal system in which the lowbrows do the work and create folk arts, and the highbrows do the thinking and create fine arts. All middlebrows, presumably, would have their radios taken away, be suspended from society until they had agreed to give up their subscriptions to the Book-of-the-Month, turned their color reproductions over to a Commission for the Dissolution of Middlebrow Taste, and renounced their affiliation with all educational and other cultural institutions whatsoever. They would be taxed for the support of all writers, artists, musicians, critics, and critics-of-criticism whose production could be certified "serious"—said writers, artists, musicians, and critics to be selected by representatives of qualified magazines with circulations of not more than five thousand copies. Middlebrows, both upper and lower, who persisted in "devaluating the precious, infecting the healthy, corrupting the honest, and stultifying the wise" would be disposed of forthwith.

But the highbrows haven't a chance; things have gone too far. Everybody but the genuine lowbrow (who is more wooed than wedded by the highbrow) is jockeying for position in the new cultural class order. *Life* magazine, sensing the trend, has been catching us up on the past of Western Civilization in sixteen-page, four-color capsules. *Mademoiselle* walks off with the first prizes in the annual short-story contests. The Pepsi-Cola Company stages the most elaborate and highest-paying art competition in the country. Even *Partisan Review,* backed by a new angel, runs full-page ads in the *New York Times* Book Review. The Book-of-the-Month Club ships out a couple of hundred thousand copies of Toynbee's *A Study of History* as "dividends."

If life for grandmother, who wouldn't dine with the Cartiers, was simple in its social distinctions, life is becoming equally simple for us. The rungs of the ladder may be different, it may even be a different ladder, but it's onward and upward just the same. You may not be known by which fork you use for the fish these days, but you will be known by which key you use for your *Finnegans Wake.*

Problems for Thought and Writing

I

1. Are Russell Lynes's distinctions between the high, low, and middlebrow drawn facetiously or seriously? Is his purpose classification or criticism or both? How does one serve the other here?

2. Go through the articles in this volume and discover what ones are drawn from magazines designated as "highbrow" by Russell Lynes. (The acknowledgments are given at the bottom of title-pages.) Do they, in your opinion, correspond with Lynes' classification?

3. What are the grounds for the contention between the highbrow and the middlebrow? Are there any important values at stake here, or is the difference based simply (as Lynes seems to imply) on class prejudices?

4. Middlebrow culture, writes Clement Greenberg, "attacks distinctions as such and insinuates itself everywhere" (page 481). On what grounds does Lynes take issue with this statement?

5. In which of Lynes's classifications would you prefer to be included? Why? Is your decision determined by the content of this article or only by the connotations of the words themselves?

6. Is there much difference between "reading" the comics and being a "connoisseur" of the comics? Why should the highbrow admire the lowbrow?

7. In your opinion, who gets the most fun out of life, the highbrow or the lowbrow?

8. Classify your professors on the basis set forth by Lynes. Is a concern for "mass education" a valid differentiating characteristic between the upper-middlebrow and the highbrow in education?

II

9. Is Lynes's style too "flip"? Do you remember his "gags" and anecdotes and illustrations more or less readily than you do the classification itself? Was he addressing, in your opinion, a high, low, or middlebrow audience? Russell Lynes is one of the senior editors of *Harper's Magazine*. Is his style of writing the kind usually found in that highbrow journal?

10. Apart from proper nouns with which you may not be familiar, would you call Lynes's style complicated or obscure?

11. Identify or define: Milliken, Toynbee, *hoi polloi*, Proust, Picasso, Parnassus, Kierkegaard, Ortega y Gasset, dilettante, Braque, meticulously, sonata, E. M. Forster, Stravinsky, phalanx, *fauteuil*, artifacts, effete, *infra dig*.

~

4 Process and Narration

If we use the term "definition" descriptively rather than logically, we can think of a *process* as a definition of how something functions, happens, or is made. It is, so to speak, the definition of a verb rather than of a noun. It orders the elements of some moving sequence of events rather than those of a specific class of objects. It asks, "How does it go?" rather than "What is it?"

But our section is called "Process and Narration." *Narrative* comes in here not because all processes are narratives, but because all narratives are, in a sense, processes. E. M. Forster defined a story as a "narrative of events arranged in their time sequence"; that is virtually a definition of process as well. And in all the selections which follow, except that by Erich Fromm, the "story" quality is evident—especially in Bell's moving sketch of the last flight of a drake. By so broadening the scope of process, we are of course stretching it from its strictly logical or formal meaning, and allowing a large admixture of the human element. But these liberties let us include richer selections, and avoid pieces on the dullness level of "How to Play Marbles" or "The Operation of a Postage Meter."

These essays and sketches provide samples of *mechanical, natural,* and *psychological* processes; it would have been as easy to include *historical, scientific,* and *intellectual* processes as well. But no such divisions are airtight and none of the selections fits snugly in the category we have assigned it. But the divisions we have used provide a fair sampling of some possible forms which process in writing can take. And inasmuch as the problem of limiting and ordering the elements of a process differs somewhat according to the subjects dealt with, we need some focus on each of these groups.

MECHANICAL PROCESS

How do you build a hot-rod, blast a stump, or fly a jet? How do you train a dog, build a pool table, or split an atom? How does a blimp fly, a transistor work, or a calculator "think"? Ours is a machine age, and a considerable share of our energy is spent in learning or passing on the answers to such questions. Strictly speaking, the above are not all *mechanical* problems, just as that flood of popular literature telling us how to bring up babies, how to get along with relatives, how to find God and a million dollars, are not really native to this category. We let the broad label stand, however, because it seems descriptive of a modern tendency: to want rules, instructions, and explicit directions for every phase of living, to find security in reducing the flux of life as much as possible to a series of mechanical steps. John A. Kouwenhoven [in *Harper's Magazine*, July 1956, "What's American

About America?"] after asking what is the "central quality" of American life replied: "That quality I would define as a concern with process rather than with product . . . a concern with the manner of handling experience or materials rather than with the experience of materials themselves." But whether you encourage or resist the pressures making us robots, you will be well instructed to know the processes at work.

Let us assume our problem is: "How does a blimp fly?" There is no one right way of meeting this problem, but the following steps are usually indispensable.

(1) *A basic image.* Your audience will probably not be a technical one, so they will want to know, in a general way, what your device looks like. A real or word picture (both if possible) will be needed. In this case it might be enough to say that a blimp looks like a big silver cigar.

(2) *Naming of tools or working parts.* What materials are essential for the operation of the device? In this instance you will need to mention helium (and perhaps discuss briefly the merits of helium over hydrogen), the airfoil shape of the blimp (which gives it part of its lifting capacity), the envelope which contains the gas, the engines, steering apparatus, instruments. Your list will be limited by the thoroughness you want to achieve.

(3) *Describing how the parts work.* How does helium serve as a lifting medium? You will need to discuss its specific gravity relative to other gases and perhaps to explain its lifting power in terms of Archimedes' Principle (a body is buoyed up by a force equal to the weight of the volume displaced). What happens to an airfoil when a stream of air is passed over it? How do these two lifting forces work together to put a blimp in the air? How does the power of the engines join with these other forces, and how much power is needed? Are regular or reversible-pitch propellers required? These and other questions will have to be answered before the *operation* of the device is adequately explained.

(4) *Demonstrating.* This is, or can be, a completion of step three, with, perhaps, a little human drama added. Show the pilot entering the ship, checking the instruments, "weighing-off," checking the controls, clearing the tower, making the take-off. In flight show him maintaining pressure, controlling altitude and direction, and all the other actions relevant to your assignment. Finally, have him bring the airship back to earth.

Your process is now probably complete, although there are inevitably other interesting aspects of it that could be included. But certain *patterns of thought* are involved in those four steps that need to be looked at separately. A process resembles a definition in that it is controlled and limited by many of the same devices—such as enumeration of parts, comparison and contrast, and description. But the logic of a process always involves three other rather special aspects.

First, a *time sequence.* A process always has a history, a beginning and ending in time, and first things must come first. In the process of running a Model-T (see White, page 498) this fact is obvious; but it is not so obvious (and harder to demonstrate) in processes involving, say, a psychological movement like the discovery of love (see Fromm, page 505). We must, to be sure, avoid the *post hot* fallacy (see Davis, page 82), but in subtle processes like the above we must also not forget that cause always precedes effect and that the links in the time-chain must be delicately forged. But in whatever kind of process, chronology is important and should be kept clear and systematic.

Second, *spatial relations*. A process occupies space as well as time; a moving elbow needs elbow-room. Say you were describing not a mechanical process, but that of settling the American frontier. You could not avoid the spatial facts of geography; neither could you avoid the historic fact of movement in time. Nor can Carson in describing the creation of the oceans (page 526) divorce the great movements in space from the movements in time.

Third, *cause and effect*. In the assembly of a machine, the very fact that this piston fits in that cylinder is usually an indication that this causes that to move, or at least that this supports that. In the total system every part is interdependent, thus causing other parts, so to speak, to know their job and do it. But it is in the *functioning* of the machine that cause and effect are most evident—as in the steam pressure that causes the locomotive's pistons to move or the explosions that drive a combustion engine.

In listing these ways of ordering and limiting elements in a mechanical process, we have necessarily anticipated much that applies to natural, historical, and logical processes as well. But a few observations still must be made.

The one essay in this collection which illustrates a mechanical process is Lee Strout White's "Farewell My Lovely." It is, obviously, not a *formal* process, and though it contains mechanical operations, it does not stop there. Its title might be "How to Repair, Operate, and *Adjust to* a Model-T." But the human interest does not, in our opinion, detract from its value as an illustration of process. Many students make the mistake of writing a process analysis as if it were a manual of instructions or a long recipe. Try to avoid the imperative voice: *describe* a process, don't order the reader around. And don't forget that the point where man's humanity touches the machine may be one of the most important and interesting conjunctions in modern history.

NATURAL PROCESS

The natural scientists, in attempting to analyze the record of nature, have insistently asked where a thing came from, how it got there, why it left home. The evolution, the history, of development through time is one of the most fascinating processes we can contemplate. A geologist can hardly define a piece of igneous rock without describing the geologic processes which formed it. A zoologist in identifying a marsupial would certainly mention the evolutionary process which produced it. Likewise, Rachel Carson in describing the nature of the oceans, recreates in our imagination the *processes* that formed them. If our world were as static as most people in the Middle Ages believed, then natural phenomena could perhaps be dealt with in other ways. But science has made us unusually aware of the mutability of things, of the *processes* of change. Today we wonder not only where the universe came from but also where it is going.

PSYCHOLOGICAL PROCESS

How does the mind and spirit of man rise to meet trials of courage, endurance, intelligence, generosity, and tenderness? Such processes are little understood, but who can deny that we are in desperate need of enlightenment? By what process does man love instead of hate? By what means can he act as a whole and not divided person? In what ways can intuition rival reason as a means to truth? How may self-knowledge permit the unleashing of creative energies? Even to guess at answers to these questions or to discuss intelligently the wheels within wheels of the human psyche requires learning and insight. Few possess Fromm's wisdom and intuitive understanding. But amateurs or no, most of us try our hand at such questions simply because we are involved in them.

Self-knowledge, by definition, is something the individual must acquire for himself. And the educated man who has some idea *why* he smokes three packs a day, bites his fingernails, and beats his wife, is better off than the Yahoo who does them all "naturally." At least that's one of the guesses colleges and universities are founded on. So, if you are asked to write a process theme, don't shy off a psychological process just because you aren't an expert. No one is, not even the experts. Your description of the accumulation of nervous tension leading to a flunked swimming test may, in fact, be full of wisdom and insight. You ought to be a good witness, for probably you were the only one really "there." To be sure, the self-appointed psychoanalyst, trained by the movies, is not a pleasant type. We are not suggesting that you be anything so fake or pretentious. But we need all the honest self-knowledge we can get, and probing the processes that make us love, hate, fear, worry, distrust, sympathize, must—for most of us—be done sitting up. The process of writing can itself sharpen insight and sensitivity; the perception of the artist is often as valid as the analyst's. It is still not bad advice to "Look into thy heart and write."

Definition answers the question "What?" Process answers the question "How?" In any single piece of writing, the two inevitably work hand in hand. But if you know the difficulties involved in answering these as independent questions, you will write with more form and precision when you bring them together.

~

FAREWELL, MY LOVELY!* *Lee Strout White*

I see by the new Sears Roebuck catalogue hat it is still possible
to buy an axle for a 1909 Model T Ford, but I am not deceived.
The great days have faded, the end is in sight. Only one page in
the current catalogue is devoted to parts and accessories for the
Model T; yet everyone remembers springtimes when the Ford gadget
section was larger than men's clothing, almost as large as household
furnishings. The last Model T was built in 1927, and the car is
fading from what scholars call the American scene—which is an
understatement, because to a few million people who grew up
with it, the old Ford practically *was* the American scene.

It was the miracle God had wrought. And it was patently the
sort of thing that could only happen once. Mechanically uncanny,
it was like nothing that had ever come to the world before. Flourishing industries rose and fell with it. As a vehicle, it was hard-working,
commonplace, heroic; and it often seemed to transmit those qualities
to the persons who rode in it. My own generation identifies it with
Youth, with its gaudy, irretrievable excitements; before it fades into
the mist, I would like to pay it the tribute of the sigh that is not a
sob, and set down random entries in a shape somewhat less cumber-
some than a Sears Roebuck catalogue.

The Model T was distinguished from all other makes of cars by
the fact that its transmission was of a type known as planetary—
which was half metaphysics, half sheer friction. Engineers accepted
the word "planetary" in its epicyclic sense, but I was always conscious that it also meant "wandering," "erratic." Because of the
peculiar nature of this planetary element, there was always, in Model
T, a certain dull rapport between engine and wheels, and even when
the car was in a state known as neutral, it trembled with a deep
imperative and tended to inch forward. There was never a moment
when the bands were not faintly egging the machine on. In this
respect it was like a horse, rolling the bit on its tongue, and country
people brought to it the same technique they used with draft
animals.

* By permission. Copr. © 1936 The New Yorker Magazine, Inc. Published
in book form by G. P. Putnam's Sons under the title "Farewell to Model T."

Its most remarkable quality was its rate of acceleration. In its palmy days the Model T could take off faster than anything on the road. The reason was simple. To get under way, you simply hooked the third finger of the right hand around a lever on the steering column, pulled down hard, and shoved your left foot forcibly against the low-speed pedal. These were simple, positive motions; the car responded by lunging forward with a roar. After a few seconds of this turmoil, you took your toe off the pedal, eased up a mite on the throttle, and the car, possessed of only two forward speeds, catapulted directly into high with a series of ugly jerks and was off on its glorious errand. The abruptness of this departure was never equalled in other cars of the period. The human leg was (and still is) incapable of letting in a clutch with anything like the forthright abandon that used to send Model T on its way. Letting in a clutch is a negative, hesitant motion, depending on delicate nervous control; pushing down the Ford pedal was a simple, country motion—an expansive act, which came as natural as kicking an old door to make it budge.

The driver of the old Model T was a man enthroned. The car, with top up, stood seven feet high. The driver sat on top of the gas tank, brooding it with his own body. When he wanted gasoline, he alighted, along with everything else in the front seat; the seat was pulled off, the metal cap unscrewed, and a wooden stick thrust down to sound the liquid in the well. There were always a couple of these sounding sticks kicking around in the ratty sub-cushion regions of a flivver. Refuelling was more of a social function then, because the driver had to unbend, whether he wanted to or not. Directly in front of the driver was the windshield—high, uncompromisingly erect. Nobody talked about air resistance, and the four cylinders pushed the car through the atmosphere with a simple disregard of physical law.

There was this about a Model T: the purchaser never regarded his purchase as a complete, finished product. When you bought a Ford, you figured you had a start—a vibrant, spirited framework to which could be screwed an almost limitless assortment of decorative and functional hardware. Driving away from the agency, hugging the new wheel between your knees, you were already full of creative worry. A Ford was born naked as a baby, and a flourishing industry grew up out of correcting its rare deficiencies and combatting its fascinating diseases. Those were the great days of lily-painting.

I have been looking at some old Sears Roebuck catalogues, and they bring everything back so clear.

First you bought a Ruby Safety Reflector for the rear, so that your posterior would glow in another car's brilliance. Then you invested thirty-nine cents in some radiator Moto Wings, a popular ornament which gave the Pegasus touch to the machine and did something godlike to the owner. For nine cents you bought a fan-belt guide to keep the belt from slipping off the pulley.

You bought a radiator compound to stop leaks. This was as much a part of everybody's equipment as aspirin tablets are of a medicine cabinet. You bought special oil to prevent chattering, a clamp-on dash light, a patching outfit, a tool box which you bolted to the running board, a sun visor, a steering-column brace to keep the column rigid, and a set of emergency containers for gas, oil, and water—three thin, disc-like cans which reposed in a case on the running board during long, important journeys—red for gas, gray for water, green for oil. It was only a beginning. After the car was about a year old, steps were taken to check the alarming disintegration. (Model T was full of tumors, but they were benign.) A set of anti-rattlers (98¢) was a popular panacea. You hooked them on to the gas and spark rods, to the brake pull rod, and to the steering-rod connections. Hood silencers, of black rubber, were applied to the fluttering hood. Shock-absorbers and snubbers gave "complete relaxation." Some people bought rubber pedal pads, to fit over the standard metal pedals. (I didn't like these, I remember.) Persons of a suspicious or pugnacious turn of mind bought a rear-view mirror; but most Model T owners weren't worried by what was coming from behind because they would soon enough see it out in front. They rode in a state of cheerful catalepsy. Quite a large mutinous clique among Ford owners went over to a foot accelerator (you could buy one and screw it to the floor board), but there was a certain madness in these people, because the Model T, just as she stood, had a choice of three foot pedals to push, and there were plenty of moments when both feet were occupied in the routine performance of duty and when the only way to speed up the engine was with the hand throttle.

Gadget bred gadget. Owners not only bought ready-made gadgets, they invented gadgets to meet special needs. I myself drove my car directly from the agency to the blacksmith's, and had the smith affix two enormous iron brackets to the port running board to support an army trunk.

People who owned closed models builded along different lines:

they bought ball grip handles for opening doors, window anti-rattlers, and de-luxe flower vases of the cut-glass anti-splash type. People with delicate sensibilities garnished their car with a device called the Donna Lee Automobile Disseminator—a porous vase guaranteed, according to Sears, to fill the car with a "faint clean odor of lavender." The gap between open cars and closed cars was not as great then as it is now: for $11.95, Sears Roebuck converted your touring car into a sedan and you went forth renewed. One agreeable quality of the old Fords was that they had no bumpers, and their fenders softened and wilted with the years and permitted the driver to squeeze in and out of tight places.

Tires were 30 x 3½, cost about twelve dollars, and punctured readily. Everybody carried a Jiffy patching set, with a nutmeg grater to roughen the tube before the goo was spread on. Everybody was capable of putting on a patch, expected to have to, and did have to.

During my association with Model T's, self-starters were not a prevalent accessory. They were expensive and under suspicion. Your car came equipped with a serviceable crank, and the first thing you learned was how to Get Results. It was a special trick, and until you learned it (usually from another Ford owner, but sometimes by a period of appalling experimentation) you might as well have been winding up an awning. The trick was to leave the ignition switch off, proceed to the animal's head, pull the choke (which was a little wire protruding through the radiator), and give the crank two or three nonchalant upward lifts. Then, whistling as though thinking about something else, you would saunter back to the driver's cabin, turn the ignition on, return to the crank, and this time, catching it on the down stroke, give it a quick spin with plenty of That. If this procedure was followed, the engine almost always responded—first with a few scattered explosions, then with a tumultuous gunfire, which you checked by racing around to the driver's seat and retarding the throttle. Often, if the emergency brake hadn't been pulled all the way back, the car advanced on you the instant the first explosion occurred and you would hold it back by leaning your weight against it. I can still feel my old Ford nuzzling me at the curb, as though looking for an apple in my pocket.

In zero weather, ordinary cranking became an impossibility, except for giants. The oil thickened, and it became necessary to jack up the rear wheels, which, for some planetary reason, eased the throw.

The lore and legend that governed the Ford were boundless. Owners had their own theories about everything; they discussed mutual problems in that wise, infinitely resourceful way old women discuss rheumatism. Exact knowledge was pretty scarce, and often proved less effective than superstition. Dropping a camphor ball into the gas tank was a popular expedient; it seemed to have a tonic effect on both man and machine. There wasn't much to base exact knowledge on. The Ford driver flew blind. He didn't know the temperature of his engine, the speed of his car, the amount of his fuel, or the pressure of his oil (the old Ford lubricated itself by what was amiably described as the "splash system"). A speedometer cost money and was an extra, like a windshield-wiper. The dashboard of the early models was bare save for an ignition key; later models, grown effete, boasted an ammeter which pulsated alarmingly with the throbbing of the car. Under the dash was a box of coils, with vibrators which you adjusted, or thought you adjusted. Whatever the driver learned of his motor, he learned not through instruments but through sudden developments. I remember that the timer was one of the vital organs about which there was ample doctrine. When everything else had been checked, you "had a look" at the timer. It was an extravagantly odd little device, simple in construction, mysterious in function. It contained a roller, held by a spring, and there were four contact points on the inside of the case against which, many people believed, the roller rolled. I have had a timer apart on a sick Ford many times, but I never really knew what I was up to— I was just showing off before God. There were almost as many schools of thought as there were timers. Some people, when things went wrong, just clenched their teeth and gave the timer a smart crack with a wrench. Other people opened it up and blew on it. There was a school that held that the timer needed large amounts of oil; they fixed it by frequent baptism. And there was a school that was positive it was meant to run dry as a bone; these people were continually taking it off and wiping it. I remember once spitting into a timer; not in anger, but in a spirit of research. You see, the Model T driver moved in the realm of metaphysics. He believed his car could be hexed.

One reason the Ford anatomy was never reduced to an exact science was that, having "fixed" it, the owner couldn't honestly claim that the treatment had brought about the cure. There were too many authenticated cases of Fords fixing themselves—restored naturally to health after a short rest. Farmers soon discovered this, and it fitted nicely with their draft-horse philosophy: "Let 'er cool off and she'll snap into it again."

A Ford owner had Number One Bearing constantly in mind. This bearing, being at the front end of the motor, was the one that always burned out, because the oil didn't reach it when the car was climbing hills. (That's what I was always told, anyway.) The oil used to recede and leave Number One dry as a clam flat; you had to watch that bearing like a hawk. It was like a weak heart—you could hear it start knocking, and that was when you stopped and let her cool off. Try as you would to keep the oil supply right, in the end Number One always went out. "Number One Bearing burned out on me and I had to have her replaced," you would say, wisely; and your companions always had a lot to tell about how to protect and pamper Number One to keep her alive.

Sprinkled not too liberally among the millions of amateur witch doctors who drove Fords and applied their own abominable cures were the heaven-sent mechanics who could really make the car talk. These professionals turned up in undreamed-of spots. One time, on the banks of the Columbia River in Washington, I heard the rear end go out of my Model T when I was trying to whip it up a steep incline onto the deck of a ferry. Something snapped; the car slid backward into the mud. It seemed to me like the end of the trail. But the captain of the ferry, observing the withered remnant, spoke up.

"What's got her?" he asked.

"I guess it's the rear end," I replied, listlessly. The captain leaned over the rail and stared. Then I saw that there was a hunger in his eyes that set him off from other men.

"Tell you what," he said, carelessly, trying to cover up his eagerness, "let's pull the son of a bitch up onto the boat, and I'll help you fix her while we're going back and forth on the river."

We did just this. All that day I plied between the towns of Pasco and Kennewick, while the skipper (who had once worked in a Ford garage) directed the amazing work of resetting the bones of my car.

Springtime in the heyday of the Model T was a delirious season. Owning a car was still a major excitement, roads were still wonderful and bad. The Fords were obviously conceived in madness: any car which was capable of going from forward into reverse without any perceptible mechanical hiatus was bound to be a mighty challenging thing to the human imagination. Boys used to veer them off the highway into a level pasture and run wild with them, as though they were cutting up with a girl. Most everybody used the reverse pedal quite as much as the regular foot brake—it distributed the wear over the bands and wore them all down evenly. That was the big trick, to wear all the bands down evenly, so that the final chattering would be total and the whole unit scream for renewal.

The days were golden, the nights were dim and strange. I still recall with trembling those loud, nocturnal crises when you drew up to a signpost and raced the engine so the lights would be bright enough to read destinations by. I have never been really planetary since. I suppose it's time to say good-bye. Farewell, my lovely!

Problems for Thought and Writing

I

1. Would you call this as much a sociological study as a description of a process? Why or why not? Is it written in too light a vein to be regarded seriously as a contribution to historical Americana?

2. Is the title, "Farewell, My Lovely!" a good one? Do you think the authors (E. B. White and Richard Lee Strout) are sentimental or too unguarded about showing their nostalgia for the "good old days"? If not, how do they avoid this danger? (See Richard Altick, page 109.)

3. Are we tired of the complications of machines and the problems of living with them? Can this feeling account in part for the appeal of this essay?

II

4. Identify or define: irretrievable, planetary, epicyclic, rapport, vibrant, Pegasus, benign, panacea, pugnacious, nonchalant, expedient, ammeter, hiatus, nocturnal.

5. Humor and sympathy are usually antithetical, for when we laugh we usually laugh *at* something. Are we here laughing *at* the Model-T or are our sympathies aroused in its favor, as for a living character we love or admire? How do the authors manage to create this ambivalent feeling in the reader?

6. The title of this essay might have been, "How to Live with a Model-T." Yet it is as much a description of a *mechanical* process as it is of a life situation. To combine the two is no mean achievement, and these authors have succeeded largely through their skillful use of concrete details. Would the essay have had much life without those details? Why is it that generalizations can almost never make us laugh, but that the details of a situation almost always can?

7. Colloquialisms and clichés abound in this essay, but they are obviously used deliberately. Why? How do the writers make these devices work usefully for them? Under what conditions may such devices, usually scorned as stylistic diseases, serve an artistic purpose?

~

THE ACHIEVEMENT
OF LOVE*

Erich Fromm

Any theory of love must begin with a theory of man, of human existence. While we find love, or rather, the equivalent of love, in animals, their attachments are mainly a part of their instinctual equipment; only remnants of this instinctual equipment can be seen operating in man. What is essential in the existence of man is the fact that he has emerged from the animal kingdom, from instinctive adaptation, that he has transcended nature—although he never leaves it; he is a part of it—and yet once torn away from nature, he cannot return to it; once thrown out of paradise—a state of original oneness with nature—cherubim and flaming swords block his way, if he should try to return. Man can only go forward by developing his reason, by finding a new harmony, a human one, instead of the pre-human harmony which is irretrievably lost.

When man is born, the human race as well as the individual, he is thrown out of a situation which was definite, as definite as the instincts, into a situation which is indefinite, uncertain and open. There is certainty only about the past—and about the future only as far as that it is death.

Man is gifted with reason; he is *life being aware of itself;* he has awareness of himself, of his fellow man, of his past, and of the possibilities of his future. This awareness of himself as a separate entity, the awareness of his own short life span, of the fact that without his will he is born and against his will he dies, that he will die before those whom he loves, or they before him, the awareness of his aloneness and separateness, of his helplessness before the forces of nature and of society, all this makes his separate, disunited existence an unbearable prison. He would become insane could he not liberate himself from this prison and reach out, unite himself in some form or other with men, with the world outside.

The experience of separateness arouses anxiety; it is, indeed, the source of all anxiety. Being separate means being cut off, without any capacity to use my human powers. Hence to be separate means to be helpless, unable to grasp the world—things and people—actively; it means that the world can invade me without my ability to react. Thus, separateness is the source of intense anxiety. Beyond that, it arouses shame and the feeling of guilt. This experience of guilt and shame in separateness is expressed in the Biblical story of Adam and Eve. After Adam and Eve have eaten of the "tree of knowledge of good and evil," after they have disobeyed (there is no good and evil unless there is freedom to disobey), after they have become human by having emancipated themselves from the original animal harmony with nature, i.e., after their birth as human beings— they saw "that they were naked—and they were ashamed." Should we assume that a myth as old and elementary as this has the prudish morals of the nineteenth-century outlook, and that the important point the story wants to convey to us in the embarrassment that their genitals were visible? This can hardly be so, and by understanding the story in a Victorian spirit, we miss the main point, which seems to be the following: after man and woman have become aware of themselves and of each other, they are aware of their separateness, and of their difference, inasmuch as they belong to different sexes. But while recognizing their separateness they remain strangers, because they have not yet learned to love each other (as is also made very clear by the fact that Adams defends himself by blaming Eve, rather than by trying to defend her). *The awareness of human separation, without reunion by love—is the source of shame. It is at the same time the source of guilt and anxiety.*

The deepest need of man, then, is the need to overcome his separateness, to leave the prison of his aloneness. The *absolute* failure to achieve this aim means insanity, because the panic of complete isolation can be overcome only by such a radical withdrawal from the world outside that the feeling of separation disappears—because the world outside, from which one is separated, has disappeared.

Man—of all ages and cultures—is confronted with the solution of one and the same question: the question of how to overcome separateness, how to achieve union, how to transcend one's own individual life and find at-onement. The question is the same for primitive man living in caves, for nomadic man taking care of his flocks, for the peasant in Egypt, the Phoenician trader, the Roman soldier, the medieval monk, the Japanese samurai, the modern clerk and factory hand. The question is the same, for it springs from the same ground: the human situation, the conditions of human existence. The answer varies. The question can be answered by animal worship, by human sacrifice or military conquest, by indulgence in luxury, by ascetic renunciation, by obsessional work, by artistic creation, by the love of God, and by the love of Man. While there are many answers—the record of which is human history—they are nevertheless not innumerable. On the contrary, as soon as one ignores smaller differences which belong more to the periphery than to the center, one discovers that there is only a limited number of answers which have been given, and only could have been given by man in the various cultures in which he has lived. The history of religion and philosophy is the history of these answers, of their diversity, as well as of their limitation in number.

The answers depend, to some extent, on the degree of individuation which an individual has reached. In the infant I-ness has developed by little yet; he still feels one with mother, has no feeling of separateness as long as mother is present. Its sense of aloneness is cured by the physical presence of the mother, her breasts, her skin. Only to the degree that the child develops his sense of separateness and individuality is the physical presence of the mother not sufficient any more, and does the need to overcome separateness in other ways arise.

Similarly, the human race in its infancy still feels one with nature. The soil, the animals, the plants are still man's world. He identifies himself with animals, and this is expressed by the wearing of animal masks, by the worshiping of a totem animal or animal gods. But the more the human race emerges from these primary bonds, the more it separates itself from the natural, the more intense becomes the need to find new ways of escaping separateness.

One way of achieving this aim lies in all kinds of *orgiastic states*. These may have the form of an auto-induced trance, sometimes with the help of drugs. Many rituals of primitive tribes offer a vivid picture of this type of solution. In a transitory state of exaltation the world outside disappears, and with it the feeling of separateness from it. Inasmuch as these rituals are practiced in common, an experience of fusion with the group is added which makes this solution all the more effective. Closely related to, and often blended with this orgiastic solution, is the sexual experience. The sexual orgasm can produce a state similar to the one produced by a trance, or to the effects of certain drugs. Rites of communal sexual orgies were a part of many primitive rituals. It seems that after the orgiastic experience, man can go on for a time without suffering too much from his separateness. Slowly the tension of anxiety mounts, and then is reduced again by the repeated performance of the ritual.

As long as these orgiastic states are a matter of common practice in a tribe, they do not produce anxiety or guilt. To act in this way is right, and even virtuous, because it is a way shared by all, approved and demanded by the medicine men or priests; hence there is no reason to feel guilty or ashamed. It is quite different when the same solution is chosen by an individual in a culture which has left behind these common practices. Alcoholism and drug addiction are the forms which the individual chooses in a non-orgiastic culture. In contrast to those participating in the socially patterned solution, such individuals suffer from guilt feelings and remorse. While they try to escape from separateness by taking refuge in alcohol or drugs, they feel all the more separate after the orgiastic experience is over, and thus are driven to take recourse to it with increasing frequency and intensity. Slightly different from this is the recourse to a sexual orgiastic solution. To some extent it is a natural and normal form of overcoming separateness, and a partial answer to the problem of isolation. But in many individuals in whom separateness is not relieved in other ways, the search for the sexual orgasm assumes a function which makes it not very different from alcoholism and drug addiction. It becomes a desperate attempt to escape the anxiety engendered by separateness, and it results in an ever-increasing sense of separateness, since the sexual act without love never bridges the gap between two human beings, except momentarily.

All forms of orgiastic union have three characteristics: they are intense, even violent; they occur in the total personality, mind *and* body; they are transitory and periodical. Exactly the opposite holds true for that form of union which is by far the most frequent solution chosen by man in the past and in the present: the union based on *conformity* with the group, its customs, practices and beliefs. Here again we find a considerable development.

In a primitive society the group is small; it consists of those with whom one shares blood and soil. With the growing development of culture, the group enlarges; it becomes the citizenry of a *polis*, the citizenry of a large state, the members of a church. Even the poor Roman felt pride because he could say *"civis romanus sum"*; Rome and the Empire were his family, his home, his world. Also in contemporary Western society the union with the group is the prevalent way of overcoming separateness. It is a union in which the individual self disappears to a large extent, and where the aim is to belong to the herd. If I am like everybody else, if I have no feelings or thoughts which make me different, if I conform in custom, dress, ideas, to the pattern of the group, I am saved; saved from the frightening experience of aloneness. The dictatorial systems use threats and terror to induce this conformity; the democratic countries, suggestion and propaganda. There is, indeed, one great difference between the two systems. In the democracies non-conformity is possible and, in fact, by no means entirely absent; in the totalitarian systems, only a few unusual heroes and martyrs can be expected to refuse obedience. But in spite of this difference the democratic societies show an overwhelming degree of conformity. The reason lies in the fact that there *has* to be an answer to the quest for union, and if there is no other or better way, then the union of herd conformity becomes the predominant one. One can only understand the power of the fear to be different, the fear to be only a few steps away from the herd, if one understands the depths of the need not to be separated. Sometimes this fear of non-conformity is rationalized as fear of practical dangers which could threaten the non-conformist. But actually, people *want* to conform to a much higher degree than they are *forced* to conform, at least in the Western democracies.

Most people are not even aware of their need to conform. They live under the illusion that they follow their own ideas and inclinations, that they are individualists, that they have arrived at their opinions as the result of their own thinking—and that it just happens that their ideas are the same as those of the majority. The consensus of all serves as a proof for the correctness of "their" ideas. Since there is still a need to feel some individuality, such need is satisfied with regard to minor differences; the initials on the handbag or the sweater, the name plate of the bank teller, the belonging to the Democratic as against the Republican party, to the Elks instead of to the Shriners become the expression of individual differences. The advertising slogan of "it is different" shows up this pathetic need for difference, when in reality there is hardly any left.

This increasing tendency for the elimination of differences is closely related to the concept and the experience of equality, as it is developing in the most advanced industrial societies. Equality had meant, in a religious context, that we are all God's children, that we all share in the same human-divine substance, that we are all one. It meant also that the very differences between individuals must be respected, that while it is true that we are all one, it is also true that each one of us is a unique entity, is a cosmos by itself. Such conviction of the uniqueness of the individual is expressed for instance in the Talmudic statement: "Whosoever saves a single life is as if he had saved the whole world; whosoever destroys a single life is as if he had destroyed the whole world." Equality as a condition for the development of individuality was also the meaning of the concept in the philosophy of the Western Enlightenment. It meant (most clearly formulated by Kant) that no man must be the means for the ends of another man. That all men are equal inasmuch as they are ends, and only ends, and never means to each other. Following the ideas of the Enlightenment, Socialist thinkers of various schools defined equality as abolition of exploitation, of the use of man by man, regardless of whether this use were cruel or "human."

In contemporary capitalistic society the meaning of equality has been transformed. By equality one refers to the equality of automatons; of men who have lost their individuality. *Equality today means "sameness," rather than "oneness."* It is the sameness of abstractions, of the men who work in the same jobs, who have the same amusements, who read the same newspapers, who have the same feelings and the same ideas. In this respect one must also look with some skepticism at some achievements which are usually praised as signs of our progress, such as the equality of women. Needless to say I am not speaking against the equality of women; but the positive aspects of this tendency for equality must not deceive one. It is part of the trend toward the elimination of differences. Equality is bought at this very price: women are equal because they are not different any more. The proposition of Enlightenment philosophy, *l'âme n'a pas de sexe,* the soul has no sex, has become the general practice. The polarity of the sexes is disappearing, and with it erotic love, which is based on this polarity. Men and women become the *same,* not *equals* as opposite poles. Contemporary society preaches this ideal of unindividualized equality because it needs human atoms, each one the same, to make them function in a mass aggregation, smoothly, without friction; all obeying the same commands, yet everybody being convinced that he is following his own desires. Just as modern mass production requires the standardization of commodities, so the social process requires standardization of man, and this standardization is called "equality."

Union by conformity is not intense and violent; it is calm, dictated by routine, and for this very reason often is insufficient to pacify the anxiety of separateness. The incidence of alcoholism, drug addiction, compulsive sexualism, and suicide in contemporary Western society are symptoms of this relative failure of herd conformity. Furthermore, this solution concerns mainly the mind and not the body, and for this reason too is lacking in comparison with the orgiastic solutions. Herd conformity has only one advantage: it is permanent, and not spasmodic. The individual is introduced into the conformity pattern at the age of three or four, and subsequently never loses his contact with the herd. Even his funeral, which he anticipates as his last great social affair, is in strict conformance with the pattern.

In addition to conformity as a way to relieve the anxiety springing from separateness, another factor of contemporary life must be considered: the role of the work routine and of the pleasure routine. Man becomes a "nine to fiver"; he is part of the labor force, or the bureaucratic force of clerks and managers. He has little initiative, his tasks are prescribed by the organization of the work; there is even little difference between those high up on the ladder and those on the bottom. They all perform tasks prescribed by the whole structure of the organization, at a prescribed speed, and in a prescribed manner. Even the feelings are prescribed: cheerfulness, tolerance, reliability, ambition, and an ability to get along with everybody without friction. Fun is routinized in similar, although not quite as drastic ways. Books are selected by the book clubs, movies by the film and theater owners and the advertising slogans paid for by them; the rest is also uniform: the Sunday ride in the car, the television session, the card game, the social parties. From birth to death, from Monday to Monday, from morning to evening—all activities are routinized, and not prefabricated. How should a man caught in this net of routine not forget that he is a man, a unique individual, one who is given only this one chance of living, with hopes and disappointments, with sorrow and fear, with longing for love and the dread of the nothing and of separateness?

A third way of attaining union lies in *creative activity*, be it that of the artist, or of the artisan. In any kind of creative work the creating person unites himself with his material, which represents the world outside of himself. Whether a carpenter makes a table, or a goldsmith a piece of jewelry, whether the peasant grows his corn or the painter paints a picture, in all types of creative work the worker and his object become one, man unites himself with the world in the process of creation. This, however, holds true only for productive work, for work in which *I* plan, produce, see the result of my work. In the modern work process of a clerk, the worker on the endless belt, little is left of this uniting quality of work. The worker becomes an appendix to the machine or to the bureaucratic organization. He has ceased to be he—hence no union takes place beyond that of conformity.

The unity achieved in productive work is not interpersonal; the unity achieved in orgiastic fusion is transitory; the unity achieved by conformity is only pseudo-unity. Hence, they are only partial answers to the problem of existence. The full answer lies in the achievement of interpersonal union, of fusion with another person, in *love.*

This desire for interpersonal fusion is the most powerful striving in man. It is the most fundamental passion, it is the force which keeps the human race together, the clan, the family, society. The failure to achieve it means insanity or destruction—self-destruction or destruction of others. Without love, humanity could not exist for a day. Yet, if we call the achievement of interpersonal union "love," we find ourselves in a serious difficulty. Fusion can be achieved in different ways—and the differences are not less significant than what is common to the various forms of love. Should they all be called love? Or should we reserve the word "love" only for a specific kind of union, one which has been the ideal virtue in all great humanistic religions and philosophical systems of the last four thousand years of Western and Eastern history?

As with all semantic difficulties, the answer can only be arbitrary. What matters is that we know what kind of union we are talking about when we speak of love. Do we refer to love as the mature answer to the problem of existence, or do we speak of those immature forms of love which may be called *symbiotic union?* In the following pages I shall call love only the former. I shall begin the discussion of "love" with the latter.

Symbiotic union has its biological pattern in the relationship between the pregnant mother and the foetus. They are two, and yet one. They live "together," (*sym-biosis*), they need each other. The foetus is a part of the mother, it receives everything it needs from her; mother is its world, as it were; she feeds it, she protects it, but also her own life is enhanced by it. In the *psychic* symbiotic union, the two bodies are independent, but the same kind of attachment exists psychologically.

The *passive* form of the symbiotic union is that of submission, or if we use a clinical term, of *masochism.* The masochistic person escapes from the unbearable feeling of isolation and separateness by making himself part and parcel of another person who directs him, guides him, protects him; who is his life and his oxygen, as it were. The power of the one to whom one submits is inflated, may he be a person or a god; he is everything, I am nothing, except inasmuch as I am part of him. As a part, I am a part of greatness, of power, of certainty. The masochistic person does not have to make decisions, does not have to take any risks; he is never alone—but he is not independent; he has no integrity; he is not yet fully born. In a religious context the object of worship is called an idol; in a secular context of a masochistic love relationship the essential mechanism, that of idolatry, is the same. The masochistic relationship can be blended with physical, sexual desire; in this case it is not only a submission in which one's mind participates, but also one's whole body. There can be masochistic submission to fate, to sickness, to rhythmic music, to the orgiastic state produced by drugs or under hypnotic trance—in all these instances the person renounces his integrity, makes himself the instrument of somebody or something outside of himself; he need not solve the problem of living by productive activity.

The *active* form of symbiotic fusion is domination or, to use the psychological term corresponding to masochism, *sadism*. The sadistic person wants to escape from his aloneness and his sense of imprisonment by making another person part and parcel of himself. He inflates and enhances himself by incorporating another person, who worships him.

The sadistic person is as dependent on the submissive person as the latter is on the former; neither can live without the other. The difference is only that the sadistic person commands, exploits, hurts, humiliates, and that the masochistic person is commanded, exploited, hurt, humiliated. This is a considerable difference in a realistic sense; in a deeper emotional sense, the difference is not so great as that which they both have in common: fusion without integrity. If one understands this, it is also not surprising to find that usually a person reacts in both the sadistic and the masochistic manner, usually toward different objects. Hitler reacted primarily in a sadistic fashion toward people, but masochistically toward fate, history, the "higher power" of nature. His end—suicide among general destruction—is as characteristic as was his dream of success—total domination.[1]

In contrast to symbiotic union, mature *love* is *union under the condition of preserving one's integrity*, one's individuality. *Love is an active power in man;* a power which breaks through the walls which

---

[1] Cf. a more detailed study of sadism and masochism in E. Fromm, *Escape from Freedom*, Rinehart & Company, New York, 1941.

separate man from his fellow men, which unites him with others; love makes him overcome the sense of isolation and separateness, yet it permits him to be himself, to retain his integrity. In love the paradox occurs that two beings become one and yet remain two.

If we say love is an activity, we face a difficulty which lies in the ambiguous meaning of the word "activity." By "activity," in the modern usage of the word, is usually meant an action which brings about a change in an existing situation by means of an expenditure of energy. Thus a man is considered active if he does business, studies medicine, works on an endless belt, builds a table, or is engaged in sports. Common to all these activities is that they are directed toward an outside goal to be achieved. What is *not* taken into account is the *motivation* of activity. Take for instance a man driven to incessant work by a sense of deep insecurity and loneliness; or another one driven by ambition, or greed for money. In all these cases the person is the slave of a passion, and his activity is in reality a "passivity" because he is driven; he is the sufferer, not the "actor." On the other hand, a man sitting quiet and contemplating, with no purpose or aim except that of experiencing himself and his oneness with the world, is considered to be "passive," because he is not "doing" anything. In reality, this attitude of concentrated meditation is the highest activity there is, an activity of the soul, which is possible only under the condition of inner freedom and independence. One concept of activity, the modern one, refers to the use of energy for the achievement of external aims; the other concept of activity refers to the use of man's inherent powers, regardless of whether any external change is brought about. The latter concept of activity has been formulated most clearly by Spinoza. He differentiates among the affects between active and passive affects, "actions" and "passions." In the exercise of an active affect, man is free, he is the master of his affect; in the exercise of a passive affect, man is driven, the object of motivations of which he himself is not aware. Thus Spinoza arrives at the statement that virtue and power are one and the same.[2] Envy, jealousy, ambition, any kind of greed are passions; love is an action, the practice of a human power, which can be practiced only in freedom and never as the result of a compulsion.

Love is an activity, not a passive affect; it is a "standing in," not a "falling for." In the most general way, the active character of love can be described by stating that love is primarily *giving*, not receiving.

[2] Spinoza, *Ethics* IV, Def. 8.

What is giving? Simple as the answer to this question seems to be, it is actually full of ambiguities and complexities. The most widespread misunderstanding is that which assumes that giving is "giving up" something, being deprived of, sacrificing. The person whose character has not developed beyond the stage of the receptive, exploitative, or hoarding orientation, experiences the act of giving in this way. The marketing character is willing to give, but only in exchange for receiving; giving without receiving for him is being cheated.[3] People whose main orientation is a non-productive one feel giving as an impoverishment. Most individuals of this type therefore refuse to give. Some make a virtue out of giving in the sense of a sacrifice. They feel that just because it is painful to give, one *should* give; the virtue of giving to them lies in the very act of acceptance of the sacrifice. For them, the norm that it is better to give than to receive means that it is better to suffer deprivation than to experience joy.

For the productive character, giving has an entirely different meaning. Giving is the highest expression of potency. In the very act of giving, I experience my strength, my wealth, my power. This experience of heightened vitality and potency fills me with joy. I experience myself as overflowing, spending, alive, hence as joyous.[4] Giving is more joyous than receiving, not because it is a deprivation, but because in the act of giving lies the expression of my aliveness.

It is not difficult to recognize the validity of this principle by applying it to various specific phenomena. The most elementary example lies in the sphere of sex. The culmination of the male sexual function lies in the act of giving; the man gives himself, his sexual organ, to the woman. At the moment of orgasm he gives his semen to her. He cannot help giving it if he is potent. If he cannot give, he is impotent. For the woman the process is not different; although somewhat more complex. She gives herself too; she opens the gates to her feminine center; in the act of receiving, she gives. If she is incapable of this act of giving, if she can only receive, she is frigid. With her the act of giving occurs again, not in her function as a lover, but in that as a mother. She gives of herself to the growing child within her, she gives her milk to the infant, she gives her bodily warmth. Not to give would be painful.

In the sphere of material things giving means being rich. Not he

---

[3] Cf. a detailed discussion of these character orientations in E. Fromm, *Man for Himself*, Rinehart & Company, New York, 1947, Chap. III, pp. 54-117.

[4] Compare the definition of joy given by Spinoza.

who *has* much is rich, but he who *gives* much. The hoarder who is anxiously worried about losing something is, psychologically speaking, the poor, impoverished man, regardless of how much he has. Whoever is capable to giving of himself is rich. He experiences himself as one who can confer of himself to others. Only one who is deprived of all that goes beyond the barest necessities for subsistence would be incapable of enjoying the act of giving material things. But daily experience shows that what a person considers the minimal necessities depends as much on his character as it depends on his actual possessions. It is well known that the poor are more willing to give than the rich. Nevertheless, poverty beyond a certain point may make it impossible to give, and is so degrading, not only because of the suffering it causes directly, but because of the fact that it deprives the poor of the joy of giving.

The most important sphere of giving, however, is not that of material things, but lies in the specifically human realm. What does one person give to another? He gives of himself, of the most precious he has, he gives of his life. This does not necessarily mean that he sacrifices his life for the other—but that he gives him of that which is alive in him; he gives him of his joy, of his interest, of his understanding, of his knowledge, of his humor, of his sadness—of all expressions and manifestations of that which is alive in him. In thus giving of his life, he enriches the other person, he enhances the other's sense of aliveness by enhancing his own sense of aliveness. He does not give in order to receive; giving is in itself exquisite joy. But in giving he cannot help bringing something to life in the other person, and this which is brought to life reflects back to him; in truly giving, he cannot help receiving that which is given back to him. Giving implies to make the other person a giver also and they both share in the joy of what they have brought to life. In the act of giving something is born, and both persons involved are grateful for the life that is born for both of them. Specifically with regard to love this means: love is a power which produces love; impotence is the inability to produce love. This thought has been beautifully expressed by Marx: "Assume," he says, "*man* as *man,* and his relation to the world as a human one, and you can exchange love only for love, confidence for confidence, etc. If you wish to enjoy art, you must be an artistically trained person; if you wish to have influence on other people, you must be a person who has a really stimulating and furthering influence on other people. Every one of your relationships to man and to nature must be a definite expression of your *real, individual* life corresponding to the object of your will. If you love without calling forth love, that is, if your love as such does not produce love, if by means of an *expression of life* as a loving person you do not make of yourself a *loved person*, then your love is impotent, a misfortune." [5] But not only in love does giving mean receiving. The teacher is taught by his students, the actor is stimulated by his audience, the psychoanalyst is cured by his patient—provided they do not treat each other as objects, but are related to each other genuinely and productively.

It is hardly necessary to stress the fact that the ability to love as an act of giving depends on the character development of the person. It presupposes the attainment of a predominantly productive orientation; in this orientation the person has overcome dependency, narcissistic omnipotence, the wish to exploit others, or to hoard, and has acquired faith in his own human powers, courage to rely on his powers in the attainment of his goals. To the degree that these qualities are lacking, he is afraid of giving himself—hence of loving.

Beyond the element of giving, the active character of love becomes evident in the fact that it always implies certain basic elements, common to all forms of love. These are *care, responsibility, respect* and *knowledge.*

That love implies *care* is most evident in a mother's love for her child. No assurance of her love would strike us as sincere if we saw her lacking in care for the infant, if she neglected to feed it, to bathe it, to give it physical comfort; and we are impressed by her love if we see her caring for the child. It is not different even with the love for animals or flowers. If a woman told us that she loved flowers, and we saw that she forgot to water them, we would not believe in her "love" for flowers. *Love is the active concern for the life and the growth of that which we love.* Where this active concern is lacking, there is no love. This element of love has been beautifully described in the book of Jonah. God has told Jonah to go to Nineveh to warn its inhabitants that they will be punished unless they mend their evil ways. Jonah runs away from his mission because he is afraid that the people of Nineveh will repent and that God will forgive them. He is a man with a strong sense of order and law, but without love. However, in his attempt to escape, he finds himself in the belly of a whale, symbolizing the state of isolation and imprisonment which his

[5] "Nationalökonomie und Philosophie," 1844, published in Karl Marx' *Die Frühschriften*, Alfred Kröner Verlag, Stuttgart, 1953, pp. 300, 301. (My translation, E. F.)

lack of love and solidarity has brought upon him. God saves him, and Jonah goes to Nineveh. He preaches to the inhabitants as God had told him, and the very thing he was afraid of happens. The men of Nineveh repent their sins, mend their ways, and God forgives them and decides not to destroy the city. Jonah is intensely angry and disappointed; he wanted "justice" to be done, not mercy. At last he finds some comfort in the shade of a tree which God had made to grow for him to protect him from the sun. But when God makes the tree wilt, Jonah is depressed and angrily complains to God. God answers: "Thou hast had pity on the gourd for the which thou hast not labored neither madest it grow; which came up in a night, and perished in a night. And should I not spare Nineveh, that great city, wherein are more than sixscore thousand people that cannot discern between their right hand and their left hand; and also much cattle?" God's answer to Jonah is to be understood symbolically. God explains to Jonah that the essence of love is to "labor" for something and "to make something grow," that love and labor are inseparable. One loves that for which one labors, and one labors for that which one loves.

Care and concern imply another aspect of love; that of *responsibility*. Today responsibility is often meant to denote duty, something imposed upon one from the outside. But responsibility, in its true sense, is an entirely voluntary act; it is my response to the needs, expressed or unexpressed, of another human being. To be "responsible" means to be able and ready to "respond." Jonah did not feel responsible to the inhabitants of Nineveh. He, like Cain, could ask: "Am I my brother's keeper?" The loving person responds. The life of his brother is not his brother's business alone, but his own. He feels responsible for his fellow men, as he feels responsible for himself. This responsibility, in the case of the mother and her infant, refers mainly to the care for physical needs. In the love between adults it refers mainly to the psychic needs of the other person.

Responsibility could easily deteriorate into domination and possessiveness, were it not for a third component of love, *respect*. Respect is not fear and awe; it denotes, in accordance with the root of the word (*respicere* = to look at), the ability to see a person as he is, to be aware of his unique individuality. Respect means the concern that the other person should grow and unfold as he is. Respect, thus, implies the absence of exploitation. I want the loved person to grow and unfold for his own sake, and in his own ways, and not for the purpose of serving me. If I love the other person, I feel one with him or her, but with him *as he is*, not as I need him to be as an object for my use. It is clear that respect is possible only if *I* have achieved independence; if I can stand and walk without needing crutches, without having to dominate and exploit anyone else. Respect exists only on the basis of freedom: "l'amour est l'enfant de la liberté" as an old French song says; love is the child of freedom, never that of domination.

To respect a person is not possible without *knowing* him; care and responsibility would be blind if they were not guided by knowledge. Knowledge would be empty if it were not motivated by concern. There are many layers of knowledge; the knowledge which is an aspect of love is one which does not stay at the periphery, but penetrates to the core. It is possible only when I can transcend the concern for myself and see the other person in his own terms. I may know, for instance, that a person is angry, even if he does not show it overtly; but I may know him more deeply than that; then I know that he is anxious, and worried; that he feels lonely, that he feels guilty. Then I know that his anger is only the manifestation of something deeper, and I see him as anxious and embarrassed, that is, as the suffering person, rather than as the angry one.

Knowledge has one more, and a more fundamental, relation to the problem of love. The basic need to fuse with another person so as to transcend the prison of one's separateness is closely related to another specifically human desire, that to know the "secret of man." While life in its merely biological aspects is a miracle and a secret, man in his human aspects is an unfathomable secret to himself— and to his fellow man. We know ourselves, and yet even with all the efforts we may make, we do not know ourselves. We know our fellow man, and yet we do not know him, because we are not a thing, and our fellow man is not a thing. The further we reach into the depth of our being, or someone else's being, the more the goal of knowledge eludes us. Yet we cannot help desiring to penetrate into the secret of man's soul, into the innermost nucleus which is "he."

There is one way, a desperate one, to know the secret: it is that of complete power over another person; the power which makes him do what we want, feel what we want, think what we want; which transforms him into a thing, our thing, our possession. The ultimate degree of this attempt to know lies in the extremes of sadism, the desire and ability to make a human being suffer; to torture him, to force him to betray his secret in his suffering. In this craving for penetrating man's secret, his and hence our own, lies an essential motivation for the depth and intensity of cruelty and destructiveness. In a very succinct way this idea has been expressed by Isaac Babel. He quotes a fellow officer in the Russian civil war, who has just stamped his former master to death, as saying: "With shooting—I'll put it this way—with shooting you only get rid of a chap. . . . With shooting you'll never get at the soul, to where it is in a fellow and how it shows itself. But I don't spare myself, and I've more than once trampled an enemy for over an hour. You see, I want to get to know what life really is, what life's like down our way." [6]

In children we often see this path to knowledge quite overtly. The child takes something apart, breaks it up in order to know it; or it takes an animal apart; cruelly tears off the wings of a butterfly in order to know it, to force its secret. The cruelty itself is motivated by something deeper: the wish to know the secret of things and of life.

The other path to knowing "the secret" is love. Love is active penetration of the other person, in which my desire to know is stilled by union. In the act of fusion I know you, I know myself, I know everybody—and I "know" nothing. I know in the only way knowledge of that which is alive is possible for man—by experience of union—not by any knowledge our thought can give. Sadism is motivated by the wish to know the secret, yet I remain as ignorant as I was before. I have torn the other being apart limb from limb, yet all I have done is to destroy him. Love is the only way of knowledge, which in the act of union answers my quest. In the act of loving, of giving myself, in the act of penetrating the other person, I find myself, I discover myself, I discover us both, I discover man.

The longing to know ourselves and to know our fellow man has been expressed in the Delphic motto: "Know thyself." It is the mainspring of all psychology. But inasmuch as the desire is to know all of man, his innermost secret, the desire can never be fulfilled in knowledge of the ordinary kind, in knowledge only by thought. Even if we knew a thousand times more of ourselves, we would never reach bottom. We would still remain an enigma to ourselves, as our fellow man would remain an enigma to us. The only way of full knowledge lies in the *act* of love: this act transcends thought, it transcends words. It is the daring plunge into the experience of union. However, knowledge in thought, that is psychological knowledge, is a necessary condition for full knowledge in the act of love. I have to know the other person and myself objectively, in order to be able to see his

[6] I. Babel, *The Collected Stories*, Criterion Books, New York, 1955.

reality, or rather, to overcome the illusions, the irrationally distorted picture I have of him. Only if I know a human being objectively, can I know him in his ultimate essence, in the act of love.[7]

The problem of knowing man is parallel to the religious problem of knowing God. In conventional Western theology the attempt is made to know God by thought, to make statements *about* God. It is assumed that I can know God in my thought. In mysticism, which is the consequent outcome of monotheim (as I shall try to show later on), the attempt is given up to know God by thought, and it is replaced by the experience of union with God in which there is no more room—and no need—for knowledge *about* God.

The experience of union, with man, or religiously speaking, with God, is by no means irrational. On the contrary, it is as Albert Schweitzer has pointed out, the consequence of rationalism, its most daring and radical consequence. It is based on our knowledge of the fundamental, and not accidental, limitations of our knowledge. It is the knowledge that we shall never "grasp" the secret of man and of the universe, but that we can know, nevertheless, in the act of love. Psychology as a science has its limitations, and, as the logical consequence of theology is mysticism, so the ultimate consequence of psychology is love.

Care, responsibility, respect and knowledge are mutually interdependent. They are a syndrome of attitudes which are to be found in the mature person; that is, in the person who develops his own powers productively, who only wants to have that which he has worked for, who has given up narcissistic dreams of omniscience and omnipotence, who has acquired humility based on the inner strength which only genuine productive activity can give.

Thus far I have spoken of love as the overcoming of human separateness, as the fulfillment of the longing for union. But above the universal, existential need for union rises a more specific, biological one: the desire for union between masculine and feminine poles. The idea of this polarization is most strikingly expressed in the myth that originally man and woman were one, that they were cut in half, and from then on each male has been seeking for the lost female part of himself in order to unite again with her. (The same idea of

---

[7] The above statement has an important implication for the role of psychology in contemporary Western culture. While the great popularity of psychology certainly indicates an interest in the knowledge of man, it also betrays the fundamental lack of love in human relations today. Psychological knowledge thus becomes a substitute for full knowledge in the act of love, instead of being a step toward it.

the original unity of the sexes is also contained in the Biblical story
of Eve being made from Adam's rib, even though in this story, in the
spirit of patriarchalism, woman is considered secondary to man.)
The meaning of the myth is clear enough. Sexual polarization leads
man to seek union in a specific way, that of union with the other
sex. The polarity between the male and female principles exists also
within each man and each woman. Just as physiologically man and
woman each have hormones of the opposite sex, they are bisexual
also in the psychological sense. They carry in themselves the principle of receiving and of penetrating, of matter and of spirit. Man—
and woman—finds union within himself only in the union of his female
and his male polarity. This polarity is the basis for all creativity.

The male-female polarity is also the basis for interpersonal creativity.
This is obvious biologically in the fact that the union of sperm and
ovum is the basis for the birth of a child. But in the purely psychic
realm it is not different; in the love between man and woman, each
of them is reborn. (The homosexual deviation is a failure to attain
this polarized union, and thus the homosexual suffers from the pain
of never-resolved separateness, a failure, however, which he shares
with the average heterosexual who cannot love.)

The same polarity of the male and female principle exists in nature;
not only, as is obvious in animals and plants, but in the polarity of
the two fundamental functions, that of receiving and that of penetrating. It is the polarity of the earth and rain, of the river and the
ocean, of night and day, of darkness and light, of matter and spirit.
This idea is beautifully expressed by the great Muslim poet and
mystic, Rūmī:

> Never, in sooth, does the lover seek without being sought by his beloved.
> When the lightning of love has shot into *this* heart, know that there is
>   love in *that* heart.
> When love of God waxes in thy heart, beyond any doubt God hath love
>   for thee.
> No sound of clapping comes from one hand without the other hand.
> Divine Wisdom is destiny and decree made us lovers of one another.
> Because of that fore-ordainment every part of the world is paired with
>   its mate.
> In the view of the wise, Heaven is man and Earth woman: Earth fosters
>   what Heaven lets fall.
> When Earth lacks heat, Heaven sends it; when she has lost her freshness
>   and moisture, Heaven restores it.
> Heaven goes on his rounds, like a husband foraging for the wife's sake;

And Earth is busy with housewiferies: she attends to births and suckling
that which she bears.
Regard Earth and Heaven as endowed with intelligence, since they do
the work of intelligent beings.
Unless these twain taste pleasure from one another, why are they creep-
ing together like sweethearts?
Without the Earth, how should flower and tree blossom? What, then,
would Heaven's water and heat produce?
As God put desire in man and woman to the end that the world should
be preserved by their union,
So hath He implanted in every part of existence the desire for another
part.
Day and Night are enemies outwardly; yet both serve one purpose,
Each in love with the other for the sake of perfecting their mutual work,
Without Night, the nature of Man would receive no income, so there
would be nothing for Day to spend.[8]

The problem of the male-female polarity leads to some further
discussion on the subject matter of love and sex. I have spoken
before of Freud's error in seeing in love exclusively the expression
—or a sublimation—of the sexual instinct, rather than recognizing that
the sexual desire is one manifestation of the need for love and union.
But Freud's error goes deeper. In line with his physiological materialism, he sees in the sexual instinct the result of a chemically
produced tension in the body which is painful and seeks for relief.
The aim of the sexual desire is the removal of this painful tension;
sexual satisfaction lies in the accomplishment of this removal. This
view has its validity to the extent that the sexual desire operates in
the same fashion as hunger or thirst do when the organism is undernourished. Sexual desire, in this concept, is an itch, sexual satisfaction
the removal of the itch. In fact, as far as this concept of sexuality
is concerned, masturbation would be the ideal sexual satisfaction.
What Freud, paradoxically enough, ignores, is the psycho-biological
aspect of sexuality, the masculine-feminine polarity, and the desire
to bridge this polarity by union. This curious error was probably
facilitated by Freud's extreme patriarchalism, which led him to the
assumption that sexuality per se is masculine, and thus made him
ignore the specific female sexuality. He expressed this idea in the
Three Contributions to the Theory of Sex, saying that the libido has
regularly "a masculine nature," regardless of whether it is the libido

[8] R. A. Nicholson, *Rūmī*, George Allen and Unwin, Ltd., London, 1950, pp.
122-3.

in a man or in a woman. The same idea is also expressed in a rationalized form in Freud's theory that the little boy experiences the woman as a castrated man, and that she herself seeks for various compensations for the loss of the male genital. But woman is not a castrated man, and her sexuality is specifically feminine and not of "a masculine nature."

Sexual attraction between the sexes is only partly motivated by the need for removal of tension; it is mainly the need for union with the other sexual pole. In fact, erotic attraction is by no means only expressed in sexual attraction. There is masculinity and femininity in *character* as well as in *sexual function*. The masculine character can be defined as having the qualities of penetration, guidance, activity, discipline and adventurousness; the feminine character by the qualities of productive receptiveness, protection, realism, endurance, motherliness. (It must always be kept in mind that in each individual both characteristics are blended, but with the preponderance of those appertaining to "his" or "her" sex.) Very often if the masculine *character* traits of a man are weakened because emotionally he has remained a child, he will try to compensate for this lack by the exclusive emphasis on his male role in *sex*. The result is the Don Juan, who needs to prove his male prowess in sex because he is unsure of his masculinity in a characterological sense. When the paralysis of masculinity is more extreme, sadism (the use of force) becomes the main—a perverted—substitute for masculinity. If the feminine sexuality is weakened or perverted, it is transformed into masochism, or possessiveness.

Freud has been criticized for his overevaluation of sex. This criticism was often prompted by the wish to remove an element from Freud's system which aroused criticism and hostility among conventionally minded people. Freud keenly sensed this motivation and for this very reason fought every attempt to change his theory of sex. Indeed, in his time, Freud's theory had a challenging and revolutionary character. But what was true around 1900 is not true any more fifty years later. The sexual mores have changed so much that Freud's theories are not any longer shocking to the Western middle classes, and it is a quixotic kind of radicalism when orthodox analysts today still think they are courageous and radical in defending Freud's sexual theory. In fact, their brand of psychoanalysis is conformist, and does not try to raise psychological questions which would lead to a criticism of contemporary society.

My criticism of Freud's theory is not that he overemphasized sex, but his failure to understand sex deeply enough. He took the first step in discovering the significance of interpersonal passions; in accordance with his philosophic premises he explained them physiologically. In the further development of psychoanalysis it is necessary to correct and deepen Freud's concept by translating Freud's insights from the physiological into the biological and existential dimension.[9]

Problems for Thought and Writing

I

1. The title of the book from which this selection has been taken is *The Art of Loving*. Fromm's thesis is clearly that love is not just an enjoyable sensation, something one experiences by chance or "falls into"; it is instead an art that requires knowledge in order to be understood and effort in order to be practiced. Does he convince you that the real problem of love is that of *loving*, of one's capacity to love, and not, as most people in our culture assume, that of *being loved?*

2. Would Fromm argue that the *object* of love is of primary or secondary importance as contrasted with the ability *to love?*

3. Does Fromm seem to you to be arguing in behalf of "Platonic love"? What does that expression mean to you? If you have not done so, read the *Symposium* to discover what Plato actually wrote on the subject of love.

4. Consider the song (there are thousands like it) that goes: "This can't be love because I feel so well. . . ." It reflects one of our culture's commonest assumptions about love, namely that it is a kind of sickness, often accompanied by exterior manifestations, i.e., sleeplessness, loss of appetite, etc. Being "in love" is, according to countless songwriters and poets, an infirmity by definition. Does the view make sense? Does it mean that a person in love looks forward to living in misery for the rest of his life? If not, and if sickness is a necessary first symptom of true love, how is the translation to joy accomplished?

5. Greek, Roman, and Medieval Christian philosophers and theologians were all in substantial agreement that contemplation—what Fromm calls the "attitude of concentrated meditation"—represented the noblest activity of which man is capable. Fromm seems to agree. Do you? Why or why not?

6. Examine Christ's admonition closely: "Love thy neighbor as thyself." Was he saying the same thing Fromm is saying?

7. "It is well known that the poor are more willing to give than the rich." Would you contest Fromm's statement?

8. Fromm's point of view is clearly at odds with countless related conventions within our culture, viz., courtship, the placing of woman on a pedestal,

[9] Freud himself made a first step in this direction in his later concept of the life and death instincts. His concept of the former (*eros*) as a principle of synthesis and unification is on an entirely different plane from that of his libido concept. But in spite of the fact that the theory of life and death instincts was accepted by orthodox analysts, this acceptance did not lead to a fundamental revision of the libido concept, especially as far as clinical work is concerned.

Mother's Day, the responsibility of the husband to remember his wife with a gift every anniversary, etc. Would you willingly sacrifice them for the kind of equality-in-love that Fromm describes? If not, what makes the conventions more desirable? Does asking this question seem to you a fair way of testing Fromm's statement that "Most people are not even aware of their need to conform"?

II

9. Fromm is a psychoanalyst. From his style, references, and allusions what else might you have guessed him to be?

10. Identify: syndrome, exploitative, narcissistic, patriarchalism, polarity, Muslim.

~

THE GRAY BEGINNINGS*   *Rachel Carson*

And the earth was without form, and void; and darkness was upon the face of the deep.   GENESIS

Beginnings are apt to be shadowy, and so it is with the beginnings of that great mother of life, the sea. Many people have debated how and when the earth got its ocean, and it is not surprising that their explanations do not always agree. For the plain and inescapable truth is that no one was there to see, and in the absence of eyewitness accounts there is bound to be a certain amount of disagreement. So if I tell here the story of how the young planet Earth acquired an ocean, it must be a story pieced together from many sources and containing whole chapters the details of which we can only imagine. The story is founded on the testimony of the earth's most ancient rocks, which were young when the earth was young; on other evidence written on the face of the earth's satellite, the moon; and on hints contained in the history of the sun and the whole universe of star-filled space. For although no man was there to witness this cosmic birth, the stars and the moon and the rocks were there, and, indeed, had much to do with the fact that there is an ocean.

The events of which I write must have occurred somewhat more than 2 billion years ago. As nearly as science can tell that is the approximate age of the earth, and the ocean must be very nearly as old. It is possible now to discover the age of the rocks that compose the crust of the earth by measuring the rate of decay of the radioactive materials they contain. The oldest rocks found anywhere on earth —in Manitoba—are about 2.3 billion years old. Allowing 100 million years or so for the cooling of the earth's materials to form a rocky crust, we arrive at the supposition that the tempestuous and violent events connected with our planet's birth occurred nearly 2½ billion years ago. But this is only a minimum estimate, for rocks indicating an even greater age may be found at any time.

The new earth, freshly torn from its parent sun, was a ball of whirling gases, intensely hot, rushing through the black spaces of the universe on a path and at a speed controlled by immense forces. Gradually the ball of flaming gases cooled. The gases began to liquefy, and Earth became a molten mass. The materials of this mass eventually became sorted out in a definite pattern: the heaviest in the center, the less heavy surrounding them, and the least heavy forming the outer rim. This is the pattern which persists today— a central sphere of molten iron, very nearly as hot as it was 2 billion years ago, an intermediate sphere of semiplastic basalt, and a hard outer shell, relatively quite thin and composed of solid basalt and granite.

The outer shell of the young earth must have been a good many millions of years changing from the liquid to the solid state, and it is believed that, before this change was completed, an event of the greatest importance took place—the formation of the moon. The next time you stand on a beach at night, watching the moon's bright path across the water, and conscious of the moon-drawn tides, re-member that the moon itself may have been born of a great tidal wave of earthly substance, torn off into space. And remember that if the moon was formed in this fashion, the event may have had much to do with shaping the ocean basins and the continents as we know them.

There were tides in the new earth, long before there was an ocean. In response to the pull of the sun the molten liquids of the earth's whole surface rose in tides that rolled unhindered around the globe and only gradually slackened and diminished as the earthly shell cooled, congealed, and hardened. Those who believe that the moon is a child of earth say that during an early stage of the earth's develop-ment something happened that caused this rolling, viscid tide to gather speed and momentum and to rise to unimaginable heights. Apparently the force that created these greatest tides the earth has ever known was the force of resonance, for at this time the period of the solar tides had come to approach, then equal, the period of the free oscillation of the liquid earth. And so every sun tide was given increased momentum by the push of the earth's oscillation, and each of the twice-daily tides was larger than the one before it. Physicists have calculated that, after 500 years of such monstrous, steadily increasing tides, those on the side toward the sun became too high for stability, and a great wave was torn away and hurled into space. But immediately, of course, the newly created satellite became subject to physical laws that sent it spinning in an orbit of its own about the earth.

There are reasons for believing that this event took place after the earth's crust had become slightly hardened, instead of during its partly liquid state. There is to this day a great scar on the surface of the globe. This scar or depression holds the Pacific Ocean. According to some geophysicists, the floor of the Pacific is composed of basalt, the substance of the earth's middle layer, while all other oceans are floored with a thin layer of granite. We immediately wonder what became of the Pacific's granite covering and the most convenient assumption is that it was torn away when the moon was formed. There is supporting evidence. The mean density of the moon is much less than that of the earth (3.3 compared with 5.5), suggesting that the moon took away none of the earth's heavy iron core, but that it is composed only of the granite and some of the basalt of the outer layers.

The birth of the moon probably helped shape other regions of the world ocean besides the Pacific. When part of the crust was torn away, strains must have been set up in the remaining granite envelope. Perhaps the granite mass cracked open on the side opposite the moon scar. Perhaps, as the earth spun on its axis and rushed on its orbit through space, the cracks widened and the masses of granite began to drift apart, moving over a tarry, slowly hardening layer of basalt. Gradually the outer portions of the basalt layer became solid and the wandering continents came to rest, frozen into place with oceans between them. In spite of theories to the contrary, the weight of geologic evidence seems to be that the locations of the major ocean basins and the major continental land masses are today much the same as they have been since a very early period of the earth's history.

But this is to anticipate the story, for when the moon was born there was no ocean. The gradually cooling earth was enveloped in heavy layers of cloud, which contained much of the water of the new planet. For a long time its surface was so hot that no moisture could fall without immediately being reconverted to steam. This dense, perpetually renewed cloud covering must have been thick enough that no rays of sunlight could penetrate it. And so the rough outlines of the continents and the empty ocean basins were sculptured out of the surface of the earth in darkness, in a Stygian world of heated rock and swirling clouds and gloom.

As soon as the earth's crust cooled enough, the rains began to fall. Never have there been such rains since that time. They fell continuously, day and night, days passing into months, into years, into centuries. They poured into the waiting ocean basins, or, falling upon the continental masses, drained away to become sea.

That primeval ocean, growing in bulk as the rains slowly filled its basins, must have been only faintly salt. But the falling rains were the symbol of the dissolution of the continents. From the moment the rains began to fall, the lands began to be worn away and carried to the sea. It is an endless, inexorable process that has never stopped —the dissolving of the rocks, the leaching out of their contained minerals, the carrying of the rock fragments and dissolved minerals to the ocean. And over the eons of time, the sea has grown ever more bitter with the salt of the continents.

In what manner the sea produced the mysterious and wonderful stuff called protoplasm we cannot say. In its warm, dimly lit waters the unknown conditions of temperature and pressure and saltiness must have been the critical ones for the creation of life from non-life. At any rate they produced the result that neither the alchemists with their crucibles nor modern scientists in their laboratories have been able to achieve.

Before the first living cell was created, there may have been many trials and failures. It seems probable that, within the warm saltiness of the primeval sea, certain organic substances were fashioned from carbon dioxide, sulphur, phosphorus, potassium, and calcium. Perhaps these were transition steps from which the complex molecules of protoplasm arose—molecules that somehow acquired the ability to reproduce themselves and begin the endless stream of life. But at present no one is wise enough to be sure.

Those first living things may have been simple microorganisms rather like some of the bacteria we know today—mysterious borderline forms that were not quite plants, not quite animals, barely over the intangible line that separates the non-living from the living. It is doubtful that this first life possessed the substance chlorophyll, with

which plants in sunlight transform lifeless chemicals into the living
stuff of their tissues. Little sunshine could enter their dim world,
penetrating the cloud banks from which fell the endless rains. Probably the sea's first children lived on the organic substances then
present in the ocean waters, or, like the iron and sulphur bacteria
that exist today, lived directly on inorganic food.

All the while the cloud cover was thinning, the darkness of the
nights alternated with palely illumined days, and finally the sun for
the first time shone through upon the sea. By this time some of the
living things that floated in the sea must have developed the magic
of chlorophyll. Now they were able to take the carbon dioxide of
the air and the water of the sea and of these elements, in sunlight,
build the organic substances they needed for life. So the first true
plants came into being.

Another group of organisms, lacking the chlorophyll but needing
organic food, found they could make a way of life for themselves by
devouring the plants. So the first animals arose, and from that day
to this, every animal in the world has followed the habit it learned
in the ancient seas and depends, directly or through complex food
chains, on the plants for food and life.

As the years passed, and the centuries, and the millions of years,
the stream of life grew more and more complex. From simple, one-
celled creatures, others that were aggregations of specialized cells
arose, and then creatures with organs for feeding, digesting, breathing, reproducing. Sponges grew on the rocky bottom of the sea's
edge and coral animals built their habitations in warm, clear waters.
Jellyfish swam and drifted in the sea. Worms evolved, and starfish,
and hard-shelled creatures with many-jointed legs. The plants, too,
progressed, from the microscopic algae to branched and curiously
fruiting seaweeds that swayed with the tides and were plucked from
the coastal rocks by the surf and cast adrift.

During all this time the continents had no life. There was little
to induce living things to come ashore, forsaking their all-providing,
all-embracing mother sea. The lands must have been bleak and
hostile beyond the power of words to describe. Imagine a whole
continent of naked rock, across which no covering mantle of green
had been drawn—a continent without soil, for there were no land
plants to aid in its formation and bind it to the rocks with their roots.
Imagine a land of stone, a silent land, except for the sound of the
rains and winds that swept across it. For there was no living voice,
and nothing moved over its surface except the shadows of the clouds.

Meanwhile, the gradual cooling of the planet, which had first given the earth its hard granite crust, was progressing into its deeper layers; and as the interior slowly cooled and contracted, it drew away from the outer shell. This shell, accommodating itself to the shrinking sphere within it, fell into folds and wrinkles—the earth's first mountain ranges.

Geologists tell us that there must have been at least two periods of mountain building (often called "revolutions") in that dim period, so long ago that the rocks have no record of it, so long ago that the mountains themselves have long since been worn away. Then there came a third great period of upheaval and readjustment of the earth's crust, about a billion years ago, but of all its majestic mountains the only reminders today are the Laurentian hills of eastern Canada, and a great shield of granite over the flat country around Hudson Bay.

The epochs of mountain building only served to speed up the processes of erosion by which the continents were worn down and their crumbling rock and contained minerals returned to the sea. The uplifted masses of the mountains were prey to the bitter cold of the upper atmosphere and under the attacks of frost and snow and ice the rocks cracked and crumbled away. The rains beat with greater violence upon the slopes of the hills and carried away the substance of the mountains in torrential streams. There was still no plant covering to modify and resist the power of the rains.

And in the sea, life continued to evolve. The earliest forms have left no fossils by which we can identify them. Probably they were soft-bodied, with no hard parts that could be preserved. Then, too, the rock layers formed in those early days have since been so altered by enormous heat and pressure, under the foldings of the earth's crust, that any fossils they might have contained would have been destroyed.

For the past 500 million years, however, the rocks have preserved the fossil record. By the dawn of the Cambrian period, when the history of living things was first inscribed on rock pages, life in the sea had progressed so far that all the main groups of backboneless or invertebrate animals had been developed. But there were no animals with backbones, no insects or spiders, and still no plant or animal had been evolved that was capable of venturing onto the forbidding land. So for more than three-fourths of geologic time the continents were desolate and uninhabited, while the sea prepared the life that was later to invade them and make them habitable.

Meanwhile, with violent tremblings of the earth and with the fire
and smoke of roaring volcanoes, mountains rose and wore away,
glaciers moved to and fro over the earth, and the sea crept over the
continents and again receded.

It was not until Silurian time, some 350 million years ago, that the
first pioneer of land life crept out on the shore. It was an arthropod,
one of the great tribe that later produced crabs and lobsters and
insects. It must have been something like a modern scorpion, but,
unlike its descendants, it never wholly severed the ties that united
it to the sea. It lived a strange life, half-terrestrial, half-aquatic,
something like that of the ghost crabs that speed along the beaches
today, now and then dashing into the surf to moisten their gills.

Fish, tapered of body and stream-molded by the press of running
waters, were evolving in Silurian rivers. In times of drought, in the
drying pools and lagoons, the shortage of oxygen forced them to
develop swim bladders for the storage of air. One form developed
an air-breathing lung and by its air could live buried in the mud for
long periods.

It is very doubtful that the animals alone would have succeeded
in colonizing the land, for only the plants had the power to bring
about the first amelioration of its harsh conditions. They helped
make soil of the crumbling rocks, they held back the soil from the
rains that would have swept it away, and little by little they softened
and subdued the bare rock, the lifeless desert. We know very little
about the first land plants, but they must have been closely related
to some of the larger seaweeds that had learned to live in the coastal
shallows, developing strengthened stems and grasping, rootlike hold-
fasts to resist the drag and pull of the waves. Perhaps it was in some
coastal lowlands, periodically drained and flooded, that some such
plants found it possible to survive, though separated from the sea.
This also seems to have taken place in the Silurian period.

The mountains that had been thrown up by the Laurentian revolution gradually wore away, and as the sediments were washed from
their summits and deposited on the lowlands, great areas of the
continents sank under the load. The seas crept out of their basins
and spread over the lands. Life fared well and was exceedingly
abundant in those shallow, sunlit seas. But with the later retreat
of the ocean water into the deeper basins, many creatures must
have been left stranded in shallow, landlocked bays. Some of these
animals found means to survive on land. The lakes, the shores of
the rivers, and the coastal swamps of those days were the testing

grounds in which plants and animals either became adapted to the new conditions or perished.

As the lands rose and the seas receded, a strange fishlike creature emerged on the land, and over the thousands of years its fins became legs, and instead of gills it developed lungs. In the Devonian sandstone this first amphibian left its footprint.

On land and sea the stream of life poured on. New forms evolved; some old ones declined and disappeared. On land the mosses and the ferns and the seed plants developed. The reptiles for a time dominated the earth, gigantic, grotesque, and terrifying. Birds learned to live and move in the ocean of air. The first small mammals lurked inconspicuously in hidden crannies of the earth as though in fear of the reptiles.

When they went ashore the animals that took up a land life carried with them a part of the sea in their bodies, a heritage which they passed on to their children and which even today links each land animal with its origin in the ancient sea. Fish, amphibian, and reptile, warm-blooded bird and mammal—each of us carries in our veins a salty stream in which the elements sodium, potassium, and calcium are combined in almost the same proportions as in sea water. This is our inheritance from the day untold millions of years ago, when a remote ancestor, having progressed from the one-celled to the many-celled stage, first developed a circulatory system in which the fluid was merely the water of the sea. In the same way, our lime-hardened skeletons are a heritage from the calcium-rich ocean of Cambrian time. Even the protoplasm that streams within each cell of our bodies has the chemical structure impressed upon all living matter when the first simple creatures were brought forth in the ancient sea. And as life itself began in the sea, so each of us begins his individual life in a miniature ocean within his mother's womb, and in the stages of his embryonic development repeats the steps by which his race evolved, from gill-breathing inhabitants of a water world to creatures able to live on land.

Some of the land animals later returned to the ocean. After perhaps 50 million years of land life, a number of reptiles entered the sea in Mesozoic time. They were huge and formidable creatures. Some had oarlike limbs by which they rowed through the water; some were web-footed, with long, serpentine necks. These grotesque monsters disappeared millions of years ago, but we remember them when we come upon a large sea turtle swimming many miles at sea, its barnacle-encrusted shell eloquent of its marine life. Much later, perhaps no more than 50 million years ago, some of the mammals, too, abandoned a land life for the ocean. Their descendants are the sea lions, seals, sea elephants, and whales of today.

Among the land mammals there was a race of creatures that took to an arboreal existence. Their hands underwent remarkable development, becoming skilled in manipulating and examining objects, and along with this skill came a superior brain power that compensated for what these comparatively small mammals lacked in strength. At last, perhaps somewhere in the vast interior of Asia, they descended from the trees and became again terrestrial. The past million years have seen their transformation into beings with the body and brain and the mystical spirit of man.

Eventually man, too, found his way back to the sea. Standing on its shores, he must have looked out upon it with wonder and curiosity, compounded with an unconscious recognition of his lineage. He could not physically re-enter the ocean as the seals and whales had done. But over the centuries, with all the skill and ingenuity and reasoning powers of his mind, he has sought to explore and investigate even its most remote parts, so that he might re-enter it mentally and imaginatively.

He fashioned boats to venture out on its surface. Later he found ways to descend to the shallow parts of its floor, carrying with him the air that, as a land mammal long unaccustomed to aquatic life, he needed to breathe. Moving in fascination over the deep sea he could not enter, he found ways to probe its depths, he let down nets to capture its life, he invented mechanical eyes and ears that could re-create for his senses a world long lost, but a world that, in the deepest part of his subconscious mind, he had never wholly forgotten.

And yet he has returned to his mother sea only on her own terms. He cannot control or change the ocean as, in his brief tenancy of earth, he has subdued and plundered the continents. In the artificial world of his cities and towns, he often forgets the true nature of his planet and the long vistas of its history, in which the existence of the race of men has occupied a mere moment of time. The sense of all these things comes to him most clearly in the course of a long ocean voyage, when he watches day after day the receding rim of the horizon, ridged and furrowed by waves; when at night he becomes aware of the earth's rotation as the stars pass overhead; or when, alone in this world of water and sky, he feels the loneliness of his earth in space. And then, as never on land, he knows the truth that his world is a water world, a planet dominated by its covering mantle of ocean, in which the continents are but transient intrusions of land above the surface of the all-encircling sea.

Problems for Thought and Writing

I

1. The "process" here recounted is clearly a reconstruction by inference and conjecture. Does the author write in such a way as to forestall accusations that she is being dogmatic about her evidence? Support your answer.

2. What is the advantage of employing the image of the mother in writing about the sea here? Is this sentimentality (see Richard Altick, page 109)? What would Jung (page 333) think of this image?

3. This selection has been taken from what was the author's best-selling book *The Sea Around Us*. A few oceanographic experts have disparaged it as "popularization." It is clearly not a textbook on marine biology, and in that sense it may be called an example of "popular science." Is it therefore guilty of oversimplification or distortion? Only an expert could judge reliably, but what is your impression? Can you detect any evidence of sensationalism (like a newspaper account of flying saucers, for example)?

4. There is a great similarity between the author's attitude toward her subject, especially at the beginning, and the "Once upon a time, long before any of us were ever born . . ." technique of the traditional fairy tale. Is there any special fitness between that technique and Carson's actual subject matter, suggesting that she chose deliberately to employ it?

II

5. What kind of expository order is used: logical, chronological, or biological?

6. Does the author seem to rely more upon adjectives or verbs in rendering her subject matter clear to the reader? Depending upon your answer, do you think her choice was a wise one?

7. Comment upon the analogy between the beginning of evolutionary life in the ocean and the beginning of individual life in the sea of the womb. Is this an analogy properly used? Is the author trying to *prove* something with it? (See "Comparison and Contrast," page 418.)

~

IN THE DARK*   *Neil Bell*

Darkness had long since fallen over the November landscape. The air of the marshes was still and frosty and faintly odorous of rotting vegetation and of the smoke drifting over from a village three miles away at the edge of the moor.

The man stood still, cursing slowly and monotonously and without zest; he kicked his toes against his heels to stir the blood in his numbed and sodden feet. He shifted his gun and blew upon his fingers, and at the sound the mongrel bitch behind him lifted her muzzle and whined softly. He bent to cuff her, felt her nose against his knee and the excited tension of her body. And then overhead he heard the whir of wings and, taking but the most random aim, fired both barrels.

The mallard duck, fifty feet up and invisible in the blackness, folded its wings jerkily, lowered its head, tipped its stern, and fell like a stooping hawk. The drake swerved, dipped, rose again, and then went on in a laboring switchback flight, its left eye sheared away.

The mongrel retrieved the duck, and the man thrust it into his bag, stood hesitating a few moments, and then, shaking his head, he tucked the gun under his arm, mumbled something to the bitch, and set off at a brisk walk, squelching heedlessly through ankle-deep slush, his head down, his shoulders hunched, his hands deep in his pockets.

It was nearly an hour before he reached his cottage. He stamped his feet on the concrete slab outside the kitchen door and then, opening the door, entered. A woman looked up from her ironing. "Any luck?" she said.

The man shook his head. "Nothing much; a duck, that's all." He tossed his bag on to a chair. "Drake got away. Too perishin' cold, so I turned it in. My boots leak like a sieve. Grub ready?"

"It's in the oven. Take your boots and socks off, and I'll lay the table 's soon as I've done these shirts."

The drake continued its stumbling flight toward the moors; it did not fly in a straight line but in long straggling arcs as if it unconsciously corrected its veer to the left. Presently it came round in a wide sweeping curve and flew back the way it had come, only to return an hour later as if it were pursuing a search or were bewildered or lost. At last, toward morning, it came down on to the still, weedy water of a dyke, some twenty miles from where its mate had been shot down.

All the next day and night it quartered the countryside, its flight more and more erratic as the sight of its other eye began to fail and the world slowly darkened. At the end of the fourth night it woke just before dawn and took wing in a strange blackness which did not lift with the coming of the sun. It flew now in great circles of three or four miles in diameter, plunging ever and again on to the surface of water, resting awhile, and then flapping up again in panic flight.

Toward evening that day it circled about the sedgy reach of a great river, nearly two hundred miles from the place where darkness had shut down upon it. The twisted skeletons of alders and willows overhung the banks of the river. The drake shot down toward the water, flying clumsily, its brain confused, the swift play of its nerves and muscles dulled and leaden. An outstretched wing struck an alder branch, and the bird, with a squawk of terror, dropped heavily into the water, trailing a broken wing.

It slept and woke and swam round in small circles endlessly throughout three nights and days, its sleep lengthening as hunger and the pain of its broken wing weakened it.

Late in the afternoon of the third day some boys coming home from school saw it, tried to reach it with long sticks, and failing, began to pelt it with mud and turf and bits of stick, none of them being lucky enough to find anything more lethal. At each impact of a missile on the water near it the drake fluttered its sound wing desperately, attempting to rise from the water, but succeeding only in driving its body round and round in panic circles.

Presently it drifted into a current and was borne out of the boys' range, and with a final volley and a chorus of hallooing they abandoned the sport and went off in search of other excitement.

The drake drifted on in the current, its broken wing trailing, its head drooped. It was bedraggled and thin; all the bright beauty of its plumage was faded; all its colors, the greenish black of the head and neck, the white collar, the chestnut breast and gray-brown back, seemed to have merged into a mired dinginess. It might have been a bundle of dirty feathers floating on the tideway.

An eddy took it and swept it round and brought it toward the river bank. Ambushed under a submerged root two bright, beadlike eyes watched it. An eel, five feet in length and as thick at the shoulders as a man's calf, slid out of the rooty blackness and shot swiftly upward. Its jaws closed about the drake's feet. The bird squawked on a note that was almost a scream and beat a frantic wing upon the water. The eel, retaining its grip, sounded, and the waters sucked over the drake as it went under. Presently, a few feathers rose slowly to the surface and drifted away on the tide.

Problems for Thought and Writing

1. Is this story art or a piece of propaganda? Might it not be used by the S.P.C.A. to promote better sportsmanship? How do you distinguish between art and propaganda?

2. Compare this story with Carrighar's "The Cutthroat Trout." In which piece is the point of view more rigorously kept? What is meant by "point of view"?

3. Is this story at all sentimental? Is there any "emotion in excess of the fact" here? (See Altick, page 109.)

4. Are there any overtones in the title that add to the resonance of the story, to its emotional vibrations?

~

5 Argument and Persuasion

A great deal of what we loosely call thinking is really informal arguing. How many times in a day's discourse do we hear the expressions: "I don't accept your premises," "You can't prove it by me," "Give me an example," "Who says so?" "What's the proposition?" Premises, proofs, examples, authorities, propositions are all terms involved in the vocabulary of argument, and even the untutored conversationalist is, without knowing it, probably adept at many of the practices and precepts we are about to explain.

More formal argument is equally prevalent. The lawyer laying a case before the jury, the preacher "proving" that virtue is its own reward, the politician viewing with alarm his opponent's personality, the salesman plugging his product, the teacher defending the merits of a poem, the dormitory caucus debating whether to study or go to the basketball game—all are engaged in argument. The study of rhetoric is no longer widely undertaken, and it is doubtful that any of the above arguments would contain all the elements of a formal and traditional argument: exordium, exposition, proposition, division of proofs, confirmation, refutation, summary, conclusion. But though much of our arguing today may be less systematic and stentorian than in the past, it still—when it is effective—requires some knowledge of the traditional rules and techniques.

Formal argument is a form of logical discourse which aims, through the presentation of evidence, to gain assent to a proposition. Its appeal is primarily to the reason.

Persuasion differs from formal argument in that (1) its appeal is mainly to the emotions, and (2) its purpose is less to convince than to gain support for some cause or course of action.

We shall elaborate on those distinctions later, but first we need to recognize that argument is quite different from the other rhetorical modes we have thus far considered. Definition, classification, comparison, and contrast are basically modes of *exposition;* ways of explaining, ordering, and clarifying. Argument, however, is a way of *convincing,* of making someone change his mind. Those expository modes are, of course, included in argument and indispensable to it, but the motive behind argument is basically different from that behind exposition.

Argument is born in *conflict* and exists to resolve it. Conflict can, of course, be dealt with by bullets or fists or brooding, but the most civilized instrument for dealing with it is argument, which uses *words* as its weapons

539

and reason as its umpire. In democracies the instrument has been perfected perhaps more than elsewhere, for such nations have assumed that contention is one of the facts of life and one of the conditions of freedom.

But the false and specious guises that argument can wear are legion. A certain tobacco company, for example, bases their advertising appeal on the gimmick that "thinking men" like and smoke its cigarettes. In one TV ad they show a man sitting next to an electronic computer and smoking this brand of filter cigarette. "Are you an electronics engineer?" the announcer asks. The smoker laughs nonchalantly—no, he is an English teacher; computers are just a hobby for him. Here, clearly, is a man who "thinks for himself"! What cigarette does he smoke? The answer is obvious.

But if we try to get underneath this sales pitch and the argument that it implies, what do we have? We might frame it as a series of syllogisms:

> Men who think for themselves act reasonably.
> Mr. X thinks for himself.
> Mr. X acts reasonably.

Now, to develop fully the conclusion above (for this is a fairly complicated argument) we need a further syllogism:

> One who acts reasonably does nothing to hurt himself.
> Mr. X acts reasonably.
> Mr. X does nothing to hurt himself.

And a third:

> One who does nothing to hurt himself would not smoke harmful cigarettes.
> Mr. X does nothing to hurt himself.
> Mr. X would not smoke harmful cigarettes.

The syllogisms could be handled in a number of different ways, but it is easy to see that the argument, as framed above, depends largely on the particular words chosen to cast it in. (The syllogism is a special form of *deductive* argument which we shall consider later.) But let's examine those words. First, "men who think for themselves." What evidence do we have that the man shown us does think for himself? If he *is* an English teacher, he must have to spend much of his time reading books, writing articles, and grading papers; where does he find the time for building computers? And if he *is* smart enough to build his own computer, what is he doing as an English teacher? He could presumably be earning a fortune working for industry. In short, the first syllogism is shaky as a leaf. Even if we grant the first premise (and it is really too vague to be defensible), the second premise falls down completely: Mr. X has not been proved to be a man who thinks for himself, so we cannot say he acts reasonably. Space doesn't permit a thorough examination of the other syllogisms, but obviously they won't stand up if the premises are false. In short, Mr. X, so far as we know from the evidence presented us, may be a perfect ass— an incompetent who should not even be trusted with matches, to say nothing of cigarettes and computers.

We might say that no "thinking man" would be taken in by such an argument as that. But that's where we came in. The prosperity of advertising in our country indicates that millions of people, thinkers or not, are susceptible to what they must in some sense regard as the "arguments" of the hucksters.

But when the argument involves not the sale of a cigarette or soap product but of, say, a presidential candidate, then it is even more important that we be able to tell a good argument from a false one. "The idea," declared Adlai Stevenson, "that you can merchandise candidates for high office like breakfast cereal . . . is the ultimate indignity to the democratic process." We can prevent the indignity only by knowing when argument is showing its true face and not a mask. The following are some of the essential ingredients.

THE PROPOSITION

The proposition of an argument is simply the main issue at stake, the thesis to be proved. It is called a proposition because it states what the writer or speaker *proposes* to prove. All arguments either begin with a proposition or imply a proposition in their context, and all propositions declare, implicitly or explicitly, that (1) something is a fact, or (2) something should be done. The statement of a debate topic—such as "Resolved: That Capital Punishment Be Abolished"—on which a clear positive or negative stand can be taken, is probably the most formal kind of proposition. In most arguments it is less explicitly delineated. The following assertions of judgment can all be regarded as propositions—matters subject to proof. Although they all, on the surface, state matters of *fact*, there is hardly one of them that does not imply the need for a proposition of action based on the fact, once it is established.

> The want of a feeling for aristocracy, among the rich as well as the poor . . . constitutes the most signal failure of the American spirit.
> Oscar Mandel, "Nobility and the United States," page 171

> The test of a first-rate intelligence is the ability to hold two opposed ideas in the mind at the same time, and still retain the ability to function.
> F. Scott Fitzgerald, "The Crack-Up," page 292

> History has no meaning, in the sense of a clear pattern or determinate plot; but it is not simply meaningless or pointless.
> Herbert J. Muller, "The Meaning of History," page 653

Some of the above are the central statements of whole arguments; some are no more than the thesis sentences of minor paragraphs. But every extended argument has, as well as its main propositions, a number of minor or subsidiary propositions—all of which require proof if the argument is to be won.

Half of any argument lies in the precise and intelligent phrasing of the proposition. To do so gives rise to some special problems.

The Common Ground in Reason

The first question to ask is: Do you really *have* an argument? Obviously you have no argument unless there is a conflict, unless there is a possibility of differing attitudes toward the proposition. Also, you have no argument unless both sides agree to submit to the arbitration of *reason*. Let us take the example of two students debating the merits of foreign sports cars, say Mercedes-Benz and Porsche. After some heated exchanges one of the students says, "I really don't care which is better. Give me either one and I'll be happy!" There is no argument, for one contestant simply had no proposition to make; he was just arguing to hear himself talk. But say, on the other hand, that we have a man so emotionally committed to a position that he cannot see it reasonably. In that remarkable film, *Twelve Angry Men*, we are shown a jury deliberating over the fate of a boy accused of murder. At first only one juryman insists that there is a "reasonable doubt" about the boy's guilt; finally he brings all the others, save one, to share his doubt. As our attention narrows to that last member of the jury, we gradually realize that he is entirely in the grip of irrational—indeed murderous—passions. In the end we learn that he was, unconsciously, trying to take out on the accused an anger which he felt toward his own son. So long as revenge was his motive and not justice, so long as he was ruled by emotions and not reason, there was no common ground between himself and the other jurymen on which argument could be based. Only when, in a dramatic final scene, he breaks down and realizes what he has been doing, is it possible for a decision to be reached. The proposition ("This boy is legally innocent of murder") was meaningless until all the jurymen agreed to the *argument*: that is, to submitting the proposition to reason.

Or take the following instance. Recently at Stanford University two eminent men debated the question whether "the university" (in a generic sense) should officially adhere to a religious orthodoxy (or be secular). The man upholding the affirmative (a recent convert to Catholicism) based his argument on an appeal to "tradition"—that the Church was *the* tradition in the Western world and that universities, by maintaining a secular nonpartisanship, were really denying the richest part of their Western inheritance. His opponent (a Protestant clergyman and scholar) met him on that *common ground*. Yes indeed, he argued, tradition is what we need as our standard. But what exactly *is* the tradition? He pointed out that one of the medieval Popes had settled the issue definitively by drawing clear and distinct lines of jurisdiction between the Church, the State, and the "Academy": the possession of the one was *holiness*, of the second *power*, of the third *knowledge*. The affirmative was clearly defeated *on his own ground*.

Let us take still a different kind of case. A man is arguing with a friend that the Empire State Building is taller than the "Queen Mary" is long. This is no argument simply because there is no opportunity for differences of opinion: all they have to do is look up the statistics in the *World Almanac*. But if the question were whether a springer spaniel is a better hunting dog than a cocker spaniel, an argument is possible, for there is evidence to be weighed and a chance to arrive at a *common ground in reason*.

A final case: suppose two gourmets were disputing the relative merits of minestrone and French onion soup. No argument is possible. *De gustibus non est disputandem:* it is impossible to argue about taste. The ancient adage is still valid. Although such arguments are often enjoyable—and useful in developing one's artistic sensitivity—they cannot be settled with any finality because there is no common ground in reason that both parties can accept.

The Specific Issue or Issues

Often a proposition cannot be proved in the terms in which it is first stated. In the debate which follows between Allan Nevins and Matthew Josephson (page 580) the proposition as stated on the title page is "Should American History Be Rewritten?" Very likely this phrasing was supplied by the magazine editors and not by the two historians, but let us suppose that either man were presented with the proposition in these terms. Immediately there is a necessity to clarify—*in what sense* should American history be rewritten? Most of us are aware that Communist China has recently "rewritten" her history, throwing out those facts and interpretations distasteful to the present regime. Surely that is not what these eminent scholars propose! For this or other reasons, Professor Nevins, in the first part of his argument, translates the general proposition into the specifics that make it up. These are the points on which the argument (or at least the first part of it) will turn; to argue in terms of the general (title) proposition is impossible: it is simply too vague a statement to be defined or refuted. Here are the specific issues listed by Nevins:

1. Every generation needs to reinterpret history to suit its own preconceptions, ideas, and outlook.
2. Historians now have research tools they didn't formerly have and can, consequently, see history in wider perspective.
3. The discovery of new historical materials constantly necessitates a recasting of our view of the past.

These are the specific grounds on which Josephson met the first part of Nevins' argument. He agreed with most of them but replied that Nevins' proposals for "revision" were "ill conceived" and "ill timed."

Or take a dispute over the proposition: Charles Dickens was a great novelist. One asks: "What do you mean by *great?* I can show you passages in his novels that are as melodramatic and sentimental as anything I've ever read. Besides, his private life was certainly not all it should be." The other answers: "But that's not what I mean. I mean by *great* (1) that he wrote more best sellers than any other English author, and (2) that he wrote, even at his worst, with a power and gusto displayed only by the greatest geniuses." Those two points, if they are accepted by the second party, are the *specific issues* of the argument, the points to be argued. The breakdown of the proposition can be outlined in this way:

> *Proposition:* Charles Dickens was a great novelist.
> *Specific Issues:* Because he (1) wrote more best sellers than any other English author, and (2) wrote with a power and gusto that is displayed only by the greatest geniuses.
> *General Assumption:* Any man who has written more best sellers than any other English author and who wrote with a power and gusto displayed only by the greatest geniuses is entitled to be called a great novelist.

The general assumption is implied in any proof of the specific issue or issues, and the whole process (the analytic breakdown of the proposition) is a movement from a particular to a general statement, from a statement about Dickens to a statement about any man. In any extended argument there may be a number of propositions, all deriving from the thesis proposition, which can be analyzed into the specific issues and outlined in the above way. A series of such outlines should delineate the argument's *plan of action.* But there may be another consequence of thus breaking down the thesis proposition. The second party may say: "Oh, if you mean 'great' in *just those two senses,* we've got no argument. I agree completely." Many futile arguments can be traced to the simple fact that the disputants have not phrased the issues precisely, have not posed the questions that really were agitating them.

But most arguments are not conducted on formal lines, and often the proposition is embedded in a context that we don't even think of as argument, but simply as a piece of reasoning or even description. Take this excerpt from the column of a TV critic:

> Monday night, the [X] Playhouse repeated another one of its hour-long films, titled "Silent Thunder." It was the story of a young Apache who becomes the innocent object of a sadistic young ranch foreman's wrath. During the 60 minutes he horsewhipped him, shot him, beat him unmercifully with his fists, kicked him in the stomach and ran

him down with his horse. It was enough to put the Apaches on the warpath again.

Each time the boy comes back like a whipped dog. In the last two minutes, he dons a gun belt and outdraws the bum but lets him go unharmed in the finale. If we are to believe the first 58 minutes, we certainly cannot be expected to accept the last two. It's a cinch the foreman shot the lad in the back just after the curtain went down.

[Terence O'Flaherty, "Slaughter of the Innocents," San Francisco *Chronicle*, July 22, 1959, p. 35]

This is obviously not just a description of the film. It is an argument, the proposition of which is that "Silent Thunder" is a revolting spectacle. That proposition might be broken down into these specific issues: the film (1) insults any normal man's intelligence, (2) is disgustingly sadistic, and (3) ought never to be shown. No detailed proof is offered for these implied statements of issue other than the words reproduced above, but the sensitive reader is probably satisfied with the evidence, incomplete though it is.

Occasionally, especially with professionals at argument, the proposition will require no breaking down into implied or included issues, but will be stated in finished form at the start. Such is the case with Thomas Henry Huxley's "Science and Culture" (page 556), one side of a famous debate with Matthew Arnold on the question of scientific *vs.* classical education. Huxley's thesis proposition is divided into its two component issues in the very first sentence:

. . . I hold very strongly by two convictions:—the first is that neither the discipline nor the subject-matter of classical education is of such direct value to the student of physical sciences as to justify the expenditure of valuable time upon either; and the second is, that for the purpose of attaining real culture, an exclusively scientific education is at least as effectual as an exclusively literary education.

Later, in debating the second proposition, Huxley breaks it into two further parts. But he is not, in so doing, redefining the proposition or its specific issues—as is the case in the breakdown of the Charles Dickens argument. He is just being systematic in his analysis of the question at stake.

We have here to deal with two distinct propositions. The first, that a criticism of life is the essence of culture; the second, that literature contains the materials which suffice for the construction of such a criticism.

As we have observed earlier, most extended arguments contain many propositions besides the thesis proposition, and they must all be reduced—if the argument is to get anywhere—to the *specific terms* on which both parties agree to meet. It is just as important, at the start of an argument, to be able to say: *Here is where we differ,* as it is to be able to say at the end of it· *Here is where we agree.*

PROOF AND EVIDENCE

Once we have established the *specific issues* to be proved and have decided in what order they are to be considered, we are ready to *argue* those issues.

We argue those issues in terms of the *evidence*, and evidence is an appeal to reason consisting mainly of (1) *facts* and (2) *authoritative opinion*. Let us consider the two *specific issues* of the proposition: Charles Dickens was a great novelist. The first (He wrote more best sellers than any other English author) is a question of *fact*. The second (He wrote with a power and gusto displayed only by the greatest geniuses) is a question of *opinion*. How can we substantiate this fact and this opinion?

A question of fact is normally established by (1) *verification*, or (2) *testimony*. The fact concerning the best sellers can be established by verification; any competent biography or scholarly study would confirm the point. Knowledge such as this is virtually in the public domain, almost like the information that the earth is an oblate spheroid or that light travels about 186,300 miles per second. But if the fact to be established were not so cut-and-dried, but concerned, say, the question of whether a captain was or was not insane at the time of a mutiny (see *The Caine Mutiny* by Herman Wouk), then *testimony* would have to be gathered, heard, checked, analyzed. Such testimony, of course, is often dramatic and full of human interest. If, in writing an argument, you have occasion to employ such evidence, don't scorn or avoid it because it makes an appeal to the emotions. Evidence must, of course, make its first and essential appeal to *reason*—and is not evidence unless it does so—but there is no law saying it can't be interesting and exciting too.

To establish evidence by authoritative opinion is no easier, for authorities do not always agree and it is sometimes hard to identify an authority in the first place. The second specific issue (Charles Dickens wrote with a power and gusto displayed only by the greatest geniuses) can only be established by examining all the leading critical assessments of Dickens. Perhaps they speak to the point of his gusto and power but say nothing about those qualities belonging only to the greatest geniuses. In that case, you will be forced to regard your second issue as having two parts and proceed accordingly. Or perhaps two leading authorities speak to the whole point but disagree between themselves. In such a case we should have to submit the matter to the arbitration of our own reason, or perhaps consult further authorities.

There are no simple rules for establishing the validity of either a fact or an authority. Seeking some facts is like peeling an onion: you take off layer after layer and when you finish you have nothing. And "authorities" can be employed in an infinite number of illegitimate ways. If a voluptuous lady eating Blast-Off breakfast food appears on TV to tell you that she owes her health, wealth, and talent to Blast-Off, she is, needless to say, not an *authority* and her *opinion* is—from a reasonable standpoint—almost worthless. What *caused* her health, wealth, and talent is an enormously complicated question; it certainly was not any *one* thing and it certainly could not be determined short of intense and prolonged study. That she had made such a study is beyond belief. Again, if you are trying to win an argument on the basis of *authoritative opinion*, it is extremely important that both parties to the conflict accept the authority. In a recent murder trial in San Francisco, the prosecution employed a handwriting "expert," and, as a surprise move, the defense also produced one. The two experts completely disagreed in their interpretations. The result was that all testimony involving handwriting was thrown out of court—a tactical victory, actually, for the defense. Finally, remember that a big name is not always a big brain. The fact that something is in print, or that its author is in all the newspapers, national-circulation magazines, and other mass media, is no sign that he can't be a fool. We live in an age of publicity and it is often hard to tell truth from advertising or honesty from a loud noise. We must take a great deal on faith, but that is not the same thing as being gullible. We may, for example, be incapable of determining the competence of an Egyptologist or a nuclear physicist, but we can certainly determine what responsible and leading men in their fields think of them. By using and keeping our heads, we can close in on truth though we may not capture her.

REASONING

The purpose of argument is to move from the evidence (or data) to a conclusion, and the process making that movement possible is *reasoning*. The subject of reasoning is an enormous one and we can in this space only touch on its more familiar features, but we need to have some acquaintance with its three major forms: *induction, deduction,* and *analogy.*

Induction

The word "induction" derives from the Latin *in-ducere,* to lead into, and it is a process of thought that leads us from a number of particular truths to a general truth. One of the most famous descriptions of induction (and how it can lead to deduction) is that by Thomas Henry Huxley in *The Method of Scientific Investigation:*

> Suppose you go into a fruiterer's shop, wanting an apple—you take one up, and, on biting, you find it is sour; you look at it, and see that it is hard, and green. You take up another one and that too is hard, green, and sour. The shop man offers you a third; but, before biting it, you examine it, and find that it is hard and green, and you immediately say that you will not have it, as it must be sour, like those that you have already tried.

Nothing can be more simple than that, you think; but if you will take the trouble to analyze and trace out into its logical elements what has been done by the mind, you will be greatly surprised. In the first place, you have performed the operation of induction. You found that, in two experiences, hardness and greenness in apples went together with sourness. It was so in the first case, and it was confirmed by the second. True, it is a very small basis, but still it is enough to make an induction from; you generalize the facts, and you expect to find sourness in apples where you get hardness and greenness. You found upon that a general law, that all hard green apples are sour; and that, so far as it goes, is a perfect induction. Well, having got your natural law in this way, when you are offered another apple which you find is hard and green, you say, "All hard and green apples are sour; this apple is hard and green, therefore this apple is sour." That train of reasoning is what logicians call a syllogism and has all its various parts and terms—its major premise, its minor premise, and its conclusion. And, by the help of further reasoning, which, if drawn out, would have to be exhibited in two or three other syllogisms, you arrive at your final determination: "I will not have that apple." So that, you see, you have, in the first place, established a law by induction, and upon that you have founded a deduction and reasoned out the special conclusion of the particular case. Well now, suppose, having got your law, that at some time afterwards, you are discussing the qualities of apples with a friend; you will say to him, "It is a very curious thing—but I find that all hard and green apples are sour!" Your friend says to you, "But how do you know that?" You at once reply, "Oh, because I have tried them over and over again and have always found them to be so." Well, if we're talking science instead of common sense, we should call that an experimental verification.

Such experimental verifications are a common occurrence in both daily life and science. In fact almost any generalization based upon experience may be called an induction, though it may not always be a good one. If, for example, you make the general statement that "all blondes are untrustworthy," just because you were jilted by one, your inductive reasoning is unsound because you have not based your generalization on enough observed cases. Or if you make the generalization that "American men are poor providers" on the basis of twenty observed instances, you still have an unsound induction because your investigation has considered only an infinitesimal fraction of all American men. But let us assume that a board of physicians and psychiatrists, gathering data and case histories from all over the country, concluded that "Cigarette smoking is a major cause of ulcers." That would be a warrantable generalization, for a statistically representative sampling of all cigarette smokers and ulcer patients would have been taken. National public opinion polls have, indeed, so refined their sampling techniques that, in the 1956 presidential election, the results were accurately foretold on the basis of sample data fed a Univac machine.

But no matter how carefully you examine or select your particular instances, no matter how exhaustive a sampling they represent, your generalization is never more than a probability. No reasoning from *some* to *all* can yield *absolute* assurance of validity. There is always a limit to the number of instances human beings can observe, and there is always a point where the gathering of specific instances must stop and some conclusions be reached. The bridging of this gap between the statement that *some* observed instances have certain qualities and the statement that *all* instances have certain qualities is called the *inductive leap*. The result of the leap is, of course, the generalization. Even such well-observed phenomena as the "laws" of acceleration or gravity are only, in the strictest sense, probabilities. One of the most spectacular inductions in recent medical science was that connected with the Salk polio vaccine. Before it was released to the public, exhaustive laboratory tests were made and the public was warned that it could be effective only with a certain percentage of cases. But even that prediction was an educated guess—and so it is with most inductions. The old adage, "The exception proves the rule," is not the piece of illogic it is commonly taken to be; it means "The exception *tests* the rule." Hence, if my observation of ten swarthy Italians has led me to the generalization that "all Italians are swarthy," my meeting a blond Italian with blue eyes *tests* that rule. My generalization has been hasty, so I qualify it and become wiser and humbler.

Some useful rules for testing an induction are as follows:

(1) You must have investigated a fair sampling of instances.

(2) The instance must be typical and not unique.

(3) Any exceptions that "test" the generalization must be carefully considered and honestly admitted.

A scientific induction is often complex and requires a thorough grounding in statistics as well as in the discipline concerned, but when we use the term rhetorically we use it much more loosely. An inductive piece of writing may be one—like Arnold's "Literature and Science"—that simply moves from particulars to a conclusion. Or it may be one in which we make no pretense of citing exhaustive evidence; our "instances" may be chosen for artistic or descriptive rather than logical reasons. Or it may be a generalization which, though arising out of particular instances, is one that can never be verified by logic. For example, in Charles Morgan's novel, *The Fountain*, the author has one of the characters—who had been carefully observing a group of fellow prisoners for many months—make this generalization:

> Never before had he been so strongly aware that in each instant of
> their lives men die to that instant. It is not time that passes away from
> them but they who recede from the constancy, the immutability of
> time, so that when afterwards they look back upon themselves they

see . . . but strange ghosts made in their image, with whom they
have no communication.

[Macmillan & Co., Ltd., London, 1932, p. 47]

The character has made an inductive leap, but it is a leap into a generalization that must be understood and tested by feeling and the imagination
more than by reason and logic.

Deduction

Deduction (from the Latin *de-ducere*, to lead from) is a process of reasoning proceeding *from* general truths or assumed truths (premises) *to* a particular truth or assumed truth (conclusion). One can think of deduction, therefore, as the opposite of induction, but the two are anything but mutually
exclusive. As Huxley demonstrated, deduction coexists with induction
wherever an extensive chain of reasoning takes place, although in most informal argument we probably *deduce* considerably more than we *induce*.
But there is one difference that totally distinguishes the two.

Induction, as we have seen, can lead only to *probability*, but deduction
can—within the terms of its own system—lead to *certainty*. The conclusion
of a sound deductive argument is a *necessary* conclusion. It is a closed
system. The whole study of Euclidian geometry, for example, is that of a
deductive system. We start with axioms from which we deduce theorems
from which we deduce more theorems; if we make no errors in reasoning or
calculation, then our conclusions must always be valid—in terms of the system—even though they may be wrong outside it. In a much looser sense,
our system of common law is also deductive; a judge's decision in a particular case is made in terms of previous cases or of "law" (established premises), and if that judge never made an error in fact, logic, or interpretation,
his decision could not be wrong. The law recognizes, of course, that humans are fallible and has set up a system of appellate courts to review decisions, but *in theory* a judge's ruling should be authoritative and final. Or
an orthodox theologian, beginning with certain basic premises assumed on
faith, can deduce an entire system which, within its own ordinances, is
infallible.

Medieval scholastics developed deduction to a fine art, and their favorite
instrument (derived from Aristotle) was the syllogism and some of its
variant forms. The syllogism is a logical figure with two premises and a
conclusion which, if the premises are valid and the reasoning correct, is
necessarily valid. Syllogistic reasoning is not particularly well received by
modern logicians, but nonetheless much of our normal thinking and arguing can be reduced to syllogistic form. For example, we use deductive
reasoning—probably without knowing it—almost every time we test or apply
the conclusion of an induction; the *probable* inductive conclusion becomes
the unqualified first premise of the syllogism. This is Huxley's conclusion
about apples cast in syllogistic form.

Major premise: All hard green apples are sour.
Minor premise: This apple is a hard green apple.
Conclusion: This apple is sour.

We have no space to consider in detail this complex subject,* but a few salient features should be noted. What if we had, for example, phrased the above syllogism this way?

Major premise: All hard green apples are sour.
Minor premise: This object is sour.
Conclusion: Therefore, this object is a hard green apple.

Clearly the conclusion is not *necessarily* valid: all sour objects are not hard green apples. What went wrong?

The particular error above is called the error of the "undivided middle term," and to understand it is to understand a fundamental fact about all syllogistic and deductive reasoning: it is reasoning in terms of *classes*. The major premise states that all hard green apples fit into the *class* of things which are sour. Then along comes an object, X, which also fits into that class. Is it a hard green apple? Obviously it can be some other member of the class sour, for the class by definition contains more than just hard green apples. If it did not we should merely be saying, "The class hard green apples contains hard green apples," which would get us nowhere. The class into which any subject fits must be larger than that subject and must include it. A classic syllogism is the following:

Major premise: All men are mortal.
Minor premise: Socrates is a man.
Conclusion: Socrates is mortal.

This can be rephrased:

All members of the class *men* are included in the class of *mortal* beings.
Socrates [individual] is included in the class *men*.
Therefore, Socrates is included in the class of *mortal* beings.

Note the grammatical difficulties in the rephrasing above. The word *mortal* had to change slightly its grammatical function in the sentence. In this case the meaning was not fundamentally affected, but in rephrasing a more complex syllogism it might well have been. And that is one real trouble with syllogisms: they are made up of words, and words, as Alice reminded us, are often ambiguous and cantankerous. Moreover, premises may appear in a confusing variety of forms—as definitions, inductive conclusions, deductive conclusions, resolutions, hypotheses, pious wishes. Sometimes it may be impossible to reduce them to a phrase form we can handle. Sometimes the key words will mean several things. Sometimes the premises will be statements of sentiment rather than of reason. And when we come to those cousin forms of the syllogism, the *disjunction* (either/ or), the *dilemma,* or the *condition,* the difficulties can be multiplied many times. Consider this conditional syllogism, derived from the billboard admonition: "The family that prays together stays together."

> *If* a family prays together, then it stays together.
> A family I know [in which several of the members shot down the others] prayed together.
> Therefore the family stayed together.

In this instance, of course, there is no *necessary* cause-effect relationship between the two terms of the conditional premise, between praying and staying. Too much is left out. Many things keep families together besides prayer—companionship, love, economics, habit, sex. But the difficulty of establishing the certainty of any cause-effect relationship is—as any reader of the philosopher David Hume knows—not to be underestimated.

Consider this crude dilemma offered in the article (page 618) by William Fulton: "Inclusion of a professor or instructor in this list [a list of presumed subversives entitled, "Red-ucators at Harvard"] is not conclusive evidence that he is a Communist. He may be simply naive." The dilemma (a "forced option," or disjunction containing two equally unwelcome alternatives) might be phrased as follows:

> Any professor listed as one of the "Red-ucators at Harvard" is guilty of being (1) a Communist, or (2) naive. If he is a Communist he is unfit to be a teacher. If he is naive he is unfit to be a teacher.

But another way to interpret the vague phrasing of the accusation is to understand "naive" as meaning "innocent." Then we end up, in effect, with the meaningless disjunction: All professors whose name are on that list are either guilty (Communists are equivalent to guilt in the writer's mind) or innocent. That is as much as to say that all men are alive or dead.

But in ordinary writing we do not often phrase an argument in syllogistic form. Normally we have recourse instead to the *enthymeme,* a truncated syllogism in which one or more of the premises has been omitted. "College is just a racket. Look at the successful men who never went!" The implied premise on which that "argument" is based would read something like this: "Anything successful men never did is a racket"—obviously a confused argument.

So while we may not use syllogisms much in ordinary argument or reasoning, they may come in handy as means of analyzing and testing such enthymemes as that above. Most of our arguing is the process of assuming certain premises and discovering the implications of those premises. That process, in whatever form it occurs, is deduction and *can* be expressed as a syllogism. Study the following enthymemes and expand them to syllogistic form. Doing so is a kind of parlor game, but it is also a way of reminding ourselves that behind most of our thinking and arguing lurk hidden and unexpressed assumptions.

I oppose having Negroes in this fraternity because I think the guys in it have a right to choose their own friends.

Maybe they didn't convict him, but where there's smoke there's fire.

Jesus loves me, this I know, for the Bible tells me so.

If they put you in jail for doing it, it can't be right.

Analogy

We have already discussed analogy under "Comparison and Contrast," but an additional word or two may be entered here. An analogy is simply a comparison between two things together with the argument that, if they are alike in several ways, they are probably alike in another. For example, many people argued that because Eisenhower was a great and successful general he should be elected President of the United States. Behind this argument lay an analogy: the implied statement that the job of being a general and that of being President were alike. But do both positions require the same talents? A notable flaw in this particular analogy lay in the fact that Mr. Eisenhower, until his campaign, knew almost nothing about politics and had never aligned himself with a political party. This is a *loose* analogy. Had the question been Eisenhower's assignment from one to another military post, then the analogy would have been a *strict* one, for the talents required in both jobs would have doubtless been similar. An analogy increases in validity in proportion to the number of likenesses that can be established between the two things compared. When an analogy becomes strict enough, it is properly termed a *comparison* and not an analogy at all.

But analogy is perhaps more useful by way of illustration and description than for argument. Consider Milton's statement (page 158):

I cannot praise a fugitive and cloistered virtue, unexercised and unbreathed, that never sallies out and sees her adversary, but slinks out of the race where that immortal garland is to be run for, not without dust and heat.

Here the analogy is between a kind of withdrawn, introverted, monkish figure (which we deduce from the imagery) and an ethical condition which we can descriptively associate with that character. In short, virtue is something to be used—like a weapon—and not just saved up, like a museum piece. The analogy appeals mainly to emotion, not to reason, but the context in which it appeared was a powerful appeal to reason.

Robert Gorham Davis (page 77) has reminded us about the dangers of false analogy, as well as about other common fallacies encountered in reasoning. He should be consulted carefully when you are dealing with such problems. But, to quote Milton again (pages 157-58):

Good and evil we know in the field of this world grow up together almost inseparably; and the knowledge of good is so involved and interwoven with the knowledge of evil, and in so many cunning resemblances hardly to be discerned, that those confused seeds which were imposed upon Psyche as an incessant labor to cull out, and sort asunder, were not more intermixed.

That being the case, we need to remember that one of our fallacies may lie in the very process of always putting reason and good on the same side of the argument and emotion and evil on the other. It is a mixed world of value we inhabit, as a discussion of persuasion may remind us.

PERSUASION

Persuasion is argument which (1) directs its appeal more to the emotions than to the reason, and (2) tries to win support for some cause or course of action. It strives not just to change the mind of its audience but to change its heart, to get at those springs of motive and will and vested interest and prejudice and sentiment and pride that lie beneath intelligence and stimulate us most often to action. It is still a *form of argument,* for reasons are given and they must make sense, but the proof is cast in a heightened style of language and the evidence adduced is often equally heightened, sometimes appealing to lofty ethical motives and exalted ideals, sometimes to anger and passion.

Obviously, persuasion in the hands of a demagogue or charlatan can be a dangerous instrument. In the hands of a man of high rational conviction it can be a powerful force for good. It can arouse men to witch hunts or to cancer drives, to acts of hate or acts of love, to war or to peace. But the aim of persuasion is always to *get results,* to *win*—and often to win at any cost. It is an ill-informed young lady who does not know that in saying "Persuade me if you can" she is saying something quite different from "Convince me if you can." Persuasion often has a hint of the illicit about it, for it is never disinterested. The political propagandist or the advertiser, for example, want you to *vote* or to *buy,* and their concern with truth is bound to be somewhat tangential to these objectives.

Some years ago, for example, when television was first invading the American scene, an advertisement appeared showing a young brother and sister tearfully comforting each other. They did not have a television set whereas the other kids on the block did. These were the words of the ad:

> *Do you expect a seven-year-old to find words for the deep loneliness he's feeling?*

Following this it was pointed out that every decent parent provides adequate sunshine and vitamins for his child's body, but . . .

> *How about sunshine for his morale? How about vitamins for his mind?*

Television, we were to assume, provides such benefits. Many of the parents reading this advertisement protested and called this assault on their pocket-books nothing short of emotional blackmail. It demonstrates, however, some of the aims and techniques of a persuasive argument, and had the subject and timing of the ad been different, it might not have misfired at all. Let us analyze some of its elements.

Its emotional appeal is obvious. Most parents have a natural solicitude for their children's frustrations and sorrows, and here that sympathy is squeezed hard. As Richard D. Altick reminds us in "Sentimentality" (page 109) there are certain "cliché situations," sure-fire tear-jerkers, which "apply a pressure pump to our lachrymal glands." Sentimentality is *emotion in excess of the fact*, and here we have a clear case of it. In real life, of course, an unhappy or abandoned child can evoke *genuine* sympathy, but when a copywriter induces that sympathy on the basis of an exaggerated fiction de-signed only to empty our pockets, we are foolish indeed to fall for it. The advertisement was loaded with such cliché words and phrases as "deep loneliness," "a bruise deep inside," and "blurt out the truth"—all designed to stimulate stock emotional responses. "Do you expect a seven-year-old to find words for the deep loneliness he's feeling?" The adman wants the stock response: "Of course not!" But a little sober thought will suggest that "Certainly!" might as well be the answer. Most seven-year-olds blurt out anything that's on their minds, and if they want a television set they aren't going to keep the fact a secret. Perhaps we spoil the story-book quality by being so sensible, but we can at times pay a very high price for living in a make-believe world.

Part of this emotional argument is likewise based on a tricky use of analogy. You can talk about a "bruised finger," reads the ad, but "How can a little girl describe a bruise deep inside?" We have already seen the analogy between "vitamins for the body" and "vitamins for the mind." That these are false or at least questionable analogies is obvious. What are some of the characteristics of a "bruised finger"? Swelling, discoloration, blood blisters, muscular pain (usually short-lived). Can we transfer those characteristics to "a bruise deep inside"? Considering that "deep inside" can be anything from the pancreas to the lower intestine, it's pretty hard. But even if we located them in, say, the "heart" (understood in the roman-tic sense) we still don't get very far. Obviously the "hurt" was the main point of the analogy, but the kind of hurt that is sharp at first and then passes away is hardly anything to shed bitter tears about. And what about "vitamins for the mind"? A good many critics would have difficulty equat-ing the daily TV slaughter of cowboys and Indians with vitamins of any kind.

The piece also contains an *appeal to authority* in that vague testimonial statement: "Educators agree—television is all that and more for a growing child." What educators? How many? Did they put their endorsement in just those terms? Without verification the statement is completely invalid in the argument. Needless to say, however, such testimonials are stock equipment in the adman's arsenal.

But persuasion is not always put to such ignoble uses. Mark Antony's funeral oration (page 622) from Shakespeare's *Julius Caesar* is perhaps the greatest example of a persuasive argument in literary history. In this famous speech, Antony stirs the Roman people to revolt against Brutus, who had recently assassinated Caesar. The real question was whether or not Caesar had entertained revolutionary designs against the Republic, but not one fact relevant to this question was brought forth by Antony. He was a friend of Caesar and wished to avenge his death; but he knew that the people would not support him unless he could arouse them to a frenzy. His appeal, therefore, was mainly cast in the form of an *argumentum ad populum* (see Davis, page 86). By planting the idea that Caesar was a generous friend to the people of Rome and that Brutus was a deceitful friend, and by such histrionics as pointing to the wounds of Caesar and his own tears, he accomplished his design. Was Caesar a traitor to Rome or not? The question was never touched on.

Dangerous as it may be, persuasion nonetheless performs a vital and useful function in the world's work. Although the consumer pays for it, advertising has without a doubt stimulated the production and distribution of wealth. Although a politician may—to our minds—be persuasive on the wrong side of an issue, he is nevertheless doing part of democracy's essential work. Moreover, there are few sound arguments that don't mix reasoning and persuasion, for the very obvious reason that intellectual conviction usually involves a degree of emotional excitement. It is, after all, hard to believe anything on conviction without wanting others to believe it too. It is a foolish young man (see Shulman, p. 88) who proposes to his lady in syllogisms.

~

SCIENCE AND
CULTURE*   *Thomas Henry Huxley*

I hold very strongly by two convictions:—The first is, that neither the discipline nor the subject-matter of classical education is of such direct value to the student of physical science as to justify the expenditure of valuable time upon either; and the second is, that for

* From an address delivered in 1880.

the purpose of attaining real culture, an exclusively scientific education is at least as effectual as an exclusively literary education.

I need hardly point out to you that these opinions, especially the latter, are diametrically opposed to those of the great majority of educated Englishmen, influenced as they are by school and university traditions. In their belief, culture is obtainable only by a liberal education; and a liberal education is synonymous, not merely with education and instruction in literature, but in one particular form of literature, namely, that of Greek and Roman antiquity. They hold that the man who has learned Latin and Greek, however little, is educated; while he who is versed in other branches of knowledge, however deeply, is a more or less respectable specialist, not admissible into the cultured caste. The stamp of the educated man, the University degree, is not for him.

I am too well acquainted with the generous catholicity of spirit, the true sympathy with scientific thought, which pervades the writings of our chief apostle of culture, to identify him with these opinions; and yet one may cull from one and another of those epistles to the Philistines, which so much delight all who do not answer to that name, sentences which lend them some support.

Mr. Arnold tells us that the meaning of culture is "to know the best that has been thought and said in the world." It is the criticism of life contained in literature. That criticism regards "Europe as being, for intellectual and spiritual purposes, one great confederation, bound to a joint action and working to a common result; and whose members have, for their common outfit, a knowledge of Greek, Roman, and Eastern antiquity, and of one another. Special, local, and temporary advantages being put out of account, that modern nation will in the intellectual and spiritual sphere make most progress, which most thoroughly carries out this programme. And what is that but saying that we too, all of us, as individuals, the more thoroughly we carry it out, shall make the more progress?"

We have here to deal with two distinct propositions. The first, that a criticism of life is the essence of culture; the second, that literature contains the materials which suffice for the construction of such a criticism.

I think that we must all assent to the first proposition. For culture certainly means something quite different from learning or technical skill. It implies the possession of an ideal, and the habit of critically estimating the value of things by comparison with a theoretic standard. Perfect culture should supply a complete theory of life, based upon a clear knowledge alike of its possibilities and of its limitations.

But we may agree to all this, and yet strongly dissent from the assumption that literature alone is competent to supply this knowledge. After having learnt all that Greek, Roman, and Eastern antiquity have thought and said, and all that modern literatures have to tell us, it is not self-evident that we have laid a sufficiently broad and deep foundation for that criticism of life which constitutes culture.

Indeed, to any one acquainted with the scope of physical science, it is not at all evident. Considering progress only in the "intellectual and spiritual sphere," I find myself wholly unable to admit that either nations or individuals will really advance, if their common outfit draws nothing from the stores of physical science. I should say that an army, without weapons of precision and with no particular base of operations, might more hopefully enter upon a campaign on the Rhine, than a man, devoid of a knowledge of what physical science has done in the last century, upon a criticism of life.

When a biologist meets with an anomaly, he instinctively turns to the study of development to clear it up. The rationale of contradictory opinions may with equal confidence be sought in history.

It is, happily, no new thing that Englishmen should employ their wealth in building and endowing institutions for educational purposes. But, five or six hundred years ago, deeds of foundation expressed or implied conditions as nearly as possible contrary to those which have been thought expedient by Sir Josiah Mason. That is to say, physical science was practically ignored, while a certain literary training was enjoined as a means to the acquirement of knowledge which was essentially theological.

The reason of this singular contradiction between the actions of men alike animated by a strong and disinterested desire to promote the welfare of their fellows, is easily discovered.

At that time, in fact, if any one desired knowledge beyond such as could be obtained by his own observation, or by common conversation, his first necessity was to learn the Latin language, inasmuch as all the higher knowledge of the western world was contained in works written in that language. Hence, Latin grammar, with logic and rhetoric, studied through Latin, were the fundamentals of education. With respect to the substance of the knowledge imparted through this channel, the Jewish and Christian Scriptures, as interpreted and supplemented by the Romish Church, were held to contain a complete and infallibly true body of information.

Theological dicta were, to the thinkers of those days, that which the axioms and definitions of Euclid are to the geometers of these. The business of the philosophers of the middle ages was to deduce, from the data furnished by the theologians, conclusions in accordance with ecclesiastical decrees. They were allowed the high privilege of showing, by logical process, how and why that which the Church said was true, must be true. And if their demonstrations fell short of or exceeded this limit, the Church was maternally ready to check their aberrations,—if need were, by the help of the secular arm.

Between the two, our ancestors were furnished with a compact and complete criticism of life. They were told how the world began and how it would end; they learned that all material existence was but a base and insignificant blot upon the fair face of the spiritual world, and that nature was, to all intents and purposes, the playground of the devil; they learned that the earth is the centre of the visible universe, and that man is the cynosure of things terrestrial; and more especially was it inculcated that the course of nature had no fixed order, but that it could be, and constantly was, altered by the agency of innumerable spiritual beings, good and bad, according as they were moved by the deeds and prayers of men. The sum and substance of the whole doctrine was to produce the conviction that the only thing really worth knowing in this world was how to secure that place in a better which, under certain conditions, the Church promised.

Our ancestors had a living belief in this theory of life, and acted upon it in their dealings with education, as in all other matters. Culture meant saintliness—after the fashion of the saints of those days; the education that led to it was, of necessity, theological; and the way to theology lay through Latin.

That the study of nature—further than was requisite for the satisfaction of everyday wants—should have any bearing on human life was far from the thoughts of men thus trained. Indeed, as nature had been cursed for man's sake, it was an obvious conclusion that those who meddled with nature were likely to come into pretty close contact with Satan. And, if any born scientific investigator followed his instincts, he might safely reckon upon earning the reputation, and probably upon suffering the fate, of a sorcerer.

Had the western world been left to itself in Chinese isolation, there is no saying how long this state of things might have endured. But, happily, it was not left to itself. Even earlier than the thirteenth century, the development of Moorish civilization in Spain and the great movement of the Crusades had introduced the leaven which, from that day to this, has never ceased to work. At first, through the intermediation of Arabic translations, afterwards by the study of the originals, the western nations of Europe became acquainted with the writings of the ancient philosophers and poets, and, in time, with the whole of the vast literature of antiquity.

Whatever there was of high intellectual aspiration or dominant capacity in Italy, France, Germany, and England, spent itself for centuries in taking possession of the rich inheritance left by the dead civilizations of Greece and Rome. Marvelously aided by the invention of printing, classical learning spread and flourished. Those who possessed it prided themselves on having attained the highest culture then within the reach of mankind.

And justly. For, saving Dante on his solitary pinnacle, there was no figure in modern literature, at the time of the Renascence, to compare with the men of antiquity; there was no art to compete with their sculpture; there was no physical science but that which Greece had created. Above all, there was no other example of perfect intellectual freedom—of the unhesitating acceptance of reason as the sole guide to truth and the supreme arbiter of conduct.

The new learning necessarily soon exerted a profound influence upon education. The language of the monks and schoolmen seemed little better than gibberish to scholars fresh from Vergil and Cicero, and the study of Latin was placed upon a new foundation. Moreover, Latin itself ceased to afford the sole key to knowledge. The student who sought the highest thought of antiquity found only a second-hand reflection of it in Roman literature, and turned his face to the full light of the Greeks. And after a battle, not altogether dissimilar to that which is at present being fought over the teaching of physical science, the study of Greek was recognized as an essential element of all higher education.

Thus the Humanists, as they were called, won the day; and the great reform which they effected was of incalculable service to mankind. But the Nemesis of all reformers is finality; and the reformers of education, like those of religion, fell into the profound, however common, error of mistaking the beginning for the end of the work of reformation.

The representatives of the Humanists, in the nineteenth century, take their stand upon classical education as the sole avenue to culture, as firmly as if we were still in the age of Renascence. Yet, surely, the present intellectual relations of the modern and the ancient worlds are profoundly different from those which obtained three centuries ago. Leaving aside the existence of a great and characteristically modern literature, of modern painting, and, especially, of modern music, there is one feature of the present state of the civilized world which separates it more widely from the Renascence than the Renascence was separated from the middle ages.

This distinctive character of our own times lies in the vast and constantly increasing part which is played by natural knowledge. Not only is our daily life shaped by it, not only does the prosperity of millions of men depend upon it, but our whole theory of life has long been influenced, consciously or unconsciously, by the general conceptions of the universe which have been forced upon us by physical science.

In fact, the most elementary acquaintance with the results of scientific investigation shows us that they offer a broad and striking contradiction to the opinion so implicitly credited and taught in the middle ages.

The notions of the beginning and the end of the world entertained by our forefathers are no longer credible. It is very certain that the earth is not the chief body in the material universe, and that the world is not subordinated to man's use. It is even more certain that nature is the expression of a definite order with which nothing interferes, and that the chief business of mankind is to learn that order and govern themselves accordingly. Moreover this scientific "criticism of life" presents itself to us with different credentials from any other. It appeals not to authority, nor to what anybody may have thought or said, but to nature. It admits that all our interpretations of natural fact are more or less imperfect and symbolic, and bids the learner seek for truth not among words but among things. It warns us that the assertion which outstrips evidence is not only a blunder but a crime.

The purely classical education advocated by the representatives of the Humanists in our day, gives no inkling of all this. A man may be a better scholar than Erasmus, and know no more of the chief causes of the present intellectual fermentation than Erasmus did. Scholarly and pious persons, worthy of all respect, favour us with allocutions upon the sadness of the antagonism of science to their mediaeval way of thinking, which betray an ignorance of the first principles of scientific investigation, an incapacity for understanding what a man of science means by veracity, and an unconsciousness of the weight of established scientific truths, which is almost comical.

There is no great force in the *tu quoque* argument, or else the advocates of scientific education might fairly enough retort upon the modern Humanists that they may be learned specialists, but that they possess no such sound foundation for a criticism of life as deserves the name of culture. And, indeed, if we were disposed to be cruel, we might urge that the Humanists have brought this reproach upon themselves, not because they are too full of the spirit of the ancient Greek, but because they lack it.

The period of the Renascence is commonly called that of the "Revival of Letters," as if the influences then brought to bear upon the mind of Western Europe had been wholly exhausted in the field of literature. I think it is very commonly forgotten that the revival of science, effected by the same agency, although less conspicuous, was not less momentous.

In fact, the few and scattered students of nature of that day picked up the clue to her secrets exactly as it fell from the hands of the Greeks a thousand years before. The foundations of mathematics were so well laid by them that our children learn their geometry from a book written for the schools of Alexandria two thousand years ago. Modern astronomy is the natural continuation and development of the work of Hipparchus and of Ptolemy; modern physics of that of Democritus and of Archimedes; it was long before modern biological science outgrew the knowledge bequeathed to us by Aristotle, by Theophrastus, and by Galen.

We cannot know all the best thoughts and sayings of the Greeks unless we know what they thought about natural phenomena. We cannot fully apprehend their criticism of life unless we understand the extent to which that criticism was affected by scientific conceptions. We falsely pretend to be the inheritors of their culture, unless we are penetrated, as the best minds among them were, with an unhesitating faith that the free employment of reason, in accordance with scientific method, is the sole method of reaching truth.

Thus I venture to think that the pretensions of our modern Humanists to the possession of the monopoly of culture and to the exclusive inheritance of the spirit of antiquity must be abated, if not abandoned. But I should be very sorry that anything I have said should be taken to imply a desire on my part to depreciate the value of a classical education, as it might be and as it sometimes is. The native capacities of mankind vary no less than their opportunities; and while culture is one, the road by which one man may best reach it is widely different from that which is most advantageous to another. Again, while scientific education is yet inchoate and tentative, classical education is thoroughly well organized upon the practical experience of generations of teachers. So that, given ample time for learning and destination for ordinary life, or for a literary career, I do not think that a young Englishman in search of culture can do better than follow the course usually marked out for him, supplementing its deficiencies by his own efforts.

But for those who mean to make science their serious occupation, or who intend to follow the profession of medicine, or who have to enter early upon the business of life,—for all these, in my opinion, classical education is a mistake; and it is for this reason that I am glad to see "mere literary education and instruction" shut out from the curriculum of Sir Josiah Mason's College, seeing that its inclusion would probably lead to the introduction of the ordinary smattering of Latin and Greek.

Nevertheless, I am the last person to question the importance of genuine literary education, or to suppose that intellectual culture can be complete without it. An exclusively scientific training will bring about a mental twist as surely as an exclusively literary training. The value of the cargo does not compensate for a ship's being out of trim; and I should be very sorry to think that the Scientific College would turn out none but lop-sided men.

There is no need, however, that such a catastrophe should happen. Instruction in English, French, and German is provided, and thus the three greatest literatures of the modern world are made accessible to the student. French and German, and especially the latter language, are absolutely indispensable to those who desire full knowledge in any department of science. But even supposing that the knowledge of these languages acquired is not more than sufficient for purely scientific purposes, every Englishman has, in his native tongue, an almost perfect instrument of literary expression; and, in his own literature, models of every kind of literary excellence. If an Englishman cannot get literary culture out of his Bible, his Shakespeare, his Milton, neither, in my belief, will the profoundest study of Homer and Sophocles, Vergil and Horace, give it to him.

Thus, since the constitution of the College makes sufficient provision for literary as well as for scientific education, and since artistic
instruction is also contemplated, it seems to me that a fairly complete culture is offered to all who are willing to take advantage of it.

But I am not sure that at this point the "practical" man, scotched
but not slain, may ask what all this talk about culture has to do
with an Institution, the object of which is defined to be "to promote
the prosperity of the manufactures and the industry of the country."
He may suggest that what is wanted for this end is not culture,
not even a purely scientific discipline, but simply a knowledge of
applied science.

I often wish that this phrase, "applied science," had never been
invented. For it suggests that there is a sort of scientific knowledge
of direct practical use, which can be studied apart from another
sort of scientific knowledge, which is of no practical utility, and
which is termed "pure science." But there is no more complete
fallacy than this. What people call applied science is nothing but
the application of pure science to particular classes of problems. It
consists of deductions from those general principles, established by
reasoning and observation, which constitute pure science. No one
can safely make these deductions until he has a firm grasp of the
principles; and he can obtain that grasp only by personal experience
of the operations of observation and of reasoning on which they
are founded.

Almost all the processes employed in the arts and manufactures
fall within the range either of physics or of chemistry. In order to
improve them, one must thoroughly understand them; and no one
has a chance of really understanding them unless he has obtained
that mastery of principles and that habit of dealing with facts,
which is given by long-continued and well-directed purely scientific
training in the physical and the chemical laboratory. So that there
really is no question as to the necessity of purely scientific discipline,
even if the work of the College were limited by the narrowest
interpretation of its stated aims.

And, as to the desirableness of a wider culture than that yielded
by science alone, it is to be recollected that the improvement of
manufacturing processes is only one of the conditions which contribute to the prosperity of industry. Industry is a means and not
an end; and mankind work only to get something which they want.
What that something is depends partly on their innate, and partly
on their acquired, desires.

If the wealth resulting from prosperous industry is to be spent upon the gratification of unworthy desires, if the increasing perfection of manufacturing processes is to be accompanied by an increasing debasement of those who carry them on, I do not see the good of industry and prosperity.

Now it is perfectly true that men's views of what is desirable depend upon their characters, and that the innate proclivities to which we give that name are not touched by any amount of instruction. But it does not follow that even mere intellectual education may not, to an indefinite extent, modify the practical manifestation of the characters of men in their actions, by supplying them with motives unknown to the ignorant. A pleasure-loving character will have pleasure of some sort, but, if you give him the choice, he may prefer pleasures which do not degrade him to those which do. And this choice is offered to every man who possesses in literary or artistic culture a never-failing source of pleasures, which are neither withered by age, nor staled by custom, nor embittered in the recollection by the pangs of self-reproach. . . .

Problems for Thought and Writing

I

1. The above selection was part of an address Huxley delivered in Birmingham, England in 1880 to commemorate the opening of the Science College (one of the earliest of such institutions) founded by Sir Josiah Mason. The cause for which Huxley was fighting now seems a dead one, for science schools abound today. But many of these issues are still vital. For example, would a modern educator distinguish as sharply as Huxley does between culture (or education) and technical skill (or training)? Do you think education and training are one and the same?

2. How would you treat the "two propositions" which Huxley extracts from Arnold's initial statement? Do you agree with his deduction?

3. Does Huxley's argument against the necessity for Latin represent, in your opinion, a narrow or catholic outlook? Has he omitted any relevant arguments pro or con?

4. Would Etienne Gilson (page 635) agree with Huxley's summary of the history of Western culture?

5. Do you think Huxley is entirely fair in his definition of "the pretensions of our modern Humanists" (page 562)? What was your reaction before and after reading Arnold's rebuttal? (See page 566.)

6. What literary echoes are sounded in the phrase, "neither withered by age, nor staled by custom. . . ." (above)? Does Huxley, in your opinion, show in his writing a knowledge of literature beyond that commonly possessed by the "scientist" of today? Does this possession have more than a decorative value? Why or why not?

II

7. Define or explain: anomaly, rationale, dicta, leaven, nemesis, *tu quoque*, inchoate, tentative, pure science, applied science, cynosure.

8. Is Huxley's an inductive or deductive argument? Outline it.

~

LITERATURE AND SCIENCE *
Matthew Arnold

I am going to ask whether the present movement for ousting letters from their old predominance in education, and for transferring the predominance in education to the natural sciences,—whether this brisk and flourishing movement ought to prevail, and whether it is likely that in the end it really will prevail. An objection may be raised which I will anticipate. My own studies have been almost wholly in letters, and my visits to the field of the natural sciences have been very slight and inadequate, although those sciences have always strongly moved my curiosity. A man of letters, it will perhaps be said, is not competent to discuss the comparative merits of letters and natural science as means of education. To this objection I reply, first of all, that his incompetence, if he attempts the discussion but is really incompetent for it, will be abundantly visible; nobody will be taken in; he will have plenty of sharp observers and critics to save mankind from that danger. But the line I am going to follow is, as you will soon discover, so extremely simple, that perhaps it may be followed without failure even by one who for a more ambitious line of discussion would be quite incompetent.

Some of you may possibly remember a phrase of mine which has been the object of a good deal of comment; an observation to the effect that in our culture, the aim being *to know ourselves and the world,* we have, as the means to this end, *to know the best which has been thought and said in the world.* A man of science, who is also an excellent writer and the very prince of debaters, Professor Huxley, in a discourse at the opening of Sir Josiah Mason's college at Birmingham, laying hold of this phrase, expanded it by quoting some more words of mine, which are these: "The civilized world is to be

* From a lecture delivered in 1882.

regarded as now being, for intellectual and spiritual purposes, one great confederation, bound to a joint action and working to a common result; and whose members have for their proper outfit a knowledge of Greek, Roman, and Eastern antiquity, and of one another. Special local and temporary advantages being put out of account, that modern nation will in the intellectual and spiritual sphere make most progress, which most thoroughly carries out this programme."

Now on my phrase, thus enlarged, Professor Huxley remarks that when I speak of the above-mentioned knowledge as enabling us to know ourselves and the world, I assert *literature* to contain the materials which suffice for thus making us know ourselves and the world. But it is not by any means clear, says he, that after having learnt all which ancient and modern literatures have to tell us, we have laid a sufficiently broad and deep foundation for that criticism of life, that knowledge of ourselves and the world, which constitutes culture. On the contrary, Professor Huxley declares that he finds himself "wholly unable to admit that either nations or individuals will really advance, if their outfit draws nothing from the stores of physical science. An army without weapons of precision, and with no particular base of operations, might more hopefully enter upon a campaign on the Rhine, than a man, devoid of a knowledge of what physical science has done in the last century, upon a criticism of life."

This shows how needful it is for those who are to discuss any matters together, to have a common understanding as to the sense of the terms they employ,—how needful, and how difficult. What Professor Huxley says, implies just the reproach which is so often brought against the study of *belles lettres,* as they are called: that the study is an elegant one, but slight and ineffectual; a smattering of Greek and Latin and other ornamental things, of little use for any one whose object is to get at truth, and to be a practical man. So, too, M. Renan talks of the "superficial humanism" of a school-course which treats us as if we were all going to be poets, writers, preachers, orators, and he opposes this humanism to positive science, or the critical search after truth. And there is always a tendency in those who are remonstrating against the predominance of letters in education, to understand by letters *belles lettres,* and by *belles lettres* a superficial humanism, the opposite of science or true knowledge.

But when we talk of knowing Greek and Roman antiquity, for instance, which is the knowledge people have called the humanities, I for my part mean a knowledge which is something more than a superficial humanism, mainly decorative. "I call all teaching *scientific*," says Wolf, the critic of Homer, "which is systematically laid out and followed up to its original sources. For example: a knowledge of classical antiquity is scientific when the remains of classical antiquity are correctly studied in the original languages." There can be no doubt that Wolf is perfectly right; that all learning is scientific which is systematically laid out and followed up to its original sources, and that a genuine humanism is scientific.

When I speak of knowing Greek and Roman antiquity, therefore, as a help to knowing ourselves and the world, I mean more than a knowledge of so much vocabulary, so much grammar, so many portions of authors in the Greek and Latin languages,—I mean knowing the Greeks and Romans, and their life and genius, and what they were and did in the world; what we get from them, and what is its value. That, at least, is the ideal; and when we talk of endeavouring to know Greek and Roman antiquity, as a help to knowing ourselves and the world, we mean endeavouring so to know them as to satisfy this ideal, however much we may still fall short of it.

The same also as to knowing our own and other modern nations, with the like aim of getting to understand ourselves and the world. To know the best that has been thought and said by the modern nations, is to know, says Professor Huxley, "only what modern *literatures* have to tell us; it is the criticism of life contained in modern literature." And yet "the distinctive character of our times," he urges, "lies in the vast and constantly increasing part which is played by natural knowledge." And how, therefore, can a man, devoid of knowledge of what physical science has done in the last century, enter hopefully upon a criticism of modern life?

Let us, I say, be agreed about the meaning of the terms we are using. I talk of knowing the best which has been thought and uttered in the world; Professor Huxley says this means knowing *literature*. Literature is a large word; it may mean everything written with letters or printed in a book. Euclid's *Elements* and Newton's *Principia* are thus literature. All knowledge that reaches us through books is literature. But by literature Professor Huxley means *belles lettres*. He means to make me say, that knowing the best which has been thought and said by the modern nations is knowing their *belles lettres* and no more. And this is no sufficient equipment, he argues, for a criticism of modern life. But as I do not mean, by knowing ancient Rome, knowing merely more or less of Latin *belles lettres,* and taking no account of Rome's military, and political, and legal, and administrative work in the world; and as, by knowing ancient Greece, I understand knowing her as the giver of Greek art, and the guide to a free and right use of reason and to scientific method, and the founder of our mathematics and physics and astronomy and biology,—I understand knowing her as all this, and not merely knowing certain Greek poems, and histories, and treatises, and speeches,—so as to the knowledge of modern nations also. By knowing modern nations, I mean not merely knowing their *belles lettres,* but knowing also what has been done by such men as Copernicus, Galileo, Newton, Darwin. "Our ancestors learned," says Professor Huxley, "that the earth is the centre of the visible universe, and that man is the cynosure of things terrestrial; and more especially was it inculcated that the course of nature had no fixed order, but that it could be, and constantly was, altered." But for us now, continues Professor Huxley, "the notions of the beginning and the end of the world entertained by our forefathers are no longer credible. It is very certain that the earth is not the chief body in the material universe and that the world is not subordinated to man's use. It is even more certain that nature is the expression of a definite order, with which nothing interferes." "And yet," he cries, "the purely classical education advocated by the representatives of the humanists in our day gives no inkling of all this!"

In due place and time I will just touch upon that vexed question of classical education; but at present the question is as to what is meant by knowing the best which modern nations have thought and said. It is not knowing their *belles lettres* merely which is meant. To know Italian *belles lettres* is not to know Italy, and to know English *belles lettres* is not to know England. Into knowing Italy and England there comes a great deal more, Galileo and Newton amongst it. The reproach of being a superficial humanism, a tincture of *belles lettres,* may attach rightly enough to some other disciplines; but to the particular discipline recommended when I proposed knowing the best that has been thought and said in the world, it does not apply. In that best I certainly include what in modern times has been thought and said by the great observers and knowers of nature.

There is, therefore, really no question between Professor Huxley and me as to whether knowing the great results of the modern scientific study of nature is not required as a part of our culture, as well as knowing the products of literature and art. But to follow the processes by which those results are reached, ought, say the friends of physical science, to be made the staple of education for the bulk of mankind. And here there does arise a question between those whom Professor Huxley calls with playful sarcasm "the Levites of culture," and those whom the poor humanist is sometimes apt to regard as its Nebuchadnezzars.

The great results of the scientific investigation of nature we are agreed upon knowing, but how much of our study are we bound to give to the processes by which those results are reached? The results have their visible bearing on human life. But all the processes, too, all the items of fact, by which those results are reached and established, are interesting. All knowledge is interesting to a wise man, and the knowledge of nature is interesting to all men. It is very interesting to know that from the albuminous white of the egg the chick in the egg gets the materials for its flesh, bones, blood, and feathers, while from the fatty yolk of the egg it gets the heat and energy which enable it at length to break its shell and begin the world. It is less interesting, perhaps, but still it is interesting, to know that when a taper burns, the wax is converted into carbonic acid and water. Moreover, it is quite true that the habit of dealing with facts, which is given by the study of nature, is, as the friends of physical science praise it for being, an excellent discipline. The appeal, in the study of nature, is constantly to observation and experiment; not only is it said that the thing is so, but we can be made to see that it is so. Not only does a man tell us that when a taper burns the wax is converted into carbonic acid and water, as a man may tell us, if he likes, that Charon is punting his ferry-boat on the river Styx, or that Victor Hugo is a sublime poet, or Mr. Gladstone the most admirable of statesmen; but we are made to see that the conversion into carbonic acid and water does actually happen. This reality of natural knowledge it is, which makes the friends of physical science contrast it, as a knowledge of things, with the humanist's knowledge, which is, say they, a knowledge of words. And hence Professor Huxley is moved to lay it down that, "for the purpose of attaining real culture, an exclusively scientific education is at least as effectual as an exclusively literary education." And a certain President of the Section for Mechanical Science in the British Association is, in Scripture phrase, "very bold," and declares that if a man, in his mental training, "has substituted literature and

history for natural science, he has chosen the less useful alternative."
But whether we go these lengths or not, we must all admit that in
natural science the habit gained of dealing with facts is a most
valuable discipline, and that every one should have some experience
of it.

More than this, however, is demanded by the reformers. It is
proposed to make the training in natural science the main part
of education, for the great majority of mankind at any rate. And
here, I confess, I part company with the friends of physical science, with whom up to this point I have been agreeing. In differing from them, however, I wish to proceed with the utmost caution
and diffidence. The smallness of my own acquaintance with the
disciplines of natural science is ever before my mind, and I am
fearful of doing these disciplines an injustice. The ability and pugnacity of the partisans of natural science make them formidable
persons to contradict. The tone of tentative inquiry, which befits
a being of dim faculties and bounded knowledge, is the tone I would
wish to take and not to depart from. At present it seems to me that
those who are for giving to natural knowledge, as they call it, the
chief place in the education of the majority of mankind, leave one
important thing out of their account: the constitution of human
nature. But I put this forward on the strength of some facts not at
all recondite, very far from it; facts capable of being stated in the
simplest possible fashion, and to which, if I so state them, the man of
science will, I am sure, be willing to allow their due weight.

Deny the facts altogether, I think, he hardly can. He can hardly
deny that when we set ourselves to enumerate the powers which
go to the building up of human life, and say that they are the
power of conduct, the power of intellect and knowledge, the power
of beauty, and the power of social life and manners,—he can hardly
deny that this scheme, though drawn in rough and plain lines
enough, and not pretending to scientific exactness, does yet give a
fairly true representation of the matter. Human nature is built up
by these powers; we have the need for them all. When we have
rightly met and adjusted the claims of them all, we shall then be in
a fair way for getting soberness and righteousness with wisdom. This
is evident enough, and the friends of physical science would admit it.

But perhaps they may not have sufficiently observed another thing:
namely, that the several powers just mentioned are not isolated,
but there is, in the generality of mankind, a perpetual tendency to
relate them one to another in divers ways. With one such way of

relating them I am particularly concerned now. Following our instinct for intellect and knowledge, we acquire pieces of knowledge; and presently, in the generality of men, there arises the desire to relate these pieces of knowledge to our sense for conduct, to our sense for beauty,—and there is weariness and dissatisfaction if the desire is balked. Now in this desire lies, I think, the strength of that hold which letters have upon us.

All knowledge is, as I said just now, interesting; and even items of knowledge which from the nature of the case cannot well be related, but must stand isolated in our thoughts, have their interest. Even lists of exceptions have their interest. If we are studying Greek accents, it is interesting to know that *pais* and *pas*, and some other monosyllables of the same form of declension, do not take the circumflex upon the last syllable of the genitive plural, but vary, in this respect, from the common rule. If we are studying physiology, it is interesting to know that the pulmonary artery carries dark blood and the pulmonary vein carries bright blood, departing in this respect from the common rule for the division of labour between the veins and the arteries. But every one knows how we seek naturally to combine the pieces of our knowledge together, to bring them under general rules, to relate them to principles; and how unsatisfactory and tiresome it would be to go on forever learning lists of exceptions, or accumulating items of fact which must stand isolated.

Well, that same need of relating our knowledge, which operates here within the sphere of our knowledge itself, we shall find operating, also, outside that sphere. We experience, as we go on learning and knowing,—the vast majority of us experience,—the need of relating what we have learnt and known to the sense which we have in us for conduct, to the sense which we have in us for beauty.

A certain Greek prophetess of Mantineia in Arcadia, Diotima by name, once explained to the philosopher Socrates that love, and impulse, and bent of all kinds, is, in fact, nothing else but the desire in men that good should forever be present to them. This desire for good, Diotima assured Socrates, is our fundamental desire, of which fundamental desire every impulse in us is only some one particular form. And therefore this fundamental desire it is, I suppose,—this desire in men that good should be forever present to them,—which acts in us when we feel the impulse for relating our knowledge to our sense for conduct and to our sense for beauty. At any rate, with men in general the instinct exists. Such is human nature. And the instinct, it will be admitted, is innocent, and human nature is preserved by our following the lead of its innocent instincts. Therefore, in seeking to gratify this instinct in question, we are following the instinct of self-preservation in humanity.

But, no doubt, some kinds of knowledge cannot be made to directly serve the instinct in question, cannot be directly related to the sense for beauty, to the sense for conduct. These are instrument-knowledges; they lead on to other knowledges, which can. A man who passes his life in instrument-knowledges is a specialist. They may be invaluable as instruments to do something beyond, for those who have the gift thus to employ them; and they may be disciplines in themselves wherein it is useful for every one to have some schooling. But it is inconceivable that the generality of men should pass all their mental life with Greek accents or with formal logic. My friend Professor Sylvester, who is one of the first mathematicians in the world, holds transcendental doctrines as to the virtue of mathematics, but those doctrines are not for common men. In the very Senate House and heart of our English Cambridge I once ventured, though not without an apology for my profaneness, to hazard the opinion that for the majority of mankind a little of mathematics, even, goes a long way. Of course this is quite consistent with their being of immense importance as an instrument to something else; but it is the few who have the aptitude for using them, not the bulk of mankind.

The natural sciences do not, however, stand on the same footing with these instrument-knowledges. Experience shows us that the generality of men will find more interest in learning that, when a taper burns, the wax is converted into carbonic acid and water, or in learning the explanation of the phenomenon of dew, or in learning how the circulation of the blood is carried on, than they find in learning that the genitive plural of *pais* and *pas* does not take the circumflex on the termination. And one piece of natural knowledge is added to another, and others are added to that, and at last we come to propositions so interesting as Mr. Darwin's famous proposition that "our ancestor was a hairy quadruped furnished with a tail and pointed ears, probably arboreal in his habits." Or we come to propositions of such reach and magnitude as those which Professor Huxley delivers, when he says that the notions of our forefathers about the beginning and the end of the world were all wrong, and that nature is the expression of a definite order with which nothing interferes.

Interesting, indeed, these results of science are, important they are, and we should all of us be acquainted with them. But what I now wish you to mark is, that we are still, when they are propounded to us and we receive them, we are still in the sphere of intellect and knowledge. And for the generality of men there will be found, I say, to arise, when they have duly taken in the proposition that their ancestor was "a hairy quadruped furnished with a tail and pointed ears, probably arboreal in his habits," there will be found to arise an invincible desire to relate this proposition to the sense in us for conduct, and to the sense in us for beauty. But this the men of science will not do for us, and will hardly even profess to do. They will give us other pieces of knowledge, other facts, about other animals and their ancestors, or about plants, or about stones, or about stars; and they may finally bring us to those great "general conceptions of the universe, which are forced upon us all," says Professor Huxley, "by the progress of physical science." But still it will be *knowledge* only which they give us; knowledge not put for us into relation with our sense for conduct, our sense for beauty, and touched with emotion by being so put; not thus put for us, and therefore, to the majority of mankind, after a certain while, unsatisfying, wearying.

Not to the born naturalist, I admit. But what do we mean by a born naturalist? We mean a man in whom the zeal for observing nature is so uncommonly strong and eminent, that it marks him off from the bulk of mankind. Such a man will pass his life happily in collecting natural knowledge and reasoning upon it, and will ask for nothing, or hardly anything, more. I have heard it said that the sagacious and admirable naturalist whom we lost not very long ago, Mr. Darwin, once owned to a friend that for his part he did not experience the necessity for two things which most men find so necessary to them,—religion and poetry; science and the domestic affections, he thought, were enough. To a born naturalist, I can well understand that this should seem so. So absorbing is his occupation with nature, so strong his love for his occupation, that he goes on acquiring natural knowledge and reasoning upon it, and has little time or inclination for thinking about getting it related to the desire in man for conduct, the desire in man for beauty. He relates it to them for himself as he goes along, so far as he feels the need; and he draws from the domestic affections all the additional solace necessary. But then Darwins are extremely rare. Another great and admirable master of natural knowledge, Faraday, was a Sandemanian.

That is to say, he related his knowledge to his instinct for conduct and to his instinct for beauty, by the aid of that respectable Scottish sectary, Robert Sandeman. And so strong, in general, is the demand of religion and poetry to have their share in a man, to associate themselves with his knowing, and to relieve and rejoice it, that, probably, for one man amongst us with the disposition to do as Darwin did in this respect, there are at least fifty with the disposition to do as Faraday.

Education lays hold upon us, in fact, by satisfying this demand. Professor Huxley holds up to scorn mediaeval education with its neglect of the knowledge of nature, its poverty even of literary studies, its formal logic devoted to "showing how and why that which the Church said was true must be true." But the great mediaeval Universities were not brought into being, we may be sure, by the zeal for giving a jejune and contemptible education. Kings have been their nursing fathers, and queens have been their nursing mothers, but not for this. The mediaeval Universities came into being, because the supposed knowledge, delivered by Scripture and the Church, so deeply engaged men's hearts, by so simply, easily, and powerfully relating itself to their desire for conduct, their desire for beauty. All other knowledge was dominated by this supposed knowledge and was subordinated to it, because of the surpassing strength of the hold which it gained upon the affections of men, by allying itself profoundly with their sense for conduct, their sense for beauty.

But now, says Professor Huxley, conceptions of the universe fatal to the notions held by our forefathers have been forced upon us by physical science. Grant to him that they are thus fatal, that the new conceptions must and will soon become current everywhere, and that every one will finally perceive them to be fatal to the beliefs of our forefathers. The need of humane letters, as they are truly called, because they serve the paramount desire in men that good should be forever present to them,—the need of humane letters, to establish a relation between the new conceptions, and our instinct for beauty, our instinct for conduct, is only the more visible. The Middle Age could do without humane letters, as it could do without the study of nature, because its supposed knowledge was made to engage its emotions so powerfully. Grant that the supposed knowledge disappears, its power of being made to engage the emotions will of course disappear along with it,—but the emotions themselves, and their claim to be engaged and satisfied, will remain.

Now if we find by experience that humane letters have an undeniable power of engaging the emotions, the importance of humane letters in a man's training becomes not less, but greater, in proportion to the success of modern science in extirpating what it calls "mediaeval thinking."

Have humane letters, then, have poetry and eloquence, the power here attributed to them of engaging the emotions, and do they exercise it? And if they have it and exercise it, *how* do they exercise it, so as to exert an influence upon man's sense for conduct, his sense for beauty? Finally, even if they both can and do exert an influence upon the senses in question, how are they to relate to them the results—the modern results—of natural science? All these questions may be asked. First, have poetry and eloquence the power of calling out the emotions? The appeal is to experience. Experience shows that for the vast majority of men, for mankind in general, they have the power. Next, do they exercise it? They do. But then, *how* do they exercise it so as to affect man's sense for conduct, his sense for beauty? And this is perhaps a case for applying the Preacher's words: "Though a man labour to seek it out, yet he shall not find it; yea, farther, though a wise man think to know it, yet shall he not be able to find it." Why should it be one thing, in its effect upon the emotions, to say, "Patience is a virtue," and quite another thing, in its effect upon the emotions, to say with Homer,

τλητὸν γὰρ Μοῖραι θυμὸν θέσαν ἀνθρώποισιν —

"for an enduring heart have the destinies appointed to the children of men"? Why should it be one thing, in its effect upon the emotions, to say with the philosopher Spinoza, *Felicitas in ea consistit quod homo suum esse conservare potest*—"Man's happiness consists in his being able to preserve his own essence," and quite another thing, in its effect upon the emotions, to say with the Gospel, "What is a man advantaged, if he gain the whole world, and lose himself, forfeit himself?" How does this difference of effect arise? I cannot tell, and I am not much concerned to know; the important thing is that it does arise, and that we can profit by it. But how, finally, are poetry and eloquence to exercise the power of relating the modern results of natural science to man's instinct for conduct, his instinct for beauty? And here again I answer that I do not know *how* they will exercise it, but that they can and will exercise it I am sure. I do not mean that modern philosophical poets and modern philosophical moralists are to come and relate for us, in express terms, the results of modern scientific research to our instinct for conduct, our instinct for beauty. But I mean that we shall find, as a matter of experience, if we know the best that has been thought and uttered in the world,—we shall find that the art and poetry and eloquence of men who lived, perhaps, long ago, who had the most limited natural knowledge, who had the most erroneous conceptions about many important matters,—we shall find that this art, and poetry, and eloquence, have in fact not only the power of refreshing and delighting us; they have also the power,—such is the strength and worth, in essentials, of their authors' criticism of life,—they have a fortifying, and elevating, and quickening, and suggestive power, capable of wonderfully helping us to relate the results of modern science to our need for conduct, our need for beauty. Homer's conceptions of the physical universe were, I imagine, grotesque; but really, under the shock of hearing from modern science that "the world is not subordinated to man's use, and that man is not the cynosure of things terrestrial," I could, for my own part, desire no better comfort than Homer's line which I quoted just now,

τλητὸν γὰρ Μοῖραι θυμὸν θέσαν ἀνθρώποισιν —

"for an enduring heart have the destinies appointed to the children of men"!

And the more that men's minds are cleared, the more that the results of science are frankly accepted, the more that poetry and eloquence come to be received and studied as what in truth they really are,—the criticism of life by gifted men, alive and active with extraordinary power at an unusual number of points,—so much the more will the value of humane letters, and of art also, which is an utterance having a like kind of power with theirs, be felt and acknowledged, and their place in education be secured.

Let us, therefore, all of us, avoid indeed as much as possible any invidious comparison between the merits of humane letters, as means of education, and the merits of the natural sciences. But when some President of a Section for Mechanical Science insists on making the comparison, and tells us that "he who in his training has substituted literature and history for natural science has chosen the less useful alternative," let us make answer to him that the student of humane letters only, will, at least, know also the great general conceptions brought in by modern physical science; for science, as Professor Huxley says, forces them upon us all. But the student of the natural sciences only, will, by our very hypothesis, know nothing of humane letters; not to mention that in setting himself to be perpetually accumulating natural knowledge, he sets himself to do what only specialists have in general the gift for doing genially. And so he will probably be unsatisfied, or at any rate incomplete, and even more incomplete than the student of humane letters only.

I once mentioned in a school-report, how a young man in one of our English training colleges having to paraphrase the passage in *Macbeth* beginning,

Can'st thou not minister to a mind diseased?

turned this line into, "Can you not wait upon the lunatic?" And I remarked what a curious state of things it would be, if every pupil of our national schools knew, let us say, that the moon is two thousand one hundred and sixty miles in diameter, and thought at the same time that a good paraphrase for

Can'st thou not minister to a mind diseased?

was, "Can you not wait upon the lunatic?" If one is driven to choose, I think I would rather have a young person ignorant about the moon's diameter, but aware that "Can you not wait upon the lunatic?" is bad, than a young person whose education had been such as to manage things the other way.

Or to go higher than the pupils of our national schools. I have in my mind's eye a member of our British Parliament who comes to travel here in America, who afterwards relates his travels, and who shows a really masterly knowledge of the geology of this great country and of its mining capabilities, but who ends by gravely suggesting that the United States should borrow a prince from our Royal Family, and should make him their king, and should create a House of Lords of great landed proprietors after the pattern of ours; and then America, he thinks, would have her future happily and perfectly secured. Surely, in this case, the President of the Section for Mechanical Science would himself hardly say that our member of Parliament, by concentrating himself upon geology and mineralogy, and so on, and not attending to literature and history, had "chosen the more useful alternative."

If then there is to be separation and option between humane letters on the one hand, and the natural sciences on the other, the great majority of mankind, all who have not exceptional and overpowering aptitudes for the study of nature, would do well, I cannot but think, to choose to be educated in humane letters rather than in the natural sciences. Letters will call out their being at more points, will make them live more. . . .

Problems for Thought and Writing

I

1. This essay was Arnold's reply to Huxley's "Science and Culture" (page 556) and was delivered as a lecture at Cambridge University in 1882. Does the fact that Arnold admits he is a man of letters and not a scientist strengthen or weaken his argument against Huxley?

2. Evaluate "to know the best which has been thought and said in the world" as an ideal for a nation's education and culture. How is one to determine "the best"? Does Arnold here deal with that problem?

3. Would you say that Arnold is really *arguing* with Huxley or *instructing* him? Does he anywhere take the wind out of Huxley's sails by seeming to agree with him? Is temporary or at least apparent agreement with the opposition an indispensable part of any argument that hopes for success? See Mark Antony's oration, page 622.

4. "It is very certain that the earth is not the chief body in the material universe and that the world is not subordinated to man's use" (page 569). Would an educated man of the fourteenth century agree with this statement of Arnold's? Would C. S. Lewis (page 326), or Etienne Gilson (page 635) agree with it?

5. What is Arnold's chief point of difference with Huxley?

6. Is Arnold being ironical or genuinely humble in referring to himself as a man "of dim faculties and bounded knowledge," page 571? If you think he is being ironical, explain the kind of irony involved here.

7. The desire to relate knowledge to our sense for conduct and beauty is, says Arnold, a part of our instinct for self-preservation. Do you think this is a valid proposition?

8. In the factories, on the assembly lines, in business offices—almost everywhere we look today we see men living with the results of "instrument-knowledge." Would they be better off with the kind of education Arnold suggests? Would they then have more constructive outlets for their emotions? Could literature compete with television or the movies for their attention?

II

9. Define or explain: *belles lettres,* cynosure, terrestrial, Philistines, Levites, pugnacity, option, Mr. Darwin, Robert Sandeman, circumflex, quadruped, pulmonary.

10. Study Arnold's use of repetition of word and phrase as a stylistic device. Does Huxley's prose have this characteristic? How do they differ? Which seems to you the more lucid? Which the more interesting?

SHOULD AMERICAN HISTORY BE REWRITTEN?*

A debate between Allan Nevins and Matthew Josephson

YES   *Allan Nevins*

One curious thing about history, as Philip Guedalla said, is that it really happened. Another curious fact about history is that while it was happening nobody really understood its meaning.

John Fiske, pausing one day in his young manhood before the window of Little, Brown & Co. in Boston, saw a volume within entitled "Pioneers of France in the New World" and noted that its author was identified as the man who had written "The Conspiracy of Pontiac." He remembered that when that earlier volume appeared he had wondered whether Pontiac was a barbarous chieftain of medieval Europe. He recalled also that some teacher at Harvard had once expressed the view that the French and Indian War was a dull squabble of no real significance to students of history. Passing on, Fiske wondered why anyone should write about French pioneers in America. He lived to pen an essay on Francis Parkman which not only placed that author at the head of American historians (where he yet stands), but recognized that the epic significance of the struggle of Britain and France for the mastery of North America—a significance which Parkman had first expounded—could hardly be overstated. An interpretation of our continental history which nowadays we assume no child could miss had been beyond the grasp of the brilliant young John Fiske in the 1860's.

The idea that history can ever be so well written that it does not need rewriting can be held only by those foolish people who think that history can ever ascertain exact truth. It cannot. We can go further than the assertion of that truism: we can say, "Fortunate for history that it cannot ascertain exact truth!" If history were a photograph of the past it would be flat and uninspiring. Happily, it is a painting; and, like all works of art, it fails of the highest truth

* From *The Saturday Review*, February 6, 1954. Copyright 1954 by Saturday Review of Literature. Reprinted by permission of Harold Ober Associates, Incorporated.

unless imagination and ideas are mixed with the paints. A hundred photographs of London Bridge look just alike and convey altogether a very slight percentage of the truth, but Turner's Thames and Whistler's Thames, though utterly different, both convey the river with a deeper truth.

All parts of our history are always being rewritten; no segment of it, from 1492 to 1952, is not now in need of vigorous rewriting. Whenever an expert applies himself to the scrutiny of a special area he at once sounds a lusty call for more searching exploration of the terrain. Douglas Freeman, carrying Washington through the Revolution, agreed with Bernard Knollenberg, writing a history of that war, that every part of the Revolutionary struggle needs the most searching re-examination and the boldest reinterpretation. Merrill Jensen states in the preface to his study of the Confederation that the entire period 1783-1789 demands a study that will embrace every state and every act of Congress. There are men who believe that the historical study of the Civil War period has only just begun—and they are right. Margaret Leech, now completing a study of the McKinley Administration, is convinced that a hundred research workers should be set to exploration of the dark nooks and secret crannies of the time.

"In vain the sage, with retrospective eye," wrote Pope, "would from the apparent what conclude the why." The three main reasons why history constantly needs reinterpretation include something more than the impossibility of ever learning all the truth about the motives and actions of the past.

The chief of the three reasons is the need of every generation for a reinterpretation to suit its own preconceptions, ideas, and outlook. Every era has its own climate of opinion. It thinks it knows more than the preceding era; it thinks it takes a wider view of the universe. Every era, too, is affected by cataclysmic events which shift its point of view; the French Revolution, the Metternichian reaction, the movement for national unification in Italy, the United States, and Germany, the apogee of Manchester Liberalism, and so on down to the multiple crisis of our atomic age. We see the past through a prism which glows and sparkles as new lights catch its facets. Much of the rewriting of history is a readjustment to this prism. George Bancroft's spectrum was outmoded a few years after his laborious "last revision"; Charles A. Beard's begins to be outworn today, for we now possess what Beard would have called a new frame of reference.

As a second reason, new tools of superior penetrative power are from time to time installed in the toolshed of even our rather unprogressive race of historians. Our council for research in the social sciences (it should be studies) justly emphasizes the value of overlapping disciplines. Much could be said for the contention that the best historians nowadays are prepared in some other field than that of history. Thus Wesley Clair Mitchell, the historian of the greenbacks, of business cycles, and of the ebb and flow of economic activity, whose National Bureau of Economic Research inspired so much fruitful historical writing, was trained as an economist. (He also was trained by John Dewey, who gave courses under all sorts of titles, but "every one of them dealt with the same subject—how we think.") Beard was trained as a political scientist. Parrington was trained as a student of literature. Carl Becker was trained in European history but wrote in the American field. James Henry Breasted was first trained in theology, a fact which stood him in good stead when this pioneer of Egyptology in America began to trace the development of conscience and religion in the Ancient East. Not one historian in fifty knows as much as he should of the tool called statistics, or of psychology, or of economic geography, or of ecology. The kinship between Halford J. Mackinder, the geographer, and Frederick J. Turner, the historian, in loosing seminal ideas showed what the geographer could learn from history, and the historian from geography.

But the third great reason why history is rewritten is simply because the constant discovery of new materials necessitates a recasting of our view of the past. We might think that this would one day cease, but it never does. Everyone who has laboriously mapped any historical subject appreciates the impact of new facts upon that map, blurring some lines and defining new ones. Happy are those who live to rewrite their books, as Parkman rewrote one of his—"LaSalle and the Great West." One would have said that all the materials for a history of the Revolution had been assembled in print by the innumerable agencies, local, state, and national, devoted to that effort, but Freeman assures us that the great archives like the Massachusetts Historical Society, the American Philosophical Society, and the main state libraries bulge with unstudied documents. One would have said that all the material for the history of the Confederate War Office had been studied and restudied; but, behold!, the diary of the third officer of that department, Kean, is suddenly deposited in the University of Virginia, and we find it possible to make a sweeping reassessment of the Southern military administration.

Thus, the idea that history is photography is set at naught. It is art; it constantly requires a new mixture of pigments, new points of view, new manipulation of light and shade; and as an art it presents an endless challenge to the writer who perceives that the highest truth of history will always transcend a statement of fact; that, indeed, historical fact is but a foundation for the truth won by imagination and intellectual power.

The best history is always interpretive, but this does not mean that the best history is consciously or ostentatiously interpretive. The work of the historical masters, from Thucydides to Trevelyan, illustrates the fact that interpretation is most effective when implicit rather than explicit. The true historical attitude is a search for truth about a situation, force, or event—the War of 1812, the Abolitionist impulse, Pearl Harbor—which slowly, painfully, accurately dredges up an unforeseen interpretation. That is, history properly operates by the inductive, not the deductive, method. The merit of an Olympian historian like Parkman is that he says in effect: "Let us collect and collate all the relevant facts and find what conclusions emerge from their impartial analysis." The cardinal weakness of a controversial historian like Beard is that he repeatedly gave the impression—perhaps falsely—of having said to himself: "Let us take this provocative theory of the truth, and see how impressive an array of facts we can collect in its support." Ideas in history, that is, should be applied in subordination to the ascertainment of all the facts, and not in control of the ascertainment of one picked body of facts. Hence it is that nothing could be more absurd than to try to predict in advance the interpretations to be applied to our history by future writers—who will certainly go their own way. But we may legitimately make some guesses—they are not prophecies, but mere guesses, offered with due modesty—as to the drift of some of the new interpretations.

As American history lengthens and the past falls into longer perspective, we tend not so much to discard major interpretations entirely as to place new ones beside them; not so much to substitute one simple synthesis for another as to embrace old monistic views in a new and complex synthesis. During the first century of our national history, 1775-1875, three great dominant developments lift themselves above all others. They are the establishment of American Independence, political, economic, and finally cultural, from Europe; the westward movement for the conquest and development of the continent; and the abolition of slavery and a Southern way of life in a civil war which vindicated national unity. Some students, to be sure, would select other elements in our historical fabric, but three special students out of five and nine lay readers out of ten would, I believe, choose these. Now it is evident to a cursory view that each of the three lent itself at first to a simple monistic interpretation, expounded in the work even of subtle historians; and that within one or two generations this simple view of the past was replaced by a dual or multiple interpretation. What had been a flat telescopic image was given depth and reality by a stereopticon lens.

Thus it was that the old simple view of the Revolution as a politico-military struggle was amplified and enriched by subsequent views of the Revolution as a great movement for social and institutional change of a purely internal character. The old simple view of the conflict of North and South as centering in the slavery struggle was widened and deepened by later treatments of that collision as arising also from the increasing moral, social, economic, and cultural differences between the two sections. The old simple view of westward expansion as significant for what the pioneer did in changing the wilderness was immensely enlarged by Turner's thesis that a greater significance lay in what the wilderness did in changing the pioneer.

Nowadays the character of a fourth great development, accomplished and sealed in the last fifty years of our national life, can hardly be missed. On that new phase of our history, too, general agreement will perhaps be found. We have become first a great world power, and then *the* great world power. We have moved first into the open arena of world affairs, and then into the very center of that arena. We now view our national past from the vantage-point of this new turn, and with the changed perspective which it gives us.

Just as John Fiske saw our history from 1607 to 1789 as an evolutionary preparation for the gift of practical democracy and the Anglo-American principle of self-government to the world in the shape of our Constitution and Federal system; just as Von Holst saw the whole period from 1776 to 1861 as a preparation for the vindication of human liberty and national unity; so now we have historians who view our whole national life as an unconscious preparation for the time when we should become Protector of the Faith for all democratic peoples; when, having turned away from Western European affairs until we gained first place among the nations, we returned to them as the pivot and support of Western European civilization. These writers regard American history not in terms of the Western continent, but in terms of an Atlantic community. We find, indeed, that we never left that community; that the Seven Years' War was our first world war, the Revolution our second; that we have but awakened to our consciousness of a global role. And when these historians write of our national future they speak not of short-term objects, but of what Lincoln called "man's vast future."

This tremendous change of the past forty or fifty years—this emergence of America to the leadership of the Western World—will undoubtedly affect our children's children, and the long generations to come, in the most sweeping way. It will loom up in time to come as tremendously as the great changes which preceded it—as the Revolution internal and external, the American conquest of the frontier and the frontier's conquest of the American, the death of slavery and the birth of machine industry. But the full significance of this development will not become evident until it, too, is given the dual or multiple interpretation that historians gave these older developments. We shall not understand its essential character until all the accompanying phenomena, social, economic, and intellectual, have been analyzed, and some mind as electric as Parrington's and as penetrating as Turner's has pierced nearer its heart. What then will be its significance? That is a question we cannot answer; it is for the oncoming generation of historians.

My own guess is that this great development by which America has been projected into world leadership, with all the exhilarations and perils, the opportunities and costs of that position, may in some fashion be connected by future interpreters with the advent of an age of mass action, mass production, and mass psychology in American life. From being one of the most unorganized, the most invertebrate of nations in 1860 we have grown into the most powerfully and efficiently organized people on the globe. Our population of 160,000,000 disposes of its resources through such mass combinations, political, social, and economic, as mankind never saw before. Our thinking in 1865 was still individual thinking; today it is largely mass thinking, shaped and colored by mass media of unparalleled and sometimes dismaying potency—press, radio, television, cinema. No one can go to what were recently primitive frontier communities in America—say Texas and California—without being struck, and a little appalled, by the complexity and efficiency with which they have organized their life. It was our mass production which won the two last world wars; it was our genius for making big organizations work which has built the means for saving Western democracy since the latest world war. Our national outlook, once that of the individualistic pioneer, has become a social outlook. Without this pervasive internal change our new position in the world would have been impossible.

The striking shift in our character and our world position in the last half century, of course, has some direct results, already visible, in our interpretation of history. We are evincing a greater militancy in asserting the virtues of our political and social system. The apologetic attitude of the years of the Great Depression is gone. We can henceforth be more confident, and more energetic, in asserting that our way of life, called decadent by our enemies, has proved itself historically to be freer, more flexible, and more humane than any other in history. We can be as emphatic and frank as ever in describing our past weaknesses, from slavery to slums, but we shall insist more rigorously on the fundamental healthiness of our system and on its proved ability to mend its defects and give us a constantly self-regenerating society.

We shall also evince, I think, a tendency to insist more emphatically on the fundamental unity of the United States with Western Europe and the various other nations sprung from Western Europe. All kinds of Western institutions and virtues now find their principal stronghold in the United States. The literature written in the English tongue increasingly has its main center of vitality in America, a fact well recognized by the London *Times Literary Supplement.* The Roman Catholic Church, like the Protestant churches, finds its chief springs of wealth and power in the United States. The Atlantic Community, as many publicists term it, has taken the place of the former division between Europe and the Americas. Oldtime quarrels between America and Western Europe have lost a great part of the significance which was once attached to them. What does the War of 1812 count for compared with the maintenance and growth of the political, social, and cultural ties that have made the English-speaking nations so nearly a unit? The nationalistic view of our history will increasingly be replaced by the international view, treating America as part of a great historic civilization with the Atlantic its center, as the Mediterranean was the center of the ancient world; the tides of population, power, and influence first moving from Europe to America, and then beginning to flow in the opposite direction.

We may look forward, also, to a more appreciative attitude toward our material strength, and to a more scientific treatment of the factors which have created this material power. In the past our historians were apologetic about this. They condemned our love of the dollar, our race to wealth, our interest in material objects; they deprecated our worship of size, and deplored our boastfulness about steel tonnage, grain production, and output of machinery. Clio, with her tradition of devotion to moral values, was scornful of any others. Our writers in general—for the historians but followed the poets, the novelists, and the dramatists—intimated that America had grown too fast, too coarsely, too muscularly; they exalted the rural virtues as against industrial might, the rarefied air of the study as against the smoky atmosphere of the mill.

Without denying that some accompaniments of our swift industrialization were atrociously bad we can now assert that this historical attitude was in part erroneous. The nation grew none too fast. We can see today that all its wealth, all its strength were needed to meet a succession of world crises—and we still dwell in a crisis era. Had we applied restrictions to keep our economy small, tame, and timid we would have lost World War I. Had the United States not possessed the mightiest oil industry, the greatest steel industry, the largest automotive factories, the most efficient machine-tool industry, the best technological schools, and the most ingenious working force in the world, we would indubitably have lost World War II.

Were we significantly weaker today in technical skills, in great mills and factories, and the scientific knowledge which gave us priority with the atomic bomb and hydrogen bomb, all Western Europe would perhaps be cowering—we ourselves would perhaps be cowering—before the knout held by the Kremlin. The architects of our material growth—the men like Whitney, McCormick, Westinghouse, Rockefeller, Carnegie, Hill, and Ford—will yet stand forth in their true stature as builders, for all their faults, of a strength which civilization found indispensable.

That Jay Gould deserves the unscientific term "robber baron" is doubtless true. Nobody can object if similar malisons are heaped on such other disreputable businessmen as Collis P. Huntington, Bet-a-Million Gates, and Frenzied-Finance Lawson. Industry, like politics, has its bad men and dark chapters, and it has long been easy to get a spurious reputation for "courage" by dilating on them. The *real* courage, however, is required by those who argue that we should approach our business history with discrimination, balance, and a concern for scientific analysis of all the evidence. The forthcoming multivolumed history of the Standard of New Jersey by members of

the Harvard School of Business Administration will show that Rockefeller and his successors were guiltless of many of the charges flung
at them, and in organizing the incredibly chaotic oil business performed a work not destructive, but essentially constructive. Andrew
Carnegie, who did so much to build the nation's steel industry, cannot be dismissed with the term "robber baron." Nor can James J.
Hill, whose Great Northern contributed so much to Northwestern
growth. Nor can Henry Ford, who lowered prices, raised wages,
and in 1911-1914 brought to birth at Highland Park the complex
creative process called mass production, which, widely applied, has
done so much to make life richer and Western democracy stronger.
As the era of muckraking fades the era of a true history of our industrial growth—not apologetics, not abuse, but scientific appraisal,
giving blame and credit where each is due—can open. And the
credit side of the ledger far outweighs the debit.

It will yet be realized that the industrial revolution in the United
States came none too soon, and none too fast; and that the ensuing
mass production revolution as yet so little understood by Americans
was not born a day too early. We shall also come to realize that the
turmoil and human suffering which inescapably accompanied the industrial revolution and the mass-production revolution were not, after
all, a tremendous price to pay for their benefits. The price was
smaller in the United States than in foreign lands. The industrial
revolution cost less in human travail here than it did in England,
where it first came to birth; less than in Germany or Japan; far less
than it is costing in Russia. Here is a wide field for the rewriting
of American history, and for the re-education of the American people,
who should have a fair presentation of the facts in place of tenden-
tious writing.

Our material might, to be sure, is valuable only as it supports, and
carries to victory, great moral ideas; only as it buttresses a civilization
in which spiritual forces are predominant. But the fundamental difference between the democratic world and the totalitarian world lies
precisely in the superior position which we give to moral and spiritual
values. It is we, not our enemies, who have the right to talk about
what Lincoln called man's vast future, for we really value men as
individual souls. Behind our dreams of man's vast future we mobilize
an unconquerable strength. In time, when future historians look
back on this period, which to us is so full of struggle, sacrifice, and
anxious uncertainty, they will perhaps give it an interpretation of no

mean character. They may say: "The era in which the United States, summoning all its strength, led democracy in winning the First World War, the Second World War, and the ensuing struggle against the Communist tyranny, was one of the imposing eras of history. It stands invested, in its own fashion, with something of the radiance of the Periclean era, the Elizabethan era, and the era of Pitt and the long struggle against Napoleon."

N O   *Matthew Josephson*

When Professor Nevins read the foregoing paper before the Society of American Archivists in Dearborn, Michigan, the newspapers rose to the significance of certain passages in it as foreshadowing a new fashion in our historical writing. These were quoted very widely, in some cases, under fairly alarming headlines, such as that in *The New York Times* for September 20, 1953:

REWRITING HISTORY IS URGED BY NEVINS

Our writers and scholars had been growing a bit edgy at reports of the banning and burning of books and of the predations of Senator McCarthy and his "literary department" in the republic of letters. Now came news that Professor Nevins was out to "rewrite" some of our recent history and it gave many persons quite a turn. He has been saying much the same things for several years and with less reservation or prudence than in the Dearborn lecture. In the 1953 edition of his biography of John D. Rockefeller ("A Study in Power"), as earlier, in August 1951, before a meeting of history teachers at Stanford University, he had asserted that many of our contemporary writers had done grave injustice to

. . . the leaders of our material growth—the Rockefellers, Carnegies, Hills, and Morgans. . . . In the past our historians tended to a feminine idealism. They were apologetic about our dollars, our race to wealth, our materialism. . . . They spoke scornfully of the robber barons who were not robber barons at all: they intimated that America had grown too fast.

Professor Samuel Eliot Morison, president of the American Historical Association, sounded the same notes last year in an address before that learned body. He assailed the tendency to the "economic interpretation" of our history as exemplified by Charles Beard, and he went to great lengths to castigate the "debunkers" who in the 1930's and 1940's, by their excessively critical spirit, as he argued, often insulted our "folk-memories," stripped America's "great figures" of all virtue, all nobility, and in fact of their greatness. Mr. Morison, therefore, urged that our damaged heroes should be salvaged from the historical junk heaps where they had been consigned, that they be patched up, varnished, and made to look like real antiques. ·At the same time *Fortune* magazine, which candidly glorifies our large corporate enterprises, in April 1952 published a long article by E. N. Saveth surveying the many injuries done to the repute of our business class by American historians old and new, from Parkman and Prescott, down to Henry Adams, Beard, and the other so-called "muckrakers." All this had made for "bad" public relations and needed much correcting, *Fortune* noted, if businessmen were to avoid new reform measures by the Government.

These facts are mentioned to indicate the context in which Professor Nevins dropped his latest remarks on how our history should be rewritten. It has all added up to quite a campaign. Assuredly, "every era has its own climate of opinion," as he observes. The present (though by a narrow electoral margin) has assumed some of the character of a Restoration, with our own Stuarts and Bourbons coming in again where they left off. The "revisionists" of history are now much concerned that our masters of heavy industry and finance be given their due.

How different was the climate of 1933 when, as it happened, I wrote my own study of our nineteenth-century industrialists and, in a spirit of good clean fun, entitled it "The Robber Barons." There were some fifteen millions unemployed in our cities; our farmers were up in arms literally; our most prominent financiers were being investigated or tried or were in flight abroad. Never were the creative contributions of our big business leadership rated so low. As for the term "robber barons," it was not of my own coinage, but was drawn from the folklore of the Kansas Greenbackers and Populists of the 1880's who had their experience with the Jay Gould type.

Today is a different day, and the prevailing trade winds in this country drive us toward mental conformity. Our university scholars are but made of flesh. Even the Justices of the Supreme Court, it has been long said, "follow the election returns" in handing down their opinions. Should historians lag far behind in judging the shift of political power to conservative hands? Reflecting upon Mr.

Nevins's timely advice that we assume "a more appreciative attitude" toward the architects of our prosperity and progress, we can imagine whole flocks of historians, large and small, hastening to change their old liberal lights for new. Where only a decade or two ago they, like Mr. Nevins himself, were fairly strong for the New Deal, we may fancy them, henceforth, writing panegyrics on the wisdom, courage, and moral beauty of FDR's enemies, the economic royalists.

The talk of rewriting our history inevitably brings to mind the nightmare vision of George Orwell's "Nineteen Eighty-Four," with its regiments of poor intellectuals helots in the labyrinthine sky-scrapers of the Ministry of Truth retouching records, destroying old documents, removing all trace of liberal and democratic ideas. Or-well's anti-utopian fantasy was, of course, based on the Nazi creation of a Federal Institute for the History of the New Germany and on the revision of the history of Soviet Russia under Stalin's direction. Will the New History of this country, too, be rewritten as crude propaganda for the party in power? Will Franklin Roosevelt be trimmed down to size—say that of Calvin Coolidge—and Henry Ford be given wings and a harp? Will the art of Tacitus, Voltaire, and Gibbon be reduced to a public-relations job?

Perish the thought. The last person to recommend such a pro-gram would be Allan Nevins, who has long conducted himself as a sincere democrat. But his proposals for "revision" have been to my mind ill conceived and ill timed. Ill timed because these are days when the works and ideas of some of our most creative thinkers, such as Oliver Wendell Holmes, Veblen, and John Dewey, have come under suspicion and attack by overheated patriots. Ill timed because history books long esteemed and profitably studied have been banned; because many writers and teachers of history show increasing fear to use their faculties on the materials and lessons of the past. Mr. Nevins's example, termed in some university circles "a harbinger of coming revisionism," will scarcely spread courage.

To be sure, history is always being rewritten. As Benedetto Croce said: "All true history is contemporary history." We write not for the dead but for the living. Yet in the past, change in the art has been a slow alembic process carrying it away from myth, romance, and superstition toward an ever more rational chronicle of the past. Thucydides vowed that he would eschew romance. Gibbon, as a man of the Enlightenment, rewrote the early Christian historians; and the men of the "scientific" school of Ranke in the next century tried to correct Gibbon. But seldom before have serious historians come with proposals to lay aside the tools of exact knowledge and place important figures of the past in the setting of romance or myth.

The revisionists have singled out Beard for punishment, because he was stubbornly unromantic about our tycoons and, as they contend, contributed more than almost any other to the formation of a skeptical attitude toward our institutions among the intellectuals of the 1930's and 1940's. His highly documented "Economic Interpretation of the American Constitution," as Dr. Morison would now say, "debunked" the Founding Fathers. Here, by a semantic device, the word "debunk" is used in the pejorative sense. But is it not honorable to eliminate bunk or buncombe? Is America not great and strong enough to do without Washington's cherry tree and Sheridan's fictitious ride? Beard's best-known work, "The Rise of American Civilization," done in collaboration with his wife, described the industrial revolution after the Civil War and the coming of the great monopolies in a coolly critical spirit. Most intelligent Americans of that era generally regarded the men of the trusts and the railway combinations with intense fear and said, with Henry Adams, that Rockefeller, Morgan, and the trusts were "doing their best" to bring on a social revolution. The masters of industry and finance were, after all, hauled into court year after year as "conspirators" against the rights of other American businessmen and farmers to engage in competitive enterprise; and the politicians of both major parties vied with each other in enacting laws regulating the monopolists. Nevins does not deny all this, but holds that Beard was not "objective"; that he wrote of the "barons" of pork, oil, or sugar with the *partipris* of an economic determinist; that the Rockefellers were "better" than Beard and his intellectual kin believed, or worked better than they knew to build up empires in industry or mass-production plants that transformed an agrarian America into the world's most powerful industrial nation.

To be sure, Charles Beard began his studies during the spectacular industrial and political conflicts of the 1890's; he was influenced, moreover, when he studied at Oxford, by the Fabian Socialists, as well as by the reading of Marx. In those days the concept of economic determinism, broadly speaking, was embraced even by scions of banking families like Professor E. R. A. Seligman. It seemed to be embodied in the career of John D. Rockefeller himself, as even Nevins pictures it. By means regarded as "morally indefensible," he relates, by use of secret railroad debates and espionage, the "anarchy" of small, competitive oil producers was ended and order and efficiency introduced into their field. A business world of small weak units was made "inevitably" to give way to a world of concentration and highly organized power. "Great business aggregations are not built without frustrating, crushing, or absorbing multitudinous small enterprises," concludes the modern apologist of Rockefeller. The historical concepts of Marx—aside from his advocacy of Socialism—have permeated our culture so generally for a hundred years that one finds Nevins unconsciously echoing one of the most familiar of Marxian doctrines: that which sees the rising capitalist class as an agency of progress leading to the triumph of "scientific" and large-scale industry.

Our Rockefellers, then, were not "morally worse" than their contemporaries of the Gilded Age, in Nevins's view, and above all should not be judged by the ethical standards of the present era. By their very ruthlessness in business, terrible even for that "loose period," he holds, they were enabled to build with all the greater speed a vast oil empire that would one day, in wartime, help save our country. Here one finds a philosophy of economic materialism in no way different from that which Beard, in earlier life, embraced—save that Beard preserved always a moral balance somewhat wanting in our current crop of revisionists. And if Dr. Nevins is going to teach us to "appreciate" or condone the moral ruthlessness of our older captains of industry, if he is going to let the end always justify the means, then I fail to see what arguments we can bring to bear against the Russian Communists. Reinhold Niebuhr was quite right in his recent observation (in "The Irony of American History") that our conservative apologists for unbridled monopoly, for the American way of materialistic life, are little better than the Communists.

There was nothing "effeminate" about Beard's idealism. That, incidentally, was the kind of accusation usually directed at reformers by the old corrupt political bosses of the General Grant era, like Roscoe Conkling. Beard was a prodigious worker, forever mining for his facts. He was not "any one thing" in his beliefs, and with time his views changed. But in writing the history of a country where most people had come to improve their material lot he would have been a dull-witted historian indeed if he had ignored the economic motive. In the long run his work stands in the mainstream of the modern pragmatists and sociologists. He desired to turn historical writing away from the mere chronicle of "past politics" or the doings of "great men" or famous diplomats and write of the people, of man in society, of the many-sided growth of a national culture or "civiliza-tion." And, far from belittling the role of those who, for private gain, usurped natural resources, acquired or built railroads nets, and or-ganized huge industries, he insisted that they were in truth the prime actors, the dominant figures in the post-Civil War scene, beside whom Presidents and Senators were but animated shadows. Long years before Nevins approached the oil or automotive industries Beard asserted that the rise of a House of Rockefeller or Morgan was as important a subject for American historians as that of the House of Howard or Burleigh for the English.

Nevins's books, like his article urging the rewriting of our history, are after all but the expressions of his own partiality for the "leaders" of our industrial progress. In truth, they were never beloved or popular as folk-heroes as were our military leaders, great inventors, famous preachers, silver-tongued orators, and picturesque newspaper editors of the Horace Greeley type. If we would return to our folk-lore then the real American tradition is after all reflected by our earlier "literary" historians as well as by the later social-minded ones who expressed habitual distaste rather than adulation for the men of fortune. Charles Francis Adams, Jr., who as a railroad president saw a good deal of them, wrote in his autobiography: "Not one that I have ever known would I care to meet again either in this world or the next . . ." And in these days of the "businessmen's Adminis-tration" in Washington it is well to recall the statement of one in-tensely American historian of half a century ago who said: "In no other country was such power held by the men who had gained these fortunes, the mighty industrial overlords. . . . The Government was practically impotent. . . . Of all forms of tyranny the least attractive and the most vulgar is the tyranny of mere wealth." Was it a Socialist who spoke? No, it was a Republican, a President of the United States, Theodore Roosevelt. He preferred as his heroes men like Peary, the explorer, or Bury, the historian, not the financial magnates. It was Roosevelt who said: "I am simply unable to make myself take the attitude of respect toward the very wealthy men that many per-sons show nowadays . . ."

Beard, the chief target of the revisionists, maintained in his later years, in quite un-Marxist fashion, that the writing of completely "objective" history was an impossibility in view of the problem of selection, proportion, and emphasis that came into play. History thus became something like an "act of faith." The historian began always with an "assumption" or a "scheme of reference." One might fix upon the theme of the struggle of church and state as the *leitmotiv* of the period studied; another upon the clash of great interest groups and institutions. But we can never reproduce the past, in Ranke's words, "as it really was."

Nor does Allan Nevins. In the concluding part of his article one finds a series of historical guesses or "assumptions" about the past and future that seem as visionary or speculative as anything in George Bancroft or Parson Weems. In his closing vaticinal phrases everything comes out all white or all black. On the one side are the plumed knights of business who were "the architects of our material progress"; on the other the dragons of totalitarianism, German, Russian and Chinese. Had we applied "restrictions," that is, state controls, upon the masters of industry, he writes, we should have lost World War I. And but for the men who organized "the mightiest oil industry, the greatest steel industry, the largest automotive factories . . . we would indubitably have lost World War II." Thus, he paints a picture all dripping with glamour of the Rockefellers, Carnegies, and Fords, conjuring up the industrial arms with which to defend democracy and lead the "Atlantic Community" in a crusade against the totalitarians of the East. This is a fairly *simpliste*, big-business version of the American Century. And this, he tells us, is the direction in which the rewriting of our history is to be carried out.

But what does the corpus of ascertainable facts reveal? To those who were in a position to study the defense program being launched in 1940-1941 it was plain that all too many leaders of our industry for two years after war had come to Europe stubbornly resisted the conversion of their plants for the manufacture of arms, or delayed providing added plant capacity, until the Government, under Franklin Roosevelt, agreed to subsidize a large part of such conversion or expansion by allowing very rapid depreciation rates for tax purposes. Today even conservative economists, such as Galbraith of Harvard University, acknowledge the truth that the swiftest and greatest expansion of our industry and our labor productivity took place *not* under the free-enterprise rules of peacetime, but in wartime under the indispensable Government planning, control, and priority restrictions.

Was "Uncle Henry" Ford thinking of the American Century when

—prior to Pearl Harbor—he flatly refused to build aircraft engines for the hard-pressed British? One wonders what Ford's idea of history was. "The bunk," he said.

Problems for Thought and Writing

I

Here, as in the famous argument between Huxley and Arnold (pages 556 and 566), we have a debate between two learned and eminent American scholars. This is an argument in its proper sense: both men are informed, both men accept the premises of logical discourse and know and respect evidence, both men differ fundamentally in their interpretation of the facts. As we might expect, there is heat produced by the exchange. But there is more light than heat, and the differences never emerge as a wrangle.

1. Are you, in reading first one side and then the other, convinced by both men? If so, that is one indication that you probably are meeting a good argument. How can this stalemate be resolved?

2. Nevins' main points are: (1) there is a need for rewriting history in general, (2) there is a specific need for rewriting the history of America's first hundred years and (3) there is a particularly urgent need to rewrite the history of the last hundred years—particularly the role played in it by the so-called "robber barons." Does Josephson meet these points squarely and clearly?

3. Which side of this controversy would Muller (page 653) have taken?

4. Who, in your opinion, wins the argument about the role of the historian Charles A. Beard?

5. In what way does Josephson question the purity of Nevins' motives? Is it only the truth that is impelling Nevins to be a "revisionist," according to Nevins?

6. Is Josephson opposed to the rewriting of history? What are the grounds for his disagreement with Nevins on this point?

7. Who, in your opinion, wins the argument about the respectability and morality of the role of the "robber barons" in American history?

8. Does Josephson meet Nevins' argument about the usefulness of our great corporations in meeting the materiel needs of our two great wars? Is the fact that the corporations seemed to put profits before patriotism an answer or an evasion?

9. "Our thinking in 1865 was still individual thinking; today it is largely mass thinking, shaped and colored by mass media of unparalleled and sometimes dismaying potency—press, radio, television, cinema." From his argument would you say Nevins is dismayed or basically proud of these developments? How do you suppose Ortega y Gasset (page 188) or Chiaromonte (page 225) would answer him?

10. Do you think that both Nevins and Josephson would agree that history is not "photography" but "art"? What, in your judgment, would Henry Adams (page 260) say?

II

11. Outline both arguments. Test them one against the other, point by point. Do your outlines look at all lopsided? Why?

12. What differences do you detect in the styles of the two adversaries? Which, in your opinion, would have been more effective on a public platform? Why?

13. Identify: Francis Parkman, John Fiske, Douglas Freeman, Charles A. Beard, Metternich, Vernon L. Parrington, William Turner, Oliver Wendell Holmes, Benedetto Croce, Reinhold Niebuhr, Horace Greeley.

~

FREEDOM AT HARVARD *

AN EXCHANGE OF LETTERS BY FRANK B. OBER OF BALTIMORE, PRESIDENT CONANT, AND GRENVILLE CLARK, FELLOW OF HARVARD COLLEGE

EXPLANATORY NOTE IN *Harvard Bulletin,* June 25, 1949

On April 27 President Conant received from Frank B. Ober, LL.B. '13, prominent member of the Maryland Bar, a letter making serious charges against Professor Harlow Shapley and Assistant Professor John Ciardi of Harvard, because of their part in certain recent public meetings. Mr. Ober was chairman of a Maryland Commission on Subversive Activities which drafted legislation, recently adopted in that state, directed against Communism. He told Mr. Conant that, because of Harvard's "apparent attitude" toward "extracurricular activities of professors," he had decided not to subscribe to the Law School Fund, and he recommended that the University modify its attitude toward the rights of its Professors to self-expression and change its policies concerning academic tenure.

President Conant answered this letter on his own behalf, and then referred it to Grenville Clark, '03, a senior member of the Corporation, who responded in a detailed argument. In this special section, the *Bulletin* prints these three letters, together with Mr. Ober's comments on Mr. Clark's reply, and a short rebuttal by Mr. Clark. In the letter columns of the current issue will be found letters also from Dean Erwin N. Griswold of the Law School, John B. Marsh, '08, LL.B. '10, Chairman of the Law School Fund, Professor

* Reprinted from the *Harvard Alumni Bulletin* of June 25, 1949. Copyright 1950, Harvard Bulletin, Inc.

Shapley, and Professor Ciardi. The Editors of the *Bulletin* believe that this entire correspondence has historical significance which extends far beyond the boundaries of the Harvard Yard.

Mr. Ober to President Conant

Baltimore, Md.
April 26, 1949

Two recent incidents reflecting the apparent attitude of Harvard toward extracurricular activities of professors giving aid and comfort to Communism have made me decide not to subscribe to the Harvard Law School Fund.

The first was an appeal made by one Professor Ciardi at a so-called "Progressive" rally for funds to fight laws directed at Communism proposed by a Maryland Commission of which I was Chairman—and which incidentally passed our General Assembly substantially as written, with but one dissenting vote. Copy of report is enclosed.

I concede the right of self-appointed "liberals" to fight particular laws against Communism, as there can be honest debate as to the method of handling the question.

But the so-called "Progressive" campaign against the laws enacted in Maryland was not debate, but vilification and falsehood—the usual Communist weapons. They attempted to foment hatred and prejudice in the typical Communist way by stating the proposed laws would send people to jail for activities intended to aid Negroes, Jews, Labor, Catholics, etc., etc. No one reading our report or the law could possibly so construe it with any semblance of honesty. Communists were actually using the Progressive Party, and the meeting Ciardi was reported to have attended was addressed by Marcantonio and other fellow travelers in the usual way—so he must have been aware of its nature. His own speech was not reported to any extent, and I do not know what he said, nor do I know whether he is a Communist, but I do know the meeting gained some respectability by the statement that a Harvard professor took part in it.

The other incident is, of course, the New York Peace meeting of which Professor Shapley was Chairman.

I do not believe a great university can properly permit the prestige which its name gives its professors to be used in a manner hostile to our own country. Anyone has a right to fight the Atlantic Alliance.

Indeed, a good argument can be made against it on honestly debatable grounds. But to my mind it is quite a different matter to join in a propaganda effort with the agents of a foreign hostile power which is engaged in efforts to subvert this country by conspiratorial methods.

The vast majority of our people have gradually reached the conclusion that Communism is not a political movement—but is a criminal conspiracy. (See Md. Report, pp. 17-20.) Even the Baltimore *Sun*, with all its ultra "liberalism" and almost fanatic devotion to free speech, has recently reached this conclusion. Our national defense policy is directed at Communism and the time has arrived when we can no longer risk our national survival by applying a "double standard," as *Life* recently said, to its conspiratorial agents in this country. The Smith Act of 1940 makes it criminal to advocate the violent overthrow of the government, and this is the law of the land. Yet, most thoughtful people who have examined Communist actions and documents know that is precisely what they are seeking to do. The laws just passed in this and some seventeen other states show an increasing awareness of this basic truth.

Surely, Harvard would not permit its professors to remain on the payrolls if they engage in conferences encouraging other types of conspiracies looking toward other crimes as part of their extracurricular activity. Why then the distinction because the conspiracy is directed toward the forcible overthrow of our government—in short, sedition or peacetime "treason"? The test of a professor's actions ought not to be whether he can be actually proved guilty of a crime. Reasonable grounds to doubt his loyalty to our government should disqualify him, for the position is one of trust, and the government has, if it chooses to exercise it, regulatory power over education.

Anyone familiar with Communist methods knows that most of the damage from teachers is done outside of the classroom, made possible by the influence gained in the classroom. Similarly, I believe a professor's efforts to aid Communists gain greatly from his prestige as a professor, and it is not reasonable to close one's eyes to such extracurricular activities.

As to academic freedom, I agree with Hook as against Meiklejohn in the recent New York *Times Magazine* debate, and think its limits are well stated in the Coudert Report (quoted p. 52 of Md. Report).

As to "tenure," I believe that:

(a) Every contract is subject to an implied obligation (if not expressly stated) to avoid aiding and abetting sedition or peacetime treason. The philosophy of our Commission was to give the colleges an opportunity to police themselves—rather than providing for governmental supervision, which might be greatly abused. The collegiate authorities already pass upon whether a man's teaching effectively covers a subject, and it would be no broader exercise of discretion to determine whether it is, on the whole, encouraging "treason" or not.

(b) Even if contracts are not subject to such an implied condition, at least future contracts, including any required by a raise in salary, should include appropriate conditions.

(c) I see no reason why the need of security of position in collegiate professorships to attract applicants to take such a position of trust is any greater than in government positions, where "reasonable grounds on all the evidence" to believe an employee is disloyal is a ground for discharge under the President's Executive Order.

In any event, I am adding my protest of what seems to me a very grave danger that the colleges are not alive to the nature or dangers arising from Communism. I know there are exceptions. I understand Dr. Bronk recently added the prestige of his presence to an anti-Communist lecture. I wonder if the group of students at Harvard organized to combat Communism received any official encouragement. I have not seen it stated in the press. Such a group, if given proper stimulation and properly organized, might attain national influence by spreading the movement to all colleges, which would do much to combat Communism so prevalent there, but only if the authorities at the same time kept a closer watch on what its professors are doing.

FRANK B. OBER

~

President Conant to Mr. Ober

Cambridge, Mass.
May 11, 1949

The attitude of Harvard toward the extracurricular activities of its professors is a policy of long standing. The fact that certain incidents have led you to refuse to subscribe to the Harvard Law School Fund does not surprise me. During the past forty years, to my personal knowledge, from time to time people have come to similar decisions because of their dislike of things Harvard professors have said publicly.

Nevertheless, we believe that our way of operating the University is not only in the best interests of Harvard but of importance to the entire country. On this point I think the case has never been better stated than by Mr. Lowell in his Annual Report of 1916-17, of which I am enclosing a copy. May I likewise take the liberty of referring you to my Annual Report for 1948, in which I set forth some of the basic premises of University operation.

Since your comments go to the heart of the nature of a university and have broad implications, I have asked Mr. Grenville Clark, a senior member of the Corporation and a leader in your profession, to write to you. I am sure you will be interested in his account of the history and significance of the traditional Harvard policy.

James B. Conant

~

The Professor Outside the Classroom

The gravest questions, and the strongest feelings, arise from action by a professor beyond his chosen field and outside of his classroom. Here he speaks only as a citizen. By appointment to a professorship he acquires no rights that he did not possess before; but there is a real difference of opinion today on the question whether he loses any rights that he would otherwise enjoy. The argument in favor of a restraining power on the part of the governing boards of universities and colleges is based upon the fact that by extreme, or injudicious, remarks that shock public sentiment a professor can do great harm to the institution with which he is connected. That is true, and sometimes a professor thoughtlessly does an injury that is without justification. If he publishes an article on the futility and harmfulness of vaccination, and signs it as professor in a certain university, he leads the public to believe that his views are those of an authority on the subject, approved by the institution and taught to its students. If he is really a professor of Greek, he is misleading the public and misrepresenting his university, which he would not do if he gave his title in full.

In spite of the risk of injury to the institution, the objections to restraint upon what professors may say as citizens seem to me far greater than the harm done by leaving them free. In the first place, to impose upon the teacher in a university restrictions to which the members of other professions, lawyers, physicians, engineers, and so forth, are not subjected, would produce a sense of irritation and humiliation. In accepting a chair under such conditions a man would surrender a part of his liberty; what he might say would be submitted to the censorship of a board of trustees, and he would cease to be a free citizen. The lawyer, physician, or engineer may express his views as he likes on the subject of the protective tariff; shall the professor of astronomy not be free to do the same? Such a policy would tend seriously to discourage some of the best men from taking up the scholar's life. It is not a question of academic freedom, but of personal liberty from constraint, yet it touches the dignity of the academic career.

That is an objection to restraint on freedom of speech from the standpoint of the teacher. There is another, not less weighty, from that of the institution itself. If a university or college censors what its professors may say, if it restrains them from uttering something that it does not approve, it thereby assumes responsibility for that which it permits them to say. This is logical and inevitable, but it is a responsibility which an institution of learning would be very unwise in assuming. It is sometimes suggested that the principles are different in time of war; that the governing boards are then justified in restraining unpatriotic expressions injurious to the country. But the same problem is presented in wartime as in time of peace. If the university is right in restraining its professors, it has a duty to do so, and it is responsible for whatever it permits. There is no middle ground. Either the university assumes full responsibility for permitting its professors to express certain opinions in public, or it assumes no responsibility whatever, and leaves them to be dealt with like other citizens by the public authorities according to the laws of the land. [From President Lowell's Annual Report of 1916-1917]

~

Mr. Clark to Mr. Ober

Dublin, N. H.
May 27, 1949

Mr. Conant sent me your letter to him of April 26 and his reply of May 11. He suggested that I might care to write you regarding the "history and significance of the traditional Harvard policy" on freedom of expression for the faculties and students. I am willing to do this because I think your letter raises questions that go to the very life of Harvard and all other colleges and are, therefore, of vital consequence to the country at large. While I write at Mr. Conant's suggestion, I do so only as an individual—although I do believe that my convictions are held by the vast majority of Harvard men.

Let me say at once that your proposals—apparently to dismiss or

censure two professors, and certainly to impose drastic controls on
the activities as citizens of all professors—cannot and will not be
adopted at Harvard, so long as Harvard remains true to her principles.

Those proposals are absolutely contrary to Harvard's tradition and
all she stands for. By reviewing the history of freedom at Harvard
under Mr. Eliot, Mr. Lowell, and Mr. Conant, I will try to make
clear why this is so.

I. Analysis of your complaint and opinions.

At the outset, I summarize your letter—I hope adequately and
fairly.

You first state your intention not to subscribe to the Harvard Law
School Fund because of the part taken by Professor Ciardi (Assistant
Professor of English Composition), and by Professor Harlow Shapley,
in two recent public meetings. It seems that you want them both
disciplined. And then you go on with some general observations
and recommendations for basic changes in Harvard policy in respect
of the "extracurricular activities" of all professors.

Concerning the two professors, your complaint as to Professor
Ciardi relates to his speaking at a Progressive Party meeting in Maryland called in opposition to certain bills "directed at Communism"
proposed by a Commission of which you were Chairman. You say:
"But the so-called 'Progressive' campaign against the laws enacted in
Maryland was not debate, but vilification and falsehood—the usual
Communist weapons," and "they attempted to foment hatred and
prejudice in the typical Communist way . . ." As to what Professor Ciardi said at the meeting, you say: "His own speech was not
reported to any extent and I do not know what he said . . ." So
you do not complain of anything he said; nor do you question his
motives. But you indicate that he ought not to have addressed that
meeting at all because "Communists were actually using the Progressive Party, and the meeting Ciardi was reported to have attended
was addressed by Marcantonio and other fellow-travelers in the usual
way—so he must have been aware of its nature." You add that "the
meeting gained some respectability by the statement that a Harvard
professor took part in it."

It seems, therefore, that the essence of what you complain of on
this count lies in the mere fact of Professor Ciardi's having spoken
at that particular meeting, without regard to his purpose or any utterance of his.

Your other specific complaint—about Professor Shapley—concerns his part in the recent Cultural and Scientific Conference for World Peace in New York. You do not elaborate on that and do not complain of anything he said, nor do you criticize his motives. So it seems that here, too, the offense, in your eyes, is the mere fact of his having presided at that meeting, and his part in its organization, as distinguished from anything said by him or any unworthy motive.

Both the Maryland and New York meetings were on public issues and were open to the press. You do not question the complete legality of either meeting. And yet you seem to say that the two professors committed some sort of grave offense. You seem to base this idea upon the following line of thought: "Communism is not a political movement—but is a criminal conspiracy"; hence if Communists or "fellow travelers" have any material part in a particular meeting, that meeting, although entirely legal and open, is a part of a criminal conspiracy; and hence all persons, including these professors, who engage actively in such meetings, whatever the purpose of the meetings or the motives of the participants or what they said, are involved in a criminal conspiracy.

On this basis, you appear to recommend, although your letter is not absolutely explicit on this point, that these two professors should somehow be disciplined—presumably by dismissal or at least by rebuke.

It is at first hard to believe that you intend to go to such lengths. But on re-reading your letter again and again, one is forced to this conclusion. For you seem directly to identify engaging in such public meetings with "other types of conspiracies looking towards other crimes as part of their extracurricular activity" (I suppose, for example, arson or robbery); and ask: "Why then the distinction because the conspiracy is directed toward the forcible overthrow of our government—in short, sedition or peacetime 'treason'?"

I do not see how you can expect reasonable men to think of participation in open and legal meetings on public subjects as the equivalent of secret plotting to commit crime, merely because Communists or "fellow travelers" take part in such meetings. On this line of reasoning, literally thousands of reputable citizens would have offended. By no possibility could Harvard adopt a view which, to put it mildly, is so extreme. To do so would, I believe, call for conclusions which offend common sense and for efforts at repression that would be out of place anywhere in our country and are inconceivable at Harvard.

Concerning your broader proposals for control of the outside activities of all professors, you want all the present agreements for their
services so construed and future agreements so drafted that "aiding
and abetting sedition or peacetime treason" shall be cause for discipline. Thus you say that in "future contracts, including any required
by a raise in salary" there should be "appropriate conditions" on this
subject. You also mention that: "Reasonable grounds to doubt his
[a professor's] loyalty to our government should disqualify him . . ."
and "see no reason" why professors should be treated any differently
in this regard than government employees where " 'reasonable grounds
on all the evidence' to believe an employee is disloyal is a ground
for discharge under the President's Executive Order."

From the context it is clear that you would like to have the "appropriate conditions" cover all matters that might in your view furnish
the above "reasonable grounds"—including, no doubt, involvement
in any meeting materially influenced by Communists or "fellow
travelers" and, I suppose, a good many other things. And you evidently want violation of any "appropriate" conditions cause for dismissal or discipline.

In addition you want the authorities to keep a "closer watch on
what its professors are doing." On this point you evidently want
a watch kept pretty much all the time—presumably day and night,
in term and in vacation. For you say that "most of the damage from
teachers is done outside of the classroom" and that "it is not reasonable to close one's eyes to such extracurricular activities."

As to the students, you want the Harvard governing authorities
to give "official encouragement" to students who organize to oppose
Communism.

I hope you will agree that this is a fair summary and interpretation
of your complaint and recommendations.

*II. Harvard conviction and tradition utterly opposed to your pro-
gram: history and significance of the tradition.*

I repeat that the things you ask for will not and cannot be done
at Harvard—at least as long as Harvard retains its basic principles
and holds by its tradition. And if the day ever came that such things
were done at the physical place on which the Harvard buildings
stand or anywhere by the Harvard authorities, it would not be "Harvard" doing them; it would be an institution of an entirely different
sort, with wholly different ideas and purposes.

The fundamental reason is that for Harvard to take the course you recommend would be to repudiate the very essence of what Harvard stands for—the search for truth by a free and uncoerced body of students and teachers. And it would be to make a mockery of a long tradition of Harvard freedom for both its students and its faculties.

As to the history of that tradition, while it is much more than eighty years old, it is sufficient, I think, to go back to President Charles W. Eliot's inaugural address in 1869 and follow down from there.

Mr. Eliot then said: "A university must be indigenous; it must be rich; but, above all, it must be free. The winnowing breeze of freedom must blow through all its chambers . . . This University aspires to serve the nation by training men to intellectual honesty and independence of mind. The Corporation demands of all its teachers that they be grave, reverent, and high-minded; but it leaves them, like their pupils, free."

The tradition so expressed was well understood and applied under President Eliot. It was then carried on and emphasized during the more controversial term of President A. Lawrence Lowell from 1909 to 1933.

In his report for 1916–17 (from which Mr. Conant sent you an extract) Mr. Lowell took notice that the war had "brought to the front" questions of academic freedom, especially "liberty of speech on the part of the professor." He then went on to make so discriminating an analysis of the subject that in the opinion of many, including myself, the writing of those few pages was the most lasting public service of his long career.

As applied to the "extracurricular" activities that you stress, the essence of the report is that "beyond his chosen field and outside of his classroom" the professor "speaks only as a citizen"; that his professorship gives him no rights that he did not possess before; but, on the other hand, it is unwise to restrict those rights because "the objections to restraint upon what professors may say as citizens seem to me far greater than the harm done by leaving them free." Mr. Lowell declared that by accepting a chair under restrictive conditions, the professor "would cease to be a free citizen" and that "such a policy would tend seriously to discourage some of the best men from taking up the scholar's life." "It is not," he emphasized, "a question of academic freedom, but of personal liberty from constraint . . ." Beyond that, he made a point very applicable to what you propose, i.e., that: "If a university or college censors what its professors may say, if it restrains them from uttering something that it does not approve, it thereby assumes responsibility for that which it permits them to say . . . There is no middle ground." And, therefore, he concluded, the University, assuming the sincerity of the professor's utterances on public matters, should take "no responsibility whatever" but should leave "them to be dealt with like other citizens by the public authorities according to the laws of the land."

I have tried to state only the essence of Mr. Lowell's thought as applied to your letter. Doubtless you are familiar with his report and I can only commend a restudy of its closely reasoned pages. The point is that this report, which became famous, stands today as part of the Harvard tradition of freedom of expression, and as a definite guide for Harvard policy.

Coming now to President Conant's term, we find the same basic thought expressed with equal clarity and force. In his address at the Harvard Tercentenary Celebration in 1936, he said:

"We must have a spirit of tolerance which allows the expression of all opinions however heretical they may appear. . . . Unfortunately there are ominous signs that a new form of bigotry may arise. This is most serious, for we cannot develop the unifying educational forces we so sorely need unless all matters may be openly discussed. . . . On this point there can be no compromise; we are either afraid of heresy or we are not."

These declarations of three Harvard presidents are, as you observe, all of a piece. They embody a consistent doctrine that can, I think, be summed up as follows:

(1) *Harvard believes in the "free trade in ideas" of Justice Holmes —a graduate of 1861—which is no more than saying that she believes in the principles of Milton's Areopagitica (1644), of Jefferson's First Inaugural (1801), and of Mill's "Essay on Liberty" (1859). She thinks that repression is not wise or workable under our system, that wide latitude for conflicting views affords the best chance for good government, and that in suppression usually lies the greater peril. Harvard is not afraid of freedom, and believes adherence to this principle to be fundamental for our universities and for the integrity of our institutions.*

(2) *She believes that the members of the faculties, in their capacity as citizens, have the same rights to express themselves as other citizens, and that those rights should not be restricted by the University by trying to keep a "watch" on professors or otherwise.*

(3) *She believes that wide limits for free expression by professors
are in the interest of her students as well as the teachers. The teachers have rights as citizens to speak and write as men of independence;
the students also have their rights to be taught by men of independent mind.*

(4) *Harvard, like any great privately supported university, badly
needs money; but Harvard will accept no gift on the condition, express or implied, that it shall compromise its tradition of freedom.*

These beliefs are not a matter of lip service. They have been
applied in practice at Harvard for a long time. Thus there certainly prevailed at Harvard during the forty years of Mr. Eliot's
term, an atmosphere highly favorable to free expression by both
students and teachers. I know that when I was at Cambridge 1899–
1906, one felt it in the very air that neither the students nor professors were under constraint. The absence of restriction on free
expression by faculty and students at that time, and during the early
years of Mr. Lowell's term, was implicit rather than something needing constant assertion; but it was nonetheless real.

In later years of the Lowell administration, however, in what has
been called the period of "uneasy fears"—much like the present—
during and after the first World War, cases arose which provided
an acid test for the Harvard doctrine.

The two best-known incidents were those of Professor Zechariah
Chafee, Jr., and of Harold J. Laski. They are related in Professor
Yeomans' recent life of Mr. Lowell.

In the former case, Professor Chafee wrote an article condemning
the conduct of the trial judge in the famous Abrams sedition case.
This was in 1920 at the height of the post-war alarm about sedition
and Bolshevism. It was the period of Attorney General Palmer's
"raids," and of the expulsion of duly elected Socialist members from
the New York Legislature, in the face of powerful opposition led
by Charles E. Hughes. Some Harvard men in New York accused
Professor Chafee of inaccuracies in his article and, without specifying
exactly what should be done, asked the Overseers to take notice of
his conduct. The Overseers' Committee to Visit the Law School
took up the matter and there occurred what was known as "The
Trial at the Harvard Club." Mr. Lowell appeared and in effect acted
as counsel for Professor Chafee. He took an unequivocal position
in defense of the professor's right to espouse an unpopular cause,

and the net result was a dismissal or dropping of the complaint. That case remains a landmark in Harvard's course.

In the Laski case, Mr. Laski, then a young lecturer at Harvard, spoke up for the side of the police strikers in Boston in 1919. Feeling on that issue was terrific; emotion ran high against anyone taking the strikers' side and there were insistent demands for the dismissal of Mr. Laski. Nevertheless, Mr. Lowell stood firmly for Mr. Laski's right to speak his mind; there was no dismissal and that set another great precedent.

Since then there have been various other incidents in which the principle has been vindicated. Perhaps the very latest was the permission given a month ago to the Harvard Law School Forum to have Mr. Laski (now, thirty years later, Professor Laski of the University of London) speak in Sanders Theater. Because of the Cambridge School Board's objections to Mr. Laski, the Forum had been denied the use of a public school auditorium, where its meetings had customarily been held. The Forum then asked for the use of Sanders Theater and, in accordance with established practice on student meetings, the request was granted.

It is, I think, unnecessary to go into more detail. For it is well-established and known that Harvard has a long-declared and, on the whole, well-adhered-to tradition favoring a wide degree of freedom for teacher and student and, therefore, as you must perceive, a tradition utterly at variance with what you recommend.

Mr. Conant mentioned the "significance" as well as the "history" of the tradition.

To my mind, its fundamental significance lies in the thought that the principles back of it are essential to the American Idea—to the workability of our free institutions and to enabling Americans to live satisfactory lives.

The professor's right to speak his mind and to espouse unpopular causes should not be regarded as something separate and apart from the maintenance of our civil rights in general. I think what is usually called academic freedom is simply part and parcel of American freedom—merely a segment of the whole front.

I believe, however, that it is an especially vital segment because it concerns the students quite as much as the professors. If the professors are censored, constrained, or harassed, it affects not only themselves; it affects also those whom they teach—the future voters and leaders upon whose integrity and independence of mind will

depend the institutions by which we live and breathe a free air.
For if the professors have always to conform and avoid unpopular
views whether in class or out, what kind of men will they be? And
where will our young men and women go to hear and weigh new
ideas, to consider both sides and acquire balance and integrity?

In *The Wild Flag* the essayist E. B. White has defined democracy
in a way closely touching this point. "Democracy," he said, "is the
recurrent suspicion that more than half of the people are right more
than half of the time." This is about it, is it not—the very basis of
our system? But how can we possibly expect most of the people to
be right most of the time if they are taught by men and women of
a sort who are constrained to work under conditions where they may
lose their jobs if, pursuant to conviction, they attend meetings that
some, or even the majority of the moment, do not approve?

In that inaugural address of Mr. Eliot's, it is also said: "In the
modern world the intelligence of public opinion is the one indispensable condition of social progress." And further: "The student
should be made acquainted with all sides of these [philosophical
and political] controversies, with the salient points of each system . . . The notion that education consists in the authoritative
inculcation of what the teacher deems true may be logical and appropriate in a convent, or a seminary for priests, but it is intolerable
in universities and public schools, from primary to professional."

But how can we fulfill the "indispensable condition" of intelligent
opinion; and how can we have non-dogmatic and excellent instruction for our leaders if their teachers are coerced or harassed?

It is impossible; and since I believe that the very existence of our
free institutions depends on the independence and integrity of our
teachers, the main significance for me of the Harvard tradition is
that it powerfully helps to sustain those institutions.

No doubt there are other more specialized significances. No
doubt the Harvard tradition has significance because, if abandoned,
it would make many good people, members of our faculties, very
unhappy. No doubt it is significant because its abandonment would
force others—administrators and Governing Boards—either to resign
or, against conscience, to engage in work bitterly hateful to them.
These things are true and important. But it is enough for me that
the tradition is in harmony with and necessary to the maintenance
of the free institutions of America, and to the values that make life
in our country most worth while.

III. Practical implications.

I cannot help wondering whether you have thought through the implications of what you propose.

Since you wish to discipline professors for taking active part in meetings such as those at which Professors Ciardi and Shapley spoke, would it not be fair to pass in advance on the kind of meetings professors could safely attend? Would this not call for a University licensing board? And would not such a board have an obnoxious and virtually impossible task?

The very cases you mention illustrate this. The Maryland meeting was called by the Maryland branch of the official Progressive Party (the Wallace party) which is a legal organization for whose ticket over a million citizens voted in 1948. The New York meeting was to advocate peace and was sponsored by many reputable citizens whose motives were above question.

If the University should undertake to decide whether or not a professor, in his capacity as a citizen, could take part in these or other meetings, what Mr. Lowell referred to would necessarily occur. If attendance at the meeting were disapproved, the professor would be deprived, under penalty of discipline, of a right enjoyed by other citizens; while if approved, the University would assume the responsibility for endorsing the meeting.

Moreover, I think you will agree that there would be little sense in censoring attendance at meetings and leaving free from censorship speeches on the radio or writings in the press, magazines, pamphlets, and books. Would not your proposals call for a censorship of all these?

Take, for example, the recent book, *Military and Political Consequences of Atomic Energy,* by Professor Blackett of Manchester University. That is a highly controversial book because it sought to justify the Soviet position on atomic energy control. I have not heard that Professor Blackett's loyalty to Britain has been questioned. But suppose that book to have been written by a Harvard professor, is it not probable that in our more tense and excited atmosphere someone would charge that it raised "reasonable doubts" about his loyalty? I think it would have been quite certain that such a charge would have been forthcoming. And, if so, would it not be fair to the professor, and also necessary to make your proposals effective, that such a book be submitted for censorship before its publication?

Beyond that, however, how could an effective "closer watch" on "extracurricular activities" be maintained unless the watch extended to conversations and correspondence? And how could that be done without a system of student and other informers—the classic and necessary method of watching for "subversive" utterances?

You may not have realized the full implications of what you ask. But if you will stop to consider what would necessarily be involved if your point of view were accepted, you must agree, I think, that these things are precisely what would be required.

What I have just said applies to the professors. But how about the students? Would it be sensible to have the teachers censored and watched while the students remain at liberty freely to speak and write and to attend such meetings as they choose, subject only to the laws of the land? On your philosophy are you not driven on to restrict, censor, and discipline the students also?

What sort of a place would Harvard be if it went down this road? It would, I think, not require six months to destroy the morale of both our teachers and students, and thereby our usefulness to the country. I think one need do no more than state the necessary implications of what you ask to demonstrate that nothing could be more alien to the principle of free expression that Harvard stands for.

IV. Harvard money and Harvard freedom.

I want to add a comment on your decision not to subscribe to the Law School Fund. As Mr. Conant wrote you, it has happened before that subscriptions have been withheld because of objections to the acts or opinions of professors or because of disapproval of University policy. This is natural and normal, I think; and it is certainly the right of anyone not to aid an institution with which he is as out of harmony as you now seem to be with Harvard. But it is also true, I am sure you will agree, that Harvard cannot be influenced at all to depart from her basic tradition of freedom by any fear that gifts will be withheld.

An interesting test case on this point came up during the first World War. It related to Professor Hugo Münsterberg, who was a German and very pro-German, and is described in Professor Yeomans' biography of President Lowell. It appears that the press reported that a certain Harvard man had, in Professor Yeomans' words, "threatened to annul a bequest to the University of $10,000,000 unless Münsterberg was immediately deprived of his professorship." Thereupon Professor Münsterberg wrote to the Harvard Corporation offering to resign if the graduate would immediately remit $5,000,000 to the Corporation. The Professor's letter was returned and the Corporation issued, as Professor Yeomans puts it, "one of its rare public pronouncements," as follows: "It is now officially stated that, at the instance of the authorities, Professor Münsterberg's resignation has been withdrawn, and that the University cannot tolerate any suggestion that it would be willing to accept money to abridge free speech, to remove a professor or to accept his resignation."

I think it will always be Harvard policy not to be influenced in any way "to abridge free speech" by the withholding of any subscription. And if $5,000,000 or any sum were offered tomorrow as the price of the removal of Professor Ciardi or Professor Shapley, or of instituting the "closer watch" that you recommend, nothing is more certain than that the Corporation would again reply that it "cannot tolerate" the suggestion.

On this money matter, the practical question has always interested me as to whether Harvard's adherence to this principle has in fact been to her financial detriment. Certainly one can point to some specific cases, besides your own, where gifts have not been made because the possible donors thought Harvard should have disciplined professors or students for their supposed "sedition" or "radicalism." I well remember how much was said on that score during the early days of the New Deal as relating to the activities, actual or supposed, of Professor Felix Frankfurter. So I do not doubt that some gifts have been withheld for reasons of this sort. On the other hand, less is heard, usually nothing at all, of those others who instead of being repelled by the steadiness of Harvard's adherence to free expression, find in it the true glory of Harvard and a principal reason for supporting her finances.

Thus I am quite sure that there are many Harvard men and others who, if they read your letter and were told that Harvard must firmly decline to follow your views, would find in that very refusal a strong reason for adding to their gifts. I think that many such would say: "If Harvard is again under pressure to depart from its tradition but is holding to it as solidly as ever, that is the place on which I want to put my money, because if we want to preserve the essence of the American Idea we must encourage those who adhere consistently to uncoerced teaching."

So I just don't know, and no one can know, whether, *on balance*, Harvard gains or loses money by its policy in this regard. But, although it cannot be proved, I have a shrewd suspicion that, while

Harvard may for a few years, in times of emotion like the present, lose some gifts and bequests by its adherence to free expression, it loses no money at all over a generation by holding to this principle.

In any case, while that is an intriguing question, it is not the real one. For whether the policy gains money or loses it, Harvard, in order to *be* Harvard, has to hew to the line. That is what Mr. Eliot meant, I am sure, when he said, in 1869, that while a university "must be rich" it must "above all" be free. That choice is as clear today as eighty years ago.

I am under no illusion that this letter, or any similar argument, is likely to affect your attitude in this matter, at least for some time. For my observation in the corresponding period after the first World War was that in a period of alarm, proposals to restrict free expression rest on strong feelings which for the time being override sound judgment. That was certainly true of the above-mentioned successful effort to oust the Socialist Assemblymen in New York, and the unsuccessful effort to discipline Professor Chafee. Several years later, I think that some of those who promoted those efforts came to see that they had been impairing the very values which, no doubt sincerely, they purported to preserve. But during the period of stress, they found it hard even to comprehend the other side.

I hope, though, that I may have convinced you that there is another side, and that there is a deep-rooted tradition at Harvard utterly opposed to your view—a tradition that must and will be upheld as long as Harvard remains true to herself.

GRENVILLE CLARK

~

Mr. Ober to Mr. Clark

Baltimore, Md.
June 8, 1949

I have read with considerable surprise your letter, which misconstrues mine of April 26 to Mr. Conant, and completely disregards the Maryland Commission report enclosed therein, explaining my views and recommendations with respect to meeting the Communist problem in schools and colleges. Had you read the report carefully you could scarcely call your letter "a fair summary" of my views. That report recommended and explained a statute requiring and providing means for investigating the loyalty of prospective teachers in State institutions, and for discharging those already employed only if, *after notice and hearing*, it is found there are "reasonable grounds on all the evidence" to believe a teacher disloyal, thus adopting a procedure similar to the President's Loyalty Order now governing millions of Federal employees.

As you know, my letter was not written for publication, and the brief space allowed me for reply to your lengthy letter does not permit me to explain my views in detail, or to specifically refer to and answer many statements and inferences as to my position, which are unjustified.

I believe that colleges have a duty to the Nation, and to their students and alumni, to take *practical* steps to see that Communists and other disloyal teachers are eliminated from the faculties. The problem is a difficult one, and there is difference of opinion as to the best means of handling it fairly and adequately, but I believe a program similar to the Federal program offers the best solution. This assumes: that academic freedom does not justify employing originally, or retaining in employment, disloyal teachers; that colleges have continuing responsibility to investigate loyalty (including motives and purposes) when they receive credible evidence that their professors are aiding Communism; and that this is justified not only on the ground of national security, but also by the fact that teachers hold a position of trust and most Americans do not want their children educated or influenced by disloyal teachers. The Federal program is not extreme; nor does it involve your implications of censorship, coercion, and continuous watching. It will *usually* prevent teachers from abusing the prestige of their position by aiding and abetting Communism, but not *always*, because the *only* procedure suggested contemplates discharge if found *disloyal after* notice and hearing.

The substitution of "reasonable grounds on all the evidence" as a criterion of loyalty for the criminal test of "proof beyond a reasonable doubt" seems required by the nature of the problem and the practical difficulties of an employer sustaining such a burden. It should not depend upon proof of crime; nor should the technical legality of meetings or organizations be conclusive as a defense. The Communist Party itself is legal in many states and constantly operates through legal "fronts."

The basic difference between us is that your essay on academic freedom completely fails to distinguish Socialism, or other unpopular radical issues, from Communism, which to most Americans means providing the fifth column for a foreign power plotting our destruction. Academic freedom, under your interpretation, would apparently permit a Harvard professor to advocate and to aid and abet Communism, in the same manner you would permit him to advocate any other cause. Your position must be due to your failure to recognize the implications of Communism and that one of the primary objects of the fifth column in the present cold war is infiltration of colleges, so that Communists can be close to scientific developments, corrupt the next generation and, incidentally, give prestige to front organizations. You would hardly say, if *reasonable grounds on all the evidence* indicates a professor is incompetent, or publicly leads a scandalous life—though not violating laws—he should be protected by academic freedom. Communism is not lesser evil, and threatens national security. Your letter gave no assurances whatsoever that *you* are concerned about Communist teachers.

Mr. Conant's joinder in a splendid public statement on Communist teachers today gives the reassurance I was seeking—that Harvard *is* alive to that menace. *Appropriate steps to implement that policy are now in order.* I sincerely hope that the principle of our statute, taken from the Federal loyalty program, may contribute to the solution of this exceedingly difficult problem.

FRANK B. OBER

~

Mr. Clark to Mr. Ober

Dublin, N. H.
June 11, 1949

The Editor confines me, quite properly, to 300 words. So I reply almost telegraphically.

Did I misconstrue your first letter? The reader can judge by carefully comparing it with my summary. I did not disregard the Maryland report. I stand upon my analysis as accurate and fair. The reader must decide.

You mention Mr. Conant's joinder in a recent report, one point of which is that a Communist Party Member is disqualified to teach. But you want to reach far beyond Communists. You want to discipline any teacher if, after hearing, "reasonable grounds on all the evidence" are found to doubt his "loyalty." These are slippery terms.

I affirm again that your plan implies an extensive system of detection and trial. Nothing of this character will happen under Mr. Conant. There will be no harassment of professors for engaging in open and legal meetings. There will be no apparatus of inquiry and "closer watch." The harm done by the effort necessary to discover even a single clandestine Party Member would outweigh any possible benefit. To go beyond that by searching for "reasonable grounds" concerning "loyalty," would still more disrupt Harvard or any free university. No greater mistake could be made than to suppose that because a proved Party Member, bound by Party discipline, should not teach, all professors are to be policed or watched. I know these to be Mr. Conant's firm convictions.

Your sincerity is unquestioned. But that very fact is disturbing. The framers of the Sedition Act of 1798 had conviction. Those who led in ousting the Socialist Assemblymen were also sincere. So, while I believe you misguided, I do not question your motives.

These issues run deep. Their ventilation is healthy. Therefore, I hope that this correspondence—all of it—will be read and pondered.

GRENVILLE CLARK

Problems for Thought and Writing

I

1. In the light of the material here presented, read William Fulton's article, "Happy Hunting for Red Front at Harvard U." (page 618). Are his allegations, in your opinion, justified? It is interesting to note that "Freedom at Harvard" was distributed free to the alumni attending commencement exercises at Harvard in June, 1949, and that President Conant at that occasion asked for contributions totalling 90 million dollars.

2. How would you answer the following argument by Mr. Ober in his letter of April 26, 1949: "I do not believe a great university can properly permit the prestige which its name gives its professors to be used in a manner hostile to our country" (page 598)? Did you feel that Mr. Clark answered it adequately? Itemize the points Mr. Ober raises and Mr. Clark's replies to them. Which are *legally* the stronger arguments? Which are more ethical? Which are more expedient in view of present conditions?

3. Do you agree or disagree with the spirit of the Harvard "tradition" as Mr. Ober outlines it? Compare that tradition with John Milton's position in *Areopagitica* (page 157), and with J. S. Mill's in "On Liberty" (page 378). Compare it with the intellectual tradition at your college or university.

4. Do you agree with President Lowell that the issue at stake in controversies like this is not "academic freedom" but "personal liberty from constraint . . ."?

5. Could one fairly call Mr. Ober's withholding of money until certain conditions were met a form of blackmail? Why or why not?

6. Are the objections in Mr. Ober's letter of June 8 well taken? Does Mr. Clark's rejoinder of June 11 answer them?

II

7. Write your own argument in answer to Mr. Ober on the basis of the traditions prevailing at your college or university.

8. Compare this exchange with that between Huxley and Arnold in "Science and Culture" and "Literature and Science" (pages 556-79). Are these *arguments* or examples of *persuasion?*

~

HAPPY HUNTING
FOR RED FRONT   *William Fulton*
AT HARVARD U.*

LEFTIST PROFS PUSH IDEAS THERE

[Chicago Tribune Press Service]

CAMBRIDGE, MASS., April 7—Harvard university, now in its fourth century of operation as a brains factory, is a happy hunting ground for Communists, doctrinaire pinks, and radicals of all hues. Many of the professors are leftists who subtly instill their propaganda into the budding brains of the students.

Under the protective umbrella of "academic freedom" the fomenting of subversive alien theories is allowed to go unmolested. President James Bryant Conant, a red hot interventionist and globalist, has refused to curb radicalism on the grounds his pedagogs should have "freedom to search for the truth."

In the opinion of local law enforcement officers and members of the legislature, the matter goes far beyond a mere question of academic discussion among radical professors and credulous students.

"FOCAL POINT" FOR SUBVERSIVES

Recalling the various spy trials, investigators point out Cambridge is a "focal point for subversive activity" because of the many atomic energy specialists here and work going forward on atomic energy projects. The projects are under way not only at Harvard, but also

* From the Chicago Sunday *Tribune,* April 8, 1951. Reprinted by permission

at the neighboring Massachusetts Institute of Technology, which has its share of fellow travelers.

In their assessment of the dangers involved, local investigators have not forgotten that Alger Hiss, former top state department official and Roosevelt adviser, went thru Harvard law school. Hiss is now serving a five year sentence for perjury, in which his clandestine peddling of war secrets to a soviet spy ring was involved.

It is the law school that is particularly under fire today. Samuel P. Sears, an alumnus of both the law school and Harvard college, now president of the Massachusetts Bar association, recently said he thought it "about time Harvard cleaned house and stopped encouraging and playing host to the Communist party."

GUILD CALLED RED BULWARK

Dean Erwin N. Griswold denied Sears' demand for disbanding the Harvard Lawyers' guild. This cell of the law school students is affiliated with the National Lawyers' guild, which has been described as "the foremost legal bulwark of the Communist party, its front organizations, and controlled unions" by the congressional committee on un-American activities.

Sears is not the only Harvard alumnus hot under the collar over the way affairs are conducted back on the campus, or "yard" as they call it here. There is increasing criticism, particularly among Harvard men who have sons fighting against communism in Korea while the Red doctrine is allowed to flourish back at the old alma mater.

Alumni have refused to make donations because of their strong feeling over the situation at Harvard.

STUDENTS MINIMIZE DANGER

Undergraduates in Harvard college with whom this correspondent talked admitted they knew of Communists among their fellow students but were inclined to minimize the danger. They parroted their professors' phrases about "academic freedom," "search for truth," "liberalism," and the like.

One student said when a leftist professor's subject was remote from the political field, as for example, geology, the pedagog carried on his propaganda at "bull sessions" outside the classroom or by other activities, such as getting youths to attend meetings for some cause or other.

This corroborated the findings of City Councilman John D. Lynch, banker and former mayor of Cambridge.

"I've talked with students," he said. "They tell me about professors inviting them to leftwing meetings and then the first thing you know they are filled up with this evil stuff."

"RED-UCATORS AT HARVARD"

Lynch, who says the city of Cambridge is controlled by Harvard influence, vainly attempted last fall to force the registration of all Communists in the vicinity. He did, however, succeed in having a copy of the dossier, "Red-ucators at Harvard University," placed on file for public perusal at the city clerk's office a few months ago.

"Red-ucators at Harvard," an expose of the communist front affiliations and connections of 76 faculty members was compiled by the National Council for American Education, with offices at 2 Maiden Lane, New York City. It shows affiliation with Stalinoid movements during recent years, principally since the end of World War II.

. . . .

"MAY BE SIMPLY NAIVE"

"Inclusion of a professor or instructor in this list is not conclusive evidence that he is a Communist," observed the council. "He may be simply naive.

"Similarly, this list does not necessarily include all Harvard professors who may be pro-Communist. Some of the most malefic and dangerous persons in America are not on any communist front: They are secret members of the Communist party—sometimes high in its councils.

"The greatest indictment against the professorial fellow travelers of the Communist party is that they lend an air of harmlessness, even respectability, to the vicious, debased movement that is communism.

SNIPERS AT CAPITALISM

"Neither does this list include the names of other members of the faculty who extol the glories of socialism, collectivism, and planned economy, who snipe and sneer at capitalism, and who are unalterably opposed to the American system of freedom and free enterprise."

The council recognized the contention that professors have a right to join any organization they wish, but added:

"But the alumni, contributors to the university, parents of students themselves, have a right to know to what un-American organizations their professors belong."

[The rest of the article goes on to explain that the "Red-ucators" list was checked against the "Guide to Subversive Organizations and Publications," a collection of information from the files of the congressional committee on un-American activities. Harvard faculty members turned up with affiliations on 124 "fronts." Some of the organizations were then listed by the *Tribune*. In the pages of the "Guide" the names of 68 faculty members listed in the "Red-ucators" document were found. The names of all 68, their ranks and departments, and the number of communist fronts with which each one had been associated were then listed—the article continuing into several columns on a later page. The entire article concluded by reminding readers of the suicides of F. O. Matthiessen, professor of English, and Laurence Duggan, 1927 graduate of Harvard and at the time of his death president of the "Carnegie-financed Institute of International Education." The *Tribune* reported that Matthiessen left a note saying that he was depressed by world conditions and that Tass, Soviet news agency, referred to the event in a dispatch as "American progressive suicide—cruelly persecuted for his progressive work." Duggan, it was reported, leaped to his death from an upper window (as did Matthiessen) ten days after being questioned by the FBI.—Eds.]

Problems for Thought and Writing

This article appeared not as an editorial but as a leading news story, front page, left column, in the Chicago Sunday *Tribune* on April 8, 1951. At the top of the column there appeared a picture of Samuel P. Sears, president of the Massachusetts Bar Association, and about halfway down the column three smaller pictures were arranged in a horizontal line of (left to right) Conant, Hiss, and Griswold. Since it appeared as a news story, it deserves to be checked for accuracy and objectivity. A thorough job will require you to look up names and information in the library. The following questions may help you get started.

1. Are there any emotionally loaded words in the opening paragraph of the article? If so, what are they? What do they mean? To what, specifically, do you think the author is appealing in his readers?

2. What does the word "leftists" mean in the opening paragraph? Do you think the author means to include both left-wing Republicans and left-wing Democrats? With what word in the previous sentence are we expected to associate this one?

3. Why is "academic freedom" put in quotation marks in the opening sentence of the second paragraph? Observe the use of the word "alien" in the same

sentence. What is meant by it? What does the use of the word suggest about the *Tribune's* trust or distrust of foreigners?

4. Do you think "radicalism" should be "curbed" in the colleges? How would you define "radicalism"?

5. What are the implications of "budding brains" and "credulous" as they are used in reference to the students? If you were a Harvard student, would you welcome the author of this article as a guardian of your individual rights?

6. Is there any attempt to establish guilt by association in the fourth paragraph? If so, how? What about the next paragraph?

7. Why do you suppose the author fails to cite specific instances in claiming that "Alumni have refused to make donations because of their strong feeling over the situation at Harvard"? See "Freedom at Harvard," page 597, and look up the record of annual alumni contributions to the university since 1951.

8. Compare the appositives after the first mention of City Councilman John D. Lynch and those placed after Conant.

9. Given the title of the dossier placed on file at the Cambridge city clerk's office, do you think it is likely to be an objective study?

10. What is a "Stalinoid" movement? Does the author define the term?

11. "Inclusion of a professor or instructor in this list is not conclusive evidence that he is a Communist," observed the council. "He may be simply naive." Is this a *non sequitur* (see Davis, "Logical Fallacies," page 77)? Why or why not?

12. Study the next to the last paragraph carefully. Presumably other Harvard critics of capitalism and free enterprise are not on the list. Should they be? Is criticism of the imperfections of our own society an act of Americanism or un-Americanism?

13. What do you think is the real goal of this attack?

14. Suppose this *had* appeared as an editorial. Would it have then been justified as it stands? Why or why not?

~

MARK ANTONY'S FUNERAL ORATION*   *William Shakespeare*

   Ant. Friends, Romans, countrymen, lend me your ears!
I come to bury Cæsar, not to praise him.
The evil that men do lives after them,
The good is oft interred with their bones;
So let it be with Cæsar. The noble Brutus

---

* *Julius Caesar*, Act III, Scene 2.

Hath told you Cæsar was ambitious;
If it were so, it was a grievous fault,
And grievously hath Cæsar answer'd it.
Here, under leave of Brutus and the rest—
For Brutus is an honourable man;
So are they all, all honourable men—
Come I to speak in Cæsar's funeral.
He was my friend, faithful and just to me;
But Brutus says he was ambitious,
And Brutus is an honourable man.
He hath brought many captives home to Rome,
Whose ransoms did the general coffers fill;
Did this in Cæsar seem ambitious?
When that the poor have cried, Cæsar hath wept;
Ambition should be made of sterner stuff:
Yet Brutus says he was ambitious,
And Brutus is an honourable man.
You all did see that on the Lupercal
I thrice presented him a kingly crown,
Which he did thrice refuse. Was this ambition?
Yet Brutus says he was ambitious,
And, sure, he is an honourable man.
I speak not to disprove what Brutus spoke,
But here I am to speak what I do know.
You all did love him once, not without cause;
What cause withholds you then to mourn for him?
O judgment! thou art fled to brutish beasts,
And men have lost their reason. Bear with me;
My heart is in the coffin there with Cæsar,
And I must pause till it come back to me.

    1. Pleb. Methinks there is much reason in his sayings.
    2. Pleb. If thou consider rightly of the matter, Cæsar has had great
        wrong.
    3. Pleb.   Has he, masters?
I fear there will a worse come in his place.
    4. Pleb. Mark'd ye his words? He would not take the crown;
Therefore 'tis certain he was not ambitious.
    1. Pleb. If it be found so, some will dear abide it.
    2. Pleb. Poor soul! his eyes are red as fire with weeping.
    3. Pleb. There's not a nobler man in Rome than Antony.
    4. Pleb. Now mark him, he begins again to speak.

Ant. But yesterday the word of Cæsar might
Have stood against the world; now lies he there,
And none so poor to do him reverence.
O masters, if I were dispos'd to stir
Your hearts and minds to mutiny and rage,
I should do Brutus wrong, and Cassius wrong,
Who, you all know, are honourable men.
I will not do them wrong; I rather choose
To wrong the dead, to wrong myself and you,
Than I will wrong such honourable men.
But here's a parchment with the seal of Cæsar;
I found it in his closet; 'tis his will.
Let but the commons hear this testament—
Which, pardon me, I do not mean to read—
And they would go and kiss dead Cæsar's wounds
And dip their napkins in his sacred blood,
Yea, beg a hair of him for memory,
And, dying, mention it within their wills,
Bequeathing it as a rich legacy
Unto their issue.
   4. Pleb. We'll hear the will. Read it, Mark Antony.
   All. The will, the will! we will hear Cæsar's will.
   Ant. Have patience, gentle friends, I must not read it;
It is not meet you know how Cæsar lov'd you.
You are not wood, you are not stones, but men;
And, being men, hearing the will of Cæsar,
It will inflame you, it will make you mad.
'Tis good you know not that you are his heirs;
For, if you should, O, what would come of it!
   4. Pleb. Read the will; we'll hear it, Antony.
You shall read us the will, Cæsar's will.
   Ant. Will you be patient? Will you stay a while?
I have o'ershot myself to tell you of it.
I fear I wrong the honourable men
Whose daggers have stabb'd Cæsar; I do fear it.
   4. Pleb. They were traitors; honourable men!
   All. The will! the testament!
   2. Pleb. They were villains, murderers. The will! Read the will!
   Ant. You will compel me, then, to read the will?
Then make a ring about the corpse of Cæsar,

And let me show you him that made the will.
Shall I descend? and will you give me leave?
    All. Come down.
    2. Pleb. Descend.
    3. Pleb. You shall have leave.
                              [*Antony comes down from the pulpit.*]
    4. Pleb. A ring; stand round.
    1. Pleb. Stand from the hearse, stand from the body.
    2. Pleb. Room for Antony, most noble Antony.
    Ant. Nay, press not so upon me; stand far off.
    All. Stand back; room; bear back!
    Ant. If you have tears, prepare to shed them now.
You all do know this mantle; I remember
The first time ever Cæsar put it on.
'Twas on a summer's evening, in his tent,
That day he overcame the Nervii.
Look, in this place ran Cassius' dagger through;
See what a rent the envious Casca made;
Through this the well-beloved Brutus stabb'd,
And as he pluck'd his cursed steel away,
Mark how the blood of Cæsar followed it,
As rushing out of doors to be resolv'd
If Brutus so unkindly knock'd or no;
For Brutus, as you know, was Cæsar's angel.
Judge, O you gods, how dearly Cæsar lov'd him!
This was the most unkindest cut of all;
For when the noble Cæsar saw him stab,
Ingratitude, more strong than traitors' arms,
Quite vanquish'd him. Then burst his mighty heart;
And, in his mantle muffling up his face,
Even at the base of Pompey's statuë,
Which all the while ran blood, great Cæsar fell.
Oh, what a fall was there, my countrymen!
Then I, and you, and all of us fell down,
Whilst bloody treason flourish'd over us.
O, now you weep, and I perceive you feel
The dint of pity. These are gracious drops.
Kind souls, what, weep you when you but behold
Our Cæsar's vesture wounded? Look you here:
                                  [*Lifting Cæsar's mantle.*]
Here is himself, marr'd, as you see, with traitors.

1. Pleb. O piteous spectacle!

2. Pleb. O noble Cæsar!

3. Pleb. O woeful day!

4. Pleb. O traitors, villains!

1. Pleb. O most bloody sight!

2. Pleb. We will be reveng'd!

[*All.*]   Revenge! About!

Seek! Burn! Fire! Kill! Slay!

Let not a traitor live!

Ant.   Stay, countrymen.

1. Pleb. Peace there! hear the noble Antony.

2. Pleb. We'll hear him, we'll follow him, we'll die with him.

Ant. Good friends, sweet friends, let me not stir you up
To such a sudden flood of mutiny.
They that have done this deed are honourable.
What private griefs they have, alas, I know not,
That made them do it; they are wise and honourable
And will, no doubt, with reasons answer you.
I come not, friends, to steal away your hearts.
I am no orator, as Brutus is;
But, as you know me all, a plain blunt man
That love my friend; and that they know full well
That gave me public leave to speak of him;
For I have neither [wit], nor words, nor worth,
Action, not utterance, nor the power of speech
To stir men's blood; I only speak right on.
I tell you that which you yourselves do know;
Show you sweet Cæsar's wounds, poor, poor, dumb mouths,
And bid them speak for me. But were I Brutus,
And Brutus Antony, there were an Antony
Would ruffle up your spirits, and put a tongue
In every wound of Cæsar, that should move
The stones of Rome to rise and mutiny.

All. We'll mutiny.

1. Pleb. We'll burn the house of Brutus.

3. Pleb. Away, then! come, seek the conspirators.

Ant. Yet hear me, countrymen; yet hear me speak.

All. Peace, ho! hear Antony, most noble Antony!

Ant. Why, friends, you go to do you know not what.
Wherein hath Cæsar thus deserv'd your loves?

Alas, you know not; I must tell you, then.
You have forgot the will I told you of.
  All. Most true. The will! Let's stay and hear the will.
  Ant. Here is the will, and under Cæsar's seal.
To every Roman citizen he gives,
To every several man, seventy-five drachmas.
  2. Pleb. Most noble Cæsar! We'll revenge his death.
  3. Pleb. O Royal Cæsar!
  Ant. Hear me with patience.
  All. Peace, ho!
  Ant. Moreover, he hath left you all his walks,
His private arbours and new-planted orchards,
On this side Tiber, he hath left them you
And to your heirs forever, common pleasures,
To walk abroad and recreate yourselves.
Here was a Cæsar! When comes such another?
  1. Pleb. Never, never! Come, away, away!
We'll burn his body in the holy place,
And with the brands fire the traitors' houses.
Take up the body.
  2. Pleb. Go fetch fire.
  3. Pleb. Pluck down benches.
  4. Pleb. Pluck down forms, windows, anything.
                            [*Exeunt Plebians with the body*].
  Ant. Now let it work. Mischief, thou art afoot,
Take thou what course thou wilt!

Problems for Thought and Writing

At this point in the play the "noble Brutus" has just finished his public defense of the conspirators' murder of Caesar. Emphasizing the evidence for Caesar's ambitious and tyrannical designs against Rome, he has won their approval of the "honorableness" of the assassination, their loyalty to himself, and aroused their hatred against all who still call themselves friends of Caesar. That he might not himself seem dictatorial, however, he has given Antony leave to speak at Caesar's funeral. Brutus' final words are these: "Here comes his body mourn'd by Mark Antony; who, though he had no hand in his death shall receive the benefit of his dying, a place in the commonwealth; as which of you shall not? With this I depart, that, as I slew my best lover for the good of Rome, I have the same dagger for myself, when it shall please my country to need my death." To which the citizens respond, "Live, Brutus! live, live!"

Antony, in short, has his work cut out for him, and when he goes before the people most of the mob are ready to slit his throat before he starts speaking.

1. What is the first job of a speaker who is conscious that he is addressing a hostile audience? Why does Antony say what he does in the first two lines?

2. Does Antony rely on the audience's response to stock or "cliché" situations? If so, what are they?

3. What is the significance of the line, repeated throughout, "For Brutus is an honourable man"? Do you suppose Shakespeare intended the actor playing the part to deliver the line in each instance with the same inflection?

4. Observe Antony's statement, "I am no orator, as Brutus is," and similar utterances throughout disparaging his own weak and humble abilities. How would you characterize what is being done here? Is this sort of thing easier to detect on paper than when it is actually heard? Why or why not?

5. Where in the speech does Antony address himself directly to the question of Caesar's ambitious designs against the Republic?

6. Does Antony use any of the persuasive techniques used by William Fulton (page 618)? Specify them.

~

6 Evaluation

In our time it is almost rare to find a statesman, hero, or movie actor who resists the temptation to unveil himself in an autobiography or book of memoirs. And a war or other great public event is scarcely over before a host of historians and commentators go to work collecting, ordering, and analyzing the facts. Let a new book appear which arouses interest and it is immediately followed by a multitude of critical reviews in newspapers and magazines. Let an atomic bomb be invented and its impact upon human society will immediately be studied.

The impulse and necessity to scrutinize, to add up, to judge our experience are, to thoughtful men, almost irresistible. The man presenting the world with an account of his career is not likely to be content with a recital of the bare facts. He will want to emphasize the *significance* of this act, the *validity* of that accusation, the *importance* of this decision. Likewise, a historian will not simply collect information but will attempt to judge it and, perhaps, even to formulate an entire philosophy around it.

The impulse to judge our knowledge and experience is part of the critical activity we call *evaluation*. Unlike the rhetorical modes we have so far considered, it is not a *technique* of organizing and analyzing material. It is, rather, an attitude we bring to that material; it is the ultimate use to which all those rhetorical modes may be put in separating the true from the false, the valuable from the worthless. We cannot, therefore, talk very specifically about *methods* of evaluation, for we have already discussed most of them. Evaluation is simply the mature exercising of critical intelligence, and beyond a certain point one cannot helpfully lay down rules and procedures for so doing. We always need to define our terms, to classify carefully, to argue reasonably—and these are, or may be, acts of evaluation in themselves. If, for example, you classified your relatives into near-morons, morons, and sub-morons, you would be judging as well as dividing your subject. And all argument, from the very fact that it ends in a conclusion, is an act of judgment. But a great many human problems can never be accommodated to prefabricated patterns of organization or fixed procedures of thought. If, for example, you are trying to determine whether or not a painting is *beautiful*, you are faced with a problem that is not easily amenable to argument (see page 543) and that cannot be solved simply by analyzing pigments and details. You need, in working out such a problem, to draw upon a wide variety of means for refining and controlling thought, and, above all, you need a *standard of judgment*, a basis upon which your determination can be made and against which it may be tested.

The discovery and application of this standard of judgment is the crucial issue in any problem in evaluation. As the name implies, evaluation involves assessing the *value* of something, deciding a question of *worth*. Ultimately, of course, all such assessments involve the greatest valuational question of all: What makes life worth living? But if we are only trying to ascertain the price of a car or the market value of a stamp collection, our problem is an easy one. We look up the answers in a blue book or catalogue. If, however, we are trying to determine whether the decay of Christian orthodoxy has weakened our moral fibre (see Gilson, Stace, and Muller, pages 635, 640, and 653) or whether art and the individual have much place in a mass culture (see MacLeish, Eliot, pages 665, 677), then we are faced with complex and difficult tasks. The reason is obvious: in these cases the investigators are not provided with any precise or merely quantative standards of judgment. Their job involves not only the intelligent *use* of some measuring stick but very likely its invention as well.

Standards of judgment can be almost as various as the people possessing them, and all too often men make value judgments on the basis only of their own passions, appetites, or prejudices. Nevertheless, every time you remark that this person has good taste, or that book is vulgar, or this action is ridiculous, you are—consciously or not—using some *standard* in making the judgments. It may take a good deal of self-examination to discover what that standard is (and it may be so buried in your subconscious that you will never find it) but it is *there*. If you do find it, it may reveal nothing flattering to yourself. As we learned in earlier sections (page 461), human beings are embarrassingly rich in talents for believing as they *want* to believe and not as the evidence would dictate. But even to discover what it is that you want to believe is no small achievement. It may not be something you can justify in the cold light of reason, but it was nonetheless the *standard* which was in fact operating and serving as the basis of your judgment.

Various as standards of judgment are, however, there are at least two bases upon which questions of value are commonly determined. The first we may call judgment on the basis of a *fixed* (or absolute) standard; the second on the basis of a *relative* standard.

The individual who adheres to an absolutist religious faith, for example, is equipped to make value judgments not only in religious matters but in many related areas of human experience. If an orthodox Catholic, for example, were to encounter a book on birth control, he would come to it equipped with a clear standard for judgment, for the subject to a man of his persuasion has already been judged. Beginning as he does with a fixed theology of comprehensive proportions, he can decide nearly all questions of value within the terms of that great deductive system. Others might not agree with his basic assumptions, but the man possessing such a referent has the means to make *decisions*, to answer—for himself at least—questions of *worth* and of *right* and *wrong*.

The man, on the other hand, who is unwilling or unable to assent to any such absolute, who feels that each individual must discover his own philosophy of life or that human society cannot depend upon revelation but must "discover" its own truth, can be called relativist. He would study the book on birth control and (ideally) approve or disapprove on the basis of no authority but his own reason. Of course, operating within his decision is some standard of judgment, some conclusion drawn from the inductions or deductions (or prejudices) of his own experience. He may, like Mowrer for example (page 238), be dedicated to the fixed idea that overpopulation will be the death of all cultural values, and will read the book in the light of that conviction. But if he is a true relativist, he will hold that fixed standard as a *hypothesis* and not as a dogma.

We should not expect, however, that an investigator—absolutist or relativist—will always indicate clearly the standards operating within and behind his reasoning. Etienne Gilson, the author of *The Breakdown of Modern Philosophy*, is, for example, a prominent Catholic philosopher; yet the cursory reader would probably detect nothing in that essay to indicate his denominational allegiance. Nevertheless—and in spite of the fact that many non-Catholics would agree with his position—he charts the course of Western culture with a special and, to the perceptive reader, recognizable compass. Take this statement:

> Man is best described as a rational animal; deprive man of reason, and what is left is not man, but animal. . . . Morality is essentially normality; for a rational being to act and to behave either without reason or contrary to its dictates is to act and behave, not exactly as a beast, but as a beastly man, which is worse. For it is proper that a beast should act as a beast that is, according to its own nature—but it is totally unfitting for a man to act as a beast, because that means the complete oblivion of his own nature, and hence his final destruction.

One of the assumptions involved in this evaluation is that man is different not just in degree but *in kind* from the animals, that his God-given faculty of reason puts him in a category fundamentally *apart from* that of the beasts. This belief, deriving from Aristotle and the Greeks, is a vital part of Catholic theology, and serves in that system as an essential link in the hierarchy of values closing with man's relationship with God. Though other Christian orthodoxies share this assumption, its most consistent modern exponent is the Catholic Church. But a modern biologist, taking the view of nature which Gilson criticizes, would probably assert that man is different only *in degree* from the animals and that his reason, rather than being in any sense "God-given," is simply the evolutionary by-product of an overdeveloped nervous system. Thus does Gilson employ a fixed standard without conspicuously advertising the fact. To detect the bases for his judgments we need both to read carefully between the lines and to exercise as much scholarship as we can command. All evaluation operates in relation to some value-standard. Unless we are aware of that standard we cannot judge a piece of writing fairly—in terms of the author's assumptions as well as his explicit statements.

The entire question of absolutism vs. relativism is, of course, a philosophical problem far beyond the scope of this discussion, and we are here trying only to suggest some of its obvious manifestations. But we can profit by being aware of that problem in reading some of the essays which follow. Two of them (those by Gilson and Stace) are evaluations of the spiritual and ethical condition of modern man and society. They both deplore, in different ways, the ethical relativism that marks our contemporary world, and both betray a certain nostalgia for an age of faith when men could "know the right" and, if they had the strength, act on it. Stace agrees with the Catholic bishops of America that "the chaotic and bewildered state of the modern world is due to man's loss of faith, his abandonment of God and religion." On the face of it, this remark would seem to place Stace in the same camp as Gilson, but this is not so. Stace is a relativist, even though he is keenly aware of the dangers in relativism. Although he acknowledges the damage that has been wrought by the decay of religious faith, he can see no salvation in the "return to God" recommended by the bishops. "For my part," he writes, "I believe in no religion at all." We must simply learn to live "without the Great Illusion, the illusion of a good, kindly, and purposeful universe." He says this in spite of his conviction that

> The widespread belief in "ethical relativity" among philosophers, psychologists, ethnologists, and sociologists is the theoretical counterpart of the repudiation of principle which we see all around us, especially in international affairs, the field in which morals have always had the weakest foothold. No one any longer effectively believes in moral principles except as the private prejudices either of individual men or of nations or cultures. This is the inevitable consequence of the doctrine of ethical relativity, which in turn is the inevitable consequence of believing in a purposeless world.

In other words, says Stace, we cannot return to ethical absolutism just because we need it. We must work within the conditions which modern man has created for himself and not attempt escape through romantic or religious illusions just because they are pleasant.

In holding such a position, Stace may seem to be striking an uneasy balance between relativism and absolutism in his sense of values. But that his emphasis is toward relativism becomes obvious when we compare his position with Gilson's. Though he longs for absolutes, he does not permit that longing to translate itself into intellectual conviction; he refuses to take the recommendations of his heart for the commands of an almighty law-giver. This kind of alliance with the objective facts of a situation is the mark of the relativist. The alliance may end in divorce, for it is a taxing one, but—if Stace is right—those are the grounds for romance in our time.

The other essays in this section—by Muller and MacLeish—are all evaluations of major problems in the modern world: the meaning of history, the devaluation of art. Would you judge Muller to be an absolutist or relativist on the basis of the following remark?

> In short, our feeling about time—however vague or unconscious—ultimately involves a philosophy of history. It leads to a momentous question. Given all the drama of human history, what is the plot, the grand design, the final meaning of the whole show? Positivists will tell us that this is a meaningless question. Manifestly we cannot give it a precise, positive answer: we cannot state it in terms that permit either empirical verification or rigorous logical analysis. But neither can we escape it.

In asking for the plot, design, or meaning Muller seems to imply what Stace denied—that there is a purpose to the whole show. And his even suggesting that there is any answer at all to this fundamental question—an answer he admits cannot be verified empirically or logically—would seem to place Muller among those who claim to know truth absolutely, through faith or revelation. But this is not quite true. The historical absolutists are those who, like the communists, insist that the drama must go a certain way and culminate in a certain preordained millennium. But Muller's conclusion is that our historical future is "wide open," that we can go to triumph or disaster depending on how we use our freedom. The only assumption he makes—and this he clearly labels an assumption—is that the will is not bound, that man possesses the "freedom to make history."

> We bear the cross of consciousness. In a fuller consciousness the burden may be eased. . . . Our adventure in freedom is so recent that what appear to be our death rattles may be growing pains. But in any event the pains are unavoidable. For a society as for an individual, the hardest problems begin with freedom. Today the future of the open society is wide open, to triumphs or to disasters of a magnitude hitherto undreamed of.

The evidence for any final judgment or any historical blueprint is not yet in. The best Muller can do is to make out a case—opposed to Spengler's pessimistic one—that we are not yet done for. And this is only a hypothesis.

Clearly, Muller's essential position is that of the relativist. The evidence may not all be in but he will *go by the evidence,* even though it prove human history to be without purpose or meaning. His standard for truth is experience, inductively examined, and not a set of assumptions derived from some revealed source, which experience merely illustrates. An historian of the second sort, in Muller's estimation, is Arnold Toynbee, who reads history as a Christian drama, the theme of which is "the universal nemesis of idolatry." But to force such a moral theme upon history is, Muller believes, both to oversimplify and to torture the facts. History simply is not *like* that:

By systematically complicating all issues, stressing the defects and the excesses of all values, insisting on tension, imbalance, uncertainty, and contradiction as the essential conditions of civilization, and the source of both its glory and its tragedy—by ironically qualifying the great triumphs, and reverently qualifying the great failures, we may get both a richer appreciation of the poetry and drama of history and a clearer understanding of the fact, the 'reality' that concerns social science. We may hope to be at once more humane and more sober in our judgments.

[*The Uses of the Past,* page 31]

To this Toynbee would probably reply: But history can't be like *that!* Surely the drama must distinguish more clearly than that between virtue and its rewards, evil and its punishments! In such differences of emphasis we glimpse the value worlds of the relativist and the absolutist.

But we live in a relativistic world. The confident absolutisms of the past, as Stace describes them, are for the most part gone and done with. That being the case, is it really relevant to ask whether a writer is relativist or absolutist? Often it is not. A man most certainly can live in a relativistic age and still have fixed standards of value: the difference is that they are not likely to be shared by his whole culture—and they may be simply private. But the point is that the relativistic culture will usually stain through and will affect the evaluation in one way or another.

Archibald MacLeish, for example, is arguing that poetry should be read as poetry and not as a vehicle carrying abstract ideas. But the problem he deals with would never have arisen had it not been that science over the past three centuries has slowly undermined our ancient confidence in the prophetic voice of the poet—and in the poem as a means of "discovering" truth. MacLeish wants us to remember—or learn—that poetry can still show us ways, even in a relativistic age, of seeing experience *whole* and not in fragments, of *knowing* through insight and not analysis. So his argument is, in effect, an appeal to return to one of the values of the past without turning back the clock—without denying science but without admitting that science has superseded poetry.

On what does he base his judgment of value? On his own experience. The whole essay is an argument supported by the testimony of himself as witness, on what he *knows.* He knows, for example

. . . that the children of abstraction are wrong—and are impoverished by their error, as our entire time is impoverished by it. They are wrong on both heads. They are wrong because they think they *can* know the world through its abstractions: nothing can be known through an abstraction but the abstraction itself. They are wrong also when they think they *cannot* know the world as the world: the whole achievement of art is a demonstration to the contrary. And the reason they are wrong on both heads is the reason given, quite unintentionally, by Matthew Arnold. They are wrong because they do not realize that all true knowledge is a matter of relation: that we *really* know a thing only when we are filled with "a wonderfully full, new and intimate sense of it" and, above all, of "our relation with" it. This sense—this *knowledge* in the truest meaning of the word knowledge—art can give but abstraction cannot.

Is such a statement of faith only an example, as Stace phrases it, of romanticism's counterattack against "the scientific view of things"? Maybe so, but it is also a suggestion that the experience of the private man in a relativistic age is far from meaningless and can be fraught with value.

"The Love Song of J. Alfred Prufrock" is a poetic self-evaluation of a certain kind of modern man. Is this *everyman*, twentieth-century edition? Eliot makes no such claim, but is not Prufrock—impotent and indecisive, rudderless and bored—a possible leading character for the kind of relativistic world sketched by Gilson and Stace, and implied by the others? This poem should be read—as MacLeish reminds us all poetry should be read—for itself and not primarily as the vehicle of an "idea." But it also serves as a footnote to the essays which precede it.

To understand the difference between relative and absolute standards of judgment is to be introduced to some of the most crucial and fundamental problems facing the modern world. Few of the ancient moral props remain intact and unchallenged. In our time the question mark has assumed the urgency of an exclamation point. Have we grounds to deny Oscar Wilde's charge that we "know the price of everything and the value of nothing"? Let us hope, at least, that the accusation makes us angry.

~

THE BREAKDOWN OF MODERN PHILOSOPHY*
Etienne Gilson

When Oswald Spengler first published *The Decline of the West,* many readers of his now famous book felt at variance with more than one of its conclusions; yet few among them would have thought of questioning the fact that the West was actually declining. Most of them had already known it for a long time. Not in the least because of the World War; on the contrary, the war had been a time of enthusiasm and complete self-dedication to a sacred cause, when old

* Reprinted with the permission of Charles Scribner's Sons from *The Unity of Philosophical Experience* by Etienne Gilson, copyright 1937 Charles Scribner's Sons.

fears and solicitous misgivings as to the future of Western culture had been forgotten. I know that it is now fashionable to laugh at that sacred cause; yet there are still a few people who remember how they were then trying to redeem war by giving it a meaning and who remember what that meaning was. A certain idea of man and a corresponding ideal of social life were not to be allowed to perish. Yet it now seems clear that even at that time Western culture was steadily following its process of dissolution, and we know it from within, by a sort of immediate and personal experience. For we are the bearers of that culture; it cannot be dying, and dying in us, without our being aware of it.

In its broadest sense, what we call Western culture is essentially the culture of Greece, inherited from the Greeks by the Romans, transfused by the fathers of the church with the religious teachings of Christianity, and progressively enlarged by countless numbers of artists, writers, scientists, and philosophers from the beginning of the Middle Ages up to the first third of the nineteenth century. It would be a waste of time to look for a turning point in its history—in the continuous stream of historical events every point is a turning point— but it can safely be assumed that the French Revolution marks the time when the more clear-sighted among the representatives of Western culture began to feel that there was something wrong with it. They offered various diagnoses, and they began to suggest remedies. For the reasons we have noted, Comte failed to provide Europe with a living dogma; his new scientific religion was stillborn, and he died, a self-appointed pope, with a very small number of disciples. On the whole, his Reformation was a failure, but Comte had at least seen clearly that the European crisis was essentially a crisis of Western culture: Can a social order, begotten by a common faith in the value of certain principles, keep on living when all faith in these principles is lost?

The meaning of that question will be illustrated best by a summary description of what may be called, for brevity's sake, the Western creed. Its most fundamental feature is a firm belief in the eminent dignity of man. The Greeks of classical times never wavered in their conviction that of all the things that can be found in nature, man is by far the highest, and that of all the things important for man to know, by far the most important is man. When Socrates, after unsuccessful attempts to deal with physical problems, made up his mind to dedicate himself to the exclusive study of man, he was making a momentous decision. "Know thyself" is not only the key to Greek culture but to the classical culture of the Western world as well. What the Greeks left to their successors was a vast body of knowledge, mainly related to man's nature and his various needs: logic, which is the science of how to think; several different philosophies, all of them culminating in ethics and politics, which are the sciences of how to live; remarkable specimens of history and political eloquence, related to the life of the city. As to what we today call positive science, the greatest achievements of the Greek genius were along the lines of mathematics, a knowledge which man draws from his own mind without submitting to the degrading tyranny of material facts, and medicine, whose proper object is to insure the well-being of the human body. And they stopped there, checked by an obscure feeling that the rest was not worth having, at least not at the price which the human mind would have to pay for it: its freedom from matter, its internal liberty.

Of the heirs to Greek culture it can truly be said that while they enlarged and deepened their heritage, they always respected its nature and never thought of displacing its center of gravity. When the Romans added the lofty structure of Roman law to it, man and the betterment of human life still remained their essential interest. As to Christianity, though it be true that God was its ultimate goal and its center of reference, the fact remains that it conceived man, created by God in His own image and likeness, as the most perfect of all earthly beings, with no higher duty than to achieve his own salvation. And why is man an image of God? Because, says St. Augustine, he has a mind. All the Greek philosophers would have gladly subscribed to that statement.

Hence the second fundamental feature of Western culture, which is a definite conviction that reason is the specific difference of man. Man is best described as a rational animal; deprive man of reason and what is left is not man, but animal. This looks like a very commonplace statement; yet Western culture is dying wherever it has been forgotten, for the rational nature of man is the only conceivable foundation for a rational system of ethics. Morality is essentially normality; for a rational being to act and to behave either without reason or contrary to its dictates is to act and behave, not exactly as a beast, but as a beastly man, which is worse. For it is proper that a beast should act as a beast—that is, according to its own nature—but it is totally unfitting for a man to act as a beast, because that means the complete oblivion of his own nature, and hence his final destruction.

It is hardly possible to realize the continuity that prevails throughout the whole history of Western culture unless one keeps in mind the important part played by the church in the work of its transmission. The Greek and the Latin fathers of the church had so carefully preserved the classical notion of man that when St. Thomas Aquinas, in the thirteenth century, undertook to build up a complete exposition of the Christian truth, he did not scruple to borrow for his technical equipment from the pagan Aristotle, whose logic, physics, biology, ethics, and metaphysics were then transformed by his mediaeval disciple into as many elements of a Christian synthesis.

The Reformation of the sixteenth century was to wreck that stately edifice, whose two component elements then fell apart, Christianity on the one side and Greek culture on the other. Yet not only Catholic humanists such as Erasmus but even Protestants such as Melanchthon immediately set about rebuilding it. Luther himself, despite his fierce attacks upon pagan culture, was fond of Ovid, and he always remained partial to Cicero. The humanists who, more or less consciously, swerved from Christianity to paganism were either going back to what seemed to them the pure doctrine of Aristotle or testing the true value of the doctrines left by the Stoics and Epicureans. Throughout the Renaissance and until the middle of the nineteenth century, the classical tradition remained the common ground on which both pagans and Christians could still meet and carry on fruitful intellectual intercourse. Even the most brilliant scientific discoveries were made by men who, like Descartes, Pascal, Fermat, Leibniz, and Newton, had learned little more at school than classical Latin, a philosophy which more or less resembled that of St. Thomas or Aristotle, and the elements of mathematics. So long as, and in so far as, science itself kept faith with its own nature, it remained the healthy exercise of reason, reason seeking to know, because knowing is its natural function. Even the most stupendous progress made by the physical and biological sciences entailed no disruption in the continuity of Western culture. While man remained in control of nature, culture could still survive. It was lost from the very moment nature began to control man.

Such a development was by no means inevitable, but the progressive growth of natural science had made it more and more probable. The growing interest taken by men in the practical results of science was in itself both natural and legitimate, but it helped them to forget that science is knowledge, and practical results but its by-products. Moreover, the constant accumulation of hitherto un-

known facts and of their recently formulated laws was destroying
the old balance between the human and the physical sciences, to the
advantage of the latter. This, however, was not the main point. It
lay rather in the fact that before their unexpected success in finding
conclusive explanations of the material world, men had begun either
to despise all disciplines in which such demonstrations could not be
found or to rebuild those disciplines after the pattern of the physical
sciences. As a consequence, metaphysics and ethics had to be either
ignored or, at least, replaced by new positive sciences; in either case,
they would be eliminated.

A very dangerous move indeed, which accounts for the perilous
position in which Western culture has now found itself. The European burned his old ships before making sure that the new ones
would float. Moreover, the first article of the scientific creed is the
acceptance of nature such as it is. Far from making up for the loss
of philosophy, the discovery of the scientific substitutes for it leaves
man alone with nature such as it is and obliges him to surrender to
natural necessity. Philosophy is the only rational knowledge by
which both science and nature can be judged. By reducing philosophy to pure science, man has not only abdicated his right to judge
nature and to rule it, but he has also turned himself into a particular
aspect of nature, subjected, like all the rest, to the necessary law
which regulates its development. A world where accomplished facts
are unto themselves their own justification is ripe for the most reckless
social adventures. Its dictators can wantonly play havoc with human
institutions and human lives, for dictatorships are facts, and they
also are unto themselves their own justification.

Problems for Thought and Writing

I

1. The book from which this selection is taken was written between World
Wars I and II. Does it seem to you that the aftermath of the second of those
wars has been a period of greater or less disillusionment than the period of
which Gilson writes?

2. What does the author mean by saying in the first paragraph that some people
during World War I tried "to redeem war by giving it a meaning"? Is he
implying that war is "beyond redemption"? Is he saying that the attempt
to give war "meaning" is a rationalization?

3. In what sense is our culture the "culture of Greece"? Is not Christianity
different from paganism? See Arnold, "Hellenism and Hebraism," page 422.

4. How would you answer Gilson's question, "Can a social order, begotten by a
common faith in the value of certain principles, keep on living when all faith

in these principles is lost?" (page 636) What are the principles by which the United States of America has sustained itself? Is our common faith in those principles as "common" and as strong today as it was when the Republic was founded? Why or why not?

5. What are the two fundamental articles in the Western creed, according to Gilson? Would you say that most men still accept them without qualification? Is it possible to believe in and maintain a social order without believing that man is, essentially, a *rational* animal?

6. What does Gilson mean by science keeping "faith with its own nature" and the loss incurred when "nature began to control man"? Rather than speculate on these remarks, if you are at a loss, read C. S. Lewis' "The Abolition of Man" (page 326) for a fully developed argument that man's conquest of nature, on which the 20th century so prides itself, turns out in the last analysis to be nature's conquest of man. See Julian Huxley, "Religion as an Objective Problem" (page 315) for the other side of the argument.

7. Do you agree that "science is knowledge, and practical results but its by-products" (page 638)? In what sense is Gilson using the word "knowledge" here?

II

8. Observe Gilson's expository command of time and space in this sweeping evaluation of Western culture. How does he effect his transpositions? Is he guilty anywhere of oversimplification?

9. What relation is there between Gilson's reference to the Greek motto "Know thyself" and his subsequent use of the word *knowledge?* Is self-knowledge on Gilson's terms the same as self-knowledge as understood by Carl Jung (page 333) or William Barrett (page 348)? Why would they disagree?

~

MAN AGAINST DARKNESS *   W. T. Stace

I

The Catholic bishops of America recently issued a statement in which they said that the chaotic and bewildered state of the modern world is due to man's loss of faith, his abandonment of God and religion. For my part I believe in no religion at all. Yet I entirely agree with the bishops. It is no doubt an oversimplification to speak of *the* cause of so complex a state of affairs as the tortured condition of the world today. Its causes are doubtless multitudinous. Yet

* Reprinted by permission from *The Atlantic Monthly*, September, 1948. Copyright 1948, The Atlantic Monthly Company.

allowing for some element of oversimplification, I say that the bishops' assertion is substantially true.

M. Jean-Paul Sartre, the French existentialist philosopher, labels himself an atheist. Yet his views seem to me plainly to support the statement of the bishops. So long as there was believed to be a God in the sky, he says, men could regard him as the source of their moral ideals. The universe, created and governed by a fatherly God, was a friendly habitation for man. We could be sure that, however great the evil in the world, good in the end would triumph and the forces of evil would be routed. With the disappearance of God from the sky all this has changed. Since the world is not ruled by a spiritual being, but rather by blind forces, there cannot be any ideals, moral or otherwise, in the universe outside us. Our ideals, therefore, must proceed only from our own minds; they are our own inventions. Thus the world which surrounds us is nothing but an immense spiritual emptiness. It is a dead universe. We do not live in a universe which is on the side of our values. It is completely indifferent to them.

Years ago Mr. Bertrand Russell, in his essay *A Free Man's Worship*, said much the same thing.

Such in outline, but even more purposeless, more void of meaning, is the world which Science presents for our belief. Amid such a world, if anywhere, our ideals henceforward must find a home. . . . Blind to good and evil, reckless of destruction, omnipotent matter rolls on its relentless way; for man, condemned today to lose his dearest, tomorrow himself to pass through the gate of darkness, it remains only to cherish, ere yet the blow falls, the lofty thoughts that ennoble his little day; . . . to worship at the shrine his own hands have built; . . . to sustain alone, a weary but unyielding Atlas, the world that his own ideals have fashioned despite the trampling march of unconscious power.

It is true that Mr. Russell's personal attitude to the disappearance of religion is quite different from either that of Mr. Sartre or the bishops or myself. The bishops think it a calamity. So do I. M. Sartre finds it "very distressing." And he berates as shallow the attitude of those who think that without God the world can go on just the same as before, as if nothing had happened. This creates for mankind, he thinks, a terrible crisis. And in this I agree with him. Mr. Russell, on the other hand, seems to believe that religion has done more harm than good in the world, and that its disappearance will be a blessing. But his picture of the world, and of the modern mind, is the same as that of M. Sartre. He stresses the *purposelessness* of the universe, the facts that man's ideals are his own creations, that the universe outside him in no way supports them, that man is alone and friendless in the world.

Mr. Russell notes that it is science which has produced this situation. There is no doubt that this is correct. But the way in which it has come about is not generally understood. There is a popular belief that some particular scientific discoveries or theories, such as the Darwinian theory of evolution, or the views of geologists about the age of the earth, or a series of such discoveries, have done the damage. It would be foolish to deny that these discoveries have had a great effect in undermining religious dogmas. But this account does not at all go to the root of the matter. Religion can probably outlive any scientific discoveries which could be made. It can accommodate itself to them. The root cause of the decay of faith has not been any particular discovery of science, but rather the general spirit of science and certain basic assumptions upon which modern science, from the seventeenth century onwards, has proceeded.

II

It was Galileo and Newton—notwithstanding that Newton himself was a deeply religious man—who destroyed the old comfortable picture of a friendly universe governed by spiritual values. And this was effected, not by Newton's discovery of the law of gravitation nor by any of Galileo's brilliant investigations, but by the general picture of the world which these men and others of their time made the basis of the science, not only of their own day, but of all succeeding generations down to the present. That is why the century immediately following Newton, the eighteenth century, was notoriously an age of religious skepticism. Skepticism did not have to wait for the discoveries of Darwin and the geologists in the nineteenth century. It flooded the world immediately after the age of the rise of science.

Neither the Copernican hypothesis nor any of Newton's or Galileo's particular discoveries were the real causes. Religious faith might well have accommodated itself to the new astronomy. The real turning point between the medieval age of faith and the modern age of unfaith came when the scientists of the seventeenth century turned their backs upon what used to be called "final causes." The final cause of a thing or event meant the purpose which it was supposed to serve in the universe, its cosmic purpose. What lay back of this was the presupposition that there is a cosmic order or plan and that everything which exists could in the last analysis be explained in terms of its place in this cosmic plan, that is, in terms of its purpose.

Plato and Aristotle believed this, and so did the whole medieval Christian world. For instance, if it were true that the sun and the moon were created and exist for the purpose of giving light to man, then this fact would explain why the sun and the moon exist. We might not be able to discover the purpose of everything, but everything must have a purpose. Belief in final causes thus amounted to a belief that the world is governed by purposes, presumably the purposes of some overruling mind. This belief was not the invention of Christianity. It was basic to the whole of Western civilization, whether in the ancient pagan world or in Christendom, from the time of Socrates to the rise of science in the seventeenth century.

The founders of modern science—for instance, Galileo, Kepler, and Newton—were mostly pious men who did not doubt God's purposes. Nevertheless they took the revolutionary step of consciously and deliberately expelling the idea of purpose as controlling nature from their new science of nature. They did this on the ground that inquiry into purposes is useless for what science aims at: namely, the prediction and control of events. To predict an eclipse, what you have to know is not its purpose but its causes. Hence science from the seventeenth century onwards became exclusively an inquiry into causes. The conception of purpose in the world was ignored and frowned on. This, though silent and almost unnoticed, was the greatest revolution in human history, far outweighing in importance any of the political revolutions whose thunder has reverberated through the world.

For it came about in this way that for the past three hundred years there has been growing up in men's minds, dominated as they are by science, a new imaginative picture of the world. The world, according to this new picture, is purposeless, senseless, meaningless. Nature is nothing but matter in motion. The motions of matter are governed, not by any purpose, but by blind forces and laws. Nature in this view, says Whitehead—to whose writings I am indebted in this part of my paper—is "merely the hurrying of material, endlessly, meaninglessly." You can draw a sharp line across the history of Europe dividing it into two epochs of very unequal length. The line passes through the lifetime of Galileo. European man before Galileo—whether ancient pagan or more recent Christian—thought of the world as controlled by plan and purpose. After Galileo European man thinks of it as utterly purposeless. This is the great revolution of which I spoke.

It is this which has killed religion. Religion could survive the discoveries that the sun, not the earth, is the center; that men are descended from simian ancestors; that the earth is hundreds of millions of years old. These discoveries may render out of date some of the details of older theological dogmas, may force their restatement in new intellectual frameworks. But they do not touch the essence of the religious vision itself, which is the faith that there is plan and purpose in the world, that the world is a moral order, that in the end all things are for the best. This faith may express itself through many different intellectual dogmas, those of Christianity, of Hinduism, of Islam. All and any of these intellectual dogmas may be destroyed without destroying the essential religious spirit. But that spirit cannot survive destruction of belief in a plan and purpose of the world, for that is the very heart of it. Religion can get on with any sort of astronomy, geology, biology, physics. But it cannot get on with a purposeless and meaningless universe.

If the scheme of things is purposeless and meaningless, then the life of man is purposeless and meaningless too. Everything is futile, all effort is in the end worthless. A man may, of course, still pursue disconnected ends, money, fame, art, science, and may gain pleasure from them. But his life is hollow at the center. Hence the dissatisfied, disillusioned, restless spirit of modern man.

The picture of a meaningless world, and a meaningless human life, is, I think, the basic theme of much modern art and literature. Certainly it is the basic theme of modern philosophy. According to the most characteristic philosophies of the modern period from Hume in the eighteenth century to the so-called positivists of today, the world is just what it is, and that is the end of all inquiry. There is no reason for its being what it is. Everything might just as well have been quite different, and there would have been no reason for that either. When you have stated what things are, what things the world contains, there is nothing more which could be said, even by an omniscient being. To ask any question about *why* things are thus, or what purpose their being so serves, is to ask a senseless question, because they serve no purpose at all. For instance, there is for modern philosophy no such thing as the ancient problem of evil.

For this once famous question presupposes that pain and misery, though they seem so inexplicable and irrational to us, must ultimately subserve some rational purpose, must have their places in the cosmic plan. But this is nonsense. There is no such overruling rationality in the universe. Belief in the ultimate irrationality of everything is the quintessence of what is called the modern mind.

It is true that, parallel with these philosophies which are typical of the modern mind, preaching the meaninglessness of the world, there has run a line of idealistic philosophies whose contention is that the world is after all spiritual in nature and that moral ideals and values are inherent in its structure. But most of these idealisms were simply philosophical expressions of romanticism, which was itself no more than an unsuccessful counterattack of the religious against the scientific view of things. They perished, along with romanticism in literature and art, about the beginning of the present century, though of course they still have a few adherents.

At the bottom these idealistic systems of thought were rationalizations of man's wishful thinking. They were born of the refusal of men to admit the cosmic darkness. They were comforting illusions within the warm glow of which the more tender-minded intellectuals sought to shelter themselves from the icy winds of the universe. They lasted a little while. But they are shattered now, and we return once more to the vision of a purposeless world.

III

Along with the ruin of the religious vision there went the ruin of moral principles and indeed of all values. If there is a cosmic purpose, if there is in the nature of things a drive towards goodness, then our moral systems will derive their validity from this. But if our moral rules do not proceed from something outside us in the nature of the universe—whether we say it is God or simply the universe itself—then they must be our own inventions. Thus it came to be believed that moral rules must be merely an expression of our own likes and dislikes. But likes and dislikes are notoriously variable. What pleases one man, people, or culture displeases another. Therefore morals are wholly relative.

This obvious conclusion from the idea of a purposeless world made its appearance in Europe immediately after the rise of science, for instance in the philosophy of Hobbes. Hobbes saw at once that if there is no purpose in the world there are no values either. "Good and evil," he writes, "are names that signify our appetites and aversions; which in different tempers, customs, and doctrines of men are different. . . . Every man calleth that which pleaseth him, good; and that which displeaseth him, evil."

This doctrine of the relativity of morals, though it has recently received an impetus from the studies of anthropologists, was thus really implicit in the whole scientific mentality. It is disastrous for morals because it destroys their entire traditional foundation. That is why philosophers who see the danger signals, from the time at least of Kant, have been trying to give to morals a new foundation, that is, a secular or nonreligious foundation. This attempt may very well be intellectually successful. Such a foundation, independent of the religious view of the world, might well be found. But the question is whether it can ever be a *practical* success, that is, whether apart from its logical validity and its influence with intellectuals, it can ever replace among the masses of men the lost religious foundation. On that question hangs perhaps the future of civilization. But meanwhile disaster is overtaking us.

The widespread belief in "ethical relativity" among philosophers, psychologists, ethnologists, and sociologists is the theoretical counterpart of the repudiation of principle which we see all around us, especially in international affairs, the field in which morals have always had the weakest foothold. No one any longer effectively believes in moral principles except as the private prejudices either of individual men or of nations or cultures. This is the inevitable consequence of the doctrine of ethical relativity, which in turn is the inevitable consequence of believing in a purposeless world.

Another characteristic of our spiritual state is loss of belief in the freedom of the will. This also is a fruit of the scientific spirit, though not of any particular scientific discovery. Science has been built up on the basis of determinism, which is the belief that every event is completely determined by a chain of causes and is therefore theoretically predictable beforehand. It is true that recent physics seems to challenge this. But so far as its practical consequences are concerned, the damage has long ago been done. A man's actions, it was argued, are as much events in the natural world as is an eclipse of the sun. It follows that men's actions are as theoretically predictable as an eclipse. But if it is certain now that John Smith will murder Joseph Jones at 2:15 P.M. on January 1, 1963, what possible meaning can it have to say that when that time comes John Smith will be *free* to choose whether he will commit the murder or not? And if he is not free, how can he be held responsible?

It is true that the whole of this argument can be shown by a competent philosopher to be a tissue of fallacies—or at least I claim that it can. But the point is that the analysis required to show this is much too subtle to be understood by the average entirely unphilosophical man. Because of this, the argument against free will is generally swallowed whole by the unphilosophical. Hence the thought that man is not free, that he is the helpless plaything of forces over which he has no control, has deeply penetrated the modern mind. We hear of economic determinism, cultural determinism, historical determinism. We are not responsible for what we do because our glands control us, or because we are the products of environment or heredity. Not moral self-control, but the doctor, the psychiatrist, the educationist, must save us from doing evil. Pills and injections in the future are to do what Christ and the prophets have failed to do. Of course I do not mean to deny that doctors and educationists can and must help. And I do not mean in any way to belittle their efforts. But I do wish to draw attention to the weakening of moral controls, the greater or less repudiation of personal responsibility which, in the popular thinking of the day, result from these tendencies of thought.

IV

What, then, is to be done? Where are we to look for salvation from the evils of our time? All the remedies I have seen suggested so far are, in my opinion, useless. Let us look at some of them.

Philosophers and intellectuals generally can, I believe, genuinely do something to help. But it is extremely little. What philosophers can do is to show that neither the relativity of morals nor the denial of free will really follows from the grounds which have been supposed to support them. They can also try to discover a genuine secular basis for morals to replace the religious basis which has disappeared. Some of us are trying to do these things. But in the first place philosophers unfortunately are not agreed about these matters, and their disputes are utterly confusing to the non-philosophers. And in the second place their influence is practically negligible because their analyses necessarily take place on a level on which the masses are totally unable to follow them.

The bishops, of course, propose as remedy a return to belief in God and in the doctrines of the Christian religion. Others think that a new religion is what is needed. Those who make these proposals fail to realize that the crisis in man's spiritual condition is something unique in history for which there is no sort of analogy in the past. They are thinking perhaps of the collapse of the ancient Greek and Roman religions. The vacuum then created was easily filled by Christianity, and it might have been filled by Mithraism if Christianity had not appeared. By analogy they think that Christianity might now be replaced by a new religion, or even that Christianity itself, if revivified, might bring back health to men's lives.

But I believe that there is no analogy at all between our present state and that of the European peoples at the time of the fall of paganism. Men had at that time lost their belief only in particular dogmas, particular embodiments of the religious view of the world. It had no doubt become incredible that Zeus and the other gods were living on the top of Mount Olympus. You could go to the top and find no trace of them. But the imaginative picture of a world governed by purpose, a world driving towards the good—which is the inner spirit of religion—had at that time received no serious shock. It had merely to re-embody itself in new dogmas, those of Christianity or some other religion. Religion itself was not dead in the world, only a particular form of it.

But now the situation is quite different. It is not merely that particular dogmas, like that of the virgin birth, are unacceptable to the modern mind. That is true, but it constitutes a very superficial diagnosis of the present situation of religion. Modern skepticism is of a wholly different order from that of the intellectuals of the ancient world. It has attacked and destroyed not merely the outward forms of the religious spirit, its particularized dogmas, but the very essence of that spirit itself, belief in a meaningful and purposeful world. For the founding of a new religion a new Jesus Christ or Buddha would have to appear, in itself a most unlikely event and one for which in any case we cannot afford to sit and wait. But even if a new prophet and a new religion did appear, we may predict that they would fail in the modern world. No one for long would believe in them, for modern men have lost the vision, basic to all religion, of an ordered plan and purpose of the world. They have before their minds the picture of a purposeless universe, and such a world-picture must be fatal to any religion at all, not merely to Christianity.

We must not be misled by occasional appearances of a revival of the religious spirit. Men, we are told, in their disgust and disillusionment at the emptiness of their lives, are turning once more to religion, or are searching for a new message. It may be so. We must expect such wistful yearnings of the spirit. We must expect men to wish back again the light that is gone, and to try to bring it back. But however they may wish and try, the light will not shine again,—not at least in the civilization to which we belong.

Another remedy commonly proposed is that we should turn to science itself, or the scientific spirit, for our salvation. Mr. Russell and Professor Dewey both make this proposal, though in somewhat different ways. Professor Dewey seems to believe that discoveries in sociology, the application of scientific method to social and political problems, will rescue us. This seems to me to be utterly naïve. It is not likely that science, which is basically the cause of our spiritual troubles, is likely also to produce the cure for them. Also it lies in the nature of science that, though it can teach us the best means for achieving our ends, it can never tell us what ends to pursue. It cannot give us any ideals. And our trouble is about ideals and ends, not about the means for reaching them.

V

No civilization can live without ideals, or to put it in another way, without a firm faith in moral ideas. Our ideals and moral ideas have in the past been rooted in religion. But the religious basis of our ideals has been undermined, and the superstructure of ideals is plainly tottering. None of the commonly suggested remedies on examination seems likely to succeed. It would therefore look as if the early death of our civilization were inevitable.

Of course we know that it is perfectly possible for individual men, very highly educated men, philosophers, scientists, intellectuals in general, to live moral lives without any religious convictions. But the question is whether a whole civilization, a whole family of peoples, composed almost entirely of relatively uneducated men and women, can do this.

It follows, of course, that if we could make the vast majority of men as highly educated as the very few are now, we might save the situation. And we are already moving slowly in that direction through the techniques of mass education. But the critical question seems to concern the time-lag. Perhaps in a few hundred years most of the population will, at the present rate, be sufficiently highly educated and civilized to combine high ideals with an absence of religion. But long before we reach any such stage, the collapse of our civilization may have come about. How are we to live through the intervening period?

I am sure that the first thing we have to do is to face the truth, however bleak it may be, and then next we have to learn to live with it. Let me say a word about each of these two points. What I am urging as regards the first is complete honesty. Those who wish to resurrect Christian dogmas are not, of course, consciously dishonest. But they have that kind of unconscious dishonesty which consists in lulling oneself with opiates and dreams. Those who talk of a new religion are merely hoping for a new opiate. Both alike refuse to face the truth that there is, in the universe outside man, no spirituality, no regard for values, no friend in the sky, no help or comfort for man of any sort. To be perfectly honest in the admission of this fact, not to seek shelter in new or old illusions, not to indulge in wishful dreams about this matter, this is the first thing we shall have to do.

I do not urge this course out of any special regard for the sanctity of truth in the abstract. It is not self-evident to me that truth is the supreme value to which all else must be sacrificed. Might not the discoverer of a truth which would be fatal to mankind be justified in suppressing it, even in teaching men a falsehood? Is truth more valuable than goodness and beauty and happiness? To think so is to invent yet another absolute, another religious delusion in which Truth with a capital T is substituted for God. The reason why we must now boldly and honestly face the truth that the universe is non-spiritual and indifferent to goodness, beauty, happiness, or truth is not that it would be wicked to suppress it, but simply that it is too late to do so, so that in the end we cannot do anything else but face it. Yet we stand on the brink, dreading the icy plunge. We need courage. We need honesty.

Now about the other point, the necessity of learning to live with the truth. This means learning to live virtuously and happily, or at least contentedly, without illusions. And this is going to be extremely difficult because what we have now begun dimly to perceive is that human life in the past, or at least human happiness, has almost wholly depended upon illusions. It has been said that man lives by truth, and that the truth will make us free. Nearly the opposite seems to me to be the case. Mankind has managed to live only by means of lies, and the truth may very well destroy us. If one were a Bergsonian one might believe that nature deliberately puts illusions into our souls in order to induce us to go on living.

The illusions by which men have lived seem to be of two kinds. First, there is what one may perhaps call the Great Illusion—I mean the religious illusion that the universe is moral and good, that it follows a wise and noble plan, that it is gradually generating some supreme value, that goodness is bound to triumph in it. Secondly, there is a whole host of minor illusions on which human happiness nourishes itself. How much of human happiness notoriously comes from the illusions of the lover about his beloved? Then again we work and strive because of the illusions connected with fame, glory, power, or money. Banners of all kinds, flags, emblems, insignia, ceremonials, and rituals are invariably symbols of some illusion or other. The British Empire, the connection between mother country and dominions, is partly kept going by illusions surrounding the notion of kingship. Or think of the vast amount of human happiness which is derived from the illusion of supposing that if some nonsense syllable, such as "sir" or "count" or "lord" is pronounced in conjunction with our names, we belong to a superior order of people.

There is plenty of evidence that human happiness is almost wholly based upon illusions of one kind or another. But the scientific spirit, or the spirit of truth, is the enemy of illusions and therefore the enemy of human happiness. That is why it is going to be so difficult to live with the truth.

There is no reason why we should have to give up the host of minor illusions which render life supportable. There is no reason why the lover should be scientific about the loved one. Even the illusions of fame and glory may persist. But without the Great Illusion, the illusion of a good, kindly, and purposeful universe, we shall *have* to learn to live. And to ask this is really no more than to ask that we become genuinely civilized beings and not merely sham civilized beings.

I can best explain the difference by a reminiscence. I remember a fellow student in my college days, an ardent Christian, who told me that if he did not believe in a future life, in heaven and hell, he would rape, murder, steal, and be a drunkard. That is what I call being a sham civilized being. On the other hand, not only could a Huxley, a John Stuart Mill, a David Hume, live great and fine lives without any religion, but a great many others of us, quite obscure persons, can at least live decent lives without it.

To be genuinely civilized means to be able to walk straightly and to live honorably without the props and crutches of one or another of the childish dreams which have so far supported men. That such a life is likely to be ecstatically happy I will not claim. But that it can be lived in quiet content, accepting resignedly what cannot be helped, not expecting the impossible, and thankful for small mercies, this I would maintain. That it will be difficult for men in general to learn this lesson I do not deny. But that it will be impossible I would not admit since so many have learned it already.

Man has not yet grown up. He is not adult. Like a child he cries for the moon and lives in a world of fantasies. And the race as a whole has perhaps reached the great crisis of its life. Can it grow up as a race in the same sense as individual men grow up? Can man put away childish things and adolescent dreams? Can he grasp the real world as it actually is, stark and bleak, without its romantic or religious halo, and still retain his ideals, striving for great ends and noble achievements? If he can, all may yet be well. If he cannot, he will probably sink back into the savagery and brutality from which he came, taking a humble place once more among the lower animals.

Problems for Thought and Writing

I

1. Why does Stace maintain that our ideals, in the modern world, "must proceed only from our own minds"? In the answer to that question lies the central issue of Stace's article. What has caused this condition? Can our "own minds" be a valid reference point for a system of values, or must we root that system in some reality, or supposed reality, outside ourselves? Is Stace agreeing with Muller's declaration that "The only possible virtue in being a civilized man . . . is in being a free, responsible individual with a mind of one's own" (pages 662-63)?

2. Stace sees the loss of faith in a "cosmic purpose" as the main disruptive influence in the modern world. But was that faith in its full flower entirely good? If it was untrue *scientifically* could it possibly be good? Or are there some illusions which men should never try to live without?

3. What is the difference between inquiry into "causes" and inquiry into "purposes"? On that difference, says Stace, hangs the difference between the old world and the new. Why should the distinction be so important?

4. How is the "dissatisfied, disillusioned, restless spirit of modern man" reflected in modern art and literature? Would you say "The Love Song of J. Alfred Prufrock" (page 677) is an expression of this spirit?

5. Who were Galileo, Copernicus, Kepler, Newton, Whitehead, Bertrand Russell, Hume, Hobbes? Identify some of their more conspicuous discoveries or beliefs.

6. Stace feels that "ethical relativity" is destructive of any *practical* moral system. Why should Stace take such a serious view of the situation?

7. Stace maintains that the idea that man is "the helpless plaything of forces over which he has no control, has deeply penetrated the modern mind." Do any of Fromm's remarks (page 198) add weight to this generalization?

Do you feel that you are not free to exercise your own will? Does the psychiatrist operate on that assumption or on an opposite assumption?

8. What are Stace's solutions to the problems he raises? Stace tells us what we must live *without,* but does he tell us what we should live *for?* Has he any positive solutions?

II

9. The five parts of Stace's essay separate five distinct stages in his thought. What are those stages? Is there any rational or artistic plan apparent in this arrangement?

10. Mr. Stace is a professor of philosophy at Princeton University. A philosopher, like a scientist, strives for objectivity in his investigations and insists upon precise definition of terms. Has Stace been entirely objective here? Has he anywhere been guilty of hasty or loose generalizations?

11. Identify or define: existentialist, atheist, positivist, scepticism, final causes, omniscient, quintessence, rationalization, anthropologist, ethnologist, determinism.

~

THE MEANING OF HISTORY *
Herbert J. Muller

Time will tell, we say; but we may not be aware of the difference that is made by our very conception of time. To the Greeks and Romans time was characteristically a slow but inexorable enemy of man, telling the destruction of all his work. To the Hindu sage it was static or illusory, resembling a deep pool rather than a flow or a river; so the splash of history made ripples that vanished as they spread, distracting only the foolish. To the modern Westerner, on the contrary, time is all-important. He tells it, keeps it, lives by it punctually. In America he has a passion for making it and saving it (though what he saves it for may not be clear). It has been his great hope, in its promise of ever bigger and better things to come. And if he is now much less hopeful he has a more vivid sense of the horrors that time may bring. For him, in any event, things always keep moving. Time Marches On!

In short, our feeling about time—however vague or unconscious—

* From *The Uses of the Past* by Herbert J. Muller. Copyright 1952 by Oxford University Press, Inc. Reprinted by permission.

ultimately involves a philosophy of history. It leads to a momentous question. Given all the drama of human history, what is the plot, the grand design, the final meaning of the whole show? Positivists will tell us that this is a meaningless question. Manifestly we cannot give it a precise, positive answer: we cannot state it in terms that permit either empirical verification or rigorous logical analysis. But neither can we escape it. Although we naturally come to it as we hope to make sense of history, we are forced to consider it if only because men persist in answering it. Thus Westerners have declared that history is a progress, and in this faith have made extraordinary history. Today Communists are still so positive the drama will have a happy ending, in a classless society, that they threaten to precipitate a war which might make any society impossible, put a literal end to history. Others have therefore been led to reject the whole faith in progress—and their negations may also have positive consequences. Time will tell in any case; but what it will tell depends on what men say and do right now.

This is to reject the Indian view that history is mere appearance or illusion. In certain moods, to be sure, we all know the feeling that the 'real' reality is changeless and timeless—the feeling of eternity as a quality of the present, which is perhaps the most valid intimation of immortality. Even so worldly a philosopher as Bertrand Russell has said that 'there is some sense, easier to feel than to state, in which Time is an unimportant and superficial characteristic of reality'; and almost all the wise men have agreed that wisdom begins with a realization of its unimportance.[1] Still, Westerners have good reason for sticking to their senses as they do. The very insistence of the Hindu sages on the necessity of renouncing or transcending the temporal world, and their arduous disciplines for shaking off the illusions of sense, indicate that this world is real enough. And as students of history, at any rate, we are bound to take time seriously. The pertinent theories of history concern dramas that are played out in time, by flesh and blood actors, on a real stage. The most common theories involve three main kinds of movement in time—progress, decline, and cycle. Because the idea of progress is so familiar, we may forget that it is a very novel Western idea, only a few centuries old; so we might first consider the alternative theories, which have

[1] A further difficulty with the Western man's common-sense notion of time is that if he begins to think seriously about it, he soon runs into the unthinkable. He cannot really conceive an eternal universe: it must have a beginning, if not an end; yet neither can he conceive of the state before the beginning, or after the end. Time cannot march on forever, but neither can it stop.

the prestige of endorsement by the most illustrious thinkers of the past.

As I have already indicated, the theory of decline is the hoariest theory of history. Men used to locate Utopia in the remote past instead of the future—as in the Garden of Eden of Babylonian-Hebrew mythology, or the Golden Age of Hesiod. Even the sophisticated literature of the Greco-Roman world is shot through with the notion that civilization is a disease or degeneration. (Lovejoy and Boas offer a comprehensive account of the early career of this theory in their *Primitivism and Related Ideas in Antiquity.*) Although it was generally assumed that the utopian simple life had actually been lived somewhere, the conceptions of it varied widely. Hedonists pictured it as a carefree life in which men were good and happy; Stoics pictured it as a hard, rugged life that bred the manly virtues wanting in their effete society. Usually primitivism was an earnest criticism and exhortation, implying that man could mend his civilized ways; but the explicit conclusion was usually a gloomy belief that he lacked the sense to do so, implying that civilization is an incurable disease. A similar diversity appears in modern versions. Dostoyevsky and Tolstoy found their ideal in primitive Christianity, and their hope in the Russian peasant; whereas D. H. Lawrence glorified the intuitive, instinctive life or 'phallic consciousness,' but could never find a satisfactory historical model.

As all this implies, theories of decline cannot be taken seriously as literal outlines of history. There is no evidence whatever of the historical existence of a Garden of Eden or Golden Age, or of an ideal primitive stage in evolution. Such fictions may be useful as metaphors, symbolizing the actual corruptions of civilization and the natural corruptibility of man, but it is essential to remember that they are fictions, pure and rather too simple. Usually they reflect a shallow view of history, or a sheer ignorance of it.[2]

Hence the deepest thought of antiquity led rather to the conclusion that history is an endless cycle. Aristotle saw a continuous 'coming to be and falling away'; he speculated that there had already been countless civilizations, which had passed through a uniform

---

[2] A modern version typical of such fictions was a recent speech by the president of an alumni association. He edified the old grads with an account of the golden age of our society, which he dated about 1910—with no hint that this businessman's Eden was breeding its own serpents, and that its fruit was war and depression. Although his speech was no doubt inspired by the beery sentimentality appropriate to alumni reunions, it expressed the sober attitude of many business leaders, congressmen, and newspaper publishers.

destiny. Stoics and Epicureans alike dwelt on the inevitable recurrences. The rational soul, wrote Marcus Aurelius, 'considers the periodic destructions and rebirths of the universe, and reflects that our posterity will see nothing new, and that our ancestors saw nothing greater than we have seen.' Or in the words of Ecclesiastes, 'The thing that hath been, it is that which shall be; and that which is done is that which shall be done; and there is no new thing under the sun.' This theory of cycles has been maintained by such Western thinkers as Bodin, Vico, and Nietzsche, and in our time has been given its most systematic, comprehensive formulation in Spengler's *Decline of the West*. Spengler argued that all civilizations necessarily pass through parallel stages and necessarily die a natural death—unless (like the Aztec) they are prematurely destroyed by accident.

Whether one is comforted or depressed by this fatalistic view of history is presumably a matter of temperament. Most thinkers have chosen to dwell on its pessimistic implications. The cycles appear to be rhymes without reason, even when God is made their author. The eternal inanity of the cosmic process is most conspicuous in the Hindu and Buddhist versions, as summarized by Sir Charles Eliot: 'An infinite number of times the Universe has collapsed in flaming or watery ruin, aeons of quiescence follow the collapse, and then the Deity (he has done it an infinite number of times) emits again from himself worlds and souls of the same old kind.' Babylonian and Aztec myths likewise stressed the melancholy idea that the cycles are punctuated by universal catastrophes. Men are most disposed to take such a view of history, moreover, when they believe that their society is on the downswing, headed for catastrophe. Like the primitivists, the 'cyclists' usually believed that the best days were behind them, and they had even less hope of the future. So we have the curious spectacle of civilized man forever marching with his face turned backward—as no doubt the cave-man looked back to the good old days when men were free to roam instead of being stuck in a damn hole in the ground. And so the theory of cycles has again become seductive, as men again fear the worst. Spengler, Sorokin, and Toynbee have presented different versions of it, but all agree that the West is on the decline.

The most obvious argument for this theory is its correspondence with the processes of birth, growth, decay, and death in the natural world. Given the fate of all other higher organisms, it seems reasonable to assume that a civilization cannot maintain itself indefinitely, but in time must age and die. Offhand, the theory also corresponds with the actual history of civilizations to date: all but our own have died, or have been dying. (Thus we have unearthed several of Aristotle's 'lost' civilizations, such as the ancient Indic and the Minoan, and in the huge statues on Easter Island see evidence that there might once have been a high civilization in the South Pacific area.) Everywhere we find a monotonous recurrence of the basic themes of selfishness and greed, fear and hate. But most pertinent is the evidence of cyclical movements within civilizations, the familiar patterns of rise and fall. In *Configurations of Cultural Growth*, A. L. Kroeber surveys the major cultural achievements of all the great societies; and the most striking fact that emerges from his anthropological study is the fact of configuration and cycle.

About 1400, for example, the notable Dutch-Flemish school of painters arose suddenly, out of nowhere, with the Van Eycks; about 1700 the whole movement ended as suddenly, for Rembrandt, Hals, Teniers, Ruysdael, and the rest had died within a few years of one another; and ever since there has been practically no Dutch-Flemish painting of consequence. So it has been with all the major growths in art, literature, philosophy, and science. This phenomenon of the golden age is so familiar that we may forget how strange it is. All our knowledge of genetics indicates that the appearance of genius in any given society should be more or less constant—yet it never has been. Except for a very few isolated great men, such as John Scotus Erigena, genius has appeared only when there was a movement afoot; most potential greatness evidently goes to waste. And the movements appear to have specific limits as well as potentialities: they move to fulfilment, and then to exhaustion. All this implies a kind of predestination that Kroeber regrets. Nevertheless 'the empirical data, over and over again, and with really remarkably few exceptions, compel the conclusion that there are whole arrays of events in the history of culture which are objectively describable only in terms of the metaphors of "growth," "realization," "exhaustion," and "death," as our vocabulary stands today.'

This much seems clear. The picture as a whole, however, is not at all clear. Although we can make out configurations everywhere, they are irregular in their growth, diverse in their content, and inconstant in their associations. After medieval philosophy reached the end of its development, about 1350, there was no important philosophy in all Europe until the rise of the moderns with Descartes, after 1600; yet this long slump coincided with the Renaissance, a period of abounding intellectual activity. Kroeber's survey indicates

that such apparent anomalies are the rule. Ancient Greece has fixed
the common notion of a golden age as a rich growth in all fields of
art and thought, a whole culture on the surge; but this glory has so
profoundly impressed men because it was indeed unique. Thus the
splendid Elizabethan Age produced no painting or sculpture to
speak of, whereas the splendor of the Italian Renaissance was largely
confined to the representative arts. Similarly there are conspicuous
gaps in great civilizations. Egypt, Mesopotamia, and Japan produced no significant philosophy, Rome no science, Islam no painting,
sculpture, or drama.[3] Furthermore, the golden ages of culture appear
to have no necessary connection with national expansion. Greek culture flowered before and after the little city-states had their brief
hour of military glory; the Italians made their greatest contributions
when their cities were torn by civil war and largely dominated by
other countries; the Germans led all Europe under Beethoven, Goethe,
and Kant while they were being overrun by Napoleon's armies, and
their great creative period was over by 1870, when their great national expansion began.

Altogether, Kroeber can make out no 'true law' in cultural history:
'nothing cyclical, regularly repetitive, or necessary.' And in the
history of whole civilizations, regular cycles are still harder to find.
Civilizations are much less discrete and homogeneous than the
cyclical theory presupposes, and their geographical, political, and
cultural components do not have a uniform destiny. (We have already seen that when 'Rome' fell, its Eastern Empire lived on.) Historians cannot even agree on their location in time and space—Toynbee makes out at least twice as many civilizations as Spengler did.
Neither can they agree on criteria for marking the peak of a society,
or on the symptoms of growth and decay. And most dubious are
the neat parallels, the efforts to make all societies swing through
exactly the same cycle. On the face of it, civilizations start at different points, building on different pasts in different environments, ex-
ploiting different possibilities. Spengler, the most systematic exponent of this theory, kept his cycles orderly only by a Teutonic

---

3 With Islam, an obvious explanation is the Mohammedan law prohibiting the
representation of the human form; but since native sculpture had been dead in
this region long before this taboo, its absence might be considered the reason for
the taboo. Kroeber warns against the conventional 'explanations' in our texts.
Although Elizabethan drama, for example, is usually explained by the defeat of
the Spanish Armada, it might be as reasonable to explain the defeat by the rise of
Elizabethan poetry. The truth probably is that both were manifestations of some
deeper cause that has yet to be defined.

forcing and drilling of the facts, with a ruthless suppression of all unruly facts.

Above all, the *necessity* of the cycles is unproved, and unprovable on the basis of present knowledge. The only cause suggested by Spengler is a biological analogy that cannot bear scientific analysis. 'The Biology of the future,' he declared, 'will undoubtedly find the point of departure for an entirely new formulation of its problems in the concept of the preordained life-span of the genus and species'— a span, he added, which is 'a numerical value of almost mystical significance.' Mystical is strictly the word for it. Biology gives no signs of accommodating him; and even if it attempted this new departure (or aspired to the exaltation of a capital B) it would not prove his point, since a society is neither a genus nor a species.

What biology still does teach is the theory of evolution; and this brings us back to the modern theory of progress. Although past societies were often complacent enough about their superiority over barbarians, there are only a few scattered hints of any hope for continuous advance. The nearest thing to it was the Hebrew vision of the Messiah, which bred the Christian visions of the Millennium and the Second Coming, but these all depended upon a direct intervention by God; they stirred no hope that man, by his own efforts, could achieve a steady improvement of his earthly condition. Only with the rise of science did men begin to entertain seriously the possibility of progress. At length the possibility was transformed into a gospel, a certainty. History became a success story, of a race that was bound to make good. 'Progress is not an accident but a necessity,' proclaimed Herbert Spencer. 'What we call evil and immorality must disappear. It is certain that man must become perfect. . . . Always toward perfection is the mighty movement.'

Now in the long evolutionary view, reaching back to the caveman and ape-man, there unquestionably has been progress—always granted the assumption that it is worth being a human being. Man has achieved greater mastery of his natural environment, greater freedom of action, and thereupon has discovered the finer possibilities of life implicit in his distinctive power of consciousness. In historic times there have been clear gains in intellectual and spiritual as well as material wealth and power. Christian thinkers who now ridicule the faith in progress forget the assumption of progress in their own concept of 'higher' religions, and of the progressive revelations of God through Abraham, Moses, and Christ; and hardly any thinker will deny that the religion of Jesus is loftier than that of Moloch. If all specific gains are disputable, there remains the general advance that man has made, from blind obedience to the totems and taboos of the tribe to conscious, reasoned loyalty to ideals of humanity. All the savagery that persists seems more frightful because it no longer seems inevitable or proper. In general, the tragic failures of civilization have left substantial residues of knowledge, skills, arts, ideas, ideals —of enduring goods that men do not willingly give up, once they are known, but that we are apt to forget because we take them for granted.

Simply as we cherish the possibilities of progress, however, we must severely qualify the popular notions about them. The progress has not been steady or in a straight line: history is not a succession of civilizations rising to ever greater heights, coming ever closer to the distinction of having produced us. The progress has not been progress pure and simple: all the gains in freedom and power have enabled men to do more evil as well as good, to destroy as well as create. Above all, the progress has not been automatic and inevitable: it has resulted from arduous human effort, an 'expense of greatness' that has often been squandered by later generations. Hence continued progress is not guaranteed by any known law of nature. Nothing in history assures the success of our civilization; history tells us only that the incalculable possibilities open to us are more likely to be for worse than for better. Nothing in biology assures the indefinite progress or even the indefinite survival of the human race; devolution or extinction has been the common fate of the more complex forms of life, while the simple amoeba is a good bet to last to the end. At that, the exciting story of the evolution of life is a local affair, an interlude confined to a speck in interstellar space. Those who make 'emergent evolution' the key to the cosmic plan have little more scientific authority than the Book of Revelation; for our most certain knowledge indicates that all life on this planet is ultimately doomed to extinction, and that its disappearance will make no apparent difference to the universe. The only enduring result of man's works, Santayana has said, is that the earth may cast a slightly different shadow on the moon.

*   *   *

What, then, is the meaning of history? The answer presumably should come at the end of this work, where conclusions belong. My conclusions were in fact modified during the course of my studies, and will be restated at the end. Yet it would be idle to pretend that we are now to embark on a voyage of exploration, with no idea of our destination. My answer has been implicit in all that I have written so far, and will determine the content of the chapters that follow. It amounts to a basic assumption, a premise that should be laid face up on the table. Briefly, my answer is at once a negation and an affirmation. History has no meaning, in the sense of a clear pattern or determinate plot; but it is not simply meaningless or pointless. It has no certain meaning because man is free to give it various possible meanings.

His freedom is sharply limited, of course. Man has to choose within the conditions imposed by his biological structure, his natural environment, and his cultural heritage. He cannot do whatever he has a mind to, and at that his mind has been largely made up by his ancestors. For such reasons he is always prone to believe that history somehow makes itself, in spite of his efforts, by the automatic operation of natural laws or God's will. Still, at any moment he has a wide range of choices and is willy-nilly making more history, discovering the meanings of his past and determining the meanings of his future. The most significant 'facts' he has to face are of man's own making. Marxism, for all its theoretical determinism, is the clearest illustration of how history is made by men's beliefs about what has happened, what is happening, and what should happen.

This insistence on human freedom is not simply cheering. It means that we have to keep making history, instead of leaning on it, and that we can never count on a final solution. It means the constant possibility of foolish or even fatal choices. Yet the dignity of man lies precisely in this power to choose his destiny. We may therefore welcome the conclusion that we cannot foretell the future, even apart from the possibility that it may not bear knowing. Uncertainty is not only the plainest condition of human life but the necessary condition of freedom, of aspiration, of conscience—of all human idealism.

It is the business of the future to be dangerous, Whitehead remarked; and we can always trust it to keep on the job. I again stress the uncertainties, however, because the dangers are always intensified by the pretensions to absolute certainty or finality. These are the ultimate source of corruption, the reason why the best becomes the worst and crusaders for heaven make a hell on earth. And none is more insidious than the principle of historical predestination. Knowing in advance how history is going to turn out, men climb on the bandwagon, ride the wave of the future.[4] They can then indulge any policy, from supine resignation to ruthless violence. So the Communists can justify the most barbarous behavior: like hangmen, they are merely executing 'the verdict of history.' They corrupt morality at its very base by implying that it is man's duty to fight for the inevitable, or that historic might makes right. Even in self-sacrifice they are profoundly irresponsible. Our business as rational beings is not to argue for what is going to be but to strive for what ought to be, in the consciousness that it will never be all we would like it to be.

Among the possible 'meanings' of history—to restate my premises in these terms—the most significant is the growth of this power of self-determination, or freedom to make history. I assume that for interpreting the past and choosing a future we must begin with a full acknowledgment of the claims of reason: a humble reason that makes no claim to finality or metaphysical certitude, because such claims cannot be rationally substantiated, and that recognizes its finiteness and fallibility; a proud reason that nevertheless maintains its authority as the final judge of all claims to truth, insisting that its tested knowledge is no less real and reliable because it is not a knowledge of ultimate reality, and that only by a further exercise of reason can its limitations and its fallacies be clearly discerned. We are not forced to choose between reason and faith in the conventional sense—we may choose between more or less reasonable faiths. The ideal of rationality in turn requires the ideal of freedom, the right to be an individual. A rational person is not merely one who has good habits or right principles, but one who knows what he believes and assumes the intellectual and moral responsibilities of his beliefs; and first he must be free to think for himself, make up his own mind. Although non-rational behavior may exhibit admirable qualities, such as the loyalty, fortitude, and daring found in barbarians, or even in the animal world, these qualities are not wholly admirable, or trustworthy, unless they are conscious, responsible choices. The only possible virtue in being a civilized man instead

----

[4] James Burnham is especially agile in the performance of this feat. In the name of hard-boiled realism, he has so far ridden at least three waves—the Marxist revolution, the managerial revolution, and the imperial destiny of America. Presumably he has a weather eye open for the next wave; but meanwhile he still tends to deride visionary idealists who are more interested in making history than in predicting it.

of a barbarian, an ignoramus, or a moron is in being a free, responsible individual with a mind of one's own.

The best society, accordingly, is that which is most conducive to the growth of such persons. It is what Karl Popper has called the 'open society.'[5] It is an adventurous society that has broken with the universal, prehistoric custom of regarding ancient customs as magical or sacred, that views its institutions as man-made for human purposes and examines their suitability for these purposes, that welcomes variety and change instead of enforcing rigid conformity, and that accordingly provides its members with personal opportunities and responsibilities beyond mere obedience. It is Athens as opposed to Sparta.

Today it is us; and thereby hangs our tale. Because we have made the farthest advance toward the open society we are likely to feel more impotent than men have ever felt before. The novel idea of progress, or simply of 'opportunity,' has been so deeply engrained in our everyday thought and feeling that we are incapable of passive acceptance and endurance; in a crisis we take for granted the possibility and the need of 'doing something about it.' Having accumulated a vast deal of sociological and historical knowledge, we are also more aware of the difficulty of doing anything about it, and are more critical of the simple faiths that once made it easier for men to do or die for God, king, and country. We bear the cross of consciousness. In a fuller consciousness the burden may be eased—and this is the reason for the chapters that follow. Our adventure in freedom is so recent that what appear to be our death rattles may be growing pains. But in any event the pains are unavoidable. For a society as for an individual, the hardest problems begin with freedom. Today the future of the open society is wide open, to triumphs or to disasters of a magnitude hitherto undreamed of.

Problems for Thought and Writing

I

1. What does Muller mean by saying that our feeling about time "ultimately involves a philosophy of history"?

2. To what extent do you think the idea of "progress"—so generally held by the West—is the result of having, for the last few hundred years, an ever-expanding frontier? Do you feel that progress is inevitable or an illusion?

[5] *The Open Society and Its Enemies,* London, 1945. Popper is somewhat unfair to its enemies, of whom he makes Plato No. 1. Otherwise his book is a cogent argument for the views I am expressing here.

3. What three philosophies of history does Muller deal with?

4. What is your reaction to Muller's remark that accounts of a Garden of Eden or a Golden Age are "fictions, pure and rather too simple," and "may be useful as metaphors, symbolizing the actual corruptions of civilization and the natural corruptibility of man, but [that] it is essential to remember that they are fictions."

5. This essay, part of a chapter from Professor Muller's book, is an example of an attempt to evaluate the whole course of history. In what respect does Muller's evaluation of history correspond to that of Gilson (page 635)? Would the "decline" of modern civilization be accounted for in the same way by Gilson as by historians like Spengler?

6. Is Spengler's analogy (page 659) "false" in the sense stated by Davis (page 81)?

7. "Nothing in history assures the success of our civilization; history tells us only that the incalculable possibilities open to us are more likely to be for worse than better." Do you find any evidence that our American civilization as a whole is accepting or rejecting this idea? What is the dominant mood as expressed by radio, television, newspapers, advertisers?

8. What, in brief, does Muller think the "meaning of history" is? Does Muller believe in free will or is he a determinist? Give a carefully qualified answer.

9. "We are not forced to choose between reason or faith in the conventional sense—we may choose between more or less reasonable faiths. The ideal of rationality in turn requires the ideal of freedom, the right to be an individual." Would Muller agree with Jung (page 333) and Barrett (page 348) in their emphasis on the importance of the *irrational*? Could Muller as an historian accept Jung's idea that the modern Western world is experiencing a revolutionary change in its subconscious? Is Muller ignoring the historical problems raised by Mowrer (page 238)?

10. Why does Muller suggest that we are "incapable of passive acceptance and endurance"? How is this condition an aspect of the "open" society?

11. Would you call Muller an absolutist or a relativist? Is he an optimist or pessimist? Is there anything unexpected in the conjunction of the two positions?

II

12. Compare and/or contrast the historical styles of Muller and Adams (page 260). Are the styles in and of themselves reflections of their points of view?

13. Identify or define: intimation, open society, Hesiod, hedonist, *Ecclesiastes*, inanity, phallic, Minoan, Teniers, configurations, Herbert Spencer, Karl Popper.

~

WHY DO WE
TEACH POETRY?*
Archibald MacLeish

There is something about the art of poetry which induces a defensive posture. Even in the old days when the primacy of poetry was no more challenged than the primacy of Heaven, which is now also ·challenged, the posture was habitual. If you published your reflections on the art in those days you called them a *Defense*. Today, when the queen of sciences is Science, you do not perhaps employ that term but you mean it. It is not that the gentlemen at the long table in the Faculty Club whose brains have been officially cleared to serve as depositories of scientific secrets of the eighth and thirteenth classes are patronizing in their manner. They are still gentlemen and therefore still modest no matter how great their distinction or how greatly certified. But one knows one's place. One knows that whereas the teachers of science meet to hear of new triumphs which the newspapers will proudly report, the teachers of poetry meet to ask old questions—which no one will report: such questions as, why teach poetry anyway in a time like this?

It is a relief in this general atmosphere to come upon someone who feels no defensiveness whatever: who is perfectly certain that poetry ought to be taught now as at any other time and who is perfectly certain also that he knows why. The paragon I have in mind is a young friend of mine, a devoted teacher, who was recently made headmaster of one of the leading American preparatory schools, and who has been taking stock, for some time past, of his curriculum and his faculty. Poetry, as he sees it, ought to be taught "as a most essential form of human expression as well as a carrier throughout the ages of some of the most important values in our heritage." What troubles him is that few teachers, at least in the schools he knows, seem to share his conviction. He is not too sure that teachers themselves have "an abiding and missionary faith in poetry" which would lead them to see it as a great clarifier—a "human language" capable of competing with the languages and mathematics and science.

But though teachers lack the necessary faith, the fault, as my young friend sees it, is not wholly theirs. The fault is the fault of modern criticism, which has turned poetry into something he calls "poetry itself"—meaning, I suppose, poetry for poetry's sake. "Poetry itself" turns out to be poetry with its meanings distilled away, and poetry with its meanings distilled away is difficult if not impossible to teach in a secondary school—at least *his* secondary school. The result is that secondary school teachers have gone back, as to the lesser of two evils, to those historical and anecdotal practices sanctified by American graduate schools in generations past. They teach "poets and not poetry." With the result that "students become acquainted with poets from Homer to MacLeish" (quite a distance no matter how you measure it!) "but the experience doesn't necessarily leave them with increased confidence in what poetry has to offer." I can well believe it.

The reason why modern criticism has this disastrous effect, the reason why it produces "an almost morbid apathy toward 'content' or 'statement of idea,'" is its excessive "preoccupation with aesthetic values." Modern criticism insists that poems are primarily works of art; and when you insist that poems are primarily works of art you cannot, in my friend's view, teach them as carriers "throughout the ages of some of the most important values in our heritage." What is important about Homer and Shakespeare and the authors of the Bible is that they were "realists with great vision . . . whose work contains immensely valuable constructions of the meaning of life"; and if you talk too much about them as artists, those constructions of the meaning of life get lost.

Now this, you will observe, is not merely another walloping of the old horse who was once called the New Criticism. It goes a great deal farther. It is a frontal attack upon a general position maintained by many who never accepted the New Criticism or even heard of it. It is an attack upon those who believe—as most poets, I think, have believed—that a poem *is* primarily a work of art and must be read as a work of art if it is to be read at all. It is a high-minded and disinterested attack delivered for the noblest of purposes, but an attack notwithstanding—and an effective one. What it contends is that an approach to poetry which insists that a poem is a work of art blocks off what the poem has to say, whereas what the poem has to say is the principal reason for teaching it. What the argument comes down to, in other words, is the proposition that it is a mistake, in teaching poetry, to insist that poetry is art, because, if you do so insist, you will not be able to bring your students to the mean-

ing of the poem, the idea of the poem, what the poem has to tell
• them about man and world and life and death—and it is for these
things the teaching of the poem is important.

Now, I can understand this argument and can respect the reasons
for making it. Far too many of those who define poetry in exclusively
artistic terms use their definition as a limiting and protective statement which relieves them of all obligation to drive the poem's meanings beyond the meanings of the poem: beyond the mere translation
of the symbols and metaphors and the classical or other references—
the whole apparatus of *explication du texte*. Far too many, indeed,
of those who have to do with literature generally in our time, and
particularly with modern literature, consider that meanings in any
but a literary (which includes a Freudian) sense are not only outside,
but beneath, their proper concern—that the intrusion of questions of
morality and religion into the world of art is a kind of trespass and
that works of literary art not only should but *can* be studied in a
moral vacuum. Literature in the hands of such teachers is well on
the way to becoming again that "terrible queen" which the men of
the nineties raised above life and which Yeats, when he outgrew the
men of the nineties, rejected.

But although I can understand this argument, and although I can
respect its reasons, and although I believe it raises a true issue and
an important issue, I cannot accept it; for it rests, or seems to me to
rest, on two quite dubious assumptions. The first is the assumption,
familiar in one form or another to all of us, that the "idea" of a work
of art is somehow separable from the work of art itself. The most
recent—and most egregious—expression of this persistent notion comes
from a distinguished Dean of Humanities in a great institution of
learning who is reported by the New York *Times* to have argued in
a scholarly gathering that "the idea which the reader derives from
Ernest Hemingway's *The Old Man and the Sea* comes after the
reader has absorbed some 60,000 words. This takes at least an
hour. . . . A similar understanding could come after a few minutes'
study of a painting by a skillful artist." Precisely, one imagines, as
the Doré illustrations gave one the "idea" of the *Inferno* in a few
easy looks!

It is the second assumption, however, which divides me most emphatically from my young friend. For the second assumption seems
to be that *unless* idea and work of art are distinguished from each
other in the teaching of a poem, the idea—and so the effectiveness of

the teaching—will be lost. At this point my friend and I part company. I am ready, and more than ready, to agree that it is for the meanings of life that one reads (and teaches) poetry. But I am unable to see how there can be a distinction between a poem as a conveyer of such meanings and a poem as a work of art. In brief, the distinction between art and knowledge which is made throughout my friend's argument seems to me wholly without foundation. That it is a distinction almost universally recognized in our epoch I know well enough. Science makes it. Poetry makes it. And the world agrees with both. "Whatever can be *known*," says Bertrand Russell, "can be known by means of science." Poetry, say its professors, has no "messages" to deliver. And no one dissents from either. The exclusive proprietary right of science to know and to communicate knowledge is not only commonly recognized in our civilization: in a very real sense it is our civilization. For the characteristic of our civilization—that which distinguishes it from the civilizations which have preceded it—is the characteristic which knowledge-by-science has conferred upon it: its abstractness.

But though the agreement is general, the proposition is not one I can accept. I argue that the apologists for science are not justified in claiming, nor the apologists for poetry in admitting, the sole right of science to know. I insist that poetry is also capable of knowledge; that poetry, indeed, is capable of a kind of knowledge of which science is not capable; that it is capable of that knowledge *as poetry;* and that the teaching of poetry as poetry, the teaching of poem as work of art, is not only not incompatible with the teaching of poetry as knowledge but is, indeed, the only possible way of teaching poetry as knowledge.

To most of us, brought up as we have been in the world of abstractions which science has prepared for us, and in the kind of school which that world produces—schools in which almost all teaching is teaching of abstractions—the notion of poetry as knowledge, the notion of art as knowledge, is a fanciful notion. Knowledge by abstraction we understand. Science can abstract ideas about apple from apple. It can organize those ideas into knowledge about apple. It can then, by some means, introduce that knowledge into our heads —possibly because our heads are abstractions also. But poetry, we know, does not abstract. Poetry presents. Poetry presents the thing as the thing. And that it should be possible to *know* the thing *as the thing it is*—to *know* apple *as* apple—this we do not understand; this, the true child of the time will assure you, cannot be done. To the true child of abstraction you can't know apple as apple. You can't know tree as tree. You can't know man as man. All you can *know* is a world dissolved by analyzing intellect into abstraction—not a world composed by imaginative intellect into itself. And the result, for the generations of abstraction, is that neither poetry nor art can be a means to knowledge. To inspiration, yes: poetry can undoubtedly lead to that—whatever it is. To revelation, perhaps: there may certainly be moments of revelation in poetry. But to knowledge, no. The only connection between poetry and knowledge we can see is the burden of used abstractions—adages and old saws—which poetry, some poetry, seems to like to carry—adages most of which we knew before and some of which aren't even true.

But if all this is so, what then is the "experience of art"—the "experience of poetry"—which all of us who think about these things at all have known? What is the experience of *realization* which comes over us with those apples on a dish of Cézanne's or those three pine trees? What is the experience of realization which comes over us with Debussy's *Nuages?* What is the experience of realization which comes over us when Coleridge's robin sits and sings

> Betwixt the tufts of snow on the bare branch
> Of mossy apple-tree, while the nigh thatch
> Smokes in the sun thaw; . . .

or when his eave-drops fall

> Heard only in the trances of the blast,
> Or if the secret ministry of frost
> Shall hang them up in silent icicles,
> Quietly shining to the quiet Moon.

And if all this is so, why does one of the most effective of modern definitions of poetry (Arnold's in his letter to Maurice de Guérin) assign to that art the peculiar "power of so dealing with *things* as to awaken in us a wonderfully full, new and intimate sense of them and of our relation with them"?

The answer is, of course, that the children of abstraction are wrong —and are impoverished by their error, as our entire time is impoverished by it. They are wrong on both heads. They are wrong when they think they *can* know the world through its abstractions: nothing can be known through an abstraction but the abstraction itself. They are wrong also when they think they *cannot* know the world as the world: the whole achievement of art is a demonstration to the contrary. And the reason they are wrong on both heads is the reason given, quite unintentionally, by Matthew Arnold. They are wrong because they do not realize that all true knowledge is a matter of relation: that we *really* know a thing only when we are filled with "a wonderfully full, new and intimate sense of it" and, above all, of "our relation with" it. This sense—this *knowledge* in the truest meaning of the word knowledge—art can give but abstraction cannot.

There are as many proofs as there are successful works of art. Take, for obvious example, that unseen mysterious phenomenon, the wind. Take any attempt, by the familiar processes of abstraction, to "know" the wind. Put beside it those two familiar lines of George Meredith:—

> Mark where the pressing wind shoots javelin-like
> Its skeleton shadow on the broad-backd wave!

What will be the essential difference between the two? Will it not be that the first, the analytical, statement is or attempts to be a wholly objective statement made without reference to an observer (true everywhere and always), whereas an observer—*one's self* as observer!—is involved in the second? And will not the consequential difference be that a relation involving one's self is created by the second but not by the first? And will not the end difference be that the second, but not the first, will enable us to know the thing itself— to know what the thing is *like?*

It would be quite possible, I suppose, to semanticize this difference between knowledge by poetry and knowledge by abstraction out of existence by demonstrating that the word, know, is being used in two different senses in the two instances, but the triumph would be merely verbal, for the difference is real. It is indeed the realest of all differences, for what it touches is the means by which we come at reality. How are we to find the knowledge of reality in the world without, or in the shifting, flowing, fluid world within? Is all this a task for the techniques of abstraction—for science as it may be or as it is? Is it through abstraction alone that we are to find what is real in our experience of our lives—and so, conceivably, what is real in ourselves? Or do we need another and a different way of knowing— a way of knowing which will make that world out there, this world in here, available to us, not by translating them into something else— into abstractions of quantity and measure—but by bringing us ourselves to confront them as they are—man and tree face to face in the shock of recognition, man and love face to face?

The question, I beg you to see, is not what we *ought* to do. There is no ought. A man can "live" on abstractions all his life if he has the stomach for them, and many of us have—not the scientists only, but great numbers of the rest of us in this contemporary world, men whose days are a web of statistics, and names, and business deals, held together by the parentheses of a pair of commuting trains with three Martinis at the close. The question is not what we ought to do. The question is what we have the choice of doing—what alternatives are open to us. And it is here and in these terms that the issue presents itself to the teacher of poetry.

Colleges and universities do not exist to impose duties but to reveal choices. In a civilization like ours in which one choice has all but overwhelmed the other, a civilization dominated by abstraction, in which men are less and less able to deal with their experience of the world or of themselves unless experience and self have first been translated into abstract terms—a civilization like a foreign language—in such a civilization the need for an understanding of the alternative is urgent. What must be put before the generation of the young is the possibility of a knowledge of experience *as* experience, of self *as* self; and that possibility only the work of art, only the poem, can reveal. That it is so rarely, or so timidly, presented in our schools is one of the greatest failures of our educational system. Young men and young women graduate from American schools and colleges by the hundreds of thousands every year to whom science is the only road to knowledge, and to whom poetry is little more than a subdivision of something called "literature"—a kind of writing printed in columns instead of straight across the page and primarily intended to be deciphered by girls, who don't read it either.

This sort of thing has consequences. Abstractions are wonderfully clever tools for taking things apart and for arranging things in patterns but they are very little use in putting things together and no use at all when it comes to determining what things are *for*. Furthermore, abstractions have a limiting, a dehumanizing, a dehydrating effect on the relation to things of the man who must live with them. The result is that we are more and more left, in our scientific society, without the means of knowledge of ourselves as we truly are or of our experience as it actually is. We have the tools, all the tools—we are suffocating in tools—but we cannot find the actual wood to work or even the actual hand to work it. We begin with one abstraction (something we think of as ourselves) and a mess of other abstractions (standing for the world) and we arrange and rearrange the counters, but who we are and what we are doing we simply do not know—above all what we are doing. With the inevitable consequence that we do not know either what our purpose is or our end. So that when the latest discoveries of the cyclotron are reported we hail them with the cry that we will now be able to control nature better than ever before—but we never go on to say for what purpose, to what end, we will control her. To destroy a city? To remake a world?

It was something of this kind, I imagine, that Adlai Stevenson had in mind when he startled a Smith Commencement last spring by warning his newly graduated audience of prospective wives that the "typical Western man—or typical Western husband—operates well in the realm of means, as the Roman did before him. But outside his specialty, in the realm of ends he is apt to operate poorly or not at all. . . . The neglect of the cultivation of more mature values," Mr. Stevenson went on, "can only mean that his life, and the life of the society he determines, will lack valid purpose, however busy and even profitable it may be."

As he has so often done before, Mr. Stevenson there found words for an uneasiness which has been endemic but inarticulate in the American mind for many years—the sense that we are getting nowhere far too fast and that, if something doesn't happen soon, we may arrive. But when he came to spell out the causes for "the neglect of the cultivation of more mature values" Mr. Stevenson failed, or so it seems to me, to identify the actual villain. The contemporary environment in America, he told his young listeners, is "an environment in which 'facts,' the data of the senses, are glorified and value judgments are assigned inferior status as 'mere matters of opinion.' It is an environment in which art is often regarded as an adornment of civilization rather than a vital element of it, while philosophy is not only neglected but deemed faintly disreputable because 'it never gets you anywhere.' " It is true that philosophy is neglected, and even truer that art is regarded in this country generally as it seems to be regarded by the automobile manufacturers of Detroit: as so much enamel paint and chromium to be applied for allegedly decorative purposes to the outside of a car which would run better without it. But the explanation is not, I think, that we set facts—even facts in quotation marks—above values, or that we glorify the data of the senses, unless one means by that latter phrase not what the senses tell us of the world we live in but what the statistics that can be compiled out of the data of the senses would tell us if we were ever in touch with our senses.

In few civilizations have the senses been less alive than they are with us. Look at the cities we build and occupy—but look at them!—the houses we live in, the way we hold ourselves and move; listen to the speaking voices of the greater part of our women. And in no civilization, at least in recorded time, have human beings been farther from the *facts* if we mean by that word, facets of reality. Our indifference to ends is the result of our obsession with abstractions rather than facts: with the ideas of things rather than with things. For there can be no concern for ends without a hunger for reality. And there can be no hunger for reality without a sense of the real. And there can be no sense of the real in the world which abstraction creates, for abstraction is incapable of the real: it can neither lay hold of the real itself nor show us where to find it. It cannot, that is to say, create the *relation* between reality and ourselves which makes *knowledge* of reality possible, for neither reality nor ourselves exist in abstraction. Everything in the world of abstraction is object. And, as George Buttrick pointedly says, *we* are not objects: we are subjects.

But all this is a negative way of saying what a defender of poetry should not be afraid of saying positively. Let me say it. We have lost our concern with ends because we have lost our touch with reality and we have lost our touch with reality because we are estranged from the means to reality which is the poem—the work of art. To most members of our generation this would seem an extravagant statement but it is not extravagant in fact and would not have seemed so in another time. In ancient China the place of poetry in men's lives was assumed as matter of course; indeed, the polity was based on it. The three hundred and five odes or songs which make up the Song-word Scripture survived to the fourth century B.C., when Confucius is said to have collected them because they were part of the government records preserved in the Imperial Archive. For thousands of years the examinations for the Chinese civil service were examinations in poetry, and there is no record that the results were more disappointing to the throne than examinations of a different character might have been. Certainly there is no record that a Chinese civil servant ever attempted to deny an honor student in a

military academy his commission in the imperial army *or* navy because he was friendly with his own mother!* Idiocies which the
study of science and of other abstractions in contemporary institutions of naval education in the United States seem to nourish were
apparently cauterized from the mind by the reading of poems.

It was not for nothing that Confucius told his disciples that the
three hundred and five songs of the Song-word Scripture could be
boiled down to the commandment: "Have no twisty thoughts." You
cannot have twisty thoughts if you are real and if you are thinking
about real things. But if a mother is merely a biological event to
you and if you yourself are merely a military event called an admiral,
anything may happen: you may make your country ridiculous, humiliate a promising boy, and deprive the navy of a good officer, all
in the twisted belief that you are being a wise man and a patriot.

One can see, not only in the three hundred and five songs, but in
Chinese poetry of other periods, what Confucius meant. Consider
two Chinese poems of the second century B.C. and the sixth of our
era, both written by Emperors. The first is a poem of grief—of the
sense of loss of someone loved: a poem therefore of that inward world
of feeling, of emotion, which seems to us most nearly ourselves and
which, because it is always in flux, always shifting and changing and
flowing away, is, of all parts of our experience of our lives, most
difficult to know. We cannot know it through science. We cannot
know it by knowing things *about* it—even the shrewdest and most
intelligent things, helpful though they may be to us in other ways.
We cannot know it either by merely feeling it—by uttering its passing
urgencies, crying out "I love" meaning "I think of myself as loving"
or sobbing "I grieve" meaning "I think of myself as grieving." How
then can we know it?

The Emperor Wu-ti wrote (this is Arthur Waley's beautiful translation):—

> The sound of her silk skirt has stopped.
> On the marble pavement dust grows.
> Her empty room is cold and still.
> Fallen leaves are piled against the doors.
>
> Longing for that lovely lady
> How can I bring my aching heart to rest?

[* A reference to "loyalty" investigations of students in the military academies
during the heyday of McCarthyism.]

Four images, one of sound, two of sight, one of feeling, each like a note plucked on a stringed instrument. Then a question like the chord the four would make together. And all at once we *know*. We know this grief which no word could have described, which any abstraction the mind is capable of would have destroyed. But we know more than this grief: we know our own—or will when it shall visit us—and so know something of ourselves.

The second is a poem of that emotion, that feeling, which is even more difficult to know than grief itself. The second is a poem of delight: youth and delight—the morning of the world—the emotion, of all emotions, most difficult to stop, to hold, to see. "Joy whose hand is ever at his lips bidding adieu." How would you *know* delight in yourself and therefore yourself delighting? Will the psychiatrists tell you? Is there a definition somewhere in the folios of abstraction by which we attempt to live which will capture it for you? The Emperor Ch'ien Wen-ti (again Waley's translation) knew that there is only one mirror which will hold that vanishing smile: the mirror of art, the mirror of the poem:—

> A beautiful place is the town of Lo-yang:
> The big streets are full of spring light
> The lads go driving out with harps in their hands:
> The mulberry girls go out to the fields with their baskets
> Golden whips glint at the horses' flanks,
> Gauze sleeves brush the green boughs.
> Racing dawn the carriages come home—
> And the girls with their high baskets full of fruit.

In this world within, you see, this world which is ourselves, there is no possibility of knowing by abstracting the meaning out—or what we hope will be the meaning. There we must know things *as* themselves and it must be *we* who know them. Only art, only poetry, can bring about that confrontation, because only art, only poetry, can show us what we are and ourselves confronting it. To be ignorant of poetry is to be ignorant therefore of the one means of reaching the world of our experience of the world. And to be ignorant of *that* world is to be ignorant of who and what we are. And to be ignorant of who and what we are is to be incapable of reality no matter what tools we have, or what intelligence, or what skills. It is this incapacity, this impotence, which is the tragedy of the time we live in. We are spiritually impotent because we have cut ourselves off from the poem.

And the crowing irony is that it is only in the poem that we can know how impotent we have become.

Why do we teach poetry in this scientific age? To present the great alternative not to science but to that knowledge by abstraction which science has imposed. And what is this great alternative? Not the "messages" of poems, their interpreted "meanings," for these are abstractions also—abstractions far inferior to those of science. Not the explications of poetic texts, for the explication of a poetic text which goes no farther ends only in abstraction.

No, the great alternative is the poem as itself, the poem as a poem, the poem as a work of art—which is to say, the poem in the context in which alone the work of art exists: the context of the world, of the man and of the thing, of the infinite relationship which is our lives. To present the great alternative is to present the poem not as a message in a bottle, and not as an object in an uninhabited landscape, but as an action in the world, an action in which we ourselves are actors and our lives are known.

Problems for Thought and Writing

I

1. Does MacLeish convince you that poetry is "a 'human language' capable of competing with the languages of mathematics and science"?

2. Do you or do you not think that the intrusion of questions of morality and religion into literary art is a "kind of trespass"?

3. Why can MacLeish not accept the above argument?

4. What does MacLeish mean by saying that he cannot accept a division between "art and knowledge" in studying poetry? What does he mean by "poetry as knowledge"?

5. "To *know* the thing *as the thing it is*—to *know* apple *as* apple" is to know a world undissolved "by analyzing intellect into abstraction." To do this is to define in a new way, is it not? Should this method of definition have been included in the Introductory Discussion of this problem in this volume? Why or why not?

6. "Nothing can be known through an abstraction but the abstraction itself." What if that abstraction is God? How would a religious man respond to that problem? What is MacLeish's argument against abstraction? Can you find any flaw in his reasoning?

7. Why, according to Adlai Stevenson, are we "indifferent to ends"? What does he mean? In what way does MacLeish agree and disagree with him?

8. "In few civilizations have the senses been less alive than they are with us." Could you add instances to those MacLeish gives? Or don't you agree with the statement?

9. The reference to the student denied a commission because he was "friendly with his own mother" concerned a Naval cadet whose mother was or had been a Communist. In what way is this stupidity possible owing to the existence of an "abstracting intellect" among our officials?

10. We can never *know* an emotion through science (abstraction) or know it by knowing things *about* it, writes MacLeish. We know it only through the concrete images of a poem. Is MacLeish in agreement here with any of the basic premises of Zen, as described by Barrett (page 348)?

11. "To be ignorant of poetry is to be ignorant . . . of the one means of reaching the world of our experience of the world. And to be ignorant of *that* world is to be ignorant of who and what we are." This is a large claim and cannot, of course, be easily evaluated—especially by one unfamiliar with poetry. But what is your instinctive reaction to it? Does knowledge of "The Love Song of J. Alfred Prufrock" seem to give you this knowledge?

II

12. Compare the first two paragraphs of this article with Muller's (page 653) Which is the better written? What defects—and where—can you detect?

13. This is obviously an argument as well as an evaluation. How astutely does MacLeish handle evidence? Does he resort to the techniques of poetry to win his case, or does he argue *logically?*

~

THE LOVE SONG OF
J. ALFRED PRUFROCK* *T. S. Eliot*

> *S'io credesse che mia risposta fosse*
> *A persona che mai tornasse al mondo,*
> *Questa fiamma staria senza piu scosse.*
> *Ma perciocche giammai di questo fondo*
> *Non torno vivo alcum, s'i' odo il vero,*
> *Senza tema d'infamia ti rispondo.*[1]

Let us go then, you and I,
When the evening is spread out against the sky
Like a patient etherized upon a table;
Let us go, through certain half-deserted streets,
The muttering retreats
Of restless nights in one-night cheap hotels

* From *Collected Poems 1909–1935* by T. S. Eliot, copyright, 1936, by Harcourt, Brace and Company, Inc.

[1] "If I thought my answer were to one who ever could return to the world, this flame should shake no more; but since none ever did return alive from this depth, if what I hear be true, without fear of infamy I answer thee."—*Inferno,* XXVII, 61–66.

And sawdust restaurants with oyster-shells:
Streets that follow like a tedious argument
Of insidious intent
To lead you to an overwhelming question. . . .
Oh, do not ask, "What is it?"
Let us go and make our visit.

In the room the women come and go
Talking of Michelangelo.

The yellow fog that rubs its back upon the window-panes,
The yellow smoke that rubs its muzzle on the window-panes
Licked its tongue into the corners of the evening,
Lingered upon the pools that stand in drains,
Let fall upon its back the soot that falls from chimneys,
Slipped by the terrace, made a sudden leap,
And seeing that it was a soft October night,
Curled once about the house, and fell asleep.
And indeed there will be time
For the yellow smoke that slides along the street
Rubbing its back upon the window-panes;
There will be time, there will be time
To prepare a face to meet the faces that you meet;
There will be time to murder and create,
And time for all the works and days of hands
That lift and drop a question on your plate;
Time for you and time for me,
And time yet for a hundred indecisions,
And for a hundred visions and revisions,
Before the taking of a toast and tea.

In the room the women come and go
Talking of Michelangelo.

And indeed there will be time
To wonder, "Do I dare?" and, "Do I dare?"
Time to turn back and descend the stair,
With a bald spot in the middle of my hair—
(They will say: "How his hair is growing thin!")
My morning coat, my collar mounting firmly to the chin,
My necktie rich and modest, but asserted by a simple pin—

(They will say: "But how his arms and legs are thin!")
Do I dare
Disturb the universe?
In a minute there is time
For decisions and revisions which a minute will reverse.

For I have known them all already, known them all:
Have known the evenings, mornings, afternoons,
I have measured out my life with coffee spoons;
I know the voices dying with a dying fall
Beneath the music from a farther room.
   So how should I presume?
And I have known the eyes already, known them all—
The eyes that fix you in a formulated phrase,
And when I am formulated, sprawling on a pin,
When I am pinned and wriggling on the wall,
Then how should I begin
To spit out all the butt-ends of my days and ways?
   And how should I presume?

And I have known the arms already, known them all—
Arms that are braceleted and white and bare
(But in the lamplight, downed with light brown hair!)
Is it perfume from a dress
That makes me so digress?
Arms that lie along a table, or wrap about a shawl.
   And should I then presume?
   And how should I begin?

Shall I say, I have gone at dusk through narrow streets
And watched the smoke that rises from the pipes
Of lonely men in shirt-sleeves, leaning out of windows? . . .

I should have been a pair of ragged claws
Scuttling across the floors of silent seas.

And the afternoon, the evening, sleeps so peacefully!
Smoothed by long fingers,
Asleep . . . tired . . . or it malingers,
Stretched on the floor, here beside you and me.
Should I, after tea and cakes and ices,

Have the strength to force the moment to its crisis?
But though I have wept and fasted, wept and prayed,
Though I have seen my head (grown slightly bald) brought in upon
   a platter,
I am no prophet—and here's no great matter;
I have seen the moment of my greatness flicker,
And I have seen the eternal Footman hold my coat, and snicker,
And in short, I was afraid.

And would it have been worth it, after all,
After the cups, the marmalade, the tea,
Among the porcelain, among some talk of you and me,
Would it have been worth while,
To have bitten off the matter with a smile,
To have squeezed the universe into a ball
To roll it toward some overwhelming question,
To say: "I am Lazarus, come from the dead,
Come back to tell you all, I shall tell you all"—
If one, settling a pillow by her head,
      Should say: "That is not what I meant at all;
      That is not it, at all."

And would it have been worth it, after all,
Would it have been worth while,
After the sunsets and the dooryards and the sprinkled streets,
After the novels, after the teacups, after the skirts that trail along the
      floor—
And this, and so much more?—
It is impossible to say just what I mean!
But as if a magic lantern threw the nerves in patterns on a screen:
Would it have been worth while
If one, settling a pillow or throwing off a shawl,
And turning toward the window, should say:
      "That is not it at all,
      That is not what I meant, at all."

No! I am not Prince Hamlet, nor was meant to be;
Am an attendant lord, one that will do
To swell a progress, start a scene or two,
Advise the prince; no doubt, an easy tool,
Deferential, glad to be of use,

Politic, cautious, and meticulous;
Full of high sentence, but a bit obtuse;
At times, indeed, almost ridiculous—
Almost, at times, the Fool.

I grow old. . . . I grow old. . . .
I shall wear the bottoms of my trousers rolled.

Shall I part my hair behind? Do I dare to eat a peach?
I shall wear white flannel trousers, and walk upon the beach.
I have heard the mermaids singing, each to each.

I do not think that they will sing to me.

I have seen them riding seaward on the waves
Combing the white hair of the waves blown back
When the wind blows the water white and black.
We have lingered in the chambers of the sea
By sea-girls wreathed with seaweed red and brown
Till human voices wake us, and we drown.

Problems for Thought and Writing

We have concluded this volume with "The Love Song of J. Alfred Prufrock"
for a number of reasons. First, and most obvious, is the fact that it presents a
self-evaluation. But more important is the fact that the *quality* of that self-
evaluation reminds us of many of the issues and moods of the modern predicament
which were touched upon by the other authors in this section. Prufrock has been
taken by some critics as a symbolic figure, an embodiment of the futility, despair,
and frustration characterizing the life of modern man. Whether this is, in fact,
the character of modern existence and whether Prufrock truly represents it are,
of course, open questions. But if the testimony of most contemporary art can
be trusted, then a man in the twentieth century is indeed a rudderless and despairing figure. Prufrock comes from a leisure class, and perhaps you regard
him as somewhat fortunate in having the *opportunity* to measure out his life
with coffee spoons. But we need not view him merely as the representative of a
class. He symbolizes a psychological and spiritual condition, a quality of moral
vagabondage, which—to Eliot at least—is not primarily a social, political, or
economic problem. The problem is one to be solved in the mind and heart of
man, for it involves the discovery of life's meaning and the living in that awareness.

The poem itself is dramatic, not didactic. We are preached no sermon, we are
only shown a man walking to a drawing room where he associates with some vapid
and arty women of his own class. They "talk" of Michelangelo, but what do
they know of the vitality, discipline, and strenuous idealism that lay behind such
art? We are, however, shown these things only indirectly. Throughout most of
the poem we are actually *in* Prufrock's mind, following the free association of his

ideas as one thing suggests another. Transitions between one place and another or one idea and another are not clearly indicated, for in real life our thoughts are not necessarily sprung from present time and place, nor do our reveries follow any logical pattern of development. Again and again, Prufrock's thoughts break off in the middle, and even when he is trying to reason his philosophic "visions" are followed by "revisions."

But in spite of the fragmentary nature of his stream-of-consciousness, there is a distinct unity in the poem. It is a unity of mood. No matter what Prufrock is thinking or doing, we can read in it futility, weakness, despair, impotence. Thus we must read the poem intensively to get the meaning. Eliot brings us no confident answers, but expects us to *participate* in an experience in order that we might find some direction where Prufrock found none. The poem is, therefore, more of a question than a statement. What *values* can modern man confidently assume? If you can squeeze "the universe into a ball" and "roll it toward [that] overwhelming question," then you will be solving Prufrock's dilemma.

This book offers no scope for a careful explication of this poem, but some of the following questions might be helpful in evoking its meaning.

1. What does Prufrock mean by saying, "I should have been a pair of ragged claws"? Why are the "claws" alone mentioned?

2. Is Prufrock, in your opinion, afraid of women? Why or why not? What, precisely, is the nature of his attitude towards the "Arms that are braceleted and white and bare"?

3. What extended metaphor is apparent in Eliot's description of the fog? What artistic purpose does this serve?

4. Why, in your opinion, does Eliot have Prufrock walk through a slum to get where "the women come and go"?

5. What do the mermaids at the end symbolize?

6. What Shakespearian echoes can you detect in this poem? What character from *Hamlet* is suggested in the following lines?

> Politic, cautious, and meticulous:
> Full of high sentence, but a bit obtuse;

Index